The
Random
House
Basic Dictionary

Spanish-English
English-Spanish

The Random House Basic Dictionary

Spanish-English English-Spanish

Edited by
Donald F. Solá
Cornell University

Under the General Editorship of
Professor Frederick B. Agard
Cornell University

The Ballantine Reference Library

Ballantine Books · New York

Library of Congress Catalog Card Number: 67-20648
ISBN 0-345-29620-6
This edition published by arrangement with Random House, Inc.
Previously published as *The Spanish Vest Pocket Dictionary* and
The Random House Spanish Dictionary.

Manufactured in the United States of America
First Ballantine Books Edition: August 1981

Sixth Printing: July 1984
First Special Edition: August 1981
Second Special Edition: October 1981

Concise Pronunciation Guide

Spanish Letter	Pronunciation
a	Like English *a* in *father*.
b, v	At beginning of word group and after *m* or *n* like English *b*. Elsewhere, like English *v*, but pronounced with both lips instead of upper teeth and lower lip.
c	Before *e* or *i*, like English *th* in *thin* (in Northern Spain); like Spanish *s* (in Southern Spain and the Americas); elsewhere, like English *k* in *key*.
ch	Like English *ch* in *child*.
d	At beginning of word group and after *n* or *l*, like English *d*. Elsewhere, like English *th* in *either*.
e	Like English *e* in *bet*.
f	As in English.
g	Before *e* or *i*, the same as Spanish *j*. Elsewhere, like English *g* in *get*.
gu	Before *e* or *i*, like English *g* in *get*. Elsewhere, like English *gw* in *Gwynn*.
gü	Like English *gw* in *Gwynn*.
h	Silent.
i	Like English *i* in *machine*, but more clipped. Before or after another vowel, like English *y* (except when accented.)
j	Like English *h*, but more rasping.
k	Like English *k*.
l	Like English *l* in *like*, but with the tongue behind the upper front teeth.
ll	Like English *lli* in *million* (in Northern Spain); like Spanish *y* (in Southern Spain and the Americas).
m	As in English.
n	As in English.
ñ	Like English *ny* in *canyon*.
o	Approximately like English *o* in *vote*, but more clipped.
p	As in English.
qu	Like English *k*.
r	Not at all like American English *r*; a quick flap of the tongue-tip on the roof of the mouth.
rr	A strongly "rolled" or trilled version of Spanish *r*.
s	Like English *s* in *lease*.
t	As in English.
u	Like English *oo* in *boot*, but more clipped. Before *e* or after another vowel, like English *w* (except when accented).
v	See *b* above.
x	Like English *x*; although before consonants many speakers pronounce it like Spanish *s*; like Spanish *j* (in Mexican Indian words).
y	Approximately like English *y* in *yes*.
z	Like English *th* in *thin* (in Northern Spain); like English *s* in *lease* (in Southern Spain and the Americas).

Spanish Accentuation

In a number of words spoken stress is marked by an accent (´): *nación*, *país*, *médico*, *día*.

Words which are not so marked are, generally speaking, stressed on the next-to-the-last syllable if they end in a vowel, *n*, or *s*; and on the last syllable if they end in a consonant other than *n* or *s*.

Note: An accent is placed over some words to distinguish them from others having the same spelling and pronunciation but differing in meaning.

Irregular Verbs

Infinitive	Present	Future	Preterit	Past Part.
andar	ando	andaré	anduve	andado
caber	quepo	cabré	cupe	cabido
caer	caigo	caeré	caí	caído
conducir	conduzco	conduciré	conduje	conducido
dar	doy	daré	dí	dado
decir	digo	diré	dije	dicho
estar	estoy	estaré	estuve	estado
haber	he	habré	hube	habido
hacer	hago	haré	hice	hecho
ir	voy	iré	fuí	ido
jugar	juego	jugaré	jugué	jugado
morir	muero	moriré	morí	muerto
oír	oigo	oiré	oí	oído
poder	puedo	podré	pude	podido
poner	pongo	pondré	puse	puesto
querer	quiero	querré	quise	querido
saber	sé	sabré	supe	sabido
salir	salgo	saldré	salí	salido
ser	soy	seré	fuí	sido
tener	tengo	tendré	tuve	tenido
traer	traigo	traeré	traje	traído
valer	valgo	valdré	valí	valido
venir	vengo	vendré	vine	venido
ver	veo	veré	ví	visto

Abbreviations

a.	adjective
abbr.	abbreviation
adv.	adverb
aero.	aeronautical
agr.	agriculture
anat.	anatomy
art.	article
bot.	botany
chem.	chemistry
coll.	colloquial
com.	commercial
conj.	conjunction
dem.	demonstrative
f.	feminine
fin.	finance
geog.	geography
govt.	government
gram.	grammar
interj.	interjection
interrog.	interrogative
leg.	legal
m.	masculine
mech.	mechanics
med.	medicine
Mex.	Mexico
mus.	musical
n.	noun
naut.	nautical
pl.	plural
prep.	preposition
pron.	pronoun
punct.	punctuation
rel.	relative, religion
S.A.	Spanish American
v.	verb

Useful Phrases

Good day, Good morning.   Buenos días.
Good afternoon.   Buenas tardes.
Good night, Good evening.   Buenas noches.
Hello.   ¡Hola!
See you later.   Hasta luego.
Goodbye.   ¡Adiós!
How are you?   ¿Cómo está usted?
I am fine, thank you.   Estoy bien, gracias.
I am pleased to meet you.   Mucho gusto en conocerle.
Thank you very much.   Muchas gracias.
You're welcome.   De nada.
Please.   Por favor.
Good luck.   ¡Buena suerte!
To your health.   ¡Salud!

Please help me.   Ayúdeme, por favor.
I don't know.   No sé.
I don't understand.   No entiendo.
Do you understand?   ¿Entiende usted?
I don't speak Spanish.   No hablo español.
Do you speak English?   ¿Habla usted inglés?
How do you say...in Spanish?   ¿Cómo se dice...en español?
Speak slowly, please.   Hable despacio, por favor.
Please repeat.   Repita, por favor.
I don't like it.   No me gusta.

What is your name?   ¿Cómo se llama usted?
My name is...   Me llamo...
I am an American.   Soy norteamericano.

How is the weather?   ¿Qué tiempo hace?
It's cold (hot) today.   Hace frío (calor) hoy.
What time is it?   ¿Qué hora es?

How much is it?   ¿Cuánto es?
It is too much.   Es demasiado.
What do you wish?   ¿Qué desea usted?
I want to buy...   Quiero comprar...

I am hungry. Tengo hambre.
I am thirsty. Tengo sed.
Where is there a restaurant? ¿Dónde hay un restaurante?
The bill, please. La cuenta, por favor.
Where is there a hotel? ¿Donde hay un hotel?
Where is the post office? ¿Dónde está el correo?
Take me to… Lléveme a…
I believe I am ill. Creo que estoy enfermo.
Please call a doctor. Por favor, llame al médico.
I want to send a telegram. Quiero poner un telegrama.
As soon as possible. Cuanto antes.

Round trip Ida y vuelta.
Where can I change my money? ¿Dónde puedo cambiar mi dinero?
Can you accept my check? ¿Puede aceptar usted mi cheque?
What is the postage? ¿Cuánto es el franqueo?

Right away. ¡Pronto!
Help. ¡Socorro!
Come in. ¡Pase usted!
Pardon me. Dispense usted.
Stop. ¡Pare!
Look out. ¡Cuidado!
Hurry. ¡De prisa!
Go on. ¡Siga!
To (on, at) the right A la derecha.
To (on, at) the left A la izquierda.
Straight ahead Adelante.

Signs

Caution Precaución
Danger Peligro
Exit Salida
Entrance Entrada
Stop Alto
Closed Cerrado
Open Abierto
Slow Despacio
No smoking Prohibido fumar
No admittance Prohibida la entrada
One way una vía
Women Señoras, Mujeres, Damas
Men Señores, Hombres, Caballeros
Ladies' Room El cuarto de damas
Men's Room El servicio

Weights and Measures

The Spanish use the *Metric System* of weights and measures, which is a decimal system in which multiples are shown by the prefixes: deci- (one tenth); centi- (one hundredth); mili- (one thousandth); deca- (ten); hecto- (hundred); kilo- (thousand).

1 centímetro	=	.3937 inches
1 metro	=	39.37 inches
1 kilómetro	=	.621 mile
1 centigramo	=	.1543 grain
1 gramo	=	15.432 grains
1 kilogramo	=	2.2046 pounds
1 tonelada	=	2,204 pounds
1 centilitro	=	.338 ounces
1 litro	=	1.0567 quart (liquid); .908 quart (dry)
1 kilolitro	=	264.18 gallons

Money

	Monetary Unit		Monetary Unit
Spain	peseta	El Salvador	colón
Argentina	peso	Guatemala	quetzal
Bolivia	peso	Haiti	gourde
Brazil	cruzeiro	Honduras	lempira
Chile	escudo	Mexico	peso
Colombia	peso	Nicaragua	córdoba
Costa Rica	colón	Panama	balboa
Cuba	peso	Paraguay	guaraní
Dominican Republic	peso	Peru	sol
Ecuador	sucre	Uruguay	peso
		Venezuela	bolívar

Numerals

Cardinal

1	uno, una	30	treinta
2	dos	31	treinta y uno
3	tres	32	treinta y dos
4	cuatro	40	cuarenta
5	cincó	50	cincuenta
6	seis	60	sesenta
7	siete	70	setenta
8	ocho	80	ochenta
9	nueve	90	noventa
10	diez	100	cien
11	once	101	ciento uno
12	doce	102	ciento dos
13	trece	200	doscientos, -as
14	catorce	300	trescientos, -as
15	quince	400	cuatrocientos, -as
16	dieciséis	500	quinientos, -as
17	diecisiete	600	seiscientos, -as
18	dieciocho	700	setecientos, -as
19	diecinueve	800	ochocientos, -as
20	veinte	900	novecientos, -as
21	veinte y uno (or veintiuno)	1,000	mil
		2,000	dos mil
22	veinte y dos (or veintidos)	100,000	cien mil
		1,000,000	un millón
		2,000,000	dos millones

Ordinal

1st	primero	6th	sexto
2nd	segundo	7th	séptimo
3rd	tercero	8th	octavo
4th	cuarto	9th	noveno
5th	quinto	10th	décimo

Days of the Week

Sunday	domingo
Monday	lunes
Tuesday	martes
Wednesday	miércoles
Thursday	jueves
Friday	viernes
Saturday	sábado

Months

January	enero	July	julio
February	febrero	August	agosto
March	marzo	September	septiembre
April	abril	October	octubre
May	mayo	November	noviembre
June	junio	December	diciembre

Spanish-English

A

a, *prep.* to; at.
abacero, *m.* grocer.
abad, *m.* abbot.
abadía, *f.* abbey.
abajo, *adv.* down; downstairs.
abandonar, *v.* abandon.
abanico, *m.* fan. —abanicar, *v.*
abaratar, *v.* cheapen.
abarcar, *v.* comprise; clasp.
abastecer, *v.* supply, provision.
abatido, *a.* dejected, despondent.
abatir, *v.* depress, dishearten.
abdicar, *v.* abdicate.
abdomen, *m.* abdomen.
abeja, *f.* bee.
abejarrón, *m.* bumblebee.
abertura, *f.* opening, aperture, slit.
abeto, *m.* fir.
abierto, *a.* open; overt.
abismo, *m.* abyss, chasm.
ablandar, *v.* soften.
abochornar, *v.* embarrass.
abogado, *m.* lawyer, attorney.
abolengo, *m.* ancestry.
abolición, *f.* abolition.
abolladura, *f.* dent. —abollar, *v.*
abominable, *a.* abominable.
abominar, *v.* abhor.
abonar, *v.* pay; fertilize.
abonarse, *v.* subscribe.
abono, *m.* fertilizer; subscription.
aborrecer, *v.* hate, loathe, abhor.
aborto, *m.* abortion.
abovedar, *v.* vault.
abrasar, *v.* burn.
abrazar, *v.* embrace; clasp.
abrazo, *m.* embrace.
abreviar, *v.* abbreviate, abridge, shorten.
abreviatura, *f.* abbreviation.
abrigar, *v.* harbor, shelter.
abrigarse, *v.* bundle up.
abrigo, *m.* overcoat; shelter; *(pl.)* wraps.
abril, *m.* April.
abrir, *v.* open; (med.) lance.
abrochar, *v.* clasp.
abrojo, *m.* thorn.
abrumar, *v.* overwhelm, crush, swamp.
absceso, *m.* abscess.
absolución, *f.* absolution; acquittal.
absoluto, *a.* absolute; downright.
absolver, *v.* absolve, pardon.
absorbente, *a.* absorbent.
absorber, *v.* absorb.
absorción, *f.* absorption.
abstenerse, *v.* abstain; refrain.
abstinencia, *f.* abstinence.
abstracción, *f.* abstraction.
abstraer, *v.* abstract.
absurdo, 1. *a.* absurd. 2. *m.* absurdity.

abuela, *f.* grandmother.
abuelo, *m.* grandfather; *(pl.)* grandparents.
abultado, *a.* bulky.
abultamiento, *m.* bulge. —abultar, *v.*
abundancia, *f.* abundance, plenty.
abundante, *a.* abundant, plentiful.
abundar, *v.* abound.
aburrido, *a.* boring, tedious.
aburrimiento, *m.* boredom.
aburrir, *v.* bore.
abusar, *v.* abuse, misuse.
abusivo, *a.* abusive.
abuso, *m.* abuse.
abyecto, *a.* abject, low.
acá, *adv.* here.
acabar, *v.* finish. a. de . . ., to have just . . . .
academia, *f.* academy.
académico, *a.* academic.
acaecer, *v.* happen.
acanalar, *v.* groove.
acaparar, *v.* hoard; monopolize.
acariciar, *v.* caress, stroke.
acaso, *m.* chance. por si a., just in case.
acceder, *v.* accede.
accesible, *a.* accessible.
acceso, *m.* access, approach.
accesorio, *a.* accessory.
accidental, *a.* accidental.
accidente, *m.* accident, wreck.
acción, *f.* action, act; (com.) share of stock.
acechar, *v.* ambush, spy on.
aceite, *m.* oil.
aceitoso, *a.* oily.
aceituna, *f.* olive.
aceleración, *f.* acceleration.
acelerar, *v.* accelerate, speed up.
acento, *m.* accent.
acentuar, *v.* accent, accentuate, stress.
acepillar, *v.* brush; plane (wood).
aceptable, *a.* acceptable.
aceptación, *f.* acceptance.
aceptar, *v.* accept.
acequía, *f.* ditch.
acera, *f.* sidewalk.
acerca de, *prep.* about, concerning.
acercar, *v.* bring near.
acercarse, *v.* approach, come near, go near.
acero, *m.* steel.
acertar, *v.* guess right. a. en, hit (a mark).
acertijo, *m.* puzzle, riddle.
acidez, *f.* acidity.
ácido, 1. *a.* sour. 2. *m.* acid.
aclamación, *f.* acclamation.
aclamar, *v.* acclaim.
aclarar, *v.* brighten; clarify, clear up.
acoger, *v.* welcome, receive.
acogida, *f.* welcome, reception.
acometer, *v.* attack.

acomodador, *m.* usher.
acomodar, *v.* accommodate, fix up.
acompañamiento, *m.* accompaniment; following.
acompañar, *v.* accompany.
acondicionar, *v.* condition.
aconsejable, *a.* advisable.
aconsejar, *v.* advise.
acontecer, *v.* happen.
acontecimiento, *m.* event, happening.
acorazado, *m.* battleship.
acordarse, *v.* remember, recollect.
acortar, *v.* shorten.
acosar, *v.* beset, harry.
acostar, *v.* lay down; put to bed.
acostarse, *v.* lie down; go to bed.
acostumbrado, *a.* accustomed; customary.
acostumbrar, *v.* accustom.
acrecentar, *v.* increase.
acreditar, *v.* accredit.
acreedor -ra, *n.* creditor.
acróbata, *m.* acrobat.
actitud, *f.* attitude.
actividad, *f.* activity.
activista, *a. & n.* activist.
activo, *a.* active.
acto, *m.* act.
actor, *m.* actor.
actriz, *f.* actress.
actual, *a.* present.
actuar, *v.* act.
acuarela, *f.* watercolor.
acuario, *m.* aquarium.
acuático, *a.* aquatic.
acuchillar, *v.* slash, knife.
acudir, *v.* rally; hasten; be present.
acuerdo, *m.* accord, agreement; settlement. de a., in agreement, agreed.
acumulación, *f.* accumulation.
acumular, *v.* accumulate.
acuñar, *v.* coin, mint.
acupuntura, *f.* acupuncture.
acusación, *f.* accusation, charge.
acusado -da, *a. & n.* accused; defendant.
acusador -ra, *n.* accuser.
acusar, *v.* accuse; acknowledge.
acústica, *f.* acoustics.
achicar, *v.* diminish, dwarf; humble.
adaptación, *f.* adaptation.
adaptar, *v.* adapt.
adecuado, *a.* adequate.
adelantado, *a.* advanced; fast (clock).
adelantamiento, *m.* advancement, promotion.
adelantar, *v.* advance.
adelante, *adv.* ahead, forward, onward, on.
adelanto, *m.* advancement, progress, improvement.
adelgazar, *v.* make thin.

ademán, *m.* attitude; gesture.

además, *adv.* in addition, besides, also.

adentro, *adv.* in, inside.

adepto, *a.* adept.

aderezar, *v.* prepare; trim.

adherirse, *v.* adhere, stick.

adhesivo, *a.* adhesive.

adición, *f.* addition.

adicional, *a.* additional, extra.

adicto, *a. & m.* addicted; addict.

adiós, *m. & interj.* good-bye, farewell.

adivinar, *v.* guess.

adjetivo, *m.* adjective.

adjunto, *a.* enclosed.

administración, *f.* administration.

administrador, *m.* administrator.

administrar, *v.* administer; manage.

administrativo, *a.* administrative.

admirable, *a.* admirable.

admiración, *f.* admiration; wonder.

admirar, *v.* admire.

admisión, *f.* admission.

admitir, *v.* admit, acknowledge.

adolescencia, *f.* adolescence, youth.

adolescente, *a.* adolescent.

adónde, *adv.* where.

adondequiera, *conj.* wherever.

adopción, *f.* adoption.

adoptar, *v.* adopt.

adoración, *f.* worship, love, adoration. —**adorar,** *v.*

adormecer, *v.* drowse.

adornar, *v.* adorn; decorate.

adorno, *m.* adornment, trimming.

adquirir, *v.* acquire, obtain.

adquisición, *f.* acquisition, attainment.

aduana, *f.* custom house, customs.

aducto. *m.* input.

adujada, *f.* (naut.) coil of rope.

adulación, *f.* flattery.

adular, *v.* flatter.

adulterar, *v.* adulterate.

adulterio, *m.* adultery.

adulto, *a. & m.* adult.

adusto, *a.* gloomy; austere.

adverbio, *m.* adverb.

adversario, *m.* adversary.

adversidad, *f.* adversity.

adverso, *a.* adverse.

advertencia, *f.* warning.

advertir, *v.* warn; notice.

adyacente, *a.* adjacent.

aéreo, *a.* aerial; air.

aeromoza, *f.* stewardess, flight attendant.

aeroplano, *m.* airplane.

aeropuerto, *m.* airport.

aerosol, *m.* aerosol, spray.

afable, *a.* affable, pleasant.

afanar~ *v.* toil.

~mar, deform.

afectar, *v.* affect.

afecto, *m.* affection, attachment.

afeitada, *f.* shave. —**afeitarse,** *v.*

afeminado, *a.* effeminate.

afición, *f.* fondness, liking; hobby.

aficionado, *a.* fond.

aficionado -da, *n.* fan, devotee; amateur.

aficionarse a, *v.* become fond of.

afilada, *a.* sharp.

afilar, *v.* sharpen.

afiliación, *f.* affiliation.

afiliado, *m.* affiliate. —**afiliar,** *v.*

afinar, *v.* polish, tune up.

afinidad, *f.* relationship.

afirmación, *f.* affirmation, statement.

afirmar, *v.* affirm, assert.

afirmativa, *f.* affirmative. —**afirmativo,** *a.*

aflicción, *f.* affliction; sorrow, grief.

afligido, *a.* sorrowful, grieved.

afligir, *v.* grieve, distress.

aflojar, *v.* loosen.

afortunado, *a.* fortunate, successful, lucky.

afrenta, *f.* insult, outrage, affront. —**afrentar,** *v.*

afrentoso, *a.* shameful.

africano -na, *a. & n.* African.

afuera, *adv.* out, outside.

afueras, *f.,pl.* suburbs.

agacharse, *v.* squat, crouch, cower.

agarrar, *v.* seize, grasp, clutch.

agarro, *m.* clutch, grasp.

agencia, *f.* agency.

agente, *m.* agent, representative.

ágil, *a.* agile, spry.

agitación, *f.* agitation, ferment.

agitado, *a.* agitated; excited.

agitador, *m.* agitator.

agitar, *v.* shake, agitate, excite.

agobiar, *v.* oppress, burden.

agosto, *m.* August.

agotamiento, *m.* exhaustion.

agotar, *v.* exhaust, use up, sap.

agradable, *a.* agreeable, pleasant.

agradar, *v.* please.

agradecer, *v.* thank; appreciate, be grateful for.

agradecido, *a.* grateful, thankful.

agradecimiento, *m.* gratitude, thanks.

agravar, *v.* aggravate, make worse.

agravio, *m.* wrong. —**agraviar,** *v.*

agregado, *a. & m.* aggregate.

agregar, *v.* add; gather.

agresión, *f.* aggression; (leg.) battery.

agresivo, *a.* aggressive.

agresor, *m.* aggressor.

agrícola, *a.* agricultural.

agricultor, *m.* farmer.

agricultura, *f.* agriculture, farming.

agrio, *a.* sour.

agrupar, *v.* group.

agua, *f.* water. —**aguar,** *v.*

aguacate, *m.* avocado, alligator pear.

aguantar, *v.* endure, stand, put up with.

aguardar, *v.* await; expect.

aguardiente, *m.* brandy.

agudo, *a.* sharp, keen, shrill, acute.

agüero, *m.* omen.

águila, *f.* eagle.

aguja, *f.* needle.

agujero, *m.* hole.

aguzar, *v.* sharpen.

ahí, *adv.* there.

ahogar, *v.* drown; choke; suffocate.

ahondar, *v.* deepen.

ahora, *adv.* now.

ahorcar, *v.* hang (execute).

ahorrar, *v.* save, save up; spare.

ahorros, *m.pl.* savings.

ahumar, *v.* smoke.

airado, *a.* angry, indignant.

aire, *m.* air. —**airear,** *v.*

aislamiento, *m.* isolation.

aislar, *v.* isolate.

ajedrez, *m.* chess.

ajeno, *a.* alien; someone else's.

ají, *m.* chili.

ajo, *m.* garlic.

ajustado, *a.* adjusted; trim; exact.

ajustar, *v.* adjust.

ajuste, *m.* adjustment, settlement.

al, *contr.* of **a** + **el.**

ala, *f.* wing; brim (of hat).

alabanza, *f.* praise. —**alabar,** *v.*

alabear, *v.* warp.

alambique, *m.* still.

alambre, *m.* wire. **a. de púas,** barbed wire.

alarde, *m.* boasting, ostentation.

alargar, *v.* lengthen; stretch out.

alarma, *f.* alarm. —**alarmar,** *v.*

alba, *f.* daybreak, dawn.

albanega, *f.* hair net.

albañil, *m.* bricklayer; mason.

albaricoque, *m.* apricot.

albergue, *m.* shelter. —**albergar,** *v.*

alborotar, *v.* disturb, make noise, brawl, riot.

alboroto, *m.* brawl, disturbance, din, tumult.

álbum, *m.* album.

alcachofa, *f.* artichoke.

alcalde, *m.* mayor.

alcance, *m.* reach; range, scope.

alcanfor, *m.* camphor.

alcanzar, *v.* reach, overtake, catch.

alcayata, *f.* spike.

alce, *m.* elk.

alcoba, *f.* bedroom; alcove.

alcohol, *m.* alcohol.

alcohólico, a. alcoholic.
aldaba, f. latch.
aldea, f. village.
alegación, f. allegation.
alegar, v. allege.
alegrar, v. make happy, brighten.
alegrarse, v. be glad.
alegre, a. gay, cheerful, merry.
alegría, f. gaiety, cheer.
alejarse, v. move away, off.
alemán -ana, a. & n. German.
Alemania, f. Germany.
alentar, v. cheer up, encourage.
alergía, f. allergy.
alerta, adv. on the alert.
aleve, alevoso, a. treacherous.
alfabeto, m. alphabet.
alfalfa, f. alfalfa.
alfarería, f. pottery.
alférez, m. (naval) ensign.
alfil, m. (chess) bishop.
alfiler, m. pin.
alfombra, f. carpet, rug.
alforja, f. knapsack; saddlebag.
algarabía, f. jargon; din.
álgebra, f. algebra.
algo, pron. & adv. something, somewhat; anything.
algodón, m. cotton.
alguien, pron. somebody, someone; anybody, anyone.
algún -no -na, a. & pron. some; any.
alhaja, f. jewel.
aliado, a. & m. allied; ally. —**aliar,** v.
alianza, f. alliance.
alicates, m.pl. pliers.
aliento, m. breath. **dar a.,** encourage.
aligerar, v. lighten.
alimentar, v. feed, nourish.
alimento, m. nourishment, food.
alinear, v. line up; (pol.) align.
alisar, v. smooth.
alistamiento, m. enlistment.
alistar, v. make ready, prime. **alistarse,** v. get ready. (mil.) enlist.
aliviar, v. alleviate, relieve, ease.
alivio, m. relief.
alma, f. soul.
almacén, m. department store; storehouse.
almacenaje, m. storage.
almacenar, v. store.
almanaque, m. almanac.
almeja, f. clam.
almendra, f. almond.
almíbar, m. syrup.
almidón, m. starch. —**almidonar,** v.
almirante, m. admiral.
almohada, f. pillow.
almuerzo, m. lunch. —**almorzar,** v.
alojamiento, m. lodging, accommodations.
alojar, v. lodge, house.
alojarse, v. stay, room.

alquiler, m. rent. —**alquilar,** v.
alrededor, adv. around.
alrededores, m.pl. environs.
altanero, a. haughty.
altar, m. altar.
altavoz, m. loudspeaker.
alteración, f. alteration.
alterar, v. alter.
alternativa, f. alternative. —**alternativo,** a.
alterno, a. alternate. —**alternar,** v.
alteza, f. highness.
altivo, a. proud, haughty; lofty.
alto, 1. a. high, tall; loud. **2.** m. height, story (house).
altura, f. height, altitude.
alud, m. avalanche.
aludir, v. allude.
alumbrado, m. lighting.
alumbrar, v. light.
aluminio, m. aluminum.
alumno -na, n. student, pupil.
alusión, f. allusion.
alza, f. rise; boost.
alzar, v. raise, lift.
allá, adv. there. **más a.,** beyond, farther on.
allanar, v. flatten, smooth, plane.
allí, adv. there. **por a.,** that way.
ama, f. housewife, mistress (of house). **a. de llaves,** housekeeper.
amable, a. kind; pleasant, sweet.
amalgamar, v. amalgamate.
amamantar, v. suckle, nurse.
amanecer, 1. v. dawn, daybreak. **2.** v. dawn; awaken.
amante, m. lover.
amar, v. love.
amargo, a. bitter.
amargón, m. dandelion.
amargura, f. bitterness.
amarillo, a. yellow.
amarradero, m. mooring.
amarrar, v. hitch, moor, tie up.
amartillar, v. hammer; cock (a gun).
amasar, v. knead, mold.
ámbar, m. amber.
ambarino, a. amber.
ambición, f. ambition.
ambicionar, v. aspire to.
ambicioso, a. ambitious.
ambiente, m. environment, atmosphere.
ambigüedad, f. ambiguity.
ambiguo, a. ambiguous.
ambos, a. & pron. both.
ambulancia, f. ambulance.
amenaza, f. threat, menace.
amenazar, v. threaten, menace.
ameno, a. pleasant.
americano -na, a. & n. American.
ametralladora, f. machine gun.
amigable, a. amicable, friendly.
amígdala, f. tonsil.
amigo -ga, n. friend.

amistad, f. friendship.
amistoso, a. friendly.
amniocéntesis, m. amniocentesis.
amo, m. master.
amonestaciones, f.pl. banns.
amonestar, v. admonish.
amoníaco, m. ammonia.
amontonar, v. amass, pile up.
amor, m. love. **a. propio,** self-esteem.
amorío, m. romance, love affair.
amoroso, a. amorous; loving.
amortecer, v. deaden.
amparar, v. aid, befriend; protect, shield.
amparo, m. protection.
ampliar, v. enlarge; elaborate.
amplificar, v. amplify.
amplio, a. ample, roomy.
ampolla, f. bubble; bulb; blister.
amputar, v. amputate.
amueblar, v. furnish.
analfabeto, a. & m. illiterate.
análisis, m. or f. analysis.
analizar, v. analyze.
analogía, f. analogy.
análogo, a. similar, analogous.
anarquía, f. anarchy.
anatomía, f. anatomy.
ancho, a. wide, broad.
anchoa, f. anchovy.
anchura, f. width, breadth.
anciano -na, a. & m. old, aged (person).
ancla, f. anchor. —**anclar,** v.
anclaje, m. anchorage.
andamio, m. scaffold.
andar, v. walk; move, go.
andén, m. (railroad) platform.
andrajoso, a. ragged, uneven.
anécdota, f. anecdote.
anegar, v. flood, drown.
anestesia, f. anesthetic.
anexar, v. annex.
anexión, f. annexation.
anfitrión, m. host.
ángel, m. angel.
angosto, a. narrow.
anguila, f. eel.
angular, a. angular.
ángulo, m. angle.
angustia, f. anguish, agony.
angustiar, v. distress.
anhelar, v. long for.
anidar, v. nest, nestle.
anillo, m. ring; circle.
animación, f. animation; bustle.
animado, a. animated, lively; animate.
animal, a. & m. animal.
ánimo, m. state of mind, spirits; courage.
aniquilar, v. annihilate, destroy.
aniversario, m. anniversary.
anoche, adv. last night.
anochecer, 1. m. twilight, nightfall. **2.** v. get dark.
anónimo, a. anonymous.
anormal, a. abnormal.
anotación, f. annotation.

anotar, v. annotate.

ansia, ansiedad, f. anxiety.

ansioso, a. anxious.

antagonismo, m. antagonism.

antagonista, m. & f. antagonist, opponent.

anteayer, adv. day before yesterday.

antebrazo, m. forearm.

antecedente, a. & m. antecedent.

anteceder, v. precede.

antecesor, m. ancestor.

antemano, de a., in advance.

antena, f. antenna.

anteojos, m.pl. eyeglasses.

antepasado, m. ancestor, forefather.

anterior, a. previous, former.

antes, adv. before; formerly.

anticipación, f. anticipation.

anticipar, v. anticipate; advance.

anticuado, a. antiquated, obsolete.

antídoto, m. antidote.

antigüedad, f. antiquity; antique.

antiguo, a. former; old; ancient, antique.

antílope, m. antelope.

antinuclear, a. antinuclear.

antipatía, f. antipathy.

antipático, a. disagreeable, nasty.

antiséptico, a. & m. antiseptic.

antojarse, v. se me antoja . . . etc., I desire . . ., take a fancy to . . ., etc.

antojo, m. whim, fancy.

antorcha, f. torch.

antracita, f. anthracite.

anual, a. annual, yearly.

anudar, v. knot; tie.

anular, v. annul, void.

anunciar, v. announce; proclaim, advertise.

anuncio, m. announcement; advertisement.

añadir, v. add.

añil, m. bluing.

año, m. year.

apacible, a. peaceful, peaceable.

apaciguamiento, m. appeasement.

apaciguar, v. appease; placate.

apagado, a. dull.

apagar, v. extinguish, quench, put out.

aparador, m. buffet, cupboard.

aparato, m. apparatus; machine; appliance, set.

aparecer, v. appear, show up.

aparejo, m. rig. —**aparejar,** v.

aparentar, v. pretend; profess.

aparente, a. apparent.

apariencia, aparición, f. appearance.

apartado, 1. a. aloof; separate. **2.** m. post-office box.

apartamento, m. apartment. **a. condominium.**

apartheid, m. apartheid.

apasionado, a. passionate.

apatía, f. apathy.

apearse, v. get off, alight.

apedrear, v. stone.

apelación, f. appeal. —**apelar,** v.

apellido, m. family name.

apenas, adv. scarcely, hardly.

apéndice, m. appendix.

apercibir, v. prepare, warn.

aperitivo, m. appetizer.

aperos, m.pl. implements.

apetecer, v. desire, have appetite for.

apetito, m. appetite.

ápice, m. apex.

apilar, v. stack.

apio, m. celery.

aplacar, v. appease; placate.

aplastar, v. crush, flatten.

aplaudir, v. applaud, cheer.

aplauso, m. applause.

aplazar, v. postpone, put off.

aplicable, a. applicable.

aplicado, a. industrious, diligent.

aplicar, v. apply.

aplomo, m. aplomb, poise.

apoderado, m. attorney.

apoderarse de, v. get hold of, seize.

apodo, m. nickname. —**apodar,** v.

apologético, a. apologetic.

apoplejía, f. apoplexy.

aposento, m. room, flat.

apostar, v. bet, wager.

apóstol, m. apostle.

apoyar, v. support, prop; lean.

apoyo, m. support; prop; aid; approval.

apreciable, a. appreciable.

apreciar, v. appreciate, prize.

aprecio, m. appreciation, regard.

apremio, m. pressure, compulsion.

aprender, v. learn.

aprendiz, m. apprentice.

aprensión, f. apprehension.

aprensivo, a. apprehensive.

apresurado, a. hasty, fast.

apresurar, v. hurry, speed up.

apretado, a. tight.

apretar, v. squeeze, press; tighten.

apretón, m. squeeze.

aprieto, m. plight, predicament.

aprobación, f. approbation, approval.

aprobar, v. approve.

apropiación, f. appropriation.

apropiado, a. appropriate. —**apropiar,** v.

aprovechar, v. profit by.

aprovecharse, v. take advantage.

aproximado, a. approximate.

aproximarse a, v. approach.

aptitud, f. aptitude.

apto, a. apt.

apuesta, f. bet, wager, stake.

apuntar, v. point, aim; prompt; write down.

apunte, m. annotation, note; promptings, cue.

apuñalar, v. stab.

apurar, v. hurry; worry.

apuro, m. predicament, scrape, trouble.

aquel, aquella, dem. a. that.

aquél, aquélla, dem. pron. that (one); the former.

aquello, dem. pron. that.

aquí, adv. here. **por a.,** this way.

aquietar, v. allay; lull, pacify.

ara, f. altar.

árabe, a. & n. Arab, Arabic.

arado, m. plow. —**arar,** v.

arándano, m. cranberry.

araña, f. spider. **a. de luces,** chandelier.

arbitración, f. arbitration.

arbitrador -ra, n. arbitrator.

arbitraje, m. arbitration.

arbitrar, v. arbitrate.

arbitrario, a. arbitrary.

árbitro, m. arbiter, umpire, referee.

árbol, m. tree; mast.

arbusto, m. bush, shrub.

arca, f. chest; ark.

arcada, f. arcade.

arcaico, a. archaic.

arce, m. maple.

arcilla, f. clay.

arco, m. arc; arch; (archer's) bow. **a. iris,** rainbow.

archipiélago, m. archipelago.

archivo, m. archive; file. —**archivar,** v.

arder, v. burn.

ardid, m. stratagem, cunning.

ardiente, a. ardent, burning, fiery.

ardilla, f. squirrel.

ardor, m. ardor, fervor.

arduo, a. arduous.

área, f. area.

arena, f. sand; arena.

arenoso, a. sandy.

arenque, m. herring.

arete, n. earring.

argentino -na, a. & n. Argentine.

argüir, v. dispute, argue.

árido, a. arid.

aristocracia, f. aristocracy.

aristócrata, f. aristocrat.

aristocrático, a. aristocratic.

aritmética, f. arithmetic.

arma, f. weapon, arm.

armadura, f. armor; reinforcement; framework.

armamento, m. armament.

armar, v. arm.

armario, m. cabinet, bureau, wardrobe.

armazón, m. framework, frame.

armería, f. armory.

armisticio, m. armistice.

armonía, f. harmony.

armonioso, a. harmonious.

armonizar, v. harmonize.

arnés, m. harness.

aroma, f. aroma, fragrance.
aromático, a. aromatic.
arpa, f. harp.
arquear, v. arch.
arquitecto, m. architect.
arquitectura, f. architecture.
arquitectural, a. architectural.
arrabal, m. suburb.
arraigar, v. take root, settle.
arrancar, v. pull out, tear out; start up.
arranque, m. dash, sudden start; fit of anger.
arrastrar, v. drag.
arrebatar, v. snatch, grab.
arrebato, m. sudden attack, fit of anger.
arrecife, m. reef.
arreglar, v. arrange; repair, fix; adjust, settle.
arreglárselas, v. manage, shift for oneself.
arreglo, m. arrangement, settlement.
arremeter, v. attack.
arrendar, v. rent.
arrepentimiento, m. repentance.
arrepentirse, v. repent.
arrestar, v. arrest.
arriba, adv. up; upstairs.
arriendo, m. lease.
arriero, m. muleteer.
arriesgar, v. risk.
arrimarse, v. lean.
arrodillarse, v. kneel.
arrogancia, f. arrogance.
arrogante, a. arrogant.
arrojar, v. throw, hurl; shed.
arrollar, v. roll, coil.
arroyo, m. brook; gully; gutter.
arroz, m. rice.
arruga, f. ridge; wrinkle.
arrugar, v. wrinkle, crumple.
arruinar, v. ruin, destroy, wreck.
arsenal, m. arsenal; armory.
arsénico, m. arsenic.
arte, m. (f. in pl.) art, craft; wiliness.
arteria, f. artery.
artesa, f. trough.
artesano, m. artisan, craftsman.
ártico, a. arctic.
articulación, f. articulation; joint.
articular, v. articulate.
artículo, m. article.
artífice, m. & f. artisan.
artificial, a. artificial.
artificio, m. artifice, device.
artificioso, a. affected.
artillería, f. artillery.
artista, m. & f. artist.
artístico, a. artistic.
arzobispo, m. archbishop.
as, m. ace.
asado, m. roast.
asaltador, m. assailant.
asaltar, v. assail, attack.
asalto, m. assault. —**asaltar**, v.
asamblea, f. assembly.

asar, v. roast; broil, cook (meat).
asaz, adv. enough; quite.
ascender, v. ascend, go up; amount.
ascenso, m. ascent.
ascensor, m. elevator.
ascensorista, m. & f. (elevator) operator.
asco, m. nausea; disgusting thing. **qué a.**, how disgusting.
aseado, a. tidy. —**asear**, v.
asediar, v. besiege.
asedio, m. siege.
asegurar, v. assure; secure.
asegurarse, v. make sure.
asemejarse a, v. resemble.
asentar, v. settle; seat.
asentimiento, m. assent. — **asentir**, v.
aseo, m. neatness, tidiness.
aserción, f. assertion.
aserrar, v. saw.
asesinar, v. assassinate; murder, slay.
asesinato, m. assassination, murder.
asesino -na, n. murderer, assassin.
aseveración, f. assertion.
aseverar, v. assert.
asfalto, m. asphalt.
así, adv. so, thus, this way, that way. **a. como**, as well as. **a. que**, as soon as.
asiático -ca, a. & n. Asiatic.
asiduo, a. assiduous.
asiento, m. seat; chair; site.
asignar, v. assign; allot.
asilo, m. asylum, sanctuary.
asimilar, v. assimilate.
asir, v. grasp.
asistencia, f. attendance, presence.
asistir, v. be present, attend.
asno, m. donkey.
asociación, f. association.
asociado, m. associate, partner.
asociar, v. associate.
asolar, v. desolate; burn, parch.
asoleado, a. sunny.
asomar, v. appear, loom up, show up.
asombrar, v. astonish, amaze.
asombro, m. amazement, astonishment.
aspa, f. reel. —**aspar**, v.
aspecto, m. aspect.
aspereza, f. harshness.
áspero, a. rough, harsh.
aspiración, f. aspiration.
aspirador, m. vacuum cleaner.
aspirar, v. aspire.
aspirina, f. aspirin.
asqueroso, a. dirty, nasty, filthy.
asta, f. shaft.
asterisco, m. asterisk.
astilla, f. splinter, chip. —**astillar**, v.
astillero, m. dry dock.
astro, m. star.
astronauta, m. astronaut.

astronomía, f. astronomy.
astucia, f. cunning.
astuto, a. astute, sly, shrewd.
asumir, v. assume.
asunto, m. matter, affair, business; subject.
asustar, v. frighten, scare, startle.
atacar, v. attack, charge.
atajo, m. shortcut.
ataque, m. attack, charge; spell, stroke.
atar, v. tie, bind, fasten.
atareado, a. busy.
atascar, v. stall, stop, obstruct.
ataúd, m. casket, coffin.
atavío, m. dress; gear, equipment.
atemorizar, v. frighten.
atención, f. attention.
atender, v. heed; attend to, wait on.
atenerse a, v. count on, depend on.
atentado, m. crime, offense.
atento, a. attentive, courteous.
ateo, m. atheist.
aterrizar, v. land.
atesorar, v. hoard.
atestar, v. witness.
atestiguar, v. attest, testify.
atinar, v. hit upon.
atisbar, v. scrutinize, pry.
Atlántico, m. Atlantic.
atlántico, a. Atlantic.
atlas, m. atlas.
atleta, m. athlete.
atlético, a. athletic.
atletismo, m. athletics.
atmósfera, f. atmosphere.
atmosférico, a. atmospheric.
atómico, a. atomic.
átomo, m. atom.
atormentar, v. torment, plague.
atornillar, v. screw.
atracción, f. attraction.
atractivo, 1. a. attractive. **2.** m. attraction.
atraer, v. attract; lure.
atrapar, v. trap, catch.
atrás, adv. back; behind.
atrasado, a. belated; backward; slow (clock).
atrasar, v. delay, retard; be slow.
atraso, m. delay; backwardness; (pl.) arrears.
atravesar, v. cross.
atreverse, v. dare.
atrevido, a. daring, bold.
atrevimiento, m. boldness.
atribuir, v. attribute, ascribe.
atributo, m. attribute.
atrincherar, v. entrench.
atrocidad, f. atrocity, outrage.
atronar, v. deafen.
atropellar, v. trample; fell.
atroz, a. atrocious.
aturdir, v. daze, stun, bewilder.
audacia, f. audacity.
audaz, a. audacious, bold.
audible, a. audible.
audiovisual, a. audiovisual.
auditorio, m. audience.
aula, f. classroom, hall.

aullar, v. howl, bay.

aullido, m. howl.

aumentar, v. augment; increase, swell.

aun, aún, adv. still; even. **a. cuando,** even though, even if.

aunque, conj. although, though.

áureo, a. golden.

aureola, f. halo.

aurora, f. dawn.

ausencia, f. absence.

ausentarse, v. stay away.

ausente, a. absent.

auspicio, m. auspice.

austeridad, f. austerity.

austero, a. austere.

austriaco -ca, a. & n. Austrian.

auténtico, a. authentic.

auto, automóvil, m. auto, automobile.

autobús, m. bus.

automático, a. automatic.

autonomía, f. autonomy.

autor, m. author.

autoridad, f. authority.

autoritario, a. authoritative.

autorizar, v. authorize.

auxiliar, 1. a. auxiliary. **2.** v. assist, aid.

auxilio, m. aid, assistance.

avaluar, v. evaluate, appraise.

avance, m. advance. —**avanzar,** v.

avaricia, f. avarice.

avariento, a. miserly, greedy.

avaro -ra, a. & m. miser; miserly.

ave, f. bird.

avena, f. oat.

avenida, f. avenue; flood.

avenirse, v. compromise; agree.

aventajar, v. surpass, get ahead of.

aventar, v. fan; scatter.

aventura, f. adventure.

aventurar, v. venture, risk, gamble.

aventurero, a. & m. adventurous; adventurer.

avergonzado, a. ashamed, abashed.

avergonzar, v. shame, abash.

avería, f. damage. —**averiar,** v.

averiguar, v. ascertain, find out.

aversión, f. aversion.

avestruz, m. ostrich.

aviación, f. aviation.

aviador -ra, n. aviator.

ávido, a. avid; eager.

avión, m. airplane.

avisar, v. notify, let know; warn, advise.

aviso, m. notice, announcement; advertisement; warning.

avispa, f. wasp.

avivar, v. enliven, revive.

aya, f. governess.

ayatola, m. ayatollah.

ayer, adv. yesterday.

ayuda, f. help, aid. —**ayudar,** v.

ayudante, a. assistant, helper; adjutant.

ayuno, m. fast. —**ayunar,** v.

ayuntamiento, m. city hall.

azada, f., **azadón,** m. hoe.

azafata, f. stewardess, flight attendant.

azar, m. hazard, chance. **al a.,** at random.

azotar, v. whip, flog; belabor.

azote, m. scourge, lash.

azúcar, m. sugar.

azul, a. blue.

azulado, a. azure.

azulejo, m. tile; bluebird.

B

baba, f. drivel. —**babear,** v.

babador, m. bib.

babucha, f. slipper.

bacalao, m. codfish.

bacía, f. washbasin.

bacterias, f.pl. bacteria.

bacteriología, f. bacteriology.

bachiller -ra, n. bachelor (degree).

bahía, f. bay.

bailador -ra, n. dancer.

bailar, v. dance.

bailarín -ina, n. dancer.

baile, m. dancing, dance.

baja, f. fall (in price); (mil.) casualty.

bajar, v. lower; descend.

bajeza, f. baseness.

bajo, 1. prep. under, below. **2.** a. low; short; base.

bala, f. bullet; ball; bale.

balada, f. ballad.

balancear, v. balance; roll, swing, sway.

balanza, f. balance; scales.

balbuceo, m. stammer; babble. —**balbucear,** v.

balcón, m. balcony.

balde, m. bucket, pail. **de b.,** gratis. **en b.,** in vain.

balística, f. ballistics.

balompié, m. football.

balón, m. football; (auto.) balloon tire.

baloncesto, m. basketball.

balota, f. ballot, vote, —**balotar,** v.

balsa, f. raft.

bálsamo, m. balm.

baluarte, m. bulwark.

ballena, f. whale.

bambolearse, v. sway.

bambú, m. bamboo.

banal, a. banal, trite.

banana, f. banana.

banano, m. banana tree.

bancarrota, f. bankruptcy.

banco, m. bank; bench; school of fish.

banda, f. band.

bandada, f. covey; flock.

bandeja, f. tray.

bandera, f. flag; banner; ensign.

bandido, m. bandit.

bando, m. faction.

bandolero, m. bandit, robber.

banquero, m. banker.

banqueta, f. stool; (Mex.) sidewalk.

banquete, m. feast, banquet.

banquillo, m. stool.

bañera, f. bathtub.

baño, m. bath; bathroom.

bañar, v. bathe.

baraja, f. pack of cards; game of cards.

baranda, f. railing, banister.

barato, a. cheap.

barba, f. beard; chin.

barbacoa, f. barbecue; stretcher.

barbaridad, f. barbarity; (Am.) excess (in anything).

bárbaro, a. barbarous; crude.

barbería, f. barbershop.

barbero, m. barber.

barca, f. (small) boat.

barcaza, f. barge.

barco, m. ship, boat.

barniz, m. varnish. —**barnizar,** v.

barómetro, m. barometer.

barón, m. baron.

barquilla, f. (naut.) log.

barra, f. bar.

barraca, f. hut, shed.

barrear, v. bar, barricade.

barreno, m. blast, blasting. —**barrenar,** v.

barrer, v. sweep.

barrera, f. barrier.

barricada, f. barricade.

barriga, f. belly.

barril, m. barrel; cask.

barrio, m. district, ward, quarter.

barro, m. clay, mud.

base, f. base; basis. —**basar,** v.

bastante, 1. a. enough, plenty of. **2.** adv. enough; rather, quite.

bastar, v. suffice, be enough.

bastardo -a, a. & n. bastard.

bastear, v. baste.

bastidor, m. wing (in theater).

bastón, m. (walking) cane.

bastos, m.pl. clubs (cards).

basura, f. refuse, dirt; garbage; junk.

basurero, m. scavenger.

batalla, f. battle. —**batallar,** v.

batallón, m. battalion.

batata, f. sweet potato.

bate, m. bat. —**batear,** v.

batería, f. battery.

batido, m. (cooking) batter.

batir, v. beat; demolish; conquer.

baúl, m. trunk.

bautismo, m. baptism.

bautista, m. & f. Baptist.

bautizar, v. Christen, baptize.

bautizo, m. baptism.

baya, f. berry.

bayoneta, f. bayonet.

beato, a. blessed.

bebé, m. baby.

beber, v. drink.

bebible, a. drinkable.

bebida, f. drink, beverage.

beca, *f.* grant, scholarship.

becado -da, *n.* scholar.

becerro, *m.* calf; calfskin.

beldad, *f.* beauty.

belga, *a. & n.* Belgian.

Bélgica, *f.* Belgium.

belicoso, *a.* warlike.

beligerante, *a. & n.* belligerent.

bellaco, 1. *a.* sly, roguish. **2.** *m.* rogue.

belleza, *f.* beauty.

bello, *a.* beautiful.

bellota, *f.* acorn.

bendecir, *v.* bless.

bendición, *f.* blessing, benediction.

bendito, *a.* blessed.

beneficio, *m.* benefit. **—beneficiar,** *v.*

beneficioso, *a.* beneficial.

benevolencia, *f.* benevolence.

benévolo, *a.* benevolent.

benigno, *a.* benign.

beodo, *a.* drunk.

berenjena, *f.* eggplant.

beso, *m.* kiss. **—besar,** *v.*

bestia, *f.* beast, brute.

betabel, *m.* beet.

Biblia, *f.* Bible.

bíblico, *a.* Biblical.

biblioteca, *f.* library.

bicarbonato, *m.* bicarbonate.

bicicleta, *f.* bicycle.

bien, 1. *adv.* well. **2.** *n.* good; (*pl.*) possessions.

bienestar, *m.* well-being, welfare.

bienhechor -ra, *n.* benefactor.

bienvenida, *f.* welcome.

bienvenido, *a.* welcome.

biftec, *m.* steak.

bifurcación, *f.* fork. **—bifurcar,** *v.*

bigamía, *f.* bigamy.

bígamo -a, *n.* bigamist.

bigotes, *m.pl.* mustache.

bilis, *f.* bile.

billar, *m.* billiards.

billete, *m.* ticket; bank note, bill.

billón, *m.* billion.

biodegradable, *a.* biodegradable.

biografía, *f.* biography.

biología, *f.* biology.

biombo, *m.* screen.

bisel, *m.* bevel. **—biselar,** *v.*

bisonte, *m.* bison.

bisté, bistec, *m.* steak.

bizarro, *a.* brave; generous; smart.

bizcocho, *m.* biscuit, cake.

blanco, 1. *a.* white; blank. **2.** *m.* white; target.

blandir, *v.* brandish, flourish.

blando, *a.* soft.

blanquear, *v.* whiten; bleach.

blasfemar, *v.* blaspheme, curse.

blasfemia, *f.* blasphemy.

blindado, *a.* armored.

blindaje, *m.* armor.

bloque, *m.* block. **—bloquear,** *v.*

bloqueo, *m.* blockade. **—bloquear,** *v.*

blusa, *f.* blouse.

bobo -ba, *a. & n.* fool; foolish.

boca, *f.* mouth.

bocado, *m.* bit; bite, mouthful, morsel.

bocanada, *f.* puff (of smoke); mouthful (of liquor).

bocina, *f.* horn.

bochorno, *m.* sultry weather; embarrassment.

boda, *f.* wedding.

bodega, *f.* wine cellar; (naut.) hold; grocery store.

bofetada, f. bofetón, *m.* slap.

boga, *f.* vogue; fad.

bogar, *v.* row (a boat).

bohemio -a, *a. & n.* Bohemian.

boicoteo, *m.* boycott. **—boicotear,** *v.*

boina, *f.* beret.

bola, *f.* ball.

bolera, *f.* bowling alley.

boletín, *m.* bulletin.

boleto, *m.* ticket.

boliche, *m.* bowling alley.

boliviano -a, *a. & n.* Bolivian.

bolos, *m.pl.* bowling.

bolsa, *f.* purse; stock exchange.

bolsillo, *m.* pocket.

bollo, *m.* bun, loaf.

bomba, *f.* pump; bomb; gas station.

bombardear, *v.* bomb; bombard, shell.

bombear, *v.* pump.

bombero, *m.* fireman.

bombilla, *f.* (light) bulb.

bonanza, *f.* prosperity; fair weather.

bondad, *f.* kindness; goodness.

bondadoso, *a.* kind, kindly.

bonito, *a.* pretty.

bono, *m.* bonus; (fin.) bond.

boqueada, *f.* gasp; gape. **—boquear,** *v.*

boquilla, *f.* cigarette holder.

bordado, *m.,* **bordadura,** *f.* embroidery.

bordar, *v.* embroider.

borde, *m.* border, rim, edge, brink, ledge.

borla, *f.* tassel.

borracho, *a.* drunk.

borrachón, *m.* drunkard.

borrador, *m.* eraser.

borradura, *f.* erasure.

borrar, *v.* erase, rub out.

borrasca, *f.* squall, storm.

borrico, *m.* donkey.

bosque, *m.* forest, wood.

bostezo, *m.* yawn. **—bostezar,** *v.*

bota, *f.* boot.

botalón, *m.* (naut.) boom.

botánica, *f.* botany.

botar, *v.* throw out, throw away.

bote, *m.* boat; can, box.

botica, *f.* pharmacy, drugstore.

boticario, *m.* pharmacist, druggist.

botín, *m.* booty, plunder, spoils.

boto, *a.* dull, stupid.

botón, *m.* button.

botones, *m.* bellboy (in a hotel).

bóveda, *f.* vault.

boxeador, *m.* boxer.

boxeo, *m.* boxing. **—boxear,** *v.*

boya, *f.* buoy.

boyante, *a.* buoyant.

bozal, *m.* muzzle.

bramido, *m.* roar, bellow. **—bramar,** *v.*

brasileño -ña, *a. & n.* Brazilian.

bravata, *f.* bravado.

bravear, *v.* bully.

braza, *f.* fathom.

brazada, *f.* (swimming) stroke.

brazalete, *m.* bracelet.

brazo, *m.* arm.

brea, *f.* tar, pitch.

brecha, *f.* gap, breach.

bregar, *v.* scramble.

breña, *f.* rough country with brambly shrubs.

Bretaña, *f.* Britain.

breve, *a.* brief, short. **en b.,** shortly, soon.

brevedad, *f.* brevity.

bribón, *m.* rogue, rascal.

brida, *f.* bridle.

brigada, *f.* brigade.

brillante, 1. *a.* brilliant, shiny. **2.** *m.* diamond.

brillo, *m.* shine, glitter. **—brillar,** *v.*

brinco, *m.* jump; bounce, skip. **—brincar,** *v.*

brindis, *m.* toast. **—brindar,** *v.*

brío, *m.* vigor.

brioso, *a.* vigorous, spirited.

brisa, *f.* breeze.

británico, *a.* British.

brocado, *m.* brocade.

brocha, *f.* brush.

broche, *m.* brooch, clasp, pin.

broma, *f.* joke. **—bromear,** *v.*

bronce, *m.* bronze; brass.

bronquitis, *f.* bronchitis.

brotar, *v.* gush; sprout; bud.

brote, *m.* bud, shoot.

bruja, *f.* witch.

brújula, *f.* compass.

bruma, *f.* mist.

brumoso, *a.* misty.

brusco, *a.* brusque; abrupt, curt.

brutal, *a.* savage, brutal.

brutalidad, *f.* brutality.

bruto, 1. *a.* brutish; ignorant. **2.** *m.* blockhead.

bucear, *v.* dive.

bueno, *a.* good, fair; well (in health).

buey, *m.* ox, steer.

búfalo, *m.* buffalo.

bufanda, *f.* scarf.

bufón -ona, *n.* fool, buffoon, clown.

buho, *m.* owl.

buhonero, *m.* peddler, vender.

bujía, *f.* spark plug.

bulevar, *m.* boulevard.

bulto, *m.* bundle; lump.

bullicio, *m.* bustle, noise.

bullicioso, *a.* boisterous, noisy.

buñuelo, *m.* bun.

buque, *m.* ship.

burdo, *a.* coarse.

burgés -esa, *a. & n.* bourgeois.

burla, *f.* mockery; fun.

burlador, *m.* trickster, jokester.

burlar, *v.* mock, deride.

burlarse de, *v.* scoff at; make fun of.

burro, *m.* donkey.

busca, *f.* search, pursuit, quest.

buscar, *v.* seek, look for; look up.

busto, *m.* bust.

butaca, *f.* armchair; (theat.) orchestra seat.

buzo, *m.* diver.

buzón, *m.* mailbox.

C

cabal, *a.* exact; thorough.

cabalgar, *v.* ride horseback.

caballeresco, *a.* gentlemanly, chivalrous.

caballería, *f.* cavalry; chivalry.

caballeriza, *f.* stable.

caballero, *m.* gentleman; knight.

caballete, *m.* sawhorse; easel; ridge (of roof).

caballo, *m.* horse.

cabaña, *f.* cabin; booth.

cabecear, *v.* pitch (as a ship).

cabecera, *f.* head (of bed, table).

cabello, *m.* hair.

caber, *v.* fit into, be contained in. **no cabe duda,** there is no doubt.

cabeza, *f.* head; warhead.

cabildo, *m.* city hall.

cabizbajo, *a.* downcast.

cablegrama, *m.* cablegram.

cabo, *m.* end; (geog.) cape; (mil.) corporal. **llevar a c.,** carry out, accomplish.

cabra, *f.* goat.

cacahuete, *m.* peanut.

cacao, *m.* cocoa; chocolate.

cacerola, *f.* pan, casserole.

cachorro, *m.* cub; puppy.

cada, *a.* each, every.

cadáver, *m.* corpse.

cadena, *f.* chain.

cadera, *f.* hip.

cadete, *m.* cadet.

caer, *v.* fall.

café, *m.* coffee; café.

cafetal, *m.* coffee plantation.

cafetera, *f.* coffee pot.

caída, *f.* fall, drop; collapse.

caimán, *m.* alligator.

caja, *f.* box, case.

cajero -ra, *n.* cashier.

cajón, *m.* drawer.

cal, *f.* lime.

calabaza, *f.* calabash, pumpkin.

calabozo, *m.* jail, cell.

calambre, *m.* cramp.

calamidad, *f.* calamity, disaster.

calcetín, *m.* sock.

calcio, *m.* calcium.

calcular, *v.* calculate, figure.

cálculo, *m.* calculation, estimate.

caldera, *f.* kettle, caldron; boiler.

caldo, *m.* broth.

calefacción, *f.* heat, heating.

calendario, *m.* calendar.

calentar, *v.* heat, warm.

calidad, *f.* quality, grade.

caliente, *a.* hot, warm.

calificar, *v.* qualify.

calma, *f.* calm, quiet.

calmado, *a.* calm.

calmante, *a.* soothing, calming.

calmar, *v.* calm, quiet, lull, soothe.

calor, *n.* heat, warmth. **tener c.,** to be hot, warm; feel hot, warm. **hacer c.,** to be hot, warm (weather).

calorífero, *m.* radiator.

calumnia, *f.* slander. **—calumniar,** *v.*

caluroso, *a.* warm, hot.

calvario, *m.* Calvary.

calvo, *a.* bald.

calzado, *m.* footwear.

calzar, *v.* wear (as shoes).

calzoncillos, *m.pl.* shorts.

calzones, *m.pl.* trousers.

callado, *a.* silent, quiet.

callarse, *v.* quiet down; keep still; stop talking.

calle, *f.* street.

callejón, *m.* alley.

callo, *m.* callus, corn.

cama, *f.* bed.

cámara, *f.* chamber; camera.

camarada, *m. & f.* comrade.

camarera, *f.* chambermaid; waitress.

camarero, *m.* steward; waiter.

camarón, *m.* shrimp.

camarote, *m.* stateroom, berth.

cambiar, *v.* exchange, change, trade; cash.

cambio, *m.* change, exchange. **en c.,** on the other hand.

cambista, *m.* banker, broker.

cambur, *m.* banana.

camello, *m.* camel.

camilla, *f.* stretcher.

caminar, *v.* walk.

caminata, *f.* tramp, hike.

camino, *m.* road; way.

camión, *m.* truck.

camisa, *f.* shirt.

camisería, *f.* haberdashery.

camiseta, *f.* undershirt; T-shirt.

campamento, *m.* camp.

campana, *f.* bell.

campanario, *m.* bell tower, steeple.

campaneo, *m.* chime.

campaña, *f.* campaign.

campeón, *m.* champion.

campeonato, *m.* championship.

campesino -na, *n.* peasant.

campestre, *a.* country, rural.

campo, *m.* field; (the) country.

Canadá, *m.* Canada.

canadiense, *a. & n.* Canadian.

canal, *m.* canal; channel.

canalla, *f.* rabble.

canario, *m.* canary.

canasta, *f.* basket.

cáncer, *m.* cancer.

canciller, *m.* chancellor.

canción, *f.* song.

candado, *m.* padlock.

candela, *f.* fire; light; candle.

candelero, *m.* candlestick.

candidato -ta, *n.* candidate; applicant.

candidatura, *f.* candidacy.

canela, *f.* cinnamon.

cangrejo, *m.* crab.

caníbal, *m.* cannibal.

canje, *m.* exchange, trade. **— canjear,** *v.*

cano, *a.* gray.

canoa, *f.* canoe.

cansado, *a.* tired, weary.

cansancio, *m.* fatigue.

cansar, *v.* tire, fatigue, wear out.

cantante, *m. & f.* singer.

cantar, 1. *m.* song. 2. *v.* sing.

cántaro, *m.* pitcher.

cantera, *f.* (stone) quarry.

cantidad, *f.* quantity, amount.

cantina, *f.* bar, tavern; restaurant.

canto, *m.* chant, song, singing; edge.

caña, *f.* cane, reed; sugar cane.

cañón, *m.* canyon; cannon; gun barrel.

caoba, *f.* mahogany.

caos, *m.* chaos.

caótico, *a.* chaotic.

capa, *f.* cape, cloak; coat (of paint).

capacidad, *f.* capacity; capability.

capacitar, *v.* enable.

capataz, *m.* foreman.

capaz, *a.* capable, able.

capellán, *m.* chaplain.

caperuza, *f.* hood.

capilla, *f.* chapel.

capital, *m.* capital. *f.* capital (city).

capitalista, *a. & n.* capitalist.

capitán, *m.* captain.

capitular, *v.* yield.

capítulo, *m.* chapter.

capota, *f.* hood.

capricho, *m.* caprice; fancy, whim.

caprichoso, *a.* capricious.

cápsula, *f.* capsule.

capturar, *v.* capture.

capucha, *f.* hood.

capullo, *m.* cocoon.

cara, *f.* face.

caracol, *m.* snail.

carácter, *m.* character.

característica, *f.* characteristic.

característico, *a.* characteristic.

caramba, mild exclamation.

caramelo, *m.* caramel; candy.

carátula, *f.* dial.

caravana, *f.* caravan.

carbón, *m.* carbon; coal.

carbonizar, v. char.

carburador, m. carburetor.

carcajada, f. burst of laughter.

cárcel, f. prison, jail.

carcelero, m. jailer.

carcinogénico, a. carcinogenic.

cardenal, m. cardinal.

carecer, v. lack.

carestía, f. scarcity; famine.

carga, f. cargo; load, burden; freight.

cargar, v. carry; load; charge.

cargo, m. load; charge, office.

caricia, f. caress.

caridad, f. charity.

cariño, m. affection, fondness.

cariñoso, a. affectionate, fond.

carisma, m. charisma.

caritativo, a. charitable.

carmesí, a. & m. crimson.

carnaval, m. carnival.

carne, f. meat, flesh; pulp.

carnero, m. ram; mutton.

carnicería, f. meat market; massacre.

carnicero, m. butcher.

carnívoro, a. carnivorous.

caro, a. dear, costly, expensive.

carpa, f. tent.

carpeta, f. folder; briefcase.

carpintero, m. carpenter.

carrera, f. race; career.

carreta, f. wagon, cart.

carrete, m. reel, spool.

carretera, f. road, highway.

carril, m. rail.

carrillo, m. cart (for baggage or shopping).

carro, m. car, automobile; cart.

carroza, f. chariot.

carruaje, m. carriage.

carta, f. letter; (pl.) cards.

cartel, m. placard, poster; cartel.

cartera, f. pocketbook, handbag, wallet; portfolio.

cartero, m. mailman, postman.

cartón, m. cardboard.

cartucho, m. cartridge; cassette.

casa, f. house, dwelling; home.

casaca, f. dress coat.

casado, a. married.

casamiento, m. marriage.

casar, v. marry, marry off.

casarse, v. get married. c. con, marry.

cascabel, m. jingle bell.

cascada, f. waterfall, cascade.

cascajo, m. gravel.

cascanueces, m. nutcracker.

cascar, v. crack, break, burst.

cáscara, f. shell, rind, husk.

casco, m. helmet; hull.

casera, f. landlady; housekeeper.

caserío, m. settlement.

casero, a. 1. homemade. 2. m. landlord, superintendent.

caseta, f. cottage, hut.

casi, adv. almost, nearly.

casilla, f. booth; ticket office; pigeonhole.

casino, m. club; clubhouse.

caso, m. case. hacer c. a, pay attention to.

casorio, m. informal wedding.

caspa, f. dandruff.

casta, f. caste.

castaña, f. chestnut.

castaño, 1. a. brown. 2. m. chestnut tree.

castañuela, f. castanet.

castellano, a. & m. Castillian.

castidad, f. chastity.

castigar, v. punish.

castigo, m. punishment.

castillo, m. castle.

castizo, a. pure, genuine; noble.

casto, a. chaste.

castor, m. beaver.

casual, adj. accidental, coincidental.

casualidad, f. coincidence. por c., by chance.

casuca, f. hut, shanty, hovel.

catadura, f. act of tasting; appearance.

catalán, a. & m. Catalonian.

catálogo, m. catalogue. —catalogar, v.

catar, v. taste; examine, try; bear in mind.

catarata, f. cataract, waterfall.

catarro, m. head cold.

catástrofe, m. catastrophe.

catecismo, m. catechism.

cátedra, f. professorship.

catedral, f. cathedral.

catedrático, m. professor.

categoría, f. category.

categórico, a. categorical.

catequizar, v. catechize.

catolicismo, m. Catholicism.

católico -ca, a. & n. Catholic.

catorce, a. & pron. fourteen.

catre, m. cot.

cauce, m. riverbed; ditch.

caución, f. precaution; security, guarantee.

cauchal, m. rubber plantation.

caucho, m. rubber.

caudal, m. means, fortune; (pl.) holdings.

caudaloso, a. prosperous, rich.

caudillaje, m. leadership; tyranny.

caudillo, m. leader, chief.

causa, f. cause. —causar, v.

cautela, f. caution.

cauteloso, a. cautious.

cautivar, v. captivate.

cautiverio, m. captivity.

cautividad, f. captivity.

cautivo -va, a. & n. captive.

cauto, a. cautious.

cavar, v. dig.

caverna, f. cavern, cave.

cavernoso, a. cavernous.

cavidad, f. cavity, hollow.

cavilar, v. criticize, cavil.

cayado, m. shepherd's staff.

cayo, m. small rocky islet, key.

caza, f. hunting, pursuit, game.

cazador, m. hunter.

cazar, v. hunt.

cazatorpedero, m. destroyer.

cazo, m. ladle, dipper; pot.

cazuela, f. crock.

cebada, f. barley.

cebo, m. bait. —cebar, v.

cebolla, f. onion.

ceceo, m. lisp. —cecear, v.

cecina, f. dried beef.

cedazo, m. sieve, sifter.

ceder, v. cede; transfer; yield.

cedro, m. cedar.

cédula, f. decree. c. personal, identification card.

céfiro, m. zephyr.

cegar, v. blind.

ceguedad, ceguera, f. blindness.

ceja, f. eyebrow.

cejar, v. go backwards; yield, retreat.

celada, f. trap; ambush.

celaje, m. appearance of the sky.

celar, v. watch carefully, guard.

celda, f. cell.

celebración, f. celebration.

celebrante, m. officiating priest.

celebrar, v. celebrate, observe.

célebre, a. celebrated, noted, famous.

celebridad, f. fame; celebrity; pageant.

celeridad, f. speed, rapidity.

celeste, a. celestial.

celestial, a. heavenly.

célibe, 1. a. unmarried. 2. m. & f. unmarried person.

celo, m. zeal; (pl.) jealousy.

celosía, f. Venetian blind.

celoso, a. jealous; zealous.

céltico, a. Celtic.

célula, f. (biol.) cell.

celuloide, m. celluloid.

cellisca, f. sleet. —cellisquear, v.

cementar, v. cement.

cementerio, m. cemetery.

cemento, m. cement.

cena, f. supper.

cenagal, m. swamp, marsh.

cenagoso, a. swampy, marshy, muddy.

cenar, v. dine, eat.

cencerro, m. cowbell.

cendal, m. thin, light cloth; gauze.

cenicero, m. ashtray.

ceniciento, a. ashen.

cenit, m. zenith.

ceniza, f. ash, ashes.

censo, m. census.

censor, m. critic.

censura, f. reproof, censure; censorship.

censurable, a. objectionable.

censurar, v. censure, criticize.

centavo, m. cent.

centella, f. thunderbolt, lightning.

centellear, v. twinkle, sparkle.

centelleo, m. sparkle.

centenar, m. (a) hundred.

centenario, m. centennial, centenary.

centeno, m. rye.

centígrado, *a.* centigrade.
centímetro, *m.* centimeter.
céntimo, *m.* cent.
centinela, *m.* sentry, guard.
central, *a.* central.
centrar, *v.* center.
céntrico, *a.* central.
centro, *m.* center.
centroamericano -na, *a. & n.* Central American.
ceñidor, *m.* belt, sash; girdle.
ceñir, *v.* gird.
ceño, *m.* frown.
ceñudo, *a.* frowning, grim.
cepa, *f.* stump.
cepillo, *m.* brush; plane. — **cepillar,** *v.*
cera, *f.* wax.
cerámica, *m.* ceramics.
cerca, 1. *adv.* near. **2.** *f.* fence, hedge.
cercado, *m.* enclosure; garden.
cercamiento, *m.* enclosure.
cercanía, *f.* proximity.
cercano, *a.* near, nearby.
cercar, *v.* surround.
cercenar, *v.* clip; lessen, reduce.
cerciorar, *v.* make sure; affirm.
cerco, *m.* hoop; siege.
cerda, *f.* bristle.
cerdo, *m.* hog.
cerdoso, *a.* bristly.
cereal, *a. & m.* cereal.
cerebro, *m.* brain.
ceremonia, *f.* ceremony.
ceremonial, *a. & m.* ceremonial, ritual.
ceremonioso, *a.* ceremonious.
cereza, *f.* cherry.
cerilla, *f.* **cerillo,** *m.* match.
cerner, *v.* sift.
cero, *m.* zero.
cerrado, *a.* cloudy; obscure; stupid.
cerradura, *f.* lock.
cerrajero, *m.* locksmith.
cerrar, *v.* close, shut.
cerro, *m.* hill.
cerrojo, *m.* latch, bolt.
certamen, *m.* contest; competition.
certero, *a.* accurate, exact; certain, sure.
certeza, *f.* certainty.
certidumbre, *f.* certainty.
certificado, *m.* certificate.
certificar, *v.* certify; register (a letter).
cerúleo, *a.* cerulean, sky-blue.
cervecería, *f.* brewery; beer saloon.
cervecero, *m.* brewer.
cerveza, *f.* beer.
cesante, *a.* unemployed.
cesar, *v.* cease.
césped, *m.* sod, lawn.
cesta, *f.,* **cesto,** *m.* basket.
cetrino, *a.* yellow, lemon-colored.
cetro, *m.* scepter.
cicatero, *a.* stingy.
cicatriz, *f.* scar.
cicatrizar, *v.* heal.
ciclamato, *m.* cyclamate.

ciclo, *m.* cycle.
ciclón, *m.* cyclone.
ciego -ga, 1. *a.* blind. **2.** *n.* blind person.
cielo, *m.* heaven; sky, heavens; ceiling.
ciempiés, *m.* centipede.
cien, ciento, *a. & pron.* hundred. **por c.,** per cent.
ciénaga, *f.* swamp, marsh.
ciencia, *f.* science.
cieno, *m.* mud.
científico, 1. *a.* scientific. **2.** *n.* scientist.
cierre, *m.* fastener, snap, clasp.
cierto, *a.* certain, sure, true.
ciervo, *m.* deer.
cierzo, *m.* northerly wind.
cifra, *f.* cipher, number. — **cifrar,** *v.*
cigarra, *f.* locust.
cigarrera, cigarrillera, *f.* cigarette case.
cigarrillo, *m.* cigarette.
cigarro, *m.* cigar; cigarette.
cilíndrico, *a.* cylindrical.
cilindro, *m.* cylinder.
cima, *f.* summit, peak.
cimarrón, 1. *a.* wild, untamed. **2.** *m.* runaway slave.
címbalo, *m.* cymbal.
cimbrar, *v.* shake, brandish.
cimientos, *m.pl.* foundation.
cinc, *m.* zinc.
cincel, *m.* chisel. — **cincelar,** *v.*
cinco, *a. & pron.* five.
cincuenta, *a. & pron.* fifty.
cincha, *f.* (harness) cinch. — **cinchar,** *v.*
cine, *m.* movies; movie theater.
cíngulo, *m.* girdle.
cínico, *a. & n.* cynical; cynic.
cinta, *f.* ribbon, tape; (movie) film.
cintilar, *v.* glitter, sparkle.
cinto, *m.* belt; girdle.
cintura, *f.* waist.
cinturón, *m.* belt.
ciprés, *m.* cypress.
circo, *m.* circus.
circuito, *m.* circuit.
circulación, *f.* circulation.
circular, 1. *a. & m.* circular. **2.** *v.* circulate.
círculo *m.* circle, club.
circundante, *a.* surrounding.
circundar, *v.* encircle, surround.
circunferencia, *f.* circumference.
circunlocución, *n.* circumlocution.
circunscribir, *v.* circumscribe.
circunspección, *n.* decorum, propriety.
circunspecto, *a.* circumspect.
circunstancia, *f.* circumstance.
circunstante, *m.* bystander.
circunvecino, *a.* neighboring, adjacent.
cirio, *m.* candle.
ciruela, *f.* plum; prune.
cirugía, *f.* surgery.
cirujano, *m.* surgeon.

cisne, *m.* swan.
cisterna, *f.* cistern.
cita, *f.* citation; appointment, date.
citación, *f.* citation; (legal) summons.
citar, *v.* cite, quote; summon; make an appointment with.
ciudad, *f.* city.
ciudadanía, *f.* citizenship.
ciudadano -na, *n.* citizen.
ciudadela, *f.* fortress, citadel.
cívico, *a.* civic.
civil, *a. & n.* civil; civilian.
civilidad, *f.* politeness, civility.
civilización, *f.* civilization.
civilizador, *a.* civilizing.
civilizar, *v.* civilize.
cizallas, *f.pl.* shears. — **cizallar,** *v.*
cizaña, *f.* weed; vice.
clamar, *v.* clamor.
clamor, *m.* clamor.
clamoreo, *m.* persistent clamor.
clamoroso, *a.* clamorous.
clandestino, *a.* secret, clandestine.
clara, *f.* white (of egg).
claraboya, *m.* skylight; bull's-eye.
clarear, *v.* clarify; become light, dawn.
claridad, *f.* clarity.
clarificar, *v.* clarify.
clarín, *m.* bugle, trumpet.
clarinete, *m.* clarinet.
clarividencia, *f.* clairvoyance.
claro, *a.* clear; bright; light (in color); of course.
clase, *f.* class; classroom; kind, sort.
clásico, *a.* classic, classical.
clasificar, *v.* classify, rank.
claustro, *m.* cloister.
cláusula, *f.* clause.
clausura, *f.* cloister; inner sanctum.
clavado, *m.* dive.
clavar, *v.* nail, peg, pin.
clave, *f.* code; (mus.) key.
clavel, *m.* carnation.
clavetear, *v.* nail.
clavija, *f.* pin, peg.
clavijero, *m.* hatrack.
clavo, *m.* nail, spike.
clemencia, *f.* clemency.
clemente, *a.* merciful.
clerecía, *f.* clergy.
clerical, *a.* clerical.
clérigo, *m.* clergyman.
clero, *m.* clergy.
cliente, *m. & f.* customer, client.
clientela, *f.* clientele, practice.
clima, *m.* climate.
clímax, *m.* climax.
clínica, *f.* clinic.
clíper, *m.* clipper ship.
cloaca, *f.* sewer.
cloquear, *v.* cluck, cackle.
cloqueo, *m.* cluck.
cloro, *m.* chlorine.
club, *m.* club, association.
clueca, *f.* brooding hen.

coacción, n. compulsion.

coagular, v. coagulate, clot.

coágulo, m. clot.

coalición, f. coalition.

coartar, v. limit.

cobarde, a. & n. cowardly; coward.

cobardía, f. cowardice.

cobertizo, m. shed.

cobertor, m., **cobija,** f. blanket.

cobertura, f. cover, wrapping.

cobijar, v. cover; protect.

cobrador, m. collector.

cobranza, f. collection or recovery of money.

cobrar, v. collect; charge; cash.

cobre, m. copper.

cobrizo, a. coppery.

cobro, m. collection or recovery of money.

coca, f. coca leaves.

cocaína, f. cocaine.

cocal, m. coconut plantation.

cocear, v. kick; resist.

cocer, v. cook, boil, bake.

cocido, m. stew.

cociente, m. quotient.

cocimiento, m. cooking.

cocina, f. kitchen.

cocinar, v. cook.

cocinero -ra, n. cook.

coco, m. coconut; coconut tree.

cocodrilo, m. crocodile.

coctel, m. cocktail.

coche, m. coach; car, automobile.

cochera, f. garage.

cochero, m. coachman; cab driver.

cochinada, f. filth; herd of swine.

cochino, m. pig, swine.

codazo, m. nudge with the elbow.

codicia, f. avarice, greed; lust.

codiciar, v. covet.

codicioso, a. covetous; greedy.

código, m. (law) code.

codo, m. elbow.

codorniz, f. quail.

coetáneo, a. contemporary.

cofrade, m. fellow member of a club, etc.

cofre, m. coffer; chest; trunk.

coger, v. catch; pick; take.

cogote, m. nape.

cohecho, m. bribe. —**cohechar,** v.

coheredero, m. co-heir.

coherente, a. coherent.

cohesión, f. cohesion.

cohete, m. fire cracker, rocket.

cohibición, n. restraint; repression.

cohibir, v. restrain; repress.

coincidencia, f. coincidence.

coincidir, v. coincide.

cojear, v. limp.

cojera, m. limp.

cojín, m. cushion.

cojinete, m. small cushion, pad.

cojo, a. lame.

col, f. cabbage.

cola, f. tail; glue; line, queue. **hacer c.,** stand in line.

colaboración, f. collaboration.

colaborar, v. collaborate.

coladera, f. strainer.

colador, m. colander, strainer.

colapso, m. collapse, prostration.

colar, v. strain; drain.

colateral, a. collateral.

colcha, f. bedspread, quilt.

colchón, m. mattress.

colear, v. wag the tail.

colección, f. collection, set.

coleccionar, v. collect.

colecta, f. collection (a prayer).

colectivo, a. collective.

colector, m. collector.

colega, m. & f. colleague.

colegial, m. college student.

colegiatura, f. college scholarship.

colegio, m. (private) school, college.

colegir, v. infer, deduce.

cólera, f. rage, wrath.

colérico, adj. angry, irritated.

coleto, m. leather jacket.

colgador, m. rack, hanger.

colgaduras, f.pl. drapery.

colgante, a. hanging.

colgar, v. hang up, suspend.

colibrí, m. hummingbird.

coliflor, m. cauliflower.

coligarse, v. band together, unite.

colilla, f. butt of a cigar or cigarette.

colina, f. hill, hillock.

colinabo, m. turnip.

colindante, a. neighboring, adjacent.

colindar, v. neighbor, abut.

coliseo, m. theater; coliseum.

colisión, f. collision.

colmar, v. heap up, fill liberally.

colmena, f. hive.

colmillo, m. eyetooth; tusk; fang.

colmo, m. height, peak, extreme.

colocación, f. place, position; employment, job; arrangement.

colocar, v. place, locate, put, set.

colombiano -na, a. & n. Colombian.

colon, m. colon (of intestines).

colonia, f. colony.

colonial, a. colonial.

colonización, f. colonization.

colonizador, m. colonizer.

colonizar, v. colonize.

colono, m. colonist; tenant farmer.

coloquio, m. conversation, talk.

color, m. color. —**colorar,** v.

coloración, f. coloring.

colorado, a. red, ruddy.

colorar, v. color, paint; dye.

colorete, m. rouge.

colorido, m. color, coloring. —**colorir,** v.

colosal, a. colossal.

columbrar, v. discern.

columna, f. column, pillar, shaft.

columpiar, v. swing.

columpio, m. swing.

collado, m. hillock.

collar, m. necklace; collar.

coma, f. coma; comma.

comadre, f. midwife; gossip; close friend.

comadreja, n. weasel.

comandancia, m. command; command post.

comandante, m. commandant; commander; major.

comandar, v. command.

comandita, f. silent partnership.

comanditario, m. silent partner.

comando, m. command.

comarca, f. region; border, boundary.

comba, f. bulge.

combar, v. bend; bulge.

combate, m. combat. —**combatir,** v.

combatiente, a. & m. combatant.

combinación, f. combination; (lady's) slip.

combinar, v. combine.

combustible, 1. a. combustible. **2.** m. fuel.

combustión, f. combustion.

comedero, m. trough.

comedia, f. comedy; play.

comediante, m. actor; comedian.

comedido, a. polite, courteous; obliging.

comedirse, v. to be polite or obliging.

comedor, m. dining room. **coche c.,** dining car.

comendador, m. commander.

comensal, m. member of a household.

comentador, m. commentator.

comentario, m. commentary.

comento, m. comment. —**comentar,** v.

comenzar, v. begin, start, commence.

comer, v. eat, dine.

comercial, a. commercial.

comerciante, m. merchant, trader, businessman.

comerciar, v. trade, deal, do business.

comercio, m. commerce, trade, business.

comestible, 1. a. edible. **2.** m. (pl.) groceries, provisions.

cometa, m. comet. f. kite.

cometer, v. commit.

cometido, m. commission; duty; task.

comezón, f. itch.

comicios, m.pl. primary elections.

cómico -ca, *a. & n.* comic, comical; comedian.

comida, *f.* food; dinner; meal.

comidilla, *f.* light meal; gossip.

comienzo, *m.* beginning.

comilitona, *f.* banquet.

comilón, *m.* glutton; heavy eater.

comillas, *f.pl.* quotation marks.

comisario, *m.* commissary.

comisión, *f.* commission. — **comisionar,** *v.*

comisionado, *m.* agent, commissioner.

comisionar, *v.* commission.

comiso, *m.* (law) confiscation of illegal goods.

comistrajo, *m.* mess, hodge-podge.

comité, *m.* committee.

comitiva, *f.* retinue.

como, *conj. & adv.* like, as.

como, *adv.* how.

cómoda, *f.* bureau, chest (of drawers).

cómodamente, *adv.* conveniently.

comodatario, *m.* pawnbroker.

comodato, *m.* loan.

comodidad, *f.* convenience, comfort; commodity.

cómodo, *a.* comfortable; convenient.

comodoro, *m.* commodore.

compacto, *a.* compact.

compadecer, *v.* be sorry for, pity.

compadraje, *m.* clique.

compadre, *m.* close friend.

compaginar, *v.* put in order; arrange.

companaje, *m.* cold lunch.

compañerismo, *m.* companionship.

compañero -ra, *n.* companion, partner.

compañía, *f.* company.

comparable, *a.* comparable.

comparación, *f.* comparison.

comparar, *v.* compare.

comparativamente, *adv.* comparatively.

comparativo, *a.* comparative.

comparecer, *v.* appear.

comparendo, *m.* summons.

comparsa, *f.* carnival masquerade; retinue.

compartimiento, *m.* compartment.

compartir, *v.* share.

compás, *m.* compass; beat, rhythm.

compasar, *v.* measure exactly.

compasible, *a.* compassionate.

compasión, *f.* compassion.

compasivo, *a.* compassionate.

compatibilidad, *f.* compatibility.

compatible, *a.* compatible.

compatriota, *m. & f.* compatriot.

compeler, *v.* compel.

compendiar, *v.* summarize; abridge.

compendiariamente, *adv.* briefly.

compendio, *m.* summary; abridgment.

compendiosamente, *adv.* briefly.

compensación, *f.* compensation.

compensar, *v.* compensate.

competencia, *f.* competence; competition.

competente, *a.* competent.

competentemente, *adv.* competently.

competición, *f.* competition.

competidor, *a. & n.* competitive; competitor.

competir, *v.* compete.

compilación, *f.* compilation.

compilar, *v.* compile.

compinche, *m.* pal.

complacencia, *f.* complacency.

complacer, *v.* please, oblige, humor.

complaciente, *a.* pleasing, obliging.

complejidad, *f.* complexity.

complejo, *a. & n.* complex.

complemento, *m.* complement; (gram.) object.

completamente, *adv.* completely.

completamiento, *m.* completion, finish.

completar, *v.* complete.

completo, *a.* complete, full, perfect.

complexidad, *f.* complexity.

complexión, *f.* nature, temperament.

complexo, *a.* complex, intricate.

complicación, *f.* complication.

complicado, *a.* complicated.

complicar, *v.* complicate.

cómplice, *m. & f.* accomplice, accessory.

complicidad, *f.* complicity.

complot, *m.* conspiracy.

componedor, *m.* typesetter.

componenda, *f.* compromise; settlement.

componente, *a. & m.* component.

componer, *v.* compose; fix, repair.

componible, *a.* reparable.

comportable, *a.* endurable.

comportamiento, *m.* behavior.

comportarse, *v.* behave.

comporte, *m.* behavior.

composición, *f.* composition.

compositivo, *a.* synthetic; composite.

compositor -ra, *n.* composer.

compostura, *f.* composure; repair; neatness.

compota, *f.* (fruit) sauce.

compra, *f.* purchase. **ir de compras,** to go shopping.

comprador -ra, *n.* buyer, purchaser.

comprar, *v.* buy, purchase.

comprehensivo, *a.* comprehensive.

comprender, *v.* comprehend, understand; include, comprise.

comprensibilidad, *f.* comprehensibility.

comprensible, *a.* understandable.

comprensión, *f.* comprehension, understanding.

comprensivo, *a.* comprehensive.

compresa, *f.* medical compress.

compresión, *f.* compression.

comprimir, *v.* compress.

comprobación, *f.* proof.

comprobante, **1.** *a.* proving. **2.** *m.* proof.

comprobar, *v.* prove; verify, check.

comprometer, *v.* compromise.

comprometerse, *v.* become engaged.

compromiso, *m.* compromise; engagement.

compropietario, *m.* co-owner.

compuerta, *f.* floodgate.

compuesto, *a.* composition; compound.

compulsión, *f.* compulsion.

compulsivo, *a.* compulsive.

compunción, *f.* compunction.

compungirse, *v.* regret, feel remorse.

computación, *f.* computation.

computador, *m.* computer.

computar, *v.* compute.

cómputo, *m.* computation.

comulación, *f.* cumulation.

comulgar, *v.* take communion.

comulgatorio, *m.* communion altar.

común, *a.* common, usual.

comunal, *m.* common people.

comunero, *m.* commoner.

comunicable, *a.* communicable.

comunicación, *f.* communication.

comunicante, *m. & f.* communicant.

comunicar, *v.* communicate; convey.

comunicativo, *a.* communicative.

comunidad, *f.* community.

comunión, *f.* communion.

comunismo, *m.* communism.

comunista, *a. & n.* communistic; communist.

comúnmente, *adv.* commonly; usually; often.

con, *prep.* with.

concavidad, *f.* concavity.

cóncavo, **1.** *a.* concave. **2.** *m.* concavity.

concebible, *a.* conceivable.

concebir, *v.* conceive.

conceder, *v.* concede.

concejal, *m.* councilman.

concejo, *m.* city council.

concento, *m.* harmony.

concentración, *f.* concentration.

concentrar, *v.* concentrate.

concepción, *f.* conception.
conceptible, *a.* conceivable.
concepto, *m.* concept; opinion.
concerniente, *a.* concerning.
concernir, *v.* concern.
concertar, *v.* arrange.
concertina, *f.* concertina.
concesión, *f.* concession.
conciencia, *f.* conscience; consciousness; conscientiousness.
concienzudo, *a.* conscientious.
concierto, *m.* concert.
conciliación, *f.* conciliation.
conciliador, *m.* conciliator.
conciliar, *v.* conciliate.
concilio, *m.* council.
concisión, *f.* conciseness.
conciso, *a.* concise.
concitar, *v.* instigate, stir up.
conciudadano, *m.* fellow citizen.
concluir, *v.* conclude.
conclusión, *f.* conclusion.
conclusivo, *a.* conclusive.
concluso, *a.* concluded; closed.
concluyentemente, *adv.* conclusively.
concomitante, *a.* concomitant, attendant.
concordador, *m.* moderator; conciliator.
concordancia, *f.* agreement, concord.
concordar, *v.* agree; put or be in accord.
concordia, *f.* concord, agreement.
concretamente, *adv.* concretely.
concretar, *v.* summarize.
concretarse, *v.* limit oneself to.
concreto, *a. & m.* concrete.
concubina, *f.* concubine, mistress.
concupiscente, *a.* lustful.
concurrencia, *f.* assembly; attendance; competition.
concurrente, *a.* concurrent.
concurrido, *a.* heavily attended or patronized.
concurrir, *v.* concur; attend.
concurso, *m.* contest, competition; meeting.
concha, *f.* (sea) shell.
conde, *m.* (title) count.
condecente, *a.* appropriate, proper.
condecoración, *f.* decoration; medal; badge.
condecorar, *v.* decorate with a medal.
condena, *f.* prison sentence.
condenación, *f.* condemnation.
condenar, *v.* condemn; damn; sentence.
condensación, *f.* condensation.
condensar, *v.* condense.
condesa, *f.* countess.
condescendencia, *f.* condescension.
condescender, *v.* condescend, deign.
condescendiente, *a.* condescending.

condición, *f.* condition.
condicional, *a.* conditional.
condicionalmente, *adv.* conditionally.
condimentar, *v.* season, flavor.
condimento, *m.* condiment, seasoning, dressing.
condiscípulo, *m.* schoolmate.
condolencia, *f.* condolence, sympathy.
condolerse de, *v.* sympathize with.
condómino, *m.* co-owner.
condonar, *v.* condone.
cóndor, *m.* condor (bird).
conducción, *f.* conveyance.
conducente, *a.* conducive.
conducir, *v.* conduct, escort, lead; drive.
conducta, *f.* conduct, behavior.
conducto, *m.* pipe, conduit; sewer.
conductor, *m.* driver; conductor.
conectar, *v.* connect.
conejera, *f.* rabbit warren; place of ill repute.
conejo, *m.* rabbit.
conexión, *f.* connection; coupling.
conexivo, *a.* connective.
conexo, *a.* connected, united.
confalón, *m.* ensign, standard.
confección, *f.* workmanship; ready-made article; concoction.
confeccionar, *v.* concoct.
confederación, *f.* confederation.
confederado, *a. & m.* confederate.
confederar, *v.* confederate, unite, ally.
conferencia, *f.* lecture; conference.
conferenciante, *m. & f.* lecturer, speaker.
conferenciar, *v.* confer.
conferencista, *m. & f.* lecturer, speaker.
conferir, *v.* confer.
confesar, *v.* confess.
confesión, *f.* confession.
confesionario, *m.* confessional.
confesor, *m.* confessor.
confetti, *m.pl.* confetti.
confiable, *a.* dependable.
confiado, *a.* confident; trusting.
confianza, *f.* confidence, trust, faith.
confiar, *v.* entrust; trust, rely.
confidencia, *f.* confidence, secret.
confidencial, *a.* confidential.
confidente, *m. & f.* confidant.
confidentemente, *adv.* confidently.
confín, *m.* confine.
confinamiento, *m.* confinement.
confinar, *v.* confine, imprison; border on.
confirmación, *f.* confirmation.
confirmar, *v.* confirm.

confiscación, *f.* confiscation.
confiscar, *v.* confiscate.
confitar, *v.* sweeten; make into candy or jam.
confite, *m.* candy.
confitería, *f.* confectionery; candy store.
confitura, *f.* confection.
conflagración, *f.* conflagration.
conflicto, *m.* conflict.
confluencia, *f.* confluence, junction.
confluir, *v.* flow into each other.
conformación, *f.* conformation.
conformar, *v.* conform.
conforme, 1. *a.* acceptable, right, as agreed; in accordance, in agreement. **2.** *conj.* according as.
conformidad, *f.* conformity; agreement.
conformismo, *m.* conformism.
conformista, *m.* conformist.
confortar, *v.* comfort.
confraternidad, *m.* brotherhood, fraternity.
confricar, *v.* rub.
confrontación, *f.* confrontation.
confrontar, *v.* confront.
confucianismo, *m.* Confucianism.
confundir, *v.* confuse; puzzle, mix up.
confusamente, *adv.* confusedly.
confusión, *f.* confusion, mix-up; clutter.
confuso, *a.* confused; confusing.
confutación, *n.* disproof.
confutar, *v.* refute, disprove.
congelable, *a.* congealable.
congelación, *f.* congealment; deep freeze.
congelado, *a.* frozen, congealed.
congelar, *v.* congeal, freeze.
congenial, *a.* congenial; analogous.
congeniar, *v.* be congenial.
congestión, *f.* congestion.
conglomeración, *f.* conglomeration.
congoja, *f.* grief, anguish.
congraciamiento, *m.* flattery; ingratiation.
congraciar, *v.* flatter; ingratiate oneself.
congratulación, *f.* congratulation.
congratular, *v.* congratulate.
congregación, *f.* congregation.
congregar, *v.* congregate.
congresista, *m. & f.* congressional representative.
congreso, *m.* congress; conference.
conjetura, *f.* conjecture. **—conjeturar,** *v.*
conjetural, *a.* conjectural.
conjugación, *f.* conjugation.
conjugar, *v.* conjugate.

conjunción, *f.* union; conjunction.

conjuntamente, *adv.* together, jointly.

conjunto. 1. *a.* joint, unified. **2.** *m.* whole.

conjuración, *f.* conspiracy, plot.

conjurado, *m.* conspirator, plotter.

conjurar, *v.* conjure.

conllevador, *m.* helper, aide.

conmemoración, *f.* commemoration; remembrance.

conmemorar, *v.* commemorate.

conmemorativo, *a.* commemorative, memorial.

conmensal, *m.* messmate.

conmigo, *adv.* with me.

conmilitón, *m.* fellow soldier.

conminación, *f.* threat, warning.

conminar, *v.* threaten.

conminatorio, *a.* threatening, warning.

conmiseración, *f.* sympathy.

conmoción, *f.* commotion, stir.

conmovedor, *a.* moving, touching.

conmover, *v.* move, affect, touch.

conmutación, *f.* commutation.

conmutador, *m.* electric switch.

conmutar, *v.* exchange.

connotación, *f.* connotation.

connotar, *v.* connote.

connubial, *a.* connubial.

connubio, *m.* matrimony.

cono, *m.* cone.

conocedor -ra, *n.* expert, connoisseur.

conocer, *v.* know, be acquainted with; meet, make the acquaintance of.

conocible, *a.* knowable.

conocido -da, 1. *a.* familiar, well known. **2.** *n.* acquaintance, person known.

conocimiento, *m.* knowledge, acquaintance; consciousness.

conque, *conj.* so then; and so.

conquista, *f.* conquest.

conquistador, *m.* conqueror.

conquistar, *v.* conquer.

consabido, *a.* aforesaid.

consagración, *f.* consecration.

consagrado, *a.* consecrated.

consagrar, *v.* consecrate, dedicate, devote.

consanguinidad, *f.* consanguinity.

consciente, *a.* conscious, aware.

conscientemente, *adv.* consciously.

conscripción, *f.* conscription for military service.

consecución, *f.* attainment.

consecuencia, *f.* consequence.

consecuente, *a.* consequent; consistent.

consecuentemente, *adv.* consequently.

consecutivamente, *adv.* consecutively.

consecutivo, *a.* consecutive.

conseguir, *v.* obtain, get, secure; succeed in, manage to.

conseja, *n.* fable.

consejero -ra, *n.* adviser, counselor.

consejo, *m.* council; counsel (piece of) advice.

consenso, *m.* consensus.

consentido, *a.* spoiled, bratty.

consentimiento, *m.* consent.

consentir, *v.* allow, permit.

conserje, *m.* superintendent, keeper.

conserva, *f.* conserve, preserve.

conservación, *f.* conservation.

conservador, *a. & m.* conservative.

conservar, *v.* conserve.

conservativo, *a.* conservative, preservative.

conservatorio, *m.* conservatory.

considerable, *a.* considerable, substantial.

considerablemente, *adv.* considerably.

consideración, *f.* consideration.

consideradamente, *adv.* considerably.

considerado, *a.* considerate.

considerando, *conj.* whereas.

considerar, *v.* consider.

consigna, *f.* watchword.

consignación, *f.* consignment.

consignar, *v.* consign.

consignatario, *m.* consignee; trustee.

consigo, *adv.* with herself, with himself, with oneself, with themselves, with yourself, with yourselves.

consiguiente, 1. *a.* consequent. **2.** *m.* consequence.

consiguientemente, *adv.* consequently.

consistencia, *f.* consistency.

consistente, *a.* consistent.

consistir, *v.* consist.

consistorio, *m.* consistory.

consocio, *m.* associate; partner; comrade.

consola, *f.* console.

consolación, *f.* consolation.

consolar, *v.* console.

consolativo, *a.* consolatory.

consolidación, *n.* consolidation.

consolidado, *a.* consolidated.

consolidar, *v.* consolidate.

consonancia, *f.* agreement, accord, harmony.

consonante, *a. & n.* consonant.

consonar, *v.* rhyme.

consorte, *m. & f.* consort, mate.

conspicuo, *a.* conspicuous.

conspiración, *f.* conspiracy, plot.

conspirador -ra, *n.* conspirator.

conspirar, *v.* conspire, plot.

constancia, *f.* perseverance; record.

constante, *a.* constant.

constantemente, *adv.* constantly.

constar, *v.* consist; be clear, be on record.

constelación, *f.* constellation.

consternación, *f.* consternation.

consternar, *v.* dismay.

constipación, *f.* head cold.

constipado, *a.* having a head cold.

constitución, *f.* constitution.

constitucional, *a.* constitutional.

constitucionalidad, *f.* constitutionality.

constituir, *v.* constitute.

constitutivo, *m.* constituent.

constituyente, *a.* constituent.

constreñidamente, *adv.* compulsively; with constraint.

constreñimiento, *m.* compulsion; constraint.

constreñir, *v.* constrain.

constricción, *f.* constriction.

construcción, *f.* construction.

constructivo, *a.* constructive.

constructor, *m.* builder.

construir, *v.* construct, build.

consuelo, *m.* consolation.

cónsul, *m.* consul.

consulado, *m.* consulate.

consular, *a.* consular.

consulta, *f.* consultation.

consultación, *f.* consultation.

consultante, *m. & f.* consultant.

consultar, *v.* consult.

consultivo, *a.* consultative.

consultor, *m.* adviser.

consumación, *f.* consummation; end.

consumado, *a.* consummate, downright.

consumar, *v.* consummate.

consumidor, *m.* consumer.

consumir, *v.* consume.

consumo, *m.* consumption.

consunción, *m.* consumption, tuberculosis.

contabilidad, *f.* accounting, bookkeeping.

contabilista, contable, *m. & f.* accountant.

contacto, *m.* contact.

contado, *m.* **al c.,** (for) cash.

contador -ra, *n.* accountant, bookkeeper.

contagiar, *v.* infect.

contagio, *m.* contagion.

contagioso, *a.* contagious.

contaminación, *f.* contamination, pollution.

contaminar, *v.* contaminate, pollute.

contar, *v.* count; relate, recount, tell. **c. con,** count on.

contemperar, *v.* moderate.

contemplación, *f.* contemplation.

contemplador -ra, *n.* thinker.

contemplar, *v.* contemplate.

contemplativamente, *adv.* thoughtfully.

contemplativo, *a.* contemplative.

contemporáneo -nea, *a.* & *n.* contemporary.

contención, *f.* contention.

contencioso, *a.* quarrelsome; argumentative.

contender, *v.* cope, contend; conflict.

contendiente, *m.* & *f.* contender.

contenedor -ra, *n.* tenant.

contener, *v.* contain; curb, control.

contenido, *m.* contents.

contenta, *f.* endorsement.

contentamiento, *m.* contentment.

contentar, *v.* content, satisfy.

contentible, *a.* contemptible.

contento, 1. *a.* contented, happy. **2.** *m.* contentment, satisfaction, pleasure.

contérmino, *a.* adjacent, abutting.

contestable, *a.* disputable.

contestación, *f.* answer. —**contestar,** *v.*

contextura, *f.* texture.

contienda, *f.* combat; match; strife.

contigo, *adv.* with you.

contiguamente, *adv.* closely.

contiguo, *a.* adjoining, next.

continencia, *f.* continence, moderation.

continental, *a.* continental.

continente, *m.* continent; mainland.

continentemente, *adv.* in moderation.

contingencia, *f.* contingency.

contingente, *a.* contingent; incidental.

continuación, *f.* continuation. **a c.,** thereupon, hereupon.

continuamente, *adv.* continuously.

continuar, *v.* continue, keep on.

continuidad, *f.* continuity.

continuo, *a.* continual; continuous.

contorcerse, *v.* writhe, twist.

contorción, *f.* contortion.

contorno, *m.* contour; profile, outline; neighborhood.

contra, *prep.* against.

contraalmirante, *m.* rear admiral.

contraataque, *m.* counterattack.

contrabalancear, *v.* counterbalance.

contrabandear, *v.* smuggle.

contrabandista, *m.* smuggler.

contrabando, *m.* contraband, smuggling.

contracción, *f.* contraction.

contracepción, *f.* contraception, birth control.

contractual, *a.* contractual.

contradecir, *v.* contradict.

contradicción, *f.* contradiction.

contradictorio, *adj.* contradictory.

contraer, *v.* contract; shrink.

contrahacedor -ra, *n.* imitator.

contrahacer, *v.* forge.

contralor, *m.* comptroller.

contramandar, *v.* countermand.

contraorden, *f.* countermand.

contraparte, *f.* counterpart.

contrapesar, *v.* counterbalance, offset.

contrapeso, *m.* counterweight.

contrapunto, *m.* counterpoint.

contrariamente, *adv.* contrarily.

contrariar, *v.* contradict; vex; antagonize; counteract.

contrariedad, *f.* contrariness; opposition; contradiction; disappointment; trouble.

contrario, *a.* & *m.* contrary, opposite.

contrarrestar, *v.* resist; counteract.

contrasol, *m.* sunshade.

contraste, *m.* contrast. —**contrastar,** *v.*

contratar, *v.* engage, contract.

contratiempo, *m.* accident; misfortune.

contratista, *m.* contractor.

contrato, *m.* contract.

contribución, *f.* contribution; tax.

contribuir, *v.* contribute.

contribuyente, *m.* contributor; taxpayer.

contrición, *f.* contrition.

contristar, *v.* afflict.

contrito, *a.* contrite, remorseful.

control, *m.* control. —**controlar,** *v.*

controversia, *f.* controversy.

controversista, *m.* disputant.

controvertir, *v.* dispute.

contumacia, *f.* stubbornness.

contumaz, *adj.* stubborn.

contumelia, *f.* contumely; abuse.

conturbar, *v.* trouble, disturb.

contusión, *f.* contusion; bruise.

convalecencia, *f.* convalescence.

convalecer, *v.* convalesce.

convaleciente, *a.* convalescent.

convecino, *adj.* near, close.

convencedor, *adj.* convincing.

convencer, *v.* convince.

convencimiento, *m.* conviction, firm belief.

convención, *f.* convention.

convencional, *a.* conventional.

conveniencia, *f.* suitability; advantage, interest.

conveniente, *a.* suitable; advantageous, opportune.

convenio, *m.* pact, treaty; agreement.

convenir, *v.* assent, agree, concur; be suitable, fitting, convenient.

convento, *m.* convent.

convergencia, *f.* convergence.

convergir, *v.* converge.

conversación, *f.* conversation.

conversar, *v.* converse.

conversión, *f.* conversion.

convertible, *a.* convertible.

convertir, *v.* convert.

convexidad, *f.* convexity.

convexo, *a.* convex.

convicción, *f.* conviction.

convicto, *adj.* guilty.

convidado -da, *n.* guest.

convidar, *v.* invite.

convincente, *a.* convincing.

convite, *m.* invitation, treat.

convocación, *f.* convocation.

convocar, *v.* convoke, assemble.

convoy, *m.* convoy, escort.

convoyar, *v.* convey; escort.

convulsión, *f.* convulsion.

convulsivo, *adj.* convulsive.

conyugal, *adj.* conjugal.

cónyuge, *n.* spouse, mate.

coñac, *m.* cognac, brandy.

cooperación, *f.* cooperation.

cooperador, *adj.* cooperative.

cooperar, *v.* cooperate.

cooperativo, *a.* cooperative.

coordinación, *f.* coordination.

coordinar, *v.* coordinate.

copa, *f.* goblet.

copartícipe, *m.* partner.

copete, *m.* tuft; toupee.

copia, *f.* copy. —**copiar,** *v.*

copiadora, *f.* copier.

copioso, *a.* copious.

copista, *m.* copyist.

copla, *f.* popular song.

coplero, *m.* poetaster.

cópula, *f.* connection.

coqueta, *f.* flirt. —**coquetear,** *v.*

coraje, *m.* courage, bravery; anger.

coral, 1. *a.* choral. **2.** *m.* coral.

coralino, *a.* coral.

corazón, *m.* heart.

corazonada, *f.* foreboding.

corbata, *f.* necktie.

corbeta, *f.* corvette.

corcova, *f.* hump, hunch.

corcovado, *m.* hunchback.

corcho, *m.* cork.

cordaje, *m.* rigging.

cordel, *m.* string, cord.

cordero, *m.* lamb.

cordial, *a.* cordial, hearty.

cordialidad, *f.* cordiality.

cordillera, *f.* mountain range.

cordón, *m.* cord; (shoe) lace.

cordura, *f.* sanity.

coreografía, *f.* choreography.

corista, *f.* chorus girl.

corneja, *f.* crow.

córneo, *a.* horny.

corneta, *f.* bugle, horn, cornet.

corniforme, *a.* horn-shaped.

cornisa, *f.* cornice.

cornucopia, *f.* cornucopia.

coro, *m.* chorus; choir.

corola, *f.* corolla.

corolario, *m.* corollary.

corona, *f.* crown, halo, wreath.

coronación, *f.* coronation.

coronamiento, *f.* completion of a task.

coronar, v. crown.
coronel, m. colonel.
coronilla, f. small crown.
corporación, f. corporation.
corporal, adj. corporeal, bodily.
corpóreo, a. corporeal.
corpulencia, f. corpulence.
corpulento, a. corpulent, stout.
corpuscular, a. corpuscular.
corpúsculo, m. corpuscle.
corral, m. corral, pen, yard.
correa, f. belt, strap.
corrección, f. correction.
correcto, a. correct, proper, right.
corrector, m. corrector, proofreader.
corredera, f. race course.
corredizo, a. easily untied.
corredor, m. corridor; runner.
corregible, a. corrigible.
corregidor, m. corrector; magistrate, mayor.
corregir, v. correct.
correlación, f. correlation.
correlacionar, v. correlate.
correlativo, a. correlative.
correo, m. mail.
correoso, a. leathery.
correr, v. run.
correría, f. raid; escapade.
correspondencia, f. correspondence.
corresponder, v. correspond.
correspondiente, a. & m. corresponding; correspondent.
corresponsal, m. correspondent.
corretaje, m. brokerage.
correvedile, m. tale bearer; gossip.
corrida, f. race. **c. (de toros),** bullfight.
corrido, a. abashed; expert.
corriente, 1. a. current, standard. **2.** f. current, stream. **m. al c.,** informed, up to date.
corroboración, f. corroboration.
corroborar, v. corroborate.
corroer, v. corrode.
corromper, v. corrupt.
corrompido, adj. corrupt.
corrupción, f. corruption.
corruptela, f. corruption, vice.
corruptibilidad, f. corruptibility.
corruptor, m. corrupter.
corsario, m. corsair.
corsé, m. corset.
corso, m. piracy.
cortadillo, m. small glass.
cortado, a. cut.
cortadura, f. cut.
cortante, a. cutting, sharp, keen.
cortapisa, f. obstacle.
cortaplumas, m. penknife.
cortar, v. cut, cut off, cut out.
corte, f. court, m. cut.
cortedad, f. smallness; shyness.
cortejar, v. pay court to, woo.
cortejo, m. court, courtship; sweetheart.

cortés, a. civil, courteous, polite.
cortesana, f. courtesan.
cortesano. 1. a. courtly, courteous. **2.** m. courtier.
cortesía, f. courtesy.
corteza, f. bark; rind; crust.
cortijo, m. farmhouse.
cortina, f. curtain.
corto, a. short.
corva, f. bend of the knee.
cosa, f. thing. **c. de,** a matter of, roughly.
cosecha, f. crop, harvest. **—cosechar,** v.
coser, v. sew, stitch.
cosmético, a. & m. cosmetic.
cosmopolita, a. & n. cosmopolitan.
coso, m. arena for bull fights.
cosquilla, f. tickle. **—cosquillar,** v.
cosquilloso, a. ticklish.
costa, f. coast; cost, expense.
costado, m. side.
costal, m. sack, bag.
costanero, a. coastal.
costar, v. cost.
costarricense, a. & n. Costa Rican.
coste, m. cost, price.
costear, v. defray, sponsor; sail along the coast of.
costilla, f. rib; chop.
costo, m. cost, price.
costoso, a. costly.
costra, f. crust.
costumbre, f. custom, practice, habit.
costura, f. sewing; seam.
costurera, f. seamstress, dressmaker.
cota de malla, coat of mail.
cotejar, v. compare.
coteleta, f. cutlet.
cotidiano, a. daily; everyday.
cotillón, m. cotillion.
cotización, f. quotation.
cotizar, v. quote (a price).
coto, m. enclosure; boundary.
cotón, m. printed cotton cloth.
cotufa, f. Jerusalem artichoke.
coturno, m. buskin.
covacha, f. small cave.
coxal, a. of the hip.
coy, m. hammock.
coyote, m. coyote.
coyuntura, f. joint; juncture.
coz, f. kick.
crac, m. failure.
cráneo, m. skull.
craniano, a. cranial.
crapuloso, a. drunken.
crasiento, a. greasy, oily.
craso, a. fat; gross.
cráter, m. crater.
craza, f. crucible.
creación, f. creation.
creador -ra, a. & n. creative; creator.
crear, v. create.
creativo, a. creative.
crébol, m. holly tree.
crecer, v. grow, grow up; increase.

creces, f.pl. increase, addition.
crecidamente, adv. abundantly.
crecido, a. increased, enlarged; swollen.
creciente, 1. a. growing. **2.** f. crescent.
crecimiento, m. growth.
credenciales, f.pl. credentials.
credibilidad, f. credibility.
crédito, m. credit.
credo, m. creed, belief.
crédulamente, adv. credulously, gullibly.
credulidad, f. credulity.
crédulo, a. credulous.
creedero, a. credible.
creedor, a. credulous, believing.
creencia, f. belief.
creer, v. believe; think.
creíble, a. credible, believable.
crema, f. cream.
cremación, f. cremation.
cremar, v. cremate.
crémor tártaro, cream of tartar.
creosota, f. creosote.
crepitar, v. crackle.
crepuscular, a. of or like the dawn or dusk.
crepúsculo, m. dusk, twilight.
crescendo, m. crescendo.
crespo, a. crisp; curly.
crespón, m. crepe.
cresta, f. crest.
crestado, a. crested.
creta, f. chalk.
cretáceo, a. chalky.
cretinismo, m. cretinism.
cretino, n. & a. cretin.
cretona, f. cretonne.
creyente, 1. a. believing. **2.** n. believer.
creyón, m. crayon.
cría, f. (stock) breeding; young (of an animal), litter.
criada, f. girl servant, maid.
criadero, m. (agr.) nursery.
criado -da, m. servant.
criador, a. fruitful, prolific.
crianza, f. breeding; upbringing.
criar, v. raise, rear, bring up; breed.
criatura, f. creature; infant.
criba, f. sieve; crib.
cribado, a. sifted.
cribar, v. sift.
crimen, m. crime.
criminal, a. & m. criminal.
criminalidad, f. criminality.
criminalmente, adv. criminally.
criminoso, a. criminal.
crin, f. mane of a horse.
crinolina, f. crinoline.
criocirugía, f. cryosurgery.
criollo -lla, a. & n. native; creole.
cripta, f. crypt.
criptografía, f. cryptography.
crisantemo, m. chrysanthemum.
crisis, f. crisis.
crisma, f. chrism.

crisol, m. crucible.
crispamiento, m. twitch, contraction.
crispar, v. contract (the muscles); twitch.
crista, f. heraldic crest.
cristal, m. crystal; lens.
cristalería, f. glassware.
cristalino, a. crystalline.
cristalización, f. crystallization.
cristalizar, v. crystallize.
cristianar, v. baptize.
cristiandad, f. Christendom.
cristianismo, m. Christianity.
cristiano -na, a. & n. Christian.
Cristo, m. Christ.
criterio, m. criterion; judgment.
crítica, f. criticism; critique.
criticable, a. blameworthy.
criticador, a. critical.
criticar, v. criticize.
crítico, a. & m. critical; critic.
croar, v. croak.
crocante, m. peanut brittle.
crocidar, v. crow.
crocodilo, m. crocodile.
cromático, a. chromatic.
cromo, m. chromium.
cromotipia, f. color printing.
crónica, f. chronicle.
crónico, a. chronic.
cronicón, m. concise chronicle.
cronista, m. chronicler.
cronología, f. chronology.
cronológicamente, adv. chronologically.
cronológico, a. chronologic.
cronometro, m. chronometer.
croqueta, f. croquette.
croquis, m. sketch; rough outline.
crótalo, m. rattlesnake; castanet.
cruce, m. crossing, crossroads, junction.
crucero, m. cruiser.
crucífero, a. cross-shaped.
crucificado, a. crucified.
crucificar, v. crucify.
crucifijo, m. crucifix.
crucifixión, f. crucifixion.
crudamente, adv. crudely.
crudeza, f. crudeness.
crudo, a. crude, raw.
cruel, a. cruel.
crueldad, f. cruelty.
cruelmente, adv. cruelly.
cruentamente, adv. bloodily.
cruento, a. bloody.
crujía, f. corridor.
crujido, m. creak.
crujir, v. crackle, creak; rustle.
cruórico, a. bloody.
crup, m. croup.
crustáceo, m. & a. crustacean.
cruz, f. cross.
cruzada, f. crusade.
cruzado -da, n. crusader.
cruzamiento, m. crossing.
cruzar, v. cross.
cruzarse con, v. to (meet and) pass.
cuaderno, m. notebook.

cuadra, f. block; (hospital) ward.
cuadradamente, adv. exactly, precisely; completely, in full.
cuadradillo, m. lump of sugar.
cuadrado, a. & m. square.
cuadrafónico, a. quadraphonic.
cuadragésima, f. Lent.
cuadragesimal, a. Lenten.
cuadrángulo, m. quadrangle.
cuadrante, m. quadrant; dial.
cuadrar, v. square; suit.
cuadricular, a. in squares.
cuadrilátero, a. quadrilateral.
cuadrilla, f. band, troop, gang.
cuadrinieto, n. great-grandchild.
cuadro, m. picture; painting; frame. a cuadros, checked, plaid.
cuadro de servicio, timetable.
cuadrupedal, a. quadruped.
cuádruplo, a. fourfold.
cuajada, f. curd.
cuajamiento, m. coagulation.
cuajar, v. coagulate; overdecorate.
cuajo, m. rennet; coagulation.
cuakerismo, m. Quakerism.
cuákero, n. & a. Quaker.
cual, rel. pron. which.
cuál, a. & pron. what, which.
cualidad, f. quality.
cualitativo, a. qualitative.
cualquiera, a. & pron. whatever, any; anyone.
cuando, conj. when.
cuando, adv. when. de cuando en cuando, from time to time.
cuantía, f. quantity; amount.
cuantiar, v. estimate.
cuantidad, f. quantity.
cuantiosamente, adv. abundantly.
cuantioso, a. abundant.
cuantitativo, a. quantitative.
cuanto, a., adv. & pron. as much as, as many as; all that which. en c., as soon as. en c., as for. c. antes, as soon as possible. c. más . . . tanto más, the more . . . the more. unos cuantos, a few.
cuánto, a. & adv. how much, how many.
cuaquerismo, m. Quakerism.
cuáquero, n. & a. Quaker.
cuarenta, a. & pron. forty.
cuarentena, f. quarantine.
cuaresma, f. Lent.
cuaresmal, a. Lenten.
cuarta, f. quarter; quadrant; quart.
cuartana, f. ague.
cuartear, v. divide into quarters.
cuartel, m. (mil.) quarters; barracks; (naut.) hatch. c. general, headquarters. sin c., giving no quarter.
cuartelada, f. military uprising.
cuarterón, n. & a. quadroon.
cuarteto, m. quartet.
cuartillo, m. pint.

cuarto, 1. a. fourth. 2. m. quarter; room.
cuarto de baño, bathroom.
cuarto de dormir, bedroom.
cuarzo, m. quartz.
cuasi, adv. almost, nearly.
cuate, a. & n. twin.
cuatrero, m. cattle rustler.
cuatrillón, m. quadrillion.
cuatro, a. & pron. four.
cuatrocientos, a. & pron. four hundred.
cuba, f. cask, tub, vat.
cubano -na, a. & n. Cuban.
cubero, m. cooper.
cubertura, f. cover.
cubeta, f. small barrel, keg.
cúbico, a. cubic.
cubierta, f. cover; envelope; wrapping; tread (of a tire); deck.
cubiertamente, adv. secretly, stealthily.
cubierto, m. place (at table).
cubil, m. lair.
cubo, m. cube; bucket.
cubrecama, f. bedspread.
cubrir, v. cover.
cubrirse, v. put on one's hat.
cucaracha, f. cockroach.
cuclillo, m. cuckoo.
cuco, a. sly.
cuculla, f. hood, cowl.
cuchara, f. spoon, tablespoon.
cucharada, f. spoonful.
cucharita, cucharilla, f. teaspoon.
cucharón, m. dipper, ladle.
cuchicheo, m. whisper. —cuchichear, v.
cuchilla, f. cleaver.
cuchillada, f. slash.
cuchillería, f. cutlery.
cuchillo, m. knife.
cucho, m. fertilizer.
cuchufleta, f. jest.
cuelga, f. cluster, bunch.
cuelgacapas, m. coat rack.
cuello, m. neck; collar.
cuenca, f. socket; (river) basin; wooden bowl.
cuenco, m. earthen bowl.
cuenta, f. account; bill. darse c., to realize. tener en c., to keep in mind.
cuentagotas, m. dropper (for medicine).
cuentista, m. informer.
cuento, m. story, tale.
cuerda, f. cord; chord; rope; string; spring (of clock). dar c. a, to wind (clock).
cuerdamente, adv. sanely; prudently.
cuerdo, a. sane; prudent.
cuerno, m. horn.
cuero, m. leather; hide.
cuerpo, m. body; corps.
cuervo, m. crow, raven.
cuesco, m. pit, stone (of fruit).
cuesta, f. hill, slope. llevar a cuestas, to carry on one's back.
cuestación, f. solicitation for charity.

cuestión, *f.* question; affair; argument.

cuestionable, *a.* questionable.

cuestionar, *v.* question; discuss; argue.

cuestionario, *m.* questionnaire.

cuete, *m.* firecracker.

cuetzale, *m.* quetzal.

cueva, *f.* cave; cellar.

cugujada, *f.* lark.

cuidado, *m.* care, caution, worry. **tener c.,** to be careful.

cuidadosamente, *adv.* carefully.

cuidadoso, *a.* careful, painstaking.

cuidante, *n.* caretaker, custodian.

cuidar, *v.* take care of.

cuita, *f.* trouble, care, grief.

cuitado, *a.* unfortunate; shy, timid.

cuitamiento, *m.* timidity.

culata, *f.* haunch, buttock; butt of a gun.

culatada, *f.* recoil.

culatazo, *m.* blow with the butt of a gun; recoil.

culebra, *f.* snake.

culero, *a.* lazy, indolent.

culinario, *a.* culinary.

culminación, *f.* culmination.

culminar, *v.* culminate.

culpa, *f.* fault, guilt, blame. **tener la c.,** to be at fault. **echar la culpa a,** to blame.

culpabilidad, *f.* guilt, fault, blame.

culpable, *a.* at fault, guilty, to blame.

culpar, *v.* blame, accuse.

cultamente, *adv.* politely, elegantly.

cultivable, *a.* arable.

cultivación, *f.* cultivation.

cultivador, *m.* cultivator.

cultivar, *v.* cultivate.

cultivo, *m.* cultivation; (growing) crop.

culto, 1. *a.* cultured, cultivated. **2.** *m.* cult; worship.

cultura, *f.* culture; refinement.

cultural, *a.* cultural.

culturar, *v.* cultivate.

cumbre, *m.* summit, peak.

cumpleaños, *m.pl.* birthday.

complidamente, *adv.* completely.

cumplido, *a.* polite, polished.

cumplimentar, *v.* compliment.

cumplimiento, *m.* fulfillment; compliment.

cumplir, *v.* comply; carry out, fulfill; reach (years of age).

cumular, *v.* accumulate.

cumulativo, *a.* cumulative.

cúmulo, *m.* heap, pile.

cuna, *f.* cradle.

cundir, *v.* spread; expand; propagate.

cuneiforme, *a.* cuneiform, wedge-shaped.

cuneo, *m.* rocking.

cuña, *f.* wedge.

cuñada, *f.* sister-in-law.

cuñado, *m.* brother-in-law.

cuñete, *m.* keg.

cuociente, *m.* quotient.

cuota, *f.* quota; dues.

cuotidiano, *a.* daily.

cupé, *m.* coupé.

cupido, *m.* lover.

cupo, *m.* share; assigned quota.

cupón, *m.* coupon.

cúpula, *f.* dome.

cura, *m.* priest. *f.* treatment, (medical) care. **c. de urgencia,** first aid.

curable, *a.* curable.

curación, *f.* healing; cure; (surgical) dressing.

curado, *a.* cured, healed.

curador, *m.* custodian; curator.

curandero, *m.* healer, medicine man.

curar, *v.* cure, heal, treat.

curativo, *a.* curative, healing.

curia, *f.* ecclesiastical court.

curiosear, *v.* snoop, pry, meddle.

curiosidad, *f.* curiosity.

curioso, *a.* curious.

curro, *a.* showy, loud, flashy.

cursante, *n.* student.

cursar, *v.* frequent; attend to.

cursi, *a.* vulgar, shoddy, in bad taste.

curso, *m.* course.

curtidor, *m.* tanner.

curtir, *v.* tan.

curva, *f.* curve; bend.

curvatura, *f.* curvature.

cúspide, *f.* top, peak.

custodia, *f.* custody.

custodiar, *v.* guard, watch.

custodio, *m.* custodian.

cutáneo, *a.* cutaneous.

cutícula, *f.* cuticle.

cutis, *m.* or *f.* skin, complexion.

cuyo, *a.* whose.

CH

chabancano, *a.* clumsy.

chacal, *m.* jackal.

chacó, *m.* shako.

chacona, *f.* chaconne.

chacota, *f.* fun, mirth.

chacotear, *v.* joke.

chacra, *f.* small farm.

chafallar, *v.* mend badly.

chagra, *m.* rustic; rural person.

chal, *m.* shawl.

chalán, *m.* horse trader.

chaleco, *m.* vest.

chalet, *m.* chalet.

challí, *m.* challis.

chamada, *f.* brushwood.

chamarillero, *m.* gambler.

chamarra, *f.* coarse linen jacket.

chambelán, *m.* chamberlain.

champaña, *m.* champagne.

champú, *m.* shampoo.

chamuscar, *v.* scorch.

chancaco, *a.* brown.

chancear, *v.* jest, joke.

chanciller, *m.* chancellor.

chancillería, *f.* chancery.

chancla, *f.* old shoe.

chancleta, *f.* slipper.

chanclos, *m.pl.* galoshes.

chancro, *m.* chancre.

changador, *m.* porter, handyman.

chantaje, *m.* blackmail.

chantajista, *n.* blackmailer.

chanto, *m.* flagstone.

chantre, *m.* precentor.

chanza, *f.* joke, jest. **—chancear,** *v.*

chanzoneta, *f.* chansonette.

chapa, *f.* (metal) sheet, plate; lock.

chaparrada, *f.* shower.

chaparral, *m.* chaparral.

chaparreras, *f.pl.* chaps.

chaparrón, *m.* downpour.

chapear, *v.* veneer.

chapeo, *m.* hat.

chapitel, *m.* spire, steeple; (architecture) capital.

chapodar, *v.* lop.

chapón, *m.* inkblot.

chapotear, *v.* paddle or splash in the water.

chapoteo, *m.* splash.

chapucear, *v.* fumble, bungle.

chapucero, *a.* sloppy, bungling.

chapurrear, *v.* speak (a language) brokenly.

chapuz, *m.* dive; ducking.

chapuzar, *v.* dive, duck.

chaqueta, *f.* jacket, coat.

charada, *f.* charade.

charamusca, *f.* twisted candy stick.

charanga, *f.* military band.

charanguero, *m.* peddler.

charca, *f.* pool, pond.

charco, *m.* pool, puddle.

charla, *f.* chat; chatter, prattle. **—charlar,** *v.*

charladuría, *f.* chatter.

charlatán, *m.* charlatan.

charlatanismo, *m.* charlatanism.

charol, *m.* varnish.

charolar, *v.* varnish; polish.

charquear, *v.* jerk (beef).

charquí, *m.* jerked beef.

charrán, *a.* roguish.

chascarrillo, *m.* risqué story.

chasco, *m.* disappointment, blow; practical joke.

chasis, *m.* chassis.

chasquear, *v.* fool, trick; disappoint; crack (a whip).

chasquido, *m.* crack (sound).

chata, *f.* bedpan.

chato, *a.* flat-nosed, pug-nosed.

chauvinismo, *m.* chauvinism.

chauvinista, *n. & a.* chauvinist.

chelín, *m.* shilling.

cheque, *m.* (bank) check.

chica, *f.* girl.

chicana, *f.* chicanery.

chicle, *m.* chewing gum.

chico, 1. *a.* a little. **2.** *m.* boy.

chicote, *m.* cigar; cigar butt.
chicotear, *v.* whip, flog.
chicha, *f.* an alcoholic drink.
chícharo, *f.* pea.
chicharra, *f.* cicada; talkative person.
chicharrón, *m.* crisp fried scrap of meat.
chichear, *v.* hiss in disapproval.
chichón, *m.* bump, bruise, lump.
chifladura, *f.* mania; whim; jest.
chiflar, *v.* whistle; become insane.
chiflido, *m.* shrill whistle.
chile, *m.* chili.
chileno -na, *a.* & *n.* Chilean.
chillido, *m.* shriek, scream, screech. —**chillar,** *v.*
chillón, *a.* shrill.
chimenea, *f.* chimney, smoke-stack; fireplace.
china, *f.* pebble; maid; Chinese woman.
chinarro, *m.* large pebble, stone.
chinche, *f.* bedbug; thumbtack.
chinchilla, *f.* chinchilla.
chinchorro, *m.* fishing net.
chinela, *f.* slipper.
chinero, *m.* china closet.
chino -na, *a.* & *n.* Chinese.
chiquero, *m.* pen for pigs, goats, etc.
chiquito, 1. *a.* small, tiny. **2.** *m.* small child.
chiribitil, *m.* small room, den.
chirimía, *f.* flageolet.
chiripa, *f.* stroke of good luck.
chirla, *f.* mussel.
chirle, *a.* insipid.
chirona, *f.* prison, jail.
chirrido, *m.* squeak, chirp. —**chirriar,** *v.*
chis, *interj.* hush!
chisgarabís, *n.* meddler; unimportant person.
chisguete, *m.* squirt, splash.
chisme, *m.* gossip. —**chismear,** *v.*
chismero, *m.* gossiper.
chismoso, *adj.* gossiping.
chispa, *f.* spark.
chispeante, *a.* sparkling.
chispear, *v.* sparkle.
chisporrotear, *v.* emit sparks.
chistar, *v.* mumble.
chiste, *m.* joke, gag; witty saying.
chistera, *f.* fish basket; top hat.
chistoso, *a.* funny, comic, amusing.
chito, *interj.* hush!
chiva, *f.* female goat.
chivato, *m.* kid, young goat.
chivo, *m.* male goat.
chocante, *a.* striking; shocking; unpleasant.
chocar, *v.* collide, clash, crash; shock.
chocarrear, *v.* joke, jest.

choclo, *m.* clog; overshoe; ear of corn.
chocolate, *m.* chocolate.
chocolatería, *f.* chocolate shop.
chochear, *v.* be in one's dotage.
chochera, *f.* dotage, senility.
chofer, chófer, *m.* chauffeur, driver.
chofeta, *f.* chafing dish.
cholo, *m.* half-breed.
chopo, *m.* black poplar.
choque, *m.* collision, clash, crash; shock.
chorizo, *m.* sausage.
chorrear, *v.* spout; drip.
chorro, *m.* spout; spurt, jet. **llover a chorros,** to pour (rain).
choto, *m.* calf, kid.
choza, *f.* hut, cabin.
chozno, *m.* great-grandson.
chubasco, *m.* shower, squall.
chubascoso, *a.* squally.
chuchería, *f.* trinket, knick-knack.
chulería, *f.* pleasant manner.
chuleta, *f.* chop, cutlet.
chulo, *m.* rascal, rogue; joker.
chupa, *f.* jacket.
chupada, *f.* suction.
chupado, *a.* very thin.
chupaflor, *m.* hummingbird.
chupar, *v.* suck.
churrasco, *m.* roasted meat.
chuscada, *f.* joke, jest.
chusco, *a.* funny, humorous.
chusma, *f.* mob, rabble.
chuzo, *m.* pike.

D

dable, *a.* possible.
dactilógrafo, *m.* typewriter.
dádiva, *f.* gift.
dadivosamente, *adv.* generously.
dadivoso, *a.* generous, bountiful.
dador, *m.* giver.
dados, *m.pl.* dice.
daga, *f.* dagger.
dalia, *f.* dahlia.
daltonismo, *m.* color blindness.
dallador, *m.* lawn mower.
dallar, *v.* mow.
dama, *f.* lady.
damasco, *m.* apricot.
damisela, *f.* young lady, girl.
danés -esa, *a.* & *n.* Danish, Dane.
danza, *f.* (the) dance. —**danzar,** *v.*
danzante, *m.* dancer.
dañable, *a.* condemnable.
dañar, *v.* hurt, harm; damage.
dañino, dañoso, *a.* harmful.
daño, *m.* damage; harm.
dañoso, *a.* harmful.
dar, *v.* give; strike (clock). **d. a,** face, open on. **d. con,** find, locate.
dardo, *m.* dart.
dársena, *f.* dock.
datar, *v.* date.

dátil, *m.* date (fruit).
dativo, *m.* & *a.* dative.
datos, *m.pl.* data.
de, *prep.* of; from; than.
debajo, *adv.* underneath. **d. de,** under.
debate, *m.* debate.
debatir, *v.* debate, argue.
debe, *m.* debit.
debelación, *f.* conquest.
debelar, *v.* conquer.
deber, 1. *v.* owe; must; be to, be supposed to. **2.** *m.* obligation.
debido, *a.* due.
débil, *a.* weak, faint.
debilidad, *f.* weakness.
debilitación, *f.* weakness.
debilitar, *v.* weaken.
débito, *m.* debit.
debutante, *f.* debutante.
debutar, *v.* make a debut.
década, *f.* decade.
decadencia, *f.* decadence, decline, decay.
decadente, *a.* decadent, declining, decaying.
decaer, *v.* decay, decline.
decalitro, *m.* decaliter.
decálogo, *m.* decalogue.
decámetro, *m.* decameter.
decano, *m.* dean.
decantado, *a.* much discussed; overexalted.
decapitación, *f.* beheading.
decapitar, *v.* behead.
decencia, *f.* decency.
decenio, *m.* decade.
decente, *a.* decent.
decentemente, *adv.* decently.
decepción, *f.* disappointment; delusion.
decepcionar, *v.* disappoint, disillusion.
decibelio, *m.* decibel.
decididamente, *adv.* decidedly.
decidir, *v.* decide.
decigramo, *m.* decigram.
decilitro, *m.* deciliter.
décima, *f.* ten-line stanza.
decimal, *a.* decimal.
décimo, *a.* tenth.
decir, *v.* tell, say. **es d.,** that is (to say).
decisión, *f.* decision.
decisivamente, *adv.* decisively.
decisivo, *a.* decisive.
declamación, *f.* declamation, speech.
declamar, *v.* declaim.
declaración, *f.* declaration; statement; plea.
declarar, *v.* declare, state.
declarativo, *a.* declarative.
declinación, *f.* descent; decay; decline; declension.
declinar, *v.* decline.
declive, *m.* declivity, slope.
decocción, *f.* decoction.
decomiso, *m.* seizure, confiscation.
decoración, *f.* decoration, trimming.
decorado, *m.* (theat.) scenery, set.

decorar, v. decorate, trim.

decorativo, a. decorative, ornamental.

decoro, m. decorum; decency.

decoroso, a. decorous.

decrecer, v. decrease.

decrépito, a. decrepit.

decreto, m. decree. **—decretar,** v.

dechado, m. model; sample; pattern; example.

dedal, m. thimble.

dédalo, m. labyrinth.

dedicación, f. dedication.

dedicar, v. devote; dedicate.

dedicatoria, f. dedication, inscription.

dedo, m. finger, toe.

deducción, f. deduction.

deducir, v. deduce; subtract.

defectivo, a. defective.

defecto, m. defect, flaw.

defectuoso, a. defective, faulty.

defender, v. defend.

defensa, f. defense.

defensivo, a. defensive.

defensor, m. defender.

deferencia, f. deference.

deferir, v. defer.

deficiente, a. deficient.

déficit, m. deficit.

definición, f. definition.

definido, a. definite.

definir, v. define; establish.

definitivamente, adv. definitely.

definitivo, a. definite; definitive.

deformación, f. deformation.

deformar, v. deform.

deforme, a. deformed; ugly.

deformidad, f. deformity.

defraudar, v. defraud.

defunción, f. death.

degeneración, f. degeneration.

degenerado, a. degenerate. **—degenerar,** v.

deglutir, v. swallow.

degollar, v. behead.

degradación, f. degradation.

degradar, v. degrade, debase.

deidad, f. deity.

deificación, f. deification.

deificar, v. deify.

deífico, a. divine, deific.

deísmo, m. deism.

dejadez, f. neglect, untidiness; laziness.

dejado, a. untidy; lazy.

dejar, v. let, allow; leave. **d. de,** stop, leave off. **no d. de,** not fail to.

dejo, m. abandonment; negligence; aftertaste; accent.

del, contr. of **de** + **el.**

delantal, m. apron.

delante, adv. ahead, forward; in front.

delantero, a. forward, front, first.

delator, m. informer; accuser.

delegación, f. delegation.

delegado -da, n. delegate. **—delegar,** v.

deleite, m. delight. **—deleitar,** v.

deleitoso, a. delightful.

deletrear, v. spell; decipher.

delfín, m. dolphin; dauphin.

delgadez, f. thinness, slenderness.

delgado, a. thin, slender, slim, slight.

deliberación, f. deliberation.

deliberadamente, adv. deliberately.

deliberar, v. deliberate.

deliberativo, a. deliberative.

delicadamente, adv. delicately.

delicadeza, f. delicacy.

delicado, a. delicate, dainty.

delicia, f. delight; deliciousness.

delicioso, a. delicious.

delincuencia, f. delinquency.

delincuente, a. & n. delinquent; culprit, offender.

delineación, f. delineation, sketch.

delinear, v. delineate, sketch.

delirante, a. delirious.

delirar, v. rave, be delirious.

delirio, m. delirium; rapture, bliss.

delito, m. crime, offense.

delta, m. delta (of river).

demagogia, f. demagogy.

demagogo, n. demagogue.

demanda, f. demand, claim.

demandador -ra, n. plaintiff.

demandar, v. sue; demand.

demarcación, f. demarcation.

demarcar, v. demarcate, limit.

demás, a. & n. other; (the) rest (of). **por d.,** too much.

demasía, f. excess; audacity; iniquity.

demasiado, a. & adv. too; too much; too many.

demencia, f. dementia; insanity.

demente, a. demented.

democracia, f. democracy.

demócrata, m. & f. democrat.

democrático, a. democratic.

demoler, v. demolish, tear down.

demolición, f. demolition.

demonio, m. demon, devil.

demontre, m. devil.

demora, f. delay, **—demorar,** v.

demostración, f. demonstration.

demostrador, m. demonstrator.

demostrar, v. demonstrate, show.

demostrativo, a. demonstrative.

demudar, v. change; disguise; conceal.

denegación, f. denial, refusal.

denegar, v. deny, refuse.

dengue, m. prudishness; dengue.

denigración, f. defamation, disgrace.

denigrar, v. defame, disgrace.

denodado, a. brave, dauntless.

denominación, f. denomination.

denominar, v. name, call.

denotación, f. denotation.

denotar, v. denote, betoken, express.

densidad, f. density.

denso, a. dense.

dentado, a. toothed; serrated; cogged.

dentadura, f. set of teeth.

dental, a. dental.

dentífrico, m. dentifrice.

dentista, m. dentist.

dentistería, f. dentistry.

dentro, adv. within, inside. **d. de poco,** in a short while.

denuedo, m. bravery, courage.

denuesto, m. insult, offense.

denuncia, f. denunciation; declaration.

denunciación, f. denunciation.

denunciar, v. denounce.

deparar, v. offer; grant.

departamento, m. department, section.

departir, v. talk, chat.

dependencia, f. dependence; branch office.

depender, v. depend.

dependiente, a. & m. dependent; clerk.

depilatorio, a. depilatory.

deplorable, a. deplorable, wretched.

deplorablemente, adv. deplorably.

deplorar, v. deplore.

deponer, v. depose.

deportación, f. deportation; exile.

deportar, v. deport.

deporte, m. sport. **—deportivo,** a.

deposición, f. assertion, deposition; removal; movement.

depositante, m. & f. depositor.

depósito, m. deposit. **—depositar,** v.

depravación, f. depravation; depravity.

depravado, a. depraved, wicked.

depravar, v. deprave, corrupt, pervert.

depreciación, f. depreciation.

depreciar, v. depreciate.

depredación, f. depredation.

depredar, v. pillage, depredate.

depresión, f. depression.

depresivo, a. depressive.

deprimir, v. depress.

depurar, v. purify.

derecha, f. right (hand, side).

derechera, f. shortcut.

derecho, 1. a. right; straight. 2. m. right; (the) law. **derechos,** (com.) duty.

derechura, f. straightness.

derelicto, a. abandoned, derelict.

deriva, f. (naut.) drift.

derivación, f. derivation.

derivar, v. derive.

derogar, v. derogate; repeal; abrogate.

derramamiento, m. overflow.

derramar, v. spill, pour, scatter.

derrame, m. overflow; discharge.

derretir, v. melt, dissolve.

derribar, v. demolish, knock down; bowl over, floor, fell.

derrocamiento, m. overthrow.

derrocar, v. overthrow; oust; demolish.

derrochar, v. waste.

derroche, v. waste.

derrota, f. rout, defeat. —**derrotar**, v.

derrumbamiento, derrumbe, m. collapse; landslide.

derrumbarse, v. collapse, tumble.

derviche, m. dervish.

desabotonar, v. unbutton.

desabrido, a. insipid, tasteless.

desabrigar, v. uncover.

desabrochar, v. unbutton, unclasp.

desacierto, m. error.

desacobardar, v. remove fear; embolden.

desacomodadamente, adv. inconveniently.

desacomodado, a. unemployed.

desacomodar, v. molest; inconvenience; dismiss.

desacomodo, m. loss of employment.

desconsejado, a. imprudent, ill advised, rash.

desaconsejar, v. dissuade.

desacordadamente, adv. unadvisedly.

desacordar, v. differ, disagree; be forgetful.

desacorde, a. discordant.

desacostumbradamente, adv. unusually.

desacostumbrado, a. unusual, unaccustomed.

desacostumbrar, v. give up a habit or custom.

desacreditar, v. discredit.

desacuerdo, m. disagreement.

desadeudar, v. pay one's debts.

desadormecer, v. waken, rouse.

desadornar, v. divest of ornament.

desadvertidamente, adv. inadvertently.

desadvertido, a. imprudent.

desadvertimiento, m. imprudence, rashness.

desadvertir, v. act imprudently.

desafección, f. disaffection.

desafecto, a. disaffected.

desafiar, v. defy; challenge.

desafinar, v. be out of tune.

desafío, m. defiance; challenge.

desaforar, v. infringe one's rights; be outrageous.

desafortunado, a. unfortunate.

desafuero, m. violation of the law; outrage.

desagraciado, a. graceless.

desagradable, a. disagreeable, unpleasant.

desagradablemente, adv. disagreeably.

desagradecido, a. ungrateful.

desagradecimiento, m. ingratitude.

desagrado, m. displeasure.

desagraviar, v. make amends.

desagregar, v. separate, disintegrate.

desagriar, v. mollify, appease.

desaguadero, m. drain, outlet; cesspool; sink.

desaguador, m. water pipe.

desaguar, v. drain.

desaguisado, m. offense; injury.

desahogadamente, adv. impudently; brazenly.

desahogado, a. impudent, brazen; cheeky.

desahogar, v. relieve.

desahogo, m. relief; nerve, cheek.

desahuciar, v. give up hope for; despair of.

desairado, a. graceless.

desaire, m. slight; scorn. —**desairar**, v.

desajustar, v. mismatch, misfit; make unfit.

desalar, v. hurry, hasten.

desalentar, v. make out of breath; discourage.

desaliento, m. discouragement.

desaliñar, v. disarrange; make untidy.

desaliño, m. slovenliness, untidiness.

desalivar, v. salivate.

desalmadamente, adv. mercilessly.

desalmado, a. merciless.

desalojamiento, m. displacement; dislodging.

desalojar, v. dislodge.

desalquilado, a. vacant, unrented.

desamar, v. cease loving.

desamasado, a. dissolve, undo.

desamistarse, v. quarrel, disagree.

desamor, m. disaffection, dislike; hatred.

desamorado, a. cruel; harsh; rude.

desamparador, m. deserter.

desamparar, v. desert, abandon.

desamparo, m. desertion, abandonment.

desamueblar, v. dismantle.

desandrajado, a. shabby, ragged.

desanimadamente, adv. in a discouraged manner; spiritlessly.

desanimar, v. dishearten, discourage.

desánimo, m. discouragement.

desanudar, v. untie; loosen; disentangle.

desapacible, a. rough, harsh; unpleasant.

desaparecer, v. disappear.

desaparición, f. disappearance.

desapasionadamente, adv. dispassionately.

desapasionado, a. dispassionate.

desapego, m. impartiality.

desapercibido, adj. unprepared.

desapiadado, a. merciless, cruel.

desaplicación, f. indolence, laziness; negligence.

desaplicado, a. indolent, lazy; negligent.

desaposesionar, v. dispossess.

desapreciar, v. depreciate.

desapretador, m. screwdriver.

desapretar, v. loosen; relieve, ease.

desaprisionar, v. set free, release.

desaprobación, f. disapproval.

desaprobar, v. disapprove.

desaprovechado, a. useless, profitless; backward.

desaprovechar, v. waste; be backward.

desarbolar, v. unmast.

desarmado, a. disarmed, defenseless.

desarmar, v. disarm.

desarme, m. disarmament.

desarraigar, v. uproot; eradicate; expel.

desarreglar, v. disarrange, mess up.

desarrollar, v. develop.

desarrollo, m. development.

desarropar, v. undress; uncover.

desarrugar, v. remove wrinkles from.

desaseado, a. dirty; disorderly.

desasear, v. make dirty or disorderly.

desaseo, m. dirtiness; disorder.

desasir, v. loosen; disengage.

desasociable, a. unsociable.

desasosegar, v. disturb.

desasosiego, m. uneasiness.

desastrado, a. ragged, wretched.

desastre, m. disaster.

desastroso, a. disastrous.

desatar, v. untie, undo.

desatención, f. inattention; disrespect; rudeness.

desatender, v. ignore; disregard.

desatentado, a. inconsiderate; imprudent.

desatinado, a. foolish; insane; wild.

desatino, m. blunder. —**desatinar**, v.

desautorizado, a. unauthorized.

desautorizar, v. deprive of authority.

desavenencia, *f.* disagreement, discord.

desaventajado, *a.* disadvantageous.

desayuno, *m.* breakfast. — **desayunarse,** *v.*

desazón, *f.* insipidity; uneasiness.

desazonado, *a.* insipid; uneasy.

desbandada, *f.* disbanding.

desbandarse, *v.* disband.

desbarajuste, *m.* disorder, confusion.

desbaratar, *v.* destroy.

desbastar, *v.* plane, smoothen.

desbocado, *a.* foul-spoken, indecent.

desbocarse, *v.* use obscene language.

desbordamiento, *m.* overflow; flood.

desbordar, *v.* overflow.

desbrozar, *v.* clear away rubbish.

descabal, *a.* incomplete.

descabalar, *v.* render incomplete; impair.

descabellado, *a.* absurd, preposterous.

descabezar, *v.* behead.

descaecimiento, *m.* weakness; dejection.

descafeinado, *a.* decaffeinated.

descalabrar, *v.* injure, wound (esp. the head).

descalabro, *m.* accident, misfortune.

descalzarse, *v.* take off one's shoes.

descalzo, *a.* shoeless; barefoot.

descaminado, *a.* wrong, misguided.

descaminar, *v.* mislead; lead into error.

descamisado, *a.* shirtless; shabby.

descanso, *m.* rest. — **descansar,** *v.*

descarado, *a.* saucy, fresh.

descarga, *f.* discharge.

descargar, *v.* discharge, unload, dump.

descargo, *m.* acquittal.

descarnar, *v.* skin.

descaro, *m.* gall, effrontery.

descarriar, *v.* lead or go astray.

descarrilamiento, *m.* derailment.

descarrilar, *v.* derail.

descartar, *v.* discard.

descascarar, *v.* peel; boast, brag.

descendencia, *f.* descent, origin; progeny.

descender, *v.* descend.

descendiente, *m.& f.* descendant.

descendimiento, *m.* descent.

descenso, *m.* descent.

descentralización, *f.* decentralizing.

descifrar, *v.* decipher, puzzle out.

descoco, *m.* boldness, brazenness.

descolgar, *v.* take down.

descolorar, *v.* discolor.

descolorido, *a.* pale, faded.

descollar, *v.* stand out; excel.

descomedido, *a.* disproportionate; rude.

descomedirse, *v.* be rude.

descomponer, *v.* decompose; break down, get out of order.

descomposición, *f.* discomposure; disorder, confusion.

descompuesto, *a.* impudent, rude.

descomulgar, *v.* excommunicate.

descomunal, *a.* extraordinary, huge.

desconcertar, *v.* disconcert, baffle.

desconcierto, *m.* confusion, disarray.

desconectar, *v.* disconnect.

desconfiado, *a.* distrustful.

desconfianza, *f.* distrust.

desconfiar, *v.* distrust, mistrust; suspect.

descongestionante, *m.* decongestant.

desconocer, *v.* ignore, fail to recognize.

desconocido -da, *n.* stranger.

desconocimiento, *m.* ingratitude; ignorance.

desconsolado, *a.* disconsolate, wretched.

desconsuelo, *m.* grief.

descontar, *v.* discount, subtract.

descontentar, *v.* dissatisfy.

descontento, *m.* discontent.

descontinuar, *v.* discontinue.

desconvenir, *v.* disagree.

descorazonar, *v.* dishearten.

descorchar, *v.* uncork.

descortés, *a.* discourteous, impolite, rude.

descortesía, *f.* discourtesy, rudeness.

descortezar, *v.* peel.

descoyuntar, *v.* dislocate.

descrédito, *m.* discredit.

describir, *v.* describe.

descripción, *f.* description.

descriptivo, *a.* descriptive.

descuartizar, *v.* dismember, disjoint.

descubridor, *m.* discoverer.

descubrimiento, *m.* discovery.

descubrir, *v.* discover; uncover; disclose.

descubrirse, *v.* take off one's hat.

descuento, *m.* discount.

descuidado, *a.* reckless, careless; slack.

descuido, *m.* neglect. — **descuidar,** *v.*

desde, *prep.* since; from. **d. luego,** of course.

desdén, *m.* disdain. — **desdeñar,** *v.*

desdeñoso, *a.* contemptuous, disdainful, scornful.

desdicha, *f.* misfortune.

deseable, *a.* desirable.

desear, *v.* desire, wish.

desecar, *v.* dry, desiccate.

desechar, *v.* scrap, reject.

desecho, *m.* remainder, residue; (*pl.*) waste.

desembalar, *v.* unpack.

desembarazado, *a.* free; unrestrained.

desembarazar, *v.* free; extricate; unburden.

desembarcar, *v.* disembark, go ashore.

desembocar, *v.* flow into.

desembolsar, *v.* disburse; expend.

desembolso, *m.* disbursement.

desemejante, *a.* unlike, dissimilar.

desempacar, *v.* unpack.

desempeñar, *v.* carry out; redeem.

desempeño, *m.* fulfillment.

desencajar, *v.* disjoint; disturb.

desencantar, *v.* disillusion.

desencanto, *m.* disillusion.

desencarcelar, *v.* set free; release.

desenfadado, *a.* free; unembarrassed; spacious.

desenfado, *m.* freedom; ease; calmness.

desengaño, *m.* disillusion. — **desengañar,** *v.*

desenlace, *m.* outcome, conclusion.

desenredar, *v.* disentangle.

desensartar, *v.* unthread.

desentenderse, *v.* overlook; avoid noticing.

desenterrar, *v.* disinter, exhume.

desenvainar, *v.* unsheath.

desenvoltura, *f.* impudence, boldness.

desenvolver, *v.* evolve, unfold.

deseo, *m.* wish, desire, urge.

deseoso, *a.* desirous.

deserción, *f.* desertion.

desertar, *v.* desert.

desertor, *m.* deserter.

desesperación, *f.* despair, desperation.

desesperado, *a.* desperate; hopeless.

desesperar, *v.* despair.

desfalcar, *v.* embezzle.

desfavorable, *a.* unfavorable.

desfigurar, *v.* disfigure, mar.

desfiladero, *m.* defile.

desfile, *m.* parade. — **desfilar,** *v.*

desgaire, *m.* slovenly appearance.

desgana, *f.* lack of appetite; repugnance.

desgarrar, *v.* tear, lacerate.

desgastar, *v.* wear away, waste, erode.

desgaste, *m.* wear; erosion.

desgracia, *f.* misfortune.

desgraciado, *a.* unfortunate.

desgranar, *v.* shell.

desgreñar, *v.* dishevel.

deshacer, *v.* undo, take apart, destroy.

deshacerse de, v. get rid of, dispose of.

deshecho, a. undone; wasted.

deshelar, v. thaw; melt.

desheredamiento, m. disinheriting.

desheredar, v. disinherit.

deshielo, m. thaw, melting.

deshinchar, v. reduce a swelling.

deshojarse, v. shed (leaves).

deshonestidad, f. dishonesty.

deshonesto, a. dishonest.

deshonra, f. dishonor.

deshonrar, v. disgrace; dishonor.

deshonroso, a. dishonorable.

desierto, m. desert, wilderness.

designar, v. appoint, name.

designio, m. purpose, intent.

desigual, a. uneven, unequal.

desigualdad, f. inequality.

desilusión, f. disappointment.

desinfección, f. disinfection.

desinfectar, v. disinfect.

desintegrar, v. disintegrate, zap.

desinterés, m. indifference.

desinteresado, a. disinterested, unselfish.

desistir, v. desist, stop.

desleal, a. disloyal.

deslealtad, f. disloyalty.

desleir, v. dilute, dissolve.

desligar, v. untie, loosen; free, release.

deslindar, v. make the boundaries of.

deslinde, m. demarcation.

desliz, m. slip; false step; weakness.

deslizarse, v. slide; slip; glide; coast.

deslumbramiento, m. dazzling glare; confusion.

deslumbrar, v. dazzle; glare.

deslustre, m. tarnish. —deslustrar, v.

desmán, m. mishap; misbehavior; excess.

desmantelar, v. dismantle.

desmañado, a. awkward, clumsy.

desmayar, v. dismay, appall.

desmayo, m. faint. —desmayarse, v.

desmejorar, v. make worse; decline.

desmembrar, v. dismember.

desmemoria, f. forgetfulness.

desmemoriado, a. forgetful.

desmentir, v. contradict, disprove.

desmenuzable, a. crisp, crumbly.

desmenuzar, v. crumble, break into bits.

desmesurado, a. excessive.

desmonetización, f. demonetization.

desmonetizar, v. demonetize.

desmontado, a. dismounted.

desmoralización, f. demoralization.

desmoralizar, v. demoralize.

desmoronar, v. crumble, decay.

desmovilizar, v. demobilize.

desnatar, v. skim.

desnaturalización, f. denaturalization.

desnaturalizar, v. denaturalize.

desnegamiento, m. denial, contradiction.

desnervar, v. enervate.

desnivel, m. unevenness or difference in elevation.

desnudamente, adv. nakedly.

desnudar, v. undress.

desnudez, f. bareness, nudity.

desnudo, a. bare, naked.

desnutrición, f. malnutrition.

desobedecer, v. disobey.

desobediencia, f. disobedience.

desobediente, a. disobedient.

desobedientemente, adv. disobediently.

desobligar, v. release from obligation; offend.

desocupado, a. idle, not busy; vacant.

desocupar, v. vacate.

desolación, f. desolation; ruin.

desolado, a. desolate. —desolar, v.

desollar, v. skin.

desorden, m. disorder.

desordenar, v. disarrange.

desorganización, f. disorganization.

desorganizar, v. disorganize.

despabilado, a. vigilant, watchful; lively.

despacio, adv. slowly.

despachar, v. dispatch, ship, send.

despacho, m. shipment; dispatch, promptness; office.

desparpajo, m. glibness; fluency of speech.

desparramar, v. scatter.

despavorido, a. terrified.

despecho, m. spite.

despedazar, v. tear up.

despedida, f. farewell; leave-taking; discharge.

despedir, v. dismiss, discharge; see off.

despedirse de, v. say good-bye to, take leave of.

despegar, v. unglue; separate.

despego, m. indifference; disinterest.

despejar, v. clear, clear up.

despejo, m. sprightly; clear; unobstructed.

despensa, f. pantry.

despensero, m. butler.

despeñar, v. throw down.

desperdicio, m. waste. —desperdiciar, v.

despertador, m. alarm clock.

despertar, v. wake, wake up.

despesar, m. dislike.

despicar, v. satisfy.

despidida, f. gutter.

despierto, a. awake; alert, wide-awake.

despilfarrado, a. wasteful, extravagant.

despilfarrar, v. waste, squander.

despilfarro, m. waste, extravagance.

despique, m. revenge.

desplazamiento, m. displacement.

desplegar, v. display; unfold.

desplome, m. collapse. —desplomarse, v.

desplumar, v. defeather, pluck.

despoblar, v. depopulate.

despojar, v. strip; despoil, plunder.

despojo, m. plunder, spoils; (pl.) remains, debris.

desposado, a. newly married.

desposar, v. marry.

desposeer, v. dispossess.

déspota, m. & f. despot.

despótico, a. despotic.

despotismo, m. despotism, tyranny.

despreciable, a. contemptible.

despreciar, v. spurn, despise, scorn.

desprecio, m. scorn, contempt.

desprender, v. detach, unfasten.

desprenderse, v. loosen, come apart. d. de, part with.

desprendido, a. disinterested.

despreocupado, a. unprejudiced.

desprevenido, a. unprepared, unready.

desproporción, f. disproportion.

despropósito, m. nonsense.

desprovisto, a. devoid.

después, adv. afterwards, later; then, next. d. de, d. que, after.

despuntar, v. blunt; remove the point of.

desquiciar, v. unhinge; disturb, unsettle.

desquitar, v. get revenge, retaliate.

desquite, m. revenge, retaliation.

destacamento, m. (mil.) detachment.

destacarse, v. stand out, be prominent.

destapar, v. uncover.

destello, m. sparkle, gleam.

destemplar, v. change; soften.

desteñir, v. fade, discolor.

desterrado -da, n. exile.

desterrar, v. banish, exile.

destierro, m. banishment, exile.

destilación, f. distillation.

destilar, v. distill.

destilería, f. distillery.

destinación, f. destination.

destinar, v. destine, intend.

destinatorio -ria, n. addressee.

destino, m. destiny, fate; destination.

destitución, f. dismissal; abandonment.

destituido, a. destitute.

destorcer, v. undo, straighten out.

destornillado, a. reckless, careless.

destornillador, m. screwdriver.

destraillar, v. unleash; set loose.

destral, m. hatchet.

destreza, f. cleverness, dexterity, skill.

destripar, v. eviscerate, disembowel.

destrísimo, a. extremely dexterous.

destronamiento, m. dethronement.

destronar, v. dethrone.

destrozador, m. destroyer, wrecker.

destrozar, v. destroy, wreck.

destrozo, m. destruction, ruin.

destrucción, f. destruction.

destructibilidad, f. destructibility.

destructible, a. destructible.

destructivamente, adv. destructively.

destructivo, a. destructive.

destruir, v. destroy; wipe out.

desuello, m. impudence.

desunión, f. disunion; discord; separation.

desunir, v. disconnect, sever.

desusadamente, adv. unusually.

desusado, a. archaic; obsolete.

desuso, m. disuse.

desvalido, a. helpless, destitute.

desvalijador, m. highwayman.

desván, m. attic.

desvanecerse, v. vanish; faint.

desvariado, a. delirious; disorderly.

desvarío, m. raving. —**desvariar,** v.

desvedado, a. free; unrestrained.

desveladamente, adv. watchfully, alertly.

desvelado, a. watchful; alert.

desvelar, v. be watchful; keep awake.

desvelo, m. vigilance; uneasiness.

desventaja, f. disadvantage.

desventar, v. let air out of.

desventura, f. misfortune.

desventurado, a. unhappy; unlucky.

desvergonzado, a. shameless, brazen.

desvergüenza, f. shamelessness.

desvestir, v. undress.

desviación, f. deviation.

desviado, a. devious.

desviar, v. divert; deviate.

desvío, m. detour; side track; indifference.

desvirtuar, v. decrease the value of.

deszumar, v. remove the juice from.

detalle, m. detail. —**detallar,** v.

detective, m. detective.

detención, f. detention, arrest.

detenedor, f. detention, arrest.

detener, v. detain, stop; arrest.

detenidamente, adv. carefully, slowly.

detenido, adv. stingy; thorough.

détente, f. detente.

detergente, a. detergent.

deterioración, f. deterioration.

deteriorar, v. deteriorate.

determinable, a. determinable.

determinación, f. determination.

determinar, v. determine.

determinismo, m. determinism.

determinista, n. & a. determinist.

detestable, a. detestable, hateful.

detestablemente, adv. detestably, hatefully, abhorrently.

detestación, f. detestation, hatefulness.

detestar, v. detest.

detonación, f. detonation.

detonar, v. detonate, explode.

detracción, f. detraction, defamation.

detractar, v. detract, defame, vilify.

detraer, v. detract.

detrás, adv. behind; in back.

detrimento, m. detriment, damage.

deuda, f. debt.

deudo -da, n. relative, kin.

deudor -ra, n. debtor.

devalar, v. drift.

devanar, v. to wind, as on a spool.

devanear, v. talk deliriously, rave.

devaneo, m. frivolity; idle pursuit; delirium.

devantal, m. apron.

devastación, f. devastation, ruin, havoc.

devastador, m. devastator.

devastar, v. devastate.

devenir, v. happen, occur; become.

devoción, f. devotion.

devocionario, m. prayer book.

devocionero, a. devotional.

devolver, v. return, give back.

devorar, v. devour.

devotamente, adv. devotedly, devoutly, piously.

devoto, a. devout; devoted.

deyección, f. depression, dejection.

día, m. day. **buenos días,** good morning.

diabetes, f. diabetes.

diabético, a. diabetic.

diablear, i. play pranks.

diablo, m. devil.

diablura, f. mischief.

diabólicamente, adv. diabolically.

diabólico, a. diabolic, devilish.

diaconado, m. deaconship.

diaconía, f. deaconry.

diácono, m. deacon.

diacrítico, a. diacritic.

diadema, f. diadem, crown.

diáfano, a. transparent.

diafragma, m. diaphragm.

diagnosticar, v. diagnose.

diagonal, f. diagonal.

diagonalmente, adv. diagonally.

diagrama, m. diagram.

dialectal, a. dialectal.

dialéctico, a. dialectic.

dialecto, m. dialect.

diálogo, m. dialogue.

diamante, m. diamond.

diamantista, m. diamond cutter; jeweler.

diametral, a. diametric.

diametralmente, adv. diametrically.

diámetro, m. diameter.

diana, f. reveille.

diapasón, m. pitch; tuning fork.

diaplejía, f. paralysis.

diariamente, adv. daily.

diario, a. & m. daily; daily paper; diary; journal.

diarrea, f. diarrhea.

diatriba, f. diatribe, harangue.

dibujo, m. drawing, sketch. — **dibujar,** v.

dicción, f. diction.

diccionario, m. dictionary.

diccionarista, n. lexicographer.

diciembre, m. December.

dicotomía, f. dichotomy.

dictado, m. dictation.

dictador, m. dictator.

dictadura, f. dictatorship.

dictamen, m. dictate.

dictar, v. dictate; direct.

dictatoría, a. dictatorial; tyrannic.

dicha, f. happiness.

dicho, m. saying.

dichoso, a. happy; fortunate.

didáctico, a. didactic.

diecinueve, a. & pron. nineteen.

dieciocho, a. & pron. eighteen.

dieciseis, a. & pron. sixteen.

diecisiete, a. & pron. seventeen.

diente, m. tooth.

diestramente, adv. skillfully, ably; ingeniously.

diestro, a. dexterous, skillful; clever.

dieta, f. diet; allowance.

dietética, f. dietetic.

diez, a. & pron. ten.

diezmal, a. decimal.

diezmar, v. decimate.

difamación, f. defamation, smear.

difamar, v. defame, smear, libel.

difamatorio, a. defamatory.

diferencia, f. difference.

diferencial, a. & f. differential.

diferenciar, v. differentiate, distinguish.

diferente, a. different.

diferentemente, adv. differently.

diferir, v. differ; defer, put off.

difícil, a. difficult, hard.

difícilmente, adv. with difficulty or hardship.

dificultad, f. difficulty.

dificultar, v. make difficult.

dificultoso, a. difficult, hard.

difidencia, f. diffidence.

difidente, a. diffident.

difteria, f. diphtheria.

difundir, v. diffuse, spread.

difunto, a. deceased, dead, late.

difusamente, adv. diffusely.

difusión, f. diffusion, spread.

digerible, a. digestible.

digerir, v. digest.

digestible, a. digestible.

digestión, f. digestion.

digestivo, a. digestive.

digesto, m. digest or code of laws.

digitado, a. digitate.

digital, 1. a. digital. **2.** f. foxglove.

dignación, f. condescension; deigning.

dignamente, adv. with dignity.

dignarse, v. condescend, deign.

dignidad, f. dignity.

dignificar, v. dignify.

dignitario, m. dignitary.

digno, a. worthy; dignified.

digresión, f. digression.

digresivo, a. digressive.

dij, dije, m. trinket, piece of jewelry.

dilación, f. delay.

dilapidación, f. dilapidation.

dilatación, f. dilatation, enlargement.

dilatar, v. dilate; delay; expand.

dilatoria, f. delay.

dilecto, a. loved.

dilema, m. dilemma.

diligencia, f. diligence, industriousness.

diligente, a. diligent, industrious.

diligentemente, adv. diligently.

dilogía, f. ambiguous meaning.

dilución, f. dilution.

diluir, v. dilute.

diluvial, a. diluvial.

diluvio, m. flood, deluge.

dimensión, f. dimension; measurement.

diminución, f. diminution.

diminuto, diminutivo, a. diminutive, little.

dimisión, f. resignation.

dimitir, v. resign.

Dinamarca, f. Denmark.

dinamarqués -esa, a. & n. Danish, Dane.

dinámico, a. dynamic.

dinamita, f. dynamite.

dinamitero, m. dynamiter.

dínamo, m. dynamo.

dinasta, m. dynast, king, monarch.

dinastía, f. dynasty.

dinástico, a. dynastic.

dinero, m. money, currency.

dinosauro, m. dinosaur.

Dios, m. God.

dios -sa, n. god, goddess.

diploma, m. diploma.

diplomacia, f. diplomacy.

diplomado -da, n. graduate.

diplomarse, v. graduate (from a school).

diplomática, f. diplomacy.

diplomático, a. & m. diplomat; diplomatic.

dipsomanía, f. dipsomania.

diptongo, m. diphthong.

diputación, f. deputation, delegation.

diputado, m. deputy.

diputar, v. depute; delegate; empower.

dique, m. dike; dam.

dirección, f. direction; address; guidance; (com.) management.

directamente, adv. directly.

directo, a. direct.

director, m. director; manager.

dirigente, a. directing, controlling, managing.

dirigible, m. dirigible.

dirigir, v. direct; lead; manage.

dirigirse a, v. address; approach, turn to; head for.

dirruir, v. destroy, devastate.

disanto, m. holy day.

discantar, v. sing (esp. in counterpoint); discuss.

disceptación, f. argument, quarrel.

disceptar, v. argue, quarrel.

discernimiento, m. discernment.

discernir, v. discern.

disciplina, f. discipline.

disciplinable, a. disciplinable.

disciplinar, v. discipline, train, teach.

discípulo -la, n. disciple, follower; pupil.

disco, m. disk; (phonograph) record.

discontinuación, f. discontinuation.

discontinuar, v. discontinue, break off, cease.

discordancia, f. discordance.

discordar, v. disagree, conflict.

discordia, f. discord.

discoteca, f. disco, discotheque.

discreción, f. discretion.

discrecional, a. optional.

discrecionalmente, adv. optionally.

discrepancia, f. discrepancy.

discretamente, adv. discreetly.

discreto, a. discreet.

discrimen, m. risk, hazard.

discriminación, f. discrimination.

discriminar, v. discriminate.

disculpa, f. excuse; apology.

disculpar, v. excuse; exonerate.

disculparse, v. apologize.

discurrir, v. roam; flow; think; plan.

discursante, n. lecturer, speaker.

discursivo, a. discursive.

discurso, m. speech, talk.

discusión, f. discussion.

discutible, a. debatable.

discutir, v. discuss; debate; contest.

disecación, f. dissection.

disecar, v. dissect.

disección, f. dissection.

diseminación, f. dissemination.

diseminar, v. disseminate, spread.

disensión, f. dissension; dissent.

disenso, m. dissent.

disentería, f. dysentery.

disentir, v. disagree, dissent.

diseñador -ra, n. designer.

diseño, m. design. —**diseñar,** v.

disertación, f. dissertation.

disfamación, f. defamation.

disforme, a. deformed, monstrous, ugly.

disformidad, f. deformity.

disfraz, m. disguise. —**disfrazar,** v.

disfrutar, v. enjoy.

disfrute, m. enjoyment.

disgustar, v. displease; disappoint.

disgusto, m. displeasure; disappointment.

disidencia, f. dissidence.

disidente, a. & n. dissident.

disímil, a. unlike.

disimilitud, f. dissimilarity.

disimulación, f. dissimulation.

disimulado, a. dissembling, feigning; sly.

disimular, v. hide, dissemble.

disimulo, m. pretense.

disipación, f. dissipation.

disipado, a. dissipated; wasted; scattered.

disipar, v. waste; scatter.

dislexia, f. dyslexia.

dislocación, f. dislocation.

dislocar, v. dislocate; displace.

disminuir, v. diminish, lessen, reduce.

disociación, f. dissociation.

disociar, v. dissociate.

disolubilidad, f. dissolubility.

disoluble, a. dissoluble.

disolución, f. dissolution.

disolutemente, adv. dissolutely.

disoluto, a. dissolute.

disolver, v. dissolve.

disonancia, f. dissonance; discord.

disonante, a. dissonant; discordant.

disonar, v. be discordant; clash in sound.

dísono, a. dissonant.

dispar, a. unlike.

disparadamente, *adv.* hastily, hurriedly.

disparar, *v.* shoot, fire (a weapon).

disparatado, *a.* nonsensical.

disparatar, *v.* talk nonsense.

disparate, *m.* nonsense, tall tale.

disparejo, *a.* uneven, unequal.

disparidad, *f.* disparity.

disparo, *m.* shot.

dispendio, *m.* extravagance.

dispendioso, *a.* expensive; extravagant.

dispensa, dispensación, *f.* dispensation.

dispensable, *a.* dispensable; excusable.

dispensar, *v.* dispense, excuse; grant.

dispensario, *m.* dispensary.

dispepsia, *f.* dyspepsia.

dispéptico, *a.* dyspeptic.

dispersar, *v.* scatter; dispel; disband.

dispersión, *f.* dispersion, dispersal.

disperso, *a.* dispersed.

displicente, *a.* unpleasant.

disponer, *v.* dispose. **d. de,** have at one's disposal.

disponible, *a.* available.

disposición, *f.* disposition; disposal.

dispuesto, *a.* disposed, inclined; attractive.

disputa, *f.* dispute, argument.

disputable, *a.* disputable.

disputador, *m.* disputant.

disputar, *v.* argue; dispute.

disquisición, *f.* disquisition.

distancia, *f.* distance.

distante, *a.* distant.

distantemente, *adv.* distantly.

distar, *v.* be distant, be far.

distención, *f.* distension, swelling.

distender, *v.* distend, swell, enlarge.

dístico, *m.* couplet.

distinción, *f.* distinction, difference.

distingo, *m.* restriction.

distinguible, *a.* distinguishable.

distinguido, *a.* distinguished, prominent.

distinguir, *v.* distinguish; make out, spot.

distintamente, *adv.* distinctly, clearly; differently.

distintivo, *a.* distinctive.

distinto, *a.* distinct, different.

distracción, *f.* distraction, pastime; absent-mindedness.

distraer, *v.* distract.

distraídamente, *adv.* absentmindedly, distractedly.

distraído, *a.* absent-minded; distracted.

distribución, *f.* distribution.

distribuidor -ra, *n.* distributor.

distribuir, *v.* distribute.

distributivo, *a.* distributive.

distributor, *m.* distributor.

distrito, *m.* district.

disturbar, *v.* disturb, trouble.

disturbio, *m.* disturbance, outbreak; turmoil.

disuadir, *v.* dissuade.

disuasión, *f.* dissuasion; deterrence.

disuasivo, *a.* dissuasive.

disyunción, *f.* disjunction.

ditirambo, *m.* dithyramb.

diurno, *a.* diurnal.

diva, *f.* singer.

divagación, *f.* digression.

divagar, *v.* digress, ramble.

diván, *m.* couch.

divergencia, *f.* divergence.

divergente, *a.* divergent, differing.

divergir, *v.* diverge.

diversamente, *adv.* diversely.

diversidad, *f.* diversity.

diversificar, *v.* diversify, vary.

diversión, *f.* diversion, pastime.

diverso, *a.* diverse, different; (*pl.*) various, several.

divertido, *a.* humorous, amusing.

divertimiento, *m.* diversion; amusement.

divertir, *v.* entertain, amuse.

divertirse, *v.* enjoy oneself, have a good time.

dividendo, *m.* dividend.

divididero, *a.* divisible.

dividir, *v.* divide, separate.

divieso, *m.* (med.) boil.

divinamente, *adv.* divinely.

divinidad, *f.* divinity.

divinizar, *v.* deify.

divino, *a.* divine; heavenly.

divisa, *f.* badge, emblem.

divisar, *v.* sight, make out.

divisibilidad, *f.* divisibility.

divisible, *a.* divisible.

división, *f.* division.

divisivo, *a.* divisive.

diviso, *a.* divided.

divo, *m.* god.

divorcio, *m.* divorce. —**divorciar,** *v.*

divulgable, *a.* divulgable.

divulgación, *f.* divulgation.

divulgar, *v.* divulge, reveal.

dobladamente, *adv.* doubly.

dobladillo, *m.* hem of a skirt or dress.

dobladura, *f.* fold, bend.

doblar, *v.* fold; bend.

doble, *a.* double.

doblegable, *a.* flexible, foldable.

doblegar, *v.* fold, bend; yield.

doblez, *m.* fold; duplicity.

doblón, *m.* doubloon.

doce, *a. & pron.* twelve.

docena, *f.* dozen.

docente, *a.* educational

dócil, *a.* docile.

docilidad, *f.* docility, tractableness.

dócilmente, *adv.* docilely, meekly.

doctamente, *adv.* learnedly, profoundly.

docto, *a.* learned, expert.

doctor, *m.* doctor.

doctorado, *m.* doctorate.

doctoral, *a.* doctoral.

doctrina, *f.* doctrine.

doctrinador, *m.* teacher.

doctrinal, *m.* catechism.

doctrinar, *v.* teach.

documentación, *f.* documentation.

documental, *a.* documentary.

documento, *m.* document.

dogal, *m.* noose.

dogma, *m.* dogma.

dogmáticamente, *adv.* dogmatically.

dogmático, *m.* dogmatic.

dogmatismo, *m.* dogmatism.

dogmatista, *m.* dogmatist.

dogo, *m.* bulldog.

dolar, *v.* cut, chop, hew.

dólar, *m.* dollar.

dolencia, *f.* pain; disease.

doler, *v.* ache, hurt, be sore.

doliente, *a.* ill; aching.

dolor, *m.* pain; grief, sorrow, woe.

dolorido, *a.* painful, sorrowful.

dolorosamente, *adv.* painfully, sorrowfully.

doloroso, *a.* painful, sorrowful.

dolosamente, *adv.* deceitfully.

doloso, *a.* deceitful.

domable, *a.* that can be tamed or managed.

domar, *v.* tame; subdue.

dombo, *m.* dome.

domesticable, *a.* that can be domesticated.

domesticación, *f.* domestication.

domésticamente, *adv.* domestically.

domesticar, *v.* tame.

domesticidad, *f.* domesticity.

doméstico, *a.* domestic.

domicilio, *m.* dwelling, home, residence.

dominación, *f.* domination.

dominador, *a.* dominating.

dominante, *a.* dominant.

dominar, *v.* rule, dominate; master.

dómine, *m.* teacher.

domingo, *m.* Sunday.

dominio, *m.* domain; rule; power.

dominó, *m.* domino.

domo, *m.* dome.

Don, *title used before a man's first name.*

don, *m.* gift.

dona, *f.* woman.

donación, *f.* donation.

donador -ra, *n.* giver, donor.

donaire, *m.* grace.

donairosamente, *adv.* gracefully.

donairoso, *a.* graceful.

donante, *n.* giver, donor.

donar, *v.* donate.

donativo, *f.* donation, contribution; gift.

doncella, *f.* lass; maid.

donde, dónde, *conj. & adv.* where.

dondequiera, *adv.* wherever, anywhere.

donosamente, *adv.* gracefully; wittily.

donoso, *a.* graceful; witty.

donosura, *f.* gracefulness; wittiness.

Doña, *title used before a lady's first name.*

dorado, *a.* gilded.

dorador, *m.* gilder.

dorar, *v.* gild.

dórico, *a.* Doric.

dormidero, *a.* sleep-inducing; soporific.

dormido, *a.* asleep.

dormir, *v.* sleep.

dormirse, *v.* fall asleep, go to sleep.

dormitar, *v.* doze.

dormitorio, *m.* dormitory; bedroom.

dorsal, *a.* dorsal.

dorso, *m.* spine.

dos, *a. & pron.* two. **los d.,** both.

dosañal, *a.* biennial.

doscientos, *a. & pron.* two hundred.

dosel, *m.* canopy; platform; dais.

dosificación, *f.* dosage.

dosis, *f.* dose.

dotación, *f.* endowment; (*naut.*) crew.

dotador, *m.* donor.

dotar, *v.* endow; give a dowry to.

dote, *m.* dowry; (*pl.*) talents.

dragaminas, *m.* mine sweeper.

dragar, *v.* dredge; sweep.

dragón, *m.* dragon; dragoon.

dragonear, *v.* pretend to be.

drama, *m.* drama; play.

dramática, *f.* dramatics.

dramáticamente, *adv.* dramatically.

dramático, *a.* dramatic.

dramatizar, *v.* dramatize.

dramaturgo, *m.* playwright, dramatist.

drástico, *a.* drastic.

drenaje, *m.* drainage.

dríada, *f.* dryad.

driza, *f.* halyard.

droga, *f.* drug.

droguería, *f.* drugstore.

droguero, *m.* druggist.

dromedario, *m.* dromedary.

druida, *m.* Druid.

dualidad, *f.* duality.

dubitable, *a.* doubtful.

dubitación, *f.* doubt.

ducado, *m.* duchy.

ducal, *a.* ducal.

dúctil, *a.* ductile.

ductilidad, *f.* ductility.

ducha, *f.* shower (bath).

duda, *f.* doubt.

dudable, *a.* doubtful.

dudar, *v.* doubt; hesitate; question.

dudosamente, *adv.* doubtfully.

dudoso, *a.* dubious; doubtful.

duela, *f.* stave.

duelista, *m.* duelist.

duelo, *m.* duel; grief; mourning.

duende, *m.* elf, hobgoblin.

dueño -ña, *n.* owner; landlord, -lady; master, mistress.

dulce, **1.** *a.* sweet. **agua d.,** fresh water. **2.** *m.* piece of candy; (*pl.*) candy.

dulcedumbre, *f.* sweetness.

dulcemente, *adv.* sweetly.

dulcería, *f.* confectionery; candy shop.

dulcificar, *v.* sweeten.

dulzura, *f.* sweetness; mildness.

duna, *f.* dune.

duodenal, *a.* duodenal.

dúo, *m.* duet.

duplicación, *f.* duplication; doubling.

duplicadamente, *adv.* doubly.

duplicado, *a. & m.* duplicate.

duplicar, *v.* double, duplicate, repeat.

duplicidad, *f.* duplicity.

duplo, *a.* double.

duque, *m.* duke.

duquesa, *f.* duchess.

durabilidad, *f.* durability.

durable, *a.* durable.

duración, *f.* duration.

duradero, *a.* lasting, durable.

duramente, *adv.* harshly, roughly.

durante, *prep.* during.

durar, *v.* last.

durazno, *m.* peach.

dureza, *f.* hardness.

durmiente, *a.* dormant.

duro, *a.* hard; stiff; stern; stale.

dux, *m.* doge.

E

e, *conj.* and.

ebanista, *m.* cabinetmaker.

ebanizar, *v.* give an ebony finish to.

ébano, *m.* ebony.

ebonita, *f.* ebonite.

ebrio, *a.* drunken, inebriated.

ebullición, *f.* boiling.

eclecticismo, *m.* eclecticism.

ecléctico, *n. & a.* eclectic.

eclesiástico, *a. & m.* ecclesiastic.

eclipse, *m.* eclipse. —**eclipsar,** *v.*

eclipsis, *f.* ellipsis.

écloga, *f.* eclogue.

eco, *m.* echo.

ecología, *f.* ecology.

ecológico, *a.* ecological.

ecologista, *m. & f.* ecologist.

economía, *f.* economy; thrift. **e. política,** economics.

económicamente, *adv.* economically.

económico, *a.* economic; economical, thrifty.

economista, *f.* economist.

economizar, *v.* save, economize.

ecuación, *f.* equation.

ecuador, *m.* equator.

ecuanimidad, *f.* equanimity.

ecuatorial, *a.* equatorial.

ecuatoriano -na, *a. & n.* Ecuadorian.

ecuestre, *a.* equestrian.

ecuménico, *a.* ecumenical.

echada, *f.* throw.

echadillo, *m.* foundling; orphan.

echar, *v.* throw, toss; pour. **e. a,** start to. **e. a perder,** spoil, ruin. **e. de menos,** miss.

echarse, *v.* lie down.

edad, *f.* age.

edecán, *m.* aide-de-camp.

Edén, *m.* Eden.

edición, *f.* edition; issue.

edicto, *m.* edict, decree.

edificación, *f.* construction.

edificador, *n.* constructor; builder.

edificar, *v.* build.

edificio, *m.* edifice, building.

editar, *v.* publish, issue.

editor, *m.* publisher.

editorial, *a.* editorial.

edredón, *m.* quilt.

educación, *f.* upbringing, breeding; education.

educador, *m.* educator.

educar, *v.* educate, bring up; train.

educativo, *a.* educational.

educción, *f.* deduction.

educir, *v.* educe.

educto, *m.* output.

efectivamente, *adv.* actually, really.

efectivo, *a.* effective; actual, real. **en e.,** (*com.*) in cash.

efecto, *m.* effect.

efectuar, *v.* effect; cash.

eferente, *a.* efferent.

efervescencia, *f.* effervescence; zeal.

eficacia, *f.* efficacy.

eficaz, *a.* efficient, effective.

eficazmente, *adv.* efficaciously.

eficiencia, *f.* efficiency.

eficiente, *a.* efficient.

efigie, *f.* effigy.

efímera, *f.* May fly.

efímero, *a.* ephemeral, passing.

efulvio, *m.* effluvium.

efundir, *v.* effuse; pour out.

efusión, *f.* effusion.

egipcio -cía, *a. & n.* Egyptian.

Egipto, *m.* Egypt.

égira, *f.* hegira.

egoísmo, *m.* egoism, egotism, selfishness.

egoísta, *a. & n.* selfish, egoistic; egoist.

egotismo, *m.* egotism.

egotista, *n.* egotist.

egreso, *m.* expense, outlay.

eje, *m.* axis; axle.

ejecución, *f.* execution; performance; enforcement.

ejecutar, *v.* execute; enforce; carry out.

ejecutivo, *a. & m.* executive.

ejecutor, *m.* executor.

ejemplar, 1. *a.* exemplary. **2.** *m.* copy.

ejemplificación, *f.* exemplification.

ejemplificar, *v.* illustrate.

ejemplo, *m.* example.

ejercer, *v.* exert; practice.

ejercicio, *m.* exercise, drill. —**ejercitar,** *v.*

ejercitación, *f.* exercise, training, drill.

ejercitar, *v.* exercise, train, drill.

ejército, *m.* army.

ejotes, *m.pl.* string beans.

el, *art. & pron.* the; the one.

él, *pron.* he, him; it.

elaboración, *f.* elaboration; working up.

elaborado, *a.* elaborate.

elaborador, *m.* manufacturer, maker.

elaborar, *v.* elaborate; manufacture; brew.

elación, *f.* elation; magnanimity; turgid style.

elasticidad, *f.* elasticity.

elástico, *m.* elastic.

elección, *f.* election; option, choice.

electivo, *a.* elective.

electo, *a.* elected, chosen, appointed.

electorado, *m.* electorate.

electoral, *a.* electoral.

electricidad, *f.* electricity.

electricista, *m.* electrician.

eléctrico, *a.* electric.

electrización, *f.* electrification.

electrocardiograma, *m.* electrocardiogram.

electrocución, *f.* electrocution.

electrocutar, *v.* electrocute.

electrodo, *m.* electrode.

electroimán, *m.* electromagnet.

electrólisis, *f.* electrolysis.

electrólito, *m.* electrolyte.

electrón, *m.* electron.

elefante, *m.* elephant.

elegancia, *f.* elegance.

elegante, *a.* elegant, smart, stylish, fine.

elegantemente, *adv.* elegantly.

elegía, *f.* elegy.

elegibilidad, *f.* eligibility.

elegible, *a.* eligible.

elegir, *v.* select, choose; elect.

elemental, *a.* elementary.

elementalmente, *adv.* elementally; fundamentally.

elementar, *a.* elementary.

elemento, *m.* element.

elevación, *f.* elevation; height.

elevador, *m.* elevator.

elevamiento, *m.* elevation.

elevar, *v.* elevate; erect, raise.

elidir, *v.* elide.

eliminación, *f.* elimination.

eliminar, *v.* eliminate.

elipse, *f.* ellipse.

elipsis, *f.* ellipsis.

elíptico, *a.* elliptic.

elocuencia, *f.* eloquence.

elocuente, *a.* eloquent.

elocuentemente, *adv.* eloquently.

elogio, *m.* praise, compliment. —**elogiar,** *v.*

elucidación, *f.* elucidation.

elucidar, *v.* elucidate.

eludir, *v.* elude.

ella, *pron.* she, her; it.

ello, *pron.* it.

ellos -as, *pron. pl.* they, them.

emaciación, *f.* emaciation.

emanar, *v.* emanate, stem.

emancipación, *f.* emancipation, freeing.

emancipador, *n.* emancipator.

emancipar, *v.* emancipate, free.

embajada, *f.* embassy; legation; (coll.) errand.

embajador, *m.* ambassador.

embalar, *v.* pack, bale.

embaldosado, *m.* tile floor.

embalsamador, *m.* embalmer.

embalsamar, *v.* embalm.

embarazada, *a.* pregnant.

embarazadamente, *adv.* embarrassedly.

embarazar, *v.* embarrass.

embarazo, *m.* embarrassment; pregnancy.

embarbascado, *a.* difficult; complicated.

embarcación, *f.* boat, ship; embarkation.

embarcadero, *m.* wharf, pier, dock.

embarcador, *m.* shipper, loader, stevedore.

embarcar, *v.* ship.

embarcarse, *v.* embark; sail.

embargador, *m.* one who impedes; one who orders an embargo.

embargante, *a.* impeding, hindering.

embargar, *v.* impede, restrain; (leg.) seize, embargo.

embargo, *m.* seizure, embargo. **sin e.,** however, nevertheless.

embarnizar, *v.* varnish.

embarque, *m.* shipment.

embarrador, *m.* plasterer.

embarrancar, *v.* get stuck in mud.

embarrar, *v.* plaster; besmear with mud.

embasamiento, *m.* foundation of a building.

embastecer, *v.* get fat.

embaucador, *m.* imposter.

embaucar, *v.* deceive, trick, hoax.

embaular, *v.* pack in a trunk.

embausamiento, *m.* amazement.

embebecer, *v.* amaze, astonish; entertain.

embeber, *v.* absorb; incorporate; saturate.

embelecador, *m.* imposter.

embeleco, *m.* fraud, perpetration.

embeleñar, *v.* fascinate, charm.

embelesamiento, *m.* rapture.

embelesar, *v.* fascinate, charm.

embeleso, *m.* rapture, bliss.

embellecer, *v.* beautify, embellish.

embestida, *f.* violent assault; attack.

emblandecer, *v.* soften; moisten; move to pity.

emblema, *m.* emblem.

emblemático, *a.* emblematic.

embocadura, *f.* narrow entrance; mouth of a river.

embocar, *v.* eat hastily; gorge.

embolia, *f.* embolism.

embolsar, *v.* pocket.

embonar, *v.* improve, fix, repair.

emborrachador, *a.* intoxicating.

emborrachar, *v.* get drunk.

emboscada, *f.* ambush.

emboscar, *v.* put or lie in ambush.

embotado, *a.* blunt, dull (edged). —**embotar,** *v.*

embotadura, *f.* bluntness; dullness.

embotellar, *v.* put in bottles.

embozado, *v.* muzzled; muffled.

embozar, *v.* muzzle; muffle.

embozo, *m.* muffler.

embrague, *m.* (auto.) clutch.

embravecer, *v.* be or make angry.

embriagado, *a.* drunken, intoxicated.

embriagar, *v.* intoxicate.

embriaguez, *f.* drunkenness.

embrión, *m.* embryo.

embrionario, *a.* embryonic.

embrochado, *a.* embroidered.

embrollo, *m.* muddle. —**embrollar,** *v.*

embromar, *v.* tease; joke.

embuchado, *m.* pork sausage.

embudo, *m.* funnel.

embuste, *m.* lie, fib.

embustear, *v.* lie, fib.

embustero -ra, *m.* liar.

embutir, *v.* stuff, cram.

emendación, *f.* emendation, change, correction.

emergencia, *f.* emergency.

emérito, *a.* emeritus.

emético, *m. & a.* emetic.

emigración, *f.* emigration.

emigrante, *a. & n.* emigrant.

emigrar, *v.* emigrate.

eminencia, *f.* eminence, height.

eminente, *a.* eminent.

emisario, *m.* emissary, spy; outlet.

emisión, *f.* issue; emission.

emisor, *m.* radio transmitter.

emitir, *v.* emit.

emoción, *f.* feeling, emotion, thrill.

emocional, *a.* emotional.

emocionante, *a.* exciting.

emocionar, *v.* touch, move, excite.

emolumento, *m.* emolument; perquisite.

empacar, *v.* pack.

empacho, *m.* shyness, timidity; embarrassment.

empadronamiento, *m.* census; list of taxpayers.

empalizada, *f.* palisade, stockade.

empanada, *f.* meat pie.

empañar, *v.* blur; soil, sully.

empapar, *v.* soak.

empapelado, *m.* wallpaper.

empaque, *m.* packing; appearance, mien.

empaquetar, *v.* pack, package.

emparejarse, *v.* match, pair off; level, even off.

emparentado, *a.* related by marriage.

emparrado, *m.* arbor.

empastadura, *f.* (dental) filling.

empastar, *v.* fill (a tooth).

empate, *m.* tie, draw. —**empatarse,** *v.*

empecer, *v.* hurt, harm, injure; prevent.

empedernir, *v.* harden.

empeine, *m.* groin; instep; hoof.

empellar, *v.* shove, jostle.

empellón, *m.* hard push, shove.

empeñar, *v.* pledge; pawn.

empeñarse en, *v.* persist in, be bent on.

empeño, *m.* persistence; pledge; pawning.

empeoramiento, *m.* deterioration.

empeorar, *v.* get worse.

emperador, *m.* emperor.

emperatriz, *f.* empress.

empernar, *v.* nail.

empero, *conj.* however.

emperramiento, *m.* stubbornness.

empezar, *v.* begin, start.

empinado, *a.* steep.

empinar, *v.* raise; exalt.

empíreo, *a.* celestial, heavenly; divine.

empíricamente, *adv.* empirically.

empírico, *a.* empirical.

empirismo, *m.* empiricism.

emplastarse, *v.* get smeared.

emplasto, *m.* salve.

emplazamiento, *m.* court summons.

emplazar, *v.* summon to court.

empleado -da, *n.* employee.

emplear, *v.* employ; use.

empleo, *m.* employment, job; use.

empobrecer, *v.* make or become impoverished.

empobrecimiento, *m.* impoverishment.

empolvado, *a.* dusty.

empolvar, *v.* powder.

empollador, *m.* incubator.

empollar, *v.* hatch.

emporcar, *v.* soil, make dirty.

emporio, *m.* emporium.

emprendedor, *a.* enterprising.

emprender, *v.* undertake.

empreñar, *v.* make pregnant; beget.

empresa, *f.* enterprise, undertaking.

empresario, *m.* impresario.

empréstito, *m.* loan.

empujón, *m.* push; shove. —**empujar,** *v.*

empuñar, *v.* grasp, seize; wield.

emulación, *f.* emulation; envy; rivalry.

emulador, *m.* emulator; rival.

émulo, *a.* rival. —**emular,** *v.*

emulsión, *f.* emulsion.

emulsionar, *v.* emulsify.

en, *prep.* in, on, at.

enaguas, *f.pl.* petticoat; skirt.

enajenable, *a.* alienable.

enajenación, *f.* alienation; derangement, insanity.

enajenar, *v.* alienate.

enamoradamente, *adv.* lovingly.

enamorado, *a.* in love.

enamorador, *m.* wooer; suitor; lover.

enamorarse, *v.* fall in love.

enano -na, *n.* midget; dwarf.

enardecer, *v.* inflame.

enastado, *a.* horned.

encabestrar, *v.* halter.

encabezado, *m.* headline.

encabezador, *m.* reaping machine.

encabezamiento, *m.* title; census; tax roll.

encabezar, *v.* head.

encachar, *v.* hide.

encadenamiento, *m.* connection, linkage.

encadenar, *v.* chain; link, connect.

encajar, *v.* fit in, insert.

encaje, *m.* lace.

encalar, *v.* whitewash.

encalvecer, *v.* lose one's hair.

encallarse, *v.* be stranded.

encallecido, *a.* hardened; calloused.

encaminar, *v.* guide; direct; be on the way to.

encandilar, *v.* dazzle; daze.

encantación, *f.* incantation.

encantado, *a.* charmed, fascinated, enchanted.

encantador, *a.* charming, delightful.

encante, *m.* public auction.

encanto, *m.* charm, delight. —**encantar,** *v.*

encapillado, *m.* clothes one is wearing.

encapotar, *v.* cover, cloak; muffle.

encaramarse, *v.* perch; climb.

encararse con, *v.* face.

encarcelación, *f.* imprisonment.

encarcelar, *v.* jail, imprison.

encarecer, *v.* recommend; extol.

encarecidamente, *adv.* extremely; ardently.

encargado, *m.* agent; attorney; representative.

encargar, *v.* entrust.

encargarse, *v.* take charge, be in charge.

encargo, *m.* errand; assignment; (com.) order.

encarnación, *f.* incarnation.

encarnado, *a.* red.

encarnar, *v.* embody.

encarnecer, *v.* grow fat or heavy.

encarnizado, *a.* bloody, fierce.

encarrilar, *v.* set right; put on the track.

encartar, *v.* ban, outlaw; summon.

encastar, *v.* improve by crossbreeding.

encastillar, *v.* be obstinate or unyielding.

encatarrado, *a.* suffering from a cold.

encausar, *v.* prosecute; take legal action against.

encauzar, *v.* channel; direct.

encefalitis, *f.* encephalitis.

encelamiento, *m.* envy, jealousy.

encenagar, *v.* wallow in mud.

encendedor, *m.* lighter.

encender, *v.* light; set fire to, kindle; turn on.

encendido, *m.* ignition.

encerado, *m.* oilcloth; tarpaulin.

encerar, *v.* wax.

encerrar, *v.* enclose; confine, shut in.

encía, *f.* gum.

encíclico, 1. *a.* encyclic. **2.** *f.* encyclical.

enciclopedia, *f.* encyclopedia.

enciclopédico, *a.* encyclopedic.

encierro, *m.* confinement; enclosure.

encima, *adv.* on top. **e. de,** on. **por e. de,** above.

encina, *f.* oak.

encinta, *a.* pregnant.

enclavar, *v.* nail.

enclenque, *a.* frail, weak, sickly.

encogerse, *v.* shrink. **e. de hombros,** shrug the shoulders.

encogido, *a.* shy, bashful, timid.

encojar, *v.* make or become lame; cripple.

encolar, *v.* glue, paste, stick.

encolerizar, *v.* make or become angry.

encomendar, *v.* commend; recommend.

encomiar, *v.* praise, laud, extol.

encomienda, *f.* commission, charge; (postal) package.

encomio, *m.* encomium, eulogy.

enconar, *v.* irritate, annoy, anger.

encono, *m.* rancor, resentment.

enconoso, *a.* rancorous, resentful.

encontrado, *a.* opposite.

encontrar, *v.* find; meet.

encorajar, v. encourage; incite.

encorralar, v. corral.

encorvadura, f. bend, curvature.

encorvar, v. arch, bend.

encorvarse, v. stoop.

encrucijada, f. crossroads.

encuadrar, v. frame.

encubierta, a. secret, fraudulent.

encubrir, v. hide, conceal.

encuentro, m. encounter; match, bout.

encurtido, m. pickle.

enchapado, m. veneer.

enchufe, m. (elec.) plug, socket.

endeble, a. rail, weak, sickly.

enderezar, v. straighten; redress.

endiablado, a. devilish.

endibia, f. endive.

endiosar, v. deify.

endorso, endoso, m. endorsement.

endosador, m. endorser.

endosar, v. endorse.

endosatario, m. endorsee.

endulzar, v. sweeten; soothe.

endurar, v. harden; endure.

endurecer, v. harden.

enemigo -ga, n. foe, enemy.

enemistad, f. enmity.

éneo, a. brass.

energía, f. energy.

enérgicamente, adv. energetically.

enérgico, a. forceful; energetic.

enero, m. January.

enervación, f. enervation.

enfadado, a. angry.

enfadar, v. anger, vex.

enfado, m. anger, vexation.

énfasis, m. or f. emphasis, stress.

enfáticamente, adv. emphatically.

enfático, a. emphatic.

enfermar, v. make ill; fall ill.

enfermedad, f. illness, sickness, disease.

enfermera, f. nurse.

enfermería, f. sanitorium.

enfermo -ma, a. & n. ill, sick; sickly; patient.

enfilar, v. line up; put in a row.

enflaquecer, v. make thin; grow thin.

enfoque, m. focus. —enfocar, v.

enfrascamiento, m. entanglement.

enfrascar, v. entangle oneself.

enfrenar, v. bridle, curb; restrain.

enfrente, adv. across, opposite; in front.

enfriadera, f. icebox; cooler.

enfriar, v. chill, cool.

enfurecer, v. infuriate, enrage.

engalanar, v. adorn, trim.

enganchar, v. hook, hitch, attach.

engañar, v. deceive, cheat.

engaño, m. deceit; delusion.

engañoso, a. deceitful.

engarce, m. connection, link.

engastar, v. to put (gems) in a setting.

engaste, m. setting.

engatusar, v. deceive, trick.

engendrar, v. engender, beget, produce.

engendro, m. fetus, embryo.

engolfar, v. be deeply absorbed.

engolosinar, v. allure, charm, entice.

engomar, v. gum.

engordador, a. fattening.

engordar, v. fatten; grow fat.

engranaje, m. (mech.) gear.

engranar, v. gear; mesh together.

engrandecer, v. increase, enlarge; exalt; exaggerate.

engrasación, f. lubrication.

engrasar, v. grease, lubricate.

engreído, a. conceited.

engreimiento, m. conceit.

engullidor, m. devourer.

engullir, v. devour.

enhebrar, v. thread.

enhestadura, f. raising.

enhestar, v. raise, erect, set up.

enhiesto, a. erect, upright.

enhorabuena, f. congratulations.

enigma, m. enigma, puzzle.

enigmáticamente, adv. enigmatically.

enigmático, a. enigmatic.

enjabonar, v. soap, lather.

enjalbegar, v. whitewash.

enjambradera, f. queen bee.

enjambre, m. swarm. —enjambrar, v.

enjaular, v. cage, coop up.

enjebe, m. lye.

enjuagar, v. rinse.

enjugar, v. wipe, dry off.

enjutez, f. dryness.

enjuto, a. dried; lean, thin.

enlace, m. attachment; involvement; connection.

enladrillador, m. bricklayer.

enlardar, v. baste.

enlazar, v. lace; join, connect; wed.

enlodar, v. cover with mud.

enloquecer, v. go insane; drive crazy.

enloquecimiento, m. insanity.

enlustrecer, v. polish, brighten.

enmarañar, v. entangle.

enmendación, f. emendation.

enmendador, m. emender, reviser.

enmendar, v. amend, correct.

enmienda, f. amendment; correction.

enmohecer, v. rust; mold.

enmohecido, a. rusty; moldy.

enmudecer, v. silence; become silent.

ennegrecer, v. blacken.

ennoblecer, v. ennoble.

enodio, m. young deer.

enojado, a. angry, cross.

enojarse, v. get angry.

enojo, m. anger. —enojar, v.

enojosamente, adv. angrily.

enorme, a. enormous, huge.

enormemente, adv. enormously; hugely.

enormidad, f. enormity; hugeness.

enraizar, v. take root, sprout.

enramada, f. bower.

enredado, a. entangled, snarled.

enredar, v. entangle, snarl; mess up.

enredo, m. tangle, entanglement.

enriquecer, v. enrich.

enrojecerse, v. color; blush.

enrollar, v. wind, coil, roll up.

enromar, v. make dull, blunt.

enronquecimiento, m. hoarseness.

enroscar, v. twist, curl, wind.

ensacar, v. put in a bag.

ensalada, f. salad.

ensaladera, f. salad bowl.

ensalmo, m. charm, enchantment.

ensalzamiento, m. praise.

ensalzar, v. praise, laud, extol.

ensamblar, v. join; unite; connect.

ensanchamiento, m. widening, expansion, extension.

ensanchar, v. widen, expand, extend.

ensangrentado, a. bloody; bloodshot.

ensañar, v. enrage, infuriate, rage.

ensayar, v. try out; rehearse.

ensayista, n. essayist.

ensayo, m. attempt; trial; rehearsal.

ensenada, f. cove.

enseña, f. ensign, standard.

enseñador, m. teacher.

enseñanza, f. education; teaching.

enseñar, v. teach, train; show.

enseres, m.pl. household goods.

ensilaje, m. ensilage.

ensillar, v. saddle.

ensordecer, v. deafen.

ensordecimiento, m. deafness.

ensuciar, v. dirty, muddy, soil.

ensueño, m. illusion, dream.

entablar, v. board up; initiate, begin.

entallador, m. sculptor, carver.

entapizar, v. upholster.

ente, m. being.

entenada, f. stepdaughter.

entenado, m. stepson.

entender, v. understand.

entendimiento, m. understanding.

entenebrecer, v. darken.

enterado, a. aware, informed.

enteramente, adv. entirely, completely.

enterar, v. inform.

enterarse, v. find out.

entereza, f. entirety; integrity; firmness.

entero, *a.* entire, whole, total.
enterramiento, *m.* burial, interment.
enterrar, *v.* bury.
entestado, *a.* stubborn, willful.
entibiar, *v.* to cool; moderate.
entidad, *f.* entity.
entierro, *m.* interment, burial.
entonación, *f.* intonation.
entonamiento, *m.* intonation.
entonar, *v.* chant; harmonize.
entonces, *adv.* then.
entono, *m.* arrogance; affectation.
entortadura, *f.* crookedness.
entortar, *v.* make crooked; bend.
entrada, *f.* entrance; admission, admittance.
entrambos, *a.* & *pron.* both.
entrante, *a.* coming, next.
entrañable, *a.* affectionate.
entrañas, *f.pl.* entrails, bowels; womb.
entrar, *v.* enter, go in, come in.
entre, *prep.* among; between.
entreabierto, *a.* ajar, half-open.
entreabrir, *v.* set ajar.
entreacto, *m.* intermission.
entrecejo, *a.* frowning.
entrecuesto, *m.* spine, backbone.
entredicho, *m.* prohibition.
entrega, *f.* delivery.
entregar, *v.* deliver, hand; hand over.
entrelazar, *v.* intertwine, entwine.
entremedias, *adv.* meanwhile; halfway.
entremés, *m.* side dish.
entremeterse, *v.* meddle, intrude.
entremetido, *m.* meddler; intermediary.
entrenador, *m.* coach. —**entrenar,** *v.*
entrenarse, *v.* train.
entrepalado, *a.* variegated; spotted.
entrerenglonar, *v.* interline.
entresacar, *v.* select, choose; sift.
entretanto, *adv.* meanwhile.
entretenedor, *m.* entertainer.
entretener, *v.* entertain, amuse; delay.
entretenimiento, *m.* entertainment, amusement.
entrevista, *f.* interview. —**entrevistar,** *v.*
entristecedor, *a.* sad.
entristecer, *v.* sadden.
entronar, *v.* enthrone.
entroncar, *v.* be related or connected.
entronización, *f.* enthronement.
entronque, *m.* relationship, connection.
entumecer, *v.* become or be numb; swell.
entusiasmado, *a.* enthusiastic.
entusiasmo, *m.* enthusiasm.

entusiasta, *m.* & *f.* enthusiast.
entusiástico, *a.* enthusiastic.
enumeración, *f.* enumeration.
enumerar, *v.* enumerate.
enunciación, *f.* enunciation; statement.
enunciar, *v.* enunciate.
envainar, *v.* sheathe.
envalentonar, *v.* encourage, embolden.
envanecimiento, *m.* conceit, vanity.
envasar, *v.* put in a container; bottle.
envase, *m.* container.
envejecer, *v.* age, grow old.
envejecimiento, *m.* oldness, age.
envenenar, *v.* poison.
envés, *m.* wrong side; back.
envestir, *v.* put in office; invest.
enviada, *f.* shipment.
enviado, *m.* envoy.
enviar, *v.* send; ship.
envidia, *f.* envy. —**envidiar,** *v.*
envidiable, *a.* enviable.
envidioso, *a.* envious.
envilecer, *v.* vilify, debase, disgrace.
envío, *m.* shipment.
envión, *m.* shove.
envoltura, *f.* wrapping.
envolver, *v.* wrap, wrap up.
enyesar, *v.* plaster.
enyugar, *v.* yoke.
eperlano, *m.* smelt (fish).
épica, *f.* epic writing.
épico, *a.* epic.
epicureísmo, *m.* Epicureanism.
epicúreo, *n.* & *a.* epicurean.
epidemia, *f.* epidemic.
epidémico, *a.* epidemic.
epidermis, *f.* epidermis.
epigrama, *m.* epigram.
epigramático, *a.* epigrammatic.
epilepsia, *f.* epilepsy.
epiléptico, *n.* & *a.* epileptic.
epílogo, *m.* epilogue.
episcopado, *m.* bishopric; episcopate.
episcopal, *a.* episcopal.
episódico, *a.* episodic.
episodio, *m.* episode.
epístola, *f.* epistle, letter.
epitafio, *m.* epitaph.
epitomadamente, *adv.* concisely.
epitomar, *v.* epitomize, summarize.
época, *f.* epoch, age.
epopeya, *f.* epic.
epsomita, *f.* Epsom salts.
equidad, *f.* equity.
equilibrado, *a.* stable.
equilibrio, *m.* equilibrium, balance.
equinoccio, *m.* equinox.
equipaje, *m.* luggage, baggage.
equipar, *v.* equip.
equiparar, *v.* compare.
equipo, *m.* equipment; team.
equitación, *f.* horsemanship.
equitativo, *a.* fair, equitable.
equivalencia, *f.* equivalence.

equivalente, *a.* equivalent.
equivaler, *v.* equal, be equivalent.
equivocación, *f.* mistake.
equivocado, *a.* wrong, mistaken.
equivocarse, *v.* make a mistake, be wrong.
equívoco, *a.* equivocal, ambiguous.
era, *f.* era, age.
erario, *m.* exchequer.
erección, *f.* erection; elevation.
eremita, *m.* hermit.
erguir, *v.* erect; straighten up.
erigir, *v.* erect, build.
erisipela, *f.* erysipelas.
erizado, *a.* bristly.
erizarse, *v.* bristle.
erizo, *m.* hedgehog; sea urchin.
ermita, *f.* hermitage.
ermitaño, *m.* hermit.
erogación, *f.* expenditure. —**erogar,** *v.*
erosión, *f.* erosion.
erótico, *a.* erotic.
erradicación, *f.* eradication.
erradicar, *v.* eradicate.
errado, *a.* mistaken, erroneous.
errante, *a.* wandering, roving.
errar, *v.* be mistaken.
errata, *f.* erratum.
errático, *a.* erratic.
erróneamente, *adv.* erroneously.
erróneo, *a.* erroneous.
error, *m.* error, mistake.
eructo, *m.* belch. —**eructar,** *v.*
erudición, *f.* scholarship, learning.
eruditamente, *adv.* learnedly.
erudito, *m.* scholar.
erupción, *f.* eruption; rash.
eruptivo, *a.* eruptive.
esbozo, *m.* outline, sketch. —**esbozar,** *v.*
escabechar, *v.* pickle; preserve.
escabel, *m.* small stool or bench.
escabroso, *a.* rough, irregular; craggy; rude.
escabullirse, *v.* steal away, sneak away.
escala, *f.* scale; ladder. **hacer e.,** to make a stop.
escalada, *f.* escalation.
escalador, *m.* climber.
escalar, *v.* climb; scale.
escaldar, *v.* scald.
escalera, *f.* stairs, staircase; ladder.
escalfado, *a.* poached.
escalofriado, *a.* chilled.
escalofrío, *m.* chill.
escalón, *m.* step.
escaloña, *f.* scallion.
escalpar, *v.* scalp.
escalpelo, *m.* scalpel.
escama, *f.* (fish) scale. —**escamar,** *v.*
escamondar, *v.* trim, cut; prune.
escampada, *f.* stampede.

escandalizar, v. shock, scandalize.

escandalizativo, a. scandalous.

escándalo, m. scandal.

escandaloso, a. scandalous; disgraceful.

escandinavo, n. & a. Scandinavian.

escandir, v. scan.

escanilla, f. cradle.

escañuelo, m. small footstool.

escapada, f. escapade.

escapar, v. escape.

escape, m. escape; (auto.) exhaust.

escápula, f. scapula.

escarabajo, m. black beetle; scarab.

escaramucear, v. skirmish; dispute.

escarbadientes, m. toothpick.

escarbar, v. scratch; poke.

escarcha, f. frost.

escardar, v. weed.

escarlata, f. scarlet.

escarmentar, v. correct severely.

escarnecedor, m. scoffer; mocker.

escarnecer, v. mock, make fun of.

escarola, f. endive.

escarpado, 1. a. steep. **2.** m. bluff.

escarpe, m. escarpment.

escasamente, adv. scarcely; sparingly; barely.

escasear, v. be scarce.

escasez, f. shortage, scarcity.

escaso, a. scant; scarce.

escatimoso, a. malicious; sly, cunning.

escena, f. scene; stage.

escenario, m. stage (of theater); scenario.

escénico, a. scenic.

escépticamente, adv. skeptically.

escepticismo, m. skepticism.

escéptico -ca, a. & n. skeptic; skeptical.

esclarecer, v. clear up.

esclavitud, f. slavery; bondage.

esclavizar, v. enslave.

esclavo -va, n. slave.

escoba, f. broom.

escocés, a. & n. Scotch, Scottish; Scot.

Escocia, f. Scotland.

escofinar, v. rasp.

escoger, v. choose, select.

escogido, a. choice, select.

escogimiento, m. choice.

escolar, 1. a. scholastic, (of) school. **2.** m. student.

escolasticismo, m. scholasticism.

escolta, f. escort. —**escoltar,** v.

escollo, m. reef.

escombro, m. mackerel.

escombros, m.pl. debris, rubbish.

esconce, m. corner.

escondedero, m. hiding place.

esconder, v. hide, conceal.

escondidamente, adv. secretly.

escondimiento, m. concealment.

escopeta, f. shotgun.

escopetazo, m. gunshot.

escoplo, m. chisel.

escorbuto, m. scurvy.

escorpena, f. grouper.

escorpión, m. scorpion.

escorzón, m. toad.

escribiente, m. & f. clerk.

escribir, v. write.

escritor -ra, n. writer, author.

escritorio, m. desk.

escritura, f. writing, handwriting.

escrófula, f. scrofula.

escroto, m. scrotum.

escrúpulo, m. scruple.

escrupuloso, a. scrupulous.

escrutinio, m. scrutiny; examination.

escuadra, f. squad; fleet.

escuadrón, m. squadron.

escualidez, f. squalor; poverty.

escuálido, a. squalid.

escualo, m. shark.

escuchar, v. listen; listen to.

escudero, m. squire.

escudo, m. shield; protection; coin of certain countries.

escuela, f. school.

escuerzo, m. toad.

esculpir, v. carve, sculpture.

escultor, m. sculptor.

escultura, f. sculpture.

escupidera, f. cuspidor.

escupir, v. spit.

escurridor, m. colander, strainer.

escurrir, v. drain off; wring out.

escurrirse, v. slip; sneak away.

ese, esa, dem. a. that.

ése, ésa, dem. pron. that (one).

esencia, f. essence; perfume.

esencial, a. essential.

esencialmente, adv. essentially.

esfera, f. sphere.

esfinge, f. sphinx.

esforzar, v. strengthen.

esforzarse, v. strive, exert oneself.

esfuerzo, m. effort, attempt; vigor.

esgrima, f. fencing.

eslabón, m. link (of a chain).

eslabonar, v. link, join, connect.

eslavo, a. & n. Slavic; Slav.

esmalte, m. enamel. —**esmaltar,** v.

esmerado, a. careful, thorough.

esmeralda, f. emerald.

esmerarse, v. take pains, do one's best.

esmeril, m. emery.

eso, dem. pron. that.

esófago, m. esophagus.

esotérico, a. esoteric.

espacial, a. spatial.

espacio, m. space. —**espaciar,** v.

espaciosidad, f. spaciousness.

espacioso, a. spacious.

espada, f. sword; spade (in cards).

espadarte, m. swordfish.

espalda, f. back.

espaldera, f. espalier.

espantar, v. frighten; scare; scare away.

espanto, m. fright.

espantoso, a. frightening, frightful.

España, f. Spain.

español -ola, a. & n. Spanish; Spaniard.

esparcir, v. scatter, disperse.

espárrago, m. asparagus.

espartano, n. & a. Spartan.

espasmo, m. spasm.

espasmódico, a. spasmodic.

espata, f. spathe.

espato, m. spar (mineral).

espátula, f. spatula.

especia, f. spice. —**especiar,** v.

especial, a. special, especial.

especialidad, f. specialty.

especialista, m. & f. specialist.

especialización, f. specialization.

especialmente, adv. especially.

especie, f. species; sort.

especiería, f. grocery store.

especiero, m. grocer.

especificar, v. specify.

específico, a. specific.

espécimen, m. specimen.

especioso, a. neat; polished; specious.

espectáculo, m. spectacle, show.

espectador -ra, n. spectator.

espectro, m. specter, ghost.

especulación, f. speculation.

especulador, m. speculator.

especular, v. speculate.

especulativo, a. speculative.

espejo, m. mirror.

espelunca, f. dark cave, cavern.

espera, f. wait.

esperanza, f. hope, expectation.

esperar, v. hope; expect; wait, wait for, watch for.

espesar, v. thicken.

espeso, a. thick, dense, bushy.

espesor, m. thickness, density.

espía, m. & f. spy. —**espiar,** v.

espigón, m. bee sting.

espina, f. thorn.

espinaca, f. spinach.

espinal, a. spinal.

espinazo, m. spine.

espineta, f. spinet.

espino, m. briar.

espinoso, a. spiny, thorny.

espión, m. spy.

espionaje, m. espionage.

espiración, f. expiration.

espiral, a. & m. spiral.

espirar, v. expire; breathe, exhale.

espíritu, m. spirit.

espiritual, a. spiritual.

espiritualidad, f. spirituality.

espiritualmente, adv. spiritually.

espita, f. faucet, spigot.
espléndido, a. splendid.
esplendor, m. splendor.
espolear, v. incite, urge on.
espoleta, f. wishbone.
esponja, f. sponge.
esponjoso, a. spongy.
esponsales, m.pl. engagement, betrothal.
esponsalicio, a. nuptial.
espontáneamente, adv. spontaneously.
espontaneidad, f. spontaneity.
espontáneo, a. spontaneous.
espora, f. spore.
esporádico, a. sporadic.
esposa, f. wife.
esposar, v. shackle.
esposo, m. husband.
espuela, f. spur. —espolear, v.
espuma, f. foam. —espumar, v.
espumadera, f. colander.
espumajear, v. foam at the mouth.
espumajo, m. foam.
espumar, v. foam, froth; skim.
espumoso, a. foamy; sparkling (wine).
espurio, a. spurious.
esputar, v. spit, expectorate.
esputo, m. spit, saliva.
esquela, f. note.
esqueleto, m. skeleton.
esquema, m. scheme; diagram.
esquero, m. leather sack or pouch.
esquiciar, v. outline, sketch roughly.
esquicio, m. rough sketch or outline.
esquife, m. skiff.
esquilar, v. fleece, shear.
esquilmo, m. harvest.
esquimal, m. & a. Eskimo.
esquina, f. corner.
esquivar, v. evade, shun.
estabilidad, f. stability.
estable, a. stable.
establecedor, m. founder, originator.
establecer, v. establish, set up.
establecimiento, m. establishment.
establero, m. groom.
establo, m. stable.
estaca, f. stake.
estación, f. station; season.
estacionar, v. station; park (a vehicle).
estacionario, a. stationary.
estadista, m. statesman.
estadística, f. statistics.
estadístico, a. statistical.
estado, m. state; condition; status.
estafa, f. swindle, fake. —estafar, v.
estafeta, f. post office.
estagnación, f. stagnation.
estallar, v. explode; burst; break out.
estallido, m. crash; crack; explosion.
estampa, f. stamp. —estampar, v.

estampado, m. printed cotton cloth.
estampida, f. stampede.
estampilla, f. (postage) stamp.
estancado, a. stagnant.
estancar, v. stanch, stop, check.
estancia, f. stay; (S.A.) small farm.
estanciero -ra, n. small farmer.
estandarte, m. banner.
estanque, m. pool; pond.
estante, m. shelf.
estaño, m. tin. —estañar, v.
estar, v. be; stand; look.
estática, f. static.
estático, a. static.
estatua, f. statue.
estatura, f. stature.
estatuto, m. statute, law.
este, m. east.
este, esta, dem. a. this.
éste, ésta, dem. pron. this (one); the latter.
estelar, a. stellar.
estenografía, f. stenography.
estenógrafo -fa, n. stenographer.
estera, f. mat, matting.
estereofónico, a. stereophonic.
estéril, a. barren; sterile.
esterilidad, f. sterility, fruitlessness.
esterilizar, v. sterilize.
estética, f. esthetics.
estético, a. esthetic.
estetoscopio, m. stethoscope.
estibador, m. stevedore.
estiércol, m. dung, manure.
estigma, m. stigma; disgrace.
estilo, m. style; sort.
estilográfica, f. (fountain) pen.
estima, f. esteem.
estimable, a. estimable, worthy.
estimación, f. estimation.
estimar, v. esteem; value; estimate; gauge.
estimular, v. stimulate.
estímulo, m. stimulus.
estío, m. summer.
estipulación, f. stipulation.
estipular, v. stipulate.
estirar, v. stretch.
estirpe, m. stock, lineage.
esto, dem. pron. this.
estocada, f. stab, thrust.
estofado, m. stew. —estofar, v.
estoicismo, m. stoicism.
estoico, m. & a. stoic.
estómago, m. stomach.
estorbar, v. bother, hinder, interfere with.
estorbo, m. hindrance.
estornudo, m. sneeze. —estornudar, v.
estrabismo, m. strabismus.
estrago, m. devastation, havoc.
estrangulación, f. strangulation.
estrangular, v. strangle.
estratagema, f. stratagem.
estrategia, f. strategy.
estratégico, a. strategic.
estrato, m. stratum.

estrechar, v. tighten; narrow.
estrechez, f. narrowness; tightness.
estrecho, 1. a. narrow, tight. 2. m. strait.
estregar, v. scour, scrub.
estrella, f. star.
estrellamar, f. starfish.
estrellar, v. shatter, smash.
estremecimiento, m. shudder. —estremecerse, v.
estrenar, v. wear for the first time; open (a play).
estreno, m. debut, first performance.
estrenuo, a. strenuous.
estreptococo, m. streptococcus.
estría, f. groove.
estribillo, m. refrain.
estribo, m. stirrup.
estribor, m. starboard.
estrictamente, adv. strictly.
estrictez, f. strictness.
estricto, a. strict.
estrofa, f. stanza.
estropajo, m. mop.
estropear, v. cripple, damage, spoil.
estructura, f. structure.
estructural, a. structural.
estruendo, m. din, clatter.
estuario, m. estuary.
estuco, m. stucco.
estudiante -ta, n. student.
estudiar, v. study.
estudio, m. study; studio.
estudioso, a. studious.
estufa, f. stove.
estulto, a. foolish.
estupendo, a. wonderful, grand, fine.
estupidez, f. stupidity.
estúpido, a. stupid.
estupor, m. stupor.
estuque, m. stucco.
esturión, m. sturgeon.
etapa, f. stage.
éter, m. ether.
etéreo, a. ethereal.
eternal, a. eternal.
eternidad, f. eternity.
eterno, a. eternal.
ética, f. ethics.
ético, a. ethical.
etimología, f. etymology.
etiqueta, f. etiquette; tag, label.
étnico, a. ethnic.
etrusco, n. & a. Etruscan.
eucaristía, f. Eucharist.
eufemismo, m. euphemism.
eufonía, f. euphony.
Europa, f. Europe.
europeo -pea, a. & n. European.
eutanasia, f. euthanasia.
evacuación, f. evacuation.
evacuar, v. evacuate.
evadir, v. evade.
evangélico, a. evangelical.
evangelio, m. gospel.
evangelista, m. evangelist.
evaporación, f. evaporation.
evaporarse, v. evaporate.

evasión, f. evasion.
evasivamente, adv. evasively.
evasivo, a. evasive.
evento, m. event, occurrence.
eventual, a. eventual.
eventualidad, f. eventuality.
evicción, f. eviction.
evidencia, f. evidence.
evidenciar, v. prove, show.
evidente, a. evident.
evitación, f. avoidance.
evitar, v. avoid, shun.
evocación, f. evocation.
evocar, v. evoke.
evolución, f. evolution.
exacerbar, v. irritate deeply.
exactamente, adv. exactly.
exactitud, f. precision, accuracy.
exacto, a. exact, accurate.
exageración, f. exaggeration.
exagerar, v. exaggerate.
exagonal, a. hexagonal.
exaltación, f. exaltation.
exaltamiento, m. exaltation.
exaltar, v. exalt.
examen, m. test, examination.
examinar, v. test, examine.
exánime, a. spiritless, weak.
exasperación, f. exasperation.
exasperar, v. exasperate.
excavación, f. excavation.
excavar, v. excavate.
exceder, v. exceed, surpass; outrun.
excelencia, f. excellence.
excelente, a. excellent.
excéntrico, a. eccentric.
excepción, f. exception.
excepcional, a. exceptional.
excepto, prep. except, except for.
exceptuar, v. except.
excesivamente, adv. excessively.
excesivo, a. excessive.
exceso, m. excess.
excitabilidad, f. excitability.
excitación, f. excitement.
excitar, v. excite.
exclamación, f. exclamation.
exclamar, v. exclaim.
excluir, v. exclude, bar, shut out.
exclusión, f. exclusion.
exclusivamente, adv. exclusively.
exclusivo, a. exclusive.
excomulgar, v. excommunicate.
excomunión, f. excommunication.
excreción, f. excretion.
excremento, m. excrement.
excretar, v. excrete.
exculpar, v. exonerate.
excursión, f. excursion.
excursionista, n. excursionist.
excusa, f. excuse. —excusar, v.
excusado, m. toilet.
excusarse, v. apologize.
exención, f. exemption.
exento, a. exempt. —exentar, v.
exhalación, f. exhalation.

exhalar, v. exhale, breathe out.
exhausto, a. exhausted.
exhibición, f. exhibit, exhibition.
exhibir, v. exhibit, display.
exhortación, f. exhortation.
exhortar, v. exhort, admonish.
exhumación, f. exhumation.
exhumar, v. exhume.
exigencia, f. requirement, demand.
exigente, a. exacting, demanding.
exigir, v. require, exact, demand.
eximir, v. exempt.
existencia, f. existence; (econ.) supply.
existente, a. existent.
existir, v. exist.
éxito, m. success.
éxodo, m. exodus.
exoneración, f. exoneration.
exonerar, v. exonerate, acquit.
exorar, v. beg, implore.
exorbitancia, f. exorbitance.
exorbitante, a. exorbitant.
exorcismo, m. exorcism.
exornar, v. adorn, decorate.
exótico, a. exotic.
expansibilidad, f. expansibility.
expansión, f. expansion.
expansivo, a. expansive; effusive.
expatriación, f. expatriation.
expatriar, v. expatriate.
expectación, f. expectation.
expectorar, v. expectorate.
expedición, f. expedition.
expediente, m. expedient, means.
expedir, v. send off, ship; expedite.
expeditivo, a. speedy, prompt.
expedito, a. speedy, prompt.
expeler, v. expel, eject.
expendedor, m. dealer.
expender, v. expend.
expensas, f.pl. expenses, costs.
experiencia, f. experience.
experimentado, a. experienced.
experimental, a. experimental.
experimentar, v. experience.
experimento, m. experiment.
expertamente, adv. expertly.
experto, a. & m. expert.
expiación, f. atonement.
expiar, v. atone for.
expiración, f. expiration.
expirar, v. expire.
explanación, f. explanation.
explanar, v. make level.
expletivo, n. & a. expletive.
explicable, a. explicable.
explicación, f. explanation.
explicar, v. explain.
explicativo, a. explanatory.
explícitamente, adv. explicitly.
explícito, adj. explicit.
exploración, f. exploration.
explorador, m. explorer; scout.
explorar, v. explore; scout.
exploratorio, a. exploratory.

explosión, f. explosion; outburst.
explosivo, a. explosive.
explotación, f. exploitation.
explotar, v. exploit.
exponer, v. expose; set forth.
exportación, f. exportation; export.
exportador, m. exporter.
exportar, v. export.
exposición, f. exhibit; exposition; exposure.
expósito, n. foundling; orphan.
expresado, a. aforesaid.
expresamente, adv. clearly, explicitly.
expresar, v. express.
expresión, f. expression.
expresivo, a. expressive; affectionate.
expreso, a. & m. express.
exprimir, v. squeeze.
expropiación, f. expropriation.
expropiar, v. expropriate.
expulsar, v. expel, eject; evict.
expulsión, f. expulsion.
expurgación, f. expurgation.
expurgar, v. expurgate.
exquisitamente, adv. exquisitely.
exquisito, a. exquisite.
éxtasi, m. ecstasy.
extemporáneo, a. extemporaneous, impromptu.
extender, v. extend; spread; widen; stretch.
extensamente, adv. extensively.
extensión, f. extension, spread, expanse.
extenso, a. extensive, widespread.
extenuación, f. weakening; emaciation.
extenuar, v. extenuate.
exterior, a. & m. exterior; foreign.
exterminar, v. exterminate.
exterminio, m. extermination, ruin.
extinción, f. extinction.
extinguir, v. extinguish.
extinto, a. extinct.
extintor, m. fire extinguisher.
extirpar, v. eradicate.
extorsión, f. extortion.
extra, n. extra.
extracción, f. extraction.
extractar, v. summarize.
extracto, m. extract; summary.
extradición, f. extradition.
extraer, v. extract.
extranjero -ra, 1. a. foreign. 2. n. foreigner; stranger.
extrañar, v. surprise; miss.
extraño, a. strange, queer.
extraordinariamente, adv. extraordinarily.
extraordinario, a. extraordinary.
extravagancia, f. extravagance.
extravagante, a. extravagant.
extraviado, a. lost, misplaced.
extraviarse, v. stray, get lost.

extravío, *m.* aberration, deviation.

extremadamente, *adv.* extremely.

extremado, *a.* extreme.

extremaunción, *f.* extreme unction.

extremidad, *f.* extremity.

extremista, *n.* & *a.* extremist.

extremo, *a.* & *m.* extreme, end.

extrínseco, *a.* extrinsic.

exuberancia, *f.* exuberance.

exuberante, *a.* exuberant.

exudación, *f.* exudation.

exudar, *v.* exude, ooze.

exultación, *f.* exultation.

F

fábrica, *f.* factory.

fabricación, *f.* manufacture, manufacturing.

fabricante, *m.* manufacturer, maker.

fabricar, *v.* manufacture, make.

fabril, *a.* making, building.

fábula, *f.* fable, myth.

fabuloso, *a.* fabulous.

facción, *f.* faction, party; (*pl.*) features.

faccioso, *a.* factious.

fácil, *a.* easy.

facilidad, *f.* facility, ease.

facilitar, *v.* facilitate, make easy.

fácilmente, *adv.* easily.

facsímil, *m.* facsimile.

factible, *a.* feasible.

factor, *m.* factor.

factótum, *m.* factotum; jack of all trades.

factura, *f.* invoice, bill.

facturar, *v.* check (baggage).

facultad, *f.* faculty; ability.

facultativo, *a.* optional.

fachada, *f.* façade, front.

faena, *f.* task; work.

faja, *f.* band; sash; zone.

falacia, *f.* fallacy; deceitfulness.

falda, *f.* skirt; lap.

falibilidad, *f.* fallibility.

falsear, *v.* falsify, counterfeit; forge.

falsedad, *f.* falsehood; lie; falseness.

falsificación, *f.* falsification; forgery.

falsificar, *v.* falsify, counterfeit, forge.

falso, *a.* false; wrong.

falta, *f.* error, mistake; fault; lack. **hacer f.,** to be lacking, to be necessary. **sin f.,** without fail.

faltar, *v.* be lacking, be missing; be absent.

faltriquera, *f.* pocket.

falla, *f.* failure, fault.

fallar, *v.* fail.

fallecer, *v.* pass away, die.

fallo, *m.* verdict.

fama, *f.* fame; reputation; glory.

familia, *f.* family; household.

familiar, *a.* familiar; domestic; (of) family.

familiaridad, *f.* familiarity, intimacy.

familiarizar, *v.* familiarize, acquaint.

famoso, *a.* famous.

fanal, *m.* lighthouse; lantern, lamp.

fanático -ca, *a.* & *n.* fanatic.

fanatismo, *m.* fanaticism.

fanfarria, *f.* bluster. **—fanfarrear,** *v.*

fango, *m.* mud.

fantasía, *f.* fantasy; fancy, whim.

fantasma, *m.* phantom; ghost.

fantástico, *a.* fantastic.

faquín, *m.* porter.

faquir, *m.* fakir.

farallón, *m.* cliff.

Faraón, *m.* Pharaoh.

fardel, *m.* bag; package.

fardo, *m.* bundle.

farináceo, *a.* farinaceous.

faringe, *f.* pharynx.

fariseo, *m.* pharisee, hypocrite.

farmacéutico, *m.* pharmacist.

farmacia, *f.* pharmacy.

faro, *m.* beacon; lighthouse; headlight.

farol, *m.* lantern; (street) light.

farra, *f.* spree.

fárrago, *m.* medley; hodgepodge.

farsa, *f.* farce.

fascinación, *f.* fascination.

fascinar, *v.* fascinate, bewitch.

fase, *f.* phase.

fastidiar, *v.* disgust; irk, annoy.

fastidio, *m.* disgust; annoyance.

fastidioso, *a.* annoying; tedious.

fatal, *a.* fatal.

fatalidad, *f.* fate; calamity, bad luck.

fatalismo, *m.* fatalism.

fatalista, *n.* & *a.* fatalist.

fatiga, *f.* fatigue. **—fatigar,** *v.*

fauno, *m.* faun.

favor, *m.* favor; behalf. **por f.,** please.

favorable, *a.* favorable.

favorablemente, *adv.* favorably.

favorecer, *v.* favor; flatter.

favoritismo, *m.* favoritism.

favorito -ta, *a.* & *n.* favorite.

faz, *f.* face.

fe, *f.* faith.

fealdad, *f.* ugliness, homeliness.

febrero, *m.* February.

febril, *a.* feverish.

fécula, *f.* starch.

fecundar, *v.* fertilize.

fecundidad, *f.* fecundity, fertility.

fecundo, *a.* fecund, fertile.

fecha, *f.* date. **—fechar,** *v.*

federación, *f.* confederacy.

federal, *a.* federal.

felicidad, *f.* happiness; bliss.

felicitación, *f.* congratulation.

felicitar, *v.* congratulate; compliment.

feligrés -esa, *n.* parishioner.

feliz, *a.* happy; fortunate.

felón, *m.* felon.

felonía, *f.* felony.

felpa, *f.* plush.

felpudo, *m.* doormat.

femenino, *a.* feminine.

feminismo, *m.* feminism.

feminista, *n.* feminist.

fenecer, *v.* conclude; die.

fénix, *m.* phoenix; model.

fenomenal, *a.* phenomenal.

fenómeno, *m.* phenomenon.

feo, *a.* ugly, homely.

feracidad, *f.* feracity, fertility.

feraz, *a.* fertile, fruitful; copious.

feria, *f.* fair; market.

feriado, *a.* **día f.,** holiday.

fermentación, *f.* fermentation.

fermento, *m.* ferment. **—fermentar,** *v.*

ferocidad, *f.* ferocity, fierceness.

feroz, *a.* ferocious, fierce.

férreo, *a.* of iron.

ferrería, *f.* ironworks.

ferretería, *f.* hardware; hardware store.

ferrocarril, *m.* railroad.

fértil, *a.* fertile.

fertilidad, *f.* fertility.

fertilizar, *v.* fertilize.

férvido, *a.* fervid, ardent.

ferviente, *a.* fervent.

fervor, *m.* fervor, zeal.

fervoroso, *a.* zealous, eager.

festejar, *v.* entertain, fete.

festejo, *m.* feast.

festín, *m.* feast.

festividad, *f.* festivity.

festivo, *a.* festive.

fétido, *adj.* fetid.

feudal, *a.* feudal.

feudo, *m.* feud.

fiado, *adj.* on trust, on credit.

fianza, *f.* bail.

fiar, *v.* trust, sell on credit; give credit.

fiarse de, *v.* trust (in), rely on.

fiasco, *m.* fiasco.

fibra, *f.* fiber; vigor.

fibroso, *a.* fibrous.

ficción, *f.* fiction.

ficticio, *a.* fictitious.

ficha, *f.* slip, card; chip.

fidedigno, *a.* trustworthy.

fideicomisario, *m.* trustee.

fideicomiso, *m.* trust.

fidelidad, *f.* fidelity.

fideo, *m.* noodle.

fiebre, *f.* fever.

fiel, *a.* faithful.

fieltro, *m.* felt.

fiera, *f.* wild animal.

fiereza, *f.* fierceness, wildness.

fiero, *a.* fierce; wild.

fiesta, *f.* festival, feast; party.

figura, *f.* figure. **—figurar,** *v.*

figurarse, *v.* imagine.

figurón, *m.* dummy.
fijar, *v.* fix; set, establish; post.
fijarse en, *v.* notice.
fijeza, *f.* firmness.
fijo, *a.* fixed, stationary, permanent, set.
fila, *f.* row, rank, file, line.
filantropía, *f.* philanthropy.
filete, *m.* fillet.
film, *m.* film. **—filmar**, *v.*
filo, *m.* (cutting) edge.
filón, *m.* vein (of ore).
filosofía, *f.* philosophy.
filosófico, *a.* philosophical.
filósofo, *m.* philosopher.
filtro, *m.* filter. **—filtrar**, *v.*
fin, *m.* end, purpose, goal. **a f. de que**, in order that. **en f.**, in short. **por f.**, finally, at last.
final, **1.** *a.* final. **2.** *m.* end.
finalidad, *f.* finality.
finalmente, *adv.* at last.
financiero, **1.** *a.* financial. **2.** *m.* financier.
finca, *f.* real estate; estate; farm.
finés, *a.* Finnish.
fineza, *f.* courtesy, politeness; fineness.
fingimiento, *m.* pretense.
fingir, *v.* feign, pretend.
fino, *a.* fine; polite, courteous.
firma, *f.* signature; (com.) firm.
firmamento, *m.* firmament, heavens.
firmar, *v.* sign.
firme, *a.* firm, fast, steady, sound.
firmemente, *adv.* firmly.
firmeza, *f.* firmness.
fisco, *m.* exchequer, treasury.
física, *f.* physics.
físico, *a. & n.* physical; physicist.
fisiología, *f.* physiology.
fláccido, *a.* flaccid, soft.
flaco, *a.* thin, gaunt.
flagelación, *f.* flagellation.
flagelar, *v.* flagellate, whip.
flagrancia, *f.* flagrancy.
flagrante, *a.* flagrant.
flama, *f.* flame; ardor, zeal.
flamante, *a.* flaming.
flamenco, *m.* flamingo.
flan, *m.* custard.
flanco, *m.* side; (mil.) flank.
flanquear, *v.* flank.
flaqueza, *f.* thinness; weakness.
flauta, *f.* flute.
flautín, *m.* piccolo.
flautista, *m. & f.* flutist, piper.
fleco, *m.* fringe; flounce.
flecha, *f.* arrow.
flechero, *m.* archer.
flema, *f.* phlegm.
flete, *m.* freight. **—fletar**, *v.*
flexibilidad, *f.* flexibility.
flexible, *a.* flexible, pliable.
flirtear, *v.* flirt.
flojo, *a.* limp; loose, flabby, slack.
flor, *f.* flower; compliment.
flora, *f.* flora.

floral, *a.* floral.
florecer, *v.* flower, bloom; flourish.
floreo, *m.* flourish.
florero, *m.* flower pot; vase.
floresta, *f.* forest.
florido, *a.* flowery; flowering.
florista, *m. & f.* florist.
flota, *f.* fleet.
flotante, *a.* floating.
flotar, *v.* float.
flotilla, *f.* flotilla, fleet.
fluctuación, *f.* fluctuation.
fluctuar, *v.* fluctuate.
fluente, *a.* fluent.
fluidez, *f.* fluency.
flúido, *a. & m.* fluid, liquid.
fluir, *v.* flow.
flujo, *m.* flow, flux.
flúor, *m.* fluorine.
fluorescencia, *f.* fluorescence.
fluorescente, *a.* fluorescent.
fobia, *f.* phobia.
foca, *f.* seal.
foco, *m.* focus, center.
fogata, *f.* bonfire.
fogón, *m.* hearth, fireplace.
fogosidad, *f.* vehemence, ardor.
fogoso, *a.* vehement, ardent.
folklore, *m.* folklore.
follaje, *m.* foliage.
folleto, *m.* pamphlet, booklet.
fomentar, *v.* develop, promote, further, foster.
fomento, *m.* fomentation.
fonda, *f.* eating house, inn.
fondo, *m.* bottom; back (part); background; (pl.) funds; finances. **a f.**, thoroughly.
fonética, *f.* phonetics.
fonético, *a.* phonetic.
fonógrafo, *m.* phonograph.
forastero -ra, **1.** *a.* foreign, exotic. **2.** *n.* stranger.
forjar, *v.* forge.
forma, *f.* form, shape. **—formar**, *v.*
formación, *f.* formation.
formal, *a.* formal.
formaldehído, *m.* formaldehyde.
formalidad, *f.* formality.
formalizar, *v.* finalize; formulate.
formidable, *a.* formidable.
formidablemente, *adv.* formidably.
formón, *m.* chisel.
fórmula, *f.* formula.
formular, *v.* formulate, draw up.
formulario, *m.* form.
foro, *m.* forum.
forraje, *m.* forage, fodder.
forrar, *v.* line.
forro, *m.* lining.
fortalecer, *v.* fortify.
fortaleza, *f.* fort, fortress; fortitude.
fortificación, *f.* fortification.
fortitud, *f.* fortitude.
fortuitamente, *adv.* fortuitously.
fortuito, *a.* fortuitous.
fortuna, *f.* fortune; luck.

forúnculo, *m.* boil.
forzar, *v.* force, compel, coerce.
forzosamente, *adv.* compulsorily; forcibly.
forzoso, *a.* compulsory; necessary. **paro f.**, unemployment.
forzudo, *a.* powerful, vigorous.
fosa, *f.* grave.
fósforo, *m.* match; phosphorus.
fósil, *m.* fossil.
foso, *m.* ditch, trench; moat.
fotocopiadora, *f.* photocopier.
fotografía, *f.* photograph. **—fotografiar**, *v.*
frac, *m.* dress coat.
fracasar, *v.* fail.
fracaso, *m.* failure.
fracción, *f.* fraction.
fractura, *f.* fracture, break.
fragancia, *f.* fragrance; perfume; aroma.
fragante, *a.* fragrant.
frágil, *a.* fragile, breakable.
fragilidad, *f.* fragility.
fragmentario, *a.* fragmentary.
fragmento, *m.* fragment, bit.
fragor, *m.* noise, clamor.
fragoso, *a.* noisy.
fragua, *f.* forge. **—fraguar**, *v.*
fraile, *m.* monk.
frambuesa, *f.* raspberry.
francamente, *adv.* frankly, candidly.
francés, -esa, *a. & n.* French; Frenchman.
Francia, *f.* France.
franco, *a.* frank.
franela, *f.* flannel.
frangible, *a.* breakable.
franqueo, *m.* postage.
franqueza, *f.* frankness.
franquicia, *f.* franchise.
frasco, *m.* flask, bottle.
frase, *f.* phrase; sentence.
fraseología, *f.* phraseology; style.
fraternal, *a.* fraternal, brotherly.
fraternidad, *f.* fraternity, brotherhood.
fraude, *m.* fraud.
fraudulento, *a.* fraudulent.
frazada, *f.* blanket.
frecuencia, *f.* frequency.
frecuente, *a.* frequent.
frecuentemente, *adv.* frequently, often.
fregadero, *m.* sink.
fregadura, *f.* scouring, scrubbing.
fregar, *v.* scour, scrub, mop.
freír, *v.* fry.
fréjol, *m.* kidney bean.
frenesí, *m.* frenzy.
frenéticamente, *adv.* frantically.
frenético, *a.* frantic, frenzied.
freno, *m.* brake. **—frenar**, *v.*
frente, **1.** *f.* forehead. **2.** *m.* front. **en f.**, **al f.**, opposite, across. **f. a**, in front of.
fresa, *f.* strawberry.
fresca, *f.* fresh, cool air.

fresco, *a.* fresh; cool; crisp.
frescura, *f.* coolness, freshness.
fresno, *m.* ash tree.
fresquería, *f.* soda fountain.
friabilidad, *f.* brittleness.
friable, *a.* brittle.
frialdad, *f.* coldness.
fríamente, *adv.* coldly; coolly.
fricandó, *m.* fricandeau.
fricar, *v.* rub together.
fricción, *f.* friction.
friccionar, *v.* rub.
friega, *f.* friction.
frigidez, *f.* frigidity.
frígido, *a.* frigid.
frijol, *m.* bean.
frío, *a.* & *n.* cold. tener f., to be cold, feel cold. hacer f., to be cold (weather).
friolento, friolero, *a.* chilly; sensitive to cold.
friolera, *f.* trifle, trinket.
friso, *m.* frieze.
fritillas, *f.pl.* fritters.
frito, *a.* fried.
fritura, *f.* fritter.
frívolamente, *adv.* frivolously.
frivolidad, *f.* frivolity.
frívolo, *a.* frivolous.
frondoso, *a.* leafy.
frontera, *f.* frontier; border.
frotar, *v.* rub.
fructífero, *a.* fruitful.
fructificar, *v.* bear fruit.
fructuosamente, *adv.* fruitfully.
fructuoso, *a.* fruitful.
frugal, *a.* frugal, thrifty.
frugalidad, *f.* frugality; thrift.
frugalmente, *adv.* frugally, thriftily.
fruncir, *v.* gather, contract. f. el entrecejo, frown.
fruslería, *f.* trinket.
frustrar, *v.* frustrate, thwart.
fruta, *f.* fruit.
fruto, *m.* fruit; product; profit.
fucsia, *f.* fuchsia.
fuego, *m.* fire.
fuelle, *m.* bellows.
fuente, *f.* fountain; source; platter.
fuera, *adv.* without, outside.
fuero, *m.* statute.
fuerte, 1. *a.* strong; loud. **2.** *m.* fort.
fuertemente, *adv.* strongly; loudly.
fuerza, *f.* force, strength.
fuga, *f.* flight, escape.
fugarse, *v.* flee, escape.
fugaz, *a.* fugitive, passing.
fugitivo -va, *a.* & *n.* fugitive.
fulcro, *m.* fulcrum.
fulgor, *m.* gleam, glow. —**fulgurar,** *v.*
fulminante, *a.* explosive.
fumador, *m.* smoker.
fumar, *v.* smoke.
fumigación, *f.* fumigation.
fumigador, *m.* fumigator.
fumigar, *v.* fumigate.
fumoso, *a.* smoky.
función, *f.* function; performance, show.

funcionar, *v.* function, work, run.
funcionario, *m.* official, functionary.
funda, *f.* case, sheath, slip-cover.
fundación, *f.* foundation.
fundador -ra, *n.* founder.
fundamental, *a.* fundamental, basic.
fundamentalmente, *adv.* fundamentally.
fundamento, *m.* base, basis, foundation.
fundar, *v.* found, establish.
fundición, *f.* foundry; melting, meltdown.
fundir, *v.* fuse; smelt.
fúnebre, *a.* dismal.
funeral, *m.* funeral.
funestamente, *adv.* sadly.
fungo, *m.* fungus.
furente, *a.* furious, enraged.
furia, *f.* fury.
furiosamente, *adv.* furiously.
furioso, *a.* furious.
furor, *m.* furor; fury.
furtivamente, *adv.* furtively.
furtivo, *a.* furtive, sly.
furúnculo, *m.* boil.
fusibilidad, *f.* fusibility.
fusible, *m.* fuse.
fusil, *m.* rifle, gun.
fusilar, *v.* shoot.
fusión, *f.* fusion; merger.
fusionar, *v.* unite, fuse, merge.
fútbol, *m.* football, soccer.
fútil, *a.* trivial.
futilidad, *f.* triviality.
futuro, *a.* & *m.* future.
futurología, *f.* futurology.

G

gabán, *m.* overcoat.
gabinete, *m.* closet; cabinet; study.
gacela, *f.* gazelle.
gaceta, *f.* gazette, newspaper.
gacetilla, *f.* personal news section of a newspaper.
gaélico, *a.* Gaelic.
gafas, *f.pl.* eyeglasses.
gaguear, *v.* stutter, stammer.
gaita, *f.* bagpipe.
gaje, *m.* salary; fee.
gala, *f.* gala, ceremony; (*pl.*) regalia. tener a g., be proud of.
galán, *m.* gallant.
galano, *a.* stylishly dressed; elegant.
galante, *a.* gallant.
galantería, *f.* gallantry, compliment.
galápago, *m.* fresh-water turtle.
galardón, *m.* prize; reward.
gáleo, *m.* swordfish.
galera, *f.* wagon; shed.
galería, *f.* gallery, (theat.) balcony.
galés, *n.* & *a.* Welsh.
galgo, *m.* greyhound.

galillo, *m.* uvula.
galocha, *f.* galosh.
galón, *m.* gallon; (mil.) stripe.
galope, *m.* gallop. —**galopar,** *v.*
gallardete, *m.* pennant.
galleta, *f.* cracker.
gallina, *f.* hen.
gallinero, *m.* chicken coop.
gallo, *m.* rooster.
gambito, *m.* gambit.
gamuza, *f.* chamois.
gana, *f.* desire, wish, mind (to). de buena g., willingly. tener ganas de, to feel like.
ganado, *m.* cattle.
ganador -ra, *n.* winner.
ganancia, *f.* gain, profit; (*pl.*) earnings.
ganapán, *m.* drudge.
ganar, *v.* earn; win; beat.
gancho, *m.* hook, hanger, clip, hairpin.
gandul -la, *n.* idler, tramp, hobo.
ganga, *f.* bargain.
gangrena, *f.* gangrene.
gansarón, *m.* gosling.
ganso, *m.* goose.
garabato, *m.* hook; scrawl, scribble.
garaje, *m.* garage.
garantía, *f.* guarantee; collateral, security.
garantizar, *v.* guarantee, secure, pledge.
garbanzo, *m.* chickpea.
garbo, *m.* grace.
garboso, *a.* graceful, sprightly.
gardenia, *f.* gardenia.
garfa, *f.* claw, talon.
garganta, *f.* throat.
gárgara, *f.* gargle. —**gargarizar,** *v.*
garita, *f.* sentry box.
garito, *m.* gambling house.
garlopa, *f.* carpenter's plane.
garra, *f.* claw.
garrafa, *f.* decanter, carafe.
garrideza, *f.* elegance, handsomeness.
garrido, *a.* elegant, handsome.
garrote, *m.* club, cudgel.
garrotillo, *m.* croup.
garrudo, *a.* powerful, brawny.
garza, *f.* heron.
gas, *m.* gas.
gasa, *f.* gauze.
gaseosa, *f.* carbonated water.
gaseoso, *a.* gaseous.
gasolina, *f.* gasoline.
gastar, *v.* spend; use up, wear out; waste.
gastritis, *f.* gastritis.
gastrómano, *m.* glutton.
gastrónomo -ma, *n.* gourmet, epicure.
gatear, *v.* creep.
gatillo, *m.* trigger.
gato -ta, *n.* cat.
gaucho, *m.* Argentine cowboy.
gaveta, *f.* drawer.
gavilla, *f.* sheaf.
gaviota, *f.* sea gull.
gayo, *a.* merry, gay.
gazapera, *f.* rabbit warren.

gazapo, *m.* rabbit.

gazmonado, *f.* prudishness.

gazmoño, *m.* prude.

gaznate, *m.* windpipe.

gelatina, *f.* gelatine.

gemelo -la, *n.* twin.

gemelos, *m.pl.* cuff links; opera glasses.

gemido, *m.* moan, groan, wail. **—gemir,** *v.*

genciana, *f.* gentian.

genealogía, *f.* genealogy, pedigree.

generación, *f.* generation.

generador, *m.* generator.

general, *a.* & *m.* general.

generalidad, *f.* generality.

generalización, *f.* generalization.

generalizar, *v.* generalize.

generalmente, *adv.* generally.

género, *m.* gender; kind; (*pl.*) goods, material.

generosidad, *f.* generosity.

generoso, *a.* generous.

génesis, *m.* genesis.

genial, *a.* genial; brilliant.

genio, *m.* genius; temper; disposition.

genitivo, *m.* genitive.

gente, *f.* people, folk.

gentil, *a.* gracious; graceful.

gentileza, *f.* grace, graciousness.

gentío, *m.* mob, crowd.

genuino, *a.* genuine.

geografía, *f.* geography.

geográfico, *a.* geographical.

geométrico, *a.* geometric.

geranio, *m.* geranium.

gerencia, *f.* management.

gerente, *m.* manager, director.

germen, *m.* germ.

germinar, *v.* germinate.

gerundio, *m.* gerund.

gesticulación, *f.* gesticulation.

gesticular, *v.* gesticulate, gesture.

gestión, *f.* conduct; effort.

gesto, *m.* gesture, facial expression.

gigante, *a.* & *m.* gigantic, giant.

gigantesco, *a.* gigantic, huge.

gimnasio, *m.* gymnasium.

gimnástica, *f.* gymnastics.

gimotear, *v.* whine.

ginebra, *f.* gin.

girado, *m.* (com.) drawee.

girador, *m.* (com.) drawer.

girar, *v.* revolve, turn, spin, whirl.

giratorio, *a.* rotary, revolving.

giro, *m.* whirl, turn, spin; (com.) draft. **g. postal,** money order.

gitano -na, *a.* & *n.* Gypsy.

glacial, *a.* glacial, icy.

gladiador, *m.* gladiator.

glándula, *f.* gland.

glasé, *m.* glacé.

glicerina, *f.* glycerine.

globo, *m.* globe; balloon.

gloria, *f.* glory.

glorieta, *f.* bower.

glorificación, *f.* glorification.

glorificar, *v.* glorify.

glorioso, *a.* glorious.

glosa, *f.* gloss. **—glosar,** *v.*

glosario, *m.* glossary.

glotón -ona, *a.* & *n.* gluttonous; glutton.

glutin, *m.* gluten; glue.

gobernación, *f.* government.

gobernador, *m.* governor.

gobernalle, *m.* rudder, tiller, helm.

gobernante, *m.* ruler.

gobernar, *v.* govern.

gobierno, *m.* government.

goce, *m.* enjoyment.

gola, *f.* throat.

golfo, *m.* gulf.

golondrina, *f.* swallow.

golosina, *f.* delicacy.

golpe, *m.* blow, stroke. **de g.,** suddenly.

golpear, *v.* strike, beat, pound.

gollete, *m.* upper portion of one's throat.

goma, *f.* rubber; gum; glue; eraser.

gonce, *m.* hinge.

góndola, *f.* gondola.

gordo, *a.* fat.

gordura, *f.* fatness.

gorila, *m.* gorilla.

gorja, *f.* gorge.

gorjeo, *m.* warble, chirp. — **gorjear,** *v.*

gorrión, *m.* sparrow.

gorro, *m.* cap.

gota, *f.* drop (of liquid).

gotear, *v.* drip, leak.

goteo, *m.* leak.

gotera, *f.* leak; gutter.

gótico, *a.* Gothic.

gozar, *v.* enjoy.

gozne, *m.* hinge.

gozo, *m.* enjoyment, delight, joy.

gozoso, *a.* joyful, joyous.

grabado, *m.* engraving, cut, print.

grabador, *m.* engraver.

grabar, *v.* engrave; record.

gracia, *f.* grace; wit, charm. **hacer g.,** to amuse, strike as funny. **tener g.,** to be funny, to be witty.

gracias, *f.pl.* thanks, thank you.

gracioso, *a.* witty, funny.

grada, *f.* step.

gradación, *f.* gradation.

grado, *m.* grade; rank; degree.

graduado -da, *n.* graduate.

gradual, *a.* gradual.

graduar, *v.* grade, graduate.

gráfico, *a.* graphic, vivid.

grafito, *m.* graphite.

grajo, *m.* jackdaw.

gramática, *f.* grammar.

gramo, *m.* gram.

gran, grande, *a.* big, large; great.

granada, *f.* grenade; pomegranate.

granar, *v.* seed.

grandeza, *f.* greatness.

grandiosidad, *f.* grandeur.

grandioso, *a.* grand, magnificent.

grandor, *m.* size.

granero, *m.* barn; granary.

granito, *m.* granite.

granizada, *f.* hailstorm.

granizo, *m.* hail. **—granizar,** *v.*

granja, *f.* grange; farm; farmhouse.

granjear, *v.* earn, gain; get.

granjero, *m.* farmer.

grano, *m.* grain; kernel.

granuja, *m.* waif, urchin.

grapa, *f.* clamp, clip.

grasa, *f.* grease, fat.

grasiento, *a.* greasy.

gratificación, *f.* gratification; reward; tip.

gratificar, *v.* gratify; reward; tip.

gratis, *adv.* gratis, free.

gratitud, *f.* gratitude.

grato, *a.* grateful; pleasant.

gratuito, *a.* gratuitous.

gravamen, *m.* tax; burden; obligation.

grave, *a.* grave, serious, severe.

gravedad, *f.* gravity, seriousness.

gravitación, *f.* gravitation.

gravitar, *v.* gravitate.

gravoso, *a.* burdensome.

graznido, *m.* croak. **—graznar,** *v.*

Grecia, *f.* Greece.

greco, *a.* & *n.* Greek.

greda, *f.* clay.

gresca, *f.* revelry; quarrel.

griego -ga, *a.* & *n.* Greek.

grieta, *f.* opening; crevice, crack.

grifo, *m.* faucet.

grillo, *m.* cricket.

grima, *f.* fright.

gringo -ga, *n.* foreigner (usually North American).

gripa, gripe, *f.* grippe.

gris, *a.* gray.

grito, *m.* shout, scream, cry. — **gritar,** *v.*

grosella, *f.* currant.

grosería, *f.* grossness; coarseness.

grosero, *a.* coarse, vulgar, discourteous.

grotesco, *a.* grotesque.

grúa, *f.* crane.

gruesa, *f.* gross.

grueso, 1. *a.* bulky; stout; coarse, thick. **2.** *m.* bulk.

grulla, *f.* crane.

gruñido, *m.* growl, snarl, mutter. **—gruñir,** *v.*

grupo, *m.* group, party.

gruta, *f.* cavern.

guadaña, *f.* scythe. **—guadañar,** *v.*

guagua, *f.* (S.A.) baby; (Carib.) bus.

gualdo, *m.* yellow, golden.

guano, *m.* guano (fertilizer).

guante, *m.* glove.

guapo, *a.* handsome.

guarda, *m.* or *f.* guard.

guardabarros, *m.* fender.

guardacostas, *m.* revenue ship.

guardar, *v.* keep, store, put away; guard.

guardarropa, *f.* coat room.

guardarse de, *v.* beware of, avoid.

guardia, 1. *f.* guard; watch. **2.** *m.* policeman.

guardián, *m.* guardian, keeper, watchman.

guardilla, *f.* attic.

guarida, *f.* den.

guarismo, *m.* number, figure.

guarnecer, *v.* adorn.

guarnición, *f.* garrison; trimming.

guasa, *f.* joke, jest.

guayaba, *f.* guava.

gubernativo, *a.* governmental.

guerra, *f.* war.

guerrero, *m.* warrior.

guía, 1. *m.* & *f.* guide. **2.** *f.* guidebook, directory.

guiar, *v.* guide; steer, drive.

guija, *f.* pebble.

guillotina, *f.* guillotine.

guindar, *v.* hang.

guinga, *f.* gingham.

guiñada, *f.,* **guiño,** *m.* wink. — **guiñar,** *v.*

guión, *m.* dash, hyphen.

guirnalda, *f.* garland, wreath.

guisa, *f.* guise, manner.

guisado, *m.* stew.

guisante, *m.* pea.

guisar, *v.* cook.

guita, *f.* twine.

guitarra, *f.* guitar.

guitarrista, *n.* guitarist.

gula, *f.* gluttony.

gurú, *m.* guru.

gusano, *m.* worm, caterpillar.

gustar, *v.* please; taste.

gusto, *m.* pleasure; taste; liking.

gustoso, *a.* pleasant, tasteful.

gutural, *a.* guttural.

H

haba, *f.* bean.

habanera, *f.* Cuban dance melody.

haber, *v.* have. **h. de,** be to, be supposed to.

haberes, *m.pl.* property; worldly goods.

habichuela, *f.* bean.

hábil, *a.* skillful; capable; clever.

habilidad, *f.* ability; skill; talent.

habilidoso, *a.* able, skillful, talented.

habilitado, *m.* paymaster.

habilitar, *v.* qualify; supply, equip.

hábilmente, *adv.* ably.

habitación, *f.* dwelling; room.

habitante, *m.* & *f.* inhabitant.

habitar, *v.* inhabit; dwell.

hábito, *m.* habit; custom.

habitual, *a.* habitual.

habituar, *v.* accustom, habituate.

habla, *f.* speech.

hablador, *a.* talkative.

hablar, *v.* talk, speak.

haca, *f.* pony.

hacedor, *m.* maker.

hacendado, *m.* hacienda owner; farmer.

hacendoso, *a.* industrious.

hacer, *v.* do; make. **hace dos años,** etc., two years ago, etc.

hacerse, *v.* become, get to be.

hacia, *prep.* toward.

hacienda, *f.* property; estate; ranch; farm; (govt.) treasury.

hacha, *f.* ax, hatchet.

hada, *f.* fairy.

hado, *m.* fate.

halagar, *v.* flatter.

halar, *v.* haul, pull.

halcón, *m.* hawk, falcon.

haleche, *m.* anchovy.

hallado, *a.* found. **bien h.,** welcome. **mal h.,** uneasy.

hallar, *v.* find, locate.

hallarse, *v.* be located; happen to be.

hallazgo, *m.* find, thing found.

hamaca, *f.* hammock.

hambre, *f.* hunger. **tener h., estar con h.,** to be hungry.

hambrear, *v.* hunger; starve.

hambriento, *a.* starving, hungry.

haragán, *m.* idler, lazy person.

haraganear, *v.* loiter.

harapo, *m.* rag, tatter.

haraposo, *a.* ragged, shabby.

harem, *m.* harem.

harina, *f.* flour, meal.

harnero, *m.* sieve.

hartar, *v.* satiate.

harto, *a.* stuffed; fed up.

hartura, *f.* superabundance, glut.

hasta, 1. *prep.* until, till; as far as, up to. **h. luego,** good-bye, so long. **2.** *adv.* even.

hastío, *m.* distaste, loathing.

hato, *m.* herd.

hay, *v.* there is, there are. **h. que,** it is necessary to. **no h. de qué,** you're welcome, don't mention it.

haya, *f.* beech tree.

haz, *f.* bundle, sheaf; face.

hazaña, *f.* deed; exploit, feat.

hebdomadario, *a.* weekly.

hebilla, *f.* buckle.

hebra, *f.* thread, string.

hebreo -rea, *a.* & *n.* Hebrew.

hechicero -ra, *n.* wizard, witch.

hechizar, *v.* bewitch.

hechizo, *m.* spell.

hecho, *m.* fact; act; deed.

hechura, *f.* workmanship, make.

hediondez, *f.* stench.

helada, *f.* frost.

helado, *m.* ice cream.

helar, *v.* freeze.

helecho, *m.* fern.

hélice, *f.* propeller.

helicóptero, *m.* helicopter.

helio, *m.* helium.

hembra, *f.* female.

hemisferio, *m.* hemisphere.

hemoglobina, *f.* hemoglobin.

henchir, *v.* stuff.

hendedura, *f.* crevice, crack.

heno, *m.* hay.

hepática, *f.* liverwort.

heraldo, *m.* herald.

herbáceo, *a.* herbaceous.

herbívoro, *a.* herbivorous.

heredar, *v.* inherit.

heredero -ra, *n.* heir; successor.

hereditario, *a.* hereditary.

hereje, *m.* & *f.* heretic.

herejía, *f.* heresy.

herencia, *f.* inheritance; heritage.

herético, *a.* heretical.

herida, *f.* wound, injury.

herir, *v.* wound, injure.

hermafrodita, *a.* & *m.* hermaphrodite.

hermana, *f.* sister.

hermano, *m.* brother.

hermético, *a.* airtight.

hermoso, *a.* beautiful, handsome.

hermosura, *f.* beauty.

hernia, *f.* hernia, rupture.

héroe, *m.* hero.

heroico, *a.* heroic.

heroína, *f.* heroine.

heroísmo, *m.* heroism.

herradura, *f.* horseshoe.

herramienta, *f.* tool; implement.

herrería, *f.* blacksmith's shop.

herrero, *m.* blacksmith.

herrumbre, *f.* rust.

hertzio, *m.* hertz.

hervir, *v.* boil.

hesitación, *f.* hesitation.

heterogéneo, *a.* heterogeneous.

heterosexual, *a.* heterosexual.

hexágono, *m.* hexagon.

hez, *f.* dregs, sediment.

híbrido, *n.* & *a.* hybrid.

hidalgo -ga, *n.* noble.

hidalguía, *f.* nobility; generosity.

hidráulico, *a.* hydraulic.

hidrofobia, *f.* rabies.

hidrógeno, *m.* hydrogen.

hidropesía, *f.* dropsy.

hiedra, *f.* ivy.

hiel, *f.* gall.

hielo, *m.* ice.

hiena, *f.* hyena.

hierba, *f.* grass; herb; marijuana.

hierbabuena, *f.* mint.

hierro, *m.* iron.

hígado, *m.* liver.

higiene, *f.* hygiene.

higiénico, *a.* sanitary, hygienic.

higo, *m.* fig.

higuera, *f.* fig tree.

hija, *f.* daughter.

hijastro, *m.* stepchild.

hijo, *m.* son.

hila, *f.* line.

hilandero, *m.* spinner.

hilar, *v.* spin.

hilera, *f.* row, line, tier.

hilo, *m.* thread; string; wire; linen.

himno, *m.* hymn.

hincar, *v.* drive, thrust, sink.

hincarse, *v.* kneel down.

hinchar, *v.* swell.

hindú, *n. & a.* Hindu.

hinojo, *m.* knee.

hipnótico, *a.* hypnotic.

hipnotismo, *m.* hypnotism.

hipnotizar, *v.* hypnotize.

hipo, *m.* hiccough.

hipocresía, *f.* hypocrisy.

hipócrita, *a. & n.* hypocritical; hypocrite.

hipódromo, *m.* race track.

hipoteca, *f.* mortgage. **—hipotecar,** *v.*

hipótesis, *f.* hypothesis.

hirsuto, *a.* hairy, hirsute.

hispano, *a.* Hispanic, Spanish American.

Hispanoamérica, *f.* Spanish America.

hispanoamericano -na, *a. & n.* Spanish American.

histerectomía, *f.* hysterectomy.

histeria, *f.* hysteria.

histérico, *a.* hysterical.

historia, *f.* history; story.

historiador, *m.* historian.

histórico, *a.* historic, historical.

histrión, *m.* actor.

hocico, *m.* snout, muzzle.

hogar, *m.* hearth; home.

hoguera, *f.* bonfire, blaze.

hoja, *f.* leaf; sheet (of paper); pane; blade.

hajalata, *f.* tin.

hojalatero, *m.* tinsmith.

hojear, *v.* scan, skim through.

hola, *interj.* hello.

Holanda, *f.* Holland, Netherlands.

holandés -esa, *a. & n.* Dutch; Hollander.

holganza, *f.* leisure; diversion.

holgazán, **1.** *a.* idle, lazy. **2.** *m.* idler, loiterer, tramp.

holgazanear, *v.* idle, loiter.

holografía, *f.* holography.

holograma, *m.* hologram.

hollín, *m.* soot.

hombre, *m.* man.

hombría, *f.* manliness.

hombro, *m.* shoulder.

homenaje, *m.* homage.

homeópata, *m.* homeopath.

homicidio, *m.* homicide.

homilía, *f.* homily.

homosexual, *a.* homosexual, gay.

honda, *f.* sling.

hondo, *a.* deep.

hondonada, *f.* ravine.

hondura, *f.* depth.

honestidad, *f.* modesty, unpretentiousness.

honesto, *a.* honest; pure; just.

hongo, *m.* fungus; mushroom.

honor, *m.* honor.

honorable, *a.* honorable.

honorario, **1.** *a.* honorary. **2.** *m.* honorarium, fee.

honorífico, *a.* honorary.

honra, *f.* honor. **—honrar,** *v.*

honradez, *f.* honesty.

honrado, *a.* honest, honorable.

hora, *f.* hour, time (of day).

horadar, *v.* perforate.

horario, *m.* timetable, schedule.

horca, *f.* gallows; pitchfork.

horda, *f.* horde.

horizontal, *a.* horizontal.

horizonte, *m.* horizon.

hormiga, *f.* ant.

hormiguear, *v.* itch.

hormiguero, *m.* ant hill.

hornero -ra, *n.* baker.

hornillo, *m.* stove.

horno, *m.* oven; kiln.

horóscopo, *m.* horoscope.

horrendo, *a.* dreadful, horrendous.

horrible, *a.* horrible, hideous, awful.

horrido, *a.* horrid.

horror, *m.* horror.

horrorizar, *v.* horrify.

horroroso, *a.* horrible, frightful.

hortelano, *m.* horticulturist.

hospedaje, *m.* lodging.

hospedar, *v.* give or take lodgings.

hospital, *m.* hospital.

hospitalario, *a.* hospitable.

hospitalidad, *f.* hospitality.

hospitalmente, *adv.* hospitably.

hostia, *f.* host.

hostil, *a.* hostile.

hostilidad, *f.* hostility.

hotel, *m.* hotel.

hoy, *adv.* today. **h. día, h. en día,** nowadays.

hoya, *f.* dale; valley.

hoyo, *m.* pit, hole.

hoyuelo, *m.* dimple.

hoz, *f.* sickle.

hucha, *f.* chest, money box; savings.

hueco, 1. *a.* hollow, empty. **2.** *m.* hole, hollow.

huelga, *f.* strike.

huella, *f.* track, trace; footprint.

huérfano -na, *a. & n.* orphan.

huero, *a.* empty.

huerta, *f.* (vegetable) garden.

huerto, *m.* orchard.

hueso, *m.* bone; fruit pit.

huésped, *m. & f.* guest.

huesudo, *a.* bony.

huevo, *m.* egg.

huida, *f.* flight, escape.

huir, *v.* flee.

hule, *m.* oilcloth.

humanidad, *f.* humanity, mankind; humaneness.

humanista, *m.* humanist.

humanitario, *a.* humane.

humano, *a.* human; humane.

humareda, *f.* dense cloud of smoke.

humedad, *f.* humidity, moisture, dampness.

humedecer, *v.* moisten, dampen.

húmedo, *a.* humid, moist, damp.

humildad, *f.* humility, meekness.

humilde, *a.* humble, meek.

humillación, *f.* humiliation.

humillar, *v.* humiliate.

humo, *m.* smoke; (*pl.*) airs, affectation.

humor, *m.* humor, mood.

humorista, *m.* humorist.

hundimiento, *m.* collapse.

hundir, *v.* sink; collapse.

húngaro -ra, *a. & n.* Hungarian.

Hungría, *f.* Hungary.

huracán, *m.* hurricane.

huraño, *a.* shy, bashful.

hurgar, *v.* stir.

hurón, *m.* ferret.

hurraca, *f.* magpie.

hurtadillas, *f.pl.* **a h.,** on the sly.

hurtador, *m.* thief.

hurtar, *v.* steal, rob of; hide.

hurtarse, *v.* hide; withdraw.

husmear, *v.* scent, smell.

huso, *m.* spindle; bobbin.

I

ibérico, *a.* Iberian.

iberoamericano -na, *a. & n.* Latin American.

ida, *f.* departure; trip out. **i. y vuelta,** round trip.

idea, *f.* idea.

ideal, *a. & m.* ideal.

idealismo, *m.* idealism.

idealista, *m. & f.* idealist.

idear, *v.* plan, conceive.

idéntico, *a.* identical.

identidad, *f.* identity; identification.

identificar, *v.* identify.

idilio, *m.* idyll.

idioma, *m.* language.

idiota, *a. & n.* idiotic; idiot.

idiotismo, *m.* idiom; idiocy.

idolatrar, *v.* idolize, adore.

ídolo, *m.* idol.

idóneo, *a.* suitable, fit, apt.

iglesia, *f.* church.

ignición, *f.* ignition.

ignominia, *f.* ignominy, shame.

ignominioso, *a.* ignominious, shameful.

ignorancia, *f.* ignorance.

ignorante, *a.* ignorant.

ignorar, *v.* be ignorant of, not know.

ignoto, *a.* unknown.

igual, 1. *a.* equal; the same; (*pl.*) alike. **2.** *a.* equal.

igualar, *v.* equal; equalize; match.

igualdad, *f.* equality.

ijada, *f.* flank (of an animal).

ilegal, *a.* illegal.

ilegítimo, *a.* illegitimate.

ileso, *a.* unharmed.

ilícito, *a.* illicit, unlawful.

iluminación, *f.* illumination.

iluminar, *v.* illuminate.

ilusión, *f.* illusion.
ilusorio, *a.* illusive.
ilustración, *f.* illustration; learning.
ilustrador, *m.* illustrator.
ilustrar, *v.* illustrate.
ilustre, *a.* illustrious, honorable, distinguished.
imagen, *f.* image.
imaginación, *f.* imagination.
imaginar, *v.* imagine.
imaginario, *a.* imaginary.
imaginativo, *a.* imaginative.
imán, *m.* magnet; imam.
imbécil, *a. & n.* imbecile; stupid, foolish; fool.
imbuir, *v.* imbue, instil.
imitación, *f.* imitation.
imitador, *m.* imitator.
imitar, *v.* imitate.
impaciencia, *f.* impatience.
impaciente, *a.* impatient.
impar, *a.* unequal, uneven, odd.
imparcial, *a.* impartial.
impasible, *a.* impassive, unmoved.
impávido, *adj.* fearless, intrepid.
impedimento, *m.* impediment, obstacle.
impedir, *v.* impede, hinder, stop, obstruct.
impeler, *v.* impel; incite.
impensado, *a.* unexpected.
imperar, *v.* reign; prevail.
imperativo, *a.* imperative.
imperceptible, *a.* imperceptible.
imperdible, *n.* safety pin.
imperecedero, *a.* imperishable.
imperfecto, *a.* imperfect, faulty.
imperial, *a.* imperial.
imperialismo, *m.* imperialism.
impericia, *f.* inexperience.
imperio, *m.* empire.
imperioso, *a.* imperious, domineering.
impermeable, 1. *a.* waterproof. **2.** *m.* raincoat.
impersonal, *a.* impersonal.
impertinencia, *f.* impertinence.
ímpetu, *m.* impulse; impetus.
impetuoso, *a.* impetuous.
impiedad, *f.* impiety.
impío, *a.* impious.
implacable, *a.* implacable, unrelenting.
implicar, *v.* implicate, involve.
implorar, *v.* implore.
imponente, *a.* impressive.
imponer, *v.* impose.
importación, *f.* import, importing.
importancia, *f.* importance.
importador, *m.* importer.
importante, *a.* important.
importar, *v.* be important, matter; import.
importe, *m.* value, amount.
importunar, *v.* beg, importune.
imposibilidad, *f.* impossibility.
imposibilitado, *a.* helpless.
imposible, *a.* impossible.

imposición, *f.* imposition.
impostor, *m.* imposter, faker.
impotencia, *f.* impotence.
impotente, *a.* impotent.
imprecar, *v.* curse.
impreciso, *adj.* inexact.
impregnar, *v.* impregnate.
imprenta, *f.* press; printing house.
imprescindible, *a.* essential.
impresión, *f.* impression.
impresionable, *a.* emotional.
impresionar, *v.* impress.
impresor, *m.* printer.
imprevisión, *f.* oversight, thoughtlessness.
imprevisto, *a.* unexpected, unforeseen.
imprimir, *v.* print; imprint.
improbable, *a.* improbable.
improbo, *a.* dishonest.
improductivo, *a.* unproductive.
improperio, *m.* insult.
impropio, *a.* improper.
improvisación, *f.* improvisation.
improvisar, *v.* improvise.
improviso, *a.* unforeseen.
imprudencia, *f.* imprudence.
imprudente, *a.* imprudent, reckless.
impuesto, *m.* tax.
impulsar, *v.* prompt, impel.
impulsivo, *a.* impulsive.
impulso, *m.* impulse.
impureza, *f.* impurity.
impuro, *a.* impure.
imputación, *f.* imputation.
imputar, *v.* impute, attribute.
inaccesible, *a.* inaccessible.
inacción, *f.* inaction; inactivity.
inaceptable, *a.* unacceptable.
inactivo, *a.* inactive; sluggish.
inadecuado, *a.* inadequate.
inadvertencia, *f.* oversight.
inadvertido, *a.* inadvertent, careless; unnoticed.
inagotable, *a.* inexhaustible.
inalterado, *a.* unchanged.
inanición, *f.* starvation.
inanimado, *adj.* inanimate.
inapetencia, *f.* lack of appetite.
inaplicable, *a.* inapplicable; unfit.
inaudito, *a.* unheard of.
inauguración, *f.* inauguration.
inaugurar, *v.* inaugurate, open.
incandescente, *a.* incandescent.
incansable, *a.* tireless.
incapacidad, *f.* incapacity.
incapacitar, *v.* incapacitate.
incapaz, *a.* incapable.
incauto, *a.* unwary.
incendiar, *v.* set on fire.
incendio, *m.* fire, conflagration.
incertidumbre, *f.* uncertainty, suspense.
incesante, *a.* continual, incessant.
incidente, *m.* incident, event.
incienso, *m.* incense.

incierto, *a.* uncertain, doubtful.
incisión, *f.* incision, cut.
incitamiento, *m.* incitement, motivation.
incitar, *v.* incite, instigate.
incivil, *a.* impolite, rude.
inclemencia, *f.* inclemency.
inclemente, *a.* inclement, merciless.
inclinación, *f.* inclination, bent; slope.
inclinar, *v.* incline; influence.
inclinarse, *v.* slope; lean, bend over; bow.
incluir, *v.* include; enclose.
inclusivo, *a.* inclusive.
incluso, *prep.* including.
incógnito, *a.* unknown.
incoherente, *a.* incoherent.
incombustible, *a.* fireproof.
incomodar, *v.* disturb, bother, inconvenience.
incomodidad, *f.* inconvenience.
incómodo, *m.* uncomfortable; cumbersome; inconvenient.
incomparable, *a.* incomparable.
incompatible, *a.* incompatible.
incompetencia, *f.* incompetence.
incompetente, *a.* incompetent.
incompleto, *a.* incomplete.
incondicional, *a.* unconditional.
inconexo, *a.* incoherent; unconnected.
incongruente, *a.* not suitable.
inconsciencia, *f.* unconsciousness.
inconsciente, *a.* unconscious.
inconsecuencia, *f.* inconsistency.
inconsecuente, *a.* inconsistent.
inconsiderado, *a.* inconsiderate.
inconstancia, *f.* changeableness.
inconstante, *a.* changeable.
inconveniencia, *f.* unsuitability.
inconveniente, 1. *a.* unsuitable. **2.** *m.* disadvantage; objection.
incorporar, *v.* incorporate, embody.
incorporarse, *v.* sit up.
incorrecto, *a.* incorrect, wrong.
incredulidad, *f.* incredulity.
incrédulo, *a.* incredulous.
increíble, *a.* incredible.
incremento, *m.* increase.
incubar, *v.* hatch.
inculto, *a.* uncultivated.
incurable, *a.* incurable.
incurrir, *v.* incur.
indagación, *f.* investigation, inquiry.
indagador, *m.* investigator.
indagar, *v.* investigate, inquire into.
indebido, *a.* undue.
indecencia, *f.* indecency.
indecente, *a.* indecent.
indeciso, *a.* undecided.

indefenso, *a.* defenseless.
indefinido, *a.* indefinite.
indeleble, *a.* indelible.
indemnizar, *v.* indemnify.
independencia, *f.* independence.
independiente, *a.* independent.
India, *f.* India.
indicación, *f.* indication.
indicar, *v.* indicate, point out.
indicativo, *a. & m.* indicative.
índice, *m.* index; forefinger.
indicio, *m.* hint, clue.
indiferencia, *f.* indifference.
indiferente, *a.* indifferent.
indígena, *a. & n.* native.
indigente, *a.* indigent, poor.
indignación, *f.* indignation.
indignado, *a.* indignant, incensed.
indignar, *v.* incense.
indigno, *a.* unworthy.
indio -dia, *a. & n.* Indian.
indirecto, *a.* indirect.
indiscreción, *f.* indiscretion.
indiscreto, *a.* indiscreet.
indiscutible, *a.* unquestionable.
indispensable, *a.* indispensable.
indisposición, *f.* indisposition, ailment; reluctance.
indistinto, *a.* indistinct, unclear.
individual, *a.* individual.
individualidad, *f.* individuality.
individuo, *a. & m.* individual.
indócil, *a.* headstrong, unruly.
índole, *f.* nature, character, disposition.
indolencia, *f.* indolence.
indolente, *a.* indolent.
indómito, *a.* untamed, wild; unruly.
inducir, *v.* induce, persuade.
indudable, *a.* certain, indubitable.
indulgencia, *f.* indulgence.
indulgente, *a.* indulgent.
indultar, *v.* free; pardon.
industria, *f.* industry.
industrial, *a.* industrial.
industrioso, *a.* industrious.
inédito, *a.* unpublished.
ineficaz, *a.* inefficient.
inepto, *a.* incompetent.
inequívoco, *a.* unmistakable.
inercia, *f.* inertia.
inerte, *a.* inert.
inesperado, *a.* unexpected.
inestable, *a.* unstable.
inevitable, *a.* inevitable.
inexacto, *a.* inexact.
inexperto, *a.* unskilled.
inexplicable, *a.* inexplicable, unexplainable.
infalible, *a.* infallible.
infame, *a.* infamous, bad.
infamia, *f.* infamy.
infancia, *f.* infancy; childhood.
infante, *m.* infant.
infantería, *f.* infantry.
infantil, *a.* infantile, childish.
infatigable, *a.* untiring.
infausto, *a.* unlucky.

infección, *f.* infection.
infeccioso, *a.* infectious.
infectar, *v.* infect.
infeliz, *a.* unhappy, miserable.
inferior, *a.* inferior; lower.
inferir, *v.* infer; inflict.
infernal, *a.* infernal.
infestar, *v.* infest.
infiel, *a.* unfaithful.
infierno, *m.* hell.
infiltrar, *v.* infiltrate.
infinidad, *f.* infinity.
infinito, *a.* infinite.
inflación, *f.* inflation.
inflamación, *f.* inflammation.
inflamar, *v.* inflame, set on fire.
inflar, *v.* inflate, pump up, puff up.
inflexible, *a.* inflexible, rigid.
inflexión, *f.* inflection.
infligir, *v.* inflict.
influencia, *f.* influence.
influenza, *f.* influenza, flu.
influir, *v.* influence, sway.
influyente, *a.* influential.
información, *f.* information.
informal, *a.* informal.
informar, *v.* inform; report.
informe, *m.* report; (*pl.*) information, data.
infortunio, *m.* misfortune.
infracción, *f.* violation.
infrascrito, *m.* signer, undersigned.
infringir, *v.* infringe, violate.
infructuoso, *a.* fruitless.
infundir, *v.* instil, inspire with.
ingeniería, *f.* engineering.
ingeniero, *m.* engineer.
ingenio, *m.* wit; talent.
ingeniosidad, *f.* ingenuity.
ingenioso, *a.* witty, ingenious.
ingenuidad, *f.* candor; naïveté.
ingenuo, *a.* ingenuous, naïve, candid.
Inglaterra, *f.* England.
ingle, *f.* groin.
inglés -esa, *a. & n.* English; Englishman.
ingratitud, *f.* ingratitude.
ingrato, *a.* ungrateful.
ingrediente, *m.* ingredient.
ingresar en, *v.* enter; join.
ingreso, *m.* entrance; (*pl.*) earnings, income.
inhábil, *a.* unskilled, incapable.
inhabilitar, *v.* disqualify.
inherente, *a.* inherent.
inhibir, *v.* inhibit.
inhumano, *a.* cruel, inhuman.
iniciador, *m.* initiator.
inicial, *a.* initial.
iniciar, *v.* initiate, begin.
iniciativa, *f.* initiative.
inicuo, *a.* wicked.
iniquidad, *f.* iniquity; sin.
injuria, *f.* insult. **—injuriar,** *v.*
injusticia, *f.* injustice.
injusto, *a.* unjust, unfair.
inmaculado, *a.* immaculate; pure.
inmediato, *a.* immediate.
inmensidad, *f.* immensity.

inmenso, *a.* immense.
inmersión, *f.* immersion.
inmigración, *f.* immigration.
inmigrante, *a. & n.* immigrant.
inmigrar, *v.* immigrate.
inminente, *a.* imminent.
inmoderado, *a.* immoderate.
inmodesto, *a.* immodest.
inmoral, *a.* immoral.
inmoralidad, *f.* immorality.
inmortal, *a.* immortal.
inmortalidad, *f.* immortality.
inmóvil, *a.* immobile, motionless.
inmundicia, *f.* dirt, filth.
inmune, *a.* immune.
inmunidad, *f.* immunity.
innato, *a.* innate, inborn.
innecesario, *a.* unnecessary, needless.
innoble, *a.* ignoble.
innocuo, *a.* innocuous.
innovación, *f.* innovation.
innumerable, *a.* innumerable, countless.
inocencia, *f.* innocence.
inocente, *a.* innocent.
inocular, *v.* inoculate.
inodoro, *m.* toilet.
inofensivo, *a.* inoffensive, harmless.
inolvidable, *a.* unforgettable.
inoportuno, *a.* inopportune.
inquietar, *v.* disturb, worry, trouble.
inquieto, *a.* anxious, uneasy, worried; restless.
inquietud, *f.* concern, anxiety, worry; restlessness.
inquilino -na, *n.* occupant, tenant.
inquirir, *v.* inquire into, investigate.
inquisición, *f.* inquisition, investigation.
insaciable, *a.* insatiable.
insalubre, *a.* unhealthy.
insano, *a.* insane.
inscribir, *v.* inscribe; record.
inscribirse, *v.* register, enroll.
inscripción, *f.* inscription; registration.
insecto, *m.* insect.
inseguro, *a.* unsure, uncertain; insecure, unsafe.
insensato, *a.* stupid, senseless.
insensible, *a.* unfeeling, heartless.
inseparable, *a.* inseparable.
inserción, *f.* insertion.
insertar, *v.* insert.
insidioso, *a.* insidious, crafty.
insigne, *a.* famous, noted.
insignia, *f.* insignia, badge.
insignificante, *a.* insignificant, negligible.
insincero, *a.* insincere.
insinuación, *f.* insinuation; hint.
insinuar, *v.* insinuate, suggest, hint.
insipidez, *f.* insipidity.
insípido, *a.* insipid.
insistencia, *f.* insistence.
insistente, *a.* insistent.

insistir, v. insist.
insolación, f. sunstroke.
insolencia, f. insolence.
insolente, a. insolent.
insólito, a. unusual.
insolvente, a. insolvent.
insomnio, m. insomnia.
insoportable, a. unbearable.
inspección, f. inspection.
inspeccionar, v. inspect, examine.
inspector, m. inspector.
inspiración, f. inspiration.
inspirar, v. inspire.
instalación, f. installation, fixture.
instalar, v. install, set up.
instantánea, f. snapshot.
instantáneo, a. instantaneous.
instante, a. & m. instant. **al i.**, at once.
instar, v. coax, urge.
instigar, v. instigate, urge.
instintivo, a. instinctive.
instinto, m. instinct.
institución, f. institution.
instituto, m. institute. **—instituir**, v.
institutriz, f. governess.
instrucción, f. instruction; education.
instructivo, a. instructive.
instructor, m. instructor.
instruir, v. instruct, teach.
instrumento, m. instrument.
insuficiente, a. insufficient.
insufrible, a. intolerable.
insular, a. island, insular.
insulto, m. insult. **—insultar**, v.
insuperable, a. insuperable.
insurgente, n. & a. insurgent, rebel.
insurrección, f. insurrection, revolt.
insurrecto, a. & m. insurgent.
intacto, a. intact.
integral, a. integral.
integridad, f. integrity; entirety.
íntegro, a. entire; upright.
intelecto, m. intellect.
intelectual, a. & n. intellectual.
inteligencia, f. intelligence.
inteligente, a. intelligent.
inteligible, a. intelligible.
intemperie, f. bad weather.
intención, f. intention.
intendente, m. manager.
intensidad, f. intensity.
intensificar, v. intensify.
intensivo, a. intensive.
intenso, a. intense.
intentar, v. attempt, try.
intento, m. intent.
interceptar, v. intercept.
intercesión, f. intercession.
interés, m. interest; concern; appeal.
interesante, a. interesting.
interesar, v. interest, appeal to.
interferencia, f. interference.
interino, a. temporary.
interior, 1. a. interior, inner; **2.** m. interior.
interjección, f. interjection.

intermedio, 1. a. intermediate.
2. m. intermediary; intermission.
interminable, a. interminable, endless.
intermisión, f. intermission.
intermitente, a. intermittent.
internacional, a. international.
internarse en, v. enter into, go into.
interno, a. internal.
interpelar, v. ask questions; quiz.
interponer, v. interpose.
interpretación, f. interpretation.
interpretar, v. interpret; construe.
intérprete, m. & f. interpreter.
interrogación, f. interrogation.
interrogar, v. question, interrogate.
interrogativo, a. interrogative.
interrumpir, v. interrupt.
interrupción, f. interruption.
intersección, f. intersection.
intervalo, m. interval.
intervención, f. intervention.
intervenir, v. intervene, interfere.
intestino, m. intestine.
intimación, f. intimation, hint.
intimar, v. suggest, hint.
intimidad, f. intimacy.
intimidar, v. intimidate.
íntimo -ma, a. & n. intimate.
intolerable, a. intolerable.
intolerancia, f. intolerance, bigotry.
intolerante, a. intolerant.
intranquilo, a. uneasy.
intravenoso, a. intravenous.
intrepidez, f. daring.
intrépido, a. intrepid.
intriga, f. intrigue, plot, scheme. **—intrigar**, v.
intrincado, a. intricate, involved.
introducción, f. introduction.
introducir, v. introduce.
intruso -sa, m. intruder.
intuición, f. intuition.
inundación, f. flood. **—inundar**, v.
inútil, a. useless.
invadir, v. invade.
inválido -da, a. & n. invalid.
invariable, a. constant.
invasión, f. invasion.
invasor, m. invader.
invencible, a. invincible.
invención, f. invention.
inventar, v. invent; devise.
inventario, m. inventory.
inventivo, a. inventive.
invento, m. invention.
inventor, m. inventor.
invernáculo, m. greenhouse.
invernal, a. wintry.
inverosímil, a. improbable, unlikely.
inversión, f. inversion; (com.) investment.
inverso, a. inverse, reverse.

invertir, v. invert; reverse; (com.) invest.
investigación, f. investigation.
investigador, m. investigator.
investigar, v. investigate.
invierno, m. winter.
invisible, a. invisible.
invitación, f. invitation.
invitar, v. invite.
invocar, v. invoke.
involuntario, a. involuntary.
inyección, f. injection.
inyectar, v. inject.
ir, v. go. **irse**, go away, leave.
ira, f. anger, ire.
iracundo, a. wrathful, irate.
iris, m. iris. **arco i.**, rainbow.
Irlanda, f. Ireland.
irlandés -esa, a. & n. Irish; Irishman.
ironía, f. irony.
irónico, a. ironical.
irracional, a. irrational; insane.
irradiación, f. radiation.
irradiar, v. radiate.
irrazonable, a. unreasonable.
irregular, a. irregular.
irreligioso, a. irreligious.
irremediable, a. irremediable, hopeless.
irresistible, a. irresistible.
irresoluto, a. irresolute, wavering.
irrespectuoso, a. disrespectful.
irreverencia, f. irreverence.
irreverente, adj. irreverent.
irrigación, f. irrigation.
irrigar, v. irrigate.
irritación, f. irritation.
irritar, v. irritate.
irrupción, f. raid, attack.
isla, f. island.
isleño -ña, n. islander.
israelita, n. & a. Israelite.
Italia, f. Italy.
italiano -na, a. & n. Italian.
itinerario, m. itinerary; timetable.
izar, v. hoist.
izquierda, f. left (hand, side).
izquierdista, n. & a. leftist.
izquierdo, a. left.

J

jabalí, m. wild boar.
jabón, m. soap.
jabonar, v. soap.
jaca, f. nag.
jacinto, m. hyacinth.
jactancia, f. boast. **—jactarse**, v.
jactancioso, a. boastful.
jadear, v. pant, puff.
jaez, m. harness; kind.
jalar, v. haul, pull.
jalea, f. jelly.
jaletina, f. gelatin.
jamás, adv. never, ever.
jamón, m. ham.
Japón, m. Japan.
japonés -esa, a. & n. Japanese.
jaqueca, f. headache.

jarabe, *m.* syrup.

jaranear, *v.* jest; carouse.

jardín, *m.* garden.

jardinero -ra, *n.* gardener.

jarra, *f.* jar; pitcher.

jarro, *m.* jug, pitcher.

jaspe, *m.* jasper.

jaula, *f.* cage; coop.

jauría, *f.* pack of hounds.

jazmín, *m.* jasmine.

jefatura, *f.* headquarters.

jefe, *m.* chief, boss.

Jehová, *m.* Jehovah.

jengibre, *m.* ginger.

jerez, *m.* sherry.

jerga, *f.* slang.

jergón, *m.* straw bed.

jerigonza, *f.* jargon.

jeringa, *f.* syringe.

jeringar, *v.* inject; annoy.

jeroglífico, *m.* hieroglyph.

jesuíta, *m.* Jesuit.

Jesús, *m.* Jesus.

jeta, *f.* snout.

jícara, *f.* cup.

jinete, *m.* horseman.

jingoísmo, *m.* jingoism.

jingoísta, *n. & a.* jingoist.

jira, *f.* tour, picnic, outing.

jirafa, *f.* giraffe.

jocundo, *a.* jovial.

jornada, *f.* journey; day's work.

jornal, *m.* day's wage.

jornalero, *m.* day laborer, workman.

joroba, *f.* hump.

jorobado, *a.* humpbacked.

joven, 1. *a.* young. 2. *m. & f.* young person.

jovial, *a.* jovial, jolly.

jovilidad, *f.* joviality.

joya, *f.* jewel, gem.

joyelero, *m.* jewel box.

joyería, *f.* jewelry; jewelry store.

joyero, *m.* jeweler.

juanete, *m.* bunion.

jubilación, *f.* retirement; pension.

jubilar, *v.* retire, pension.

jubileo, *m.* jubilee, public festivity.

júbilo, *m.* glee, rejoicing.

jubiloso, *a.* joyful, gay.

judaico, *a.* Jewish.

judaísmo, *m.* Judaism.

judía, *f.* bean, string bean.

judicial, *a.* judicial.

judío -día, *a. & n.* Jewish; Jew.

juego, *m.* game; play; gambling; set. j. de damas, checkers.

juerga, *f.* spree.

jueves, *m.* Thursday.

juez, *m.* judge.

jugador -ra, *n.* player.

jugar, *v.* play; gamble.

juglar, *m.* minstrel.

jugo, *m.* juice.

jugoso, *a.* juicy.

juguete, *m.* toy, plaything.

juguetear, *v.* trifle.

juguetón, *a.* playful.

juicio, *m.* sense, wisdom, judgment.

juicioso, *a.* wise, judicious.

julio, *m.* July.

jumento, *m.* donkey.

junco, *m.* reed, rush.

junio, *m.* June.

junípero, *m.* juniper.

junquillo, *m.* jonquil.

junta, *f.* board, council; joint, coupling.

juntamente, *adv.* jointly.

juntar, *v.* join; connect; assemble.

junto, *a.* together. j. a, next to.

juntura, *f.* joint, juncture.

jurado, *m.* jury.

juramento, *m.* oath.

jurar, *v.* swear.

jurisconsulto, *m.* jurist.

jurisdicción, *f.* jurisdiction; territory.

jurisprudencia, *f.* jurisprudence.

justa, *f.* joust. —justar, *v.*

justicia, *f.* justice, equity.

justiciero, *a.* just.

justificación, *f.* justification.

justificadamente, *adv.* justifiably.

justificar, *v.* justify, warrant.

justo, *a.* right; exact; just; righteous.

juvenil, *a.* youthful.

juventud, *f.* youth.

juzgado, *m.* court.

juzgar, *v.* judge, estimate.

K, L, LL

káiser, *m.* kaiser.

karate, *m.* karate.

kepis, *m.* military cap.

kerosena, *f.* kerosene.

kilo, kilogramo, *m.* kilogram.

kilohertzio, *m.* kilohertz.

kilolitro, *m.* kiloliter.

kilómetro, *m.* kilometer.

kiosco, *m.* newsstand; pavilion.

la, 1. *art. & pron.* the; the one. 2. *pron.* her, it, you; (*pl.*) them, you.

laberinto, *m.* labyrinth, maze.

labia, *f.* eloquence, fluency.

labio, *m.* lip.

labor, *f.* labor, work.

laborar, *v.* work; till.

laboratorio, *m.* laboratory.

laborioso, *a.* industrious.

labrador, *m.* farmer.

labranza, *f.* farming; farmland.

labrar, *v.* work, till.

labriego -ga, *n.* peasant.

laca, *f.* shellac.

lacio, *a.* withered; limp; straight.

lactar, *v.* nurse, suckle.

lácteo, *a.* milky.

ladear, *v.* tilt, tip; sway.

ladera, *f.* slope.

ladino, *a.* cunning, crafty.

lado, *m.* side. al l. de, beside. de l., sideways.

ladra, *f.* barking. —ladrar, *v.*

ladrillo, *m.* brisk.

ladrón -ona, *n.* thief, robber.

lagarto, *m.* lizard; (Mex.) alligator.

lago, *m.* lake.

lágrima, *f.* tear.

lagrimear, *v.* weep, cry.

laguna, *f.* lagoon; gap.

laico, *a.* lay.

laja, *f.* stone slab.

lamentable, *a.* lamentable.

lamentación, *f.* lamentation.

lamentar, *v.* lament; wail; regret, be sorry.

lamento, *m.* lament, wail.

lamer, *v.* lick; lap.

lámina, *f.* print, illustration.

lámpara, *f.* lamp.

lampiño, *a.* beardless.

lana, *f.* wool.

lanar, *a.* woolen.

lance, *m.* throw; episode; quarrel.

lancha, *f.* launch; small boat.

lanchón, *m.* barge.

langosta, *f.* lobster; locust.

languidecer, *v.* languish, pine.

languidez, *f.* languidness.

lánguido, *a.* languid.

lanza, *f.* lance, spear.

lanzada, *f.* thrust, throw.

lanzar, *v.* throw, hurl; launch.

lañar, *v.* cramp; clamp.

lapicero, *m.* mechanical pencil.

lápida, *f.* stone; tombstone.

lápiz, *m.* pencil; crayon.

lapso, *m.* lapse.

lardo, *m.* lard.

largar, *v.* loosen; free.

largo, 1. *a.* long. a lo l. de, along. 2. *m.* length.

largor, *m.* length.

largueza, *f.* generosity; length.

largura, *f.* length.

laringe, *f.* larynx.

larva, *f.* larva.

lascivia, *f.* lasciviousness.

lascivo, *a.* lascivious.

láser, *m.* laser.

laso, *a.* weary.

lástima, *f.* pity. ser l., to be a pity, to be too bad.

lastimar, *v.* hurt, injure.

lastimoso, *a.* pitiful.

lastre, *m.* ballast. —lastrar, *v.*

lata, *f.* tin can; tin (plate); (coll.) annoyance, bore.

latente, *a.* latent.

lateral, *a.* lateral, side.

latigazo, *m.* lash, whipping.

látigo, *m.* whip.

latín, *m.* Latin (language).

latino, *a.* Latin.

latir, *v.* bet, pulsate.

latitud, *f.* latitude.

latón, *m.* brass.

laúd, *m.* lute.

laudable, *a.* laudable.

láudano, *m.* laudanum.

laurel, *m.* laurel.

lava, *f.* lava.

lavabo, lavamanos, *m.* washroom, lavatory.

lavandera, *f.* washerwoman, laundress.
lavandería, *f.* laundry.
lavar, *v.* wash.
lavatorio, *m.* lavatory.
laya, *f.* spade. —**layar**, *v.*
lazar, *v.* lasso.
lazareto, *m.* hospital; quarantine.
lazo, *m.* tie, knot; bow; loop.
le, *pron.* him, her, you; (*pl.*) them, you.
leal, *a.* loyal.
lealtad, *f.* loyalty, allegiance.
lebrel, *m.* greyhound.
lección, *f.* lesson.
lecito, *m.* yolk.
lector -ra, *n.* reader.
lectura, *f.* reading.
leche, *f.* milk.
lechería, *f.* dairy.
lechero, *m.* milkman.
lecho, *m.* bed, couch.
lechón, *m.* pig.
lechoso, *a.* milky.
lechuga, *f.* lettuce.
lechuza, *f.* owl.
leer, *v.* read.
legación, *f.* legation.
legado, *m.* bequest.
legal, *a.* legal, lawful.
legalizar, *v.* legalize.
legar, *v.* bequeath, leave, will.
legible, *a.* legible.
legión, *f.* legion.
legislación, *f.* legislation.
legislador, *m.* legislator.
legislar, *v.* legislate.
legislativo, *a.* legislative.
legislatura, *f.* legislature.
legítimo, *a.* legitimate.
lego, *m.* layman.
legua, *f.* league (measure).
legumbres, *f.pl.* vegetables.
lejano, *a.* distant, far-off.
lejía, *f.* lye.
lejos, *adv.* far. **a lo l.**, in the distance.
lelo, *a.* stupid, foolish.
lema, *m.* theme; slogan.
lengua, *f.* tongue; language.
lenguado, *m.* sole, flounder.
lenguaje, *m.* speech, language.
lenguaraz, *a.* talkative.
lente, *m. or f.* lens. *m.pl.* eyeglasses.
lenteja, *f.* lentil.
lentitud, *f.* slowness.
lento, *a.* slow.
leña, *f.* wood, firewood.
león, *m.* lion.
leopardo, *m.* leopard.
lerdo, *a.* dull-witted.
lesbiana, *f.* lesbian.
lesión, *f.* wound; damage.
letanía, *f.* litany.
letárgico, *a.* lethargic.
letargo, *m.* lethargy.
letra, *f.* letter (of alphabet); print; words (of a song).
letrado, **1.** *a.* learned. **2.** *m.* lawyer.
letrero, *m.* sign, poster.
leva, *f.* (mil.) draft.

levadura, *f.* yeast, leavening, baking powder.
levantador, *m.* lifter; rebel, mutineer.
levantar, *v.* raise, lift.
levantarse, *v.* rise, get up; stand up.
levar, *v.* weigh (anchor).
leve, *a.* slight, light.
levita, *f.* frock coat.
léxico, *m.* lexicon, dictionary.
ley, *f.* law, statute.
leyenda, *f.* legend.
lezna, *f.* awl.
libación, *f.* libation.
libelo, *m.* libel.
libélula, *f.* dragonfly.
liberación, *f.* liberation, release.
liberal, *a.* liberal.
libertad, *f.* liberty, freedom.
libertador, *m.* liberator.
libertar, *v.* free, liberate.
libertinaje, *m.* licentiousness.
libertino, *m.* libertine.
libidine, *f.* licentiousness; lust.
libidinoso, *a.* libidinous; lustful.
libra, *f.* pound.
libranza, *f.* draft, bill of exchange.
librar, *v.* free, rid.
libre, *a.* free, unoccupied.
librería, *f.* bookstore.
librero, *m.* bookseller.
libreta, *f.* notebook; booklet.
libreto, *m.* libretto.
libro, *m.* book.
licencia, *f.* permission, license, leave; furlough.
licenciado -da, *n.* graduate.
licencioso, *a.* licentious.
lícito, *a.* lawful.
licor, *m.* liquor.
lid, *f.* fight. —**lidiar**, *v.*
líder, *m.* leader.
liebre, *f.* hare.
lienzo, *m.* linen.
liga, *f.* league, confederacy; garter.
ligadura, *f.* ligature.
ligar, *v.* tie, bind, join.
ligero, *a.* light; fast, nimble.
ligustro, *m.* privet.
lija, *f.* sandpaper.
lijar, *v.* sandpaper.
lima, *f.* file; lime.
limbo, *m.* limbo.
limitación, *f.* limitation.
límite, *m.* limit. —**limitar**, *v.*
limo, *m.* slime.
limón, *m.* lemon.
limonada, *f.* lemonade.
limonero, *m.* lemon tree.
limosna, *f.* alms.
limosnero -ra, *n.* beggar.
limpiabotas, *m.* bootblack.
limpiadientes, *m.* toothpick.
limpiar, *v.* clean, wash, wipe.
límpido, *a.* limpid, clear.
limpieza, *f.* cleanliness.
limpio, *a.* clean.
linaje, *m.* lineage, ancestry.
linaza, *f.* linseed.

lince, *a.* sharp-sighted, observing.
linchamiento, *m.* lynching.
linchar, *v.* lynch.
lindar, *v.* border, bound.
linde, *m.* boundary; landmark.
lindero, *m.* boundary.
lindo, *a.* pretty, lovely, nice.
línea, *f.* line.
lineal, *a.* lineal.
linfa, *f.* lymph.
lingüista, *m. & f.* linguist.
lingüístico, *a.* linguistic.
linimento, *m.* liniment.
lino, *m.* linen; flax.
linóleo, *m.* linoleum.
linterna, *f.* lantern; flashlight.
lío, *m.* pack, bundle; mess, scrape; hassle.
liquidación, *f.* liquidation.
liquidar, *v.* liquidate; settle up.
líquido, *a. & m.* liquid.
lira, *f.* lyre.
lírico, *a.* lyric.
lirio, *m.* lily.
lirismo, *m.* lyricism.
lis, *f.* lily.
lisiar, *v.* cripple, lame.
liso, *a.* smooth, even.
lisonja, *f.* flattery.
lisonjear, *v.* flatter.
lisonjero -ra, *n.* flatterer.
lista, *f.* list; stripe; menu.
listar, *v.* list; put on a list.
listo, *a.* ready; smart, clever.
listón, *m.* ribbon.
litera, *f.* litter, bunk, berth.
literal, *a.* literal.
literario, *a.* literary.
literato, *m.* literary person, writer.
literatura, *f.* literature.
litigación, *f.* litigation.
litigio, *m.* litigation; lawsuit.
litoral, *m.* coast.
litro, *m.* liter.
liturgia, *f.* liturgy.
liviano, *a.* light (in weight).
lívido, *a.* livid.
lo, *pron.* the; him, it, you; (*pl.*) them, you.
loar, *v.* praise, laud.
lobina, *f.* striped bass.
lobo, *m.* wolf.
lóbrego, *a.* murky; dismal.
local, **1.** *a.* local. **2.** *m.* site.
localidad, *f.* locality, location; seat (in theater).
localizar, *v.* localize.
loción, *f.* lotion.
loco -ca, **1.** *a.* crazy, insane, mad. **2.** *n.* lunatic.
locomotora, *f.* locomotive.
locuaz, *a.* loquacious.
locución, *f.* locution, expression.
locura, *f.* folly; madness, insanity.
lodo, *m.* mud.
lodoso, *a.* muddy.
lógica, *f.* logic.
lógico, *a.* logical.
lograr, *v.* achieve; succeed in.
logro, *m.* accomplishment.
lombriz, *f.* earthworm.

lomo, *m.* loin; back (of an animal).

lona, *f.* canvas.

longevidad, *f.* longevity.

longitud, *f.* longitude; length.

lonja, *f.* shop; market.

lontananza, *f.* distance.

loro, *m.* parrot.

losa, *f.* slab.

lote, *m.* lot, share.

lotería, *f.* lottery.

loza, *f.* china, crockery.

lozanía, *f.* freshness, vigor.

lozano, *a.* fresh, spirited.

lubricación, *f.* lubrication.

lubricar, *v.* lubricate.

lucero, *m.* (bright) star.

lúcido, *a.* lucid, clear.

luciente, *a.* shining, bright.

luciérnaga, *f.* firefly.

lucimiento, *m.* success; splendor.

lucir, *v.* shine, sparkle; show off.

lucrativo, *a.* lucrative, profitable.

lucha, *f.* fight, struggle; wrestling. **—luchar,** *v.*

luchador, *m.* fighter, wrestler.

luego, *adv.* right away; afterwards, next. **l. que,** as soon as. **desde l.,** of course. **hasta l.,** good-bye, so long.

lugar, *m.* place, spot; space, room.

lúgubre, *a.* gloomy; dismal.

lujo, *m.* luxury. **de l.,** de luxe.

lujoso, *a.* luxurious.

lumbre, *f.* fire; light.

luminoso, *a.* luminous.

luna, *f.* moon.

lunar, *m.* beauty mark, mole; polka dot.

lunático, *a. & n.* lunatic.

lunes, *m.* Monday.

luneta, *f.* (theat.) orchestra seat.

lustre, *m.* polish, shine. **—lustrar,** *v.*

lustroso, *a.* shiny.

luto, *m.* mourning.

luz, *f.* light. **dar a l.,** give birth to.

llaga, *f.* sore.

llama, *f.* flame; llama.

llamada, *f.* call; knock. **—llamar,** *v.*

llamarse, *v.* be called, be named. **se llama . . .** etc., his name is . . . etc.

llamativo, *a.* gaudy, showy.

llamear, *v.* blaze.

llaneza, *f.* simplicity.

llano, 1. *a.* flat, level; plain. **2.** *m.* plain.

llanta, *f.* tire.

llanto, *m.* crying, weeping.

llanura, *f.* prairie, plain.

llave, *f.* key; wrench; faucet; (elec.) switch. **ll. inglesa,** monkey wrench.

llegada, *f.* arrival.

llegar, *v.* arrive; reach. **ll. a ser,** become, come to be.

llenar, *v.* fill.

lleno, *a.* full.

llenura, *f.* abundance.

llevadero, *a.* tolerable.

llevar, *v.* take, carry, bear; wear (clothes); **ll. a cabo,** carry out.

llevarse, *v.* take away, run away with. **ll. bien,** get along well.

llorar, *v.* cry, weep.

lloroso, *a.* sorrowful, tearful.

llover, *v.* rain.

llovido, *m.* stowaway.

llovizna, *f.* drizzle, sprinkle. **—lloviznar,** *v.*

lluvia, *f.* rain.

lluvioso, *a.* rainy.

M

maca, *f.* blemish, flaw.

macaco, *a.* ugly, horrid.

macareno, *a.* boasting.

macarrones, *m.pl.* macaroni.

macear, *v.* molest, push around.

maceta, *f.* vase; mallet.

macizo, 1. *a.* solid. **2.** *m.* bulk; flower bed.

macular, *v.* stain.

machacar, *v.* pound; crush.

machina, *f.* derrick.

machista, *a.* macho.

macho, *m.* male.

machucho, *a.* mature, wise.

madera, *f.* lumber; wood.

madero, *m.* beam, timber.

madrastra, *f.* stepmother.

madre, *f.* mother. **m. política,** mother-in-law.

madreperla, *f.* mother-of-pearl.

madriguera, *f.* burrow; lair, den.

madrina, *f.* godmother.

madroncillo, *m.* strawberry.

madrugada, *f.* daybreak.

madrugar, *v.* get up early.

madurar, *v.* ripen.

madurez, *f.* maturity.

maduro, *a.* ripe; mature.

maestría, *f.* mastery.

maestro, *m.* master; teacher.

mafia, *f.* mafia.

maganto, *a.* lethargic, dull.

magia, *f.* magic.

mágico, *a. & m.* magic; magician.

magistrado, *m.* magistrate.

magnánimo, *a.* magnanimous.

magnético, *a.* magnetic.

magnetismo, *m.* magnetism.

magnetófono, *m.* tape recorder.

magnificar, *v.* magnify.

magnificencia, *f.* magnificence.

magnífico, *a.* magnificent.

magnitud, *f.* magnitude.

magno, *a.* great, grand.

magnolia, *f.* magnolia.

mago, *m.* magician; wizard.

magosto, *m.* picnic, outing.

magro, *a.* meager; thin.

magullar, *v.* bruise.

mahometano, *n. & a.* Mohammedan.

mahometismo, *m.* Mohammedanism.

maíz, *m.* corn.

majadero, *a. & m.* foolish; fool.

majar, *v.* mash.

majestad, *f.* majesty.

majestuoso, *a.* majestic.

mal, 1. *adv.* badly; wrong. **2.** *m.* evil, ill; illness.

mala, *f.* mail.

malacate, *m.* hoist.

malandanza, *f.* misfortune.

malaventura, *f.* misfortune.

malcomido, *a.* underfed; malnourished.

malcontento, *a.* disssatisfied.

maldad, *f.* badness; wickedness.

maldecir, *v.* curse, damn.

maldición, *f.* curse.

maldito, *a.* accursed, damned.

malecón, *m.* embankment.

maledicencia, *f.* slander.

maleficio, *m.* spell, charm.

malestar, *m.* indisposition.

maleta, *f.* suitcase, valise.

malevolo, *a.* malevolent.

maleza, *f.* weeds; underbrush.

malgastar, *v.* squander.

malhechor, *m.* malefactor, evildoer.

malhumorado, *a.* morose, ill-humored.

malicia, *f.* malice.

maliciar, *v.* suspect.

malicioso, *a.* malicious.

maligno, *a.* malignant, evil.

malo, *a.* bad; evil, wicked; naughty; ill.

malograr, *v.* miss, lose.

malparto, *m.* abortion, miscarriage.

malquerencia, *f.* hatred.

malquerer, *v.* dislike; bear ill will.

malsano, *a.* unhealthy; unwholesome.

malsín, *m.* malicious gossip.

malta, *f.* malt.

maltratar, *v.* mistreat.

malvado, 1. *a.* wicked. **2.** *m.* villain.

malviz, *m.* redwing.

malla, *f.* mesh, net.

mallete, *m.* mallet.

mamá, *f.* mama, mother.

mamar, *v.* suckle; suck.

mamífero, *m.* mammal.

mampara, *f.* screen.

mampostería, *f.* masonry.

mamut, *m.* mammoth.

manada, *f.* flock, herd, drove.

manatial, *m.* spring (of water).

manar, *v.* gush, flow out.

mancebo, *m.* young man.

mancilla, *f.* stain; blemish.

manco, *a.* armless; one-armed.

mancha, *f.* stain, smear, blemish, spot. **—manchar,** *v.*

mandadero, *m.* messenger.

mandado, *m.* order, command.

mandamiento, *m.* commandment; command.

mandar, v. send; order, command.

mandatario, m. attorney; representative.

mandato, m. mandate, command.

mandíbula, f. jaw; jawbone.

mando, m. command, order; leadership.

mandón, a. domineering.

mandril, m. baboon.

manejar, v. handle, manage; drive (a car).

manejo, m. management; horsemanship.

manera, f. way, manner, means. **de m. que,** so, as a result.

manga, f. sleeve.

mangana, f. lariat, lasso.

manganeso, m. manganese.

mango, m. handle; mango (fruit).

mangosta, f. mongoose.

manguera, f. hose.

manguito, m. muff.

maní, m. peanut.

manía, f. mania, madness; hobby.

maníaco, maniático, a. & m. maniac.

manicomio, m. insane asylum.

manicura, f. manicure.

manifactura, f. manufacture.

manifestación, f. manifestation.

manifestar, v. manifest, show.

manifiesto, a. & m. manifest.

manija, f. handle; crank.

maniobra, f. maneuver. —**maniobrar,** v.

manipulación, f. manipulation.

manipular, v. manipulate.

maniquí, m. mannequin.

manivela, f. (mech.) crank.

manjar, m. food, dish.

manlieve, m. swindle.

mano, f. hand.

manojo, m. handful; bunch.

manómetro, m. gauge.

manopla, f. gauntlet.

manosear, v. handle, feel, touch.

manotada, f. slap, smack. —**manotear,** v.

mansedumbre, f. meekness, tameness.

mansión, f. mansion; abode.

manso, a. tame, gentle.

manta, f. blanket.

manteca, f. fat, lard; butter.

mantecado, m. ice cream.

mantecoso, a. buttery.

mantel, m. tablecloth.

mantener, v. maintain, keep; sustain; support.

mantenimiento, m. maintenance.

mantequera, f. butter dish; churn.

mantequilla, f. butter.

mantilla, f. mantilla; baby clothes.

mantillo, m. humus; manure.

manto, m. mantle, cloak.

manual, a. & m. manual.

manubrio, m. handle; crank.

manufacturar, v. manufacture; make.

manuscrito, m. manuscript.

manzana, f. apple; block (of street).

manzano, m. apple tree.

maña, f. skill; cunning; trick.

mañana, 1. adv. tomorrow. **2.** f. morning.

mañanear, v. rise early in the morning.

mañero, a. clever; skillful; lazy.

mapa, m. map, chart.

mapache, m. raccoon.

mapurito, m. skunk.

máquina, f. machine.

maquinación, f. machination; plot.

maquinador, m. plotter, schemer.

maquinal, a. mechanical.

maquinar, v. scheme, plot.

maquinaria, f. machinery.

maquinista, m. machinist; engineer.

mar, m. or f. sea.

marabú, m. marabou.

maraña, f. tangle; maze; snarl; plot.

maravilla, f. marvel, wonder. —**maravillarse,** v.

maravilloso, a. marvelous, wonderful.

marbete, m. tag, label; check.

marca, f. mark, sign; brand, make.

marcar, v. mark; observe, note.

marcial, a. martial.

marco, m. frame.

marcha, f. march, progress. —**marchar,** v.

marchante, m. merchant; customer.

marcharse, v. go away, depart.

marchitable, a. perishable.

marchitar, v. fade, wilt, wither.

marchito, a. faded, withered.

marea, f. tide.

mareado, a. seasick.

marearse, v. get dizzy; be seasick.

mareo, m. dizziness, seasickness.

marfil, m. ivory.

margarita, f. pearl; daisy.

margen, m. or f. margin, edge, rim.

marido, m. husband.

marijuana, f. marijuana, pot, grass.

marimba, f. marimba.

marina, f. navy; seascape.

marinero, m. sailor, seaman.

marino, a. & m. marine, (of) sea; mariner, seaman.

marión, m. sturgeon.

mariposa, f. butterfly.

mariquita, f. ladybird.

mariscal, m. marshal.

marisco, m. shellfish; mollusk.

marital, a. marital.

marítimo, a. maritime.

marmita, f. pot, kettle.

mármol, m. marble.

marmóreo, a. marble.

maroma, f. rope.

marqués, m. marquis.

marquesa, f. marquise.

Marte, m. Mars.

martes, m. Tuesday.

martillo, m. hammer. —**martillar,** v.

mártir, m. & f. martyr.

martirio, m. martyrdom.

martirizar, v. martyrize.

marzo, m. March.

mas, conj. but.

más, a. & adv. more, most; plus. **no m.,** only.

masa, f. mass; dough.

masaje, m. massage.

mascar, v. chew.

máscara, f. mask.

mascarada, f. masquerade.

mascota, f. mascot; good-luck charm.

masculino, a. masculine.

mascullar, v. mumble.

masón, m. Freemason.

masticar, v. chew.

mástil, m. mast; post.

mastín, m. mastiff.

mastuerzo, m. fool, ninny.

mata, f. plant; bush.

matadero, m. slaughterhouse.

matador, m. matador.

matanza, f. killing, bloodshed, slaughter.

matar, v. kill, slay; slaughter.

matasanos, m. quack.

mate, m. checkmate; Paraguayan tea.

matemáticas, f.pl. mathematics.

matemático, a. mathematical.

materia, f. material; subject (matter).

material, a. & m. material.

materialismo, m. materialism.

materializar, v. materialize.

maternal, materno, a. maternal.

maternidad, f. maternity.

matiné, m. matinee.

matiz, m. hue, shade.

matizar, v. blend; tint.

matón, m. bully.

matorral, m. thicket.

matoso, a. weedy.

matraca, f. rattle. —**matraquear,** v.

matrícula, f. registration; tuition.

matricularse, v. enroll, register.

matrimonio, m. matrimony, marriage, married couple.

matriz, f. womb; (mech.) die, mold.

matrona, f. matron.

maullar, v. mew.

máxima, f. maxim.

máxime, a. principally.

máximo, a. & m. maximum.

maya, f. daisy.

mayo, m. May.

mayonesa, f. mayonnaise.

mayor, 1. a. larger, largest;

greater, greatest; elder, eldest, senior. **m. de edad**, major, of age. **al por m.**, at wholesale. **2.** *m.* major.

mayoral, *m.* head shepherd; boss; foreman.

mayordomo, *m.* manager; butler, steward.

mayoría, *f.* majority, bulk.

mazmorra, *f.* dungeon.

mazorca, *f.* ear of corn.

me, *pron.* me; myself.

mecánico, *a. & m.* mechanical; mechanic.

mecanismo, *m.* mechanism.

mecanizar, *v.* mechanize.

mecanografía, *f.* typewriting.

mecanógrafo -fa, *n.* typist.

mecedor, *m.* swing.

mecedora, *f.* rocking chair.

mecer, *v.* rock; swing, sway.

mecha, *f.* wick; fuse.

mechón, *m.* lock (of hair).

medalla, *f.* medal.

médano, *m.* sand dune.

media, *f.* stocking.

mediación, *f.* mediation.

mediador, *m.* mediator.

mediados, *m.pl.* **a m. de**, about the middle of (a period of time).

medianero, *m.* mediator.

medianía, *f.* mediocrity.

mediano, *a.* medium; moderate; mediocre.

medianoche, *f.* midnight.

mediante, *prep.* by means of.

mediar, *v.* mediate.

medicamento, *m.* medicine, drug.

medicastro, *m.* quack.

medicina, *f.* medicine.

medicinar, *v.* treat (as a doctor).

médico, **1.** *a.* medical. **2.** *m.* doctor, physician.

medida, *f.* measure, step.

medidor, *m.* meter.

medio, **1.** *a.* half; mid, middle of. **2.** *m.* middle; means.

mediocre, *a.* mediocre.

mediocridad, *f.* mediocrity.

mediodía, *m.* midday, noon.

medioeval, *a.* medieval.

medir, *v.* measure, gauge.

meditación, *f.* meditation.

meditar, *v.* meditate.

mediterráneo, *a.* Mediterranean.

medrar, *v.* thrive.

medroso, *a.* fearful, cowardly.

megáfono, *m.* megaphone.

megahertzio, *f.* megahertz.

mejicano, *a. & m.* Mexican.

mejilla, *f.* cheek.

mejor, *a. & adv.* better; best. **a lo m.**, perhaps.

mejora, *f.*, **mejoramiento**, *m.* improvement.

mejorar, *v.* improve, better.

mejoría, *f.* improvement; superiority.

melancolía, *f.* melancholy.

melancólico, *a.* melancholy.

melaza, *f.* molasses.

melena, *f.* mane; long or loose hair.

melindroso, *a.* fussy.

melocotón, *m.* peach.

melodía, *f.* melody.

melodioso, *a.* melodious.

melón, *m.* melon.

meloso, *a.* like honey.

mella, *f.* notch; dent. **—mellar**, *v.*

mellizo -za, *n. & a.* twin.

membrana, *f.* membrane.

membrete, *m.* memorandum; letterhead.

membrillo, *m.* quince.

membrudo, *a.* strong, muscular.

memorable, *a.* memorable.

memorándum, *m.* memorandum; notebook.

memoria, *f.* memory; memoir; memorandum.

mención, *f.* mention. **—mencionar**, *v.*

mendigar, *v.* beg (for alms).

mendigo -a, *n.* beggar.

mendrugo, *m.* crumb, bit.

menear, *v.* shake, wag; stir.

menester, *m.* need, want; duty, task. **ser m.**, to be necessary.

menesteroso, *a.* needy.

mengua, *f.* decrease; lack; poverty.

menguar, *v.* abate, decrease.

menor, *a.* smaller, smallest; lesser, least; younger, youngest, junior. **m. de edad**, minor, under age. **al por m.**, at retail.

menos, *a. & adv.* less; least; minus. **a m. que**, unless. **echar de m.**, to miss.

menospreciar, *v.* cheapen; despise; slight.

mensaje, *m.* message.

mensajero -ra, *n.* messenger.

menstruar, *v.* menstruate.

mensual, *a.* monthly.

mensualidad, *f.* monthly income or allowance; monthly payment.

menta, *f.* mint, peppermint.

mentado, *a.* famous.

mental, *a.* mental.

mentalidad, *f.* mentality.

mente, *f.* mind.

mentecato, *a.* foolish, stupid.

mentir, *v.* lie, tell a lie.

mentira, *f.* lie, falsehood. **parece m.**, it seems impossible.

mentiroso, *a.* lying, untruthful.

mentol, *m.* menthol.

menú, *m.* menu.

menudeo, *m.* retail.

menudo, *a.* small, minute. **a m.**, often.

meñique, *a.* tiny.

meple, *m.* maple.

merca, *f.* purchase.

mercader, *m.* merchant.

mercaderías, *f.pl.* merchandise, commodities.

mercado, *m.* market.

mercancía, *f.* merchandise; (*pl.*) wares.

mercante, *a.* merchant.

mercantil, *a.* mercantile.

merced, *f.* mercy, grace.

mercenario -ria, *a. & m.* mercenary.

mercurio, *m.* mercury.

merecedor, *a.* worthy.

merecer, *v.* merit, deserve.

merecimiento, *m.* merit.

merendar, *v.* eat lunch.

merendero, *m.* lunchroom.

meridional, *a.* southern.

merienda, *f.* midday meal, lunch.

mérito, *m.* merit, worth.

meritorio, *a.* meritorious.

merla, *f.* blackbird.

merluza, *f.* haddock.

mermelada, *f.* marmalade.

mero, *a.* mere.

mes, *m.* month.

mesa, *f.* table.

meseta, *f.* plateau.

mesón, *m.* inn.

mesonero, *m.* innkeeper.

mestizo -za, *a. & n.* half-caste.

meta, *f.* goal, objective.

metabolismo, *m.* metabolism.

metafísica, *f.* metaphysics.

metáfora, *f.* metaphor.

metal, *m.* metal.

metálico, *a.* metallic.

metalurgia, *f.* metallurgy.

meteoro, *m.* meteor.

meteorología, *f.* meteorology.

meter, *v.* put (in).

meterse, *v.* interfere, meddle.

metódico, *a.* methodic.

método, *m.* method, approach.

metralla, *f.* shrapnel.

métrico, *a.* metric.

metro, *m.* meter (measure); subway.

metrópoli, *f.* metropolis.

mexicano -na, *a. & n.* Mexican.

mezcla, *f.* mixture; blend.

mezclar, *v.* mix; blend.

mezcolanza, *f.* mixture; hodgepodge.

mezquino, *a.* stingy; petty.

mi, *a.* my.

mí, *pron.* me; myself.

microbio, *m.* microbe, germ.

microficha, *f.* microfiche.

micrófono, *m.* microphone.

microforma, *f.* microform.

microscópico, *a.* microscopic.

microscopio, *m.* microscope.

miedo, *m.* fear. **tener m.**, fear, be afraid.

miedoso, *a.* fearful.

miel, *f.* honey.

miembro, *m.* member; limb.

mientras, *conj.* while. **m. tanto**, meanwhile. **m. más . . . más**, the more . . . the more.

miércoles, *m.* Wednesday.

miga, **migaja**, *f.* scrap, crumb.

migración, *f.* migration.

migratorio, *a.* migratory.

mil, *a. & pron.* thousand.

milagro, *m.* miracle.

milagroso, *a.* miraculous.

milicia, *f.* militia.

militante, *a.* militant.

militar, 1. *a.* military. 2. *m.* military man.

militarismo, *m.* militarism.

milla, *f.* mile.

millar, *m.* (a) thousand.

millón, *m.* million.

millonario -ria, *n.* millionaire.

mimar, *v.* pamper, spoil (a child).

mimbre, *m.* willow; wicker.

mímico, *a.* mimic.

mimo, *m.* mime, mimic.

mina, *f.* mine. —minar, *v.*

mineral, *a.* & *m.* mineral.

minero, *m.* miner.

miniatura, *f.* miniature.

miniaturizar, *v.* miniaturize.

mínimo, *a.* & *m.* minimum.

ministerio, *m.* ministry; cabinet.

ministro, *m.* (govt.) minister, secretary.

minoría, *f.* minority.

minoridad, *f.* minority; nonage.

minucioso, *a.* minute; thorough.

minué, *m.* minuet.

minuta, *f.* minute; draft.

mío, *a.* mine.

miopía, *f.* myopia.

mira, *f.* gunsight.

mirada, *f.* look; gaze, glance.

miramiento, *m.* consideration; respect.

mirar, *v.* look, look at; watch. m. a, face.

miríada, *f.* myriad.

mirlo, *m.* blackbird.

mirón, *m.* bystander, observer.

mirra, *f.* myrrh.

mirto, *m.* myrtle.

misa, *f.* mass, church service.

misceláneo, *a.* miscellaneous.

miserable, *a.* miserable, wretched.

miseria, *f.* misery.

misericordia, *f.* mercy.

misericordioso, *a.* merciful.

misión, *f.* assignment; mission.

misionario -ria, misionero -ra, *n.* missionary.

mismo, 1. *a.* & *pron.* same; -self, -selves. 2. *adv.* right, exactly.

misterio, *m.* mystery.

misterioso, *a.* mysterious, weird.

místico, *a.* & *m.* mystical, mystic.

mitad, *f.* half.

mítico, *a.* mythical.

mitigar, *v.* mitigate.

mitín, *m.* meeting.

mito, *m.* myth.

mitón, *m.* mitten.

mitra, *f.* miter (bishop's).

mixto, *a.* mixed.

mixtura, *f.* mixture.

mobiliario, *m.* household goods.

mocasín, *m.* moccasin.

mocedad, *f.* youthfulness.

moción, *f.* motion.

mocoso -sa, *a.* brat.

mochila, *f.* knapsack, backpack.

mocho, *a.* cropped, trimmed, shorn.

moda, *f.* mode, fashion, style.

modales, *m.pl.* manners.

modelo, *m.* model, pattern.

moderación, *f.* moderation.

moderado, *a.* moderate. — moderar, *v.*

modernizar, *v.* modernize.

moderno, *a.* modern.

modestia, *f.* modesty.

modesto, *a.* modest.

módico, *a.* reasonable, moderate.

modificación, *f.* modification.

modificar, *v.* modify.

modismo, *m.* (gram.) idiom.

modista, *f.* dressmaker; milliner.

modo, *m.* way, means.

modular, *v.* modulate.

mofarse, *v.* scoff, sneer.

mofletudo, *a.* fat-cheeked.

mohín, *m.* grimace.

moho, *m.* mold, mildew.

mohoso, *a.* moldy.

mojar, *v.* wet.

mojón, *m.* landmark; heap.

molde, *m.* mold, form.

molécula, *f.* molecule.

moler, *v.* grind, mill.

molestar, *v.* molest, bother, disturb, annoy, trouble.

molestia, *f.* bother, annoyance, trouble; hassle.

molesto, *a.* bothersome; annoyed; uncomfortable.

molicie, *f.* softness.

molinero, *m.* miller.

molino, *m.* mill.

molusco, *m.* mollusk.

mollera, *f.* top of the head.

momentáneo, *a.* momentary.

momento, *m.* moment.

mona, *f.* female monkey.

monarca, *m.* monarch.

monarquía, *f.* monarchy.

monarquista, *n.* & *a.* monarchist.

monasterio, *m.* monastery.

mondadientes, *m.* toothpick.

moneda, *f.* coin; money.

monetario, *a.* monetary.

monición, *f.* warning.

monigote, *m.* puppet.

monja, *f.* nun.

monje, *m.* monk.

mono -na, 1. *a.* (coll.) cute. 2. *m.* & *f.* monkey.

monólogo, *m.* monologue.

monopatín, *m.* skateboard.

monopolio, *m.* monopoly.

monopolizar, *v.* monopolize.

monosílabo, *m.* monosyllable.

monotonía, *f.* monotony.

monótono, *a.* monotonous, dreary.

monstruo, *m.* monster.

monstruosidad, *f.* monstrosity.

monstruoso, *a.* monstrous.

monta, *f.* amount; price.

montaña, *f.* mountain.

montañoso, *a.* mountainous.

montar, *v.* mount, climb; amount; (mech.) assemble. m. a caballo, ride horseback.

montaraz, *a.* wild, barbaric.

monte, *m.* mountain, forest.

montón, *m.* heap, pile.

montuoso, *a.* mountainous.

montura, *f.* riding horse, mount.

monumental, *a.* monumental.

monumento, *m.* monument.

mora, *f.* blackberry.

morada, *f.* residence, dwelling.

morado, *a.* purple.

moral, 1. *a.* moral. 2. *f.* morale.

moraleja, *f.* moral.

moralidad, *f.* morality, morals.

moralista, *m.* & *f.* moralist.

morar, *v.* dwell, live, reside.

mórbido, *a.* morbid.

mordaz, *a.* caustic; sarcastic.

mordedura, *f.* bite.

morder, *v.* bite.

moreno -na, *a.* & *n.* brown; dark-skinned; dark-haired, brunette.

morfina, *f.* morphine.

moribundo, *a.* dying.

morir, *v.* die.

morisco -ca, moro -ra, *a.* & *n.* Moorish; Moor.

morriña, *f.* sadness.

morro, *m.* bluff.

mortaja, *f.* shroud.

mortal, *a.* & *m.* mortal.

mortalidad, *f.* mortality.

mortero, *m.* mortar.

mortífero, *a.* fatal, mortal.

mortificar, *v.* mortify.

mortuario, *a.* funereal.

mosaico, *a.* & *m.* mosaic.

mosca, *f.* fly.

mosquito, *m.* mosquito.

mostacho, *m.* mustache.

mostaza, *f.* mustard.

mostrador, *m.* counter; showcase.

mostrar, *v.* show, display.

mote, *m.* nickname; alias.

motín, *m.* mutiny; riot.

motivo, *m.* motive, reason.

motocicleta, *f.* motorcycle.

motor, *m.* motor.

motorista, *n.* motorist.

movedizo, *a.* movable; shaky.

mover, *v.* move; stir.

movible, *a.* movable.

móvil, *a.* mobile.

movilización, *f.* mobilization.

movilizar, *v.* mobilize.

movimiento, *m.* movement, motion.

mozo, *m.* boy; servant, waiter, porter.

muaré, *m.* moiré.

mucoso, *a.* mucous.

muchacha, *f.* girl; maid (servant).

muchachez, *m.* boyhood, girlhood.

muchacho, *m.* boy.

muchedumbre, *f.* crowd, mob.

mucho, 1. *a.* much, many. 2. *adv.* much.

muda, *f.* change.

N, Ñ

mudanza, *f.* change; change of residence.
mudar, *v.* change, shift.
mudarse, *v.* change residence, move.
mudo -da, *a. & n.* mute.
mueble, *m.* piece of furniture; (*pl.*) furniture.
mueca, *f.* grimace.
muela, *f.* (back) tooth.
muelle, *m.* pier, wharf; (mech.) spring.
muerte, *f.* death.
muerto -ta, 1. *a.* dead. **2.** *n.* dead person.
muesca, *f.* notch; groove.
muestra, *f.* sample, specimen, sign.
mugido, *m.* lowing; mooing.
mugir, *v.* low, moo.
mugre, *f.* filth, dirt.
mugriento, *a.* dirty.
mujer, *f.* woman; wife.
mujeril, *a.* womanly, feminine.
mula, *f.* mule.
mulato, *a. & m.* mulatto.
muleta, *f.* crutch; prop.
mulo, *m.* mule.
multa, *f.* fine, penalty.
multicolor, *a.* many-colored.
multinacional, *a.* multinational.
múltiple, *a.* multiple.
multiplicación, *f.* multiplication.
multiplicar, *v.* multiply.
multiplicidad, *f.* multiplicity.
multitud, *f.* multitude, crowd.
mundanal, *a.* worldly.
mundano, *a.* worldly, mundane.
mundial, *a.* worldwide; (of the) world.
mundo, *m.* world.
munición, *f.* ammunition.
municipal, *a.* municipal.
muñeca, *f.* doll; wrist.
muñeco, *m.* doll; puppet.
mural, *a. & m.* mural.
muralla, *f.* wall.
murciélago, *m.* bat.
murga, *f.* musical band.
murmullo, *m.* murmur; rustle.
murmurar, *v.* murmur; rustle; grumble.
murta, *f.* myrtle.
musa, *f.* muse.
muscular, *a.* muscular.
músculo, *m.* muscle.
muselina, *f.* muslin.
museo, *m.* museum.
música, *f.* music.
musical, *a.* musical.
músico, *a. & m.* musical; musician.
muslo, *m.* thigh.
mustio, *a.* sad.
muta, *f.* pack of hounds.
mutabilidad, *f.* mutability.
mutación, *f.* mutation.
mutilación, *f.* mutilation.
mutilar, *v.* mutilate; mangle.
mutuo, *a.* mutual.
muy, *adv.* very.

nabo, *m.* turnip.
nacar, *m.* mother-of-pearl.
nacarado, *a.* pearly.
nacer, *v.* be born.
naciente, *a.* rising.
nacimiento, *m.* birth.
nación, *f.* nation.
nacional, *a.* national.
nacionalidad, *f.* nationality.
nacionalismo, *m.* nationalism.
nacionalista, *n. & a.* nationalist.
nacionalización, *f.* nationalization.
nacionalizar, *v.* nationalize.
nada, 1. *pron.* nothing; anything. **de n.,** you're welcome. **2.** *adv.* at all.
nadador, *m.* swimmer.
nadar, *v.* swim.
nadie, *pron.* no one, nobody; anyone, anybody.
nafta, *f.* naphtha.
naipe, *m.* (playing) card.
naranja, *f.* orange.
naranjada, *f.* orangeade.
naranjo, *m.* orange tree.
narciso, *m.* daffodil; narcissus.
narcótico, *a. & m.* narcotic.
nardo, *m.* spikenard.
nariz, *f.* nose; (*pl.*) nostrils.
narración, *f.* narration.
narrador, *m.* narrator.
narrar, *v.* narrate.
narrativo, *f.* narrative.
nata, *f.* cream.
natal, *a.* native, natal.
natalicio, *m.* birthplace.
natalidad, *f.* birth rate.
natilla, *f.* custard.
nativo, *a.* native; innate.
natural, 1. *a.* natural. **2.** *m. & f.* native. *m.* nature, disposition.
naturaleza, *f.* nature.
naturalidad, *f.* naturalness; nationality.
naturalista, *a. & m.* naturalistic; naturalist.
naturalización, *f.* naturalization.
naturalizar, *v.* naturalize, accustom.
naufragar, *v.* be shipwrecked; fail.
naufragio, *m.* shipwreck; disaster.
náufrago -ga, *a. & n.* shipwrecked (person).
náusea, *f.* nausea.
nausear, *v.* feel nauseous.
náutico, *a.* nautical.
navaja, *f.* razor; pen knife.
naval, *a.* naval.
nave, *f.* ship.
navegable, *a.* navigable.
navegación, *f.* navigation.
navegador, *m.* navigator.
navegante, *m.* navigator.
navegar, *v.* sail; navigate.
Navidad, *f.* Christmas.
navío, *m.* ship.

neblina, *f.* mist, fog.
nebuloso, *a.* misty; nebulous.
necedad, *f.* stupidity; nonsense.
necesario, *a.* necessary.
necesidad, *f.* necessity, need, want.
necesitado, *a.* needy, poor.
necesitar, *v.* need.
necio -cia, 1. *a.* stupid, silly. **2.** *n.* fool.
néctar, *m.* nectar.
nefando, *a.* nefarious.
negable, *a.* deniable.
negación, *f.* denial, negation.
negar, *v.* deny.
negarse, *v.* refuse, decline.
negativa, *f.* negative, refusal.
negativamente, *adv.* negatively.
negativo, *a.* negative.
negligencia, *f.* negligence, neglect.
negligente, *a.* negligent.
negociación, *f.* negotiation, deal.
negociador, *m.* negotiator.
negociante, *m.* businessman.
negociar, *v.* negotiate, trade.
negocio, *m.* trade; business.
negro -gra, 1. *a.* black. **2.** *m.* Black.
nene -na, *m.* baby.
neo, neón, *m.* neon.
nervio, *m.* nerve.
nervioso, *a.* nervous.
nervosamente, *adv.* nervously.
nesciencia, *f.* ignorance.
nesciente, *a.* ignorant.
neto, *a.* net.
neumático, 1. *a.* pneumatic. **2.** *m.* (pneumatic) tire.
neumonía, *f.* pneumonia.
neurótico, *a.* neurotic.
neutral, *a.* neutral.
neutralidad, *f.* neutrality.
neutro, *a.* neuter; neutral.
neutrón, *m.* neutron.
nevada, *f.* snowfall.
nevado, *a.* snow-white; snow-capped.
nevar, *v.* snow.
nevera, *f.* icebox.
nevoso, *a.* snowy.
ni, 1. *conj.* nor. **ni . . . ni,** neither . . . nor. **2.** *adv.* not even.
nicho, *m.* recess.
nido, *m.* nest.
niebla, *f.* fog; mist.
nieto -ta, *m.* grandchild.
nieve, *f.* snow.
nilón, *m.* nylon.
nimio, *adj.* stingy.
ninfa, *f.* nymph.
ningún -no -na, *a. & pron.* no, none, neither (one); any, either (one).
niñera, *f.* nursemaid.
niñez, *f.* childhood.
niño -ña 1. *a.* young; childish; childlike. **2.** *n.* child.
níquel, *m.* nickel.
niquelado, *a.* nickel-plated.
nítido, *a.* neat, clean, bright.
nitrato, *m.* nitrate.
nitro, *m.* niter.

nitrógeno, *m.* nitrogen.
nivel, *m.* level; grade. **—nivelar,** *v.*
no, 1. *adv.* not. **no más,** only. **2.** *interj.* no.
noble, *a. & n.* noble; nobleman.
nobleza, *f.* nobility; nobleness.
noción, *f.* notion, idea.
nocivo, *a.* harmful.
noctiluca, *f.* glowworm.
nocturno, *a.* nocturnal.
noche, *f.* night; evening.
Nochebuena, *f.* Christmas Eve.
nodriza, *f.* wet nurse.
nogal, *m.* walnut.
nombradía, *f.* fame.
nombramiento, *m.* appointment, nomination.
nombrar, *v.* name, appoint, nominate; mention.
nombre, *m.* name; noun.
nómina, *f.* list; payroll.
nominación, *f.* nomination.
nominal, *a.* nominal.
nominar, *v.* name.
non, *a.* uneven, odd.
nonada, *f.* trifle.
nordeste, *m.* northeast.
nórdico, *a.* Nordic.
norma, *f.* norm, standard.
normal, *a.* normal, standard.
normalidad, *f.* normality.
normalizar, *v.* normalize; standardize.
noroeste, *m.* northwest.
norte, *m.* north.
norteamericano -na, *a. & n.* North American.
Noruega, *f.* Norway.
noruego -ga, *a. & n.* Norwegian.
nos, *pron.* us; ourselves.
nosotros -as, *pron.* we, us; ourselves.
nostalgia, *f.* nostalgia, homesickness.
nostálgico, *a.* nostalgic.
nota, *f.* note; grade, mark.
notable, *a.* notable, remarkable.
notación, *f.* notation; note.
notar, *v.* note, notice.
notario, *m.* notary.
noticia, *f.* notice; piece of news; *(pl.)* news.
notificación, *f.* notification.
notificar, *v.* notify.
notorio, *a.* well-known.
novato -ta, *n.* novice.
novecientos, *a. & pron.* nine hundred.
novedad, *f.* novelty; piece of news.
novel, *a.* new, inexperienced.
novela, *f.* novel.
novelista, *m. & f.* novelist.
novena, *f.* novena.
noveno, *a.* ninth.
noventa, *a. & pron.* ninety.
novia, *f.* bride; sweetheart, fiancée.
noviazgo, *m.* engagement, match.

novicio -cia, *n.* novice, beginner.
noviembre, *m.* November.
novilla, *f.* heifer.
novio, *m.* bridegroom; sweetheart, fiancé.
nube, *f.* cloud.
nubile, *a.* marriageable.
nublado, *a.* cloudy.
nuclear, *a.* nuclear.
núcleo, *m.* nucleus.
nudo, *m.* knot.
nuera, *f.* daughter-in-law.
nuestro, *a.* our, ours.
nueva, *f.* news.
nueve, *a. & pron.* nine.
nuevo, *a.* new. **de n.,** again, anew.
nuez, *f.* nut; walnut.
nulidad, *f.* nonentity.
nulo, *a.* null, void.
numeración, *f.* numeration.
numerar, *v.* number.
numérico, *a.* numerical.
número, *m.* number; size (of shoe, etc.)
numeroso, *a.* numerous.
numismática, *f.* numismatics.
nunca, *adv.* never; ever.
nupcial, *a.* nuptial.
nupcias, *f.pl.* nuptials, wedding.
nutrición, *f.* nutrition.
nutrimiento, *m.* nourishment.
nutrir, *v.* nourish.
nutritivo, *a.* nutritious.
ñame, *m.* yam.
ñapa, *f.* something extra.
ñoñería, *f.* dotage.
ñoño, *a.* feeble-minded, senile.

O

o, *conj.* or. **o . . . o,** either . . . or.
oasis, *m.* oasis.
obedecer, *v.* obey, mind.
obediencia, *f.* obedience.
obediente, *a.* obedient.
obelisco, *m.* obelisk.
obertura, *f.* overture.
obeso, *a.* obese.
obispo, *m.* bishop.
obituario, *m.* obituary.
objeción, *f.* objection.
objetivo, *a. & m.* objective.
objeto, *m.* object. **—objetar,** *v.*
oblicuo, *a.* oblique.
obligación, *f.* obligation, duty.
obligar, *v.* oblige, require, compel; obligate.
obligatorio, *a.* obligatory, compulsory.
oblongo, *a.* oblong.
oboe, *m.* oboe.
obra, *f.* work. **—obrar,** *v.*
obrero -ra, *n.* worker, laborer.
obscenidad, *f.* obscenity.
obsceno, *a.* obscene.
obscurecer, *v.* obscure; darken.
obscuridad, *f.* obscurity; darkness.
obscuro, *a.* obscure; dark.

obsequiar, *v.* court; make presents to, fete.
obsequio, *m.* obsequiousness; gift; attention.
observación, *f.* observation.
observador, *m.* observer.
observancia, *f.* observance.
observar, *v.* observe, watch.
observatorio, *m.* observatory.
obsesión, *f.* obsession.
obstáculo, *m.* obstacle.
obstante, *adv.* **no o.,** however, yet, nevertheless.
obstar, *v.* hinder, obstruct.
obstetricia, *f.* obstetrics.
obstinación, *f.* obstinacy.
obstinado, *a.* obstinate, stubborn.
obstinarse, *v.* persist, insist.
obstrucción, *f.* obstruction.
obstruir, *v.* obstruct, clog, block.
obtener, *v.* obtain, get, secure.
obtuso, *a.* obtuse.
obvio, *a.* obvious.
ocasión, *f.* occasion; opportunity, chance. **de o.,** second-hand.
ocasional, *a.* occasional.
ocasionalmente, *adv.* occasionally.
ocasionar, *v.* cause, occasion.
occidental, *a.* western.
occidente, *m.* west.
océano, *m.* ocean.
ocelote, *m.* ocelot.
ocio, *m.* idleness, leisure.
ociosidad, *f.* idleness, laziness.
ocioso, *a.* idle, lazy.
ocre, *a.* ochre.
octava, *f.* octave.
octavo, *a.* eighth.
octogonal, *a.* octagonal.
octubre, *m.* October.
oculista, *m.* oculist.
ocultación, *f.* concealment.
ocultar, *v.* hide, conceal.
oculto, *a.* hidden.
ocupación, *f.* occupation.
ocupado, *a.* occupied; busy.
ocupante, *m.* occupant.
ocupar, *v.* occupy.
ocuparse de, *v.* take care of, take charge of.
ocurrencia, *f.* occurrence; witticism.
ocurrir, *v.* occur, happen.
ochenta, *a. & pron.* eighty.
ocho, *a. & pron.* eight.
ochocientos, *a. & pron.* eight hundred.
oda, *f.* ode.
odio, *m.* hate. **—odiar,** *v.*
odiosidad, *f.* odiousness; hatred.
odioso, *a.* obnoxious, odious.
odisea, *f.* odyssey.
oeste, *m.* west.
ofender, *v.* offend, wrong.
ofenderse, *v.* be offended, take offense.
ofensa, *f.* offense.
ofensiva, *f.* offensive.
ofensivo, *a.* offensive.
ofensor -ra, *n.* offender.

oferta, f. offer, proposal.
ofertorio, m. offertory.
oficial, a. & m. official; officer.
oficialmente, adv. officially.
oficiar, v. officiate.
oficina, f. office.
oficio, m. office; trade; church service.
oficioso, a. officious.
ofrecer, v. offer.
ofrecimiento, m. offer, offering.
ofrenda, f. offering.
oftalmía, f. ophthalmia.
ofuscamiento, m. obfuscation; bewilderment.
ofuscar, v. obfuscate; bewilder.
ogro, m. ogre.
oído, m. ear; hearing.
oír, v. hear; listen.
ojal, m. buttonhole.
ojalá, interj. expressing wish or hope. **o. que . . .** would that . . .
ojeada, f. glance; peep; look.
ojear, v. eye, look at, glance at, stare at.
ojeriza, f. spite; grudge.
ojiva, f. pointed arch; ogive.
ojo, m. eye. **¡Ojo!** Look out!
ola, f. wave.
olaje, m. surge of waves.
oleada, f. swell.
oleo, m. oil; holy oil; extreme unction.
oleomargarina, f. oleomargarine.
oleoso, a. oily.
oler, v. smell.
olfatear, v. smell.
olfato, m. scent, smell.
oliva, f. olive.
olivar, m. olive grove.
olivo, m. olive tree.
olmo, m. elm.
olor, m. odor, smell, scent.
oloroso, a. fragrant, scented.
olvidadizo, a. forgetful.
olvidar, v. forget.
olvido, m. omission; forgetfulness.
olla, f. pot, kettle. **o. podrida**, stew.
ombligo, m. navel.
ominar, v. foretell.
ominoso, a. ominous.
omisión, f. omission.
omitir, v. omit, leave out.
ómnibus, m. bus.
omnipotencia, f. omnipotence.
omnipotente, a. almighty.
omnipresencia, f. omnipresence.
omnisciencia, f. omniscience.
omnívoro, a. omnivorous.
once, a. & pron. eleven.
onda, f. wave, ripple.
ondear, v. ripple.
ondulación, f. wave, undulation.
ondular, v. undulate, ripple.
onza, f. ounce.
opaco, a. opaque.
ópalo, m. opal.
opción, f. option.

ópera, f. opera.
operación, f. operation.
operar, v. operate; operate on.
operario -ria, n. operator; (skilled) worker.
operarse, v. have an operation.
operativo, a. operative.
opereta, f. operetta.
opiato, m. opiate.
opinar, v. opine.
opinión, f. opinion, view.
opio, m. opium.
oponer, v. oppose.
oporto, m. port (wine).
oportunidad, f. opportunity.
oportunismo, m. opportunism.
oportunista, n. & a. opportunist.
oportuno, a. opportune, expedient.
oposición, f. opposition.
opresión, f. oppression.
opresivo, a. oppressive.
oprimir, v. oppress.
oprobio, m. infamy.
optar, v. select, choose.
óptica, f. optics.
óptico, a. optic.
optimismo, m. optimism.
optimista, a. & n. optimistic; optimist.
óptimo, a. best.
opuesto, a. opposite; opposed.
opugnar, v. attack.
opulencia, f. opulence, wealth.
opulento, a. opulent, wealthy.
oración, f. sentence; prayer; oration.
oráculo, m. oracle.
orador, m. orator, speaker.
oral, a. oral.
orangután, m. orangutan.
orar, v. pray.
oratoria, f. oratory.
oratorio, a. oratorical.
orbe, m. orb; globe.
órbita, f. orbit.
orden, m. or f. order.
ordenador, m. computer; regulator.
ordenanza, f. ordinance.
ordenar, v. order; put in order; ordain.
ordeñar, v. milk.
ordinal, n. & a. ordinal.
ordinario, a. ordinary; common, usual.
oreja, f. ear.
orejera, f. earmuff.
orfanato, m. orphanage.
organdí, m. organdy.
orgánico, a. organic.
organismo, m. organism.
organista, m. & f. organist.
organización, f. organization.
organizar, v. organize.
órgano, m. organ.
orgía, f. orgy, revel.
orgullo, m. pride.
orgulloso, a. proud.
orientación, f. orientation.
oriental, a. Oriental; eastern.
orientar, v. orient.
oriente, m. orient, east.

orificación, f. gold filling (for tooth).
origen, m. origin; parentage, descent.
original, a. original.
originalidad, f. originality.
originalmente, adv. originally.
originar, v. originate.
orilla, f. shore; bank; edge.
orín, m. rust.
orina, f. urine.
orinar, v. urinate.
orines, n.pl. urine.
oriol, m. oriole.
orla, f. border; edging.
ornado, a. ornate.
ornamentación, f. ornamentation.
ornamento, m. ornament. — **ornamentar**, v.
ornar, v. ornament, adorn.
oro, m. gold.
oropel, m. tinsel.
orquesta, f. orchestra.
ortiga, f. nettle.
ortodoxo, a. orthodox.
ortografía, f. orthography, spelling.
ortóptero, a. orthopterous.
oruga, f. caterpillar.
orzuelo, m. sty.
os, pron. you (pl.); yourselves.
osadía, f. daring.
osar, v. dare.
oscilación, f. oscillation.
oscilar, v. oscillate, rock.
ósculo, m. kiss.
oscurecer, oscuridad, oscuro = obscur-.
oso, osa, n. bear.
ostentación, f. ostentation, showiness.
ostentar, v. show off.
ostentoso, a. ostentatious, flashy.
ostra, f. oyster.
ostracismo, m. ostracism.
otalgia, f. earache.
otero, m. hill, knoll.
otoño, m. autumn, fall.
otorgar, v. grant, award.
otro, a. & pron. other, another. **o. vez**, again. **el uno al o.**, one another, each other.
ovación, f. ovation.
oval, ovalado, a. oval.
óvalo, m. oval.
ovario, m. ovary.
oveja, f. sheep.
ovejero, m. shepherd.
ovillo, m. ball of yarn.
oxidación, f. oxidation.
oxidar, v. oxidize; rust.
óxido, m. oxide.
oxígeno, m. oxygen.
oyente, m. hearer; (pl.) audience.
ozono, m. ozone.

P

pabellón, m. pavilion.
pabilo, m. wick.
paciencia, f. patience.

paciente, *a. & n.* patient.

pacificar, *v.* pacify.

pacífico, *a.* pacific.

pacifismo, *m.* pacifism.

pacifista, *n. & a.* pacifist.

pacto, *m.* pact, treaty.

padecer, *v.* suffer.

padrastro, *m.* stepfather.

padre, *m.* father; priest; *(pl.)* parents.

padrenuestro, *m.* paternoster.

padrino, *m.* godfather; sponsor.

paella, *f.* dish of rice with meat or chicken.

paga, *f.* pay, wages.

pagadero, *a.* payable.

pagador, *m.* payer.

paganismo, *m.* paganism.

pagano -na, *a. & n.* heathen, pagan.

pagar, *v.* pay, pay for.

página, *f.* page.

pago, *m.* pay, payment.

país, *m.* country, nation.

paisaje, *m.* landscape, scenery, countryside.

paisano -na, *n.* countryman; compatriot; civilian.

paja, *f.* straw.

pajar, *m.* barn.

pájaro, *m.* bird.

paje, *m.* page (person).

pala, *f.* shovel, spade.

palabra, *f.* word.

palabrero, *a.* talkative.

palabrista, *m.* talkative person.

palacio, *m.* palace.

paladar, *m.* palate.

paladear, *v.* taste; relish.

palanca, *f.* lever.

palangana, *f.* washbasin.

palco, *m.* theater box.

palenque, *m.* palisade.

palidecer, *v.* turn pale.

palidez, *f.* paleness.

pálido, *a.* pale.

paliza, *f.* beating.

palizada, *m.* palisade.

palma, palmera, *f.* palm (tree).

palmada, *f.* slap, clap.

palmear, *v.* applaud.

palo, *m.* pole, stick; suit (in cards); (naut.) mast.

paloma, *f.* dove, pigeon.

palpar, *v.* touch, feel.

palpitación, *f.* palpitation.

palpitar, *v.* palpitate.

paludismo, *m.* malaria.

palleta, *f.* mat, pallet.

pampa, *f.* (South America) prairie, plain.

pan, *m.* bread; loaf.

pana, *f.* corduroy.

pánacea, *f.* panacea.

panadería, *f.* bakery.

panadero -ra, *n.* baker.

panameño -ña, *a. & n.* Panamanian, of Panama.

panamericano, *a.* Pan-American.

páncreas, *m.* pancreas.

pandeo, *m.* bulge.

pandilla, *f.* band, gang.

panecillo, *m.* roll, muffin.

panegírico, *m.* panegyric.

pánico, *m.* panic.

panocha, *f.* ear of corn.

panorámico, *a.* panoramic.

pantalones, *m.pl.* trousers, pants.

pantalla, *f.* (movie) screen; lamp shade.

pantano, *m.* bog, marsh, swamp.

pantanoso, *a.* swampy, marshy.

pantera, *f.* panther.

pantomima, *f.* pantomime.

panza, *f.* belly, paunch.

pañal, *m.* diaper.

paño, *m.* piece of cloth.

pañuelo, *m.* handkerchief.

Papa, *m.* Pope.

papa, *f.* potato.

papá, *m.* papa, father.

papado, *m.* papacy.

papagayo, *m.* parrot.

papal, *a.* papal.

papel, *m.* paper; role, part.

papelera, *f.* file or folder for papers.

papelería, *f.* stationery store.

papera, *f.* mumps.

paquete, *m.* package.

par, 1. *a.* even, equal. **2.** *m.* pair; equal, peer. **abierto de p. en p.,** wide open.

para, *prep.* for; in order to. **p. que,** in order that. **estar p.,** to be about to.

parabién, *m.* greeting; congratulation.

parabrisa, *f.* windshield.

paracaídas, *m.* parachute.

parachoques, *m.* (auto.) bumper.

parada, *f.* stop, halt; parade.

paradero, *m.* whereabouts; stopping place.

paradigma, *m.* paradigm.

paradoja, *f.* paradox.

parafina, *f.* paraffin.

parafrasear, *v.* paraphrase.

paraguas, *m.* umbrella.

paraguayano -na, *n. & a.* Paraguayan.

paraíso, *m.* paradise.

paralelo, *a. & m.* parallel.

parálisis, *f.* paralysis.

paralizar, *v.* paralyze.

paramédico, *m.* paramedic.

parámetro, *m.* parameter.

parapeto, *m.* parapet.

parar, *v.* stop, stem, ward off; stay.

pararse, *v.* stop; stand up.

parasismo, *m.* paroxysm.

parasítico, *a.* parasitic.

parásito, *m.* parasite.

parcela, *f.* plot of ground.

parcial, *a.* partial.

parcialidad, *f.* partiality; bias.

parcialmente, *adv.* partially.

pardo, *a.* brown.

parear, *v.* pair, match, mate.

parecer, 1. *m.* opinion. **2.** *v.* seem, appear, look.

parecerse, *v.* look alike. **p. a,** look like.

parecido, *a.* similar.

pared, *f.* wall.

pareja, *f.* pair, couple; (dancing) partner.

parentela, *f.* kinfolk.

parentesco, *m.* parentage, lineage; kin.

paréntesis, *m.* parenthesis.

paria, *m.* outcast.

paridad, *f.* parity.

pariente, *m. & f.* relative.

parir, *v.* give birth to young.

parisiense, *n. & a.* Parisian.

parlamentario, *a.* parliamentary.

parlamento, *m.* parliament.

paro, *m.* stoppage; strike. **p. forzoso,** unemployment.

parodia, *f.* parody.

parodista, *m.* parodist.

paroxismo, *m.* paroxysm.

párpado, *m.* eyelid.

parque, *m.* park.

parra, *f.* grapevine.

párrafo, *m.* paragraph.

parranda, *f.* spree.

parrandear, *v.* carouse.

parrilla, *f.* grill.

párroco, *m.* parish priest.

parroquia, *f.* parish.

parroquial, *a.* parochial.

parsimonia, *f.* economy, thrift.

parsimonioso, *a.* economical, thrifty.

parte, *f.* part. **de p. de,** on behalf of. **alguna p.,** somewhere. **por otra p.,** on the other hand. **dar p. a,** to notify.

partera, *f.* midwife.

partición, *f.* distribution.

participación, *f.* participation.

participante, *m. & f.* participant.

participar, *v.* participate; announce.

participio, *m.* participle.

partícula, *f.* particle.

particular, 1. *a.* particular; private. **2.** *m.* particular; detail; individual.

particularmente, *adv.* particularly.

partida, *f.* departure; (mil.) party; (sport) game.

partidario -ria, *n.* partisan.

partido, *m.* side, party, faction; game, match.

partir, *v.* leave, depart; part, cleave, split.

parto, *m.* delivery, childbirth.

pasa, *f.* raisin.

pasado, 1. *a.* past; last. **2.** *m.* past.

pasaje, *m.* passage, fare.

pasajero -ra, 1. *a.* passing, transient. **2.** *n.* passenger.

pasamano, *m.* banister.

pasaporte, *m.* passport.

pasar, *v.* pass; happen; spend (time). **p. por alto,** overlook. **p. lista,** call the roll. **p. sin,** do without.

pasatiempo, *m.* pastime, hobby.

pascua, *f.* religious holiday;

(*pl.*) Christmas (season). **P. Florida,** Easter.

paseo, *m.* walk, stroll; drive. —**pasear,** *v.*

pasillo, *m.* aisle; hallway.

pasión, *f.* passion.

pasivo, *a.* passive.

pasmar, *v.* astonish, astound, stun.

pasmo, *m.* spasm; wonder.

paso, 1. *a.* dried (fruit). **2.** *m.* pace, step; (mountain) pass.

pasta, *f.* paste; batter; plastic.

pastar, *v.* graze.

pastel, *m.* pastry; pie.

pastelería, *f.* pastry; pastry shop.

pasteurización, *f.* pasteurization.

pasteurizar, *v.* pasteurize.

pastilla, *f.* tablet, lozenge, drop.

pasto, *m.* pasture; grass.

pastor, *m.* pastor, shepherd.

pastorear, *v.* pasture, tend (a flock).

pastura, *f.* pasture.

pata, *f.* foot (of animal).

patada, *f.* kick.

patán, *m.* boor.

patanada, *f.* rudeness.

patata, *f.* potato.

patear, *v.* stamp, tramp, kick.

patente, *a. & m.* patent. —**patentar,** *v.*

paternal, paterno, *a.* paternal.

paternidad, *f.* paternity, fatherhood.

patético, *a.* pathetic.

patíbulo, *m.* scaffold, gallows.

patín, *m.* skate. —**patinar,** *v.*

patio, *m.* yard, court, patio.

pato, *m.* duck.

patria, *f.* native land.

patriarca, *m.* patriarch.

patrimonio, *m.* inheritance.

patriota, *m. & f.* patriot.

patriótico, *a.* patriotic.

patriotismo, *m.* patriotism.

patrocinar, *v.* patronize, sponsor.

patrón, *m.* patron; boss; (dress) pattern.

patrulla, *f.* patrol. —**patrullar,** *v.*

pausa, *f.* pause. —**pausar,** *v.*

pavesa, *f.* embers.

pavimentar, *v.* pave.

pavimento, *m.* pavement.

pavo, *m.* turkey. **p. real,** peacock.

payaso, *m.* clown.

paz, *f.* peace.

peatón -na, *n.* pedestrian.

peca, *f.* freckle.

pecado, *m.* sin. —**pecar,** *v.*

pecador -ra, *a. & n.* sinful; sinner.

pecera, *f.* aquarium, fishbowl.

peculiar, *a.* peculiar.

peculiaridad, *f.* peculiarity.

pechera, *f.* shirt front.

pecho, *m.* chest; breast; bosom.

pedagogía, *f.* pedagogy.

pedagogo, *m.* pedagogue, teacher.

pedal, *m.* pedal.

pedantesco, *a.* pedantic.

pedazo, *m.* piece.

pedernal, *m.* flint.

pedestal, *m.* pedestal.

pediatría, *f.* pediatrics.

pedicuro, *m.* chiropodist.

pedir, *v.* ask, ask for, request; apply for; order.

pedregoso, *a.* rocky.

pegajoso, *a.* sticky.

pegar, *v.* beat, strike; adhere, fasten, stick.

peinado, *m.* coiffure, hairdo.

peine, *m.* comb. —**peinar,** *v.*

peineta, *f.* (ornamental) comb.

pelagra, *f.* pellagra.

pelar, *v.* skin, pare, peel.

pelea, *f.* fight, row. —**pelearse,** *v.*

pelícano, *m.* pelican.

película, *f.* movie, motion picture, film.

peligrar, *v.* be in danger.

peligro, *m.* peril, danger.

peligroso, *a.* perilous, dangerous.

pelo, *m.* hair.

pelota, *f.* ball.

peltre, *m.* pewter.

peluca, *f.* wig.

peludo, *a.* hairy.

peluquería, *f.* hairdresser's shop, beauty parlor.

peluquero, *m.* hairdresser.

pellejo, *m.* skin, peel (of fruit).

pellizco, *m.* pinch. —**pellizcar,** *v.*

pena, *f.* pain, grief, trouble, woe; penalty. **valer la p.,** to be worthwhile.

penacho, *m.* plume.

penalidad, *f.* trouble; penalty.

pender, *v.* hang, dangle; be pending.

pendiente, 1. *a.* hanging; pending. **2.** *m.* incline, slope; earring, pendant.

pendón, *m.* pennant, flag.

penetración, *f.* penetration.

penetrar, *v.* penetrate, pierce.

penicilina, *f.* penicillin.

península, *f.* peninsula.

penitencia, *f.* penitence, penance.

penitenciaría, *f.* penitentiary.

penoso, *a.* painful, troublesome, grievous.

pensador -ra, *n.* thinker.

pensamiento, *m.* thought.

pensar, *v.* think; intend, plan.

pensativo, *a.* pensive, thoughtful.

pensión, *f.* pension; boarding-house.

pensionista, *m. & f.* boarder.

pentagonal, *a.* pentagonal.

penuria, *f.* penury, poverty.

peña, *f.* rock.

peñascoso, *a.* rocky.

peón, *m.* unskilled laborer; infantryman.

peonada, *f.* group of laborers.

peonía, *f.* peony.

peor, *a.* worse, worst.

pepino, *m.* cucumber.

pepita, *f.* seed (in fruit).

pequeñez, *f.* smallness; trifle.

pequeño -ña, 1. *a.* small, little, short, slight. **2.** *n.* child.

pera, *f.* pear.

peral, *m.* pear tree.

perca, *f.* perch (fish).

percal, *m.* calico, percale.

percentaje, *m.* percentage.

percepción, *f.* perception.

perceptivo, *a.* perceptive.

percibir, *v.* perceive, sense; collect.

percha, *f.* perch; clothes hanger, rack.

perder, *v.* lose; miss; waste. **echar a p.,** spoil.

perdición, *f.* perdition, downfall.

pérdida, *f.* loss.

perdiz, *f.* partridge.

perdón, *m.* pardon, forgiveness.

perdonar, *v.* forgive, pardon; spare.

perdurable, *a.* enduring, everlasting.

perdurar, *v.* endure, last.

perecedero, *a.* perishable.

perecer, *v.* perish.

peregrinación, *f.* peregrination; pilgrimage.

peregrino -na, *n.* pilgrim.

perejil, *m.* parsley.

perenne, *a.* perennial.

pereza, *f.* laziness.

perezoso, *a.* lazy, sluggish.

perfección, *f.* perfection.

perfeccionar, *v.* perfect.

perfectamente, *adv.* perfectly.

perfecto, *a.* perfect.

perfidia, *f.* falseness, perfidy.

pérfido, *a.* perfidious.

perfil, *m.* profile.

perforación, *f.* perforation.

perforar, *v.* pierce, perforate.

perfume, *m.* perfume, scent. —**perfumar,** *v.*

pergamino, *m.* parchment.

pericia, *f.* skill, expertness.

perico, *m.* parakeet.

perímetro, *m.* perimeter.

periódico, 1. *a.* periodic. **2.** *m.* newspaper.

periodista, *m.* journalist.

período, *m.* period.

periscopio, *m.* periscope.

perito -ta, *a. & n.* experienced; expert, connoisseur.

perjudicar, *v.* damage, hurt; impair.

perjudicial, *a.* harmful, injurious.

perjuicio, *m.* injury, damage.

perjurar, *v.* commit perjury.

perjurio, *m.* perjury.

perla, *f.* pearl.

permanecer, *v.* remain, stay.

permanencia, *f.* permanence; stay.

permanente, *a.* permanent.

permiso, *m.* permission; permit; furlough.

permitir, *v.* permit, enable, let, allow.

permuta, *f.* exchange; barter.

pernicioso, *a.* pernicious.

perno, *m.* bolt.

pero, *conj.* but.

peróxido, *m.* peroxide.

perpendicular, *m. & a.* perpendicular.

perpetración, *f.* perpetration.

perpetrar, *v.* perpetrate.

perpetuar, *v.* perpetuate.

perpetuidad, *f.* perpetuity.

perpetuo, *a.* perpetual.

perplejo, *a.* perplexed, puzzled.

perro -rra, *n.* dog.

persecución, *f.* persecution.

perseguir, *v.* pursue; persecute.

perseverancia, *f.* perseverance.

perseverar, *v.* persevere.

persiana, *f.* shutter, Venetian blind.

persistente, *a.* persistent.

persistir, *v.* persist.

persona, *f.* person.

personaje, *m.* personage; (theat.) character.

personal, 1. *a.* personal. **2.** *m.* personnel, staff.

personalidad, *f.* personality.

personalmente, *adv.* personally.

perspectiva, *f.* perspective; prospect.

perspicaz, *a.* perspicacious, acute.

persuadir, *v.* persuade.

persuasión, *f.* persuasion.

persuasivo, *a.* persuasive.

pertenecer, *v.* pertain, belong.

pertinencia, *f.* pertinence.

pertinente, *a.* pertinent; relevant.

perturbar, *v.* perturb, disturb.

peruano -na, *a. & n.* Peruvian.

perversidad, *f.* perversity.

perverso, *a.* perverse.

pesadez, *f.* dullness, importunity.

pesadilla, *f.* nightmare.

pesado, *a.* heavy; dull, dreary, boring.

pésame, *m.* condolence.

pesar, 1. *m.* sorrow; regret. **a p. de,** in spite of. **2.** *v.* weigh.

pesca, *f.* fishing; catch (of fish).

pescado, *m.* fish. —**pescar,** *v.*

pescador, *m.* fisherman.

pesebre, *m.* stall, manger, crib.

peseta, *f.* monetary unit of Spain.

pesimismo, *m.* pessimism.

pesimista, *a. & n.* pessimistic; pessimist.

peso, *m.* weight; load; peso (monetary unit).

pesquera, *f.* fishery.

pesquisa, *f.* investigation.

pestaña, *f.* eyelash.

pestañeo, *m.* wink, blink. —**pestañear,** *v.*

peste, *f.* plague.

pestilencia, *f.* pestilence.

pétalo, *m.* petal.

petición, *f.* petition.

petirrojo, *m.* robin.

petrel, *m.* petrel.

pétreo, *a.* rocky.

petrificar, *v.* petrify.

petróleo, *m.* petroleum.

petunia, *f.* petunia.

pez, *m.* fish (in the water). *f.* pitch, tar.

pezuña, *f.* hoof.

piadoso, *a.* pious.

pianista, *m. & f.* pianist.

piano, *m.* piano.

picadura, *f.* sting, bite, prick.

picamaderos, *m.* woodpecker.

picante, *a.* hot, spicy.

picaporte, *m.* latch.

picar, *v.* sting, bite, prick; itch; chop up, grind up.

pícaro -ra, 1. *a.* knavish, mischievous. **2.** *n.* rogue, rascal.

picarse, *v.* be offended, piqued.

picazón, *f.* itch.

pícea, *f.* spruce.

pico, *m.* peak; pick; beak; spout; small amount.

picotazo, *m.* peck. —**picotear,** *v.*

pictórico, *a.* pictorial.

pichón, *m.* pigeon, squab.

pie, *m.* foot. **al p. de la letra,** literally; thoroughly.

piedad, *f.* piety; pity, mercy.

piedra, *f.* stone.

piel, *f.* skin, hide; fur.

pierna, *f.* leg.

pieza, *f.* piece; room; (theat.) play.

pijamas, *m. or f.pl.* pajamas.

pila, *f.* pile, stack; battery; sink.

pilar, *m.* pillar, column.

píldora, *f.* pill.

piloto, *m.* pilot.

pillo, *m.* thief; rascal.

pimienta, *f.* pepper (spice).

pimiento, *m.* pepper (vegetable).

pináculo, *m.* pinnacle.

pincel, *m.* (artist's) brush.

pinchazo, *m.* puncture. —**pinchar,** *v.*

pingajo, *m.* rag, tatter.

pino, *m.* pine.

pinta, *f.* pint.

pintar, *v.* paint; portray, depict.

pintor -ra, *n.* painter.

pintoresco, *a.* picturesque.

pintura, *f.* paint; painting.

pinzas, *f.pl.* pincers, tweezers; claws.

piña, *f.* pineapple.

pío, *a.* pious; merciful.

piojo, *m.* louse.

pionero -ra, *n.* pioneer.

pipa, *f.* tobacco pipe.

pique, *m.* resentment, pique. **echar a p.,** sink (ship).

pira, *f.* pyre.

pirámide, *f.* pyramid.

pirata, *m.* pirate. **p. de aviones,** hijacker.

pisada, *f.* tread, step. —**pisar,** *v.*

piscina, *f.* fishpond; swimming pool.

piso, *m.* floor.

pista, *f.* trace, clue, track; racetrack.

pistola, *f.* pistol.

pistón, *m.* piston.

pitillo, *m.* cigarette.

pito, *m.* whistle. —**pitar,** *v.*

pizarra, *f.* slate; blackboard.

pizca, *f.* bit, speck; pinch.

pizza, *f.* pizza.

placentero, *a.* pleasant.

placer, 1. *m.* pleasure. **2.** *v.* please.

plácido, *a.* placid.

plaga, *f.* plague, scourge.

plagio, *m.* plagiarism; (S.A.) kidnapping.

plan, *m.* plan. —**planear,** *v.*

plancha, *f.* plate, slab, flatiron.

planchar, *v.* iron, press.

planeta, *m.* planet.

plano, 1. *a.* level, flat. **2.** *m.* plan; plane.

planta, *f.* plant; sole (of foot).

plantación, *f.* plantation.

plantar, *v.* plant.

plantear, *v.* pose, present.

plantel, *m.* educational institution; (agr.) nursery.

plasma, *m.* plasma.

plástico, *a. & m.* plastic.

plata, *f.* silver; (coll.) money.

plataforma, *f.* platform.

plátano, *m.* plantain, cooking banana.

platel, *m.* platter.

plática, *f.* chat, talk. —**platicar,** *v.*

platillo, *m.* saucer.

plato, *m.* plate, dish.

playa, *f.* beach, shore.

plaza, *f.* square. **p. de toros,** bullring.

plazo, *m.* term, deadline; installment.

plebe, *f.* common people; masses.

plebiscito, *m.* plebiscite.

plegadura, *f.* fold, pleat. —**plegar,** *v.*

pleito, *m.* lawsuit; dispute.

plenitud, *f.* fullness; abundance.

pleno, *a.* full. **en pleno . . .** in the middle of . . .

pliego, *m.* sheet of paper.

pliegue, *m.* fold, pleat, crease.

plomería, *f.* plumbing.

plomero, *m.* plumber.

plomizo, *a.* leaden.

plomo, *m.* lead; fuse.

pluma, *f.* feather; (writing) pen.

plumafuente, *f.* fountain pen.

plumaje, *m.* plumage.

plumero, *m.* feather duster; plume.

plumoso, *a.* feathery.

plural, *a. & m.* plural.

población, f. population; town.
poblador -ra, n. settler.
poblar, v. populate; settle.
pobre, a. & n. poor; poor person.
pobreza, f. poverty, need.
pocilga, f. pigpen.
poción, f. drink; potion.
poco, 1. a. & adv. little, not much, (pl.) few. **por p.,** almost, nearly. **2.** m. **un p. (de),** a little, a bit (of).
poder, 1. m. power. **2.** v. be able to, can; be possible, may, might. **no p. menos de,** not be able to help.
poderío, m. power, might.
poderoso, a. powerful, mighty, potent.
podrido, a. rotten.
poema, m. poem.
poesía, f. poetry; poem.
poeta, m. poet.
poético, a. poetic.
polaco -ca, a. & n. Polish; Pole.
polar, a. polar.
polaridad, f. polarity.
polea, f. pulley.
polen, m. pollen.
policía, f. police. m. policeman.
poligamia, f. polygamy.
polígloto -ta, n. polyglot.
polilla, f. moth.
política, f. politics; policy.
político, a. & m. politic; political; politician.
póliza, f. (insurance) policy; permit, ticket.
polizonte, m. policeman.
polo, m. pole; polo.
polonés, a. Polish.
Polonia, f. Poland.
polvera, f. powder box; powder puff.
polvo, m. powder; dust.
pólvora, f. powder, gunpowder.
pollada, f. brood.
pollería, f. poultry shop.
pollino, m. donkey.
pollo, m. chicken.
pompa, f. pomp.
pomposo, a. pompous.
ponche, m. punch (beverage).
ponchera, f. punch bowl.
ponderar, v. ponder.
ponderoso, a. ponderous.
poner, v. put, set, lay, place.
ponerse, v. put on; become, get; set (sun). **p. a,** start to.
poniente, m. west.
pontífice, m. pontiff.
popa, f. stern.
popular, a. popular.
popularidad, f. popularity.
populazo, m. populace; masses.
por, prep. by, through, because of; via; for. **p. qué,** why?
porcelana, f. porcelain, chinaware.
porcentaje, m. percentage.
porción, f. portion, lot.
porche, m. porch; portico.

porfiar, v. persist; argue.
pormenor, m. detail.
pornografía, f. pornography.
poro, m. pore.
poroso, a. porous.
porque, conj. because.
porqué, m. reason, motive.
porra, f. stick, club.
porrazo, m. blow.
portaaviones, m. aircraft carrier.
portador -ra, n. bearer.
portal, m. portal.
portar, v. carry.
portarse, v. behave, act.
portátil, a. portable.
portavoz, m. megaphone.
porte, m. bearing; behavior; postage.
portero, m. porter; janitor.
pórtico, m. porch.
portorriqueño -ña, n. & a. Puerto Rican.
portugués -esa, a. & n. Portuguese.
posada, f. lodge, inn.
posar, v. pose.
posdata, f. postscript.
poseer, v. possess, own.
posesión, f. possession.
posibilidad, f. possibility.
posible, a. possible.
posiblemente, adv. possibly.
posición, f. position, stand.
positivo, a. positive.
posponer, v. postpone.
postal, a. postal.
poste, m. post, pillar.
posteridad, f. posterity.
posterior, a. posterior, rear.
postizo, a. false, artificial.
postrado, a. prostrate. **—postrar,** v.
postre, m. dessert.
póstumo, a. posthumous.
postura, f. posture, pose; bet.
potable, a. drinkable.
potaje, m. porridge; pot stew.
potasa, f. potash.
potasio, m. potassium.
pote, m. pot, jar.
potencia, f. potency, power.
potencial, a. & f. potential.
potentado, m. potentate.
potente, a. potent, powerful.
potestad, f. power.
potro, m. colt.
pozo, m. well.
práctica, f. practice. **—practicar,** v.
práctico, a. practical.
pradera, f. prairie, meadow.
prado, m. meadow; lawn.
pragmatismo, m. pragmatism.
preámbulo, m. preamble.
precario, a. precarious.
precaución, f. precaution.
precaverse, v. beware.
precavido, a. cautious, guarded, wary.
precedencia, f. precedence, priority.
precedente, a. & m. preceding; precedent.
preceder, v. precede.

precepto, m. precept.
preciar, v. value, prize.
preciarse de, v. take pride in.
precio, m. price.
precioso, a. precious; beautiful, gorgeous.
precipicio, m. precipice, cliff.
precipitación, f. precipitation.
precipitar, v. precipitate, rush; throw headlong.
precipitoso, a. precipitous; rash.
precisar, v. fix, specify; be necessary.
precisión, f. precision; necessity.
preciso, a. precise; necessary.
precocidad, f. precocity.
precoz, a. precocious.
precursor -ra 1. a. preceding. **2.** n. precursor, forerunner.
predecesor, -ra, a. & n. predecessor.
predecir, v. predict, foretell.
predicación, f. sermon.
predicador, m. preacher.
predicar, v. preach; publish.
predicción, f. prediction.
predilecto, a. favorite, preferred.
predisponer, v. predispose.
predisposición, f. predisposition; bias.
predominante, a. prevailing, prevalent, predominant.
predominar, v. prevail, predominate.
predominio, m. predominance, sway.
prefacio, m. preface.
preferencia, f. preference.
preferentemente, adv. preferably.
preferible, a. preferable.
preferir, v. prefer.
prefijo, m. prefix; area code. **—prefijar,** v.
pregón, m. proclamation, cry.
pregonar, v. proclaim, cry out.
pregunta, f. question, inquiry. **hacer una p.,** to ask a question.
preguntar, v. ask, inquire.
preguntarse, v. wonder.
prehistórico, a. prehistoric.
prejuicio, m. prejudice.
prelacía, f. prelacy.
preliminar, a. & m. preliminary.
preludio, m. prelude.
prematuro, a. premature.
premeditación, f. premeditation.
premeditar, v. premeditate.
premiar, v. reward; award a prize to.
premio, m. prize, award; reward.
premisa, f. premise.
premura, f. pressure; urgency.
prenda, f. jewel; (personal) quality. **p. de vestir,** garment.
prender, v. seize, arrest, catch; attack, pin, clip. **p. fuego a,** set fire to.

prensa, f. printing press; (the) press.

prensar, v. press, compress.

preñado, a. pregnant.

preocupación, f. worry, preoccupation.

preocupar, v. worry, preoccupy.

preparación, f. preparation.

preparar, v. prepare.

preparativo, m. preparation.

preparatorio, m. preparatory.

preponderante, a. preponderant.

preposición, f. preposition.

prerrogativa, f. prerogative, privilege.

presa, f. capture; prey; (water) dam.

presagiar, v. presage, forebode.

presbiteriano -na, n. & a. Presbyterian.

presbítero, m. priest.

prescindir de, v. dispense with; omit.

prescribir, v. prescribe.

prescripción, f. prescription.

presencia, f. presence.

presenciar, v. witness, be present at.

presentable, a. presentable.

presentación, f. presentation; introduction.

presentar, v. present; introduce.

presente, a. & m. present.

preservación, f. preservation.

preservar, v. preserve, keep.

preservativo, a. & m. preservative.

presidencia, f. presidency.

presidencial, a. presidential.

presidente -ta, n. president.

presidio, m. prison; garrison.

presidir, v. preside.

presión, f. pressure.

preso, m. prisoner.

presta, f. mint (plant).

prestador, m. lender.

prestamista, m. & f. money lender.

préstamo, m. loan.

prestar, v. lend.

presteza, f. haste, promptness.

prestidigitación, f. sleight of hand.

prestigio, m. prestige.

presto, 1. a. quick, prompt; ready. 2. adv. quickly; at once.

presumido, a. conceited, presumptuous.

presumir, v. presume; boast; claim; be conceited.

presunción, f. presumption; conceit.

presunto, a. presumed; prospective.

presuntuoso, a. presumptuous.

presupuesto, m. motive, pretext; budget.

pretender, v. pretend; intend; aspire.

pretendiente, m. suitor; pretender (to throne).

pretensión, f. pretension; claim.

pretérito, a. & m. preterit, past (tense).

pretexto, m. pretext.

prevalecer, v. prevail.

prevención, f. prevention.

prevenir, v. prevent; forewarn; prearrange.

preventivo, a. preventive.

prever, v. foresee.

previamente, adv. previously.

previo, a. previous.

previsión, f. foresight. **p. social,** social security.

prieto, a. blackish, very dark.

primacía, f. primacy.

primario, a. primary.

primavera, f. spring (season).

primero, a. & adv. first.

primitivo, a. primitive.

primo -ma, n. cousin.

primor, m. beauty; excellence; lovely thing.

primoroso, a. exquisite, elegant; graceful.

princesa, f. princess.

principal, 1. a. principal, main. 2. m. chief, head, principal.

principalmente, adv. principally.

príncipe, m. prince.

principiar, v. begin, initiate.

principio, m. beginning, start; principle.

prioridad, f. priority.

prisa, f. hurry, haste. **darse p.,** hurry, hasten. **tener p.,** be in a hurry.

prisión, f. prison; imprisonment.

prisionero -ra, n. captive, prisoner.

prisma, m. prism.

prismático, a. prismatic.

privación, f. privation, want.

privado, a. private, secret; deprived.

privar, v. deprive.

privilegio, m. privilege.

pro, m. or f. benefit, advantage. **en p. de,** in behalf of. **en p. y en contra,** pro and con.

proa, f. prow, bow.

probabilidad, f. probability.

probable, a. probable, likely.

probablemente, adv. probably.

probar, v. try, sample; taste; test; prove.

probarse, v. try on.

probidad, f. honesty, integrity.

problema, m. problem.

probo, a. honest.

procaz, a. impudent, saucy.

proceder, v. proceed.

procedimiento, m. procedure.

procesar, v. prosecute; sue; process.

procesión, f. procession.

proceso, m. process; (court) trial.

proclama, proclamación, f. proclamation.

proclamar, v. proclaim.

procreación, f. procreation.

procrear, v. procreate.

procurar, v. try; see to it; get, procure.

prodigalidad, f. prodigality.

prodigar, v. lavish, squander, waste.

prodigio, m. prodigy.

pródigo, a. prodigal, profuse, lavish.

producción, f. production.

producir, v. produce.

productivo, a. productive.

producto, m. product.

proeza, f. prowess.

profanación, f. profanation.

profanar, v. defile, desecrate.

profanidad, f. profanity.

profano, a. profane.

profecía, f. prophecy.

proferir, v. utter, express.

profesar, v. profess.

profesión, f. profession.

profesional, a. professional.

profesor -ra, n. professor, teacher.

profeta, m. prophet.

profético, a. prophetic.

profetizar, v. prophesy.

proficiente, a. proficient.

profundamente, adv. profoundly, deeply.

profundidad, f. profundity, depth.

profundizar, v. deepen.

profundo, a. profound, deep.

profuso, a. profuse.

progenie, f. progeny, offspring.

programa, m. program; schedule.

progresar, v. progress, advance.

progresión, f. progression.

progresista, progresivo, a. progressive.

progreso, m. progress.

prohibición, f. prohibition.

prohibir, v. prohibit, forbid.

prohibitivo, a. prohibitive.

prole, f. progeny.

proletariado, m. proletariat.

proliferación, f. proliferation.

prolijo, a. prolix, tedious; long-winded.

prólogo, m. prologue; preface.

prolongar, v. prolong.

promedio, m. average.

promesa, f. promise.

prometer, v. promise.

prometido, a. promised; engaged (to marry).

prominencia, f. prominence.

promiscuamente, adv. promiscuously.

promiscuo, a. promiscuous.

promisorio, a. promissory.

promoción, f. promotion.

promover, v. promote, further.

promulgación, f. promulgation.

promulgar, v. promulgate.

pronombre, m. pronoun.

pronosticación, f. prediction, forecast.

pronosticar, v. predict, forecast.

pronóstico, m. prediction.

prontamente, *adv.* promptly.
prontitud, *f.* promptness.
pronto, 1. *a.* prompt; ready. **2.** *adv.* soon; quickly. **de p.,** abruptly.
pronunciación, *f.* pronunciation.
pronunciar, *v.* pronounce.
propagación, *f.* propagation.
propaganda, *f.* propaganda.
propagandista, *n.* propagandist.
propagar, *v.* propagate.
propicio, *a.* propitious, auspicious, favorable.
propiedad, *f.* property.
propietario -ria, *n.* proprietor; owner; landlord, landlady.
propina, *f.* gratuity, tip.
propio, *a.* proper, suitable; typical; (one's) own; -self.
proponer, *v.* propose.
proporción, *f.* proportion.
proporcionado, *a.* proportionate.
proporcionar, *v.* provide with, supply, afford.
proposición, *f.* proposition, offer; proposal.
propósito, *m.* purpose; plan; **a p.,** by the way, apropos; **on purpose.**
propuesta, *f.* proposal, motion.
prorrata, *f.* quota.
prórroga, *f.* renewal, extension.
prorrogar, *v.* renew, extend.
prosa, *f.* prose.
prosaico, *a.* prosaic.
proscribir, *v.* prohibit, proscribe, ban.
prosecución, *f.* prosecution.
proseguir, *v.* pursue; proceed, go on.
prosélito, *m.* proselyte.
prospecto, *m.* prospectus.
prosperar, *v.* prosper, thrive, flourish.
prosperidad, *f.* prosperity.
próspero, *a.* prosperous, successful.
prosternado, *a.* prostrate.
prostitución, *f.* prostitution.
prostituir, *v.* prostitute; debase.
prostituta, *f.* prostitute.
protagonista, *n. & f.* protagonist, hero, heroine.
protección, *f.* protection.
protector -ra, *a. & n.* protective; protector.
proteger, *v.* protect, safeguard.
protegido -da, *n.* protégé.
proteína, *f.* protein.
protesta, *f.* protest. **—protestar,** *v.*
protestante, *a. & n.* Protestant.
protocolo, *m.* protocol.
protuberancia, *f.* protuberance, lump.
provecho, *m.* profit, gain, benefit. **¡Buen provecho!** May you enjoy your meal!
provechoso, *a.* beneficial, advantageous, profitable.
proveer, *v.* provide, furnish.

provenir de, *v.* originate in, be due to, come from.
proverbial, *a.* proverbial.
proverbio, *m.* proverb.
providencia, *f.* providence.
providente, *a.* provident.
provincia, *f.* province.
provincial, *a.* provincial.
provinciano -na, *a. & n.* provincial.
provisión, *f.* provision, supply, stock.
provisional, *a.* provisional.
provocación, *f.* provocation.
provocador, *m.* provoker.
provocar, *v.* provoke, excite.
provocativo, *a.* provocative.
proximidad, *f.* proximity, vicinity.
próximo, *a.* next; near.
proyección, *f.* projection.
proyectar, *v.* plan, project.
proyectil, *m.* projectile, missile, shell.
proyecto, *m.* plan, project, scheme.
proyector, *m.* projector.
prudencia, *f.* prudence.
prudente, *a.* prudent.
prueba, *f.* proof; trial; test.
psicoanálisis, *m. or f.* psychoanalysis.
psicología, *f.* psychology.
psicológico, *a.* psychological.
psicólogo, *m.* psychologist.
psiquedélico, *a.* psychedelic.
psiquiatra, *m.* psychiatrist.
psiquiatría, *f.* psychiatry.
publicación, *f.* publication.
publicar, *v.* publish.
publicidad, *f.* publicity.
público, *a. & m.* public.
puchero, *m.* pot.
pudiente, *a.* powerful; wealthy.
pudín, *m.* pudding.
pudor, *m.* modesty.
pudoroso, *a.* modest.
pudrirse, *v.* rot.
pueblo, *m.* town, village; (the) people.
puente, *m.* bridge.
puerco -ca, *n.* pig.
pueril, *a.* childish.
puerilidad, *f.* puerility.
puerta, *f.* door; gate.
puerto, *m.* port, harbor.
puertorriqueño -ña, *a. & n.* Puerto Rican.
pues, 1. *adv.* well . . . **2.** *conj.* as, since, for.
puesto, *m.* appointment, post, job; place; stand. **p. que,** since.
pugilato, *m.* boxing.
pugna, *f.* conflict.
pugnacidad, *f.* pugnacity.
pugnar, *v.* fight; oppose.
pulcritud, *f.* beauty.
pulga, *f.* flea.
pulgada, *f.* inch.
pulgar, *m.* thumb.
pulir, *v.* polish; beautify.
pulmón, *m.* lung.
pulmonía, *f.* pneumonia.
pulpa, *f.* pulp.

púlpito, *m.* pulpit.
pulque, *m.* pulque (fermented maguey juice).
pulsación, *f.* pulsation, beat.
pulsar, *v.* pulsate, beat.
pulsera, *f.* wristband; bracelet; wristwatch.
pulso, *m.* pulse.
pulverizar, *v.* pulverize.
puma, *m.* puma.
pundonor, *m.* point of honor.
punta, *f.* point, tip, end.
puntada, *f.* stitch.
puntapié, *m.* kick.
puntería, *f.* (marksman's) aim.
puntiagudo, *a.* sharp-pointed.
puntillas, *f.pl.* **de p., en p.,** on tiptoe.
punto, *m.* point; period; spot, dot. **dos puntos,** (punct.) colon. **a p. de,** about to. **al p.,** instantly.
puntuación, *f.* punctuation.
puntual, *a.* punctual, prompt.
puntuar, *v.* punctuate.
puñada, *f.* fist, blow.
puñado, *m.* handful.
puñal, *m.* dagger.
puñalada, *f.* stab.
puñetazo, *m.* punch, fist blow.
puño, *m.* fist; cuff; handle.
pupila, *f.* pupil (of eye).
pupitre, *m.* writing desk, school desk.
pureza, *f.* purity; chastity.
purgante, *m.* laxative.
purgar, *v.* purge, cleanse.
purgatorio, *m.* purgatory.
puridad, *f.* purity.
purificación, *f.* purification.
purificar, *v.* purify.
purismo, *m.* purism.
purista, *n.* purist.
puritanismo, *m.* puritanism.
puro, 1. *a.* pure. **2.** *m.* cigar.
púrpura, *f.* purple.
purpúreo, *a.* purple.
purulencia, *f.* purulence.
purulento, *a.* purulent.
pus, *m.* pus.
pusilánime, *a.* pusillanimous.
puta, *f.* prostitute.
putrefacción, *f.* putrefaction, rot.
putrefacto, *a.* putrid, rotten.
pútrido, *a.* putrid.
puya, *f.* goad.

Q

que, 1. *rel. pron.* who, whom; that, which. **2.** *conj.* than.
qué, 1. *a. & pron.* what. **por q., para q.,** why? **2.** *adv.* how.
quebrada, *f.* ravine, gully, gulch; stream.
quebradizo, *a.* fragile, brittle.
quebrar, *v.* break.
queda, *f.* curfew.
quedar, *v.* remain, be located; be left. **q. bien a,** be becoming to.
quedarse, *v.* stay, remain. **q. con,** keep, hold on to.

quedo, *a.* quiet; gentle.

quehacer, *m.* task; chore.

queja, *f.* complaint.

quejarse, *v.* complain, grumble.

quejido, *m.* moan.

quejoso, *a.* complaining.

quema, *f.* burning.

quemadura, *f.* burn.

quemar, *v.* burn.

querella, *f.* quarrel; complaint.

querencia, *f.* affection, liking.

querer, *v.* want, wish; will; love (a person). **q. decir,** mean. **sin q.,** without meaning to; unwillingly.

querido, *a.* dear, loved, beloved.

quesería, *f.* dairy.

queso, *m.* cheese.

quiebra, *f.* break, fracture; damage; bankruptcy.

quien, *rel. pron.* who, whom.

quién, *interrog. pron.* who, whom.

quienquiera, *pron.* whoever, whomever.

quietamente, *adv.* quietly.

quieto, *a.* quiet, still.

quietud, *f.* quiet, quietude.

quijada, *f.* jaw.

quijotesco, *a.* quixotic.

quilate, *m.* carat.

quilla, *f.* keel.

quimera, *f.* chimera, vision; quarrel.

química, *f.* chemistry.

químico, *a. & m.* chemical; chemist.

quimoterapía, *f.* chemotherapy.

quincalleri, *f.* hardware store.

quince, *a. & pron.* fifteen.

quinientos, *a. & pron.* five hundred.

quinina, *f.* quinine.

quintana, *f.* country home.

quinto, *a.* fifth.

quirúrgico, *m.* surgeon.

quiste, *m.* cyst.

quitamanchas, *m.* stain remover.

quitanieve, *m.* snowplow.

quitar, *v.* take away, remove.

quitarse, *v.* take off; get rid of.

quitasol, *m.* parasol, umbrella.

quizá, quizás, *adv.* perhaps, maybe.

quórum, *m.* quorum.

R

rábano, *m.* radish.

rabí, rabino, *m.* rabbi.

rabia, *f.* rage; grudge; rabies.

rabiar, *v.* rage, be furious.

rabieta, *f.* tantrum.

rabioso, *a.* furious; rabid.

rabo, *m.* tail.

racimo, *m.* bunch, cluster.

ración, *f.* ration. **—racionar,** *v.*

racionabilidad, *f.* rationality.

racional, *a.* rational.

racionalismo, *m.* rationalism.

racionalmente, *adv.* rationally.

racha, *f.* streak.

radar, *m.* radar.

radiación, *f.* radiation.

radiador, *m.* radiator.

radiante, *a.* radiant.

radical, *a. & m.* radical.

radicalismo, *m.* radicalism.

radicoso, *a.* radical.

radio, *m. or f.* radio.

radioactividad, *f.* radioactivity.

radioactivo, *a.* radioactive.

radiodifundir, *v.* broadcast.

radiodifusión, *f.* (radio) broadcasting.

ráfaga, *f.* gust (of wind).

raíz, *f.* root.

raja, *f.* rip; split, crack. **—rajar,** *v.*

ralea, *f.* stock, breed.

ralo, *a.* thin, scattered.

rama, *f.* branch, bough.

ramillete, *m.* bouquet.

ramo, *m.* branch, bough.

ramonear, *v.* browse.

rampa, *f.* ramp.

rana, *f.* frog.

rancidez, *f.* rancidity.

rancio, *a.* rancid, rank, stale, sour.

ranchero -ra, *n.* small farmer.

rancho, *m.* ranch.

rango, *m.* rank.

ranúnculo, *m.* ranunculus; buttercup.

ranura, *f.* slot.

rapacidad, *f.* rapacity.

rapaz, 1. *a.* rapacious. **2.** *m.* young boy.

rapé, *m.* snuff.

rápidamente, *adv.* rapidly.

rapidez, *f.* rapidity, speed.

rápido, 1. *a.* rapid, fast, speedy. **2.** *m.* express (train).

rapiña, *f.* robbery, plundering.

rapsodia, *f.* rhapsody.

raqueta, *f.* (tennis) racket.

rareza, *f.* rarity, freak.

raridad, *f.* rarity.

raro, *a.* rare, strange, unusual, odd, queer.

rasar, *v.* skim.

rascar, *v.* scrape; scratch.

rasgadura, *f.* tear, rip. **—rasgar,** *v.*

rasgo, *m.* trait.

rasgón, *m.* tear.

rasguño, *m.* scratch. **—rasguñar,** *v.*

raso, 1. *a.* plain. **soldado r.,** (mil.) private. **2.** *m.* satin.

raspar, *v.* scrape; erase.

rastra, *f.* trail, track. **—rastrear,** *v.*

rastrillar, *v.* rake.

rastro, *m.* track, trail, trace; rake.

rata, *f.* rat.

ratificación, *f.* ratification.

ratificar, *v.* ratify.

rato, *m.* while, spell, short time.

ratón, *m.* mouse.

ratonera, *f.* mousetrap.

raya, *f.* dash, line, streak, stripe.

rayar, *v.* rule, stripe; scratch; cross out.

rayo, *m.* lightning bolt; ray; flash.

rayón, *m.* rayon.

raza, *f.* race; breed, stock.

razón, *f.* reason; ratio. **a r. de,** at the rate of. **tener r.,** to be right.

razonable, *a.* reasonable, sensible.

razonamiento, *m.* argument.

razonar, *v.* reason.

reacción, *f.* reaction.

reaccionar, *v.* react.

reaccionario, *m.* reactionary.

reacondicionar, *v.* recondition.

reactivo, *a. & m.* reactive; (chem.) reagent.

reactor, *m.* reactor.

real, *a.* royal, regal; real, actual.

realdad, *f.* royal authority.

realeza, *f.* royalty.

realidad, *f.* reality.

realista, *a. & n.* realistic; realist.

realización, *f.* achievement, accomplishment.

realizar, *v.* accomplish; fulfill; effect; (com.) realize.

realmente, *adv.* in reality.

realzar, *v.* enhance.

reata, *f.* rope; lasso, lariat.

rebaja, *f.* reduction.

rebajar, *v.* cheapen; reduce (in price); lower.

rebanada, *f.* slice. **—rebanar,** *v.*

rebaño, *m.* flock, herd.

rebato, *m.* alarm; sudden attack.

rebelarse, *v.* rebel, revolt.

rebelde, *a. & n.* rebellious; rebel.

rebelión, *f.* rebellion, revolt.

reborde, *m.* border.

rebotar, *v.* rebound.

rebozo, *m.* shawl.

rebuscar, *v.* search thoroughly.

rebuznar, *v.* bray.

recado, *m.* message; errand.

recaída, *f.* relapse. **—recaer,** *v.*

recalcar, *v.* stress, emphasize.

recámara, *f.* (Mex.) bedroom.

recapitulación, *f.* recapitulation.

recapitular, *v.* recapitulate.

recatado, *m.* coy; prudent.

recelar, *v.* fear, distrust.

receloso, *a.* distrustful.

recepción, *f.* reception.

receptáculo, *m.* receptacle.

receptividad, *f.* receptivity.

receptivo, *a.* receptive.

receptor, *m.* receiver.

receta, *f.* recipe; prescription.

recetar, *v.* prescribe.

recibimiento, *m.* reception; cordiality.

recibir, *v.* receive.

recibo, *m.* receipt.

reciclar, *v.* recycle.

recidiva, *f.* relapse.

recién, *adv.* recently, newly, just.

reciente, *a.* recent.

recinto, *m.* enclosure.

recipiente, *m.* recipient.

reciprocación, *f.* reciprocation.

recíprocamente, *adv.* reciprocally.

reciprocar, *v.* reciprocate.

reciprocidad, *f.* reciprocity.

recitación, *f.* recitation.

recitar, *v.* recite.

reclamación, *f.* claim; complaint.

reclamar, *v.* claim; complain.

reclamo, *m.* claim; advertisement, advertising; decoy.

reclinar, *v.* recline, repose, lean.

recluta, *m.* recruit.

reclutar, *v.* recruit, draft.

recobrar, *v.* recover, salvage, regain.

recobro, *m.* recovery.

recoger, *v.* gather; collect; pick up.

recogerse, *v.* retire (for night).

recolectar, *v.* gather, assemble; harvest.

recomendación, *f.* recommendation; commendation.

recomendar, *v.* recommend; commend.

recompensa, *f.* recompense; compensation.

recompensar, *v.* reward; compensate.

reconciliación, *f.* reconciliation.

reconciliar, *v.* reconcile.

reconocer, *v.* recognize; acknowledge; inspect, examine; (mil.) reconnoiter.

reconocimiento, *m.* recognition; appreciation, gratitude.

reconstituir, *v.* reconstitute.

reconstruir, *v.* reconstruct, rebuild.

record, *m.* (sports) record.

recordar, *v.* recall, recollect; remind.

recorrer, *v.* go over; read over; cover (distance).

recorte, *m.* clipping, cutting.

recostarse, *v.* recline, lean back, rest.

recreación, *f.* recreation.

recreo, *m.* recreation.

recriminación, *f.* recrimination.

rectangular, *a.* rectangular.

rectángulo, *m.* rectangle.

rectificación, *f.* rectification.

rectificar, *v.* rectify.

recto, *a.* straight; just, fair. **ángulo r.,** right angle.

recuento, *m.* recount.

recuerdo, *m.* memory, souvenir, remembrance; (*pl.*) regards.

reculada, *f.* recoil. **—recular,** *v.*

recuperación, *f.* recuperation.

recuperar, *v.* recuperate.

recurrir, *v.* revert; resort, have recourse.

recurso, *m.* resource; recourse.

rechazar, *v.* reject, spurn, discard.

rechinar, *v.* chatter.

red, *f.* net; trap.

redacción, *f.* (editorial) staff; composition (of written material).

redactar, *v.* draft, draw up; edit.

redactor, *m.* editor.

redada, *f.* netful, catch, haul.

redargución, *f.* retort. **—redargüir,** *v.*

redención, *f.* redemption, salvation.

redentor, *m.* redeemer.

redimir, *v.* redeem.

redoblante, *m.* drummer.

redonda, *f.* neighborhood, vicinity.

redondo, *a.* round, circular.

reducción, *f.* reduction.

reducir, *v.* reduce.

reembolso, *m.* refund. **—reembolsar,** *v.*

reemplazar, *v.* replace, supersede.

reencarnación, *f.* reincarnation.

reexaminar, *v.* reexamine.

reexpedir, *v.* forward (mail).

referencia, *f.* reference.

referéndum, *m.* referendum.

referir, *v.* relate, report on.

referirse, *v.* refer.

refinamiento, *m.* refinement.

refinar, *v.* refine.

refinería, *f.* refinery.

reflejar, *v.* reflect; think, ponder.

reflejo, *m.* reflection; glare.

reflexión, *f.* reflection, thought.

reflexionar, *v.* reflect, think.

reflujo, *m.* ebb; ebb tide.

reforma, *f.* reform. **—reformar,** *v.*

reformación, *f.* reformation.

reformador, *m.* reformer.

reforzar, *v.* reinforce, strengthen; encourage.

refractario, *a.* refractory.

refrán, *m.* proverb, saying.

refrenar, *v.* curb, rein; restrain.

refrescar, *v.* refresh, freshen, cool.

refresco, *m.* refreshment; cold drink.

refrigeración, *f.* refrigeration.

refrigerador, *m.* refrigerator.

refrigerar, *v.* refrigerate.

refuerzo, *m.* reinforcement.

refugiado -da, *f.* refugee.

refugiarse, *v.* take refuge.

refugio, *m.* refuge, asylum, shelter.

refulgencia, *f.* refulgence.

refulgente, *a.* refulgent.

refulgir, *v.* shine.

refunfuñar, *v.* mutter, grumble, growl.

refutación, *f.* refutation; rebuttal.

refutar, *v.* refute.

regadizo, *a.* irrigable.

regadura, *f.* irrigation.

regalar, *v.* give (a gift), give away.

regalo, *m.* gift, present, **con r.,** in luxury.

regañar, *v.* reprove; scold.

regaño, *m.* reprimand, scolding.

regar, *v.* water, irrigate.

regatear, *v.* haggle.

regateo, *m.* bargaining, haggling.

regazo, *m.* lap.

regencia, *f.* regency.

regeneración, *f.* regeneration.

regenerar, *v.* regenerate.

regente, *m.* regent.

régimen, *m.* regime; diet.

regimentar, *v.* regiment.

regimiento, *m.* regiment.

región, *f.* region.

regional, *a.* regional, sectional.

regir, *v.* rule; be in effect.

registrar, *v.* register; record; search.

registro, *m.* register; record; search.

regla, *f.* rule, regulation. **en r.,** in order.

reglamento, *m.* code of regulations.

regocijarse, *v.* rejoice, exult.

regocijo, *f.* rejoicing; merriment, joy.

regordete, *a.* chubby, plump.

regresar, *v.* go back, return.

regresión, *f.* regression.

regresivo, *a.* regressive.

regreso, *m.* return.

regulación, *f.* regulation.

regular, 1. *a.* regular; fair, middling. **2.** *v.* regulate.

regularidad, *f.* regularity.

regularmente, *adv.* regularly.

rehabilitación, *f.* rehabilitation.

rehabilitar, *v.* rehabilitate.

rehén, *m.* hostage.

rehusar, *v.* refuse; decline.

reina, *f.* queen.

reinado, *m.* reign. **—reinar,** *v.*

reino, *m.* kingdom; realm; reign.

reír, *v.* laugh.

reiteración, *f.* reiteration.

reiterar, *v.* reiterate.

reja, *f.* grating, grillwork.

relación, *f.* relation; account, report.

relacionar, *v.* relate, connect.

relajamiento, *m.* laxity, laxness.

relajar, *v.* relax, slacken.

relámpago, *m.* lightning; flash (of lightning).

relatador, *m.* teller.

relatar, *v.* relate, recount.

relativamente, *adv.* relatively.

relatividad, *f.* relativity.

relativo, *a.* relative.

relato, *m.* account, story.

relegación, *f.* relegation.

relegar, *v.* relegate.

relevar, *v.* relieve.

relicario, *m.* reliquary; locket.

relieve, *m.* (sculpture) relief.

religión, *f.* religion.

religiosidad, *f.* religiosity.

religioso -sa, 1. *a.* religious. **2.** *m.* member of a religious order.

reliquia, *f.* relic.

reloj, *m.* clock; watch.

relojería, *f.* watchmaker's shop.

relojero, *m.* watchmaker.

relucir, *v.* glow, shine; excel.

relumbrar, *v.* glitter, sparkle.

rellenar, *v.* refill; fill up, stuff.

relleno, *m.* filling; stuffing.

remache, *m.* rivet. —**remachar,** *v.*

remar, *v.* row (a boat).

rematado, *a.* finished; sold.

remate, *m.* end, finish; auction. **de r.,** utterly.

remedador, *m.* imitator.

remedar, *v.* imitate.

remedio, *m.* remedy. —**remediar,** *v.*

remendar, *v.* mend, patch.

remesa, *f.* shipment; remittance.

remiendo, *m.* patch.

remilgado, *a.* prudish; affected.

reminiscencia, *f.* reminiscence.

remitir, *v.* remit.

remo, *m.* oar.

remolacha, *f.* beet.

remolcador, *m.* tug (boat).

remolino, *m.* whirl; whirlpool; whirlwind.

remolque, *m.* tow. —**remolcar,** *v.*

remontar, *v.* ascend, go up.

remontarse, *v.* get excited; soar. **r. a,** date from; go back to (in time).

remordimiento, *m.* remorse.

remotamente, *adv.* remotely.

remoto, *a.* remote.

remover, *v.* remove; stir; shake; loosen.

rempujar, *v.* jostle.

remuneración, *f.* remuneration.

remunerar, *v.* remunerate.

renacido, *a.* reborn, born-again.

renacimiento, *m.* rebirth; renaissance.

rencor, *m.* rancor, bitterness, animosity; grudge.

rencoroso, *a.* rancorous, bitter.

rendición, *f.* surrender.

rendido, *a.* weary, worn out.

rendir, *v.* yield; surrender, give up; win over.

renegado, *m.* renegade.

renglón, *m.* line; (com.) item.

reno, *m.* reindeer.

renombre, *m.* renown.

renovación, *f.* renovation, renewal.

renovar, *v.* renew; renovate.

renta, *f.* income; rent.

rentar, *v.* yield; rent for.

renuencia, *f.* reluctance.

renuente, *a.* reluctant.

renuncia, *f.* resignation; renunciation.

renunciar, *v.* resign; renounce, give up.

reñir, *v.* scold, berate; quarrel, wrangle.

reo, *a.* & *n.* criminal; convict.

reorganizar, *v.* reorganize.

reparación, *f.* reparation, atonement; repair.

reparar, *v.* repair; mend; stop, stay over. **r. en,** notice; consider.

reparo, *m.* repair; remark; difficulty; objection.

repartición, *f.,* **repartimiento, reparto,** *m.* division, distribution.

repartir, *v.* divide, apportion, distribute; (theat.) cast.

repaso, *m.* review. —**repasar,** *v.*

repatriación, *f.* repatriation.

repatriar, *v.* repatriate.

repeler, *v.* repel.

repente, *m.* **de r.,** suddenly; unexpectedly.

repentinamente, *adv.* suddenly.

repentino, *a.* sudden.

repercusión, *f.* repercussion.

repertorio, *m.* repertoire.

repetición, *f.* repetition.

repetidamente, *adv.* repeatedly.

repetir, *v.* repeat.

repisa, *f.* shelf.

réplica, *f.* reply; objection.

replicar, *v.* reply; answer back.

repollo, *m.* cabbage.

reponer, *v.* replace; repair.

reponerse, *v.* recover, get well.

reporte, *m.* report; news.

repórter, reportero, *m.* reporter.

reposado, *a.* tranquil, peaceful, quiet.

reposo, *m.* repose, rest. —**reposar,** *v.*

reposte, *f.* pantry.

represalia, *f.* reprisal.

representación, *f.* representation; (theat.) performance.

representante, *m.* representative, agent.

representar, *v.* represent, depict; (theat.) perform.

representativo, *a.* representative.

represión, *f.* repression.

represivo, *a.* repressive.

reprimenda, *f.* reprimand.

reprimir, *v.* repress, quell.

reproche, *m.* reproach. —**reprochar,** *v.*

reproducción, *f.* reproduction.

reproducir, *v.* reproduce.

reptil, *m.* reptile.

república, *f.* republic.

republicano -na, *a.* & *n.* republican.

repudiación, *f.* repudiation.

repudiar, *v.* repudiate; disown.

repuesto, *m.* spare part. **de r.,** spare.

repugnancia, *f.* repugnance.

repugnante, *a.* repugnant, repulsive.

repugnar, *v.* disgust.

repulsa, *f.* refusal; repulse.

repulsivo, *a.* repulsive.

reputación, *f.* reputation.

reputar, *v.* repute; appreciate.

requerir, *v.* require.

requesón, *m.* cottage cheese.

requisición, *f.* requisition.

requisito, *m.* requisite, requirement.

res, *f.* head of cattle.

resbalar, *v.* slide; slip.

resbaloso, *a.* slippery.

rescate, *m.* rescue, ransom. —**rescatar,** *v.*

rescindir, *v.* rescind.

resentimiento, *m.* resentment.

resentirse, *v.* resent.

reserva, *f.* reserve. —**reservar,** *v.*

reservación, *f.* reservation.

resfriado, *m.* (med.) cold.

resfriarse, *v.* catch cold.

resguardar, *v.* guard, protect.

residencia, *f.* residence, seat.

residente, *a.* & *n.* resident.

residir, *v.* reside.

residuo, *m.* remainder.

resignación, *f.* resignation.

resignar, *v.* resign.

resina, *f.* resin; rosin.

resistencia, *f.* resistance.

resistir, *v.* resist; endure.

resolución, *f.* resolution.

resolutivamente, *adv.* resolutely.

resolver, *v.* resolve; solve.

resonante, *a.* resonant.

resonar, *v.* resound.

resorte, *m.* (mech.) spring.

respaldar, *v.* endorse; back.

respaldo, *m.* back (of a seat).

respectivo, *a.* respective.

respecto, *m.* relation, proportion; **r. a,** concerning, regarding.

respetabilidad, *f.* respectability.

respetable, *a.* respectable.

respeto, *m.* respect. —**respetar,** *v.*

respetuosamente, *adv.* respectfully.

respetuoso, *a.* respectful.

respiración, *f.* respiration, breath.

respirar, *v.* breathe.

resplandeciente, *a.* resplendent.

resplandor, *m.* brightness, glitter.

responder, *v.* respond, answer.

responsabilidad, *f.* responsibility.

responsable, *a.* responsible.

respuesta, *f.* answer, response, reply.

resquicio, *m.* crack, slit.

resta, *f.* subtraction, remainder.

restablecer, *v.* restore, reestablish.

restablecerse, v. recover, get well.

restar, v. remain; subtract.

restauración, f. restoration.

restaurante, m. restaurant.

restaurar, v. restore.

restitución, f. restitution.

restituir, v. restore, give back.

resto, m. remainder, rest; (pl.) remains.

restorán, m. restaurant.

restregar, v. scrape.

restricción, f. restriction.

restrictivo, a. restrictive.

restringir, v. restrict, curtail.

resucitar, v. resuscitate; resurrect.

resuelto, a. resolute.

resultado, m. result.

resultar, v. result; turn out; ensue.

resumen, m. résumé, summary, **en r.,** in brief.

resumir, v. sum up.

resurgir, v. resurge, reappear.

resurrección, f. resurrection.

retaguardia, f. rear guard.

retal, m. remnant.

retardar, v. retard, show.

retardo, m. delay.

retención, f. retention.

retener, v. retain, keep, withhold.

reticencia, f. reticence.

reticente, a. reticent.

retirada, f. retreat, retirement.

retirar, v. retire, retreat, withdraw.

retiro, m. retirement.

retorcer, v. wring.

retórica, f. rhetoric.

retórico, a. rhetorical.

retorno, m. return.

retozo, m. frolic, romp. —**retozar,** v.

retozón, a. frisky.

retracción, f. retraction.

retractor, v. retract.

retrasar, v. delay, set back; be slow.

retraso, m. delay, lag, slowness.

retratar, v. portray; photograph.

retrato, m. portrait, picture; photograph.

retreta, f. (mil.) retreat.

retrete, m. alcove; toilet.

retribución, f. retribution.

retroactivo, a. retroactive.

retroalimentación, f. feedback.

retroceder, v. recede, go back, draw back, back up.

retumbar, v. resound, rumble.

reumático, a. rheumatic.

reumatismo, m. rheumatism.

reunión, f. gathering, meeting, party; reunion.

reunir, v. gather, collect, bring together.

reunirse, v. meet, assemble, get together.

revelación, f. revelation.

revelar, v. reveal, betray; (phot.) develop.

reventa, f. resale.

reventar, v. burst; split apart.

reventón, m. blowout (of tire).

reverencia, f. reverence.

reverendo, a. reverend.

reverente, a. reverent.

revertir, v. revert.

revés, m. reverse; back, wrong side. **al r.,** just the opposite; inside out.

revisar, v. revise; review.

revisión, f. revision.

revista, f. magazine, periodical; review.

revivir, v. revive.

revocación, f. revocation.

revocar, v. revoke, reverse.

revolotear, v. hover.

revolución, f. revolution.

revolucionario -ria, a. & n. revolutionary.

revolver, v. revolve; stir, agitate.

revólver, m. revolver, pistol.

revuelta, f. revolt; turn.

rey, m. king.

reyerta, f. quarrel, wrangle.

rezar, v. pray.

rezongar, v. grumble; mutter.

ría, f. estuary.

riachuelo, m. creek.

riba, f. embankment.

rico, a. rich, wealthy; delicious.

ridículamente, adv. ridiculously.

ridiculizar, v. ridicule.

ridículo, a. & m. ridiculous; ridicule.

riego, m. irrigation.

rienda, f. rein.

riesgo, m. risk, gamble.

rifa, f. raffle; lottery; scuffle.

rifle, m. rifle.

rígidamente, adv. rigidly.

rigidez, f. rigidity.

rígido, a. rigid, stiff.

rigor, m. rigor.

riguroso, a. rigorous, strict.

rima, f. rhyme. —**rimar,** v.

rincón, m. corner, nook.

rinoceronte, m. rhinoceros.

riña, f. quarrel, feud.

riñón, m. kidney.

río, m. river.

ripio, m. debris.

riqueza, f. wealth.

risa, f. laugh; laughter.

risco, m. cliff.

risibilidad, f. risibility.

risotada, f. peal of laughter.

risueño, a. cheerful, smiling.

rítmico, a. rhythmical.

ritmo, m. rhythm.

rito, m. rite.

ritual, a. & m. ritual.

rivalidad, f. rivalry.

rivera, f. brook.

rizado, a. curly.

rizo, m. curl. —**rizar,** v.

robar, v. rob, steal.

roble, m. oak.

roblón, m. rivet. —**roblar,** v.

robo, m. robbery, theft.

robustamente, adv. robustly.

robusto, a. robust.

roca, f. rock; cliff.

rociada, f. spray, sprinkle. —**rociar,** v.

rocío, m. dew.

rodar, v. roll; roam.

rodear, v. surround, encircle.

rodeo, m. turn, winding; roundup.

rodilla, f. knee.

rodillo, m. roller.

rodio, m. rhodium.

rododendro, m. rhododendron.

roedor, m. rodent.

roer, v. gnaw.

rogación, f. request, entreaty.

rogar, v. beg, plead with, supplicate.

rojizo, a. reddish.

rojo, a. red.

rollo, m. roll; coil.

romadizo, m. head cold.

romance, m. romance, ballad.

románico, a. Romance.

romano -na, a. & n. Roman.

romántico, a. romantic.

romería, f. pilgrimage; picnic.

romero -ra, n. pilgrim.

rompecabezas, m. puzzle (pastime).

romper, v. break, smash, shatter; sever; tear.

rompible, a. breakable.

ron, m. rum.

roncar, v. snore.

ronco, a. hoarse.

ronda, f. round.

rondar, v. prowl.

ronquido, m. snore.

ronzal, m. halter.

roña, f. scab; filth.

ropa, f. clothes, clothing. **r. blanca,** linen. **r. interior,** underwear.

ropero, m. closet.

rosa, f. rose. **r. náutica,** compass.

rosado, a. pink, rosy.

rosal, m. rose bush.

rosario, m. rosary.

rosbif, m. roast beef.

rosca, f. thread (of screw).

róseo, a. rosy.

rostro, m. face, countenance.

rota, f. defeat; (naut.) course.

rotación, f. rotation.

rotatorio, a. rotary.

rótulo, m. label. —**rotular,** v.

rotundo, a. round; sonorous.

rotura, f. break, fracture, rupture.

rozar, v. rub against, chafe; graze.

rubí, m. ruby.

rubio -bia, a. & n. blond.

rubor, m. blush; bashfulness.

rúbrica, f. caption; scroll.

rucho, m. donkey.

rudeza, f. rudeness; roughness.

rudimento, m. rudiment.

rudo, a. rude, rough.

rueda, f. wheel.

ruego, m. plea; entreaty.

rufián, m. ruffian.

rufo, a. sandy (colored).

rugir, v. bellow, roar.
rugoso, a. wrinkled.
ruibarbo, m. rhubarb.
ruido, m. noise.
ruidoso, a. noisy.
ruina, f. ruin, wreck.
ruinar, v. ruin, destroy.
ruinoso, a. ruinous.
ruiseñor, m. nightingale.
ruleta, f. roulette.
rumba, f. rumba (dance or music).
rumbo, m. course, direction.
rumor, m. rumor; murmur.
runrún, m. rumor.
ruptura, f. rupture, break.
rural, a. rural.
Rusia, f. Russia.
ruso -sa, a. & n. Russian.
rústico -ca, a. & n. rustic. **en r.,** paperback f.
ruta, f. route.
rutina, f. routine.
rutinario, a. routine.

S

sábado, m. Saturday.
sábalo, m. shad.
sábana, f. sheet.
sabañon, m. chilblain.
saber, 1. n. knowledge. **2.** v. know; learn, find out; know how to; taste. **a s.,** namely, to wit.
sabiduría, f. wisdom; learning.
sabio, 1. a. wise; scholarly. **2.** m. sage; scholar.
sable, m. saber.
sabor, m. flavor, taste, savor.
saborear, v. savor, relish.
sabotaje, m. sabotage.
sabroso, a. savory, tasty.
sabuesco, m. hound.
sacacorchos, m. corkscrew.
sacar, v. draw out; take out; take.
sacerdocio, m. priesthood.
sacerdote, m. priest.
saciar, v. satiate.
saco, m. sack, bag, pouch; suit coat, jacket.
sacramento, m. sacrament.
sacrificio, m. sacrifice. **—sacrificar,** v.
sacrilegio, m. sacrilege.
sacristán, m. sexton.
sacro, a. sacred, holy.
sacrosanto, a. sacrosanct.
sacudir, v. shake, jerk, jolt.
sádico, a. sadistic.
sadismo, m. sadism.
sagacidad, f. sagacity.
sagaz, a. sagacious, sage.
sagrado, a. sacred, holy.
sal, f. salt; (coll.) wit.
sala, f. room; living room, parlor; hall, auditorium.
salado, a. salted, salty; (coll.) witty.
salar, v. salt; steep in brine.
salario, m. salary, wages.
salchicha, f. sausage.

saldo, m. remainder, balance; (bargain) sale.
salero, m. salt shaker.
salida, f. exit, outlet; departure.
salir, v. go out, come out; set out, leave, start; turn out, result.
salirse de, v. get out of. **s. con la suya,** have one's own way.
salitre, m. saltpeter.
saliva, f. saliva.
salmo, m. psalm.
salmón, m. salmon.
salmuera, f. pickle; brine.
salobre, a. salty.
salón, m. parlor, living room; hall.
salpicar, v. spatter, splash.
salpullido, m. rash.
salsa, f. sauce; gravy.
saltamontes, m. grasshopper.
salteador, m. highwayman.
salto, m. jump, leap, spring. **—saltar,** v.
saltón, m. grasshopper.
salubre, a. salubrious, healthful.
salubridad, f. health.
salud, f. health.
saludable, a. healthful, wholesome.
saludar, v. greet; salute.
saludo, m. greeting; salutation; salute.
salutación, f. salutation.
salva, f. salvo.
salvación, f. salvation; deliverance.
salvador -ra, n. savior; rescuer.
salvaguardia, m. safeguard.
salvaje, a. & m. savage, wild (man).
salvamento, m. salvation; rescue.
salvar, v. save; salvage; rescue; jump over.
salvavidas, m. life preserver.
salvia, f. sage (plant).
salvo, 1. a. safe. **2.** prep. except, save (for). **s. que,** unless.
San, title. Saint.
sanar, v. heal, cure.
sanatorio, m. sanatorium.
sanción, f. sanction. **—sancionar,** v.
sandalia, f. sandal.
sandez, f. stupidity.
sandía, f. watermelon.
saneamiento, m. sanitation.
sangrar, v. bleed.
sangre, f. blood.
sangriento, a. bloody.
sanguinario, a. bloodthirsty.
sanidad, f. health.
sanitario, a. sanitary.
sano, a. healthy, sound, sane; healthful, wholesome.
santidad, f. sanctity, holiness.
santificar, v. sanctify.
santo -ta, 1. a. holy, saintly. **2.** m. saint.
Santo -ta, title. Saint.
santuario, m. sanctuary, shrine.

saña, f. rage, anger.
sapiente, a. wise.
sapo, m. toad.
saquera, v. sack, ransack, plunder.
sarampión, m. measles.
sarape, m. (Mex.) woven blanket; shawl.
sarcasmo, m. sarcasm.
sarcástico, a. sarcastic.
sardina, f. sardine.
sargento, m. sergeant.
sarna, f. itch.
sartén, m. frying pan.
sastre, m. tailor.
satánico, a. satanic.
satélite, m. satellite.
sátira, f. satire.
satírico, a. & m. satirical; satirist.
satirizar, v. satirize.
sátiro, m. satyr.
satisfacción, f. satisfaction.
satisfacer, v. satisfy.
satisfactorio, a. satisfactory.
saturación, f. saturation.
saturar, v. saturate.
sauce, m. willow.
savia, f. sap.
saxófono, m. saxophone.
saya, f. skirt.
sazón, f. season; seasoning. **a la s.,** at that time.
sazonar, v. flavor, season.
se, pron. -self, -selves.
seca, f. drought.
secante, a. **papel s.,** blotting paper.
secar, v. dry.
sección, f. section.
seco, a. dry; curt.
secreción, f. secretion.
secretar, v. secrete.
secretaria, f. secretary's office; secretariat.
secretario -ra, n. secretary.
secreto, a. & m. secret.
secta, f. denomination, sect.
secuela, f. result; sequel.
secuestrar, v. abduct, kidnap; hijack.
secuestro, m. abduction, kidnapping.
secular, a. secular.
secundario, a. secondary.
sed, f. thirst. **tener s., estar con s.,** to be thirsty.
seda, f. silk.
sedar, v. quiet, allay.
sedativo, a. & m. sedative.
sede, f. seat, headquarters.
sedentario, a. sedentary.
sedición, f. sedition.
sedicioso, a. seditious.
sediento, a. thirsty.
sedimento, m. sediment.
sedoso, a. silky.
seducir, v. seduce.
seductivo, a. seductive, alluring.
segar, v. reap, harvest; mow.
seglar, m. layman.
segmento, m. segment.
segregar, v. segregate.

seguida, f. succession. **en s.,** right away, at once.

seguido, a. consecutive.

seguir, v. follow; continue, keep on, go on.

según, **1.** prep. according to, **2.** conj. as.

segundo, a. & m. second. —**segundar**, v.

seguridad, f. safety; security; assurance.

seguro, **1.** a. safe, secure; sure, certain. **2.** m. insurance.

seis, a. & pron. six.

seiscientos, a. & pron. six hundred.

selección, f. selection, choice.

seleccionar, v. select, choose.

selecto, a. select, choice, elite.

selva, f. forest; jungle.

selvoso, a. sylvan.

sello, m. seal; stamp. —**sellar**, v.

semáforo, m. semaphore.

semana, f. week.

semanal, a. weekly.

semántica, f. semantics.

semblante, m. look, expression.

sembrado, m. sown field.

sembrar, v. sow, seed.

semejante, a. like, similar; such (a). **2.** m. fellowman.

semejanza, f. similarity, likeness.

semejar, v. resemble.

semilla, f. seed.

seminario, m. seminary.

senado, m. senate.

senador -ra, n. senator.

sencillez, f. simplicity; naturalness.

sencillo, a. simple, natural; single.

senda, f. **sendero**, m. path.

senectud, f. old age.

senil, a. senile.

seno, m. breast, bosom.

sensación, f. sensation.

sensacional, a. sensational.

sensato, a. sensible, wise.

sensibilidad, f. sensibility; sensitiveness.

sensible, a. sensitive; emotional.

sensitivo, a. sensitive.

sensual, a. sensual.

sensualidad, f. sensuality.

sentar, v. seat. **s. bien**, fit well, be becoming.

sentarse, v. sit, sit down.

sentencia, f. (court) sentence.

sentidamente, adv. feelingly.

sentido, m. meaning, sense; consciousness.

sentimental, a. sentimental.

sentimiento, m. sentiment, feeling.

sentir, v. feel, sense; hear; regret, be sorry.

seña, f. sign, indication; (pl.) address.

señal, f. sign, signal; mark.

señalar, v. designate, point out; mark.

señor, m. gentleman; lord; (title) Mr., Sir.

señora, f. lady; wife; (title) Mrs., Madam.

señorita, f. young lady; (title) Miss.

sépalo, m. sepal.

separación, f. separation, parting.

separadamente, adv. separately.

separado, a. separate. —**separar**, v.

septentrional, a. northern.

septiembre, m. September.

séptimo, a. seventh.

sepulcro, m. sepulcher.

sepultar, v. bury, entomb.

sepultura, f. grave.

sequedad, f. dryness.

sequía, f. drought.

ser, v. be.

serenata, f. serenade.

serenidad, f. serenity.

sereno, **1.** a. serene, calm. **2.** m. dew; watchman.

serie, f. series, sequence.

seriedad, f. seriousness.

serio, a. serious. **en s.,** seriously.

sermón, m. sermon.

seroso, a. watery.

serpiente, f. serpent, snake.

serrano, m. mountaineer.

serrar, v. saw.

serrín, m. sawdust.

servicial, a. helpful, of service.

servicio, m. service; toilet.

servidor -ra, n. servant.

servidumbre, f. bondage; staff of servants.

servil, a. servile, menial.

servilleta, f. napkin.

servir, v. serve. **s. para**, be good for.

servirse, v. help oneself.

sesenta, a. & pron. sixty.

sesgo, m. slant. —**sesgar**, v.

sesión, f. session; sitting.

seso, m. brain.

seta, f. mushroom.

setecientos, a. & pron. seven hundred.

setenta, a. & pron. seventy.

seto, m. hedge.

severamente, adv. severely.

severidad, f. severity.

severo, a. severe, strict, stern.

sexismo, m. sexism.

sexista, m. & a. sexist.

sexo, m. sex.

sexto, a. sixth.

sexual, a. sexual.

si, conj. if; whether.

sí, **1.** pron. -self, -selves. **2.** interj. yes.

sicómoro, m. sycamore.

sidra, f. cider.

siempre, adv. always. **para s.,** forever. **s. que**, whenever; provided that.

sierra, f. saw; mountain range.

siervo, m. slave; serf.

siesta, f. (afternoon) nap.

siete, a. & pron. seven.

sifón, m. siphon; siphon bottle.

siglo, m. century.

signatura, f. signature.

significación, f. significance.

significado, m. meaning.

significante, a. significant.

significar, v. signify, mean.

significativo, a. significant.

signo, m. sign, symbol; mark.

siguiente, a. following, next.

sílaba, f. syllable.

silbar, v. whistle; hiss, boo.

silbato, **silbido**, m. whistle.

silencio, m. silence, stillness.

silenciosamente, a. silently.

silencioso, a. silent, still.

silicato, m. silicate.

silicio, m. silicon.

silueta, f. silhouette.

silvestre, a. wild, uncultivated. **fauna s.,** wildlife.

silla, f. chair; saddle.

sillón, m. armchair.

sima, f. chasm; cavern.

simbólico, a. symbolic.

símbolo, m. symbol.

simetría, f. symmetry.

simétrico, a. symmetrical.

símil, **similar**, a. similar, alike.

similitud, f. similarity.

simpatía, f. congeniality; friendly feeling.

simpático, a. likeable, nice, congenial.

simple, a. simple.

simpleza, f. silliness; trifle.

simplicidad, f. simplicity.

simplificación, f. simplification.

simplificar, v. simplify.

simular, v. simulate.

simultáneo, a. simultaneous.

sin, prep. without.

sinagoga, f. synagogue.

sinceridad, f. sincerity.

sincero, a. sincere.

sincronizar, v. synchronize.

sindicato, m. syndicate; labor union.

síndrome, m. syndrome.

sinfonía, f. symphony.

sinfónico, a. symphonic.

singular, a. & m. singular.

siniestro, a. sinister, ominous.

sino, conj. but.

sinónimo, m. synonym.

sinrazón, f. wrong, injustice.

sinsabor, m. displeasure, distaste.

sintaxis, f. syntax.

síntesis, f. synthesis.

sintético, a. synthetic.

síntoma, m. symptom.

siquiera, adv. **ni s.,** not even.

sirena, f. siren.

sirviente -ta, n. servant.

sistema, m. system.

sistemático, a. systematic.

sistematizar, v. systematize.

sitiar, v. besiege.

sitio, m. site, location, place, spot.

situación, f. situation; location.

situar, *v.* situate; locate.
smoking, *m.* tuxedo, dinner jacket.
so, *prep.* under.
soba, *f.* massage. **—sobar,** *v.*
sobaco, *m.* armpit.
sobaquero, *f.* armhole.
soberano -na, *a.* & *m.* sovereign.
soberbia, *f.* arrogance.
soberbio, *a.* superb; arrogant.
soborno, *m.* bribe. **—sobornar,** *v.*
sobra, *f.* excess, surplus. **de sobra,** to spare.
sobrado, *m.* attic.
sobrante, *a.* & *m.* surplus.
sobre, 1. *prep.* about; above, over. **2.** *m.* envelope.
sobrecama, *f.* bedspread.
sobrecargo, *m.* supercargo.
sobredicho, *a.* aforesaid.
sobrehumano, *a.* superhuman.
sobrenatural, *a.* supernatural, weird.
sobrepasar, *v.* surpass.
sobresalir, *v.* excel.
sobretodo, *m.* overcoat.
sobrevivir, *v.* survive, outlive.
sobriedad, *f.* sobriety; moderation.
sobrina, *f.* niece.
sobrino, *m.* nephew.
sobrio, *a.* sober, temperate.
socarrén, *m.* eaves.
sociable, *a.* sociable.
social, *a.* social.
socialismo, *m.* socialism.
socialista, *a.* & *m.* socialistic; socialist.
sociedad, *f.* society; association.
socio -cia, *n.* associate, partner; member.
sociología, *f.* sociology.
socorro, *m.* help, aid. **—socorrer,** *v.*
soda, *f.* soda.
sodio, *m.* sodium.
sofá, *m.* sofa, couch.
sofisma, *m.* sophism.
sofista, *m.* sophist.
sofocación, *f.* suffocation.
sofocar, *v.* smother, suffocate, stifle, choke.
soga, *f.* rope.
soja, *f.* soybean.
sol, *m.* sun.
solada, *f.* dregs.
solanera, *f.* sunbath.
solapa, *f.* lapel.
solar, 1. *a.* solar. **2.** *m.* building lot.
solaz, *m.* solace, comfort. **—solazar,** *v.*
soldado, *m.* soldier.
soldar, *v.* solder, weld.
soledad, *f.* solitude, privacy.
solemne, *a.* solemn.
solemnemente, *adv.* solemnly.
solemnidad, *f.* solemnity.
soler, *v.* be in the habit of.
solicitador, *m.* solicitor.
solicitar, *v.* solicit; apply for.
solícito, *a.* solicitous.

solicitud, *f.* solicitude; application.
sólidamente, *adv.* solidly.
solidaridad, *f.* solidarity.
solidez, *f.* solidity.
solidificar, *v.* solidify.
sólido, *a.* & *m.* solid.
soliloquio, *m.* soliloquy.
solitario, *a.* solitary, lone.
solo, 1. *a.* only; single; alone; lonely. **a solas,** alone. **2.** *m.* solo.
sólo, *adv.* only, just.
soltar, *v.* release; loosen.
soltero -ra, *a.* & *n.* single, unmarried (person).
soltura, *f.* poise, ease, facility.
solubilidad, *f.* solubility.
solución, *f.* solution.
solucionar, *v.* solve, settle.
solvente, *a.* solvent.
sollozo, *m.* sob. **—sollozar,** *v.*
sombra, *f.* shade; shadow. **—sombrear,** *v.*
sombrero, *m.* hat.
sombrilla, *f.* parasol.
sombrío, *a.* somber, bleak, gloomy.
sombroso, *a.* shady.
someter, *v.* subject; submit.
somnolencia, *f.* drowsiness.
son, *m.* sound. **—sonar,** *v.*
sonata, *f.* sonata.
sondar, *v.* sound, fathom.
sonido, *m.* sound.
sonoridad, *f.* sonority.
sonoro, *a.* sonorous.
sonrisa, *f.* smile. **—sonreír,** *v.*
sonrojo, *m.* flush, blush. **—sonrojarse,** *v.*
soñador -ra, *a.* & *n.* dreamy; dreamer.
soñar, *v.* dream.
soñoliento, *a.* sleepy.
sopa, *f.* soup.
soplar, *v.* blow.
soplete, *m.* blowtorch.
soplo, *m.* breath; puff, gust.
soportar, *v.* abide, bear, stand.
soprano, *m.* & *f.* soprano.
sorbete, *m.* sherbet.
sorbo, *m.* sip. **—sorber,** *v.*
sordera, *f.* deafness.
sórdidamente, *adv.* sordidly.
sordidez, *f.* sordidness.
sórdido, *a.* sordid.
sordo, *a.* deaf; muffled, dull.
sordomudo -da, *a.* & *n.* deaf-mute.
sorpresa, *f.* surprise. **—sorprender,** *v.*
sorteo, *m.* drawing lots; raffle.
sortija, *f.* ring.
sosa, *f.* (chem.) soda.
soso, *a.* dull, insipid, tasteless.
sospecha, *f.* suspicion.
sospechar, *v.* suspect.
sospechoso, *a.* suspicious.
sostén, *m.* support; brassiere.
sostener, *v.* hold, support; maintain.
sostenimiento, *m.* sustenance.
sota, *f.* jack (in cards).
sótano, *m.* basement, cellar.
soto, *m.* grove.

soviet, *m.* soviet.
soya, *f.* soybean.
su, *a.* his, her, its, their, your.
suave, *a.* smooth; gentle, soft, mild.
suavidad, *f.* smoothness; gentleness, softness, mildness.
suavizar, *v.* soften.
subalterno, *a.* & *m.* subordinate.
subasta, *f.* auction.
subconsciencia, *f.* subconscious.
súbdito -ta, *n.* subject.
subida, *f.* ascent, rise.
subilla, *f.* awl.
subir, *v.* rise, climb, ascend, mount. **s. a,** amount to.
súbito, *a.* sudden.
subjetivo, *a.* subjective.
subjuntivo, *a.* & *m.* subjunctive.
sublimación, *f.* sublimation.
sublimar, *v.* elevate; sublimate.
sublime, *a.* sublime.
submarino, *a.* & *m.* submarine.
subordinación, *f.* subordination.
subordinado, *a.* & *m.* subordinate. **—subordinar,** *v.*
subrayar, *v.* underline.
subscribirse, *v.* subscribe; sign one's name.
subscripción, *f.* subscription.
subsecuente, *a.* subsequent.
subsidiario, *a.* subsidiary.
subsiguiente, *a.* subsequent.
substancia, *f.* substance.
substancial, *a.* substantial.
substantivo, *m.* substantive, noun.
substitución, *f.* substitution.
substituir, *v.* replace; substitute.
substitutivo, *a.* substitute.
substituto -ta, *m.* substitute.
substraer, *v.* subtract.
subterfugio, *m.* subterfuge.
subterráneo, 1. *a.* subterranean, underground. **2.** *m.* place underground; subway.
suburbio, *m.* suburb.
subvención, *f.* subsidy, grant.
subversión, *f.* subversion.
subversivo, *a.* subversive.
subvertir, *v.* subvert.
subyugación, *f.* subjugation.
subyugar, *v.* subjugate, quell.
succión, *f.* suction.
suceder, *v.* happen, occur, befall. **s. a,** succeed, follow.
sucesión, *f.* succession.
sucesivo, *a.* successive. **en lo s.,** in the future.
suceso, *m.* event.
sucesor -ra, *n.* successor.
suciedad, *f.* filth, dirt.
sucio, *a.* filthy, dirty.
suculento, *a.* succulent.
sucumbir, *v.* succumb.
sud, *m.* south.
sudamericano -na, *a.* & *n.* South American.
sudar, *v.* perspire, sweat.
sudeste, *m.* southeast.

sudoeste, *m.* southwest.

sudor, *m.* perspiration, sweat.

Suecia, *f.* Sweden.

sueco -ca, *a.* & *n.* Swedish; Swede.

suegra, *f.* mother-in-law.

suegro, *m.* father-in-law.

suela, *f.* sole.

sueldo, *m.* salary, wages.

suelo, *m.* soil; floor; ground.

suelto, *a.* loose; free; odd, separate.

sueño, *m.* sleep; sleepiness; dream. **tener s.,** to be sleepy.

suero, *m.* serum.

suerte, *f.* luck; chance; lot.

suéter, *m.* sweater.

suficiente, *a.* sufficient.

sufragio, *m.* suffrage.

sufrimiento, *m.* suffering, agony.

sufrir, *v.* suffer; undergo; endure.

sugerencia, *f.* suggestion.

sugerir, *v.* suggest.

sugestión, *f.* suggestion.

sugestionar, *v.* influence; hypnotize.

suicida, *m.* & *f.* suicide (person).

suicidarse, *v.* commit suicide.

suicidio, *m.* (act of) suicide.

Suiza, *f.* Switzerland.

suizo -za, *a.* & *n.* Swiss.

sujeción, *f.* subjection.

sujetar, *v.* hold, fasten, clip.

sujeto, 1. *a.* subject, liable. **2.** *m.* (gram.) subject.

sulfato, *m.* sulfate.

sulfuro, *m.* sulfide.

sultán, *m.* sultan.

suma, *f.* sum, amount. **en s.,** in short.

sumar, *v.* add up.

sumaria, *f.* indictment.

sumario, *m.* & *a.* summary.

sumergir, *v.* submerge.

sumersión, *f.* submersion.

sumisión, *f.* submission.

sumiso, *a.* submissive.

sumo, *a.* great, high, utmost.

suntuoso, *a.* sumptuous.

superar, *v.* overcome, surpass.

superficial, *a.* superficial, shallow.

superficie, *f.* surface.

superfluo, *a.* superfluous.

superhombre, *m.* superman.

superintendente, *m.* superintendent.

superior, 1. *a.* superior; upper, higher. **2.** *m.* superior.

superioridad, *f.* superiority.

superlativo, *m.* & *a.* superlative.

superstición, *f.* superstition.

supersticioso, *a.* superstitious.

supervisar, *v.* supervise.

supervivencia, *f.* survival.

suplantar, *v.* supplant.

suplementario, *a.* supplementary.

suplemento, *m.* supplement. — **suplementar,** *v.*

suplente, *a.* & *m.* substitute.

súplica, *f.* request, entreaty, plea.

suplicación, *f.* supplication; request, entreaty.

suplicar, *v.* request, entreat; implore.

suplicio, *m.* torture, ordeal.

suplir, *v.* supply.

suponer, *v.* suppose, pressume, assume.

suposición, *f.* supposition, assumption.

supremacía, *f.* supremacy.

supremo, *a.* supreme.

supresión, *f.* suppression.

suprimir, *v.* suppress; abolish.

supuesto, *a.* supposed. **por s.,** of course.

sur, *m.* south.

surco, *m.* furrow. —**surcar,** *v.*

surgir, *v.* arise; appear suddenly.

surtido, *m.* assortment; supply, stock.

surtir, *v.* furnish, supply.

susceptibilidad, *f.* susceptibility.

susceptible, *a.* susceptible.

suscitar, *v.* stir up.

suscri- = **subscri-**

suspender, *v.* withhold; suspend; fail (in a course).

suspensión, *f.* suspension.

suspenso, *m.* failing grade. **en s.,** in suspense.

suspicacia, *f.* suspicion, distrust.

suspicaz, *a.* suspicious.

suspicazmente, *adv.* suspiciously.

suspiro, *m.* sigh. —**suspirar,** *v.*

sustan- = **substan-**

sustentar, *v.* sustain, support.

sustento, *m.* sustenance, support, living.

susti- = **substi-**

susto, *m.* fright, scare.

sustraer = **substraer.**

susurro, *m.* rustle; whisper. — **susurrar,** *v.*

sutil, *a.* subtle.

sutileza, sutilidad, *f.* subtlety.

sutura, *f.* suture.

suyo, *a.* his, hers, theirs, yours.

T

tabaco, *m.* tobacco.

tábano, *m.* horsefly.

taberna, *f.* tavern, bar.

tabernáculo, *m.* tabernacle.

tabique, *m.* dividing wall, partition.

tabla, *f.* board, plank; table, list.

tablado, *m.* stage, platform.

tablero, *m.* panel.

tableta, *f.* tablet.

tablilla, *f.* bulletin board.

tabú, *m.* taboo.

tabular, *a.* tabular.

tacaño, *a.* stingy.

tácitamente, *adv.* tacitly.

tácito, *a.* tacit.

taciturno, *a.* taciturn.

taco, *m.* heel (of shoe); billiard cue.

tacón, *m.* heel (of shoe).

táctico, *a.* tactical.

tacto, *m.* (sense of) touch; tact.

tacha, *f.* fault, defect.

tachar, *v.* find fault with; cross out.

tachuela, *f.* tack.

tafetán, *m.* taffeta.

taimado, *a.* sly.

tajada, *n.* cut, slice, chop. — **tajar,** *v.*

tajea, *f.* channel.

tal, *a.* such. **con t. que.,** provided that. **t. vez,** perhaps.

taladrar, *v.* drill.

taladro, *m.* (mech.) drill.

talante, *m.* humor, disposition.

talco, *m.* talc.

talega, *f.* bag, sack.

talento, *m.* talent.

talón, *m.* heel (of foot); (baggage) check, stub.

talla, *f.* engraving; stature; size (of suit).

tallador -ra, *n.* engraver; dealer (at cards).

talle, *m.* figure; waist; fit.

taller, *m.* workshop, factory.

tallo, *m.* stem, stalk.

tamal, *m.* tamale.

tamaño, *m.* size.

tambalear, *v.* stagger, totter.

también, *adv.* also, too.

tambor, *m.* drum.

tamiz, *m.* sieve, sifter.

tampoco, *adv.* neither, either.

tan, *adv.* so.

tanda, *f.* turn, relay.

tándem, *m.* tandem bicycle.

tangencia, *f.* tangency.

tangible, *a.* tangible.

tango, *m.* tango (dance or music).

tanque, *m.* tank.

tanteo, *m.* estimate. —**tantear,** *v.*

tanto, 1. *a.* & *pron.* so much, so many; as much, as many. **entre t., mientras t.,** meanwhile. **por lo t.,** therefore. **un t.,** somewhat, a bit. **2.** *m.* point (in games); (*pl*) score. **estar al t.,** to be up to date.

tañer, *v.* play (an instrument); ring (bells).

tapa, *f.* cap, cover. —**tapar,** *v.*

tapadero, *m.* stopper, lid.

tápara, *f.* caper.

tapete, *m.* small rug, mat, cover.

tapia, *f.* wall.

tapicería, *f.* tapestry.

tapioca, *f.* tapioca.

tapiz, *m.* tapestry; carpet.

tapizado (de pared), *m.* (wall) covering.

tapón, *m.* plug; cork.

taquigrafía, *f.* shorthand.

taquilla, *f.* ticket office; ticket window.

tara, *f.* hang-up.

tarántula, *f.* tarantula.

tararear, v. hum.

tardanza, f. delay; lateness.

tardar, v. delay; be late; take (of time). **a más t.,** at the latest.

tarde, 1. adv. late. **2.** f. afternoon; early evening.

tardío, a. late, belated.

tarea, f. task, assignment.

tarifa, f. rate; tariff; price list.

tarjeta, f. card.

tarta, f. tart.

tartamudear, v. stammer, falter.

tasa, f. rate.

tasación, f. valuation.

tasar, v. assess, appraise.

tasugo, m. badger.

tautología, f. tautology.

taxi, taxímetro, m. taxi.

taxonomía, f. taxonomy.

taza, f. cup.

te, pron. you; yourself.

té, m. tea.

teátrico, a. theatrical.

teatro, m. theater.

tecla, f. key (of a piano, etc.).

técnica, f. technique.

técnicamente, adv. technically.

técnico, a. technical.

tecnología, f. technology.

techo, m. roof. —**techar,** v.

tedio, m. tedium, boredom.

tedioso, a. tedious.

teísmo, m. theism.

teja, f. tile.

tejado, m. roof.

tejer, v. weave; knit.

tejido, m. fabric; weaving.

tejón, m. badger.

tela, f. cloth, fabric, web. **t. metálica,** screen; screening.

telar, m. loom.

telaraña, f. cobweb.

telefonista, m. & f. (telephone) operator.

teléfono, m. telephone. —**telefonear,** v.

telégrafo, m. telegraph. —**telegrafiar,** v.

telegrama, m. telegram.

telescopio, m. telescope.

televisión, f. television.

telón, m. (theat.) curtain.

telurio, m. tellurium.

tema, m. theme, subject.

temblar, v. tremble, quake; shake, shiver.

temblor, m. tremor; shiver.

temer, v. fear, be afraid of, dread.

temerario, a. rash.

temeridad, f. temerity.

temerosamente, adv. timorously.

temeroso, a. fearful.

temor, m. fear.

témpano, m. kettledrum; iceberg.

temperamento, m. temperament.

temperancia, f. temperance.

temperatura, f. temperature.

tempestad, f. tempest, storm.

tempestuoso, a. tempestuous, stormy.

templado, a. temperate, mild, moderate.

templanza, f. temperance; mildness.

templar, v. temper; tune (an instrument).

templo, m. temple.

temporada, f. season, time, spell.

temporal, temporáneo, a. temporary.

temprano, a. & adv. early.

tenacidad, f. tenacity.

tenaz, a. tenacious, stubborn.

tenazmente, adv. tenaciously.

tendencia, f. tendency, trend.

tender, v. stretch, stretch out.

tendero -ra, n. shopkeeper, storekeeper.

tendón, m. tendon, sinew.

tenebrosidad, f. gloom.

tenebroso, a. dark, gloomy.

tenedor, m. keeper; holder; fork.

tener, v. have; own; hold. **t. que,** have to, must.

teniente, m. lieutenant.

tenis, m. tennis.

tenor, m. tenor.

tensión, f. tension, stress, strain.

tenso, a. tense.

tentación, f. temptation.

tentáculo, m. tentacle.

tentador, a. alluring, tempting.

tentar, v. tempt, lure; grope, probe.

tentativa, f. attempt.

tentativo, a. tentative.

teñir, v. tint, dye.

teología, f. theology.

teológico, a. theological.

teoría, f. theory.

teórico, a. theoretical.

terapéutico, a. therapeutic.

tercero, a. third.

tercio, m. third.

terciopelo, m. velvet.

terco, a. obstinate, stubborn.

termal, a. thermal.

terminación, f. termination; completion.

terminar, v. terminate, finish.

término, m. term; end.

terminología, f. terminology.

termómetro, m. thermometer.

termos, m. thermos.

ternero -ra, n. calf.

ternura, f. tenderness.

terquedad, f. stubbornness.

terraza, f. terrace.

terremoto, m. earthquake.

terreno, 1. a. earthly, terrestrial. **2.** m. ground, terrain; lot, plot.

terrible, a. terrible, awful.

terrífico, a. terrific.

territorio, m. territory.

terrón, m. clod, lump; mound.

terror, m. terror.

terso, a. smooth, glossy; terse.

tertulia, f. social gathering, party.

tesis, f. thesis.

tesorería, f. treasury.

tesorero -ra, n. treasurer.

tesoro, m. treasure.

testamento, m. will, testament.

testarudo, a. stubborn.

testificar, v. testify.

testigo, m. witness; testimony.

testimonial, a. testimonal.

testimonio, m. testimony.

teta, f. teat.

tetera, f. teapot.

tétrico, a. sad; gloomy.

texto, m. text.

textura, f. texture.

tez, f. complexion.

ti, pron. you; yourself.

tía, f. aunt.

tibio, a. lukewarm.

tiburón, m. shark.

tiemblo, m. aspen.

tiempo, m. time; weather; (gram.) tense.

tienda, f. shop, store; tent.

tientas, f.pl. **andar a t.,** to grope (in the dark).

tierno, a. tender.

tierra, f. land; ground; earth, dirt, soil.

tieso, a. taut, stiff, hard, strong.

tiesto, m. flower pot.

tiesura, f. stiffness; harshness.

tifo, m. typhus.

tifoideo, f. typhoid fever.

tigre, m. tiger.

tijeras, f.pl. scissors.

tila, f. linden.

timbre, m. seal, stamp; tone; (electric) bell.

timidamente, adv. timidly.

timidez, f. timidity.

tímido, a. timid, shy.

timón, m. rudder, helm.

tímpano, m. kettledrum; eardrum.

tina, f. tub, vat.

tinaja, f. jar.

tinta, f. ink.

tinte, m. tint, shade.

tintero, m. inkwell.

tinto, a. wine-colored; red (of wine).

tintorería, f. dry cleaning shop.

tintorero -ra, n. dyer; dry cleaner.

tintura, f. tincture; dye.

tiñoso, a. scabby; stingy.

tío, m. uncle.

tiovivo, m. merry-go-round.

típico, a. typical.

tipo, m. type, sort; (interest) rate; (coll.) guy, fellow.

tira, f. strip.

tirabuzón, m. corkscrew.

tirada, f. edition.

tiranía, f. tyranny.

tiránico, m. tyrannical; domineering.

tirano, m. tyrant.

tirante, 1. a. tight, taut; tense. **2.** m. (pl.) suspenders.

tirar, v. throw; draw; pull; fire (a weapon).

tiritar, v. shiver.

tiro, *m.* throw; shot.

tirón, *m.* pull. **de un t.,** at a stretch, at one stroke.

tísico, *n.* & *a.* consumptive.

tisis, *f.* consumption, tuberculosis.

titania, *m.* titanium.

títere, *m.* puppet.

titilación, *f.* twinkle.

titubear, *v.* stagger; totter; waver.

titulado, *a.* entitled; so-called.

titular, 1. *a.* titular. 2. *v.* entitle.

título, *m.* title, headline.

tiza, *f.* chalk.

tiznar, *v.* smudge; stain.

toalla, *f.* towel.

toalleta, *f.* small towel.

tobillo, *m.* ankle.

tocadiscos, *m.* record player.

tocado, *m.* hairdo.

tocador, *m.* boudoir; dressing table.

tocante, *a.* touching. **t. a,** concerning, relative to.

tocar, *v.* touch; play (an instrument). **t. a uno,** be one's turn; be up to one.

tocayo, *m.* namesake.

tocino, *m.* bacon.

todavía, *adv.* yet, still.

todo, 1. *a.* all, whole. **todos los,** every. 2. *pron.* all, everything. **con t.,** still, however. **del t.,** wholly; at all.

todopoderoso, *a.* almighty.

toldo, *m.* awning.

tolerancia, *f.* tolerance.

tolerante, *a.* tolerant.

tolerar, *v.* tolerate.

toma, *f.* taking, capture, seizure.

tomaína, *f.* ptomaine.

tomar, *v.* take; drink.

tomate, *m.* tomato.

tomillo, *m.* thyme.

tomo, *m.* volume.

tonada, *f.* tune.

tonel, *m.* barrel, cask.

tonelada, *f.* ton.

tonelaje, *m.* tonnage.

tónico, *a.* & *m.* tonic.

tono, *m.* tone, pitch, shade. **darse t.,** to put on airs.

tonsila, *f.* tonsil.

tonsilitis, *f.* tonsilitis.

tontería, *f.* nonsense, foolishness.

tonto -ta, *a.* & *n.* foolish, silly; fool.

topacio, *m.* topaz.

topar, *v.* run into. **t. con,** come upon.

tópico, 1. *a.* topical. 2. *m.* topic.

topo, *m.* mole (animal).

toque, *m.* touch.

tórax, *m.* thorax.

torbellino, *m.* whirlwind.

torcer, *v.* twist; wind; distort.

toreador, *m.* toreador.

torero, *m.* bullfighter.

torio, *m.* thorium.

tormenta, *f.* storm.

tormento, *m.* torment.

tornado, *m.* tornado.

tornar, *v.* return; turn.

tornarse en, *v.* turn into, become.

torneo, *m.* tournament.

tornillo, *m.* screw.

toro, *m.* bull.

toronja, *f.* grapefruit.

torpe, *a.* awkward, clumsy; sluggish.

torpedero, *m.* torpedo boat.

torpedo, *m.* torpedo.

torre, *f.* tower.

torrente, *m.* torrent.

tórrido, *a.* torrid.

torta, *f.* cake; loaf.

tortilla, *f.* omelet; (Mex.) tortilla, pancake.

tórtola, *f.* dove.

tortuga, *f.* turtle.

tortuoso, *a.* tortuous.

tortura, *f.* torture. **—torturar,** *v.*

tos, *m.* cough. **—toser,** *v.*

tosco, *a.* coarse, rough, uncouth.

tosquedad, *f.* coarseness, roughness.

tostar, *v.* toast; tan.

total, *a.* & *m.* total.

totalidad, *f.* totality, entirety, whole.

totalitario, *a.* totalitarian.

totalmente, *adv.* totally; entirely.

tótem, *m.* totem.

tóxico, *a.* toxic.

trabajador -ra, 1. *a.* hardworking. 2. *n.* worker.

trabajo, *m.* work; labor. **—trabajar,** *v.*

trabar, *v.* fasten, shackle; grasp; strike up.

tracción, *f.* traction.

tracto, *m.* tract.

tractor, *m.* tractor.

tradición, *f.* tradition.

tradicional, *a.* traditional.

traducción, *f.* translation.

traducir, *v.* translate.

traductor, *m.* translator.

traer, *v.* bring; carry; wear.

tráfico, *m.* traffic. **—traficar,** *v.*

tragar, *v.* swallow.

tragedia, *f.* tragedy.

trágicamente, *adv.* tragically.

trágico -ca, 1. *a.* tragic. 2. *n.* tragedian.

trago, *m.* swallow; drink.

traición, *f.* treason, betrayal.

traicionar, *v.* betray.

traidor -ra, *a.* & *n.* traitorous; traitor.

traje, *m.* suit; dress; garb, apparel.

trama, *v.* plot (of a story).

tramador, *m.* weaver; plotter.

tramar, *v.* weave; plot, scheme.

trámite, *m.* (business) deal, transaction.

tramo, *m.* span, stretch, section.

trampa, *f.* trap, snare.

trampista, *m.* cheater; swindler.

trance, *m.* critical moment or stage. **a todo t.,** at any cost.

tranco, *m.* stride.

tranquilidad, *f.* tranquility, calm, quiet.

tranquilizar, *v.* quiet, calm down.

tranquilo, *a.* tranquil, calm, quiet.

transacción, *f.* transaction.

transbordador, *m.* ferry.

transcribir, *v.* transcribe.

transcripción, *f.* transcription.

transcurrir, *v.* elapse.

transeúnte, *a.* & *n.* transient; passerby.

transexual, *a.* transsexual.

transferencia, *f.* transference.

transferir, *v.* transfer.

transformación, *f.* transformation.

transformar, *v.* transform.

transfusión, *f.* transfusion.

transgresión, *f.* transgression.

transgresor, *m.* transgressor.

transición, *f.* transition.

transigir, *v.* compromise, settle; agree.

transitivo, *a.* transitive.

tránsito, *m.* transit, passage.

transitorio, *a.* transitory.

transmisión, *f.* transmission; broadcast.

transmisora, *f.* broadcasting station.

transmitir, *v.* transmit; broadcast.

transparencia, *f.* transparency.

transparente, 1. *a.* transparent. 2. *m.* (window) shade.

transportación, *f.* transportation.

transportar, *v.* transport, convey.

transporte, *m.* transportation; transport.

tranvía, *m.* streetcar, trolley.

trapacero, *n.* cheat; swindler.

trapo, *m.* rag.

tráquea, *f.* trachea.

tras, *prep.* after; behind.

trasegar, *v.* upset, overturn.

trasero, *a.* rear, back.

traslado, *m.* transfer. **—trasladar,** *v.*

traslapo, *m.* overlap. **—traslapar,** *v.*

trasnochar, *v.* sit up all night.

traspalar, *v.* shovel.

traspasar, *v.* go beyond; cross; violate; pierce.

trasquilar, *v.* shear; clip.

trastornar, *v.* overturn, overthrow, upset.

trastorno, *m.* overthrow; upheaval.

tratado, *m.* treaty; treatise.

tratamiento, *m.* treatment.

tratar, *v.* treat, handle. **t. de,** deal with; try to; call (a name).

tratarse de, *v.* be a question of.

trato, *m.* treatment; manners; (com.) deal.

través, *adv.* a t. de, through, across. de t., sideways.
travesía, *f.* crossing; voyage.
travesti, *m.* transvestite.
travestido, *a.* disguised.
travesura, *f.* prank; mischief.
travieso, *a.* naughty, mischievous.
trayectoria, *f.* trajectory.
trazar, *v.* plan, devise; trace; draw.
trazo, *n.* plan, outline; line, stroke.
trébol, *m.* clover.
trece, *a. & pron.* thirteen.
trecho, *m.* space, distance, stretch.
tregua, *f.* truce, respite, lull.
treinta, *a. & pron.* thirty.
tremendo, *a.* tremendous.
tremer, *v.* tremble.
tren, *m.* train.
trenza, *f.* braid. —trenzar, *v.*
trepar, *v.* climb, mount.
trepidación, *f.* trepidation.
tres, *a. & pron.* three.
trescientos, *a. & pron.* three hundred.
triángulo, *m.* triangle.
tribu, *f.* tribe.
tribulación, *f.* tribulation.
tribuna, *f.* rostrum, stand; (*pl.*) grandstand.
tribunal, *m.* court, tribunal.
tributario, *a. & m.* tributary.
tributo, *m.* tribute.
triciclo, *m.* tricycle.
trigo, *m.* wheat.
trigonometría, *f.* trigonometry.
trigueño, *a.* swarthy, dark.
trilogía, *f.* trilogy.
trimestral, *a.* quarterly.
trinchar, *v.* carve (meat).
trinchera, *f.* trench, ditch.
trineo, *m.* sled; sleigh.
trinidad, *f.* trinity.
tripa, *f.* tripe, entrails.
triple, *a.* triple. —triplicar, *v.*
tripulación, *f.* (ship's) crew.
triste, *a.* sad, sorrowful; dreary.
tristemente, *adv.* sadly.
tristeza, *f.* sadness; gloom.
triunfal, *a.* triumphal.
triunfante, *a.* triumphant.
triunfo, *m.* triumph, trump. —triunfar, *v.*
trivial, *a.* trivial, commonplace.
trivialidad, *f.* triviality.
trocar, *v.* exchange, switch; barter.
trofeo, *m.* trophy.
trombón, *m.* trombone.
trompa, trompeta, *f.* trumpet, horn.
tronada, *f.* thunderstorm.
tronar, *v.* thunder.
tronco, *m.* trunk, stump.
trono, *m.* throne.
tropa, *f.* troop.
tropel, *m.* crowd, throng.
tropezar, *v.* trip, stumble. t. con, come upon, run into.

trópico, *a. & m.* tropical; tropics.
tropiezo, *m.* stumble; obstacle; slip, error.
trote, *m.* trot. —trotar, *v.*
trovador, *m.* troubadour.
trozo, *m.* piece, portion, fragment, selection, passage.
trucha, *f.* trout.
trueco, trueque, *m.* exchange, barter.
trueno, *m.* thunder.
tu, *a.* your.
tú, *pron.* you.
tuberculosis, *f.* tuberculosis.
tubo, *m.* tube, pipe.
tuerca, *f.* (mech.) nut.
tulipán, *m.* tulip.
tumba, *f.* tomb, grave.
tumbar, *v.* knock down.
tumbarse, *v.* tumble.
tumbo, *m.* tumble; somersault.
tumor, *m.* tumor; growth.
tumulto, *m.* tumult, commotion.
tumultuoso, *a.* tumultuous, boisterous.
tunante, *m.* rascal, rogue.
tunda, *f.* spanking, whipping.
túnel, *m.* tunnel.
tungsteno, *m.* tungsten.
túnica, *f.* tunic, robe.
tupir, *v.* pack tight, stuff; stop up.
turbación, *f.* confusion, turmoil.
turbamulta, *f.* mob; crowd.
turbar, *v.* disturb, upset; embarrass.
turbina, *f.* turbine.
turbio, *a.* turbid; muddy.
turco -ca, *a. & n.* Turkish; Turk.
turismo, *m.* touring, (foreign) travel.
turista, *m. & f.* tourist.
turno, *m.* turn; (work) shift.
turquesa, *f.* turquoise.
Turquía, *f.* Turkey.
turrón, *m.* nougat.
tusa, *f.* corncob; corn.
tutear, *v.* use the pronoun tú, etc., in addressing a person.
tutela, *f.* guardianship; aegis.
tutor, *m.* tutor; guardian.
tuyo, *a.* your, yours.

U

u, *conj.* or.
ubre, *f.* udder.
ufano, *a.* proud, haughty.
úlcera, *f.* ulcer.
ulterior, *a.* ulterior.
último, *a.* last, final; ultimate; latest. por ú., finally.
ultraje, *m.* outrage. —ultrajar, *v.*
umbral, *m.* threshold.
umbroso, *a.* shady.
un, una, *art. & a.* a, an; one; (*pl.*) some.
unánime, *a.* unanimous.
unanimidad, *f.* unanimity.

unción, *f.* unction.
ungüento, *m.* ointment, salve.
único, *a.* only, sole; unique.
unicornio, *m.* unicorn.
unidad, *f.* unit; unity.
unificar, *v.* unify.
uniforme, *a. & m.* uniform.
uniformidad, *f.* uniformity.
unión, *f.* union; joining.
unir, *v.* unite, join.
universal, *a.* universal.
universalidad, *f.* universality.
universidad, *f.* university; college.
universo, *m.* universe.
uno, una, *pron.* one; (*pl.*) some.
untar, *v.* spread; grease; anoint.
uña, *f.* fingernail.
urbanidad, *f.* urbanity; good breeding.
urbano, *a.* urban; urbane; well-bred.
urbe, *f.* large city.
urgencia, *f.* urgency.
urgente, *a.* urgent, pressing. entrega u., special delivery.
urgir, *v.* be urgent.
urna, *f.* urn; ballot box; (*pl.*) polls.
usanza, *f.* usage, custom.
usar, *v.* use; wear.
uso, *m.* use; usage; wear.
usted, *pron.* you.
usual, *a.* usual.
usualmente, *adv.* usually.
usura, *f.* usury.
usurero, *m.* usurer.
usurpación, *f.* usurpation.
usurpar, *v.* usurp.
utensilio, *m.* utensil.
útero, *m.* uterus.
útil, *a.* useful, handy.
utilidad, *f.* utility, usefulness.
utilizar, *v.* use, utilize.
útilmente, *adv.* usefully.
utópico, *a.* utopian.
uva, *f.* grape.

V

vaca, *f.* cow; beef.
vacaciones, *f.pl.* vacation, holidays.
vacancia, *f.* vacancy.
vacante, 1. *a.* vacant. 2. *f.* vacancy.
vaciar, *v.* empty; pour out.
vacilación, *f.* vacillation, hesitation.
vacilante, *a.* vacillating.
vacilar, *v.* falter, hesitate; waver; stagger.
vacío, 1. *a.* empty. 2. *m.* void, empty space.
vacuna, *f.* vaccine.
vacunación, *f.* vaccination.
vacunar, *v.* vaccinate.
vacuo, 1. *a.* empty, vacant. 2. *m.* vacuum.
vadear, *v.* wade through, ford.
vado, *m.* ford.
vagabundo, *a. & m.* vagabond.

vagar, *v.* wander, rove, roam; loiter.

vago -ga, 1. *a.* vague, hazy; wandering, vagrant. **2.** *n.* vagrant, tramp.

vagón, *m.* railroad car.

vahído, *m.* dizziness.

vaina, *f.* sheath; pod.

vainilla, *f.* vanilla.

vaivén, *m.* vibration, sway.

vajilla, *f.* (dinner) dishes.

valentía, *f.* valor, courage.

valer, 1. *m.* worth. **2.** *v.* be worth.

valerse de, *v.* make use of, avail oneself of.

valía, *f.* value.

validez, *f.* validity.

válido, *a.* valid.

valiente, *a.* valiant, brave, courageous.

valija, *f.* valise.

valioso, *a.* valuable.

valor, *m.* value, worth; bravery, valor; (*pl.*, com.) securities.

valoración, *f.* appraisal.

valorar, *v.* value, appraise.

vals, *m.* waltz.

valsar, *v.* waltz.

valuación, *f.* valuation.

valuar, *v.* value; rate.

válvula, *f.* valve.

valla, *f.* fence, barrier.

valle, *m.* valley.

vándalo, *m.* vandal.

vanidad, *f.* vanity.

vanidoso, *a.* vain, conceited.

vano, *a.* vain; inane.

vapor, *m.* vapor; steam; steamer, steamship.

vaquero, *m.* cowboy.

vara, *f.* wand, stick, switch.

varadero, *m.* shipyard.

varar, *v.* launch; be stranded; run aground.

variable, *a.* variable.

variación, *f.* variation.

variar, *v.* vary.

variedad, *f.* variety.

varios, *a. & pron. pl.* various; several.

varón, *m.* man; male.

varonil, *a.* manly, virile.

vasallo, *m.* vassal.

vasectomía, *f.* vasectomy.

vasija, *f.* bowl, container (for liquids).

vaso, *m.* water glass; vase.

vástago, *m.* bud, shoot; twig; offspring.

vasto, *a.* vast.

vecindad, *f.* **vecindario,** *m.* neighborhood, vicinity.

vecino -na, *a. & n.* neighboring; neighbor.

vedar, *v.* forbid; impede.

vega, *f.* meadow.

vegetación, *f.* vegetation.

vegetal, *m.* vegetable.

vehemente, *a.* vehement.

vehículo, *m.* vehicle; conveyance.

veinte, *a. & pron.* twenty.

vejez, *f.* old age.

vejiga, *f.* bladder.

vela, *f.* vigil, watch; candle; sail.

velar, *v.* stay up, sit up; watch over.

velo, *m.* veil.

velocidad, *f.* velocity, speed; rate.

velomotor, *m.* motorbike, moped.

veloz, *a.* speedy, fast, swift.

vellón, *m.* fleece.

velloso, *a.* hairy; fuzzy.

velludo, *a.* downy.

vena, *f.* vein.

venado, *m.* deer.

vencedor -ra, *n.* victor.

vencer, *v.* defeat, overcome, conquer; (com.) become due, expire.

vencimiento, *m.* defeat.

venda, *f.* **vendaje,** *m.* bandage. **—vendar,** *v.*

vendedor -ra, *m.* seller, trader; sales clerk.

vender, *v.* sell.

vendimia, *f.* vintage.

veneno, *m.* poison.

venenoso, *a.* poisonous.

veneración, *f.* veneration.

venerar, *v.* venerate, revere.

venero, *m.* spring, origin.

véneto, *a.* Venetian.

venezolano, *a. & n.* Venezuelan.

vengador, *m.* avenger.

venganza, *f.* vengeance, revenge.

vengar, *v.* avenge.

venida, *f.* arrival, advent, coming.

venidero, *a.* future; coming.

venir, *v.* come.

venta, *f.* sale; sales.

ventaja, *f.* advantage; profit.

ventajoso, *a.* advantageous; profitable.

ventana, *f.* window.

ventero, *m.* innkeeper.

ventilación, *f.* ventilation.

ventilador, *m.* ventilator, fan.

ventilar, *v.* ventilate, air.

ventoso, *a.* windy.

ventura, *f.* venture; happiness; luck.

ver, *v.* see. **tener que v. con,** have to do with.

vera, *f.* edge.

veracidad, *f.* truthfulness, veracity.

verano, *m.* summer. **—veranear,** *v.*

veras, *f.pl.* **de v.,** really, truly.

veraz, *a.* truthful.

verbigracia, *adv.* for example.

verbo, *m.* verb.

verboso, *a.* verbose.

verdad, *f.* truth. **ser v.,** to be true.

verdadero, *a.* true, real.

verde, *a.* green; risqué, off-color.

verdor, *m.* greenness, verdure.

verdugo, *m.* hangman.

verdura, *f.* verdure, vegetation; (*pl.*) vegetables.

vereda, *f.* path.

veredicto, *m.* verdict.

vergonzoso, *a.* shameful, embarrassing; shy, bashful.

vergüenza, *f.* shame; disgrace; embarrassment.

verificar, *v.* verify, check.

verja, *f.* grating, railing.

verosímil, *a.* likely, plausible.

verraco, *m.* boar.

verruga, *f.* wart.

versátil, *a.* versatile.

verse, *v.* look, appear.

versión, *f.* version.

verso, *m.* verse, stanza; line (of poetry).

verter, *v.* pour, spill; shed; empty.

vertical, *a.* vertical.

vertiente, *f.* slope; watershed.

vertiginoso, *a.* dizzy.

vértigo, *m.* vertigo, dizziness.

vestíbulo, *m.* vestibule, lobby.

vestido, *m.* dress; clothing.

vestigio, *m.* vestige, trace.

vestir, *v.* dress, clothe.

veterano -na, *a. & n.* veteran.

veterinario, *m.* veterinary.

veto, *m.* veto.

vetusto, *a.* ancient, very old.

vez, *f.* time; turn. **tal v.,** perhaps. **a la v.,** at the same time. **en v. de,** instead of. **una v.,** once. **otra v.,** again.

vía, *f.* track; route, way.

viaducto, *m.* viaduct.

viajante, *a. & n.* traveling; traveler.

viajar, *v.* travel; journey, tour.

viaje, *m.* trip, journey, voyage; (*pl.*) travels.

viajero -ra, *n.* traveler; passenger.

viandas, *f.pl.* victuals, food.

víbora, *f.* viper.

vibración, *f.* vibration.

vibrar, *v.* vibrate.

vicepresidente, *m.* vice president.

vicio, *m.* vice.

vicioso, *a.* vicious; licentious.

víctima, *f.* victim.

victoria, *f.* victory.

victorioso, *a.* victorious.

vid, *f.* grapevine.

vida, *f.* life; living.

video, *m.* videotape.

videodisco, *m.* videodisc.

vidrio, *m.* glass.

viejo -ja, *a. & n.* old; old person.

viento, *m.* wind. **hacer v.,** to be windy.

vientre, *m.* belly.

viernes, *m.* Friday.

viga, *f.* beam, rafter.

vigente, *a.* in effect (prices, etc.).

vigilante, *a. & m.* vigilant, watchful; watchman.

vigilar, *v.* guard, watch over.

vigilia, *f.* vigil, watchfulness; (rel.) fast.

vigor, *m.* vigor. **en v.,** in effect, in force.

vil, *a.* vile, low, contemptible.

vileza, *f.* baseness; vileness.

villa, *f.* town; country house.

villancico, *m.* Christmas carol.

villanía, *f.* villainy.

villano, *m.* boor.

vinagre, *m.* vinegar.

vínculo, *m.* link. —**vincular,** *v.*

vindicar, *v.* vindicate.

vino, *m.* wine.

viña, *f.* vineyard.

violación, *f.* violation.

violar, *v.* violate.

violencia, *f.* violence.

violento, *a.* violent; impulsive.

violeta, *f.* violet.

violín, *m.* violin.

violón, *m.* bass viol.

virar, *v.* veer, change course.

virgen, *f.* virgin.

viril, *a.* virile, manly.

virilidad, *f.* virility; manhood.

virtual, *a.* virtual.

virtud, *f.* virtue; efficacy, power.

virtuoso, *a.* virtuous.

viruela, *f.* smallpox.

visa, *f.* visa.

visaje, *m.* grimace.

visera, *f.* visor.

visible, *a.* visible.

visión, *f.* vision.

visionario -ria, *a. & n.* visionary.

visita, *f.* visit; visitor, caller.

visitación, *f.* visitation.

visitante, *a. & n.* visiting; visitor.

visitar, *v.* visit; inspect, examine.

vislumbre, *m.* glimpse.

viso, *m.* looks; outlook.

víspera, *f.* eve, day before.

vista, *f.* view; scene; sight.

vistazo, *m.* glance, glimpse.

vistoso, *a.* beautiful; showy.

visual, *a.* visual.

vital, *a.* vital.

vitalidad, *f.* vitality.

vitamina, *f.* vitamin.

vitando, *a.* hateful.

vituperar, *v.* vituperate; revile.

viuda, *f.* widow.

viudo, *m.* widower.

vivaz, *a.* vivacious, buoyant; clever.

víveres, *m.pl.* provisions.

viveza, *f.* animation, liveliness.

vívido, *a.* vivid, bright.

vivienda, *f.* (living) quarters, dwelling.

vivificar, *v.* vivify, enliven.

vivir, *v.* live.

vivo, *a.* live, alive, living; vivid; animated, brisk.

vocablo, *m.* word.

vocabulario, *m.* vocabulary.

vocación, *f.* vocation, calling.

vocal, 1. *a.* vocal. **2.** *f.* vowel.

vocear, *v.* vociferate.

vodevil, *m.* vaudeville.

volante, 1. *a.* flying. **2.** *m.* memorandum; (steering) wheel.

volar, *v.* fly; explode.

volcán, *m.* volcano.

volcar, *v.* upset, capsize.

voltear, *v.* turn, whirl; overturn.

voltio, *m.* volt.

volumen, *m.* volume.

voluminoso, *a.* voluminous.

voluntad, *f.* will.

voluntario -ria, *a. & n.* voluntary; volunteer.

voluntarioso, *a.* willful.

volver, *v.* turn; return, go back, come back. **v. a hacer** (etc.), do (etc.) again.

volverse, *v.* turn around; turn, become.

vómito, *m.* vomit. —**vomitar,** *v.*

voracidad, *f.* voracity; greed.

voraz, *a.* greedy, ravenous.

vórtice, *m.* whirlpool.

vosotros -as, *pron.pl.* you; yourselves.

votación, *f.* voting, vote.

voto, *m.* vote; vow. —**votar,** *v.*

voz, *f.* voice; word. **a voces,** by shouting. **en v. alta,** aloud.

vuelco, *m.* upset.

vuelo, *m.* flight. **v. libre,** hang gliding.

vuelta, *f.* turn, bend; return. **a la v. de,** around. **dar una v.,** to take a walk.

vuestro, *a.* your, yours.

vulgar, *a.* vulgar, common.

vulgaridad, *f.* vulgarity.

vulgo, *m.* (the) masses, (the) common people.

vulnerable, *a.* vulnerable.

Y, Z

y, *conj.* and.

ya, *adv.* already; now; at once. **y. no,** no longer, any more. **y. que,** since.

yacer, *v.* lie.

yanqui, *a. & n.* North American.

yate, *m.* yacht.

yegua, *f.* mare.

yelmo, *m.* helmet.

yema, *f.* yolk (of an egg).

yerba, *f.* grass; herb.

yerno, *m.* son-in-law.

yerro, *m.* error, mistake.

yeso, *m.* plaster.

yo, *pron.* I.

yodo, *m.* iodine.

yoduro, *m.* iodide.

yugo, *m.* yoke.

yunque, *m.* anvil.

yunta, *f.* team (of animals).

zafarse, *v.* run away, escape. **z. de,** get rid of.

zafio, *a.* coarse, uncivil.

zafiro, *m.* sapphire.

zaguán, *m.* vestibule, hall.

zalamero -ra, *n.* flatterer, wheedler.

zambullir, *v.* plunge, dive.

zanahoria, *f.* carrot.

zanja, *f.* ditch, trench.

zapatería, *f.* shoe store; shoemaker's shop.

zapatero, *m.* shoemaker.

zapato, *m.* shoe.

zar, *m.* czar.

zaraza, *f.* calico; chintz.

zarza, *f.* bramble.

zarzuela, *f.* musical comedy.

zodíaco, *m.* zodiac.

zona, *f.* zone.

zoología, *f.* zoology.

zoológico, *a.* zoological.

zorro -rra, *n.* fox.

zozobra, *f.* worry, anxiety; capsizing.

zozobrar, *v.* capsize.

zumba, *f.* spanking.

zumbido, *m.* buzz, hum. —**zumbar,** *v.*

zumo, *m.* juice, sap.

zurcir, *v.* darn, mend.

zurdo, *a.* left-handed.

zurrar, *v.* flog, drub.

English-Spanish

A

a, *art.* un, una.

abacus, *n.* ábaco *m.*

abandon, 1. *n.* desenfreno, abandono *m.* 2. *v.* abandonar, desamparar.

abandoned, *a.* abandonado.

abandonment, *n.* abandono, desamparo *m.*

abase, *v.* degradar, humillar.

abasement, *n.* degradación, humillación *f.*

abash, *v.* avergonzar.

abate, *v.* menguar, moderarse.

abatement, *n.* disminución *f.*

abbess, *n.* abadesa *f.*

abbey, *n.* abadía *f.*

abbot, *n.* abad *m.*

abbreviate, *v.* abreviar.

abbreviation, *n.* abreviatura *f.*

abdicate, *v.* abdicar.

abdication, *n.* abdicación *f.*

abdomen, *n.* abdomen *m.*

abdominal, *a.* abdominal.

abduct, *v.* secuestrar.

abduction, *n.* secuestración *f.*

abductor, *n.* secuestrador *m.*

aberrant, *a.* extraviada.

aberration, *n.* error, extravío *m.*

abet, *v.* apoyar, favorecer.

abetment, *n.* apoyo *m.*

abettor, *n.* cómplice *m. & f.*

abeyance, *n.* suspensión *f.*

abhor, *v.* abominar, odiar.

abhorrence, *n.* detestación *f.*; aborrecimiento *m.*

abhorrent, *a.* detestable, aborrecible.

abide, *v.* soportar. **to a. by,** cumplir con.

abiding, *a.* perdurable.

ability, *n.* habilidad *f.*

abject, *a.* abyecto; desanimado.

abjuration, *n.* renuncia *f.*

abjure, *v.* renunciar.

ablative, *a. & n.* (gram.) ablativo *m.*

ablaze, *a.* en llamas.

able, *a.* capaz; competente. **to be a.,** poder.

able-bodied, *a.* robusto.

ablution, *n.* ablución *f.*

ably, *adv.* hábilmente.

abnegate, *v.* repudiar; negar.

abnegation, *n.* abnegación; repudiación *f.*

abnormal, *a.* anormal.

abnormality, *n.* anormalidad, deformidad *f.*

abnormally, *adv.* anormalmente.

aboard, *adv.* a bordo.

abode, *n.* residencia *f.*

abolish, *v.* suprimir.

abolishment, *n.* abolición *f.*

abolition, *n.* abolición *f.*

abominable, *a.* abominable.

abominate, *v.* abominar, detestar.

abomination, *n.* abominación; enormidad *f.*

aboriginal, *a.* primitivo.

abortion, *n.* aborto *m.*

abortive, *a.* abortivo.

abound, *v.* abundar.

about, 1. *adv.* como. **about to,** para; a punto de. 2. *prep.* de, sobre, acerca de.

about-face, *n.* (mil.) media vuelta.

above, 1. *adv.* arriba. 2. *prep.* sobre; por encima de.

aboveboard, 1. *a. & adv.* sincero, franco.

abrasion, *n.* raspadura *f.*; (med.) abrasión *f.*

abrasive, 1. *a.* raspante. 2. *n.* abrasivo *m.*

abreast, *adv.* de frente.

abridge, *v.* abreviar.

abridgment, *n.* abreviación *f.*; compendio *m.*

abroad, *adv.* en el extranjero, al extranjero.

abrogate, *v.* abrogar, revocar.

abrogation, *n.* abrogación, revocación *f.*

abrupt, *a.* repentino; brusco.

abruptly, *adv.* bruscamente, precipitadamente.

abruptness, *n.* precipitación; brusquedad *f.*

abscess, *n.* absceso *m.*

abscond, *v.* fugarse.

absence, *n.* ausencia, falta *f.*

absent, *a.* ausente.

absentee, *a. & n.* ausente *m.*

absent-minded, *a.* distraído.

absolute, *a.* absoluto.

absolutely, *adv.* absolutamente.

absoluteness, *n.* absolutismo *m.*

absolution, *n.* absolución *f.*

absolutism, *n.* absolutismo, despotismo *m.*

absolve, *v.* absolver.

absorb, *v.* absorber; preocupar.

absorbed, *a.* absorbido; absorto.

absorbent, *a.* absorbente.

absorbing, *a.* interesante.

absorption, *n.* absorción; preocupación *f.*

abstain, *v.* abstenerse.

abstemious, *a.* abstemio, sobrio.

abstinence, *n.* abstinencia *f.*

abstract, 1. *n.* resumen *m.* 2. *v.* abstraer.

abstracted, *a.* distraído.

abstraction, *n.* abstracción *f.*

abstruse, *a.* abstruso.

absurd, *a.* absurdo, ridículo.

absurdity, *n.* absurdo *m.*

absurdly, *adv.* absurdamente.

abundance, *n.* abundancia *f.*

abundant, *a.* abundante.

abundantly, *adv.* abundantemente.

abuse, 1. *n.* abuso *m.* 2. *v.* abusar de; maltratar.

abusive, *a.* abusivo.

abusively, *adv.* abusivamente, ofensivamente.

abut (on), *v.* terminar (en); lindar (con).

abutment, *n.* (building) estribo, contrafuerte *m.*

abyss, *n.* abismo *m.*

Abyssinian, *a. & n.* abisinio - nia.

academic, *a.* académico.

academy, *n.* academia *f.*

acanthus, *n.* (bot.) acanto *m.*

accede, *v.* acceder; consentir.

accelerate, *v.* acelerar.

acceleration, *n.* aceleración *f.*

accelerator, *n.* (auto.) acelerador *m.*

accent, 1. *n.* acento *m.* 2. *v.* acentuar.

accentuate, *v.* acentuar.

accept, *v.* aceptar.

acceptability, *n.* aceptabilidad *f.*

acceptable, *a.* aceptable.

acceptably, *adv.* aceptablemente.

acceptance, *n.* aceptación *f.*

access, *n.* acceso *m.*, entrada *f.*

accessible, *a.* accesible.

accessory, 1. *a.* accesorio. 2. *n.* cómplice *m. & f.*

accident, *n.* accidente *m.* **by a.,** por casualidad.

accidental, *a.* accidental.

accidentally, *adv.* accidentalmente, casualmente.

acclaim, *v.* aclamar.

acclamation, *n.* aclamación *f.*

acclimate, *v.* aclimatar.

acclivity, *n.* subida *f.*

accolade, *n.* acolada *f.*

accommodate, *v.* acomodar.

accommodating, *a.* bondadoso, complaciente.

accommodation, *n.* servicio *m.*; (pl.) alojamiento *m.*

accompaniment, *n.* acompañamiento *m.*

accompanist, *n.* acompañador *m.*

accompany, *v.* acompañar.

accomplice, *n.* cómplice *m. & f.*

accomplish, *v.* llevar a cabo; realizar.

accomplished, *a.* acabado, cumplido; culto.

accomplishment, *n.* realización *f.*; logro *m.*

accord, 1. *n.* acuerdo *m.* 2. *v.* otorgar.

accordance, *n.*: **in a. with,** de acuerdo con.

accordingly, *adv.* en conformidad.

according to, *prep.* según.

accordion, *n.* (mus.) acordeón *m.*

accost, *v.* dirigirse a.

account, 1. *n.* relato *m.*; (com.) cuenta *f.* **on a. of,** a causa de.

on no a., de ninguna manera.
2. v. a. for, explicar.
accountable, a. responsable.
accountant, n. contador -ra.
accounting, n. contabilidad f.
accouter, v. equipar, ataviar.
accouterments, n. equipo, atavío m.
accredit, v. acreditar.
accretion, n. aumento m.
accrual, n. aumento, incremento m.
accrue, v. provenir; acumularse.
accumulate, v. acumular.
accumulation, n. acumulación f.
accumulative, a. acumulativo.
accumulator, n. acumulador m.
accuracy, n. exactitud, precisión f.
accurate, a. exacto.
accursed, a. maldito.
accusation, n. acusación f., cargo m.
accusative, a. & n. acusativo m.
accuse, v. acusar.
accused, a. & n. acusado, procesado m.
accuser, n. acusador -ra.
accustom, v. acostumbrar.
accustomed, a. acostumbrado.
ace, 1. a. sobresaliente. 2. n. as m.
acerbity, n. acerbidad, amargura f.
acetate, n. (chem.) acetato m.
acetic, a. acético.
acetylene, 1. a. acetilénico. 2. n. (chem.) acetileno m.
ache, 1. n. dolor m. 2. v. doler.
achieve, v. lograr, llevar a cabo.
achievement, n. realización f.; hecho notable.
acid, a. & n. ácido m.
acidify, v. acidificar.
acidity, n. acidez f.
acidosis, n. (med.) acidismo m.
acid test, prueba decisiva.
acidulous, a. agrio, acídulo.
acknowledge, v. admitir (receipt) acusar.
acme, n. apogeo, colmo m.
acne, n. (med.) acne m. & f.; barros m.pl.
acolyte, n. acólito m.
acorn, n. bellota f.
acoustics, n. acústica f.
acquaint, v. familiarizar. to be acquainted with, conocer.
acquaintance, n. conocimiento m. (person known) conocido -da. to make the a. of, conocer.
acquainted, be acquainted with, v. conocer.
acquiesce, v. consentir.
acquiescence, n. consentimiento m.
acquire, v. adquirir.
acquirement, n. adquisición f.; (pl.) conocimientos m.pl.
acquisition, n. adquisición f.
acquisitive, a. adquisitivo.

acquit, v. exonerar, absolver.
acquittal, n. absolución f.
acre, n. acre m.
acreage, número de acres.
acrid, a. acre, picante.
acrimonious, a. acrimonioso, mordaz.
acrimony, n. acrimonia, aspereza f.
acrobat, n. acróbata m.
across, 1. adv. a través, al otro lado. 2. prep. al otro lado de, a través de.
acrostic, n. acróstico m.
act, 1. n. acción f.; acto m. 2. v. actuar, portarse. act as, hacer de. act on, decidir sobre.
acting, 1. a. interino. 2. n. acción f.; (theat.) representación f.
actinism, n. actinismo m.
actinium, n. (chem.) actinio m.
action, n. acción f. take a., tomar medidas.
activate, v. activar.
activation, n. activación f.
activator. n. (chem.) activador m.
active, a. activo.
activity, n. actividad f.
actor, n. actor m.
actress, n. actriz f.
actual, a. real, efectivo.
actuality, n. realidad, actualidad f.
actually, adv. en realidad.
actuary, n. actuario m.
actuate, v. impulsar, mover.
acumen, n. cacumen m., perspicacia f.
acupuncture, n. acupuntura f.
acute, a. agudo; perspicaz.
acutely, adv. agudamente.
acuteness, n. agudeza f.
adage, n. refrán, proverbio m.
adamant, a. firme.
Adam's apple, nuez de la garganta.
adapt, v. adaptar.
adaptable, a. adaptable.
adaptability, n. adaptabilidad f.
adaptation, n. adaptación f.
adapter, n. (tech.) adaptador m.; (mech.) ajustador m.
adaptive, a. adaptable, acomodable.
add, v. agregar, añadir. a. up, sumar.
adder, n. víbora f.; serpiente m.
addict, n. adicto f.; ('fan') aficionado m.
addition, n. adición f. in a. to, además de.
additional, a. adicional.
addle, v. confundir.
address, 1. n. dirección f.; señas f.pl. (speech) discurso. 2. v. dirigirse a.
addressee, n. destinatario -ia.
adduce, v. aducir.
adenoid, a. adenoideo.
adept, a. adepto.
adeptly, adv. diestramente.

adeptness, n. destreza f.
adequacy, n. suficiencia f.
adequate, a. adecuado.
adequately, adv. adecuadamente.
adhere, v. adherirse, pegarse.
adherence, n. adhesión f.; apego m.
adherent, n. adherente, partidario m.
adhesion, n. adhesión f.
adhesive, a. adhesivo. a. tape, esparadrapo m.
adhesiveness, n. adhesividad f.
adieu, 1. interj. adiós. 2. n. despedida f.
adjacent, a. adyacente.
adjective, n. adjetivo m.
adjoin, v. lindar (con).
adjoining, a. contiguo.
adjourn, v. suspender, levantar.
adjournment, n. suspensión f.; (leg.) espera f.
adjunct, n. adjunto m.; (gram.) atributo m.
adjust, v. ajustar, acomodar; arreglar.
adjuster, n. ajustador m.
adjustment, n. ajuste; arreglo m.
adjutant, n. (mil.) ayudante m.
administer, v. administrar.
administration, n. administración f.; gobierno m.
administrative, a. administrativo.
administrator, n. administrador m.
admirable, a. admirable.
admirably, adv. admirablemente.
admiral, n. almirante m.
admiralty, n. ministerio de marina.
admiration, n. admiración f.
admire, v. admirar.
admirer, n. admirador -ra; enamorado -da.
admiringly, adv. admirativamente.
admissible, a. admisible, aceptable.
admission, n. admisión; entrada f.
admit, v. admitir.
admittance, n. entrada f.
admittedly, adv. reconocidamente.
admixture, n. mezcla f.
admonish, v. amonestar.
admonition, n. admonición f.
adolescence, n. adolescencia f.
adolescent, n. & a. adolescente m.
adopt, v. adoptar.
adoption, n. adopción f.
adorable, a. adorable.
adoration, n. adoración f.
adore, v. adorar.
adorn, v. adornar.
adornment, n. adorno m.
adrenalin, n. adrenalina f.
adrift, adv. a la ventura.
adroit, a. diestro.

adulate, v. adular.

adulation, n. adulación f.

adult, a. & n. adulto m.

adulterant, a. & n. adulterante m.

adulterate, v. adulterar.

adulterer, n. adúltero m.

adulteress, n. adúltera f.

adultery, n. adulterio m.

advance, 1. n. avance; adelanto m. in a., de antemano, antes. 2. v. avanzar, adelantar.

advanced, a. avanzado, adelantado.

advancement, n. adelantamiento m.; promoción f.

advantage, n. ventaja f. take a. of, aprovecharse de.

advantageous, a. provechoso, ventajoso.

advantageously, adv. ventajosamente.

advent, n. venida, llegada f.

adventitious, a. adventicio, espontáneo.

adventure, n. aventura f.

adventurer, n. aventurero m.

adventurous, a. aventurero, intrépido.

adventurously, adv. arriesgadamente.

adverb, n. adverbio m.

adverbial, a. adverbial.

adversary, n. adversario m.

adverse, a. adverso.

adversely, adv. adversamente.

adversity, n. adversidad f.

advert, v. hacer referencia a.

advertise, v. avisar, anunciar.

advertisement, n. aviso, anuncio m.

advertiser, n. anunciante, avisador m.

advertising, n. publicidad f.

advice, n. consejos m.pl.

advisability, n. prudencia, propiedad f.

advisable, a. aconsejable, prudente.

advisably, adv. prudentemente.

advise, v. aconsejar.

advisedly, adv. avisadamente, prudentemente.

advisement, n. consideración f.; take under a., someter a estudio.

adviser, n. consejero m.

advocacy, n. abogacía; defensa f.

advocate, 1. n. abogado m. 2. v. apoyar.

aegis, n. amparo m.

aerate, v. airear, ventilar.

aeration, n. aeración, ventilación f.

aerial, a. aéreo.

aerie, n. nido de águila.

aeronautics, n. aeronáutica f.

aerosol bomb, n. bomba insecticida.

afar, adv. lejos. from a., de lejos, desde lejos.

affability, n. afabilidad, amabilidad f.

affable, a. afable.

affably, adv. afablemente.

affair, n. asunto m. love a., aventura amorosa.

affect, v. afectar; (emotionally) conmover.

affectation, n. afectación f.

affected, a. artificioso.

affecting, a. conmovedor.

affection, n. cariño m.

affectionate, a. afectuoso, cariñoso.

affectionately, adv. afectuosamente, con cariño.

affiance, v. dar palabra de casamiento; become affianced, comprometerse.

affidavit, n. (leg.) declaración, deposición f.

affiliate, 1. n. afiliado m. 2. v. afiliar.

affiliation, n. afiliación f.

affinity, n. afinidad f.

affirm, v. afirmar.

affirmation, n. afirmación, aserción f.

affirmative, 1. n. afirmativa f. 2. a. afirmativo.

affirmatively, adv. afirmativamente, aseveradamente.

affix, 1. n. (gram.) afijo m. 2. v. fijar, pegar, poner.

afflict, v. afligir.

affliction, n. aflicción f.; mal m.

affluence, n. abundancia, opulencia f.

affluent, a. opulento, afluente.

afford, v. proporcionar. be able to a., tener con que comprar.

affront, 1. n. afrenta f. 2. v. afrentar, insultar.

afield, adv. lejos de casa; lejos del camino; lejos del asunto.

afire, adv. ardiendo.

afloat, adv. (naut.) a flote.

aforementioned, aforesaid, a. dicho, susodicho.

afraid, a. to be a., tener miedo, temer.

African, n. & a. africano -na.

aft, adv. (naut.) a popa, en popa.

after, 1. prep. después de. 2. conj. después que.

aftermath, n. resultados m.pl, consecuencias f.pl.

afternoon, n. tarde f. good a., buenas tardes.

afterthought, n. idea tardía.

afterward(s), adv. después.

again, adv. otra vez, de nuevo. to do a., volver a hacer.

against, prep. contra; en contra de.

agape, adv. con la boca abierta.

agate, n. ágata f.

age, 1. n. edad f. of a., mayor de edad. old a., vejez f. 2. v. envejecer.

aged, a. viejo, anciano, añejo.

ageism, n. discriminación contra las personas de edad.

ageless, a. sempiterno.

agency, n. agencia f.

agenda, n. agenda f., orden m.

agent, n. agente; representante m.

agglutinate, v. aglutinar.

agglutination, n. aglutinación f.

aggrandize, v. agrandar; elevar.

aggrandizement, n. engrandecimiento m.

aggravate, v. agravar; irritar.

aggravation, n. agravamiento; empeoramiento m.

aggregate, a. & n. agregado m.

aggregation, n. agregación f.

aggression, n. agresión f.

aggressive, n. agresivo.

aggressively, adv. agresivamente.

aggressiveness, n. agresividad f.

aggressor, n. agresor m.

aghast, a. horrorizado.

agile, a. ágil.

agility, n. agilidad, ligereza, prontitud f.

agitate, v. agitar.

agitation, n. agitación f.

agitator, n. agitador m.

agnostic, a. & n. agnóstico m.

ago, adv. hace. two days a., hace dos días.

agonized, v. angustioso.

agony, n. sufrimiento m.; angustia f.

agrarian, a. agrario.

agree, v. estar de acuerdo; convenir. a. with one, sentar bien.

agreeable, a. agradable.

agreeably, adv. agradablemente.

agreement, n. acuerdo m.

agriculture, n. agricultura f.

ahead, adv. adelante.

aid, 1. n. ayuda f. 2. v. ayudar.

aide, n. ayudante m.

ailing, adj. enfermo.

ailment, n. enfermedad f.

aim, 1. n. puntería f.; (purpose) propósito m. 2. v. apuntar.

aimless, a. sin objeto.

air, n. aire m. by a. por avión. 2. v. ventilar, airear.

airbag, n. (in automobiles) saco de aire m.

air-conditioned, a. enfriado por aire.

air-conditioning, acondicionamiento del aire.

aircraft, n. máquina de volar.

aircraft carrier, n. portaaviones m.

airing, n. ventilación f.

airline, n. línea aérea.

airliner, n. avión de transporte.

airmail, n. correo aéreo.

airplane, n. avión, aeroplano m.

air pollution, contaminación atmosférica.

airport, n. aeropuerto m.

air pressure, presión atmosférica.

air raid, ataque aéreo.

airsick, *a.* mareado.

airtight, *a.* hermético.

aisle, *n.* pasillo *m.*

ajar, *a.* entreabierto.

akin, *a.* emparentado, semejante.

alacrity, *n.* alacridad, presteza *f.*

alarm, 1. *n.* alarma *f.* **2.** *v.* alarmar.

alarmist, *n.* alarmista *m. & f.*

albino, *n.* albino -na.

album, *n.* album *m.*

alcohol, *n.* alcohol *m.*

alcoholic, *a.* alcohólico.

alcove, *n.* alcoba *f.*

ale, *n.* cerveza inglesa.

alert, 1. *n.* alarma *f.* **on the a.,** alerta, sobre aviso. **2.** *a.* listo, vivo. **3.** *v.* poner sobre aviso.

alfalfa, *n.* alfalfa *f.*

algebra, *n.* álgebra *f.*

alias, *n.* alias *m.*

alibi, *n.* excusa *f.;* (leg.) coartada *f.*

alien, 1. *a.* ajeno, extranjero. **2.** *n.* extranjero -ra.

alienate, *v.* enajenar.

alight, *v.* bajar, apearse.

align, *v.* alinear.

alike, 1. *a.* semejante, igual. **2.** *adv.* del mismo modo, igualmente.

alimentary canal, tubo digestivo.

alive, *a.* vivo; animado.

alkali, *n.* (chem.) álcali, cali *m.*

alkaline, *a.* alcalino.

all, *a. & pron.* todo. **not at a.,** de ninguna manera, nada.

allay, *v.* aquietar.

allegation, *n.* alegación *f.*

allege, *v.* alegar; pretender.

allegiance, *n.* lealtad *f.;* (to country) homenaje *m.*

allegory, *n.* alegoría *f.*

allergy, *n.* alergia *f.*

alleviate, *v.* aliviar.

alley, *n.* callejón *m.* **bowling a.,** bolera *f.,* boliche *m.*

alliance, *n.* alianza *f.*

allied, *a.* aliado.

alligator, *n.* caimán *m.;* (Mex.) lagarto *m.* **a. pear,** aguacate *m.*

allocate, *v.* colocar, asignar.

allot, *v.* asignar.

allotment, *n.* lote, porción *f.*

allow, *v.* permitir, dejar.

allowance, *n.* abono *m.;* dieta *f.* **make a. for,** tener en cuenta.

alloy, *n.* mezcla *f.* (metal) aleación *f.*

all right, está bien.

allude, *v.* aludir.

allure, 1. *n.* atracción *f.* **2.** *v.* atraer, tentar.

alluring, *a.* tentador, seductivo.

allusion, *n.* alusión *f.*

ally, 1. *n.* aliado *m.* **2.** *v.* aliar.

almanac, *n.* almanaque *m.*

almighty, *a.* todopoderoso.

almond, *n.* almendra *f.*

almost, *adv.* casi.

alms, *n.* limosna *f.*

aloft, *adv.* arriba, en alto.

alone, *adv.* solo, a solas. **to leave a.,** dejar en paz.

along, *prep.* por; a lo largo de. **a. with,** junto con.

alongside, 1. *adv.* al lado. **2.** *prep.* junto a.

aloof, *a.* apartado.

aloud, *adv.* en voz alta.

alpaca, *n.* alpaca *f.*

alphabet, *n.* alfabeto *m.*

alphabetical, *a.* alfabético.

alphabetize, *v.* alfabetizar.

already, *adv.* ya.

also, *adv.* también.

altar, *n.* altar *m.*

alter, *v.* alterar.

alteration, *n.* alteración *f.*

alternate, 1. *a.* alterno. **2.** *n.* substituto -ta. **3.** *v.* alternar.

alternative, 1. *a.* alternativo. **2.** *n.* alternativa *f.*

although, *conj.* aunque.

altitude, *n.* altura *f.*

alto, *n.* contralto *m.*

altogether, *adv.* en junto; enteramente.

altruism, *n.* altruismo *m.*

alum, *n.* alumbre *m.*

aluminum, *n.* aluminio *m.*

always, *adv.* siempre.

amalgam, *n.* amalgama *f.*

amalgamate, *v.* amalgamar.

amass, *v.* amontonar.

amateur, *n.* aficionado -da.

amaze, *v.* asombrar; sorprender.

amazement, *n.* asombro *m.*

amazing, *a.* asombroso, pasmoso.

ambassador, *n.* embajador *m.*

amber, 1. *a.* ambarino. **2.** *n.* ámbar *m.*

ambidextrous, *a.* ambidextro.

ambiguity, *n.* ambigüedad *f.*

ambiguous, *a.* ambiguo.

ambition, *n.* ambición *f.*

ambitious, *a.* ambicioso.

ambulance, *n.* ambulancia *f.*

ambush, 1. *n.* emboscada *f.* **2.** *v.* acechar.

ameliorate, *v.* mejorar.

amenable, *a.* tratable, dócil.

amend, *v.* enmendar.

amendment, *n.* enmienda *f.*

amenity, *n.* amenidad *f.*

American, *a. & n.* americano -na, norteamericano -na.

amethyst, *n.* amatista *f.*

amiable, *a.* amable.

amicable, *a.* amigable.

amid, *prep.* entre, en medio de.

amidships, *adv.* (naut.) en medio del navío.

amiss, *adv.* mal. **to take a.,** llevar a mal.

amity, *n.* amistad, armonía *f.*

ammonia, *n.* amoníaco *m.*

ammunition, *n.* munición *f.*

amnesia, *n.* (med.) amnesia *f.*

amnesty, *n.* amnistía *f.,* indulto *m.*

amniocentesis, *n.* amniocéntesis *m.*

amoeba, *n.* amiba *f.*

among, *prep.* entre.

amoral, *a.* amoral.

amorous, *a.* amoroso.

amorphous, *a.* amorfo.

amortize, *v.* (com.) amortizar.

amount, 1. *n.* cantidad, suma *f.* **2.** *v.* **a. to,** subir a.

ampere, *n.* (elec.) amperio *m.*

amphibian, *a. & n.* anfibio *m.*

amphitheater, *n.* anfiteatro, circo *m.*

ample, *a.* amplio; suficiente.

amplify, *v.* amplificar.

amputate, *v.* amputar.

amuse, *v.* entretener, divertir.

amusement, *n.* diversión *f.*

an, *art.* un, una.

anachronism, *n.* anacronismo, *m.*

analogous, *a.* análogo, parecido.

analogy, *n.* analogía *f.*

analysis, *n.* análisis *m. & f.*

analyst, *n.* analizador *m.*

analytic, *a.* analítico.

analyze, *v.* analizar.

anarchy, *n.* anarquía *f.*

anatomy, *n.* anatomía *f.*

ancestor, *n.* antepasado *m.*

ancestral, *a.* de los antepasados, hereditario.

ancestry, *n.* linaje, abolengo *m.*

anchor, 1. *n.* ancla *f.* **to weigh a.,** levar el ancla. **2.** *v.* anclar.

anchorage, *n.* (naut.) ancladero, anclaje *m.*

anchovy, *n.* anchoa *f.*

ancient, *a. & n.* antiguo.

and, *conj.* y, (before *i-*, *hi-*) e.

anecdote, *n.* anécdota *f.*

anemia, *n.* (med.) anemia *f.*

anesthetic, *n.* anestesia *f.*

anew, *adv.* de nuevo.

angel, *n.* ángel *m.*

anger, 1. *n.* ira *f.,* enojo *m.* **2.** *v.* enfadar, enojar.

angle, *n.* ángulo *m.*

angry, *a.* enojado, enfadado.

anguish, *n.* angustia *f.*

angular, *a.* angular.

aniline, *n.* (chem.) anilina *f.*

animal, *a. & n.* animal *m.*

animate, 1. *adj.* animado. **2.** *v.* animar.

animated, *a.* vivo, animado.

animation, *n.* animación, viveza *f.*

animosity, *n.* rencor *m.*

anise, *n.* anís *m.*

ankle, *n.* tobillo *m.*

annals, *n.pl.* anales *m.pl.*

annex, 1. *n.* anexo *m.,* adición *f.* **2.** *v.* anexar.

annexation, *n.* anexión, adición *f.*

annihilate, *v.* aniquilar, destruir.

anniversary, *n.* aniversario *m.*

annotate, *v.* anotar.

annotation, *n.* anotación *f.,* apunte *m.*

announce, *v.* anunciar.

announcement, *n.* anuncio, aviso *m.*

announcer, *n.* anunciador *m.;* (radio) anunciador, noticiador *m.*

annoy, *v.* molestar.

annoyance, *n.* molestia, incomodidad *f.*

annual, *a.* anual.

annuity, *n.* anualidad, pensión *f.*

annul, *v.* anular, invalidar.

anode, *n.* (elec.) ánodo *m.*

anoint, *v.* untar; (rel.) ungir.

anomalous, *a.* anómalo, irregular.

anonymous, *a.* anónimo.

another, *a.* & *pron.* otro.

answer, **1.** *n.* contestación, respuesta *f.* **2.** *v.* contestar, responder. **a. for,** ser responsable de.

answerable, *a.* discutible, refutable.

ant, *n.* hormiga *f.*

antacid, *a.* & *n.* antiácido *m.*

antagonism, *n.* antagonismo *m.*

antagonist, *n.* antagonista *m.*

antagonistic, *a.* antagónico, hostil.

antagonize, *v.* contrariar.

antarctic, *a.* & *n.* antártico *m.*

antecedent, *a.* & *n.* antecedente *m.*

antedate, *v.* antedatar.

antelope, *n.* antílope *m.,* gacela *f.*

antenna, *n.* antena *f.*

anterior, *a.* anterior.

anteroom, *n.* antecámara *f.*

anthem, *n.* himno *m.;* (religious) antífona *f.*

anthology, *n.* antología *f.*

anthracite, *n.* antracita *f.*

anthrax, *n.* (med.) ántrax *m.*

anthropology, *n.* antropología *f.*

antiaircraft, *a.* antiaéreo.

antibody, *n.* anticuerpo *m.*

anticipate, *v.* esperar, anticipar.

anticipation, *n.* anticipación *f.*

anticlerical, *a.* anticlerical.

anticlimax, *n.* anticlímax *m.*

antidote, *n.* antídoto *m.*

antimony, *n.* antimonio *m.*

antinuclear, *a.* antinuclear.

antipathy, *n.* antipatía *f.*

antiquated, *a.* anticuado.

antique, **1.** *a.* antiguo. **2.** *n.* antigüedad *f.*

antiquity, *n.* antigüedad *f.*

antiseptic, *a.* & *n.* antiséptico *m.*

antisocial, *a.* antisocial.

antitoxin, *n.* (med.) antitoxina *f.*

antler, *n.* asta *f.*

anvil, *n.* yunque *m.*

anxiety, *n.* ansia, ansiedad *f.*

anxious, *a.* inquieto, ansioso.

any, *a.* alguno; (at all) cualquiera; (after *not*) ninguno.

anybody, *pron.* alguien; (at all) cualquiera; (after *not*) nadie.

anyhow, *adv.* de todos modos; en todo caso.

anyone, *pron.* = anybody.

anything, *pron.* algo; (at all) cualquier cosa; (after *not*) nada.

anyway, *adv.* = anyhow.

anywhere, *adv.* en alguna parte; (at all) dondequiera; (after *not*) en ninguna parte.

apart, *adv.* aparte. **to take a.,** deshacer.

apartheid, *n.* apartheid *m.*

apartment, *n.* apartamento, piso *m.*

apathetic, *a.* apático.

apathy, *n.* apatía *f.*

ape, **1.** *n.* mono *m.* **2.** *v.* imitar.

aperture, *n.* abertura *f.*

apex, *n.* ápice *m.*

aphorism, *n.* aforismo *m.*

apiary, *n.* apiario, abejar *m.*

apiece, *adv.* por persona; cada uno.

apologetic, *a.* apologético.

apologist, *n.* apologista *m.* & *f.*

apologize, *v.* excusarse, disculparse.

apology, *n.* excusa; apología *f.*

apoplectic, *a.* apoplético.

apoplexy, *n.* apoplejía *f.*

apostate, *n.* apóstata *m.* & *f.*

apostle, *n.* apóstol *m.*

apostolic, *a.* apostólico.

appall, *v.* espantar; desmayar.

apparatus, *n.* aparato *m.*

apparel, *n.* ropa *f.*

apparent, *a.* aparente; claro.

apparition, *n.* fantasma *f.*

appeal, **1.** *n.* súplica *f.;* interés *m.;* (leg.) apelación *f.* **2.** *v.* apelar, suplicar; interesar.

appear, *v.* aparecer, asomar; (seem) parecer; (leg.) comparecer.

appearance, *n.* apariencia *f.,* aspecto *m.*

appease, *v.* aplacar, apaciguar.

appeasement, *n.* apaciguamiento *m.*

appeaser, *n.* apaciguador, pacificador *m.*

appellant, *n.* apelante, demandante *m.*

appellate, *a.* (leg.) de apelación.

appendage, *n.* pertenencia *f.*

appendectomy, *n.* (med.) apendectomía *f.*

appendicitis, *n.* (med.) apendicitis *m.*

appendix, *n.* apéndice *m.*

appetite, *n.* apetito *m.*

appetizer, *n.* apertivo *m.*

appetizing, *a.* apetitivo.

applaud, *v.* aplaudir.

applause, *n.* aplauso *m.*

apple, *n.* manzana *f.* **a. tree,** manzano *m.*

applesauce, *n.* compota de manzana.

appliance, *n.* utensilio, aparato *m.*

applicable, *a.* aplicable.

applicant, *n.* suplicante *m.* & *f.;* candidato -ta.

application, *n.* solicitud *f.*

applied, *a.* aplicado. **a. for,** pedido.

appliqué, *n.* (sewing) aplicación *f.*

apply, *v.* aplicar. **a. for,** solicitar, pedir.

appoint, *v.* nombrar.

appointment, *n.* nombramiento, puesto *m.*

apportion, *v.* repartir.

apposition, *n.* (gram.) aposición *f.*

appraisal, *n.* valoración *f.;* apremio *m.*

appraise, *v.* avaluar, tasar; estimar.

appreciable, *a.* apreciable; notable.

appreciate, *v.* apreciar, estimar.

appreciation, *n.* aprecio; reconocimiento *m.*

apprehend, *v.* prender, capturar.

apprehension, *n.* aprensión *f.*

apprehensive, *a.* aprensivo.

apprentice, *n.* aprendiz *m.*

apprise, *v.* informar.

approach, **1.** *n.* acceso; método *m.* **2.** *v.* acercarse.

approachable, *a.* accesible.

approbation, *n.* aprobación *f.*

appropriate, **1.** *a.* apropiado. **2.** *v.* apropiar.

appropriation, *n.* apropiación *f.*

approval, *n.* aprobación *f.*

approve, *v.* aprobar.

approximate, **1.** *a.* aproximado. **2.** *v.* aproximar.

approximately, *adv.* aproximadamente.

approximation, *n.* aproximación *f.*

appurtenance, *n.* pertenencia *f.*

apricot, *n.* albaricoque, damasco *m.*

April, *n.* abril *m.*

apron, *n.* delantal *m.*

apropos, *adv.* a propósito.

apt, *a.* apto; capaz.

aptitude, *n.* aptitud; facilidad *f.*

aquarium, *n.* acuario *m.,* pecera *f.*

aquatic, *a.* acuático.

aqueduct, *n.* acueducto *m.*

aqueous, *a.* ácueo, acuoso, aguoso.

aquiline, *a.* aquilino, aguileño.

Arab, *a.* & *n.* árabe *m.* & *f.*

arable, *a.* cultivable.

arbitrary, *a.* arbitrario.

arbitrate, *v.* arbitrar.

arbitration, *n.* arbitraje *m.,* arbitración *f.*

arbitrator, *n.* arbitrador -ra.

arbor, *n.* emparrado *m.*

arboreal, *a.* arbóreo.

arc, n. arco m.

arch, 1. n. arco m. 2. v. arquear, encorvar.

archaeology, n. arqueología f.

archaic, a. arcaico.

archbishop, n. arzobispo m.

archdiocese, n. archidiócesis m.

archduke, n. archiduque m.

archer, n. arquero m.

archery, n. ballestería f.

archipelago, n. archipiélago m.

architect, n. arquitecto m.

architectural, a. arquitectural.

architecture, n. arquitectura f.

archive, n. archivo m.

archway, n. arcada f.

arctic, a. ártico.

ardent, a. ardiente.

ardor, n. ardor m., pasión f.

arduous, a. arduo, difícil.

area, n. área; extensión f.

area code, prefijo m.

arena, n. arena f.

Argentine, a. & n. argentino - na.

argue, v. disputar; sostener.

argument, n. disputa f.; razonamiento m.

argumentative, a. argumentoso.

aria, n. (mus.) aria f.

arid, a. árido, seco.

arise, v. surgir.

aristocracy, n. aristocracia f.

aristocrat, n. aristócrata m.

aristocratic, a. aristocrático.

arithmetic, n. aritmética f.

ark, n. arca f.

arm, 1. n. brazo m.; (weapon) arma f. 2. v. armar.

armament, n. armamento m.

armchair, n. sillón m., butaca f.

armed forces, fuerzas militares.

armful, n. brazada f.

armhole, n. (sew.) sobaquera f.

armistice, n. armisticio m.

armor, n. armadura f., blindaje m.

armored, a. blindado.

armory, n. armería f., arsenal m.

armpit, n. sobaco m.

army, n. ejército m.

arnica, n. árnica f.

aroma, n. fragancia f.

aromatic, a. aromático.

around, prep. alrededor de, a la vuelta de; cerca de a. here, por aquí.

arouse, v. despertar; excitar.

arraign, v. (leg.) procesar criminalmente.

arrange, v. arreglar; concertar; (mus.) adaptar.

arrangement, n. arreglo; orden m.

array, 1. n. orden; adorno m. 2. v. adornar.

arrears, n. atrasos m.pl.

arrest, 1. n. detención f. 2. v. detener, arrestar.

arrival, n. llegada f.

arrive, v. llegar.

arrogance, n. arrogancia f.

arrogant, a. arrogante.

arrogate, v. arrogarse, usurpar.

arrow, n. flecha f.

arrowhead, n. punta de flecha.

arsenal, n. arsenal m.

arsenic, n. arsénico m.

arson, n. incendio premeditado.

art, arte m. (f. in pl.); (skill) maña f.

arterial, a. arterial.

arteriosclerosis, n. arteriosclerosis m.

artery, n. arteria f.

artesian well, pozo artesiano.

artful, a. astuto.

arthritis, n. artritis m.

artichoke, n. alcachofa f.

article, n. artículo m.

articulate, v. articular.

articulation, n. articulación f.

artifice, n. artificio m.

artificial, a. artificial.

artificially, adv. artificialmente.

artillery, n. artillería f.

artisan, n. artesano m.

artist, n. artista m. & f.

artistic, a. artístico.

artistry, n. arte m. & f.

artless, a. natural, cándido.

as, adv. & conj. como; as ... as ... tan ... como.

asbestos, n. asbesto m.

ascend, v. ascender.

ascendancy, n. ascendiente m.

ascendant, a. ascendente.

ascent, n. subida f., ascenso m.

ascertain, v. averiguar.

ascetic, 1. a. ascético. 2. n. asceta m. & f.

ascribe, v. atribuir.

ash, n. ceniza f.

ashamed, a. avergonzado.

ashen, a. pálido.

ashore, adv. a tierra. go a., desembarcar.

ashtray, n. cenicero m.

Asiatic, a. & n. asiático -ca.

aside, adv. al lado. a. from. aparte de.

ask, v. preguntar; invitar; (request) pedir. a. for, pedir. a. a question, hacer una pregunta.

askance, adv. de soslayo; con recelo.

asleep, a. dormido. to fall a., dormirse.

asparagus, n. espárrago m.

aspect, n. aspecto m., apariencia f.

asperity, n. aspereza f.

aspersion, n. calumnia f.

asphalt, n. asfalto m.

asphyxia, n. asfixia f.

asphyxiate, v. asfixiar, sofocar.

aspirant, a. & n. aspirante.

aspirate, v. aspirar.

aspiration, n. aspiración f.

aspirator, n. aspirador m.

aspire, v. aspirar. a. to, ambicionar.

aspirin, n. aspirina f.

ass, n. asno, burro m.

assail, v. asaltar, acometer.

assailant, n. asaltador m.

assassin, n. asesino m.

assassinate, v. asesinar.

assassination, n. asesinato m.

assault, 1. n. asalto m. 2. v. asaltar, atacar.

assay, v. examinar; ensayar.

assemblage, n. asamblea f.

assemble, v. juntar, convocar; (mechanism) montar.

assembly, n. asamblea, concurrencia f.

assent, 1. n. asentimiento m. 2. v. asentir, convenir.

assert, v. afirmar, aseverar. a. oneself, hacerse sentir.

assertion, n. aserción, aseveración f.

assertive, a. asertivo.

assess, v. tasar, avaluar.

assessor, n. asesor m.

asset, n. ventaja f. assets, (com.) capital m.

asseverate, v. aseverar, afirmar.

asseveration, n. aseveración f.

assiduous, a. asiduo.

assiduously, adv. asiduamente.

assign, v. asignar; destinar.

assignable, a. asignable, transferible.

assignation, n. asignación f.

assignment, n. misión; tarea f.

assimilate, v. asimilar.

assimilation, n. asimilación f.

assimilative, a. asimilativo.

assist, v. ayudar, auxiliar.

assistance, n. ayuda f., auxilio m.

assistant, n. ayudante, asistente m.

associate, 1. n. socio m. 2. v. asociar.

association, n. asociación; sociedad f.

assonance, n. asonancia f.

assort, v. surtir con variedad.

assorted, a. variado, surtido.

assortment, n. surtido m.

assuage, v. mitigar, aliviar.

assume, v. suponer; asumir.

assuming, a. presuntuoso. a. that, dado que.

assumption, n. suposición; (rel.) asunción f.

assurance, n. seguridad; confianza f.

assure, v. asegurar; dar confianza.

assured, 1. a. seguro. 2. a. & n. (com.) asegurado m.

assuredly, adv. ciertamente.

aster, n. (bot.) aster m.

asterisk, n. asterisco m.

astern, adv. (naut.) a popa.

asteroid, n. asteroide m.

asthma, n. (med.) asma f.

astigmatism, n. astigmatismo m.

astir, adv. en movimiento.

astonish, v. asombrar, pasmar.

astonishment, n. asombro m., sorpresa f.

astound, v. pasmar, sorprender.

astral, a. astral, estelar.

astray, a. desviado.

astride, adv. a horcajadas.

astringent, a. & n. astringente m.

astrology, n. astrología f.

astronaut, n. astronauta m.

astronomy, n. astronomía f.

astute, a. astuto; agudo.

asunder, adv. en dos.

asylum, n. asilo, refugio m.

asymmetry, n. asimetría f.

at, prep. a, en; cerca de.

ataxia, n. (med.) ataxia f.

atheist, n. ateo m.

athlete, n. atleta m.

athletic, a. atlético.

athletics, n. atletismo m., deportes m.pl.

athwart, prep. á través de.

Atlantic, 1. a. atlántico. 2. n. Atlántico m.

Atlantic Ocean, el mar atlántico.

atlas, n. atlas m.

atmosphere, n. atmósfera f.; (fig.) ambiente m.

atmospheric, a. atmosférico.

atoll, n. atolón m.

atom, n. átomo m.

atomic, a. atómico.

atomic bomb, bomba atómica.

atomic energy, energía atómica.

atomic theory, teoría atómica.

atomic weight, peso atómico.

atonal, a. (mus.) atonal.

atone, v. expiar, compensar.

atonement, n. expiación; reparación f.

atrocious, a. atroz.

atrocity, n. atrocidad f.

atrophy, 1. n. (med.) atrofia f. 2. v. atrofiar.

atropine, n. (chem.) atropina f.

attach, v. juntar; prender; (hook) enganchar; (fig.) atribuir.

attaché, n. agregado m.

attachment, 1. enlace m.; accesorio m.; (emotional) afecto, cariño m.

attack, 1. n. ataque m. 2. v. atacar.

attacker, n. asaltador m.

attain, v. lograr, alcanzar.

attainable, a. accesible, realizable.

attainment, n. logro; (pl.) dotes f.pl.

attempt, 1. n. ensayo; esfuerzo m.; tentativa f. 2. v. ensayar, intentar.

attend, v. atender; (a meeting) asistir a.

attendance, n. asistencia; presencia f.

attendant, 1. a. concomitante. 2. n. servidor -ra.

attention, n. atención f.; obsequio m. **to pay a. to,** hacer caso a.

attentive, a. atento.

attentively, adv. atentamente.

attenuate, v. atenuar, adelgazar.

attest, v. confirmar, atestiguar.

attic, n. desván m., guardilla f.

attire, 1. n. traje m. 2. v. vestir.

attitude, n. actitud f., ademán m.

attorney, n. abogado, apoderado m.

attract, v. atraer. **a. attention,** llamar la atención.

attraction, n. atracción f., atractivo m.

attractive, a. atractivo; simpático.

attributable, a. atribuible, imputable.

attribute, 1. n. atributo m. 2. v. atribuir.

attrition, n. roce, desgaste m.; atrición f.

attune, v. armonizar.

auction, n. subasta f., (S.A.) venduta f.

auctioneer, n. subastador m., (S.A.) martillero m.

audacious, a. audaz.

audacity, n. audacia f.

audible, a. audible.

audience, n. auditorio, público m.; entrevista f.

audiovisual, a. audiovisual.

audit, v. revisar cuentas.

audition, n. audición f.

auditor, n. interventor, revisor m.

auditorium, n. sala f.; teatro m.

auditory, a. & n. auditorio m.

augment, v. aumentar.

augur, v. augurar, pronosticar.

August, n. agosto m.

aunt, n. tía f.

auspice, n. auspicio m.

auspicious, a. favorable; propicio.

austere, a. austero.

austerity, n. austeridad, severidad f.

Austrian, a. & n. austríaco -ca.

authentic, a. auténtico.

authenticate, v. autenticar.

authenticity, n. autenticidad f.

author, n. autor, escritor m.

authoritarian, a. & n. autoritario m.

authoritative, a. autoritario; autorizado.

authoritatively, adv. autorizadamente.

authority, n. autoridad f.

authorization, n. autorización f.

authorize, v. autorizar.

auto, n. auto, automóvil m.

autobiography, n. autobiografía f.

autocracy, n. autocracia f.

autocrat, n. autócrata m. & f.

autograph, n. autógrafo m.

automatic, a. automático.

automatically, adv. automáticamente.

automobile, n. automóvil, coche m.

automotive, a. automotriz.

autonomy, n. autonomía f.

autopsy, n. autopsia f.

autumn, n. otoño m.

auxiliary, a. auxiliar.

avail, 1. n. of **no a.,** en vano. 2. v. **a. oneself of,** aprovechar.

available, a. disponible.

avalanche, n. alud m.

avarice, n. avaricia, codicia f.

avariciously, adv. avaramente.

avenge, v. vengar.

avenger, n. vengador -ra.

avenue, n. avenida f.

average, 1. a. medio; común. 2. n. promedio, término medio m. 3. v. calcular el promedio.

averse, a. adverso.

aversion, n. aversión f.

avert, v. desviar; impedir.

aviary, n. pajarera, avería f.

aviation, n. aviación f.

aviator, n. aviador -ra.

aviatrix, n. aviatriz f.

avid, a. ávido.

avocation, n. pasatiempo f.

avoid, v. evitar.

avoidable, a. evitable.

avoidance, n. evitación f.; (leg.) anulación f.

avow, v. declarar; admitir.

avowal, n. admisión f.

avowed, a. reconocido; admitido.

avowedly, adv. reconocidamente; confesadamente.

await, v. esperar, aguardar.

awake, a. despierto.

awaken, v. despertar.

award, 1. n. premio m. 2. v. otorgar.

aware, a. enterado, consciente.

awash, a. & adv. (naut.) a flor de agua.

away, adv. (see under verb: **go away, put away, take away,** etc.)

awe, n. pavor m.

awesome, a. pavoroso; aterrador.

awful, a. horrible, terrible, muy malo.

awhile, adv. por un rato.

awkward, a. torpe, desmañado; (fig.) delicado, embarazoso.

awning, n. toldo m.

awry, a. oblicuo, torcido.

ax, axe, n. hacha f.

axiom, n. axioma m.

axis, n. eje m.

axle, n. eje m.

ayatollah, n. ayatola m.

azure, a. azulado.

B

babble, 1. n. balbuceo, murmullo m. 2 v. balbucear.

babbler, n. hablador -ra, charlador -ra.

baboon, n. mandril m.

baby, n. nene, bebé m.

babyish, *a.* infantil.

bachelor, *n.* soltero *m.*

bacillus, *n.* bacilo, microbio *m.*

back, 1. *adv.* atrás. **to be b.,** estar de vuelta. **b. of,** detrás de. 2. *n.* espalda *f.;* (of animal) lomo *m.*

backbone, *n.* espinazo *m.;* (fig.) firmeza *f.*

backer, *n.* sostenedor -ra.

background, *n.* fondo *m.* antecedentes *m.pl.*

backing, *n.* apoyo *m.,* garantía *f.*

backlash, *n.* repercusión negativa.

backlog, *n.* rezago *m.*

backpack, *n.* mochila *f.*

backstage, *n.* entre bastidores *m.*

backward, 1. *a.* atrasado. 2. *adv.* hacia atrás.

backwardness, *n.* atraso *m.*

backwater, *n.* remolino *m.;* contracorriente *f.*

backwoods, *n.* monte *m.;* región apartada.

bacon, *n.* tocino *m.*

bacteria, *n.* bacterias *f.pl.*

bacteriologist, *n.* bacteriólogo *m.*

bacteriology, *n.* bacteriología *f.*

bad, *a.* malo.

badge, *n.* insignia, divisa *f.*

badger, 1. *n.* tejón *m.* 2. *v.* atormentar.

badly, *adv.* mal.

badness, *n.* maldad *f.*

bad-tempered, *a.* de mal humor.

baffle, *v.* desconcertar.

bafflement, *n.* contrariedad; confusión *f.*

bag, 1. *n.* saco *m.;* bolsa *f.* 2. *v.* ensacar, cazar.

baggage, *n.* equipaje *m.* **b. check,** talón *m.*

baggage cart (airport), carrillo para llevar equipaje.

baggy, *a.* abotagado; bolsudo; hinchado.

bagpipe, *n.* gaita *f.*

bail, 1. *n.* fianza *f.* 2. *v.* desaguar.

bailiff, *n.* alguacil *m.*

bait, 1. *n.* cebo *m.* 2. *v.* cebar.

bake, *v.* cocer en horno.

baker, *n.* panadero, hornero *m.*

bakery, *n.* panadería *f.*

baking, *n.* hornada *f.* **b. powder,** levadura *f.*

balance, *n.* balanza *f.;* equilibrio *m.;* (com.) saldo *m.*

balcony, *n.* balcón *m.;* (theat.) galería *f.*

bald, *a.* calvo.

baldness, *n.* calvicie *f.*

bale, 1. *n.* bala *f.* 2. *v.* embalar.

balk, *v.* frustrar; rebelarse.

balky, *a.* rebelón.

ball, *n.* bola, pelota *f.;* (dance) baile *m.*

ballad, *n.* romance, *m.;* balada *f.*

ballast, 1. *n.* lastre *m.* 2. *v.* lastrar.

ball bearing, *n.* cojinete de bolas *m.*

ballerina, *n.* bailarina *f.*

ballet, *n.* danza *f.;* ballet *m.*

ballistics, *n.* balística *f.*

balloon, *n.* globo *m.* **b. tire,** neumático de balón.

ballot, 1. *n.* balota *f.,* voto *m.* 2. *v.* balotar, votar.

ballroom, *n.* salón de baile *m.*

balm, *n.* bálsamo; ungüento *m.*

balmy, *a.* fragante; reparador; calmante.

balsa, *n.* bálsamo *m.*

balsam, *n.* bálsamo *m.*

balustrade, *n.* barandilla *f.*

bamboo, *n.* bambú *m.,* caña *f.*

ban, 1. *n.* prohibición *f.* 2. *v.* prohibir; proscribir.

banal, *a.* trivial; vulgar.

banana, *n.* banana *f.,* cambur *m.* **b. tree,** banano, plátano *m.*

band, 1. *n.* venda *f.;* (of men) banda, cuadrilla, partida *f.* 2. *v.* asociarse.

bandage, 1. *n.* vendaje *m.* 2. *v.* vendar.

bandanna, *n.* pañuelo (grande) *m.;* bandana *f.*

bandbox, *n.* caja de cartón *m.*

bandit, *n.* bandido -da.

bandmaster, *n.* músico mayor *m.*

bandstand, *n.* kiosco de música *m.*

bang, 1. *interj.* ¡pum! 2. *n.* ruido de un golpe. 3. *v.* golpear ruidosamente.

banish, *v.* desterrar.

banishment, *n.* destierro *m.*

banister, *n.* pasamano *m.*

bank, 1. *n.* banco *m.;* (of a river) margen *m.* or *f.* 2. *v.* depositar.

bankbook, *n.* libreta de depositos *f.*

banker, *n.* banquero *m.*

banking, 1. *a.* bancaria. 2. *n.* banca *f.*

bank note, *n.* billete de banco *m.*

bankrupt, *n.* insolvente.

bankruptcy, *n.* bancarrota *f.*

banner, *n.* bandera *f.;* estandarte *m.*

banquet, *n.* banquete *f.*

banter, 1. *n.* choteo *m.;* zumba; burla *f.* 2. *v.* chotear; zumbar; burlarse.

baptism, *n.* bautismo, bautizo *m.*

baptismal, *a.* bautismal.

Baptist, *n.* bautista *m.*

baptize, *v.* bautizar.

bar, 1. *n.* barra *f.;* obstáculo *m.;* (tavern) taberna *f.,* bar *m.* 2. *v.* barrear; prohibir, excluir.

barbarian, 1. *a.* bárbaro. 2. *n.* bárbaro -ra.

barbarism, *n.* barbarismo *m.,* barbarie *f.*

barbarous, *n.* bárbaro, cruel.

barbecue, *n.* animal asado entero; (Mex.) barbacoa *f.*

barber, *n.* barbero *m.* **b. shop,** barberéa *f.*

barbiturate, *n.* barbiturado *m.*

bare, 1. *a.* desnudo; descubierto. 2. *v.* desnudar; descubrir.

bareback, *adv.* sin silla.

barefoot(ed), *a.* descalzo.

barely, *adv.* escasamente, apenas.

bareness, *n.* desnudez *f.;* pobreza *f.*

bargain, 1. *n.* ganga *f.,* compra ventajosa *f.;* contrato *m.* 2. *v.* regatear; negociar.

barge, *n.* lanchón *m.,* barcaza *f.*

baritone, *n.* barítono *m.*

barium, *n.* bario *m.*

bark, 1. *n.* corteza *f.;* (of dog) ladra *f.* 2. *v.* ladrar.

barley, *n.* cebada *f.*

barn, *n.* granero *m.*

barnacle, *n.* lapa *f.*

barnyard, *n.* corral *m.*

barometer, *n.* barómetro *m.*

barometric, *a.* barométrico.

baron, *n.* barón *m.*

baroness, *n.* baronesa *f.*

baronial, *a.* baronial.

baroque, *a.* barroco.

barracks, *n.* cuartel *m.*

barrage, *n.* cortina de fuego *f.*

barred, *a.* excluido; prohibido.

barrel, *n.* barril *m.;* (of gun) cañón *m.*

barren, *a.* estéril.

barrenness, *n.* esterilidad *f.*

barricade, *n.* barricada, barrera *f.*

barrier, *n.* barrera *f.;* obstáculo *m.*

barroom, *n.* cantina *f.*

bartender, *n.* tabernero; cantinero *m.*

barter, 1. *n.* cambio, trueque *m.* 2. *v.* cambiar, trocar.

base, 1. *a.* bajo, vil. 2. *n.* base *f.* 3. *v.* basar.

baseball, *n.* beisbol *m.*

baseboard, *n.* tabla de resguardo.

basement, *n.* sótano *m.*

baseness, *n.* bajeza, vileza *f.*

bashful, *a.* vergonzoso, tímido.

bashfully, *adv.* timidamente; vergonzosamente.

bashfulness, *n.* vergüenza; timidez *f.*

basic, *a.* fundamental, básico.

basin, *n.* bacía *f.;* (of river) cuenca *f.*

basis, *n.* base *f.*

bask, *v.* tomar el sol.

basket, *n.* cesta, canasta *f.*

bass, *n.* (fish) lobina *f.;* (mus.) bajo profundo *m.* **b. viol.** violón *m.*

bassinet, *n.* bacinete *m.*

bassoon, *n.* bajón *m.*

bastard, *a.* & *n.* bastardo; hijo natural *m.*

baste, v. (sew) bastear; (cooking) pringar.

bat, 1. n. (animal) murciélago m.; (baseball) bate m. **2.** v. batear.

batch, n. cantidad de cosas.

bath, n. baño m.

bathe, v. bañar.

bather, n. bañista.

bathing resort, n. balneario m.

bathrobe, n. bata de baña f., peinador m.

bathroom, n. cuarto de baño.

bathtub, n. bañera f.

baton, n. bastón m.; (mus.) batuta f.

battalion, n. batallón m.

batter, 1. n. (cooking) batido m.; (baseball) voleador m. **2.** v. batir; derribar.

battery, n. batería f.; (elec.) pila f.

batting, n. agramaje, moldeaje m.

battle, 1. n. batalla f.; combate m. **2.** v. batallar.

battlefield, n. campo de batalla.

battleship, n. acorazado m.

bauxite, n. bauxita f.

bawl, v. gritar; vocear.

bay, 1. n. bahía f. **2.** v. aullar.

bayonet, n. bayoneta f.

bazaar, n. bazar m., feria f.

be, v. ser; estar. (See hacer; hay; tener in Sp.-Eng. section).

beach, n. playa f.

beacon, n. faro m.

bead, n. cuenta f.; pl. (rel.) rosario m.

beading, n. abalorio m.

beady, a. globuloso; burbujoso.

beak, n. pico m.

beaker, n. vaso con pico m.

beam, n. viga f.; (of wood) madero m.; (of light) rayo m.

beaming, a. radiante.

bean, n. haba, habichuela f., frijol m.

bear, 1. n. oso -sa. **2.** v. llevar; (endure) aguantar.

bearable, a. sufrible; suportable.

beard, n. barba f.

bearded, a. barbado; barbudo.

beardless, a. lampiño; imberbe.

bearer, n. portador -ra.

bearing, n. porte, aguante m.

bearskin, n. piel de oso f.

beast, n. bestia f.; bruto m.

beat, 1. v. golpear; batir; pulsar; (in games) ganar, vencer.

beaten, a. vencido; batido.

beatify, v. beatificar.

beating, n. paliza f.

beau, n. novio m.

beautiful, a. hermoso, bello.

beautifully, adv. bellamente.

beautify, v. embellecer.

beauty, n. hermosura, belleza f.

beaver, n. castor m.

becalm, v. calmar; sosegar; encalmarse.

because, conj. porque. **b. of,** a causa de.

beckon, v. hacer señas.

become, v. hacerse; ponerse.

becoming, a. propio, correcto; **be b.,** quedar bien, sentar bien.

bed, n. cama f.; lecho m.; (of river) cauce m.

bedbug, n. chinche m.

bedclothes, n. ropa de cama.

bedding, n. colchones m.pl.

bedfellow, n. compañero de cama m.

bedizen, v. adornar; aderezar.

bedridden, a. postrado (en cama).

bedrock, n. (mining) lecho de roca m.; (fig.) fundamento m.

bedroom, n. alcoba f.; (Mex.) recámara f.

bedside, n. lado de cama m.

bedspread, n. cubrecama, sobrecama f.

bedstead, n. armadura de cama f.

bedtime, n. hora de acostarse.

bee, n. abeja f.

beef, n. carne de vaca.

beefsteak, n. bistec, bisté m.

beehive, n. colmena f.

beer, n. cerveza f.

beeswax, n. cera de abejas.

beet, n. remolacha f.; (Mex.) betabel m.

beetle, n. escarabajo m.

befall, v. suceder, sobrevenir.

befitting, a. conveniente; propio; digno.

before, 1. adv. antes. **2.** prep. antes de; (in front of) delante de. **3.** conj. antes que.

beforehand, adv. de antemano.

befriend, v. amparar.

befuddle, v. confundir; aturdir.

beg, v. rogar, suplicar; (for alms) mendigar.

beget, v. engendrar; producir.

beggar, n. mendigo -ga; (Sp. Am.) limosnero -ra.

beggarly, a. pobre, miserable.

begin, v. empezar, comenzar, principiar.

beginner, n. principiante m.

beginning, n. principio, comienzo m.

begrudge, v. envidiar.

behalf: in, on b. of, a favor de, en pro de.

behave, v. portarse comportarse.

behavior, n. conducta f.; comportamiento m.

behead, v. decapitar.

behind, 1. adv. atrás, detrás. **2.** prep. detrás de.

behold, v. contemplar.

beige, a. crema.

being, n. existencia f.; (person) ser m.

bejewel, v. adornar con joyas.

belated, a. atrasado, tardío.

belch, 1. n. eructo m. **2.** v. vomitar; eructar.

belfry, n. campanario m.

Belgian, 1. a. belga. **2.** n. belga m. & f.

Belgium, n. Bélgica f.

belie, v. desmentir.

belief, n. creencia f.; parecer m.

believable, a. creíble.

believe, v. creer.

believer, n. creyente m.

belittle, v. dar poca importancia a.

bell, n. campana f.; (of house) campanilla f.; (electric) timbre m.

bellboy, n. mozo, botones m.

bellicose, a. guerrero.

belligerence, n. beligerancia f.

belligerent, a. & n. beligerante.

belligerently, adv. belicosamente.

bellow, v. bramar, rugir.

bellows, n. fuelle m.

belly, n. vientre m.; panza, barriga f.

belong, v. pertenecer.

belongings, n. propiedad f.

beloved, a. querido, amado.

below, 1. adv. debajo, abajo. **2.** prep. debajo de.

belt, n. cinturón m.

bench, n. banco m.

bend, 1. n. vuelta; curva f. **2.** v. encorvar, doblar.

beneath, 1. adv. debajo, abajo. **2.** prep. debajo de.

benediction, n. bendición f.

benefactor, n. bienhechor -ra.

benefactress, n. bienhechora f.

beneficial, a. provechoso, beneficioso.

beneficiary, n. beneficiario, beneficiado m.

benefit, 1. n. provecho, beneficio m. **2.** v. beneficiar.

benevolence, n. benevolencia f.

benevolent, a. benévolo.

benevolently, adv. benignamente.

benign, a. benigno.

benignity, n. benignidad; bondad f.

bent, 1. a. encorvado. **b. on,** resuelto a. **2.** n. inclinación f.

benzene, n. bencina f.

bequeath, v. legar.

bequest, n. legado m.

berate, v. reñir, regañar.

bereave, v. despojar; desolar.

bereavement, n. privación f.; despojo m.

berry, n. baya f.

berth, n. camarote m.; (naut.) litera f.; (for vessel) amarradero m.

beseech, v. suplicar; implorar.

beseechingly, adv. suplicantemente.

beset, v. acosar; rodear.

beside, prep. al lado de.

besides, adv. además, por otra parte.

besiege, v. sitiar; asediar.

besieged, *a.* sitiado.

besieger, *n.* sitiador *m.*

besmirch, *v.* manchar; deshonrar.

best, *a. & adv.* mejor. **at b.**, a lo más.

bestial, *a.* bestial; brutal.

bestir, *v.* incitar; intrigar.

best man, *n.* padrino de boda.

bestow, *v.* conferir.

bestowal, *n.* dádiva; presentación *f.*

bet, **1.** *n.* apuesta *f.* **2.** *v.* apostar.

betoken, *v.* denotar, significar.

betray, *v.* traicionar; revelar.

betrayal, *n.* traición *f.*

betroth, *v.* contraer esponsales; prometer.

betrothal, *n.* esponsales *m.pl.*

better, **1.** *a. & adv.* mejor. **2.** *v.* mejorar.

between, *prep.* entre, en medio de.

bevel, **1.** *n.* cartabón *m.* **2.** *v.* cortar al sesgo.

beverage, *n.* bebida *f.;* (cold) refresco *m.*

bewail, *v.* llorar; lamentar.

beware, *v.* guardarse, precaverse.

bewilder, *v.* aturdir.

bewildered, *a.* descarriado.

bewildering, *a.* aturdente.

bewilderment, *n.* aturdimiento *m.;* perplejidad *f.*

bewitch, *v.* hechizar; embrujar.

beyond, *prep.* más allá de.

biannual, *a.* semianual; semestral.

bias, **1.** *n.* parcialidad *f.;* prejuicio *m.* **on the b.**, al sesgo. **2.** *v.* predisponer, influir.

bib, *n.* babador *m.*

Bible, *n.* Biblia *f.*

Biblical, *a.* bíblico.

bibliography, *n.* bibliografía *f.*

bicarbonate, *n.* bicarbonato *m.*

bicentennial, *a. & n.* bicentenario *m.*

biceps, *n.* biceps *m.*

bicker, *v.* altercar.

bicycle, *n.* bicicleta *f.*

bicyclist, *n.* biciclista *m.*

bid, **1.** *n.* proposición, oferta *f.* **2.** *v.* mandar; ofrecer.

bidder, *n.* postor *m.*

bide, *v.* aguardar; esperar.

bier, *n.* ataúd *m.*

bifocal, *a.* bifocal.

big, *a.* grande.

bigamist, *n.* bígamo -ma.

bigamy, *n.* bigamia *f.*

bigot, *n.* persona intolerante.

bigotry, *n.* intolerancia *f.*

bilateral, *a.* bilateral.

bile, *n.* bilis *f.*

bilingual, *a.* bilingüe.

bilious, *a.* bilioso.

bill, **1.** *n.* cuenta, factura *f.;* (money) billete *m.;* (of bird) pico *m.* **2.** *v.* facturar.

billet, **1.** *n.* billete *m.;* (mil.) boleta *f.* **2.** *v.* aposentar.

billfold, *n.* cartera *f.*

billiard balls, *n.* bolas de billar.

billiards, *n.* billar *m.*

billion, *n.* billón *m.*

bill of health, *n.* certificado de sanidad.

bill of lading, *n.* conocimiento de embarque.

bill of sale, *n.* escritura de venta.

billow, *n.* ola; oleada *f.*

bimetallic, *a.* bimetálico.

bimonthly, *a. & adv.* bimestral.

bin, *n.* hucha *f.;* depósito *m.*

bind, *v.* atar; obligar; (book) encuadernar.

bindery, *n.* taller de encuadernación *m.*

binding, *n.* encuadernación *f.*

binocular, **1.** *a.* binocular. **2.** *n.pl.* gemelos *m.pl.*

biochemistry, *n.* bioquímica *f.*

biodegradable, *a.* biodegradable.

biofeedback, *n.* retroalimentación biológica.

biographer, *n.* biógrafo *m.*

biographical, *a.* biográfico.

biography, *n.* biografía *f.*

biological, *a.* biológico.

biologically, *adv.* biológicamente.

biology, *n.* biología *f.*

bipartisan, *a.* bipartito.

biped, *n.* bípedo *m.*

bird, *n.* pájaro *m.;* ave *f.*

bird of prey, *n.* ave de rapiña *m.*

birth, *n.* nacimiento *m.* **give b. to**, dar a luz.

birth control, *n.* contracepción *f.*

birthday, *n.* cumpleaños *m.*

birthmark, *n.* estigma *f.*, marca de nacimiento.

birthplace, *n.* natalicio *m.*

birth rate, *n.* natalidad *f.*

birthright, *n.* primogenitura *f.*

biscuit, *n.* bizcocho *m.*

bisect, *v.* bisecar.

bishop, *n.* obispo *m.;* (chess) alfil *m.*

bishopric, *n.* obispado *f.*

bismuth, *n.* bismuto *m.*

bison, *n.* bisonte *m.*

bit, *n.* pedacito *m.;* (mech.) taladro *m.;* (for horse) bocado *m.;* (computer) bit *m.*

bitch, *n.* perra *f.*

bite, **1.** *n.* bocado *m.;* picada *f.* **2.** *v.* morder; picar.

biting, *a.* penetrante; mordaz.

bitter, *a.* amargo.

bitterly, *adv.* amargamente; agriamente.

bitterness, *n.* amargura *f.;* rencor *m.*

bivouac, **1.** *n.* vivaque *m.* **2.** *v.* vivaquear.

biweekly, *a.* quincenal.

black, *a.* negro.

Black, *n.* (person) negro -gra; persona de color.

blackberry, *n.* mora *f.*

blackbird, *n.* mirlo *m.*

blackboard, *n.* pizarra *f.*

blacken, *v.* ennegrecer.

black eye, *n.* ojo amoratado.

blackguard, *n.* tunante; pillo *m.*

blackmail, **1.** *n.* chantaje *m.* **2.** *v.* amenazar con chantaje.

black market, *n.* mercado negro.

blackout, *n.* oscurecimiento, apagamiento *m.*

blacksmith, *n.* herrero *m.*

bladder, *n.* vejiga *f.*

blade, *n.* (sword) hoja *f.;* (oar) pala *f.;* (grass) brizna *f.*

blame, *v.* culpar, echar la culpa a.

blameless, *a.* inculpable.

blanch, *v.* blanquear; escaldar.

bland, *a.* blando.

blank, *a. & n.* blanco.

blanket, *n.* manta *f.;* cobertor *m.*

blare, **1.** *n.* sonido de trompeta. **2.** *v.* sonar como trompeta.

blaspheme, *v.* blasfemar.

blasphemer, *n.* blasfemo, blasfemador *m.*

blasphemous, *a.* blasfemo, impío.

blasphemy, *n.* blasfemia *f.*

blast, **1.** *n.* barreno *m.;* (wind) ráfaga *f.* **2.** *v.* barrenar.

blatant, *a.* bramante.

blaze, **1.** *n.* llama, hoguera *f.* **2.** *v.* encenderse en llama.

blazing, *a.* flamante.

bleach, *v.* blanquear.

bleachers, *n.* asientos al aire libre.

bleak, *a.* frío y sombrío.

bleakness, *n.* intemperie *f.*

bleed, *v.* sangrar.

blemish, **1.** *n.* mancha *f.;* lunar *m.* **2.** *v.* manchar.

blend, **1.** *n.* mezcla *f.* **2.** *v.* mezclar, combinar.

blended, *a.* mezclado.

bless, *v.* bendecir.

blessed, *a.* bendito.

blessing, *n.* bendición *f.*

blight, **1.** *n.* plaga *f.;* tizón *m.* **2.** *v.* atizonar.

blind, *a.* ciego.

blindfold, *v.* vendar los ojos.

blinding, *a.* deslumbrante; ofuscante.

blindly, *adv.* ciegamente.

blindness, *n.* ceguedad, ceguera *f.*

blink, **1.** *n.* guiñada *f.* **2.** *v.* guiñar.

bliss, *n.* felicidad *f.*

blissful, *a.* dichoso; bienaventurado.

blissfully, *adv.* felizmente.

blister, *n.* ampolla *f.*

blithe, *a.* alegre; jovial; gozoso.

blizzard, *n.* chubasco de nieve.

bloat, *v.* hinchar.

bloc, *n.* grupo (político); bloc.

block, **1.** *n.* bloque *m.;* (street) manzana, cuadra *f.* **2.** *v.* bloquear.

blockade, 1. *n.* bloqueo *m.* **2.** *v.* bloquear.

blond, *a.* & *n.* rubio -ia.

blood, *n.* sangre *f.;* parentesco, linaje *m.*

bloodhound, *n.* sabueso *m.*

bloodless, *a.* exangüe; desangrado.

blood poisoning, *n.* envenenamiento de sangre.

blood pressure, *n.* presión arterial.

bloodshed, *n.* matanza *f.*

bloodthirsty, *a.* cruel, sanguinario.

bloody, *a.* ensangrentado, sangriento.

bloom, 1. *n.* flor *f.* **2.** *v.* florecer.

blooming, *a.* lozano; fresco.

blossom, 1. *n.* flor *f.* **2.** *v.* florecer.

blot, 1. *n.* mancha *f.* **2.** *v.* manchar.

blotch, 1. *n.* mancha, roncha *f.* **2.** *v.* manchar.

blotter, *n.* papel secante.

blouse, *n.* blusa *f.*

blow, 1. *n.* golpe *m.;* (fig.) chasco *m.* **2.** *v.* soplar.

blowout, *n.* reventón de neumático.

blubber, *n.* grasa de ballena.

bludgeon, *n.* porra *f.*

blue, *a.* azul; triste, melancólico.

bluebird, *n.* azulejo *m.*

blue jeans, *n.* jeans *m.pl.*

blueprint, *n.* heliografía *f.*

bluff, 1. *n.* risco *m.* **2.** *v.* alardear; baladronar.

bluing, *n.* añil *m.*

blunder, 1. *n.* desatino *m.* **2.** *v.* desatinar.

blunderer, *n.* desatinado *m.*

blunt, *a.* embotado; descortés. **2.** *v.* embotar.

bluntly, *adv.* bruscamente.

bluntness, *n.* grosería *f.*

blur, 1. *n.* trazo confuso. **2.** *v.* hacer indistinto.

blush, 1. *n.* rubor, sonrojo *m.* **2.** *v.* sonrojarse.

bluster, 1. *n.* fanfarria *f.* **2.** *v.* fanfarrear.

boar, *n.* verraco *m.* **wild b.,** jabalí *m.*

board, 1. *n.* tabla; (govt.) consejo *m.;* junta *f.* **b. and room,** cuarto y comida, casa y comida. **2.** *v.* (ship) abordar.

boarder, *n.* pensionista *m.* & *f.*

boardinghouse, pensión *f.,* casa de huéspedes.

boast, 1. *n.* jactancia *f.* **2.** *v.* jactarse.

boaster, *n.* fanfarrón *m.*

boastful, *a.* jactancioso.

boastfulness, *n.* jactancia *f.*

boat, *n.* barco, buque, bote *m.*

boathouse, *n.* casilla de botes *f.*

boatswain, *n.* contramaestre *m.*

bob, *v.* menear.

bobbin, *n.* bobina *f.*

bobby pin, *n.* invisible *f.,* gancho *m.*

bodice, *n.* corpiño *m.*

bodily, *a.* corporal.

body, *n.* cuerpo *m.*

bodyguard, *n.* guardia de corps.

bog, *n.* pantano *m.*

Bohemian, *a.* & *n.* bohemio -mia.

boil, 1. *n.* (med.) divieso *m.* **2.** *v.* hervir.

boiler, *n.* marmita; caldera *f.*

boisterous, *a.* tumultuoso.

boisterously, *adv.* tumultuosamente.

bold, *a.* atrevido, audaz.

boldface, *n.* (type) letra negra.

boldly, *adv.* audazmente; descaradamente.

boldness, *n.* atrevimiento *m.;* osadía *f.*

Bolivian, *a.* & *n.* boliviano -na.

bologna, *n.* salchicha *f.*

bolster, 1. *n.* travesero, cojín *m.* **2.** *v.* apoyar, sostener.

bolt, 1. *n.* perno *m.;* (of door) cerrojo *m.;* (lightning) rayo *m.* **2.** *v.* acerrojar.

bomb, 1. *n.* bomba *f.* **2.** *v.* bombardear.

bombard, *v.* bombardear.

bombardier, *n.* bombardero *m.*

bombardment, *n.* bombardeo *m.*

bomber, *n.* avión de bombardeo.

bombproof, *a.* a prueba de granadas.

bombshell, *n.* bomba *f.*

bonbon, *n.* dulce, bombón *m.*

bond, *n.* lazo *m.;* (com.) bono *m.*

bondage, *n.* esclavitud, servidumbre *f.*

bonded, *a.* garantizado.

bone, *n.* hueso *m.*

boneless, *a.* sin huesos.

bonfire, *n.* hoguera, fogata *f.*

bonnet, *n.* gorra *f.*

bonus, *n.* bono *m.*

book, *n.* libro *m.*

bookbinder, *n.* encuadernador *m.*

bookcase, *n.* armario para libros.

bookkeeper, *n.* tenedor de libros.

bookkeeping, *n.* contabilidad *f.*

booklet, *n.* folleto *m.,* libreta *f.*

bookseller, *n.* librero *m.*

bookstore, *n.* librería *f.*

boom, *n.* (naut.) botalón *m.;* prosperidad repentina.

boon, *n.* dádiva *f.*

boor, *n.* patán, rústico *m.*

boorish, *a.* villano.

boost, 1. *n.* alza; ayuda *f.* **2.** *v.* levantar, alzar; fomentar.

booster, *n.* fomentador *m.*

boot, *n.* bota *f.*

bootblack, *n.* limpiabotas *m.*

booth, *n.* cabaña; casilla *f.*

booty, *n.* botín *m.*

border, 1. *n.* borde *m.;* frontera *f.* **2.** *v.* **b. on,** lindar con.

borderline, 1. *a.* marginal. **2.** *n.* margen *m.*

bore, 1. *n.* lata *f.;* persona pesada. **2.** *v.* aburrir, fastidiar; (mech.) taladrar.

boredom, *n.* aburrimiento *m.*

boric acid, *n.* ácido bórico *m.*

boring, *a.* aburrido, pesado.

born, *a.* nacido. **be born,** nacer.

born-again, *a.* renacido.

borrow, *v.* pedir prestado.

bosom, *v.* seno, pecho *m.*

boss, *n.* jefe, patrón *m.*

botany, *n.* botánica *f.*

both, *pron.* & *a.* ambos, los dos.

bother, 1. *n.* molestia *f.* **2.** *v.* molestar, incomodar.

bothersome, *a.* molesto.

bottle, 1. *n.* botella *f.* **2.** *v.* embotellar.

bottom, *n.* fondo *m.*

boudoir, *n.* tocador *m.*

bough, *n.* rama *f.*

boulder, *n.* canto rodado.

boulevard, *n.* bulevar *m.*

bounce, 1. *n.* brinco *m.* **2.** *v.* brincar; hacer saltar.

bound, 1. *n.* salto *m.* **2.** *v.* limitar.

boundary, *n.* límite, lindero *m.*

bouquet, *n.* ramillete de flores.

bourgeois, *a.* & *n.* burgués.

bout, *n.* encuentro; combate *m.*

bow, 1. *n.* saludo *m.;* (of ship) proa *f.;* (archery) arco *m.;* (ribbon) lazo *m.* **2.** *v.* saludar, inclinar.

bowels, *n.* intestinos *m.pl.;* entrañas *f.pl.*

bowl, 1. *n.* vasija *f.;* platón *m.* **2.** *v.* jugar a los bolos. **b. over,** derribar.

bowlegged, *a.* perniabierto.

bowling, *n.* bolos *m.pl.*

box, 1. *n.* caja *f.;* (theat.) palco *m.* **2.** *v.* (sports) boxear.

boxcar, *n.* vagón *m.*

boxer, *n.* boxeador, pugilista *m.*

boxing, *n.* boxeo *m.*

box office, *n.* taquilla *f.*

boy, *n.* muchacho, chico *m.*

boycott, 1. *n.* boicoteo *m.* **2.** *v.* boicotear.

boyhood, *n.* muchachez *f.*

boyish, *a.* pueril.

boyishly, *adv.* puerilmente.

brace, 1. *n.* grapón *m.;* *pl.* tirantes *m.pl.* **2.** *v.* reforzar.

bracelet, *n.* brazalete *m.,* pulsera *f.*

bracket, *n.* ménsula *f.*

brag, *v.* jactarse.

braggart, *a.* jactancioso. **2.** *n.* jaque *m.*

braid, 1. *n.* trenza *f.* **2.** *v.* trenzar.

brain, *n.* cerebro, seso *m.*

brainy, *a.* sesudo, inteligente.

brake, 1. *n.* freno *m.* **2.** *v.* frenar.

bran, n. salvado m.

branch, n. ramo m.; (of tree) rama f.

brand, n. marca f.

brandish, v. blandir.

brand-new, a. enteramente nuevo.

brandy, n. aguardiente, coñac m.

brash, a. impetuoso.

brass, n. bronce, latón m.

brassiere, n. corpiño, sostén m.

brat, n. mocoso m.

bravado, n. bravata f.

brave, a. valiente.

bravery, n. valor m.

brawl, 1. n. alboroto m. **2.** v. alborotar.

brawn, n. músculo m.

bray, v. rebuznar.

brazen, a. desvergonzado.

Brazil, n. Brasil m.

Brazilian, a. & n. brasileño -ña.

breach, n. rotura, infracción f.

bread, n. pan m.

breadth, n. anchura f.

break, 1. n. rotura; pausa f. **2.** v. quebrar, romper.

breakable, a. rompible, frágil.

breakage, n. rotura f., destrozo m.

breakfast, 1. n. desayuno, almuerzo m. **2.** v. desayunarse, almorzar.

breakneck, a. rápido, precipitado, atropellado.

breast, n. pecho, seno m.

breath, n. aliento; soplo m.

breathe, v. respirar.

breathless, a. desalentado.

breathlessly, adv. jadeantemente, intensamente.

bred, a. criado; educado.

breeches, n.pl. calzones; pantalones, n.pl.

breed, 1. n. raza f. **2.** v. engendrar; criar.

breeder, n. criador m.

breeding, n. cría f.

breeze, n. brisa f.

breezy, a.: it is b., hace brisa.

brevity, n. brevedad f.

brew, v. fraguar, elaborar.

brewer, n. cervecero m.

brewery, n. cervecería f.

bribe, 1. n. soborno, cohecho m. **2.** v. sobornar, cohechar.

briber, n. sobornador m.

bribery, n. soborno, cohecho m.

brick, n. ladrillo m.

bricklayer, n. albañil m.

bridal, a. nupcial.

bride, n. novia f.

bridegroom, n. novio m.

bridesmaid, n. madrina de boda.

bridge, n. puente m.

bridged, a. conectado.

bridgehead, n. (mil.) cabeza de puente.

bridle, n. brida f.

brief, a. breve.

briefcase, n. maletín m.

briefly, adv. brevemente.

briefness, n. brevedad f.

brier, n. zarza f.

brig, n. bergantín m.

brigade, n. brigada f.

bright, a. claro, brillante.

brighten, v. abrillantar; alegrar.

brightness, n. resplandor m.

brilliance, n. brillantez f.

brilliant, a. brillante.

brim, n. borde m.; (of hat) ala f.

brine, n. salmuera f.

bring, v. traer. **b. about,** efectuar, llevar a cabo.

brink, n. borde m.

briny, a. salado.

brisk, a. vivo; enérgico.

briskly, adv. vivamente.

briskness, n. viveza f.

bristle, n. cerda f.

bristly, a. hirsuto.

Britain, n. **Great B.,** Gran Bretaña f.

British, a. británico.

British Empire, imperio británico.

British Isles, islas británicas.

Briton, n. inglés m.

brittle, a. quebradizo, frágil.

broad, a. ancho.

broadcast, 1. n. radiodifusión m. **2.** v. radiodifundir.

broadcaster, n. locutor m.

broadcloth, n. paño fino.

broaden, v. ensanchar.

broadly, adv. ampliamente.

broadminded, a. tolerante, liberal.

brocade, n. brocado m.

brocaded, a. espolinado.

broil, v. asar.

broiler, n. parilla f.

broken, a. roto, quebrado.

broken-hearted, a. angustiado.

broker, n. corredor, cambista m.

brokerage, n. corretaje m.

bronchial, a. bronquial.

bronchitis, n. bronquitis f.

bronze, n. bronce m.

brooch, n. broche m.

brood, 1. n. cría, progenie f. **2.** v. empollar; cobijar.

brook, n. arroyo m., quebrada f.

broom, n. escoba f.

broomstick, n. palo de escoba.

broth, n. caldo m.

brothel, n. burdel m.

brother, n. hermano m.

brotherhood, n. fraternidad f.

brother-in-law, n. cuñado m.

brotherly, a. fraternal.

brow, n. ceja; frente f.

brown, a. pardo, moreno.

browse, v. ramonear.

bruise, 1. n. contusión f. **2.** v. magullar.

brunette, a. & n. moreno -na, trigueño -ña.

brush, 1. n. cepillo m.; brocha f. **2.** v. cepillar.

brushwood, n. matorral m.

brusque, a. brusco.

brusquely, adv. bruscamente.

brutal, a. brutal.

brutality, n. brutalidad f.

brutalize, v. embrutecer.

brute, n. bruto m., bestia f.

bubble, n. ampolla f.

bucket, n. cubo m.

buckle, n. hebilla f.

buckram, n. bucarán m.

bucksaw, n. sierra de bastidor.

buckshot, n. posta f.

buckwheat, n. trigo sarraceno.

bud, 1. n. brote m. **2.** v. brotar.

budding, a. en capullo.

budge, v. moverse.

budget, n. presupuesto m.

buffalo, n. búfalo m.

buffer, n. parachoques m.

buffet, n. bufet m.; (furniture) aparador m.

buffoon, n. bufón m.

bug, n. insecto m.

bugle, n. clarín m.; corneta f.

build, v. construir.

builder, n. constructor m.

building, n. edificio m.

bulb, n. bulbo m.; (of lamp) bombilla, ampolla f.

bulge, 1. n. abultamiento m. 2. v. abultar.

bulk, n. masa f.; grueso m.; mayoría f.

bulkhead, n. frontón m.

bulky, a. grueso, abultado.

bull, n. toro m.

bulldog, n. perro de presa.

bullet, n. bala f.

bulletin, n. boletín m.

bulletproof, a. a prueba de bala.

bullfight, n. corrida de toros.

bullfighter, n. torero m.

bullfinch, n. pinzón real m.

bully, 1. n. rufián m. **2.** v. bravear.

bulwark, n. baluarte m.

bum, n. holgazán m.

bump, 1. n. golpe, choque m. **2.** v. **b. into,** chocar contra.

bumper, n. parachoques m.

bun, n. bollo m.

bunch, n. racimo; montón m.

bundle, 1. n. bulto m. **2.** v. **b. up,** abrigar.

bungalow, n. casa de un solo piso.

bungle, v. estropear.

bunion, n. juanete m.

bunk, n. litera f.

bunny, n. conejito m.

bunting, n. lanilla, banderas f.

buoy, n. boya f.

buoyant, a. boyante; vivaz.

burden, 1. n. carga f. **2.** v. cargar.

burdensome, a. gravoso.

bureau, n. (furniture) cómoda f.; departamento m.

burglar, n. ladrón m.

burglarize, v. robar.

burglary, n. robo m.

burial, n. entierro m.

burlap, n. arpillera f.

burly, a. corpulento.

burn, v. quemar; arder.
burner, n. mechero m.
burning, a. ardiente.
burnish, v. pulir; acicalar.
burrow, v. minar; horadar.
burst, v. reventar.
bury, v. enterrar.
bus, n. autobús m.
bush, n. arbusto m.
bushy, a. matoso; peludo.
business, n. negocios m.pl.; comercio m.
businesslike, a. directo.
businessman, n. comerciante m.
businesswoman, n. mujer de negocios.
bust, n. busto; pecho m.
bustle, n. bullicio m.; animación f.
busy, a. ocupado, atareado.
busybody, n. entremetido m.
but, conj. pero; sino.
butcher, n. carnicero m.
butchery, n. carnicería; matanza f.
butler, n. mayordomo m.
butt, n. punta f.; cabo extremo m.
butter, n. manteca, mantequilla f.
buttercup, n. ranúnculo m.
butterfat, n. mantequilla f.
butterfly, n. mariposa f.
buttermilk, n. suero (de leche) m.
button, n. botón m.
buttonhole, n. ojal m.
buttress, n. sostén; refuerzo m.
buxom, a. regordete.
buy, v. comprar.
buyer, n. comprador -ra.
buzz, 1. n. zumbido m. **2.** v. zumbar.
buzzard, n. gallinazo m.
buzzer, n. zumbador m.
buzz saw, n. sierra circular f.
by, prep. por; (near) cerca de, al lado de; (time) para.
by-and-by, adv. pronto; luego.
bygone, a. pasado.
bylaw, n. estatuto, reglamento m.
bypass, n. desvío m.
byproduct, n. producto accesorio m.
bystander, n. espectador; mirón m.
byte, n. en teoría de la información: ocho bits.
byway, n. camino desviado m.

C

cab, n. coche de alquiler.
cabaret, n. cabaret m.
cabbage, n. repollo m.
cabin, n. cabaña f.
cabinet, n. gabinete; ministerio m.
cabinetmaker, n. ebanista m.
cable, n. cable m.
cablegram, n. cablegrama f.
cache, n. escondite m.

cackle, 1. n. charla f., cacareo m. **2.** v. cacarear.
cacophony, n. cacofonía f.
cactus, n. cacto m.
cad, n. persona vil.
cadaver, n. cadáver m.
cadaverous, a. cadavérico.
cadence, n. cadencia f.
cadet, n. cadete m.
cadmium, n. cadmio m.
cadre, n. núcleo; (mil.) cuadro m.
café, n. café, cantina f.
cafeteria, n. cafetería f.
caffeine, n. cafeína f.
cage, 1. n. jaula f. **2.** v. enjaular.
caged, a. enjaulado.
caisson, n. arcón m.; (mil.) furgón m.
cajole, v. lisonjear; adular.
cake, n. torta f.; bizcocho m.
calamitous, a. calamitoso.
calamity, n. calamidad f.
calcify, v. calcificar.
calcium, n. calcio m.
calculable, a. calculable.
calculate, v. calcular.
calculating, a. interesado.
calculation, n. calculación f.; cálculo m.
calculus, n. cálculo m.
caldron, n. caldera f.
calendar, n. calendario m.
calf, n. ternero m.
calfskin, n. piel de becerro.
caliber, n. calibre m.
calico, n. percal m.
caliper, n. calibrador m.
calisthenics, n. calistenia, gimnasia f.
calk, v. calafatear; rellenar.
calker, n. calafate m.
call, 1. n. llamada f. **2.** v. llamar.
calligraphy, n. caligrafía f.
calling, n. vocación f.
calling card, n. tarjeta (de visita) f.
callously, adv. insensiblemente.
callow, a. sin experiencia.
callus, n. callo m.
calm, 1. a. tranquilo, calmado. **2.** n. calma f. **3.** v. calmar.
calmly, adv. serenamente.
calmness, n. calma f.
caloric, a. calórico.
calorie, n. caloría f.
calorimeter, n. calorímetro m.
calumniate, v. calumniar.
calumny, n. calumnia f.
Calvary, n. Calvario m.
calve, v. parir (la vaca).
calyx, n. cáliz m.
camaraderie, n. compañerismo m., compadrería f.
cambric, n. batista f.
camel, n. camello m.
camellia, n. camelia f.
camel's hair, n. piel de camello.
cameo, n. camafeo m.
camera, n. cámara f.
camouflage, n. camuflaje m.

camouflaging, n. simulacro, disfraz m.
camp, 1. n. campamento m. **2.** v. acampar.
campaign, n. campaña f.
camper, n. acampado m.
campfire, n. fogata de campamento.
camphor, n. alcanfor m.
camphor ball, n. bola de alcanfor.
campus, n. campo de colegio (o universidad) m.
can, v. (be able) poder.
can, 1. n. lata f. **2.** v. conservar en latas.
Canada, n. Canadá m.
Canadian, a. & n. canadiense.
canal, n. canal m.
canalize, v. canalizar.
canard, n. embuste m.
canary, n. canario m.
cancel, v. cancelar.
cancellation, n. cancelación f.
cancer, n. cáncer m.
candelabrum, n. candelabro m.
candid, a. cándido, sincero.
candidacy, n. candidatura f.
candidate, n. candidato -ta.
candidly, adv. candidamente.
candidness, n. candidez; sinceridad f.
candied, a. garapiñado.
candle, n. vela f.
candlestick, n. candelero m.
candor, n. candor m.; sinceridad f.
candy, n. dulces m.pl.
cane, n. caña f.; (for walking) bastón m.
canine, a. canino.
canister, n. frasco m.; lata f.
canker, n. llaga; úlcera f.
cankerworm, n. oruga f.
canned, a. envasado.
canner, n. envasador m.
cannery, n. fábrica de conservas alimenticias f.
cannibal, n. caníbal m.
cannon, n. cañón m.
cannonade, n. cañoneo m.
cannoneer, n. cañonero m.
canny, a. sagaz; prudente.
canoe, n. canoa f.
canon, n. canon m.; (rel.) canónigo m.
canonical, a. canónico.
canonize, v. canonizar.
canopy, n. dosel m.
cant, n. hipocresía f.
cantaloupe, n. melón m.
canteen, n. cantina f.
canter, 1. n. medio galope m. **2.** v. galopar.
cantonment, n. (mil.) acuartelamiento m.
canvas, n. lona f.
canyon, n. cañón, desfiladero m.
cap, 1. n. tapa f.; (headwear) gorro m. **2.** v. tapar.
capability, n. capacidad f.
capable, a. capaz.
capably, adv. hábilmente.
capacious, a. espacioso.

capacity, n. capacidad f.
cape, n. capa f.; (geog.) cabo m.
caper, n. zapateta f.; (bot.) alcaparra f.
capillary, a. capilar.
capital, n. capital m.; (govt.) capital f.
capitalism, n. capitalismo m.
capitalist, n. capitalista m.
capitalistic, a. capitalista.
capitalization, n. capitalización f.
capitalize, v. capitalizar.
capitulate, v. capitular.
capon, n. capón m.
caprice, n. capricho m.
capricious, a. caprichoso.
capriciously, adv. caprichosamente.
capriciousness, n. capricho m.
capsize, v. zozobrar, volcar.
capsule, n. cápsula f.
captain, n. capitán m.
caption, n. título m.; (motion pictures) subtítulo m.
captious, a. capcioso.
captivate, v. cautivar.
captivating, a. encantador.
captive, n. cautivo -va, prisionero -ra.
captivity, n. cautividad f.
captor, n. apresador m.
capture, 1. n. captura f. 2. v. capturar.
car, n. coche, carro m.; (of train) vagón, coche m. baggage c., vagón de equipajes. parlor c., coche salón.
carafe, n. garrafa f.
caramel, n. caramelo m.
carat, n. quilate m.
caravan, n. caravana f.
caraway, n. alcaravea f.
carbide, n. carburo m.
carbine, n. carabina f.
carbohydrate, n. hidrato de carbono.
carbon, n. carbón m.
carbon dioxide, anhídrido carbónico.
carbon monoxide, monóxido de carbono.
carbon paper, n. papel carbón m.
carbuncle, n. carbunclo m.
carburetor, n. carburador m.
carcinogenic, a. carcinogénico.
card, n. tarjeta f. playing c., naipe m.
cardboard, n. cartón m.
cardiac, a. cardíaco.
cardigan, n. chaqueta de punto.
cardinal, 1. a. cardinal. 2. n. cardenal m.
care, 1. n. cuidado. 2. v. c. for, cuidar.
careen, v. carenar; encharse de costado.
career, n. carrera f.
carefree, a. descuidado.
careful, a. cuidadoso. be. c., tener cuidado.

carefully, adv. cuidadosamente.
carefulness, n. esmero; cuidado m.; cautela f.
careless, a. descuidado.
carelessly, adv. descuidadamente; negligentemente.
carelessness, n. descuido m.
caress, 1. n. caricia f. 2. v. acariciar.
caretaker, n. guardián m.
cargo, n. carga f.
caricature, n. caricatura f.
caries, n. carias f.
carload, a. furgonada, vagonada.
carnal, a. carnal.
carnation, n. clavel m.
carnival, n. carnaval m.
carnivorous, a. carnívoro.
carol, n. villancico m.
carouse, v. parrandear.
carpenter, n. carpintero m.
carpet, n. alfombra f.
carpeting, n. alfombrado m.
car pool, n. uso habitual, por varias personas, de un automóvil perteneciente a una de ellas.
carriage, n. carruaje; (bearing) porte m.
carrier, n. portador -ra.
carrier pigeon, n. paloma mensajera.
carrot, n. zanahoria f.
carrousel, n. volantín m.
carry, v. llevar, cargar. c. out, cumplir, llevar a cabo.
cart, n. carreta f.
cartage, n. acarreo, carretaje m.
cartel, n. cartel m.
cartilage, n. cartílago m.
carton, n. caja de cartón.
cartoon, n. caricatura f.
cartoonist, n. caricaturista m.
cartridge, n. cartucho m.
carve, v. esculpir; (meat) trinchar.
carver, n. tallador; grabador m.
carving, n. entalladura f.; arte de trinchar. c. knife, trinchante m.
cascade, n. cascada f.
case, n. caso m.; (box) caja f. in any c., sea como sea.
cash, 1. n. dinero contante. 2. v. efectuar, cambiar.
cashier, n. cajero -ra.
cashmere, n. casimir m.
casino, n. casino m.
cask, n. barril m.
casket, n. ataúd m.
casserole, n. cacerola f.
cassette, n. cassette m., cartucho m.
cast, 1. n. (theat.) reparto de papeles. 2. v. echar; (theat.) repartir.
castanet, n. castañuela f.
castaway, n. náufrago m.
caste, n. casta f.
caster, n. tirador m.
castigate, v. castigar.

Castilian, a. castellano.
cast iron, n. hierro colado m.
castle, n. castillo m.
castoff, a. descartado.
casual, a. casual.
casually, adv. casualmente.
casualness, n. casualidad f.
casualty, n. víctima f.; (mil.) baja f.
cat, n. gato -ta.
cataclysm, n. cataclismo m.
catacomb, n. catacumba f.
catalogue, n. catálogo m.
catapult, n. catapulta f.
cataract, n. catarata f.
catarrh, n. catarro m.
catastrophe, n. catástrofe m.
catch, v. alcanzar, atrapar, coger.
catchy, a. contagioso.
catechism, n. catequismo m.
catechize, v. catequizar.
categorical, a. categórico.
category, n. categoría f.
cater, v. abastecer; proveer. c. to, complacer.
caterpillar, n. gusano m.
catgut, n. cuerda (de tripa).
catharsis, n. purga f.
cathartic, 1. a. catártico; purgante. 2. n. purgante m.
cathedral, n. catedral f.
cathode, n. cátodo m.
Catholic, 1. a. católico. 2. n. católico -ca.
Catholicism, n. catolicismo m.
catnap, n. siesta corta.
catsup, n. salsa de tomate.
cattle, n. ganado m.
cattleman, n. ganadero m.
cauliflower, n. coliflor m.
causation, n. causalidad f.
cause, n. causa f.
causeway, n. calzada f.; terraplén m.
caustic, a. cáustico.
cauterize, v. cauterizar.
cautery, n. cauterio m.
caution, n. cautela f.
cautious, a. cauteloso.
cavalcade, n. cabalgata f.
cavalier, n. caballero m.
cavalry, n. caballería f.
cave, cavern, n. caverna f.
cave-in, n. hundimiento m.
caviar, n. caviar m.
cavity, n. hueco m.
cayman, n. caimán m.
cease, v. cesar.
ceaseless, a. incesante.
cedar, n. cedro m.
cede, v. ceder.
ceiling, n. cielo m.
celebrant, n. celebrante m.
celebrate, v. celebrar.
celebration, n. celebración f.
celebrity, n. persona célebre.
celerity, n. celeridad; prontitud f.
celery, n. apio m.
celestial, a. celeste.
celibacy, n. celibato m.
celibate, a. & n. célibe m.
cell, n. celda f.; (biol.) célula f.
cellar, n. sótano m.

cellist, *a.* celista *m.*

cello, *n.* violoncelo *m.*

cellophane, *n.* celofán *m.*

cellular, *a.* celular.

celluloid, *n.* celuloide *m.*

cellulose, 1. *a.* celuloso. 2. *n.* celulosa *f.*

Celtic, *a.* céltico.

cement, *n.* cemento *m.*

cemetery, *n.* cementerio *m.;* campo santo *m.*

censor, *n.* censor *m.*

censorious, *a.* severo; crítico.

censorship, *n.* censura *f.*

censure, 1. *n.* censura *f.* 2. *v.* censurar.

census, *n.* censo *m.*

cent, *n.* centavo, céntimo *m.*

centenary, *a.* & *n.* centenario *m.*

centennial, *a.* & *n.* centenario *m.*

center, *n.* centro *m.*

centerfold, *n.* página central desplegable en una revista.

centerpiece, *n.* centro de mesa.

centigrade, *a.* centígrado.

centigrade thermometer, termómetro centígrado.

central, *a.* central.

Central American, *a.* & *n.* centroamericano -na.

centralize, *v.* centralizar.

century, *n.* siglo *m.*

century plant, *n.* maguey *f.*

ceramic, *a.* cerámico.

ceramics, *n.* cerámica *f.*

cereal, *n.* cereal *m.*

cerebral, *a.* cerebral.

ceremonial, *a.* ceremonial.

ceremonious, *a.* ceremonioso.

ceremony, *n.* ceremonia *f.*

certain, *a.* cierto, seguro.

certainly, *adv.* sin duda, seguramente.

certainty, *n.* certeza *f.*

certificate, *n.* certificado *m.*

certification, *n.* certificación *f.*

certified, *a.* certificado.

certify, *v.* certificar.

certitude, *n.* certeza *f.*

cessation, *n.* cesación *f.*, discontinuación *f.*

cession, *n.* cesión *f.*

chafe, *v.* irritar.

chafing dish, *n.* escalfador *m.*

chagrin, *n.* disgusto *m.*

chain, 1. *n.* cadena *f.* 2. *v.* encadenar.

chair, *n.* silla *f.*

chairman, *n.* presidente *m.*

chairperson, *n.* presidente -ta; persona que preside.

chalk, *n.* tiza *f.*

challenge, 1. *n.* desafío *m.* 2. *v.* desafiar.

challenger, *n.* desafiador *m.*

chamber, *n.* cámara *f.*

chamberlain, *n.* camarero *m.*

chambermaid, *n.* camarera *f.*

chameleon, *n.* camaleón *m.*

chamois, *n.* gamuza *f.*

champagne, *n.* champán *m.,* champaña *f.*

champion, 1. *n.* campeón *m.* 2. *v.* defender.

championship, *n.* campeonato *m.*

chance, *n.* oportunidad, ocasión *f.* **by c.,** por casualidad, por acaso. **take a c.,** aventurarse.

chancel, *n.* antealtar *m.*

chancellery, *n.* cancillería *f.*

chancellor, *n.* canciller *m.*

chandelier, *n.* araña de luces.

change, 1. *n.* cambio; (from a bill) moneda *f.* 2. *v.* cambiar.

changeability, *n.* mutabilidad *f.*

changeable, *a.* variable, inconstante.

changer, *n.* cambiador *m.*

channel, 1. *n.* canal *m.* 2. *v.* encauzar.

chant, 1. *n.* canto llano *m.* 2. *v.* cantar.

chaos, *n.* caos *m.*

chaotic, *a.* caótico.

chap, 1. *n.* (coll.) tipo *m.* 2. *v.* rajar.

chapel, *n.* capilla *f.*

chaperon, *n.* dueña *f.*

chaplain, *n.* capellán *m.*

chapter, *n.* capítulo *m.*

char, *v.* carbonizar.

character, *n.* carácter *m.*

characteristic, 1. *a.* característico. 2. *n.* característica *f.*

characterization, *n.* caracterización *f.*

characterize, *v.* caracterizar.

charcoal, *n.* carbón leña.

charge, 1. *n.* acusación *f.;* ataque *m.* 2. *v.* cargar; acusar; atacar.

chariot, *n.* carroza *f.*

charisma, *n.* carisma *m.*

charitable, *a.* caritativo.

charitableness, *n.* caridad *f.*

charitably, *adv.* caritativamente.

charity, *n.* caridad *f.;* (alms) limosna *f.*

charlatan, *n.* charlatán -na.

charlatanism, *n.* charlatanería *f.*

charm, 1. *n.* encanto *m.;* (witchcraft) hechizo *m.* 2. *v.* encantar; hechizar.

charming, *a.* encantador.

charred, *a.* carbonizado.

chart, *n.* mapa *m.*

charter, 1. *n.* carta *f.* 2. *v.* alquilar.

charter flight, vuelo charter *m.*

chase, 1. *n.* caza *f.* 2. *v.* cazar; perseguir.

chaser, *n.* perseguidor *m.*

chasm, *n.* abismo *m.*

chassis, *n.* chasis *m.*

chaste, *a.* casto.

chasten, *v.* corregir, castigar.

chastise, *v.* castigar.

chastisement, *n.* castigo *m.*

chastity, *n.* castidad, pureza *f.*

chat, 1. *n.* plática, charla *f.* 2. *v.* platicar, charlar.

chateau, *n.* castillo *m.*

chattels, *n.pl.* bienes *m.*

chatter, 1. *v.* cotorrear; (teeth) rechinar. 2. *n.* cotorreo *m.*

chatterbox, *n.* charlador *m.*

chauffeur, *n.* chofer *m.*

cheap, *a.* barato.

cheapen, *v.* rebajar, menospreciar.

cheaply, *adv.* barato.

cheapness, *n.* baratura *f.*

cheat, *v.* engañar.

cheater, *n.* engañador *m.*

check, 1. *n.* verificación *f.;* (bank) cheque *m.;* (restaurant) cuenta *f.;* (chess) jaque *m.* 2. *v.* verificar.

checkers, *n.* juego de damas.

checkmate, *v.* dar mate.

cheek, *n.* mejilla *f.*

cheer, 1. *n.* alegría *f.;* aplauso *m.* 2. *v.* alegrar; aplaudir.

cheerful, *a.* alegre.

cheerfully, *adv.* alegremente.

cheerfulness, *n.* alegría *f.*

cheerless, *a.* triste.

cheery, *a.* alegre.

cheese, *n.* queso *m.* **cottage c.,** requesón *m.*

chef, *n.* cocinero en jefe.

chemical, 1. *a.* químico. 2. *n.* reactivo *m.*

chemically, *adv.* químicamente.

chemist, *n.* químico *m.*

chemistry, *n.* química *f.*

chemotherapy, *n.* quimoterapía *f.*

chenille, *n.* felpilla *f.*

cherish, *v.* apreciar.

cherry, *n.* cereza *f.*

cherub, *n.* querubín *m.*

chess, *n.* ajedrez *m.*

chest, *n.* arca *f.;* (physiology) pecho *m.*

chestnut, *n.* castaña *f.*

chevron, *n.* sardineta *f.*

chew, *v.* mascar, masticar.

chewer, *n.* mascador *m.*

chic, *a.* elegante, paquete.

chicanery, *n.* trampería *f.*

chick, *n.* pollito.

chicken, *n.* pollo *m.*, gallina *f.*

chicken-hearted, *a.* cobarde.

chicken pox, *n.* viruelas locas *f.*

chicle, *n.* chicle *m.*

chicory, *n.* achicoria *f.*

chide, *v.* regañar, reprender.

chief, 1. *a.* principal. 2. *n.* jefe *m.*

chiefly, *adv.* principalmente, mayormente.

chieftain, *n.* caudillo *m.;* (Indian c.) cacique *m.*

chiffon, *n.* chifón *m.*

chilblain, *n.* sabañón *m.*

child, *n.* niño -ña; hijo -ja.

childbirth, *n.* parto *m.*

childhood, *n.* niñez *f.*

childish, *a.* pueril.

childishness, *n.* puerilidad *f.*

childless, *a.* sin hijos.

childlike, *a.* infantil.

Chilean, *a.* & *n.* chileno -na.

chili, *n.* chile ají *m.*

chill, 1. *n.* frío; escalofrío *m.* 2. *v.* enfriar.

chilliness, *n.* frialdad *f.*

chilly, *a.* frío; friolento.

chimes, *n.* juego de campanas.

chimney, *n.* chimenea *f.*

chimpanzee, *n.* chimpancé *m.*

chin, *n.* barba *f.*

china, *n.* loza *f.*

chinchilla, *n.* chinchilla *f.*

Chinese, *a.* & *n.* chino -na.

chink, *n.* grieta *f.*

chintz, *n.* zaraza *f.*

chip, 1. *n.* astilla *f.* 2. *v.* astillar.

chiropodist, *n.* pedicuro *m.*

chiropractor, *n.* quiroprático *m.*

chirp, 1. *n.* chirrido *m.* 2. *v.* chirriar, piar.

chisel, 1. *n.* cincel *m.* 2. *v.* cincelar, talar.

chivalrous, *a.* caballeroso.

chivalry, *n.* caballería *f.*

chive, *n.* cebollino *m.*

chloride, *n.* cloruro *m.*

chlorine, *n.* cloro *m.*

chloroform, *n.* cloroformo *m.*

chlorophyll, *n.* clorófila *f.*

chock-full, *a.* repleto, colmado.

chocolate, *n.* chocolate *m.*

choice, 1. *a.* selecto, escogido. 2. *n.* selección *f.;* escogimiento *m.*

choir, *n.* coro *m.*

choke, *v.* sofocar, ahogar.

cholera, *n.* cólera *f.*

choleric, *a.* colérico, irascible.

choose, *v.* elegir, escoger.

chop, 1. *n.* chuleta, costilla *f.* 2. *v.* tajar; cortar.

chopper, *n.* tajador *m.*

choppy, *a.* agitado.

choral, *a.* coral.

chord, *n.* cuerda *f.*

chore, *n.* tarea *f.*, quehacer *m.*

choreography, *n.* coreografía *f.*

chorister, *n.* corista *m.*

chorus, *n.* coro *m.*

christen, *v.* bautizar.

Christendom, *n.* cristiandad *f.*

Christian, *a.* & *n.* cristiano -na.

Christianity, *n.* cristianismo *m.*

Christmas, *n.* navidad, pascua *f.* Merry C., felices pascuas. C. Eve, nochebuena *f.*

chromatic, *a.* cromático.

chromium, *n.* cromo *m.*

chromosome, *n.* cromosoma *m.*

chronic, *a.* crónico.

chronicle, *n.* crónica *f.*

chronological, *a.* cronológico.

chronology, *n.* cronología *f.*

chrysalis, *n.* crisálida *f.*

chrysanthemum, *n.* crisantemo *m.*

chubby, *a.* regordete.

chuck, *v.* (cluck) cloquear; (throw) echar, tirar.

chuckle, *v.* reír entre dientes.

chum, *n.* amigo *m.;* compinche *m.*

chummy, *a.* íntimo.

chunk, *n.* trozo *m.*

chunky, *a.* fornido, trabado.

church, *n.* iglesia *f.*

churchman, *n.* eclesiástico *m.*

churchyard, *n.* cementerio *m.*

churn, 1. *n.* mantequera *f.* 2. *v.* agitar, revolver.

chute, *n.* conducto *m.;* canal *f.*

cicada, *n.* cigarra, chicharra *f.*

cider, *n.* sidra *f.*

cigar, *n.* cigarro, puro *m.*

cigarette, *n.* cigarrillo, pitillo *m.* **c. case,** cigarrillera *f.*

cinchona, *n.* cinchona *f.*

cinder, *n.* ceniza *f.*

cinema, *n.* cine *m.*

cinnamon, *n.* canela *f.*

cipher, *n.* cifra *f.*

circle, *n.* círculo *m.*

circuit, *n.* circuito *m.*

circuitous, *a.* tortuoso.

circuitously, *adv.* tortuosamente.

circular, *a.* circular, redondo.

circularize, *v.* hacer circular.

circulate, *v.* circular.

circulation, *n.* circulación *f.*

circulator, *n.* diseminador *m.*

circulatory, *a.* circulatorio.

circumcise, *v.* circuncidar.

circumcision, *n.* circuncisión *f.*

circumference, *n.* circunferencia *f.*

circumlocution, *n.* circunlocución *f.*

circumscribe, *v.* circunscribir; limitar.

circumspect, *a.* discreto.

circumstance, *n.* circunstancia *f.*

circumstantial, *a.* circunstancial, indirecto.

circumstantially, *adv.* minuciosamente.

circumvent, *v.* evadir, evitar.

circumvention, *n.* trampa *f.;* estratagema *f.*

circus, *n.* circo *m.*

cirrhosis, *n.* cirrosis *f.*

cistern, *n.* cisterna *f.*

citadel, *n.* ciudadela *f.*

citation, *n.* citación *f.*

cite, *v.* citar.

citizen, *n.* ciudadano -na.

citizenship, *n.* ciudadanía *f.*

citric, *a.* cítrico.

city, *n.* ciudad *f.*

civic, *a.* cívico.

civics, *n.* ciencia del gobierno civil.

civil, *a.* civil; cortés.

civilian, *a.* & *n.* civil *m.*

civility, *n.* cortesía *f.*

civilization, *n.* civilización *f.*

civilize, *v.* civilizar.

civil service, *n.* servicio civil oficial *m.*

civil war, *n.* guerra civil *f.*

clabber, 1. *n.* cuajo *m.* 2. *v.* cuajarse.

clad, *a.* vestido.

claim, 1. *n.* demanda; pretensión *f.* 2. *v.* demandar, reclamar.

claimant, *n.* reclamante *m.*

clairvoyance, *n.* clarividencia *f.*

clairvoyant, *a.* clarividente.

clam, *n.* almeja *f.*

clamber, *v.* trepar.

clamor, 1. *n.* clamor *m.* 2. *v.* clamar.

clamorous, *a.* clamoroso.

clamp, 1. *n.* prensa de sujeción *f.* 2. *v.* asegurar, sujetar.

clan, *n.* tribu *f.*

clandestine, *a.* clandestino.

clandestinely, *adv.* clandestinamente.

clangor, *n.* estruendo *m.*, estrépito *m.*

clannish, *a.* unido; exclusivista.

clap, *v.* aplaudir.

clapboard, *n.* chilla *f.*

claque, *n.* claque *f.*

claret, *n.* clarete *m.*

clarification, *n.* clarificación *f.*

clarify, *v.* clarificar.

clarinet, *n.* clarinete *m.*

clarinetist, *n.* clarinero *m.*

clarity, *n.* claridad *f.*

clash, 1. *n.* choque *m.* 2. *v.* chocar.

clasp, 1. *n.* broche *m.* 2. *v.* abrochar.

class, *n.* clase *f.*

classic, classical, *a.* clásico.

classicism, *n.* clasicismo *m.*

classifiable, *a.* clasificable, calificable.

classification, *n.* clasificación *f.*

classify, *v.* clasificar.

classmate, *n.* compañero de clase.

classroom, *n.* sala de clase.

clatter, 1. *n.* alboroto *m.* 2. *v.* alborotar.

clause, *n.* cláusula *f.*

claustrophobia, *n.* claustrofobia *f.*

claw, *n.* garra *f.*

clay, *n.* arcilla *f.;* barro *m.*

clean, 1. *a.* limpio. 2. *v.* limpiar.

cleaner, *n.* limpiador -ra.

cleanliness, *n.* limpieza *f.*

cleanse, *v.* limpiar, purificar.

cleanser, *n.* limpiador *m.*, purificador *m.*

clear, *a.* claro.

clearance, *n.* espacio libre. **c. sale,** venta de liquidación.

clearing, *n.* despejo *m.;* desmonte *m.*

clearly, *adv.* claramente, evidentemente.

clearness, *n.* claridad *f.*

cleavage, *n.* resquebradura *f.*

cleaver, *n.* partidor *m.*, hacha *f.*

clef, *n.* clave, llave *f.*

clemency, *n.* clemencia *f.*

clench, *v.* agarrar.

clergy, *n.* clero *m.*

clergyman, *n.* clérigo *m.*

clerical, *a.* clerical. **c. work,** trabajo de dependientes.

clericalism, *n.* clericalismo *m.*

clerk, *n.* dependiente, escribiente *m.*

clerkship, *n.* escribanía *f.*, secretaría *f.*

clever, a. diestro, hábil.

cleverly, adv. diestramente, hábilmente.

cleverness, n. destreza f.

cliché, n. cliché m.

client, n. cliente m.

clientele, n. clientela f.

cliff, n. precipicio, risco m.

climate, n. clima m.

climatic, a. climático.

climax, n. colmo m., culminación f.

climb, v. escalar; subir.

climber, n. trepador m., escalador m; (bot.) enredadera f.

clinch, v. afirmar.

cling, v. pegarse.

clinic, n. clínica f.

clinical, a. clínico.

clinically, adv. clinicalmente.

clip, 1. n. grapa f. **paper c.,** gancho m. **2.** v. prender; (shear) trasquilar.

clipper, n. recortador m.; (aero.) clíper m.

clipping, n. recorte m.

clique, n. camarilla f., compadraje m.

cloak, n. capa f., manto m.

clock, n. reloj m. **alarm c.,** despertador m.

clod, n. terrón m.; césped m.

clog, v. obstruir.

cloister, n. claustro m.

clone, m. ser viviente reproducido a base de las células de otro.

close, 1. a. cercano. **2.** adv. cerca. **c. to,** cerca de. **3.** v. cerrar; tapar.

closely, adv. (near) de cerca; (tight) estrechamente; (care) cuidadosamente.

closeness, n. contigüidad f., apretamiento m.; (airless) falta de ventilación f.

closet, n. gabinete m. **clothes c.,** ropero m.

clot, 1. n. coagulación f. **2.** v. coagularse.

cloth, n. paño m.; tela f.

clothe, v. vestir.

clothes, clothing, n. ropa f.

clothing, n. vestidos m., ropa f.

cloud, n. nube f.

cloudburst, n. chaparrón m.

cloudiness, n. nebulosidad f.; obscuridad f.

cloudless, a. despejado, sin nubes.

cloudy, a. nublado.

clove, n. clavo m.

clover, n. trébol m.

clown, n. bufón m.

clownish, a. grosero; bufonesco.

cloy, v. saciar.

club, 1. n. porra f.; (social) círculo, club m.; (cards) basto m. **2.** v. golpear con una porra.

clubfoot, n. pateta m., pie zambo m.

clue, n. seña, pista f.

clump, n. grupo m., masa f.

clumsiness, n. tosquedad f., desmaña f.

clumsy, a. torpe, desmañado.

cluster, 1. n. grupo m.; (fruit) racimo m. **2.** v. agrupar.

clutch, 1. n. (auto.) embrague m. **2.** v. agarrar.

clutter, 1. n. confusión f. **2.** v. poner en desorden.

coach, 1. n. coche, vagón m.; coche ordinario; (sports) entrenador m. **2.** v. entrenar.

coachman, n. cochero m.

coagulate, v. coagular.

coagulation, n. coagulación f.

coal, n. carbón m.

coalesce, v. unirse, soldarse.

coalition, n. coalición f.

coal oil, n. petróleo m.

coal tar, n. alquitrán m.

coarse, a. grosero, burdo; (material) tosco, grueso.

coarsen, v. vulgarizar.

coarseness, n. grosería; tosquedad f.

coast, 1. n. costa f., litoral m. **2.** v. deslizarse.

coastal, a. costanero.

coast guard, n. costanero f.

coat, 1. n. saco m., chaqueta f.; (paint) capa f. **2.** v. cubrir.

coat of arms, n. escudo m.

coax, v. instar.

cobalt, n. cobalto m.

cobbler, n. zapatero m.

cobblestone, n. guijarro m.

cobra, n. cobra f.

cobweb, n. telaraña f.

cocaine, n. cocaína f.

cock, n. (rooster) gallo m.; (water, etc.) llave f.; (gun) martillo m.

cockfight, n. riña de gallos f.

cockpit, n. gallera f.; reñidero de gallos m.

cockroach, n. cucaracha f.

cocktail, n. coctel m.

cocky, a. confiado, atrevido.

cocoa, n. cacao m.

coconut, n. coco m.

cocoon, n. capullo m.

cod, n. bacalao m.

code, n. código m.; clave f.

codeine, n. codeína f.

codfish, n. bacalao m.

codify, v. compilar.

coeducation, n. coeducación f.

coequal, a. mutuamente igual.

coerce, v. forzar.

coercion, n. coerción f.

coercive, a. coercitivo.

coexist, v. coexistir.

coffee, n. café m. **c. plantation,** cafetal m.

coffer, n. cofre m.

coffin, n. ataúd m.

cog, n. diente de rueda m.

cogent, a. convincente.

cogitate, v. pensar, reflexionar.

cognizance, n. conocimiento m., comprensión f.

cognizant, a. conocedor, informado.

cogwheel, n. rueda dentada f.

cohere, v. pegarse.

coherent, a. coherente.

cohesion, n. cohesión f.

cohesive, a. cohesivo.

cohort, n. cohorte f.

coiffure, n. peinado, tocado m.

coil, 1. n. rollo m.; (naut.) adujada f. **2.** v. enrollar.

coin, n. moneda f.

coinage, n. sistema monetario f.

coincide, v. coincidir.

coincidence, n. coincidencia; casualidad f.

coincident, a. coincidente.

coincidental, a. coincidental.

coincidentally, adv. coincidentalmente, al mismo tiempo.

colander, n. colador m.

cold, a. & n. frío m.; (med.) resfriado m. **to be c.,** tener frío; (weather) hacer frío.

coldly, adv. friamente.

coldness, n. frialdad f.

collaborate, v. colaborar.

collaboration, n. colaboración f.

collaborator, n. colaborador m.

collapse, 1. n. desplome m.; (med.) colapso m. **2.** v. desplomarse.

collar, n. cuello m.

collarbone, n. clavícula f.

collate, v. comparar.

collateral, 1. a. colateral. **2.** n. garantía f.

collation, n. comparación f.; (food) colación f., merienda f.

colleague, n. colega m. & f.

collect, v. cobrar; recoger; coleccionar.

collection, n. colección f.

collective, a. colectivo.

collectively, adv. colectivamente, en masa.

collector, n. colector -ra; coleccionista m. & f.

college, n. colegio m.; universidad f.

collegiate, a. colegiado m.

collide, v. chocar.

collision, n. choque m.

colloquial, a. familiar.

colloquially, adv. familiarmente.

colloquy, n. conversación f., coloquio m.

collusion, n. colusión f., connivencia f.

Colombian, a. & n. colombiano -na.

colon, n. colon m.; (punct.) dos puntos.

colonel, n. coronel m.

colonial, a. colonial.

colonist, n. colono m.

colonization, n. colonización f.

colonize, v. colonizar.

colony, n. colonia f.

color, 1. n. color; colorido m. **2.** v. colorar; colorir.

coloration, n. colorido m.

colored, a. de color.

colorful, a. vívido.

colorless, a. descolorido, sin color.

colossal, *a.* colosal.

colt, *n.* porto *m.*

column, *n.* columna *f.*

coma, *n.* coma *m.*

comb, 1. *n.* peine *m.* **2.** *v.* peinar.

combat, 1. *n.* combate *m.* **2.** *v.* combatir.

combatant, *n.* combatiente *m.*

combative, *a.* combativo.

combination, *n.* combinación *f.*

combine, *v.* combinar.

combustible, *a. & n.* combustible *m.*

combustion, *n.* combustión *f.*

come, *v.* venir. **c. back,** volver. **c. in,** entrar. **c. out,** salir. **c. up,** subir. **c. upon,** encontrarse con.

comedian, *n.* cómico -ca.

comedienne, *n.* cómica *f.,* actriz *f.*

comedy, *n.* comedia *f.*

comet, *n.* cometa *m.*

comfort, 1. *n.* confort *m.;* solaz *m.* **2.** *v.* confortar; solazar.

comfortable, *a.* cómodo.

comfortably, *adv.* cómodamente.

comforter, *n.* colcha *f.*

comfortingly, *adv.* confortantemente.

comfortless, *a.* sin consuelo; sin comodidades.

comic, comical, *a.* cómico.

coming, 1. *n.* venida *f.,* llegada *f.* **2.** *a.* próximo, que viene, entrante.

comma, *n.* coma *f.*

command, 1. *n.* mando *m.* **2.** *v.* mandar.

commandeer, *v.* reclutir forzosamente, expropiar.

commander, *n.* comandante *m.*

commander in chief, *n.* generalisimo, jefe supremo.

commandment, *n.* mandato; mandamiento *m.*

commemorate, *v.* conmemorar.

commemoration, *n.* conmemoración *f.*

commemorative, *a.* conmemorativo.

commence, *v.* comenzar, principiar.

commencement, *n.* comienzo *m.;* graduación *f.*

commend, *v.* encomendar.

commendable, *a.* recomendable.

commendably, *adv.* loablemente.

commendation, *n.* recomendación *f.*

commensurate, *a.* proporcionado.

comment, 1. *n.* comento *m.* **2.** *v.* comentar.

commentary, *n.* comentario *m.*

commentator, *n.* comentador -ra.

commerce, *n.* comercio *m.*

commercial, *a.* comercial.

commercialism, *n.* comercialismo *m.*

commercialize, *v.* mercantilizar, explotar.

commercially, *a. & adv.* comercial.

commiserate, *v.* compadecerse.

commissary, *n.* comisario *m.*

commission, 1. *n.* comisión *f.* **2.** *v.* comisionar.

commissioner, *n.* comisionista *m. & f.*

commit, *v.* cometer.

commitment, *n.* compromiso *m.*

committee, *n.* comité *m.*

commodious, *a.* cómodo.

commodity, *n.* mercadería *f.*

common, *a.* común; ordinario.

commonly, *adv.* comúnmente, vulgarmente.

commonplace, *a.* trivial, banal.

commonwealth, *n.* estado *m.;* nación *f.*

commotion, *n.* tumulto *m.*

communal, *a.* comunal, público.

commune, 1. *n.* distrito municipal *m.;* comuna *f.* **2.** *v.* conversar.

communicable, *a.* comunicativo.

communicate, *v.* comunicar.

communication, *n.* comunicación *f.*

communicative, *a.* comunicativo.

communion, *n.* comunión *f.* **take c.,** comulgar.

communiqué, *n.* comunicación *f.*

communism, *n.* comunismo *m.*

communist, *n.* comunista *m. & f.*

communistic, *a.* comunístico.

community, *n.* comunidad *f.*

commutation, *n.* conmutación *f.*

commuter, *n.* empleado que viaja diariamente desde su domicilio hasta la ciudad donde trabaja.

compact, 1. *a.* compacto. **2.** *n.* pacto *m.;* (lady's) polvera *f.*

companion, *n.* compañero -ra.

companionable, *a.* sociable.

companionship, *n.* compañerismo *m.*

company, *n.* compañía *f.*

comparable, *a.* comparable.

comparative, *a.* comparativo.

comparatively, *a.* relativamente.

compare, *v.* comparar.

comparison, *n.* comparación *f.*

compartment, *n.* compartimiento *m.*

compass, *n.* compás *m.;* (naut.) brújula *f.*

compassion, *n.* compasión *f.*

compassionate, *a.* compasivo.

compassionately, *adv.* compasivamente.

compatible, *a.* compatible.

compatriot, *n.* compatriota *m. & f.*

compel, *v.* obligar.

compensate, *v.* compensar.

compensation, *n.* compensación *f.*

compensatory, *a.* compensatorio.

compete, *v.* competir.

competence, *n.* competencia *f.*

competent, *a.* competente, capaz.

competently, *adv.* competentemente.

competition, *n.* concurrencia *f.;* concurso *m.*

competitive, *a.* competidor.

competitor, *n.* competidor -ra.

compile, *v.* compilar.

complacency, *n.* complacencia *f.*

complacent, *a.* complaciente.

complacently, *adv.* complacientemente.

complain, *v.* quejarse.

complaint, *n.* queja *f.*

complement, *n.* complemento *m.*

complete, 1. *a.* completo **2.** *v.* completar.

completely, *adv.* completamente, enteramente.

completeness, *n.* integridad *f.*

completion, *n.* terminación *f.*

complex, *a.* complejo.

complexion, *n.* tez *f.*

complexity, *n.* complejidad *f.*

compliance, *n.* consentimiento *m.* **in c. with,** de acuerdo con.

compliant, *a.* dócil; complaciente.

complicate, *v.* complicar.

complicated, *a.* complicado.

complication, *n.* complicación *f.*

complicity, *n.* complicidad *f.*

compliment, 1. *n.* flor *f.* **2.** *v.* felicitar; echar flores.

complimentary, *a.* galante, obsequioso, regaloso.

comply, *v.* cumplir.

component, *a. & n.* componente *m.*

comport, *v.* portarse.

compose, *v.* componer.

composed, *a.* tranquilo; (made up) compuesto.

composer, *n.* compositor -ra.

composite, *a.* compuesto.

composition, *n.* composición *f.*

composure, *n.* serenidad *f.;* calma *f.*

compote, *n.* compota *f.*

compound, *a. & n.* compuesto *m.*

comprehend, *v.* comprender.

comprehensible, *a.* comprensible.

comprehension, *n.* comprensión *f.*

comprehensive, *a.* comprensivo.

compress, 1. *n.* cabezal *m.* **2.** *v.* comprimir.

compressed, *a.* comprimido.

compression, *n.* compresión *f.*

compressor, *n.* compresor *m.*

comprise, v. comprender; abarcar.
compromise, 1. n. compromiso m. **2.** v. comprometer.
compromiser, n. compromisario m.
compulsion, n. compulsión f.
compulsive, a. compulsivo.
compulsory, a. obligatorio.
compunction, n. compunción f.; escrúpulo m.
computation, n. computación f.
compute, v. computar, calcular.
computer, n. computadora f., ordenador m.
computerize, v. procesar en computadora.
comrade, n. camarada m. & f.; compañero -ra.
comradeship, n. camaradería f.
concave, a. cóncavo.
conceal, v. ocultar, esconder.
concealment, n. ocultación f.
concede, v. conceder.
conceit, n. amor propio; engreimiento m.
conceited, a. engreído.
conceivable, a. concebible.
conceive, v. concebir.
concentrate, v. concentrar.
concentration, n. concentración f.
concept, n. concepto m.
conception, n. concepción f.; concepto m.
concern, 1. n. interés m.; inquietud f.; (com.) negocio m. **2.** v. concernir.
concerning, prep. respecto a.
concert, n. concierto m.
concerted, a. convenido.
concession, n. concesión f.
conciliate, v. conciliar.
conciliation, n. conciliación f.
conciliator, n. conciliador m.
conciliatory, a. conciliatorio.
concise, a. conciso.
concisely, adv. concisamente.
conciseness, n. concisión f.
conclave, n. conclave m.
conclude, v. concluir.
conclusion, n. conclusión f.
conclusive, a. conclusivo, decisivo.
conclusively, adv. concluyentemente.
concoct, v. confeccionar.
concomitant, n. & a. concomitante.
concord, n. concordia f.
concordat, n. concordato m.
concourse, n. concurso m.; confluencia f.
concrete, a. concreto.
concretely, adv. concretamente.
concubine, n. concubina, amiga f.
concur, v. concurrir.
concurrence, n. concurrencia f.; casualidad f.
concurrent, a. concurrente.
concussion, n. concusión f.; (c.

of the brain) conmoción cerebral f.
condemn, v. condenar.
condemnable, a. culpable, condenable.
condemnation, n. condenación f.
condensation, n. condensación f.
condense, v. condensar.
condenser, n. condensador m.
condescend, v. condescender.
condescension, n. condescendencia f.
condiment, n. condimento m.
condition, 1. n. condición f.; estado m. **2.** v. acondicionar.
conditional, a. condicional.
conditionally, adv. condicionalmente.
condole, v. condolerse.
condolence, n. pésame m.
condominium, n. apartamento en propiedad m.
condone, v. condonar.
conducive, a. conducente.
conduct, 1. n. conducta f. **2.** v. conducir.
conductivity, n. conductividad f.
conductor, n. conductor m.
conduit, n. caño m., canal f.; conducto m.
cone, n. cono m. **ice-cream c.,** barquillo de helado.
confection, n. confitura f.
confectioner, n. confitero m.
confectionery, n. dulcería f.
confederacy, n. federación f.
confederate, a. & n. confederado m.
confederation, n. confederación f.
confer, v. conferenciar; conferir.
conference, n. conferencia f.; congreso m.
confess, v. confesar.
confession, n. confesión f.
confessional, 1. n. confesionario m. **2.** a. confesional.
confessor, n. confesor m.
confetti, n. confetti m.
confidant, confidante, n. confidente m. & f.
confide, v. confiar.
confidence, n. confianza f.
confident, a. confiado; cierto.
confidential, a. confidencial.
confidentially, adv. confidencialmente, en secreto.
confidently, adv. confiadamente.
confine, 1. n. confín m. **2.** v. confinar; encerrar.
confirm, v. confirmar.
confirmation, n. confirmación f.
confiscate, v. confiscar.
confiscation, n. confiscación f.
conflagration, n. incendio m.
conflict, 1. n. conflicto m. **2.** v. oponerse; estar en conflicto.
conform, v. conformar.

conformation, n. conformación f.
conformer, n. conformista m. & f.
conformist, n. conformista m. & f.
conformity, n. conformidad f.
confound, v. confundir.
confront, v. confrontar.
confuse, v. confundir.
confusion, n. confusión f.
congeal, v. congelar, helar.
congealment, n. congelación f.
congenial, a. congenial.
congenital, a. congénito.
congenitally, adv. congenitalmente.
congestion, n. congestión f.
conglomerate, 1. v. conglomerar. **2.** a. conglomerado.
conglomeration, n. conglomeración f.
congratulate, v. felicitar.
congratulation, n. felicitación f.
congratulatory, a. congratulatorio.
congregate, v. congregar.
congregation, n. congregación f.
congress, n. congreso m.
conic, 1. n. cónica f. **2.** a. cónico.
conjecture, 1. n. conjetura f. **2.** v. conjeturar.
conjugal, a. conyugal, matrimonial.
conjugate, v. conjugar.
conjugation, n. conjugación f.
conjunction, n. conjunción f.
conjunctive, 1. n. (gram.) conjunción f. **2.** a. conjuntivo.
conjunctivitis, n. conjuntivitis f.
conjure, v. conjurar.
connect, v. juntar; relacionar.
connection, n. conexión f.
connivance, n. consentimiento m.
connive, v. disimular.
connoisseur, n. perito -ta.
connotation, n. connotación f.
connote, v. connotar.
connubial, a. conyugal.
conquer, v. conquistar.
conquerable, a. conquistable, vencible.
conqueror, n. conquistador m.
conquest, n. conquista f.
conscience, n. conciencia f.
conscientious, a. concienzudo.
conscientiously, adv. escrupulosamente.
conscious, a. consciente.
consciously, adv. con conocimiento.
consciousness, n. consciencia f.
conscript, 1. n. conscripto m., recluta m. **2.** v. reclutar, alistar.
conscription, n. conscripción f., alistamiento m.
consecrate, v. consagrar.

consecration, n. consagración f.

consecutive, a. consecutivo, seguido.

consecutively, adv. consecutivamente, de seguida.

consensus, n. consenso m., acuerdo general m.

consent, 1. n. consentimiento m. **2.** v. consentir.

consequence, n. consecuencia f.

consequent, a. consiguiente.

consequential, a. importante.

consequently, adv. por lo tanto, por consiguiente.

conservation, n. conservación f.

conservatism, n. conservatismo m.

conservative, a. conservador, conservativo.

conservatory, n. (plants) invernáculo m.; (school) conservatorio m.

conserve, v. conservar.

consider, v. considerar.

considerable, a. considerable.

considerably, adv. considerablemente.

considerate, a. considerado.

considerately, adv. consideradamente.

consideration, n. consideración f.

considering, prep. visto que, en vista de.

consign, v. consignar.

consignment, n. consignación f., envío m.

consist, v. consistir.

consistency, n. consistencia f.

consistent, a. consistente.

consolation, n. consolación f.

console, v. consolar.

consolidate, v. consolidar.

consommé, n. caldo m.

consonant, n. consonante f.

consort, 1. n. conyuge m. & f.; socio. **2.** v. asociarse.

conspicuous, a. conspicuo.

conspicuously, adv. visiblemente, llamativamente.

conspicuousness, n. visibilidad f.; evidencia f.; fama f.

conspiracy, n. conspiración f.; complot m.

conspirator, n. conspirador -ra.

conspire, v. conspirar.

conspirer, n. conspirante m. & f.

constancy, n. constancia f., lealtad f.

constant, a. constante.

constantly, adv. constantemente, de continuo.

constellation, n. constelación f.

consternation, n. consternación f.

constipation, n. constipación f.

constituency, n. distrito electoral m.

constituent, 1. a. constituyente. **2.** n. elector m.

constitute, v. constituir.

constitution, n. constitución f.

constitutional, a. constitucional.

constrain, v. constreñir.

constraint, n. constreñimiento m., compulsión f.

constrict, v. apretar, estrechar.

construct, v. construir.

construction, n. construcción f.

constructive, a. constructivo.

constructively, adv. constructivamente; por deducción.

constructor, n. constructor m.

construe, v. interpretar.

consul, n. cónsul m.

consular, a. consular.

consulate, n. consulado m.

consult, v. consultar.

consultant, n. consultante m. & f.

consultation, n. consulta f.

consume, v. consumir.

consumer, n. consumidor -ra.

consummation, n. consumación f.

consumption, n. consumo m.

consumptive, 1. n. tísico m. **2.** a. consuntivo.

contact, 1. n. contacto m. **2.** v. ponerse en contacto con.

contagion, n. contagio m.

contagious, a. contagioso.

contain, v. contener.

container, n. envase m.

contaminate, v. contaminar.

contemplate, v. contemplar.

contemplation, n. contemplación f.

contemplative, a. contemplativo.

contemporary, n. & a. contemporáneo -nea.

contempt, n. desprecio m.

contemptible, v. vil, despreciable.

contemptuous, a. desdeñoso.

contemptuously, adv. desdeñosamente.

contend, v. contender; competir.

contender, n. competidor m.

content, 1. a. contento. **2.** n. contenido m. **3.** v. contentar.

contented, a. contento.

contention, n. contención f.

contentment, n. contentamiento m.

contest, 1. n. concurso m. **2.** v. disputar.

contestable, a. contestable.

context, n. contexto m.

contiguous, a. contiguo.

continence, n. continencia f., castidad f.

continent, n. continente m.

continental, a. continental.

contingency, n. eventualidad f., casualidad f.

contingent, a. contingente.

continual, a. continuo.

continuation, n. continuación f.

continue, v. continuar.

continuity, n. continuidad f.

continuous, a. continuo.

continuously, adv. continualmente.

contour, n. contorno m.

contraband, n. contrabando m.

contraception, n. contracepción f.

contract, 1. n. contrato m. **2.** v. contraer.

contraction, n. contracción f.

contractor, n. contratista m.

contradict, v. contradecir.

contradiction, n. contradicción f.

contradictory, a. contradictorio, opuesto.

contralto, n. contralto m.

contrary, a. & n. contrario m.

contrast, 1. n. contraste m. **2.** v. contrastar.

contribute, v. contribuir.

contribution, n. contribución f.

contributive, contributory, a. contribuyente.

contributor, n. contribuidor m.

contrite, a. contrito.

contrition, n. contrición f.

contrivance, n. aparato m.; estratagema f.

contrive, v. inventar, tramar; darse maña.

control, 1. n. control m. **2.** v. controlar.

controllable, a. controlable, dominable.

controller, n. interventor m., contralor m.

controversial, a. contencioso.

controversy, n. controversia f.

contusion, n. contusión f.

convalesce, v. convalecer.

convalescence, n. convalecencia f.

convalescent, n. convaleciente m. & f.

convene, v. juntarse; convocar.

convenience, n. comodidad f.

convenient, a. cómodo. **to be c.,** convenir.

conveniently, adv. cómodamente.

convent, n. convento m.

convention, n. convención f.

conventional, a. convencional.

conventionally, adv. convencionalmente.

converge, v. convergir.

convergence, n. convergencia f.

convergent, a. convergente.

conversant, a. versado; entendido (de).

conversation, n. conversación, plática f.

conversational, a. de conversación.

conversationalist, n. conversador m.

converse, v. conversar.

conversely, adv. a la inversa.

convert, 1. n. convertido m. **2.** v. convertir.

converter, n. convertidor m.

convertible, a. convertible.

convex, a. convexo.

convey, v. transportar; comunicar.

conveyance, n. transporte; vehículo m.

conveyor, n. conductor m.; (mech.) transportador m.

convict, 1. n. reo m. 2. v. probar de culpa.

conviction, n. convicción f.

convince, v. convencer.

convincing, a. convincente.

convivial, a. convival.

convocation, n. convocación; asamblea f.

convoke, v. convocar, citar.

convoy, n. convoy m.; escolta f.

convulse, v. convulsionar; agitar violentamente.

convulsion, n. convulsión f.

convulsive, a. convulsivo.

cook, 1. n. cocinero -ra. 2. v. cocinar, cocer.

cookbook, n. libro de cocina m.

cooky, n. galleta dulce f.

cool, 1. a. fresco. 2. v. refrescar.

cooler, n. enfriadera f.

coolness, n. frescura f.

coop, 1. n. jaula f. chicken c., gallinero m. 2. v. enjaular.

cooperate, v. cooperar.

cooperation, n. cooperación f.

cooperative, a. cooperativo.

cooperatively, adv. cooperativamente.

coordinate, v. coordinar.

coordination, n. coordinación f.

coordinator, n. coordinador m.

cope, v. contender. c. with, superar, hacer frente a.

copier, n. copiadora f.

copious, a. copioso, abundante.

copiously, adv. copiosamente.

copiousness, n. copia f., abundancia f.

copper, n. cobre m.

copy, 1. n. copia f.; ejemplar m. 2. v. copiar.

copyist, n. copista m. & f.

copyright, n. derechos de propiedad literaria m.pl.

coquetry, n. coquetería f.

coquette, n. coqueta f.

coral, n. coral m.

cord, n. cuerda f.

cordial, a. cordial.

cordiality, n. cordialidad f.

cordially, adv. cordialmente.

cordovan, n. cordobán m.

corduroy, n. pana f.

core, n. corazón; centro m.

cork, n. corcho m.

corkscrew, n. tirabuzón m.

corn, n. maíz m.

cornea, n. córnea f.

corner, n. rincón m.; (of street) esquina f.

cornet, n. corneta f.

cornetist, n. cornetín m.

cornice, n. cornisa f.

cornstarch, n. maicena f.

corollary, n. corolario m.

coronary, a. coronario.

coronation, n. coronación f.

corporal, 1. a. corpóreo. 2. n. cabo m.

corporate, a. corporativo.

corporation, n. corporación f.

corps, n. cuerpo m.

corpse, n. cadáver m.

corpulent, a. corpulento.

corpuscle, n. corpúsculo m.

corral, 1. n. corral m. 2. v. acorralar.

correct, 1. a. correcto. 2. v. corregir.

correction, n. corrección; enmienda f.

corrective, n. & a. correctivo.

correctly, adv. correctamente.

correctness, n. exactitud f.

correlate, v. correlacionar.

correlation, n. correlación f.

correspond, v. corresponder.

correspondence, n. correspondencia f.

correspondent, a. correspondiente.

corresponding, a. correspondiente.

corridor, n. corredor, pasillo m.

corroborate, v. corroborar.

corroboration, n. corroboración f.

corroborative, a. corroborante.

corrode, v. corroer.

corrosion, n. corrosión f.

corrugate, v. arrugar; ondular.

corrupt, 1. a. corrompido. 2. v. corromper.

corruptible, a. corruptible.

corruption, n. corrupción f.

corruptive, a. corruptivo.

corset, n. corsé m.; (girdle) faja f.

cortege, n. comitiva f., séquito m.

corvette, n. corbeta f.

cosmetic, a. & n. cosmético.

cosmic, a. cósmico.

cosmopolitan, a. & n. cosmopolita m. & f.

cosmos, n. cosmos m.

cost, 1. n. coste m.; costa f. 2. v. costar.

Costa Rican, a. & n. costarricense m. & f.

costly, a. costoso, caro.

costume, n. traje; disfraz m.

cot, n. catre m.

coterie, n. camarilla f.

cotillion, n. cotillón m.

cottage, n. casita f.

cottage cheese, n. requesón m.

cotton, n. algodón m.

cottonseed, n. semilla del algodón f.

couch, n. sofá m.

cougar, n. cuguar m.

cough, 1. n. tos f. 2. v. toser.

council, n. consejo, concilio m.

counsel, 1. n. consejo; (law) abogado m. 2. v. aconsejar. to keep one's c., no decir nada.

counselor, n. consejero; (law) abogado m.

count, 1. n. cuenta f.; (title) conde m. 2. v. contar.

countenance, 1. n. aspecto m.; cara f. 2. v. aprobar.

counter, 1. adv. c. to, contra, en contra de. 2. n. mostrador m.

counteract, v. contrariar.

counteraction, n. oposición f.

counterbalance, 1. n. contrapeso m. 2. v. contrapesar.

counterfeit, 1. a. falsificado. 2. v. falsear.

countermand, v. contramandar.

counteroffensive, n. contraofensiva f.

counterpart, n. contraparte f.

countess, n. condesa f.

countless, a. innumerable.

country, n. campo m.; (pol.) país m.; (homeland) patria f.

countryman, n. paisano m. fellow c., compatriota m.

countryside, n. campo, paisaje m.

county, n. condado m.

coupé, n. cupé m.

couple, 1. n. par m. 2. v. unir.

coupon, n. cupón, talón m.

courage, n. valor m.

courageous, a. valiente.

course, n. curso m. of c., por supuesto, desde luego.

court, 1. n. corte f.; cortejo m.; (of law) tribunal m. 2. v. cortejar.

courteous, a. cortés.

courtesy, n. cortesía f.

courthouse, n. palacio de justicia m., tribunal m.

courtier, n. cortesano m.

courtly, adv. cortés, galante.

courtroom, n. sala de justicia f.

courtship, n. corte f.

courtyard, n. patio m.

cousin, n. primo -ma.

covenant, n. contrato, convenio m.

cover, 1. n. cubierta, tapa f. 2. v. cubrir, tapar.

covet, v. ambicionar, suspirar por.

covetous, a. codicioso.

cow, n. vaca f.

coward, n. cobarde m. & f.

cowardice, n. cobardía f.

cowardly, a. cobarde.

cowboy, n. vaquero, gaucho m.

cower, v. agacharse.

cowhide, n. cuero m.

coy, a. recatado, modesto.

coyote, n. coyote m.

cozy, a. cómodo y agradable.

crab, n. cangrejo m.

crab apple, n. manzana silvestre f.

crack, 1. n. hendedura f.; (noise) crujido m. 2. v. hender; crujir.

cracker, n. galleta f.

cradle, n. cuna f.

craft, n. arte m.

craftsman, *n.* artesano *m.*

craftsmanship, *n.* mano de obra *f.*

crafty, *a.* ladino.

crag, *n.* despeñadero *m.*

cram, *v.* rellenar, hartar.

cramp, *n.* calambre *m.*

cranberry, *n.* arándano *m.*

crane, 1. *n.* (bird) grulla *f.;* (mech.) grúa *f.*

cranium, *n.* cráneo *m.*

crank, *n.* (mech.) manivela *f.*

cranky, *a.* chiflado, caprichoso.

crash, 1. *n.* choque; estallido *m.* 2. *v.* estallar.

crate, *n.* canasto *m.*

crater, *n.* cráter *m.*

crave, *v.* desear; anhelar.

craven, *a.* cobarde.

craving, *n.* sed *m.,* anhelo *m.*

crawl, *v.* andar a gatas, arrastrarse.

crayon, *n.* creyón; lápiz *m.*

crazy, *a.* loco.

creak, *v.* crujir.

creaky, *a.* crujidero.

cream, *n.* crema *f.*

creamery, *n.* lechería *f.*

crease, 1. *n.* pliegue *m.* 2. *v.* plegar.

create, *v.* crear.

creation, *n.* creación *f.*

creative, *a.* creativo, creador.

creator, *n.* criador -ra.

creature, *n.* criatura *f.*

credence, *n.* creencia *f.*

credentials, *n.* credenciales *f.pl.*

credibility, *n.* credibilidad *f.*

credible, *a.* creíble.

credit, 1. *n.* crédito *m.* **on c.,** al fiado. 2. *v.* (com.) abonar.

creditable, *a.* fidedigno.

credit card, *n.* tarjeta de crédito *f.*

creditor, *n.* acreedor -ra.

credo, *n.* credo *m.*

credulity, *n.* credulidad *f.*

credulous, *a.* crédulo.

creed, *n.* credo *m.*

creek, *n.* riachuelo *m.*

creep, *v.* gatear.

cremate, *v.* cremar.

crematory, *n.* crematorio *m.*

creosote, *n.* creosota *f.*

crepe, *n.* crespón *m.*

crescent, *a. & n.* creciente *f.*

crest, *n.* cresta; cima *f.;* (heraldry) timbre *m.*

cretonne, *n.* cretona *f.*

crevice, *n.* grieta *f.*

crew, *n.* tripulación *f.*

crib, *n.* pesebre *m.;* camita de niño.

cricket, *n.* grillo *m.*

crime, *n.* crimen *m.*

criminal, *a. & n.* criminal.

criminologist, *n.* criminologo *m.*

criminology, *n.* criminología *f.*

crimson, *a. & n.* carmesí *m.*

cringe, *v.* encogerse, temblar.

cripple, 1. *n.* lisiado -da. 2. *v.* estropear, lisiar.

crisis, *n.* crisis *f.*

crisp, *a.* crespo, fresco.

crispness, *n.* encrespadura *f.*

crisscross, *a.* entrelazado.

criterion, *n.* criterio *m.*

critic, *n.* crítico *m.*

critical, *a.* crítico.

criticism, *n.* crítica; censura *f.*

criticize, *v.* criticar; censurar.

critique, *n.* crítica *f.*

croak, 1. *n.* graznido *m.* 2. *v.* graznar.

crochet, 1. *n.* crochet *m.* 2. *v.* hacer crochet.

crock, *n.* cazuela *f.;* olla de barro.

crockery, *n.* loza *f.*

crocodile, *n.* cocodrilo *m.*

crony, *n.* compinche *m.*

crooked, *a.* encorvado; deshonesto.

croon, *v.* canturrear.

crop, *n.* cosecha *f.*

croquet, *n.* juego de croquet *m.*

croquette, *n.* croqueta *f.*

cross, 1. *a.* enojado, mal humorado. 2. *n.* cruz *f.* 3. *v.* cruzar, atravesar.

crossbreed, 1. *n.* mestizo *m.* 2. *v.* cruzar.

cross-examine, *v.* interrogar.

cross-eyed, *a.* bisco.

cross-fertilization, *n.* alogamia *f.*

crossing, crossroads, *n.* cruce *m.*

cross section, *n.* corte transversal *m.*

crotch, *n.* bifurcación *f.;* (anat.) bragadura *f.*

crouch, *v.* agacharse.

croup, *n.* (med.) crup *m.*

croupier, *n.* crupié *m.*

crow, *n.* cuervo *m.*

crowd, 1. *n.* muchedumbre *f.;* tropel *m.* 2. *v.* apretar.

crowded, *a.* lleno de gente.

crown, 1. *n.* corona *f.* 2. *v.* coronar.

crown prince, *n.* príncipe heredero *m.*

crucial, *a.* crucial.

crucible, *n.* crisol *m.*

crucifix, *n.* crucifijo *m.*

crucifixion, *n.* crucifixión *f.*

crucify, *v.* crucificar.

crude, *a.* crudo; (oil) bruto.

crudeness, *n.* crudeza *f.*

cruel, *a.* cruel.

cruelty, *n.* crueldad *f.*

cruet, *n.* vinagrera *f.*

cruise, 1. *n.* viaje por mar. 2. *v.* navegar.

cruiser, *n.* crucero *m.*

crumb, *n.* miga; migaja *f.*

crumble, *v.* desmigajar; desmoronar.

crumple, *v.* arrugar; encogerse.

crusade, *n.* cruzada *f.*

crusader, *n.* cruzado *m.*

crush, *v.* aplastar.

crust, *n.* costra *f.*

crustacean, *n.* crustáceo *m.*

crutch, *n.* muleta *f.*

cry, 1. *n.* grito *m.* 2. *v.* gritar; (weep) llorar.

cryosurgery, *n.* criocirugía *f.*

crypt, *n.* gruta *f.,* cripta *f.*

cryptic, *a.* secreto.

cryptography, *n.* criptografía *f.*

crystal, *n.* cristal *m.*

crystalline, *a.* cristalino, transparente.

crystallize, *v.* cristalizar.

cub, *n.* cachorro *m.*

Cuban, *n. & a.* cubano -na.

cube, *n.* cubo *m.*

cubic, *a.* cúbico.

cubicle, *n.* cubículo *m.*

cubic measure, *n.* medida de capacidad *f.*

cubism, *n.* cubismo *m.*

cuckoo, *n.* cuco *m.*

cucumber, *n.* pepino *m.*

cuddle, *v.* abrazar.

cudgel, *n.* palo *m.*

cue, *n.* apunte *m.;* (billiards) taco *m.*

cuff, *n.* puño de camisa. **c. links**, gemelos.

cuisine, *n.* arte culinario *f.*

culinary, *a.* culinario.

culminate, *v.* culminar.

culmination, *n.* culminación *f.*

culpable, *a.* culpable.

culprit, *n.* criminal; delincuente *m.*

cult, *n.* culto *m.*

cultivate, *v.* cultivar.

cultivated, *a.* cultivado.

cultivation, *n.* cultivo *m.;* cultivación *f.*

cultivator, *n.* cultivador *m.*

cultural, *a.* cultural.

culture, *n.* cultura *f.*

cultured, *a.* culto.

cumbersome, *a.* pesado, incómodo.

cumulative, *a.* acumulativo.

cunning, 1. *a.* astuto. 2. *n.* astucia *f.*

cup, *n.* taza, jícara *f.*

cupboard, *n.* armario, aparador *m.*

cupidity, *n.* avaricia *f.*

curable, *a.* curable.

curator, *n.* guardián *m.*

curb, 1. *n.* freno *m.* 2. *v.* refrenar.

curd, *n.* cuajada *f.*

curdle, *v.* cuajarse, coagularse.

cure, 1. *n.* remedio *m.* 2. *v.* curar, sanar.

curfew, *n.* toque de queda *m.*

curio, *n.* objeto curioso.

curiosity, *n.* curiosidad *f.*

curious, *a.* curioso.

curl, 1. *n.* rizo *m.* 2. *v.* rizar.

curly, *a.* rizado.

currant, *n.* grosella *f.*

currency, *n.* circulación *f.;* dinero *m.*

current, *a. & n.* corriente *f.*

currently, *adv.* corrientemente.

curriculum, *n.* plan de estudio *m.*

curse, 1. *n.* maldición *f.* 2. *v.* maldecir.

cursory, *a.* sumario.

curt, *a.* brusco.

curtail, *v.* reducir; restringir.

curtain, *n.* cortina *f.;* (theat.) telón *m.*

curtsy, 1. *n.* reverencia *f.* **2.** *v.* hacer una reverencia.

curvature, *n.* curvatura *f.*

curve, 1. *n.* curva *f.* **2.** *v.* encorvar.

cushion, *n.* cojín *m.;* almohada *f.*

cuspidor, *n.* escupidera *f.*

custard, *n.* flan *m.;* natillas *f.pl.*

custodian, *n.* custodio *m.*

custody, *n.* custodia *f.*

custom, *n.* custumbre *f.*

customary, *a.* acostumbrado, usual.

customer, *n.* cliente *m.* & *f.*

customhouse, customs, *n.* aduana *f.*

cut, 1. *n.* corte *m.;* cortada *f.;* tajada *f.;* (printing) grabado *m.* **2.** *v.* cortar; tajar.

cute, *a.* mono, lindo.

cut glass, *n.* cristal tallado *m.*

cuticle, *n.* cutícula *f.*

cutlery, *n.* cuchillería *f.*

cutlet, *n.* coteleta, chuleta *f.*

cutter, *n.* cortador -ra; (naut.) cúter *m.*

cutthroat, *n.* asesino *m.*

cyclamate, *n.* ciclamato *m.*

cycle, *n.* ciclo *m.*

cyclist, *n.* ciclista *m.* & *f.*

cyclone, *n.* ciclón, huracán *m.*

cyclotron, *n.* ciclotrón *m.*

cylinder, *n.* cilindro *m.*

cylindrical, *a.* cilíndrico.

cymbal, *n.* címbalo *m.*

cynic, *n.* cínico *m.*

cynical, *a.* cínico.

cynicism, *n.* cinismo *m.*

cypress, *n.* ciprés *m.* **c. nut,** piñuela *f.*

cyst, *n.* quiste *m.*

D

dad, *n.* papa *m.,* papito *m.*

daffodil, *n.* narciso *m.*

dagger, *n.* puñal *m.*

dahlia, *n.* dalia *f.*

daily, *a.* diario, cotidiano.

daintiness, *n.* delicadeza *f.*

dainty, *a.* delicado.

dairy, *n.* lechería, quesería *f.*

dais, *n.* tablado *m.*

daisy, *n.* margarita *f.*

dale, *n.* valle *m.*

dally, *v.* holgar; perder el tiempo.

dam, *n.* presa *f.;* dique *m.*

damage, 1. *n.* daño *m.* **2.** *v.* dañar.

damask, *n.* damasco *m.*

damn, *v.* condenar.

damnation, *n.* condenación *f.*

damp, *a.* húmedo.

dampen, *v.* humedecer.

dampness, *n.* humedad *f.*

damsel, *n.* doncella *f.*

dance, 1. *n.* baile *m.;* danza *f.* **2.** *v.* bailar.

dancer, *n.* bailador -ra; (professional) bailarín -na.

dancing, *n.* baile *m.*

dandelion, *n.* amargón *m.*

dandruff, *n.* caspa *f.*

dandy, *n.* petimetre *m.*

danger, *n.* peligro *m.*

dangerous, *a.* peligroso.

dangle, *v.* colgar.

Danish, *a.* & *n.* danés -sa; dinamarqués -sa.

dapper, *a.* gallardo.

dare, *v.* atreverse, osar.

daredevil, *n.* atrevido *m.,* -da *f.*

daring, 1. *a.* atrevido. **2.** *n.* osadía *f.*

dark, 1. *a.* obscuro; moreno. **2.** *n.* obscuridad *f.*

darken, *v.* obscurecer.

darkness, *n.* obscuridad *f.*

darkroom, *n.* cámara obscura *f.*

darling, *a.* & *n.* querido, amado.

darn, *v.* zurcir.

darning needle, *n.* agujar de zurcir *m.*

dart, *n.* dardo *m.*

dash, *n.* arranque *m.;* (punct.) guión *m.*

data, *n.* datos *m.*

data processing, proceso de datos *m.*

date, *n.* fecha *f.;* (engagement) cita *f.;* (fruit) dátil *m.*

daughter, *n.* hija *f.*

daughter-in-law, *n.* nuera *f.*

daunt, *v.* intimidar.

dauntless, *a.* intrépido.

davenport, *n.* sofá *m.*

dawn, 1. *n.* alba, madrugada *f.* **2.** *v.* amanecer.

day, *n.* día *m.* **good d.,** buenos días.

daybreak, *n.* alba, madrugada *f.*

daydream, *n.* fantasía *f.*

daylight, *n.* luz del día.

daze, *v.* aturdir.

dazzle, *v.* deslumbrar.

deacon, *n.* diácono *m.*

dead, *a.* muerto.

deaden, *v.* amortecer.

deadline, *n.* límite absoluto *m.*

deadlock, *n.* paro *m.*

deadly, *a.* mortal.

deaf, *a.* sordo.

deafen, *v.* ensordecer.

deaf-mute, *n.* sordomudo *m.*

deafness, *n.* sordera *f.*

deal, 1. *n.* trato *m.;* negociación *f.* **a great d., a good d.,** mucho. **2.** *v.* tratar; negociar.

dealer, *n.* comerciante *m.,* (at cards) tallador -ra.

dean, *n.* decano *m.*

dear, *a.* querido; caro.

dearth, *n.* escasez *m.*

death, *n.* muerte *f.*

deathless, *a.* inmortal.

debacle, *n.* desastre *m.*

debase, *v.* degradar.

debatable, *a.* discutible.

debate, 1. *n.* debate *m.* **2.** *v.* disputar, deliberar.

debauch, *v.* corromper.

debilitate, *v.* debilitar.

debit, *n.* débito *m.*

debonair, *a.* cortés; alegre, vivo.

debris, *n.* escombros *m.pl.*

debt, *n.* deuda *f.*

debtor, *n.* deudor -ra.

debunk, *v.* traer a la realidad.

debut, *n.* debut, estreno *m.*

debutante, *n.* debutante *f.*

decade, *n.* década *f.*

decadence, *n.* decadencia *f.*

decadent, *a.* decadente.

decaffeinated, *a.* descafeinado.

decalcomania, *n.* calcomanía *f.*

decanter, *n.* garrafa *f.*

decapitate, *v.* descabezar.

decay, 1. *n.* descaecimiento *m.;* (dental) caries *f.* **2.** *v.* decaer; (dental) cariarse.

deceased, *a.* muerto, difunto.

deceit, *n.* engaño *m.*

deceitful, *a.* engañoso.

deceive, *v.* engañar.

December, *n.* diciembre *m.*

decency, *n.* decencia *f.;* decoro *m.*

decent, *a.* decente.

decentralize, *v.* descentralizar.

deception, *n.* decepción *f.*

deceptive, *a.* deceptivo.

decibel, *n.* decibelio *m.*

decide, *v.* decidir.

decimal, *a.* decimal.

decipher, *v.* descifrar.

decision, *n.* decisión *f.*

decisive, *a.* decisivo.

deck, *n.* cubierta *f.*

declamation, *n.* declamación *f.*

declaration, *n.* declaración *f.*

declarative, *a.* declarativo.

declare, *v.* declarar.

declension, *n.* declinación *f.*

decline, 1. *n.* decadencia *f.* **2.** *v.* decaer; negarse; (gram.) declinar.

decompose, *v.* descomponer.

decongestant, *n.* descongestionante *m.*

decorate, *v.* decorar, adornar.

decoration, *n.* decoración *f.*

decorative, *a.* decorativo.

decorator, *n.* decorador *m.*

decorous, *a.* correcto.

decorum, *n.* decoro *m.*

decrease, *v.* disminuir.

decree, *n.* decreto *m.*

decrepit, *a.* decrépito.

decry, *v.* descreditar.

dedicate, *v.* dedicar; consagrar.

dedication, *n.* dedicación; dedicatoria *f.*

deduce, deduct, *v.* deducir.

deduction, *n.* rebaja *f.*

deductive, *a.* deductivo.

deed, *n.* acción; hazaña *f.*

deem, *v.* estimar.

deep, *a.* hondo, profundo.

deepen, *v.* profundizar, ahondar.

deep freeze, *n.* congelación *f.*

deeply, *adv.* profundamente.

deer, *n.* venado, ciervo *m.*

deface, *v.* mutilar.

defamation, *n.* calmunia *f.*
defame, *v.* difamar.
default, 1. *n.* defecto *m.* **2.** *v.* faltar.
defeat, 1. *n.* derrota *f.* **2.** *v.* derrotar.
defect, *n.* defecto *m.*
defective, *a.* defectivo.
defend, *v.* defender.
defendant, *n.* acusado -da.
defender, *n.* defensor -ra.
defense, *n.* defensa *f.*
defensive, *a.* defensivo.
defer, *v.* aplazar; deferir.
deference, *n.* deferencia *f.*
defiance, *n.* desafío *m.*
defiant, *a.* desafiador.
deficiency, *n.* defecto *m.*
deficient, *a.* deficiente.
deficit, *n.* déficit, descubierto *m.*
defile, 1. *n.* desfiladero *m.* **2.** *v.* profanar.
define, *v.* definir.
definite, *a.* exacto; definitivo.
definitely, *adv.* definidamente.
definition, *n.* definición *f.*
definitive, *a.* definitivo.
deflation, *n.* desinflación *f.*
deflect, *v.* desviar.
deform, *v.* deformar.
deformity, *n.* deformidad *f.*
defraud, *v.* defraudar.
defray, *v.* costear.
deft, *a.* diestro.
defy, *v.* desafiar.
degenerate, 1. *a.* degenerado. **2.** *v.* degenerar.
degeneration, *n.* degeneración *f.*
degradation, *n.* degradación *f.*
degrade, *v.* degradar.
degree, *n.* grado *m.*
deign, *v.* condescender.
deity, *n.* deidad *f.*
dejected, *a.* abatido.
dejection, *n.* tristeza *f.*
delay, 1. *n.* retardo *m.*, demora *f.* **2.** *v.* tardar, demorar.
delegate, 1. *n.* delegado -da. **2.** *v.* delegar.
delegation, *n.* delegación *f.*
delete, *v.* suprimir.
deliberate, 1. *a.* premeditado. **2.** *v.* deliberar.
deliberately, *adv.* deliberadamente.
deliberation, *n.* deliberación *f.*
deliberative, *a.* deliberativo.
delicacy, *n.* delicadeza *f.*
delicate, *a.* delicado.
delicious, *a.* delicioso.
delight, *n.* deleite *m.*
delightful, *a.* deleitoso.
delinquency, *a.* delinquencia *f.*
delinquent, *a. & n.* delincuente.
delirious, *a.* delirante.
deliver, *v.* entregar.
deliverance, *n.* liberación; salvación *f.*
delivery, *n.* entrega *f.;* (med.) parto *m.*
delude, *v.* engañar.
deluge, *n.* inundación *f.*

delusion, *n.* decepción *f.;* engaño *m.*
delve, *v.* cavar, sondear.
demagogue, *n.* demagogo *m.*
demand, 1. *n.* demanda *f.* **2.** *v.* demandar; exigir.
demarcation, *n.* demarcación *f.*
demeanor, *n.* conducta *f.*
demented, *a.* demente, loco.
demilitarize, *v.* desmilitarizar.
demobilize, *v.* desmovilizar.
democracy, *n.* democracia *f.*
democrat, *n.* demócrata *m. & f.*
democratic, *a.* democrático.
demolish, *v.* demoler.
demon, *n.* demonio *m.*
demonstrate, *v.* demostrar.
demonstration, *n.* demostración *f.*
demonstrative, *a.* demostrativo.
demoralize, *v.* desmoralizar.
demure, *a.* modesto, serio.
den, *n.* caverna *f.;* retrete *m.*
denial, *n.* negación *f.*
denim, *n.* tela para jeans, azul de Vergara.
Denmark, *n.* Dinamarca *f.*
denomination, *n.* denominación; secta *f.*
denote, *v.* denotar.
denounce, *v.* denunciar.
dense, *a.* denso, espeso; estúpido.
density, *n.* densidad *f.*
dent, 1. *n.* abolladura *f.* **2.** *v.* abollar.
dental, *a.* dental.
dentist, *n.* dentista *m.*
dentistry, *n.* odontología *f.*
denture, *n.* dentadura *f.*
denunciation, *n.* denunciación *f.*
deny, *v.* negar, rehusar.
deodorant, *n.* desodorante *m.*
depart, *v.* partir; irse, marcharse.
department, *n.* departamento *m.*
departmental, *a.* departamental.
departure, *n.* salida; desviación *f.*
depend, *v.* depender.
dependability, *n.* confiabilidad *f.*
dependable, *a.* confiable.
dependence, *n.* dependencia *f.*
dependent, *a. & n.* dependiente *m.*
depict, *v.* pintar; representar.
deplete, *v.* agotar.
deplorable, *a.* deplorable.
deplore, *v.* deplorar.
deport, *v.* deportar.
deportation, *n.* deportación *f.*
deportment, *n.* conducta *f.*
depose, *v.* deponer.
deposit, 1. *n.* depósito *m.* **2.** *v.* depositar.
depositor, *n.* depositante *m. & f.*
depot, *n.* depósito *m.;* (railway) estación *f.*

depravity, *n.* depravación *f.*
deprecate, *v.* deprecar.
depreciate, *v.* depreciar.
depreciation, *n.* depreciación *f.*
depredation, *n.* depredación *f.*
depress, *v.* deprimir; desanimar.
depression, *n.* depresión *f.*
deprive, *v.* privar.
depth, *n.* profundidad, hondura *f.*
depth charge, *n.* carga de profundidad *f.*
deputy, *n.* diputado *m.*
deride, *v.* burlar.
derision, *n.* burla *f.*
derivation, *n.* derivación *f.*
derivative, *a.* derivativo.
derive, *v.* derivar.
derogatory, *a.* derogatorio.
derrick, *n.* grúa *f.*
descend, *v.* descender, bajar.
descendant, *n.* descendiente *m. & f.*
descent, *n.* descenso *m.;* origen *m.*
describe, *v.* describir.
description, *n.* descripción *f.*
descriptive, *a.* descriptivo.
desecrate, *v.* profanar.
desert, 1. *n.* desierto *m.* **2.** *v.* abandonar.
deserter, *n.* desertor *m.*
desertion, *n.* deserción *f.*
deserve, *v.* merecer.
design, 1. *n.* diseño *m.* **2.** *v.* diseñar.
designate, *v.* señalar, apuntar.
designation, *n.* designación *f.*
designer, *n.* diseñador -ra; (technical) proyectista *m. & f.*
desirability, *n.* conveniencia *f.*
desirable, *a.* deseable.
desire, 1. *n.* deseo *m.* **2.** *v.* desear.
desirous, *a.* deseoso.
desist, *v.* desistir.
desk, *n.* escritorio *m.*
desolate, 1. *a.* desolado. **2.** *v.* desolar.
desolation, *n.* desolación, ruina *f.*
despair, 1. *n.* desesperación *f.* **2.** *v.* desesperar.
despatch, dispatch, 1. *n.* despacho *m.;* prontitud *f.* **2.** *v.* despachar.
desperado, *n.* bandido *m.*
desperate, *a.* desesperado.
desperation, *n.* desesperación *f.*
despicable, *a.* vil.
despise, *v.* despreciar.
despite, *prep.* a pesar de.
despondent, *a.* abatido; desanimado.
despot, *n.* déspota *m.*
despotic, *a.* despótico.
dessert, *n.* postre *m.*
destination, *n.* destinación *f.*
destine, *v.* destinar.
destiny, *n.* destino *m.*
destitute, *a.* destituido.
destitution, *n.* destitución *f.*
destroy, *v.* destrozar, destruir.

destroyer, n. destruidor m.; (naval) destróyer m.

destruction, n. destrucción f.

destructive, a. destructivo.

desultory, a. inconexo; casual.

detach, v. separar, desprender.

detachment, n. (mil.) destacamento m.

detail, 1. n. detalle m. 2. v. detallar.

detain, v. detener.

detect, v. descubrir.

detection, n. detección f.

detective, n. detective m.

detente, n. détente f.

detention, n. detención; cautividad f.

deter, v. disuadir.

detergent, n. & a. detergente m.

deteriorate, v. deteriorar.

deterioration, n. deterioración f.

determination, n. determinación f.

determine, v. determinar.

deterrence, n. disuasión f.

detest, v. detestar.

detonate, v. detonar.

detour, n. desvío m.

detract, v. disminuir.

detriment, n. detrimento m., daño m.

detrimental, a. dañoso.

devaluate, v. depreciar.

devastate, v. devastar.

develop, v. desarrollar; (phot.) revelar.

developing nation, nación en desarrollo.

development, n. desarrollo m.

deviate, v. desviar.

deviation, n. desviación f.

device, n. aparato; artificio m.

devil, n. diablo, demonio m.

devious, a. desviado.

devise, v. inventar.

devoid, a. desprovisto.

devote, v. dedicar, consagrar.

devoted, a. devoto.

devotee, n. aficionado m.

devotion, n. devoción f.

devour, v. devorar.

devout, a. devoto.

dew, n. rocío, sereno m.

dexterity, n. destreza f.

dexterous, a. diestro.

diabetes, n. diabetes f.

diabolic, a. diabólico.

diadem, n. diadema f.

diagnose, v. diagnosticar.

diagnosis, n. diagnóstico m.

diagonal, n. diagonal f.

diagram, n. diagrama f.

dial, n. cuadrante m., carátula f.

dialect, n. dialecto m.

dialogue, n. diálogo m.

diameter, n. diámetro m.

diamond, n. diamante, brillante m.

diaper, n. pañal m.

diarrhea, n. diarrea f.

diary, n. diario m.

diathermy, n. diatermia f.

dice, n. dados m.pl.

dictate, 1. n. dictamen m. 2. v. dictar.

dictation, n. dictado m.

dictator, n. dictador m.

dictatorship, n. dictadura f.

diction, n. dicción f.

dictionary, n. diccionario m.

die, 1. n. matriz f.; (game) dado m. 2. v. morir.

diet, n. dieta f.

dietary, a. dietético.

dietitian, n. dietista m. & f.

differ, v. diferir.

difference, n. diferencia f. to make no d., no importar.

different, a. diferente, distinto.

differential, n. diferencial f.

differentiate, v. diferenciar.

difficult, a. difícil.

difficulty, n. dificultad f.

diffident, a. tímido.

diffuse, v. difundir.

diffusion, n. difusión f.

dig, v. cavar.

digest, 1. n. extracto m. 2. v. digerir.

digestible, a. digerible.

digestion, n. digestión f.

digestive, a. digestivo.

digital, a. digital.

digitalis, n. digital f.

dignified, a. digno.

dignify, v. dignificar.

dignitary, n. dignatario m.

dignity, n. dignidad f.

digress, v. divagar.

digression, n. digresión f.

dike, n. dique m.

dilapidated, a. dilapidado.

dilapidation, n. dilapidación f.

dilate, v. dilatar.

dilatory, a. dilatorio.

dilemma, n. dilema m.

dilettante, n. diletante m. & f.

diligence, n. diligencia f.

diligent, a. diligente, aplicado.

dilute, v. diluir.

dim, 1. a. oscuro. 2. v. oscurecer.

dimension, n. dimensión f.

diminish, v. disminuir.

diminution, n. disminución f.

diminutive, a. diminutivo.

dimness, n. oscuridad f.

dimple, n. hoyuelo m.

din, n. alboroto m.

dine, v. comer, cenar.

diner, n. coche comedor m.

dingy, a. deslucido, deslustrado.

dinner, n. comida, cena f.

dinosaur, n. dinosauro m.

diocese, n. diócesis m.

dip, v. sumergir, hundir.

diphtheria, n. difteria f.

diploma, n. diploma m.

diplomacy, n. diplomacia f.

diplomat, n. diplomático m.

diplomatic, a. diplomático.

dipper, n. cucharón m.

dire, a. horrendo.

direct, 1. a. directo. 2. v. dirigir.

direction, n. dirección f.

directive, n. directivo m.

directly, adv. directamente.

director, n. director -ra.

directory, n. directorio m., guía f.

dirigible, n. dirigible m.

dirt, n. basura f.; (earth) tierra f.

dirty, a. sucio.

disability, n. inhabilidad f.; invalidez m.

disable, v. incapacitar.

disabuse, v. desengañar.

disadvantage, n. desventaja f.

disagree, v. desconvenir; disentir.

disagreeable, a. desagradable.

disagreement, n. desacuerdo m.

disappear, v. desaparecer.

disappearance, n. desaparición f.

disappoint, v. disgustar, desilusionar.

disappointment, n. disgusto m., desilusión f.

disapproval, n. desaprobación f.

disapprove, v. desaprobar.

disarm, v. desarmar.

disarmament, n. desarme m.

disarrange, v. desordenar; desarreglar.

disaster, n. desastre m.

disastrous, a. desastroso.

disavow, v. repudiar.

disavowal, n. repudiación f.

disband, v. dispersarse.

disbelieve, v. descreer.

disburse, v. desembolsar, pagar.

discard, v. descartar.

discern, v. discernir.

discerning, a. discernidor, perspicaz.

discernment, n. discernimiento m.

discharge, v. descargar; despedir.

disciple, n. discípulo m.

disciplinary, a. disciplinario.

discipline, n. disciplina f.

disclaim, v. repudiar.

disclaimer, n. negador m.

disclose, v. revelar.

disclosure, n. descubrimiento m.

disco, n. discoteca f.

discolor, v. descolorar.

discomfort, n. incomodidad f.

disconcert, v. desconcertar.

disconnect, v. desunir; desconectar.

disconnected, a. desunido.

disconsolate, a. desconsolado.

discontent, n. descontento m.

discontented, a. descontento.

discontinue, v. descontinuar.

discord, n. discordia f.

discordant, a. disonante.

discotheque, n. discoteca f.

discount, n. descuento m.

discourage, v. desalentar, desanimar.

discouragement, n. desaliento, desánimo m.

discourse, n. discurso m.

discourteous, a. descortés.

discourtesy, n. descortesía f.

discover, v. descubrir.

discoverer, n. descubridor -ra.

discovery, n. descubrimiento m.

discreet, a. discreto.

discrepancy, n. discrepancia f.

discretion, n. discreción f.

discriminate, v. distinguir; diferenciar parcialmente.

discrimination, n. discernimiento m.; discriminación f.

discuss, v. discutir.

discussion, n. discusión f.

disdain, 1. n. desdén m. 2. v. desdeñar.

disdainful, a. desdeñoso.

disease, n. enfermedad f., mal m.

disembark, v. desembarcar.

disentangle, v. desenredar.

disfigure, v. desfigurar.

disgrace, 1. n. vergüenza; deshonra f. 2. v. deshonrar.

disgraceful, a. vergonzoso.

disguise, 1. n. disfraz m. 2. v. disfrazar.

disgust, 1. n. fastidio m. 2. v. fastidiar.

dish, n. plato m.

dishearten, v. desanimar; descorazonar.

dishonest, a. deshonesto.

dishonesty, n. deshonestidad f.

dishonor, 1. n. deshonra f. 2. v. deshonrar.

dishonorable, a. deshonroso.

disillusion, 1. n. desengaño m. 2. v. desengañar.

disinfect, v. desinfectar.

disinfectant, n. desinfectante m.

disinherit, v. desheredar.

disintegrate, v. desintegrar.

disinterested, a. desinteresado.

disk, n. disco m.

dislike, 1. n. antipatía f. 2. v. no gustar de.

dislocate, v. dislocar.

dislodge, v. desalojar.

disloyal, a. desleal; infiel.

disloyalty, n. deslealtad f.

dismal, a. lúgubre.

dismantle, v. desmantelar.

dismay, 1. n. consternación f. 2. v. consternar.

dismiss, v. despedir.

dismissal, n. despedida f.

dismount, v. apearse.

disobedience, n. desobediencia f.

disobedient, a. desobediente.

disobey, v. desobedecer.

disorder, n. desorden m.

disorderly, a. desarreglado, desordenado.

disown, v. repudiar.

dispassionate, a. desapasionado; templado.

dispatch, 1. n. despacho m. 2. v. despachar.

dispel, v. despersar.

dispensary, n. dispensario m.

dispensation, n. dispensación f.

dispense, v. dispensar.

dispersal, n. dispersión f.

disperse, v. dispersar.

displace, v. dislocar.

display, 1. n. despliegue m., exhibición f. 2. v. desplegar, exhibir.

displease, v. disgustar; ofender.

displeasure, n. disgusto, sinsabor m.

disposable, a. disponible.

disposal, n. disposición f.

dispose, v. disponer.

disposition, n. disposición f.; índole f., genio m.

dispossess, v. desposeer.

disproportionate, a. desproporcionado.

disprove, v. confutar.

dispute, 1. n. disputa f. 2. v. disputar.

disqualify, v. inhabilitar.

disregard, 1. n. desatención f. 2. v. desatender.

disrepair, n. descompostura f.

disreputable, a. desacreditado.

disrespect, n. falta de respecto.

disrespectful, a. irrespetuoso.

disrobe, v. desvestir.

disrupt, v. romper; desbaratar.

dissatisfaction, n. descontento m.

dissatisfy, v. descontentar.

dissect, v. disecar.

dissemble, v. disimular.

disseminate, v. diseminar.

dissension, n. disensión f.

dissent, 1. n. disensión f. 2. v. disentir.

dissertation, n. disertación f.

dissimilar, a. desemejante.

dissipate, v. disipar.

dissipation, n. disipación f.; libertinaje m.

dissolute, a. disoluto.

dissolution, n. disolución f.

dissolve, v. disolver; derretirse.

dissonant, a. disonante.

dissuade, v. disuadir.

distance, n. distancia f. **at a d.**, **in the d.**, a lo lejos.

distant, a. distante, lejano.

distaste, n. disgusto, sinsabor m.

distasteful, a. desagradable.

distill, v. destilar.

distillation, n. destilación f.

distillery, n. destilería f.

distinct, a. distinto.

distinctive, a. distintivo; característico.

distinctly, adv. distintamente.

distinction, n. distinción f.

distinguish, v. distinguir.

distinguished, a. distinguido.

distort, v. falsear; torcer.

distract, v. distraer.

distraction, n. distracción f.

distraught, a. aturrullado; demente.

distress, 1. n. dolor m. 2. v. afligir.

distribute, v. distribuir.

distribution, n. distribución f.; reparto m.

distributor, n. distribuidor -ra.

district, n. distrito m.

distrust, 1. n. desconfianza f. 2. v. desconfiar.

distrustful, a. desconfiado; sospechoso.

disturb, v. incomodar; inquietar.

disturbance, n. disturbio m.

ditch, n. zanja f.; foso m.

divan, n. diván m.

dive, 1. n. clavado m.; (coll.) leonera f. 2. v. echar un clavado; bucear.

diver, n. buzo m.

diverge, v. divergir.

divergence, n. divergencia f.

divergent, a. divergente.

diverse, a. diverso.

diversion, n. diversión f.; pasatiempo m.

diversity, n. diversidad f.

divert, v. desviar; divertir.

divest, v. desnudar, despojar.

divide, v. dividir.

dividend, n. dividendo m.

divine, a. divino.

divinity, n. divinidad f.

division, n. división f.

divorce, 1. n. divorcio m. 2. v. divorciar.

divorcee, n. divorciada f.

divulge, v. divulgar, revelar.

dizziness, n. vértigo, mareo m.

dizzy, a. mareado.

do, v. hacer.

docile, a. dócil.

dock, 1. n. muelle m. **dry d.**, astillero m. 2. v. entrar en muelle.

doctor, n. médico m.; doctor -ra.

doctrine, n. doctrina f.

document, n. documento m.

documentary, a. documental.

documentation, n. documentación f.

dodge, 1. n. evasión f. 2. v. evadir.

doe, n. gama f.

dog, n. perro m.

dogma, n. dogma m.

dogmatic, a. dogmático.

dogmatism, n. dogmatismo m.

doily, n. servilletita f.

doleful, a. triste.

doll, n. muñeca f.

dollar, n. dólar m.

dolorous, a. lastimoso.

dolphin, n. delfín m.

domain, n. dominio m.

dome, n. domo m.

domestic, a. doméstico.

domesticate, v. domesticar.

domicile, n. domicilio m.

dominance, n. dominación f.

dominant, a. dominante.

dominate, v. dominar.

domination, n. dominación f.

domineer, v. dominar.

domineering, a. tiránico, mandón.

dominion, *n.* dominio; territorio *m.*

domino, *n.* dominó *m.*

donate, *v.* donar; contribuir.

donation, *n.* donación *f.*

donkey, *n.* asno, burro *m.*

doom, **1.** *n.* perdición, ruina *f.* **2.** *v.* perder, ruinar.

door, *n.* puerta *f.*

doorman, *n.* portero *m.*

doorway, *n.* entrada *f.*

dope, *n.* narcótico *m.*

dormant, *a.* durmiente.

dormitory, *n.* dormitorio *m.*

dosage, *n.* dosificación *f.*

dose, *n.* dosis *f.*

dot, *n.* punto *m.*

double, **1.** *a.* doble. **2.** *v.* duplicar.

double-breasted, *a.* cruzado.

double-cross, *v.* traicionar.

doubly, *adv.* doblemente.

doubt, **1.** *n.* duda *f.* **2.** *v.* dudar.

doubtful, *a.* dudoso, incierto.

doubtless, **1.** *a.* indudable. **2.** *adv.* sin duda.

dough, *n.* pasta, masa *f.*

doughnut, *n.* buñuelo *m.*

dove, *n.* paloma *f.*

dowager, *n.* viuda *f.*

down, **1.** *adv.* abajo. **2.** *prep.* **d. the street**, *etc.* calle abajo, *etc.*

downcast, *a.* cabizbajo.

downfall, *n.* ruina, perdición *f.*

downhearted, *a.* descorazonado.

downpour, *n.* chaparrón *m.*

downright, *a.* absoluto, completo.

downstairs, **1.** *adv.* abajo. **2.** *n.* primer piso.

downtown, *adv.* al centro, en el centro.

downward, **1.** *a.* descendente. **2.** *adv.* hacia abajo.

dowry, *n.* dote *m.*

doze, *v.* dormitar.

dozen, *n.* docena *f.*

draft, **1.** *n.* dibujo *m.;* (com.) giro *m.;* (mil.) conscripción *f.* **2.** *v.* dibujar; (mil.) reclutar.

draftee, *n.* conscripto *m.*

drag, *v.* arrastrar.

dragon, *n.* dragón *m.*

drain, **1.** *n.* desaguadero *m.* **2.** *v.* desaguar.

drainage, *n.* drenaje *m.*

drama, *n.* drama *m.*

dramatic, *a.* dramático.

dramatics, *n.* dramática *f.*

dramatist, *n.* dramaturgo *m.*

dramatize, *v.* dramatizar.

drape, *n.* cortina *f.*

drapery, *n.* colgaduras *f.pl.;* ropaje *m.*

drastic, *a.* drástico.

draw, *v.* dibujar; atraer. **d. up**, formular.

drawback, *n.* desventaja *f.*

drawer, *n.* cajón *m.*

drawing, *n.* dibujo *m.;* rifa *f.*

dread, **1.** *n.* terror *m.* **2.** *v.* temer.

dreadful, *a.* terrible.

dreadfully, *adv.* horrendamente.

dream, **1.** *n.* sueño, ensueño *m.* **2.** *v.* soñar.

dreamer, *n.* soñador -ra; visionario -ia.

dreamy, *a.* soñador, contemplativo.

dreary, *a.* monótono y pesado.

dredge, **1.** *n.* rastra *f.* **2.** *v.* rastrear.

dregs, *n.* sedimento *m.*

drench, *v.* mojar.

dress, **1.** *n.* vestido; traje *m.* **2.** *v.* vestir.

dresser, *n.* (furniture) tocador.

dressing, *n.* (med.) curación *f.;* (cookery) condimento, relleno *m.*

dressing gown, *n.* batá *f.*

dressmaker, *n.* modista *m. & f.*

drift, **1.** *n.* tendencia *f.;* (naut.) deriva *f.* **2.** *v.* (naut.) derivar; (snow) amontonarse.

drill, **1.** *n.* ejercicio *m.;* (mech.) taladro *m.* **2.** *v.* (mech.) taladrar.

drink, **1.** *n.* bebida *f.* **2.** *v.* beber, tomar.

drinkable, *a.* potable, bebible.

drip, *v.* gotear.

drive, **1.** *n.* paseo *m.* **2.** *v.* impeler; (auto.) guiar, conducir.

driver, *n.* chofer *m.*

driveway, *n.* entrada para coches.

drizzle, **1.** *n.* llovizna *f.* **2.** *v.* lloviznar.

dromedary, *n.* dromedario *m.*

droop, *v.* inclinarse.

drop, **1.** *n.* gota *f.* **2.** *v.* soltar; dejar, caer.

dropout, *n.* joven que abandona sus estudios.

dropper, *n.* cuentagotas *f.*

dropsy, *n.* hidropesía *f.*

drought, *n.* seca, sequía *f.*

drove, *n.* manada *f.*

drown, *v.* ahogar.

drowse, *v.* adormecer.

drowsiness, *n.* somnolencia *f.*

drowsy, *a.* soñoliento.

drudge, *n.* ganapán *m.*

drudgery, *n.* trabajo penoso.

drug, **1.** *n.* droga *f.* **2.** *v.* narcotizar.

druggist, *n.* farmacéutico, boticario *m.*

drugstore, *n.* farmacia, botica, droguería *f.*

drum, *n.* tambor *m.*

drummer, *n.* tambor *m.*

drumstick, *n.* palillo *m.;* (leg) pierna *f.*

drunk, *a. & n.* borracho.

drunkard, *n.* borrachón *m.*

drunken, *a.* borracho; ebrio.

drunkenness, *n.* embriaguez *f.*

dry, **1.** *a.* seco, árido. **2.** *v.* secar.

dry cell, *n.* pila seca *f.*

dry-cleaner, *n.* tintorero *m.*

dryness, *n.* sequedad *f.*

dual, *a.* doble.

dubious, *a.* dudoso.

duchess, *n.* duquesa *f.*

duck, **1.** *n.* pato *m.* **2.** *v.* zabullir; (avoid) esquivar.

duct, *n.* canal *m.*

due, *a.* debido; (com.) vencido. **2. dues**, *n.* cuota *f.*

duel, *n.* duelo *m.*

duelist, *n.* duelista *m.*

duet, *n.* dúo *m.*

duke, *n.* duque *m.*

dull, *a.* apagado, desteñido; sin punta; (fig.) pesado, soso.

dullness, *n.* estupidez; pesadez *f.;* deslustre *m.*

duly, *adv.* debidamente.

dumb, *a.* mudo; (coll.) estúpido.

dumbwaiter, *n.* montaplatos *m.*

dumfound, *v.* confundir.

dummy, *n.* figurón *m.*

dump, **1.** *n.* depósito *m.* **2.** *v.* descargar.

dune, *n.* duna *f.*

dungeon, *n.* calabozo *m.*

dunk, *v.* mojar.

dupe, *v.* engañar.

duplicate, **1.** *a. & n.* duplicado *m.* **2.** *v.* duplicar.

duplication, *n.* duplicación *f.*

duplicity, *n.* duplicidad *f.*

durability, *n.* durabilidad *f.*

durable, *a.* durable, duradero.

duration, *n.* duración *f.*

duress, *n.* compulsión *m.;* encierro *m.*

during, *prep.* durante.

dusk, *n.* crepúsculo *m.*

dusky, *a.* oscuro; moreno.

dust, **1.** *n.* polvo *m.* **2.** *v.* polvorear; despolvorear.

dusty, *a.* empolvado.

Dutch, *a.* holandés -sa.

dutiful, *a.* respetuoso.

dutifully, *adv.* respetuosamente, obedientemente.

duty, *n.* deber *m.;* (com.) derechos *m.pl.*

duty-free, *a.* libre de derechos.

dwarf, **1.** *n.* enano -na. **2.** *v.* achicar.

dwell, *v.* habitar, residir. **d. on**, espaciarse en.

dwelling, *n.* morada, casa *f.*

dwindle, *v.* disminuirse.

dye, **1.** *n.* tintura *f.* **2.** *v.* teñir.

dyer, *n.* tintorero -ra.

dynamic, *a.* dinámico.

dynamite, *n.* dinamita *f.*

dynamo, *n.* dínamo *m.*

dynasty, *n.* dinastía *f.*

dysentery, *n.* disentería *f.*

dyslexia, *n.* dislexia *f.*

dyspepsia, *n.* dispepsia *f.*

E

each, **1.** *a.* cada. **2.** *pron.* cada uno -na. **e. other**, el uno al otro.

eager, *a.* ansioso.

eagerly, *adv.* ansiosamente.

eagerness, *n.* ansia *f.*

eagle, *n.* águila *f.*

ear, n. oído m.; (outer) oreja f.; (of corn) mazorca f.
earache, n. dolor de oído m.
earl, n. conde m.
early, a. & adv. temprano.
earn, v. ganar.
earnest, a. serio.
earnestly, adv. seriamente.
earnings, n. ganancias f.pl.; (com.) ingresos m.pl.
earphone, n. auricular m.
earring, n. pendiente, arete m.
earth, n. tierra f.
earthquake, n. terremoto m.
ease, 1. n. reposo m.; facilidad f. **2.** v. aliviar.
easel, n. caballete m.
easily, adv. fácilmente.
east, n. oriente, este m.
Easter, n. Pascua Florida.
eastern, a. oriental.
eastward, adv. hacia el este.
easy, a. fácil.
eat, v. comer.
eaves, n. socarrén m.
ebb, 1. n. menguante f. **2.** v. menguar.
ebony, n. ébano f.
eccentric, a. excéntrico.
eccentricity, n. excentricidad f.
ecclesiastic, a. & n. eclesiástico. m.
ecclesiastical, a. eclasiástico.
echelon, n. escalón m.
echo, n. eco m.
eclipse, 1. n. eclipse m. **2.** v. eclipsar.
ecological, a. ecológico.
ecology, n. ecología f.
economic, a. económico.
economical, a. económico.
economics, n. economía política.
economist, n. economista m.
economize, v. economizar.
economy, n. economía f.
ecstasy, n. éxtasis m.
Ecuadorian, a. & n. ecuatoriano -na.
ecumenical, a. ecuménico.
eczema, n. eczema f.
eddy, 1. n. remolino m. **2.** v. remolinar.
edge, 1. n. filo; borde m. **2.** v. e. one's way, abrirse paso.
edible, a. comestible.
edict, n. edicto m.
edifice, n. edificio m.
edify, v. edificar.
edition, n. edición f.
editor, n. redactor m.
editorial, n. editorial m. e. staff, redacción f.
educate, v. educar.
education, n. instrucción; enseñanza f.
educational, a. educativo.
educator, n. educador, pedagogo m.
eel, n. anguila f.
efface, v. tachar.
effect, 1. n. efecto m. in e., en vigor. **2.** v. efectuar, realizar.
effective, a. eficaz; efectivo; en vigor.

effectively, adv. eficazmente.
effectiveness, n. efectividad f.
effectual, a. eficaz.
effeminate, a. afeminado.
efficacy, n. eficacia f.
efficiency, n. eficiencia f.
efficient, a. eficaz.
efficiently, adv. eficazmente.
effigy, n. efigie m.
effort, n. esfuerzo m.
effrontery, n. impudencia f.
effusive, a. expansivo.
egg, n. huevo m. **fried e.,** huevo frito. **soft-boiled e.,** h. pasado por agua. **scrambled eggs,** huevos revueltos.
eggplant, n. berenjena f.
egoism, egotism, n. egoísmo m.
egoist, egotist, n. egoísta m. & f.
egotism, n. egotismo m.
egotist, n. egotista m.
Egypt, n. Egipto m.
Egyptian, a. & n. egipcio -ia.
eight, a. & pron. ocho.
eighteen, a. & pron. dieciocho.
eighth, a. octavo.
eightieth, n. octogésimo m.
eighty, a. & pron. ochenta.
either, 1. a. & pron. cualquiera de los dos. **2.** adv. tampoco. **3.** conj. **either . . . or,** o . . . o.
ejaculate, v. exclamar.
eject, v. expeler.
ejection, n. expulsión f.
elaborate, 1. a. elaborado. **2.** v. elaborar; ampliar.
elapse, v. transcurrir; pasar.
elastic, a. & n. elástico m.
elasticity, n. elasticidad f.
elate, v. exaltar.
elation, n. exaltación f.
elbow, n. codo m.
elder, 1. a. mayor. **2.** n. anciano m.
elderly, a. de edad.
eldest, a. mayor.
elect, v. elegir.
election, n. elección f.
elective, a. electivo.
electorate, n. electorado m.
electric, electrical, a. eléctrico.
electrician, n. electricista m.
electricity, n. electricidad f.
electrocardiogram, n. electrocardiograma m.
electrocute, v. electrocutar.
electrode, n. electrodo m.
electrolysis, n. electrólisis f.
electron, n. electrón m.
electronics, n. electrónica f.
elegance, n. elegancia f.
elegant, a. elegante.
elegy, n. elegía f.
element, n. elemento m.
elemental, a. elemental.
elementary, a. elemental.
elephant, n. elefante m.
elevate, v. elevar.
elevation, n. elevación f.
elevator, n. ascensor m.
eleven, a. & pron. once.
eleventh, a. undécimo.
elf, n. duende m.
elicit, v. sacar; despertar.

eligibility, n. elegibilidad f.
eligible, a. elegible.
eliminate, v. eliminar.
elimination, n. eliminación f.
elixir, n. elixir m.
elk, n. alce m., anta f.
elm, n. olmo m.
elocution, n. elocución f.
elongate, v. alargar.
elope, v. fugarse.
eloquence, n. elocuencia f.
eloquent, a. elocuente.
eloquently, adv. elocuentemente.
else, adv. más. **someone e.,** otra persona. **something e.,** otra cosa. **or e.,** de otro modo.
elsewhere, adv. en otra parte.
elucidate, v. elucidar.
elude, v. eludir.
elusive, a. evasivo.
emaciated, a. enflaquecido.
emanate, v. emanar.
emancipate, v. emancipar.
emancipation, n. emancipación f.
emancipator, n. libertador m.
embalm, v. embalsamar.
embankment, n. malecón, dique m.
embargo, n. embargo m.
embark, v. embarcar.
embarrass, v. avergonzar; turbar.
embarrassing, a. penoso, vergonzoso.
embarrassment, n. turbación; vergüenza f.
embassy, n. embajada f.
embellish, v. hermosear, embellecer.
embellishment, n. embellecimiento m.
embezzle, v. apropiarse dinero ilícitamente.
emblem, n. emblema m.
embody, v. incorporar.
embrace, 1. n. abrazo m. **2.** v. abrazar.
embroider, v. bordar.
embroidery, n. bordado m.
embryo, n. embrión m.
embryonic, a. embrionario.
emerald, n. esmeralda f.
emerge, v. salir.
emergency, n. emergencia f.
emergent, a. emergente.
emery, n. esmeril m.
emetic, a. emético m.
emigrant, a. & n. emigrante m. & f.
emigrate, v. emigrar.
emigration, n. emigración f.
eminence, n. altura; eminencia f.
eminent, a. eminente.
emissary, n. emisario m.
emission, n. emisión f.
emit, v. emitir.
emolument, n. emolumento m.
emotion, n. emoción f.
emotional, a. sensible.
emperor, n. emperador m.
emphasis, n. énfasis m. or f.

emphasize, v. acentuar, recalcar.

emphatic, a. enfático.

empire, n. imperio m.

empirical, a. empírico.

employ, v. emplear.

employee, n. empleado -da.

employer, n. patrón -ona.

employment, n. empleo m.

empower, v. autorizar.

emptiness, n. vaciedad; futilidad f.

empty, 1. a. vacío. 2. v. vaciar.

emulate, v. emular.

emulsion, n. emulsión f.

enable, v. capacitar; permitir.

enact, v. promulgar, decretar.

enactment, n. ley f., estatuto m.

enamel, 1. n. esmalte m. 2. v. esmaltar.

enamored, a. enamorado.

enchant, v. encantar.

enchantment, n. encanto m.

encircle, v. circundar.

enclose, v. encerrar. enclosed, (in letter) adjunto.

enclosure, n. recinto m.; (in letter) incluso m.

encompass, v. circundar.

encounter, 1. n. encuentro m. 2. v. encontrar.

encourage, v. animar.

encouragement, n. estímulo m.

encroach, v. usurpar; meterse.

encyclical, n. encíclica f.

encyclopedia, n. enciclopedia f.

end, 1. n. fin, término, cabo; extremo; (aim) propósito m. 2. v. acabar; terminar.

endanger, v. poner en peligro.

endear, v. hacer querer.

endeavor, 1. n. esfuerzo m. 2. v. esforzarse.

ending, n. conclusión f.

endless, a. sin fin.

endorse, v. endosar; apoyar.

endorsement, n. endoso m.

endow, v. dotar, fundar.

endowment, n. dotación f., fundación f.

endurance, n. resistencia f.

endure, v. soportar, resistir, aguantar.

enema, n. enema; lavativa f.

enemy, n. enemigo -ga.

energetic, a. enérgico.

energy, n. energía f.

enervate, v. enervar.

enervation, n. enervación f.

enfold, v. envolver.

enforce, v. ejecutar.

enforcement, n. ejecución f.

engage, v. emplear; ocupar.

engaged, (to marry) comprometido.

engagement, n. combate; compromiso; contrato m.; cita f.

engine, n. máquina f. (railroad) locomotora f.

engineer, n. ingeniero; maquinista m.

engineering, n. ingeniería f.

England, n. Inglaterra f.

English, a. & n. inglés m.

Englishman, n. inglés m.

Englishwoman, n. inglesa f.

engrave, v. grabar.

engraver, n. grabador m.

engraving, n. grabado m.

engross, v. absorber.

enhance, v. aumentar en valor; realzar.

enigma, n. enigma m.

enigmatic, a. enigmático.

enjoy, v. gozar de; disfrutar de. e. oneself, divertirse.

enjoyable, a. agradable.

enjoyment, n. goce m.

enlarge, v. agrandar; ampliar.

enlargement, n. ensanchamiento m., ampliación f.

enlarger, n. amplificador m.

enlighten, v. informar.

enlightenment, n. esclarecimiento m.; cultura f.

enlist, v. reclutar; alistarse.

enlistment, n. alistamiento m.

enliven, v. avivar.

enmesh, v. entrampar.

enmity, n. enemistad f.

enormity, v. enormidad f.

enormous, a. enorme.

enough, a. & adv. bastante. to be e., bastar.

enrage, v. enfurecer.

enrich, v. enriquecer.

enroll, v. registrar; matricularse.

enrollment, n. matriculación f.

ensign, n. bandera f.; (naval) sub-teniente m.

enslave, v. esclavizar.

ensue, v. seguir, resultar.

entail, v. envolver.

entangle, v. enredar.

enter, v. entrar.

enterprise, n. empresa f.

enterprising, a. emprendedor.

entertain, v. entretener; divertir.

entertainment, n. entretenimiento m.; diversión f.

enthrall, v. esclavizar.

enthusiasm, n. entusiasmo m.

enthusiast, n. entusiasta m. & f.

enthusiastic, a. entusiasmado.

entice, v. inducir.

entire, a. entero.

entirely, adv. enteramente.

entirety, n. totalidad f.

entitle, v. autorizar; (book) titular.

entity, n. entidad f.

entrails, n. entrañas f.pl.

entrance, n. entrada f.

entrant, n. competidor m.

entreat, v. rogar, suplicar.

entreaty, n. ruego m., súplica f.

entrench, v. atrincherar.

entrust, v. confiar.

entry, n. entrada f.; (com.) partida f.

enumerate, v. enumerar.

enumeration, n. enumeración f.

enunciate, v. enunciar.

enunciation, n. enunciación f.

envelop, v. envolver.

envelope, n. sobre m.; cubierta f.

enviable, a. envidiable.

envious, a. envidioso.

environment, n. ambiente m.

environmentalist, n. activista ecológico, ecologista m.

environmental protection, protección del ambiente.

environs, n. alrededores m.

envoy, n. enviado m.

envy, 1. n. envidia f. 2. v. envidiar.

eon, n. eón m.

ephemeral, a. efímero.

epic, 1. a. épico. 2. n. epopeya f.

epicure, n. epicúreo m.

epidemic, 1. a. epidémico. 2. n. epidemia f.

epidermis, n. epidermis f.

epigram, n. epigrama m.

epilepsy, n. epilepsia f.

epilogue, n. epílogo m.

episode, n. episodio m.

epistle, n. epístola f.

epitaph, n. epitafio m.

epithet, n. epiteto m.

epitome, n. epítome m.

epoch, n. época, era f.

equal, 1. a. & n. igual m. 2. v. igualar; equivaler.

equality, n. igualdad f.

equalize, v. igualar.

equanimity, n. ecuanimidad f.

equate, v. igualar.

equation, n. ecuación f.

equator, n. ecuador m.

equatorial, a. & a. ecuatorial f.

equestrian, 1. n. jinete m. 2. a. ecuestre.

equilibrium, n. equilibrio m.

equinox, n. equinoccio m.

equip, v. equipar.

equipment, n. equipo m.

equitable, a. equitativo.

equity, n. equidad, justicia f.

equivalent, a. & n. equivalente m.

equivocal, a. equívoco, ambiguo.

era, n. era, época, edad f.

eradicate, v. extirpar.

erase, v. borrar.

eraser, n. borrador m.

erasure, n. borradura f.

erect, 1. a. derecho, erguido. 2. v. erigir.

erection, erectness, n. erección f.

ermine, n. armiño f.

erode, v. corroer.

erosion, n. erosión f.

erotic, a. erótico.

err, v. equivocarse.

errand, n. encargo, recado m.

errant, a. errante.

erratic, a. errático.

erroneous, a. erróneo.

error, n. error m.

erudite, a. erudito.

erudition, n. erudición f.

eruption, n. erupción, irrupción f.

escalate, v. realizar una escalada.

escalator, n. escalera mecánica f.

escapade, n. escapada; correría f.

escape, 1. n. fuga, huída f. **fire e.,** escalera de salvamento. **2.** v. escapar; fugarse.

eschew, v. evadir.

escort, 1. n. escolta f. **2.** v. escoltar.

escrow, n. plica f.

escutcheon, n. escudo de armas m.

esophagus, n. esófago m.

esoteric, a. esotérico.

especially, adv. especialmente.

espionage, n. espionaje m.

essay, n. ensayo m.

essayist, n. ensayista m.

essence, n. esencia f.; perfume m.

essential, a. esencial.

essentially, adv. esencialmente.

establish, v. establecer.

establishment, n. establecimiento m.

estate, n. estado m.; hacienda f.; bienes m.pl.

esteem, 1. n. estima f. **2.** v. estimar.

estimable, a. estimable.

estimate, 1. n. cálculo; presupuesto m. **2.** v. estimar.

estimation, n. estimación f.; cálculo m.

estrange, v. extrañar; enajenar.

estuary, n. estuario m.

etching, n. grabado al agua fuerte.

eternal, a. eterno.

eternity, n. eternidad f.

ether, n. éter m.

ethereal, a. etéreo.

ethical, a. ético.

ethics, n. ética f.

ethnic, a. étnico.

etiquette, n. etiqueta f.

etymology, n. etimología f.

eucalyptus, n. eucalipto m.

eugenic, a. eugenésico.

eugenics, n. eugenesia f.

eulogize, v. elogiar.

eulogy, n. elogio m.

eunuch, n. eunuco m.

euphonious, a. eufónico.

Europe, n. Europa f.

European, a. & n. europeo pea.

euthanasia, n. eutanasia f.

evacuate, v. evacuar.

evade, v. evadir.

evaluate, v. avaluar.

evaluation, n. valoración f.

evangelist, n. evangelista m.

evaporate, v. evaporarse.

evaporation, n. evaporación f.

evasion, n. evasión f.

evasive, a. evasivo.

eve, n. víspera f.

even, 1. a. llano; igual. **2.** adv. aun; hasta. **not e.,** ni siquiera.

evening, n. noche, tarde f. **good e.,** buenas noches.

evenness, n. uniformidad f.

event, n. acontecimiento, suceso m.

eventful, a. memorable.

eventual, a. eventual.

ever, adv. alguna vez; (after not) nunca. **e. since,** desde que.

everlasting, a. eterno.

every, a. cada, todos los.

everybody, pron. todo el mundo; cada uno.

everyday, a. ordinario, de cada día.

everyone, pron. cada uno; cada cual; todos.

everything, pron. todo m.

everywhere, adv. por todas partes, en todas partes.

evict, v. expulsar.

eviction, n. evicción f.

evidence, n. evidencia f.

evident, a. evidente.

evidently, adv. evidentemente.

evil, 1. a. malo; maligno. **2.** n. mal m.

evince, v. revelar.

evoke, v. evocar.

evolution, n. evolución f.

evolve, v. desenvolver; desarrollar.

ewe, n. oveja f.

exact, 1. a. exacto. **2.** v. exigir.

exacting, a. exigente.

exactly, adv. exactamente.

exaggerate, v. exagerar.

exaggeration, n. exageración f.

exalt, v. exaltar.

exaltation, n. exaltación f.

examination, n. examen m.; (legal) interrogatorio m.

examine, v. examinar.

example, n. ejemplo m.

exasperate, v. exasperar.

exasperation, n. exasperación f.

excavate, v. excavar, cavar.

exceed, v. exceder.

exceedingly, adv. sumamente, extremadamente.

excel, v. sobresalir.

excellence, n. excelencia f.

Excellency, n. (title) Excelencia f.

excellent, a. excelente.

except, 1. prep. salvo, excepto. **2.** v. exceptuar.

exception, n. excepción f.

exceptional, a. excepcional.

excerpt, n. extracto.

excess, n. exceso m.

excessive, a. excesivo.

exchange, 1. n. cambio; canje m. **stock e.,** bolsa f. **telephone e.,** central telefónica f. **2.** v. cambiar, canjear.

exchangeable, a. cambiable.

excise, 1. n. sisa f. **2.** v. extirpar.

excite, v. agitar; provocar; emocionar.

excitement, n. agitación, conmoción f.

exciting, a. emocionante.

exclaim, v. exclamar.

exclamation, n. exclamación f.

exclamation point or mark, n. punto de admiración m.

exclude, v. excluir.

exclusion, n. exclusión f.

exclusive, a. exclusivo.

excommunicate, v. excomulgar, descomulgar.

excommunication, n. excomunión f.

excrement, n. excremento m.

excruciating, a. penosísimo.

exculpate, v. justificar.

excursion, n. excursión; jira f.

excuse, 1. n. excusa f. **2.** v. excusar, perdonar; dispensar; disculpar.

execrable, a. execrable.

execute, v. ejecutar.

execution, n. ejecución f.

executioner, n. verdugo m.

executive, a. & n. ejecutivo m.

executor, n. testamentario m.

exemplary, a. ejemplar.

exemplify, v. ejemplificar.

exempt, 1. a. exento. **2.** v. exentar.

exercise, 1. n. ejercicio m. **2.** v. ejercitar.

exert, v. esforzar.

exertion, n. esfuerzo m.

exhale, v. exhalar.

exhaust, 1. n. (auto.) escape m. **2.** v. agotar.

exhaustion, n. agotamiento m.

exhaustive, a. agotador.

exhibit, 1. n. exhibición, exposición f. **2.** v. exhibir.

exhibition, n. exhibición f.

exhilarate, v. alegrar; estimular.

exhort, v. exhortar.

exhortation, n. exhortación f.

exhume, v. exhumar.

exigency, n. exigencia f., urgencia f.

exile, 1. n. destierro m., (person) desterrado m. **2.** v. desterrar.

exist, v. existir.

existence, n. existencia f.

existent, a. existente.

exit, n. salida f.

exodus, n. éxodo m.

exonerate, v. exonerar.

exorbitant, a. exorbitante.

exorcise, v. exorcizar.

exotic, a. exótico.

expand, v. dilatar; ensanchar.

expanse, n. espacio m.; extensión f.

expansion, n. expansión f.

expansive, a. expansivo.

expatiate, v. espaciarse.

expatriate, 1. n. & a. expatriado m. **2.** v. expatriar.

expect, v. esperar; contar con.

expectancy, n. esperanza f.

expectation, n. esperanza f.

expectorate, v. expectorar.

expediency, n. conveniencia f.

expedient, 1. a. oportuno. **2.** n. expediente m.

expedite, v. acelerar, despachar.

expedition, *n.* expedición *f.*

expel, *v.* expeler, expulsar.

expend, *v.* desembolsar, expender.

expenditure, *n.* desembolso; gasto *m.*

expense, *n.* gasto *m.;* costa *f.*

expensive, *a.* caro, costoso.

expensively, *adv.* costosamente.

experience, 1. *n.* experiencia *f.* **2.** *v.* experimentar.

experienced, *a.* experimentado, perito.

experiment, 1. *n.* experimento *m.* **2.** *v.* experimentar.

experimental, *a.* experimental.

expert, *a.* & *n.* experto *m.*

expiate, *v.* expiar.

expiration, *n.* expiración *f.*

expire, *v.* expirar; (com.) vencerse.

explain, *v.* explicar.

explanation, *n.* explicación *f.*

explanatory, *a.* explicativo.

expletive, 1. *n.* interjección *f.* **2.** *a.* expletivo.

explicit, *a.* explícito, claro.

explode, *v.* estallar, volar; refutar.

exploit, 1. *n.* hazaña *f.* **2.** *v.* explotar.

exploitation, *n.* explotación *f.*

exploration, *n.* exploración *f.*

exploratory, *a.* exploratorio.

explore, *v.* explorar.

explorer, *n.* explorador *m.*

explosion, *n.* explosión *f.*

explosive, *a.* explosivo.

export, 1. *n.* exportación *f.* **2.** *v.* exportar.

exportation, *n.* exportación *f.*

expose, *v.* exponer; descubrir.

exposition, *n.* exposición *f.*

expository, *a.* expositivo.

expostulate, *v.* altercar.

exposure, *n.* exposición *f.*

expound, *v.* exponer, explicar.

express, 1. *a.* & *n.* expreso *m.* **e. company,** compañía de porteo. **2.** *v.* expresar.

expression, *n.* expresión *f.*

expressive, *a.* expresivo.

expressly, *adv.* expresamente.

expressman, *n.* empresario de expresos *m.*

expropriate, *v.* expropriar.

expulsion, *n.* expulsión *f.*

expunge, *v.* borrar, expurgar.

expurgate, *v.* expurgar.

exquisite, *a.* exquisito.

extant, *a.* existente.

extemporaneous, *a.* improvisado.

extend, *v.* extender.

extension, *n.* extensión *f.*

extensive, *a.* extenso.

extensively, *adv.* por extenso.

extent, *n.* extensión *f.;* grado *m.* **to a certain e.,** hasta cierto punto.

extenuate, *v.* extenuar.

exterior, *a.* & *n.* exterior *m.*

exterminate, *v.* exterminar.

extermination, *n.* exterminio *m.*

external, *a.* externo, exterior.

extinct, *a.* extinto.

extinction, *n.* extinción *f.*

extinguish, *v.* extinguir, apagar.

extol, *v.* alabar.

extort, *v.* exigir dinero sin derecho.

extortion, *n.* extorsión *f.*

extra, 1. *a.* extraordinario; adicional. **2.** *n.* (newspaper) extra *m.*

extract, 1. *n.* extracto *m.* **2.** *v.* extraer.

extraction, *n.* extracción *f.*

extraneous, *a.* extraño; ajeno.

extraordinary, *a.* extraordinario.

extravagance, *n.* extravagancia *f.*

extravagant, *a.* extravagante.

extreme, *a.* & *n.* extremo *m.*

extremity, *n.* extremidad *f.*

extricate, *v.* desenredar.

exuberant, *a.* exuberante.

exude, *v.* exudar.

exult, *v.* regocijarse.

exultant, *a.* triunfante.

eye, 1. *n.* ojo *m.* **2.** *v.* ojear.

eyeball, *n.* globo del ojo.

eyebrow, *n.* ceja *f.*

eyeglasses, *n.* lentes *m.*

eyelash, *n.* pestaña *f.*

eyelid, *n.* párpado *m.*

eyesight, *n.* vista *f.*

F

fable, *n.* fábula; ficción *f.*

fabric, *n.* tejido *m.,* tela *f.*

fabricate, *v.* fabricar.

fabulous, *a.* fabuloso.

façade, *n.* fachada *f.*

face, 1. *n.* cara *f.* **to make faces,** hacer muecas. **2.** encararse con. **t. the street,** dar a la calle.

facet, *n.* faceta *f.*

facetious, *a.* chistoso.

facial, 1. *n.* masaje facial *m.* **2.** *a.* facial.

facile, *a.* fácil.

facilitate, *v.* facilitar.

facility, *n.* facilidad *f.*

facsimile, *n.* facsímile *m.*

fact, *n.* hecho *m.* **in f.,** en realidad.

faction, *n.* facción *f.*

factor, *n.* factor *m.*

factory, *n.* fábrica *f.*

factual, *a.* verdadero.

faculty, *n.* facultad *f.*

fad, *n.* boga; novedad *f.*

fade, *v.* desteñirse; (flowers) marchitarse.

fail, 1. *n.* without f., sin falla. **2.** *v.* fallar; fracasar. **not to f. to,** no dejar de.

failure, *n.* fracaso *m.*

faint, 1. *a.* débil; vago; pálido. **2.** *n.* desmayo *m.* **3.** *v.* desmayarse.

faintly, *adv.* débilmente; indistintamente.

fair, 1. *a.* razonable, justo; (hair) rubio; (weather) bueno. **2.** *n.* feria *f.*

fairly, *adv.* imparcialmente; regularmente; claramente; bellamente.

fairness, *n.* justicia *f.*

fairy, *n.* hada *f.,* duende *m.*

faith, *n.* fe; confianza *f.*

faithful, *a.* fiel.

fake, 1. *a.* falso; postizo. **2.** *n.* imitación; estafa *f.* **3.** *v.* imitar; fingir.

faker, *n.* imitador *m.;* farsante *m.*

falcon, *n.* halcón *m.*

fall, 1. *n.* caída; catarata *f.;* (season) otoño *m.;* (in price) baja *f.* **2.** *v.* caer; bajar. **f. asleep,** dormirse; **f. in love,** enamorarse.

fallacious, *a.* falaz.

fallacy, *n.* falacia *f.*

fallible, *a.* falible.

fallout, *n.* precipitación resultante de una explosión nuclear.

fallow, *a.* sin cultivar.

false, *a.* falso; postizo.

falsehood, *n.* falsedad; mentira *f.*

falseness, *n.* falsedad, perfidia *f.*

falsetto, *n.* falsete *m.*

falsification, *n.* falsificación *f.*

falsify, *v.* falsificar.

falter, *v.* vacilar; (in speech) tartamudear.

fame, *n.* fama *f.*

familiar, 1. *a.* familiar; conocido. **to be f. with,** estar familiarizado con.

familiarity, *n.* familiaridad *f.*

familiarize, *v.* familiarizar.

family, *n.* familia; especie naje *m.*

famine, *n.* hambre; carestía *f.*

famished, *a.* muerto de hambre.

famous, *a.* famoso, célebre.

fan, *n.* abanico; ventilador *m.* (sports) aficionado -da.

fanatic, *a.* & *n.* fanático -ca.

fanatical, *a.* fanático.

fanaticism, *n.* fanatismo *m.*

fanciful, *a.* caprichoso; fantástico.

fancy, 1. *a.* fino, elegante. **f. foods,** novedades *f.pl.* **2.** *n.* fantasía; capricho *m.* **3.** *v.* imaginar.

fanfare, *n.* fanfarria *f.*

fang, *n.* colmillo *m.*

fantastic, *a.* fantástico.

fantasy, *n.* fantasía *f.*

far, 1. *a.* lejano, distante. **2.** *adv.* lejos. **how f.,** a qué distancia. **as f. as,** hasta. **so f.,** thus f., hasta aquí.

farce, *n.* farsa *f.*

fare, *n.* pasaje *m.*

farewell, 1. *n.* despedida *f.* **to**

say f. despedirse. **2.** *interj.* ¡adiós!

farfetched, *a.* forzado.

farm, 1. *n.* granja; hacienda *f.* **2.** *v.* cultivar, labrar la tierra.

farmer, *n.* labrador, agricultor *m.*

farmhouse, *n.* hacienda, alquería *f.*

farming, *n.* agricultura *f.;* cultivo *m.*

fascinate, *v.* fascinar, embelesar.

fascination, *n.* fascinación *f.*

fascism, *n.* fascismo *m.*

fashion, 1. *n.* moda; costumbre; guisa *f.* **2.** *v.* formar.

fashionable, *a.* de moda, en boga.

fast, 1. *a.* rápido, veloz; (watch) adelantado; (color) firme. **2.** *adv.* ligero, de prisa. **3.** *n.* ayuno *m.* **4.** *v.* ayunar.

fasten, *v.* afirmar, atar; fijar.

fastener, *n.* asegurador *m.*

fastidious, *a.* melindroso.

fat, 1. *a.* gordo. **2.** *n.* grasa, manteca *f.*

fatal, *a.* fatal.

fatality, *n.* fatalidad *f.*

fatally, *adv.* fatalmente.

fate, *v.* destino *m.;* suerte *f.*

fateful, *a.* fatal; ominoso.

father, *n.* padre *m.*

fatherhood, *n.* paternidad *f.*

father-in-law, *n.* suegro *m.*

fatherland, *n.* patria *f.*

fatherly, 1. *a.* paternal. **2.** *adv.* paternalmente.

fathom, 1. *n.* braza *f.* **2.** *v.* sondar; (fig.) penetrar en.

fatigue, 1. *n.* fatiga *f.*, cansancio *m.* **2.** *v.* fatigar, cansar.

fatten, *v.* engordar, cebar.

faucet, *n.* grifo *m.*, llave *f.*

fault, *n.* culpa *f.;* defecto *m.* **at f.**, culpable.

faultless, *a.* sin tacha, perfecto.

faultlessly, *adv.* perfectamente.

faulty, *a.* defectuoso, imperfecto.

favor, 1. *n.* favor *m.* **2.** *v.* favorecer.

favorable, *a.* favorable.

favorite, *a.* & *n.* favorito -ta.

favoritism, *n.* favoritismo *m.*

fawn, 1. *n.* cervato *m.* **2.** *v.* halagar, adular.

faze, *v.* desconcertar.

fear, 1. *n.* miedo, temor *m.* **2.** *v.* temer.

fearful, *a.* temeroso, medroso.

fearless, *a.* intrépido; sin temor.

fearlessness, *n.* intrepidez *f.*

feasible, *a.* factible.

feast, *n.* banquete *m.;* fiesta *f.*

feat, *n.* hazaña *f.;* hecho *m.*

feather, *n.* pluma *f.*

feature, 1. *n.* facción *f.;* rasgo *m.;* (movies) película principal. **2.** *v.* presentar como atracción especial.

February, *n.* febrero *m.*

federal, *a.* federal.

federation, *n.* confederación, federación *f.*

fee, *n.* honorarios *m.pl.*

feeble, *a.* débil.

feebleminded, *a.* imbécil.

feebleness, *a.* debilidad *f.*

feed, 1. *n.* pasto *m.* **2.** *v.* alimentar; dar de comer. **fed up with**, harto de.

feedback, *n.* feedback *m.*, retroalimentación *f.*

feel, 1. *n.* sensación *f.* **2.** *v.* sentir; palpar. **f. like**, tener ganas de.

feeling, *n.* sensación; sensibilidad *f.*

feign, *v.* fingir.

felicitate, *v.* felicitar.

felicitous, *a.* feliz.

felicity, *n.* felicidad *f.*, dicha *f.*

feline, *a.* felino.

fellow, *n.* compañero; socio *m.;* (coll.) tipo *m.*

fellowship, *n.* compañía, (for study) beca *f.*

felon, *n.* reo *m.*, felón *m.*

felony, *n.* felonía *f.*

felt, *n.* fieltro *m.*

female, *a.* & *n.* hembra *f.*

feminine, *a.* femenino.

fence, 1. *n.* cerca *f.* **2.** *v.* cercar.

fender, *n.* guardabarros *m.*

ferment, 1. *n.* fermento *m.;* (fig.) agitación *f.* **2.** *v.* fermentar.

fermentation, *n.* fermentación *f.*

fern, *n.* helecho *m.*

ferocious, *a.* feroz; fiero.

ferociously, *adv.* ferozmente.

ferocity, *n.* ferocidad, fiereza *f.*

ferry, *n.* transbordador *m.*, barca de transporte.

fertile, *a.* fecundo; (land) fértil.

fertility, *n.* fertilidad *f.*

fertilization, *n.* fertilización *f.*

fertilize, *v.* fertilizar, abonar.

fertilizer, *n.* abono *m.*

fervency, *n.* ardor *m.*

fervent, *a.* ferviente.

fervently, *adv.* fervorosamente.

fervid, *a.* férvido.

fervor, *m.* fervor *m.*

fester, *v.* ulcerarse.

festival, *n.* fiesta *f.*

festive, *a.* festivo.

festivity, *n.* festividad *f.*

festoon, 1. *n.* festón *m.* **2.** *v.* festonear.

fetch, *v.* ir por; traer.

fete, 1. *n.* fiesta *f.* **2.** *v.* festejar.

fetid, *a.* fétido.

fetish, *n.* fetiche *m.*

fetter, 1. *n.* grillete *m.* **2.** *v.* engrillar.

fetus, *n.* feto *m.*

feud, *n.* riña *f.;* feudo *m.*

feudal, *a.* feudal.

feudalism, *n.* feudalismo *m.*

fever, *n.* fiebre *f.*

feverish, *a.* febril.

feverishly, *adv.* febrilmente.

few, *a.* pocos. **a. f.**, algunos, unos cuantos.

fiancé, fiancée, *n.* novio -via.

fiasco, *n.* fiasco *m.*

fiat, *n.* fiat *m.*, orden *f.*

fib, 1. *n.* mentira *f.* **2.** *v.* mentir.

fiber, *n.* fibra *f.*

fibrous, *a.* fibroso.

fickle, *a.* caprichoso.

fickleness, *n.* inconstancia *f.*

fiction, *n.* ficción *f.;* (literature) novelas *f.pl.*

fictitious, *a.* ficticio.

fidelity, *n.* fidelidad *f.*

fidget, *v.* inquietar.

field, *n.* campo *m.*

fiend, *n.* demonio *m.*

fiendish, *a.* diabólico, malvado.

fierce, *a.* fiero, feroz.

fiery, *a.* ardiente.

fiesta, *n.* fiesta *f.*

fife, *n.* pífano *m.*

fifteen, *n.* & *a.* & *pron.* quince.

fifteenth, *n.* & *a.* décimoquinto.

fifth, *a.* quinto.

fifty, *a.* & *pron.* cincuenta.

fig, *n.* higo *m.* **f. tree**, higuera *f.*

fight, 1. *n.* lucha, pelea *f.* **2.** *v.* luchar, pelear.

fighter, *n.* peleador -ra, luchador -ra.

figment, *n.* invención *f.*

figurative, *a.* metafórico.

figuratively, *adv.* figuradamente.

figure, 1. *n.* figura; cifra *f.* **2.** *v.* figurar; calcular.

filament, *n.* filamento *m.*

file, 1. *n.* archivo *m.;* (instrument) lima *f.;* (row) fila *f.* **2.** *v.* archivar; limar.

filial, *a.* filial.

filigree, *n.* filigrana *f.*

fill, *v.* llenar.

fillet, *n.* filete *m.*

filling, *n.* relleno *m.;* (dental) empastadura *f.* **f. station**, bomba *f.*

film, 1. *n.* película *f.*, film *m.* **2.** *v.* filmar.

filter, 1. *n.* filtro *m.* **2.** *v.* filtrar.

filth, *n.* suciedad, mugre *f.*

filthy, *a.* sucio.

fin, *n.* aleta *f.*

final, 1. *a.* final, último. **2.** *n.* examen final. **finals**, (sports) final *f.*

finalist, *n.* finalista.

finally, *adv.* finalmente.

finances, *n.* recursos, fondos *m.pl.*

financial, *a.* financiero.

financier, *n.* financiero *m.*

find, 1. *n.* hallazgo *m.* **2.** *v.* hallar; encontrar. **f. out**, averiguar, enterarse, saber.

fine, 1. *a.* fino; bueno. **2.** *adv.* muy bien. **3.** *n.* multa *f.* **4.** *v.* multar.

finery, *n.* gala *f.*, adorno *m.*

finesse, 1. *n.* artificio *m.* **2.** *v.* valerse de artificio.

finger, *n.* dedo *m.*

finger bowl, *n.* enjuagatorio *m.*

fingernail, *n.* uña *f.*

fingerprint, 1. *n.* impresión digital *f.* **2.** *v.* tomar las impresiones digitales.

finicky, *a.* melindroso.

finish, 1. *n.* conclusión *f.* **2.** *v.* acabar, terminar.

finished, *a.* acabado.

finite, *a.* finito.

fir, *n.* abeto *m.*

fire, 1. *n.* fuego; incendio *m.* **2.** *v.* disparar, tirar; (coll.) despedir.

fire alarm, *n.* alarma de incendio *f.*

firearm, *n.* arma de fuego.

firecracker, *n.* triquitraque *m.,* buscapiés *m.,* petardo *m.*

fire engine, *n.* bomba de incendios *f.*

fire escape, *n.* escalera de incendios *f.*

fire extinguisher, *n.* matafuego *m.*

firefly, *n.* luciérnaga *f.*

fireman, *n.* bombero *m.;* (railway) fogonero *m.*

fireplace, *n.* hogar, fogón *m.*

fireproof, *a.* incombustible.

fireside, *n.* hogar *m.,* fogón *m.*

fireworks, *n.* fuegos artificiales.

firm, 1. *a.* firme. **2.** *n.* casa de comercio.

firmness, *n.* firmeza *f.*

first, *a.* & *adv.* primero. **at f.,** al principio.

first aid, *n.* primeros auxilios *m.*

first-class, *a.* de primera clase.

fiscal, *a.* fiscal.

fish, 1. *n.* (food) pescado *m.;* (alive) pez *m.* **2.** *v.* pescar.

fisherman, *n.* pescador *m.*

fishhook, *n.* anzuelo *m.*

fishing, *n.* pesca *f.* **to go f.,** ir de pesca.

fishmonger, *n.* pescadero *m.*

fission, *n.* fisura *f.*

fissure, *n.* grieta *f.,* quebradura *f.*

fist, *n.* puño *m.*

fit, 1. *a.* capaz; justo. **2.** *n.* corte, talle *m.;* (med.) convulsión *f.* **3.** *v.* caber; quedar bien, sentar bien.

fitful, *a.* espasmódico; caprichoso.

fitness, *n.* aptitud; conveniencia *f.*

fitting, 1. *a.* conveniente. **to be f.,** convenir. **2.** *n.* ajuste *m.*

five, *a.* & *pron.* cinco.

fix, 1. *n.* apuro *m.* **2.** *v.* fijar; arreglar; componer, reparar.

fixation, *n.* fijación *f.;* fijeza *f.*

fixed, *a.* fijo.

fixture, *n.* instalación; guarnición *f.*

flabby, *a.* flojo.

flaccid, *a.* flojo; flácido.

flag, *n.* bandera *f.*

flagellant, *n.* & *a.* flagelante *m.*

flagon, *n.* frasco *m.*

flagrant, *a.* flagrante.

flagrantly, *adv.* notoriamente.

flair, *n.* afición *f.*

flake, 1. *n.* lámina *f.;* copo de nieve. **2.** *v.* romperse en láminas.

flamboyant, *a.* flamante, llamativo.

flame, 1. *n.* llama *f.* **2.** *v.* llamear.

flaming, *a.* llameante, flamante.

flamingo, *n.* flamenco *m.*

flank, 1. *n.* ijada *f.;* (mil.) flanco *m.* **2.** *v.* flanquear.

flannel, *n.* franela *f.*

flap, 1. *n.* cartera *f.* **2.** *v.* aletear; sacudirse.

flare, 1. *n.* llamarada *f.* **2.** *v.* brillar; (fig.) enojarse.

flash, 1. *n.* resplandor *m.;* (lightning) rayo, relámpago *m.;* (fig.) instante *m.* **2.** *v.* brillar.

flashcube, *n.* cubo de flash *m.*

flashlight, *n.* linterna eléctrica.

flashy, *a.* resplandeciente; ostentoso.

flask, *n.* frasco *m.*

flat, 1. *a.* llano; (tire) desinflado. **2.** *n.* llanura *f.;* apartamiento *m.*

flatness, *n.* llanura *f.*

flatten, *v.* aplastar, allanar; abatir.

flatter, *v.* adular, lisonjear.

flatterer, *n.* lisonjero -ra. zalamero -ra.

flattery, *n.* adulación, lisonja *f.*

flaunt, *v.* ostentar.

flavor, 1. *n.* sabor *m.* **2.** *v.* sazonar.

flavoring, *n.* condimento *m.*

flaw, *n.* defecto *m.*

flax, *n.* lino *m.*

flay, *v.* despellejar; excoriar.

flea, *n.* pulga *f.*

fleck, 1. *n.* mancha *f.* **2.** *v.* varetear.

flee, *v.* huir.

fleece, 1. *n.* vellón *m.* **2.** *v.* esquilar.

fleet, 1. *a.* veloz. **2.** *n.* flota *f.*

fleeting, *a.* fugaz, pasajero.

flesh, *n.* carne *f.*

fleshy, *a.* gordo; carnoso.

flex, 1. *n.* doblez *m.* **2.** *v.* doblar.

flexibility, *n.* flexibilidad *f.*

flexible, *a.* flexible.

flier, *n.* aviador -ra.

flight, *n.* vuelo *m.;* fuga *f.*

flight attendant, *n.* azafata *f.;* ayudante de vuelo *m.*

flimsy, *a.* débil.

flinch, *v.* acobardarse.

fling, *v.* lanzar.

flint, *n.* pedernal *m.*

flip, *v.* lanzar.

flippant, *a.* impertinente.

flippantly, *adv.* impertinentemente.

flirt, 1. *n.* coqueta *f.* **2.** *v.* coquetear, flirtear.

flirtation, *n.* coqueteo *m.*

float, *v.* flotar.

flock, 1. *n.* rebaño *m.* **2.** *v.* congregarse.

flog, *v.* azotar.

flood, 1. *n.* inundación *f.* **2.** *v.* inundar.

floor, 1. *n.* suelo, piso *m.* **2.** *v.* derribar.

floral, *a.* floral.

florid, *a.* florido.

florist, *n.* florista *m.* & *f.*

flounce, 1. *n.* (sewing) volante *m.* **2.** *v.* pernear.

flounder, *n.* rodaballo *m.*

flour, *n.* harina *f.*

flourish, 1. *n.* floreo *m.* **2.** *v.* florecer; prosperar; blandir.

flow, 1. *n.* flujo *m.* **2.** *v.* fluir.

flower, 1. *n.* flor *f.* **2.** *v.* florecer.

flowerpot, *n.* maceta de flores *f.*

flowery, *a.* florido.

fluctuate, *v.* fluctuar.

fluctuation, *n.* fluctuación *f.*

flue, *n.* humero *m.*

fluency, *n.* fluidez *f.*

fluent, *a.* fluente.

fluffy, *a.* velloso.

fluid, *a.* & *n.* flúido *m.*

fluidity, *n.* fluidez *f.*

fluoroscope, *n.* fluoroscopio *m.*

flurry, *n.* agitación *f.*

flush, 1. *a.* bien provisto. **2.** *n.* sonrojo *m.* **3.** *v.* limpiar con un chorro de agua; sonrojarse.

flute, *n.* flauta *f.*

flutter, 1. *n.* agitación *f.* **2.** *v.* agitarse.

flux, *n.* flujo *m.*

fly, 1. *n.* mosca *f.* **2.** *v.* volar.

foam, 1. *n.* espuma *f.* **2.** *v.* espumar.

focal, *a.* focal.

focus, 1. *n.* enfoque *m.* **2.** *v.* enfocar.

fodder, *n.* forraje *m.*

foe, *n.* adversario -ria, enemigo -ga.

fog, *n.* niebla *f.*

foggy, *a.* brumoso.

foil, *v.* frustrar.

foist, *v.* emponer.

fold, 1. *n.* pliegue *m.* **2.** *v.* doblar, plegar.

folder, *n.* circular *m.;* (for filing) carpeta *f.*

foliage, *n.* follaje *m.*

folio, *n.* infolio; folio *m.*

folklore, *n.* folklore *m.*

folks, *n.* gente, familia *f.*

follicle, *n.* folículo *m.*

follow, *v.* seguir.

follower, *n.* partidario -ria.

folly, *n.* locura *f.*

foment, *v.* fomentar.

fond, *a.* cariñoso, tierno. **be f. of,** ser aficionado a.

fondle, *v.* acariciar.

fondly, *adv.* tiernamente.

fondness, *n.* afición *f.;* cariño *m.*

food, *n.* alimento *m.;* comida *f.*

foodstuffs, *n.pl.* comestibles, víveres *m.pl.*

fool, 1. tonto -ta; bobo -ba; bufón -ona. **2.** v. engañar.

foolhardy, a. temerario.

foolish, a. bobo, tonto, majadero.

foolproof, a. seguro.

foot, n. pie m.

footage, n. longitud en pies.

football, n. fúbol, balompié m.

foothold, n. posición establecida.

footing, n. base f., fundamento m.

footlights, n.pl. luces del proscenio.

footnote, n. nota al pie de una página.

footprint, n. huella f.

footstep, n. paso m.

footstool, n. escañuelo m., banqueta f.

fop, n. petimetre m.

for, 1. prep. para; por. **as f.,** en cuanto a. **what f.,** ¿para qué? **2.** conj. porque, pues.

forage, 1. n. forraje m. **2.** v. forrajear.

foray, n. correría f.

forbear, v. cesar; abstenerse.

forbearance, n. paciencia f.

forbid, v. prohibir.

forbidding, a. repugnante.

force, 1. n. fuerza f. **2.** v. forzar.

forceful, a. fuerte; enérgico.

forcible, a. fuerte; enérgico.

ford, 1. n. vado m. **2.** v. vadear.

fore, 1. a. delantero. **2.** n. delantera f.

fore and aft, de popa a proa.

forearm, n. antebrazo m.

forebears, n.pl. antepasados m.pl.

forebode, v. presagiar.

foreboding, n. presentimiento m.

forecast, 1. n. pronóstico m.; profecía f. **2.** v. pronosticar.

forecastle, n. (naut.) castillo de proa.

forefather, n. antepasado m.

forefinger, n. índice m.

forego, v. renunciar.

foregone, a. predeterminado.

foreground, n. primer plano.

forehead, n. frente f.

foreign, a. extranjero.

foreign aid, ayuda exterior.

foreigner, n. extranjero -ra; forastero -ra.

foreleg, n. pierna delantera.

foreman, n. capataz m.

foremost, 1. a. primero. **2.** adv. en primer lugar.

forenoon, n. mañana f.

forensic, a. forense.

forerunner, n. precursor -ra.

foresee, v. prever.

foreshadow, v. prefigurar, anunciar.

foresight, n. previsión f.

forest, n. bosque m.; selva f.

forestall, v. anticipar; prevenir.

forester, n. silvicultor; guardamonte m.

forestry, n. silvicultura f.

foretell, v. predecir.

forever, adv. por siempre, para siempre.

forevermore, adv. siempre.

forewarn, v. advertir, avisar.

foreword, n. prefacio m.

forfeit, 1. n. prenda, multa f. **2.** v. perder.

forfeiture, n. decomiso m., multa f.

forgather, v. reunirse.

forge, 1. n. fragua f. **2.** v. forjar; falsear.

forger, n. forjador; falsificador m.

forgery, n. falsificación f.

forget, v. olvidar.

forgetful, a. olvidadizo.

forgive, v. perdonar.

forgiveness, n. perdón m.

fork, 1. n. tenedor m.; bifurcación f. **2.** v. bifurcarse.

forlorn, a. triste.

form, 1. n. forma f.; (document) formulario m. **2.** v. formar.

formal, a. formal; ceremonioso. **f. dance,** baile de etiqueta. **f. dress,** traje de etiqueta.

formality, n. formalidad f.

formally, adv. formalmente.

format, n. formato m.

formation, n. formación f.

formative, a. formativo.

former, a. anterior; antiguo. **the f.,** aquél.

formerly, adv. antiguamente.

formidable, a. formidable.

formless, a. sin forma.

formula, n. fórmula f.

formulate, v. formular.

formulation, n. formulación f.; expresión f.

forsake, v. abandonar.

fort, n. fortaleza f.; fuerte m.

forte, a. & adv. (mus.) forte, fuerte.

forth, adv. adelante. **back and f.,** de aquí allá. **and so f.,** etcétera.

forthcoming, a. futuro, próximo.

forthright, a. franco.

forthwith, adv. inmediatamente.

fortification, n. fortificación f.

fortify, v. fortificar.

fortissimo, a. & adv. (mus.) fortísimo.

fortitude, n. fortaleza; fortitud f.

fortnight, n. quincena f.

fortress, n. fuerte m., fortaleza f.

fortuitous, a. fortuito.

fortunate, a. afortunado.

fortune, n. fortuna; suerte f.

fortune-teller, n. sortílego, adivino m.

forty, a. & pron. cuarenta.

forum, n. foro m.

forward, 1. a. delantero; atrevido. **2.** adv. adelante. **3.** v. trasmitir, reexpedir.

foster, 1. a. **f. child,** hijo adoptivo. **2.** v. fomentar, criar.

foul, a. sucio; impuro.

found, v. fundar.

foundation, n. fundación f.; (of building) cimientos m.pl.

founder, 1. n. fundador -ra. **2.** v. irse a pique.

foundry, n. fundición f.

fountain, n. fuente f.

four, a. & pron. cuatro.

fourteen, a. & pron. catorce.

fourth, a. & n. cuarto m.

fowl, n. ave f.

fox, n. zorro -rra.

fox trot, n. foxtrot m.

foxy, a. astuto.

foyer, n. salón de entrada.

fracas, n. riña f.

fraction, n. fracción f.

fracture, 1. n. fractura, rotura f. **2.** v. fracturar, romper.

fragile, a. frágil.

fragment, n. fragmento, trozo m.

fragmentary, a. fragmentario.

fragrance, n. fragancia f.

fragrant, a. fragante.

frail, a. débil, frágil.

frailty, n. debilidad, fragilidad f.

frame, 1. n. marco; armazón; cuadro, cuerpo m. **2.** v. fabricar; formar; encuadrar.

frame-up, n. (coll.) conspiración f.

framework, n. armazón m.

France, n. Francia f.

franchise, n. franquicia f.

frank, 1. a. franco. **2.** n. carta franca. **3.** v. franquear.

frankfurter, n. salchicha f.

frankly, adv. francamente.

frankness, n. franqueza f.

frantic, a. frenético.

fraternal, a. fraternal.

fraternity, n. fraternidad f.

fraternization, n. fraternización f.

fraternize, v. confraternizar.

fratricide, n. fratricida m. & f.

fraud, n. fraude m.

fraudulent, a. fraudulento.

fraudulently, adv. fraudulentamente.

fraught, a. cargado.

freak, n. rareza f.

freckle, n. peca f.

free, 1. a. libre; gratis. **2.** v. libertar, librar.

freedom, n. libertad f.

freeze, v. helar, congelar.

freezer, n. heladora f.

freight, 1. n. carga f.; flete m. **2.** v. cargar; fletar.

freighter, n. (naut.) fletador m.

French, a. & n. francés m.

Frenchman, n. francés m.

frenzied, a. frenético.

frenzy, n. frenesí m.

frequency, n. frecuencia f.

frequency modulation, modulación de frequencia.

frequent, a. frecuente.

frequently, *adv.* frecuentemente.

fresco, *n.* pintura al fresco.

fresh, *a.* fresco. **f. water,** agua dulce.

freshen, *v.* refrescar.

freshness, *n.* frescura *f.*

fret, *v.* quejarse, irritarse.

fretful, *a.* irritable.

fretfully, *adv.* de mala gana.

fretfulness, *n.* mal humor.

friar, *n.* fraile *m.*

fricassee, *n.* fricasé *m.*

friction, *n.* fricción *f.*

Friday, *n.* viernes *m.* **Good F.,** Viernes Santo.

fried, *a.* frito.

friend, *n.* amigo -ga.

friendless, *a.* sin amigos.

friendliness, *n.* amistad *f.*

friendly, *a.* amistoso.

friendship, *n.* amistad *f.*

fright, *n.* susto *m.*

frighten, *v.* asustar, espantar.

frightful, *a.* espantoso.

frigid, *a.* frígido, frío.

frill, *n.* (sewing) lechuga *f.*

fringe, *n.* fleco; borde *m.*

frisky, *a.* retozón.

fritter, *n.* fritura *f.*

frivolity, *n.* frivolidad *f.*

frivolous, *a.* frívolo.

frivolousness, *n.* frivolidad *f.*

frock, *n.* vestido de mujer. **f. coat,** levita *f.*

frog, *n.* rana *f.*

frolic, **1.** *n.* retozo *m.* **2.** *v.* retozar.

from, *prep.* de; desde.

front, *n.* frente; (of building) fachada *f.* **in f. of,** delante de.

frontal, *a.* frontal.

frontier, *n.* frontera *f.*

frost, *n.* helada, escarcha *f.*

frosty, *a.* helado.

froth, *n.* espuma *f.*

frown, **1.** *n.* ceño *m.* **2.** *v.* fruncir el entrecejo.

frowzy, *a.* desaliñado.

frozen, *a.* helado; congelado.

fructify, *v.* fructificar.

frugal, *a.* frugal.

frugality, *n.* frugalidad *f.*

fruit, *n.* fruta *f.;* (benefits) frutos *m.pl.* **f. tree,** árbol frutal.

fruitful, *a.* productivo.

fruition, *n.* fruición *f.*

fruitless, *a.* inútil, vano.

frustrate, *v.* frustrar.

frustration, *n.* frustración *f.*

fry, *v.* freír.

fuel, *n.* combustible *m.*

fugitive, *a. & n.* fugitivo -va.

fugue, *n.* (mus.) fuga *f.*

fulcrum, *n.* fulcro *m.*

fulfill, *v.* cumplir.

fulfillment, *n.* cumplimiento *m.;* realización *f.*

full, *a.* lleno; completo; pleno.

fullness, *n.* plenitud *f.*

fulminate, *v.* volar; fulminar.

fulmination, *n.* fulminación, detonación *f.*

fumble, *v.* chapucear.

fume, **1.** *n.* humo *m.* **2.** *v.* humear.

fumigate, *v.* fumigar.

fumigator, *n.* fumigador *m.*

fun, *n.* diversión *f.* **to make f. of,** burlarse de. **to have f.,** divertirse.

function, **1.** *n.* función *f.* **2.** *v.* funcionar.

functional, *a.* funcional.

fund, *n.* fondo *m.*

fundamental, *a.* fundamental.

funeral, *n.* funeral *m.*

fungus, *n.* hongo *m.*

funnel, **1.** *n.* embudo *m.;* (of ship) chimenea *f.*

funny, *a.* divertido, gracioso. **to be f.,** tener gracia.

fur, *n.* piel *f.*

furious, *a.* furioso.

furlough, *n.* permiso *m.*

furnace, *n.* horno *m.*

furnish, *v.* surtir, proveer; (a house) amueblar.

furniture, *n.* muebles *m.pl.*

furrow, **1.** *n.* surco *m.* **2.** *v.* surcar.

further, **1.** *a. & adv.* más. **2.** *v.* adelantar, fomentar.

furthermore, *adv.* además.

fury, *n.* furor *m.;* furia *f.*

fuse, **1.** *n.* fusible *m.* **2.** *v.* fundir.

fuss, **1.** *n.* alboroto *m.* **2.** *v.* preocuparse por pequeñeces.

fussy, *a.* melindroso.

futile, *a.* fútil.

future, **1.** *a.* futuro. **2.** *n.* porvenir *m.*

futurology, *n.* futurología *f.*

G

gag, *n.* chiste *m.*

gaiety, *n.* alegría *f.*

gain, **1.** *n.* ganancia *f.* **2.** *v.* ganar.

gait, *n.* paso *m.*

gale, *n.* ventarrón *m.*

gall, *n.* hiel *f.;* (fig.) amargura *f.;* descaro *m.*

gallant, **1.** *a.* galante. **2.** *n.* galán *m.*

gallery, *n.* galería *f.;* (theat.) paraíso *m.*

gallon, *n.* galón *m.*

gallop, **1.** *n.* galope *m.* **2.** *v.* galopar.

gallows, *n.* horca *f.*

gamble, **1.** *n.* riesgo *m.* **2.** *v.* jugar; aventurar.

game, *n.* juego *m.;* (match) partida *f.;* (hunting) caza *f.*

gang, *n.* cuadrilla; pandilla *f.*

gangster, *n.* rufián *m.*

gap, *n.* raja *f.*

gape, *v.* boquear.

garage, *n.* garaje *m.*

garbage, *n.* basura *f.*

garden, *n.* jardín *m.;* (vegetable) huerta *f.*

gardener, *n.* jardinero -ra.

gargle, **1.** *n.* gárgara *f.* **2.** *v.* gargarizar.

garland, *n.* guirnalda *f.*

garlic, *n.* ajo *m.*

garment, *n.* prenda de vestir.

garrison, *n.* guarnición *f.*

garter, *n.* liga *f.;* ataderas *f.pl.*

gas, *n.* gas *m.*

gasohol, *n.* gasohol *m.*

gasoline, *n.* gasolina *f.*

gasp, **1.** *n.* boqueada *f.* **2.** *v.* boquear.

gate, *n.* puerta; entrada *f.*

gather, *v.* recoger; inferir; reunir.

gaudy, *a.* brillante; llamativo.

gauge, **1.** *n.* manómetro, indicador *m.* **2.** *v.* medir; estimar.

gaunt, *a.* flaco.

gauze, *n.* gasa *f.*

gay, **1.** *a.* alegre; homosexual. **2.** *n.* homosexual.

gaze, **1.** *n.* mirada *f.* **2.** *v.* mirar con fijeza.

gear, *n.* engranaje *m.* **in g.,** en juego.

gem, *n.* joya *f.*

gender, *n.* género *m.*

general, *a. & n.* general *m.*

generality, *n.* generalidad *f.*

generalize, *v.* generalizar.

generation, *n.* generación *f.*

generator, *n.* generador *m.*

generosity, *n.* generosidad *f.*

generous, *a.* generoso.

genial, *a.* genial.

genius, *n.* genio *m.*

gentle, *a.* suave; manso; benigno.

gentleman, *n.* señor, caballero *m.*

gentleness, *n.* suavidad *f.*

genuine, *a.* genuino.

genuineness, *n.* pureza *f.*

geographical, *a.* geográfico.

geography, *n.* geografía *f.*

geometric, *a.* geométrico.

geranium, *n.* geranio *m.*

germ, *n.* germen; microbio *m.*

German, *a. & n.* alemán mana.

Germany, *n.* Alemania *f.*

gesticulate, *v.* gesticular.

gesture, **1.** *n.* gesto *m.* **2.** *v.* gesticular, hacer gestos.

get, *v.* obtener; conseguir; (become) ponerse. **go and g.,** ir a buscar; **g. away,** irse; escaparse; **g. together,** reunirse; **g. on,** subir; **g. off,** bajar; **g. up,** levantarse; **g. there,** llegar.

ghastly, *a.* pálido; espantoso.

ghost, *n.* espectro, fantasma *m.*

giant, *n.* gigante *m.*

gift, *n.* regalo, don; talento *m.*

gild, *v.* dorar.

gin, *n.* ginebra *f.*

ginger, *n.* jengibre *m.*

gingerbread, *n.* pan de jengibre.

gingham, *n.* guinga *f.*

gird, *v.* ceñir.

girdle, *n.* faja *f.*

girl, *n.* muchacha, niña, chica *f.*

give, *v.* dar; regalar. **g. back,**

devolver. g. up, rendirse; renunciar.

giver, *n.* dador -ra; donador -ra.

glacier, *n.* ventisquero *m.*

glad, *a.* alegre, contento. **to be g.,** alegrarse.

gladly, *adj.* con mucho gusto.

gladness, *n.* alegría *f.;* placer *m.*

glamor, *n.* encanto *m.;* elegancia *f.*

glamorous, *a.* encantador, elegante.

glance, 1. *n.* vistazo *m.,* ojeada *f.* **2.** *v.* ojear.

gland, *n.* glándula *f.*

glare, 1. *n.* reflejo; brillo *m.* **2.** *v.* deslumbrar; echar miradas indignadas.

glass, *n.* vidrio; vaso *m.;* (eyeglasses), lentes anteojos *m.pl.*

gleam, 1. *n.* fulgor *m.* **2.** *v.* fulgurar.

glee, *n.* alegría *f.;* júbilo *m.*

glide, *v.* deslizarse.

glimpse, 1. *n.* vistazo *m.* **2.** *v.* ojear.

glisten, 1. *n.* brillo *m.* **2.** *v.* brillar.

glitter, 1. *n.* resplandor *m.* **2.** *v.* brillar.

globe, *n.* globo; orbe *m.*

gloom, *n.* oscuridad; tristeza *f.*

gloomy, *a.* oscuro; sombrío, triste.

glorify, *v.* glorificar.

glorious, *a.* glorioso.

glory, *n.* gloria, fama *f.*

glossary, *n.* glosario *m.*

glove, *n.* guante *m.*

glow, 1. *n.* fulgor *m.* **2.** *v.* relucir; arder.

glue, 1. *n.* cola *f.* **2.** *v.* encolar, pegar.

glum, *a.* de mal humor.

glutton, *n.* glotón -ona.

gnaw, *v.* roer.

go, *v.* ir, irse. **g. away,** irse, marcharse. **g. back,** volver, regresar. **g. down,** bajar. **g. in,** entrar. **g. on,** seguir. **g. out,** salir. **g. up,** subir.

goal, *n.* meta *f.;* objeto *m.*

goat, *n.* cabra *f.*

goblet, *n.* copa *f.*

God, *n.* Dios *m.*

gold, *n.* oro *m.*

golden, *a.* áureo.

good, 1. *a.* bueno. **2.** *n.* bienes *m.pl.;* (com.) géneros *m.pl.*

good-bye, 1. *n.* adiós *m.* **2.** *interj.* ¡adiós! ¡hasta la vista!, ¡hasta luego! **to say g. to,** despedirse de.

goodness, *n.* bondad *f.*

goose, *n.* ganso *m.*

gooseberry, *n.* uva crespa *f.*

gooseneck, 1. *n.* cuello de cisne *m.* **2.** *a.* curvo.

goose step, *n.* paso de ganso *m.*

gore, 1. *n.* sangre *f.* **2.** *v.* acornear.

gorge, 1. *n.* gorja *f.* **2.** *v.* engullir.

gorgeous, *a.* magnífico; precioso.

gorilla, *n.* gorila *f.*

gory, *a.* sangriento.

gosling, *n.* gansarón *m.*

gospel, *n.* evangelio *m.*

gossamer, 1. *n.* telaraña *f.* **2.** *a.* delgado.

gossip, 1. *n.* chisme *m.* **2.** *v.* chismear.

Gothic, *a.* gótico.

gouge, 1. *n.* gubia *f.* **2.** *v.* escoplear.

gourd, *n.* calabaza *f.*

gourmand, *n.* glotón *m.*

gourmet, *a.* gastrónomo -ma.

govern, *v.* gobernar.

governess, *n.* aya, institutriz *f.*

government, *n.* gobierno *m.*

governmental, *a.* gubernamental.

governor, *n.* gobernador *m.*

governorship, *n.* gobernatura *f.*

gown, *n.* vestido *m.* **dressing g.,** bata *f.*

grab, *v.* agarrar, arrebatar.

grace, *n.* gracia; gentileza; merced *f.*

graceful, *a.* agraciado.

graceless, *a.* réprobo.

gracious, *a.* gentil, cortés.

grackle, *n.* grajo *m.*

grade, 1. *n.* grado; nivel *m.;* pendiente; nota; calidad *f.* **2.** *v.* graduar.

grade crossing, *n.* paso a nivel *m.*

gradual, *a.* gradual.

gradually, *adv.* gradualmente.

graduate, 1. *n.* graduado -da, diplomado-da. **2.** *v.* graduar; diplomarse.

graft, 1. *n.* injerto *m.;* soborno público. **2.** *v.* injertar.

graham, *a.* centeno; acemita.

grail, *n.* grial *m.*

grain, *n.* grano; cereal *m.*

grain alcohol, *n.* alcohol de madera *m.*

gram, *n.* gramo *m.*

grammar, *n.* gramática *f.*

grammarian, *n.* gramático *m.*

grammar school, *n.* escuela elemental *f.*

grammatical, *a.* gramatical.

gramophone, *n.* gramófono *m.*

granary, *n.* granero *m.*

grand, *a.* grande, ilustre; estupendo.

grandchild, *n.* nieto -ta.

granddaughter, *n.* nieta *f.*

grandee, *n.* noble *m.*

grandeur, *n.* grandeza *f.*

grandfather, *n.* abuelo *m.*

grandiloquent, *a.* grandílocuo.

grandiose, *a.* grandioso.

grand jury, *n.* gran jurado *m.*

grandly, *adv.* grandiosamente.

grandmother, *n.* abuela *f.*

grand opera, *n.* ópera grande *f.*

grandparents, *n.* abuelos *m.pl.*

grandson, *n.* nieto *m.*

grandstand, *n.* andanada *f.,* tribuna *f.*

grange, *n.* granja *f.*

granger, *n.* labriego *m.*

granite, *n.* granito *m.*

granny, *n.* abuelita *f.*

grant, 1. *n.* concesión; subvención *f.* **2.** *v.* otorgar; conceder; conferir. **take for granted,** tomar por cierto.

granular, *a.* granular.

granulate, *v.* granular.

granulation, *n.* granulación *f.*

granule, *n.* gránulo *m.*

grape, *n.* uva *f.*

grapefruit, *n.* toronja *f.*

grapeshot, *n.* metralla *f.*

grapevine, *n.* vid; parra *f.*

graph, *n.* gráfia *f.*

graphic, *a.* gráfico.

graphite, *n.* grafito *m.*

graphology, *n.* grafología *f.*

grapple, *v.* agarrar.

grasp, 1. *n.* puño; poder; conocimiento *m.* **2.** *v.* empuñar agarrar; comprender.

grasping, *a.* codicioso.

grass, *n.* hierba *f.;* (marijuana) marijuana *f.*

grasshopper, *n.* saltamontes *m.*

grassy, *a.* herboso.

grate, *n.* reja *f.*

grateful, *a.* agradecido.

gratify, *v.* satisfacer.

grating, 1. *n.* enrejado *m.* **2.** *a.* discordante.

gratis, *adv.* & *a.* gratis.

gratitude, *n.* agradecimiento *m.*

gratuitous, *adv.* gratismente.

gratuity, *n.* propina *f.*

grave, 1. *a.* grave. **2.** *n.* sepultura; tumba *f.*

gravel, *n.* cascajo *m.*

gravely, *adv.* gravemente.

gravestone, *n.* lápida sepulcral *f.*

graveyard, *n.* cementerio *m.*

gravitate, *v.* gravitar.

gravitation, *n.* gravitación *f.*

gravity, *n.* gravedad; seriedad *f.*

gravure, *n.* grabado *m.*

gravy, *n.* salsa *f.*

gray, *a.* gris; (hair) cano.

grayish, *a.* pardusco.

gray matter, *n.* substancia gris *f.*

graze, *v.* rozar; (cattle) pastar.

grazing, *a.* pastando.

grease, 1. *n.* grasa *f.* **2.** *v.* engrasar.

greasy, *a.* grasiento.

great, *a.* grande, ilustre; estupendo.

Great Dane, *n.* mastín danés *m.*

greatness, *n.* grandeza *f.*

Greece, *n.* Grecia *f.*

greed, greediness, *n.* codicia, voracidad *f.*

greedy, *a.* voraz.

Greek, *a.* & *n.* griego -ga.

green, *a.* & *n.* verde *m.* **greens,** *n.* verduras *f.pl.*

greenery, *n.* verdor *m.*

greenhouse, *n.* invernáculo *m.*

greet, *v.* saludar.

greeting, *n.* saludo *m.*

gregarious, *a.* gregario.

grenade, *n.* granada; bomba *f.*

greyhound, *n.* galgo *m.*

grid, *n.* parrilla *f.*

griddle, *n.* tortera *f.*

griddlecake, *n.* tortita de harina *f.*

gridiron, *n.* parrilla *f.*, campo de fútbol *m.*

grief, *n.* dolor *m.*; pena *f.*

grievance, *n.* pesar; agravio *m.*

grieve, *v.* afligir.

grievous, *a.* penoso.

grill, 1. *n.* parrilla *f.* 2. *v.* asar a la parrilla.

grillroom, *n.* restaurante de servicio rápido *m.*

grim, *a.* ceñudo.

grimace, 1. *n.* mueca *f.* 2. *v.* hacer muecas.

grime, *n.* mugre *f.*

grimy, *a.* sucio; mugroso.

grin, 1. *n.* sonrisa *f.* 2. *v.* sonreír.

grind, *v.* moler; afilar.

grindstone, *n.* esmeriladora *f.*

gringo, *n.* gringo; yanqui *m.*

grip, 1. *n.* maleta *f.* 2. *v.* agarrar.

gripe, 1. *v.* agarrar. 2. *n.* asimiento *m.*, opresión *f.*

grippe, *n.* gripe *f.*

grisly, *a.* espantoso.

grist, *n.* molienda *f.*

gristle, *n.* cartílago *m.*

grit, *n.* arena *f.*, entereza *f.*

grizzled, *a.* tordillo.

groan, 1. *n.* gemido *m.* 2. *v.* gemir.

grocer, *n.* abacero *m.*

grocery, *n.* tienda de comestibles, bodega *f.*

grog, *n.* brebaje *m.*

groggy, *a.* medio borracho; vacilante.

groin, *n.* ingle *f.*

groom, *n.* (of horses) establero; (at wedding) novio *m.*

groove, 1. *n.* estría *f.* 2. *v.* acanalar.

grope, *v.* tentar; andar a tientas.

gross, 1. *a.* grueso; grosero. 2. *n.* gruesa *f.*

grossly, *adv.* groseramente.

grossness, *n.* grosería *f.*

grotesque, *a.* grotesco.

grotto, *n.* gruta *f.*

grouch, *v.* gruñón; descontento *m.*

ground, *n.* tierra *f.*; terreno; suelo; campo; fundamento *m.*

groundhog, *n.* marmota *f.*

groundless, *a.* infundado.

groundwork, *n.* base *f.*, fundamento *m.*

group, 1. *n.* grupo *m.* 2. *v.* agrupar.

groupie, *n.* muchacha que

acompaña a un grupo de música moderna.

grouse, *n.* chachalaca *f.*

grove, *n.* arboleda *f.*

grovel, *v.* rebajarse; envilecerse.

grow, *v.* crecer; cultivar.

growl, 1. *n.* gruñido *m.* 2. *v.* gruñir.

grown, *a.* crecido; desarrollado.

grownup, *n.* adulto *m.*

growth, *n.* crecimiento; vegetación *f.*; (med.) tumor *m.*

grub, *n.* gorgojo *m.*, larva *f.*

grubby, *a.* guasarapiento.

grudge, *n.* rencor *m.* **bear a g.**, guardar rencor.

gruel, 1. *n.* atole *m.* 2. *v.* estropear.

gruesome, *a.* horripilante.

gruff, *a.* ceñudo.

grumble, *v.* quejarse.

grumpy, *a.* gruñón; quejoso.

grunt, *v.* gruñir.

guarantee, 1. *n.* garantía *f.* 2. *v.* garantizar.

guarantor, *n.* fiador *m.*

guaranty, *n.* garantía *f.*

guard, 1. *n.* guardia *m.* or *f.* 2. *v.* vigilar.

guarded, *a.* cauteloso.

guardhouse, *n.* prisión militar *f.*

guardian, *n.* guardián *m.*

guardianship, *n.* tutela *f.*

guardsman, *n.* centinela *m.*

guava, *n.* guayaba *f.*

gubernatorial, *a.* gubernativo.

guerrilla, *n.* guerrillero *m.*

guess, 1. *n.* conjetura *f.* 2. *v.* adivinar; (coll.) creer.

guesswork, *n.* conjetura *f.*

guest, *n.* huésped *m. & f.*

guffaw, *n.* risotada *f.*

guidance, *n.* dirección *f.*

guide, 1. *n.* guía *m. & f.* 2. *v.* guiar.

guidebook, *n.* guía *f.*

guidepost, *n.* poste indicador *m.*

guild, *n.* gremio *m.*

guile, *n.* engaño *m.*

guillotine, 1. *n.* guillotina *f.* 2. *v.* guillotinar.

guilt, *n.* culpa *f.*

guiltily, *adv.* culpablemente.

guiltless, *a.* inocente.

guilty, *a.* culpable.

guinea fowl, *n.* gallina de Guinea *f.*

guinea pig, *n.* cobayo *m.*

guise, *n.* modo *m.*

guitar, *n.* guitarra *f.*

gulch, *n.* quebrada *f.*

gulf, *n.* golfo *m.*

gull, *n.* gaviota *f.*

gullet, *n.* esófago *m.*, zanja *f.*

gullible, *a.* crédulo.

gully, *n.* barranca *f.*

gulp, 1. *n.* trago *m.* 2. *v.* tragar.

gum, 1. *n.* goma *f.*; (anat.) encía *f.* **chewing g.**, chicle *m.* 2. *v.* engomar.

gumbo, *n.* quimbombó *f.*

gummy, *a.* gomoso.

gun, *n.* fusil; cañón *m.*

gunboat, *n.* cañonero *m.*

gunman, *n.* bandido *m.*

gunner, *n.* artillero *m.*

gunpowder, *n.* pólvora *f.*

gunshot, *n.* escopetazo *m.*

gunwale, *n.* borda *f.*

gurgle, 1. *n.* gorgoteo *m.* 2. *v.* gorgotear.

guru, *n.* gurú *m.*

gush, 1. *n.* chorro *m.* 2. *v.* brotar, chorrear.

gusher, *n.* pozo de chorro de petróleo *m.*

gust, *n.* soplo *m.*; ráfaga *f.*

gustatory, *a.* del sentido del gusto.

gusto, *n.* gusto; placer *m.*

gusty, *a.* borrascoso.

gut, *n.* intestino *m.*, tripa *f.*

gutter, *n.* canal; zanja *f.*

guttural, *a.* gutural.

guy, *n.* tipo *m.*

guzzle, *v.* engullir; tragar.

gym, *n.* gimnasio *m.*

gymnasium, *n.* gimnasio *m.*

gymnast, *n.* gimnasta *m.*

gymnastic, *a.* gimnástico.

gymnastics, *n.* gimnasia *f.*

gynecology, *n.* ginecología *f.*

gypsum, *n.* yeso *m.*

Gypsy, *a. & n.* gitano -na.

gyrate, *v.* girar.

gyroscope, *n.* giroscopio *m.*

H

habeas corpus, *n.* habeas corpus *m.*

haberdasher, *n.* camisero *m.*

haberdashery, *n.* camisería *f.*

habiliment, *n.* vestuario *m.*

habit, *n.* costumbre *f.*, hábito *m.* **be in the h. of**, estar acostumbrado a; soler.

habitable, *a.* habitable.

habitat, *n.* habitación *f.*, ambiente *m.*

habitation, *n.* habitación *f.*

habitual, *a.* habitual.

habituate, *v.* habituar.

habitué, *n.* parroquiano *m.*

hack, 1. *n.* coche de alquiler. 2. *v.* tajar.

hackneyed, *a.* trillado.

hacksaw, *n.* sierra para cortar metal *f.*

haddock, *n.* merluza *f.*

haft, *n.* mango *m.*

hag, *n.* bruja *f.*

haggard, *a.* trasnochado.

haggle, *v.* regatear.

hail, 1. *n.* granizo; (greeting) saludo *m.* 2. *v.* granizar; saludar.

Hail Mary, *n.* Ave María *m.*

hailstone, *n.* piedra de granizo *f.*

hailstorm, *n.* granizada *f.*

hair, *n.* pelo; cabello *m.*

haircut, *n.* corte de pelo.

hairdo, *n.* peinado *m.*

hairdresser, *n.* peluquero *m.*

hairpin, *n.* horquilla *f.;* gancho *m.*

hair's-breadth, *n.* ancho de un pelo *m.*

hairspray, *n.* aerosol para cabello.

hairy, *a.* peludo.

halcyon, **1.** *n.* alcedón *m.* **2.** *a.* tranquilo.

hale, *a.* sano.

half, **1.** *a.* medio. **2.** *n.* mitad *f.*

half-and-half, *a.* mitad y mitad.

half-baked, *a.* medio crudo.

half-breed, *n.* mestizo *m.*

half brother, *n.* medio hermano *m.*

half-hearted, *a.* sin entusiasmo.

half-mast, *a. & n.* media asta *m.*

halfpenny, *n.* media penique *m.*

halfway, *adv.* a medio camino.

half-wit, *n.* bobo *m.*

halibut, *n.* hipogloso *m.*

hall, *n.* corredor *m.;* (for assembling) sala *f.* **city h.,** ayuntamiento *m.*

hallmark, *n.* marca del contraste *f.*

hallow, *v.* consagrar.

Halloween, *n.* víspera de Todos los Santos *f.*

hallucination, *n.* alucinación *f.*

hallway, *n.* pasadizo *m.*

halo, *n.* halo *m.;* corona *f.*

halt, **1.** *a.* cojo. **2.** *n.* parada *f.* **3.** *v.* parar. **4.** *interj.* ¡alto!

halter, *n.* cabestro *m.*

halve, *v.* dividir en dos partes.

halyard, *n.* driza *f.*

ham, *n.* jamón *m.*

hamburger, *n.* albóndiga *f.*

hamlet, *n.* aldea *f.*

hammer, **1.** *n.* martillo *m.* **2.** *v.* martillar.

hammock, *n.* hamaca *f.*

hamper, *n.* canasta *f.*, cesto *m.*

hamstring, **1.** *n.* tendón de la corva *m.* **2.** *v.* desjarretar.

hand, **1.** mano *f.* **on the other h.,** en cambio. *v.* pasar. **h. over,** entregar.

handbag, *n.* cartera *f.*

handball, *n.* pelota *f.*

handbook, *n.* manual *m.*

handcuff, *n.* esposas *f.*

handful, *n.* puñado *m.*

handicap, *n.* desventaja *f.*

handicraft, *n.* artífice *m.*

handiwork, *n.* artefacto *m.*

handkerchief, *n.* pañuelo *m.*

handle, **1.** *n.* mango *m.* **2.** *v.* manejar.

handmade, *n.* hecho a mano *m.*

handmaid, *n.* criada de mano *f.*

hand organ, *n.* organillo *m.*

handsome, *a.* guapo; hermoso.

hand-to-hand, *adv.* de mano a mano.

handwriting, *n.* escritura *f.*

handy, *a.* diestro; útil; a la mano.

hang, *v.* colgar; ahorcar.

hangar, *n.* hangar *m.*

hangdog, *a. & n.* camastrón *m.*

hanger, *n.* colgador, gancho *m.*

hanger-on, *n.* dependiente; mogollón *m.*

hang glider, *n.* aparato para vuelo libre.

hanging, **1.** *n.* ahorcadura *f.* **2.** *a.* colgante.

hangman, *n.* verdugo *m.*

hangnail, *n.* padrastro *m.*

hang out, *v.* enarbolar.

hangup, *n.* tara (psicológica) *f.*

hank, *n.* madeja *f.*

hanker, *v.* ansiar; apetecer.

haphazard, *a.* casual.

happen, *v.* acontecer, suceder, pasar.

happening, *n.* acontecimiento *m.*

happiness, *n.* felicidad; dicha *f.*

happy, *a.* feliz; contento; dichoso.

happy-go-lucky, *a. & n.* descuidado *m.*

harakiri, *n.* harakiri (suicidio japonés) *m.*

harangue, **1.** *n.* arenga *f.* **2.** *v.* arengar.

harass, *v.* acosar; atormentar.

harbinger, *n.* presagio *m.*

harbor, **1.** *n.* puerto; albergue *m.* **2.** *v.* abrigar.

hard, **1.** *a.* duro; difícil. **2.** *adv.* mucho.

hard coal, antracita *m.*

harden, *v.* endurecer.

hard-headed, *a.* terco.

hard-hearted, *a.* empedernido.

hardiness, *n.* vigor *m.*

hardly, *adv.* apenas.

hardness, *n.* dureza; dificultad *f.*

hardship, *n.* penalidad *f.;* trabajo *m.*

hardware, *n.* ferretería *f.*

hardwood, *n.* madera dura *f.*

hardy, *a.* fuerte, robusto.

hare, *n.* liebre *f.*

harebrained, *a.* tolondro.

harelip, **1.** *n.* labio leporino *m.* **2.** *a.* labihendido.

harem, *n.* harén *m.*

hark, *v.* escuchar; atender.

Harlequin, *n.* arlequín *m.*

harlot, *n.* ramera *f.*

harm, **1.** *n.* mal, daño; perjuicio *m.* **2.** *v.* dañar.

harmful, *a.* dañoso.

harmless, *a.* inocente.

harmonic, *n.* armónico *m.*

harmonica, *n.* armónica *f.*

harmonious, *a.* armonioso.

harmonize, *v.* armonizar.

harmony, *n.* armonía *f.*

harness, *n.* arnés *m.*

harp, *n.* arpa *f.*

harpoon, *n.* arpón *m.*

harridan, *n.* vieja regañona *f.*

harrow, **1.** *n.* rastro *m.;* grada *f.* **2.** *v.* gradar.

harry, *v.* acosar.

harsh, *a.* áspero.

harshness, *n.* aspereza *f.*

harvest, **1.** *n.* cosecha *f.* **2.** *v.* cosechar.

hash, *n.* picadillo *m.*

hashish, *n.* haxis *m.*

hasn't, *v.* no tiene (neg. + tener).

hassle, *n.* lío *m.*, molestia *f.;* controversia *f.*

hassock, *n.* cojín *m.*

haste, *n.* prisa *f.*

hasten, *v.* apresurarse, darse prisa.

hasty, *a.* apresurado.

hat, *n.* sombrero *m.*

hatch, **1.** *n.* (naut.) cuartel *m.* **2.** *v.* incubar; (fig.) tramar.

hatchery, *n.* criadero *m.*

hatchet, *n.* hacha pequeña.

hate, **1.** *n.* odio *m.* **2.** *v.* odiar, detestar.

hateful, *a.* detestable.

hatred, *n.* odio *m.*

haughtiness, *n.* arrogancia *f.*

haughty, *a.* altivo.

haul, **1.** *n.* (fishery) redada *f.* **2.** *v.* tirar, halar.

haunch, *n.* anca *f.*

haunt, **1.** *n.* lugar frecuentado. **2.** *v.* frecuentar, andar por.

have, *v.* tener; haber.

haven, *n.* puerto; asilo *m.*

haven't, *v.* no tiene (neg. + tener).

havoc, *n.* ruina *f.*

hawk, *n.* halcón *m.*

hawker, *n.* buhonero *m.*

hawser, *n.* cable *m.*

hawthorn, *n.* espino *m.*

hay, *n.* heno *m.*

hay fever, *n.* catarro anual de la nariz *m.;* alergia nasal.

hayfield, *n.* henar *m.*

hayloft, *n.* henil *m.*

haystack, *n.* hacina de heno *f.*

hazard, **1.** *n.* azar *m.* **2.** *v.* aventurar.

hazardous, *a.* peligroso.

haze, *n.* niebla *f.*

hazel, *n.* avellano *m.*

hazy, *a.* brumoso.

he, *pron.* él *m.*

head, **1.** *n.* cabeza *f.;* jefe *m.* **2.** *v.* dirigir; encabezar.

headache, *n.* dolor de cabeza.

headband, *n.* venda para cabeza *f.*

headfirst, *adv.* de cabeza.

headgear, *n.* tocado *m.*

headlight, *n.* linterna delantera *f.*, farol de tope *m.*

headline, *n.* encabezado *m.*

headlong, *a.* precipitoso.

head-on, *adv.* de frente.

headquarters, *n.* jefatura *f.;* (mil.) cuartel general.

headstone, *n.* lápida mortuoria *f.*

headstrong, *a.* terco.

headwaters, *n.* cabeceras *f.*

headway, *n.* avance *m.*, progreso *m.*

headwork, *n.* trabajo mental *m.*

heady, *a.* impetuoso.

heal, *v.* curar, sanar.

health, *n.* salud *f.*

healthful, *a.* saludable.

healthy, *a.* sano; salubre.

heap, *n.* montón *m.*

hear, *v.* oír. **h. from,** tener noticias de. **h. about, h. of,** oír hablar de.

hearing, *n.* oído *m.*

hearsay, *n.* rumor *m.*

hearse, *n.* ataúd *m.*

heart, *n.* corazón; ánimo *m.* **by h.,** de memoria.

heartache, *n.* angustia *f.*

heartbreak, *n.* angustia *f.;* pesar *m.*

heartbroken, *a.* acongojado.

heartburn, *n.* acedía *f.*

heartfelt, *a.* sentido.

hearth, *n.* hogar *m.,* chimenea *f.*

heartless, *a.* empedernido.

heartsick, *a.* desconsolado.

heart-stricken, *a.* afligido.

heart-to-heart, *adv.* franco; sincero.

hearty, *a.* cordial; vigoroso.

heat, 1. *n.* calor; ardor *m.;* calefacción *f.* 2. *v.* calentar.

heated, *a.* acalorado.

heater, *n.* calentador *m.*

heath, *n.* matorral *m.*

heathen, *a. & n.* pagano -na.

heather, *n.* brezo *m.*

heatstroke, *n.* insolación *f.*

heat wave, *n.* onda de calor *f.*

heave, *v.* tirar.

heaven, *n.* cielo *m.*

heavenly, *a.* divino.

heavy, *a.* pesado; oneroso.

Hebrew, *a. & n.* hebreo -ea.

hectic, *a.* turbulento.

hedge, *n.* seto *m.*

hedgehog, *n.* erizo *m.*

hedonism, *n.* hedonismo *m.*

heed, 1. *n.* cuidado *m.* 2. *v.* atender.

heedless, *a.* desatento; incauto.

heel, *n.* talón *m.;* (of shoe) tacón *m.*

heifer, *n.* novilla *f.*

height, *n.* altura *f.*

heighten, *v.* elevar; exaltar.

heinous, *a.* nefando.

heir, heiress, *n.* heredero -ra.

helicopter, *n.* helicóptero *m.*

heliotrope, *n.* heliotropo *m.*

helium, *n.* helio *m.*

hell, *n.* infierno *m.*

Hellenism, *n.* helenismo *m.*

hellish, *a.* infernal.

hello, *interj.* ¡hola!; (on telephone) aló; bueno.

helm, *n.* timón *m.*

helmet, *n.* yelmo, casco *m.*

helmsman, *n.* limonero *m.*

help, 1. *n.* ayuda *f.* **help!** ¡socorro! 2. *v.* ayudar. **h. oneself,** servirse. **can't help (but),** no poder menos de.

helper, *n.* ayudante *m.*

helpful, *a.* útil; servicial.

helpfulness, *n.* utilidad *f.*

helpless, *a.* imposibilitado.

hem, 1. *n.* ribete *m.* 2. *v.* ribetear.

hemisphere, *n.* hemisferio *m.*

hemlock, *n.* abeto *m.*

hemoglobin, *n.* hemoglobina *f.*

hemophilia, *n.* hemofilia *f.*

hemorrhage, *n.* hemorragia *f.*

hemorrhoid, *n.* hemorriodes *f.pl.*

hemp, *n.* cáñamo *m.*

hemstitch, 1. *n.* vainica *f.* 2. *v.* hacer una vainica.

hen, *n.* gallina *f.*

hence, *adv.* por lo tanto.

henceforth, *adv.* de aquí en adelante.

henchman, *n.* paniaguado *m.*

henna, *n.* alheña *f.*

her, 1. *a.* su. 2. *pron.* ella; la; le.

herald, *n.* heraldo *m.*

heraldic, *a.* heráldico.

heraldry, *n.* heráldica *f.*

herb, *n.* yerba, hierba *f.*

herbaceous, *a.* herbáceo.

herbarium, *n.* herbario *m.*

herd, 1. *n.* hato, rebaño *m.* 2. *v.* reunir en hatos.

here, *adv.* aquí; acá.

hereafter, *adv.* en lo futuro.

hereby, *adv.* por éstas, por la presente.

hereditary, *a.* hereditario.

heredity, *n.* herencia *f.*

herein, *adv.* aquí dentro; incluso.

heresy, *n.* herejía *f.*

heretic, 1. *a.* herético. 2. *n.* hereje *m. & f.*

heretical, *a.* herético.

heretofore, *adv.* hasta ahora.

herewith, *adv.* con esto, adjunto.

heritage, *n.* herencia *f.*

hermetic, *a.* hermético.

hermit, *n.* ermitaño *m.*

hernia, *n.* hernia *f.*

hero, *n.* héroe *m.*

heroic, *a.* heroico.

heroically, *adv.* heroicamente.

heroin, *n.* heroína *f.*

heroine, *n.* heroína *f.*

heroism, *n.* heroísmo *m.*

heron, *n.* garza *f.*

herring, *n.* arenque *m.*

hers, *pron.* suyo, de ella.

herself, *pron.* sí, sí misma, se. **she h.,** ella misma. **with h.,** consigo.

hertz, *n.* hertzio *m.*

hesitancy, *n.* hesitación *f.*

hesitant, *a.* indeciso.

hesitate, *v.* vacilar.

hesitation, *n.* duda; vacilación *f.*

heterogeneous, *a.* heterogéneo.

heterosexual, *a.* heterosexual.

hexagon, *n.* hexágono *m.*

hibernate, *v.* invernar.

hibernation, *n.* invernada *f.*

hibiscus, *n.* hibisco *m.*

hiccup, 1. *n.* hipo *m.* 2. *v.* tener hipo.

hickory, *n.* nogal americano *m.*

hidden, *a.* oculto; escondido.

hide, 1. *n.* cuero *m.;* piel *f.* 2. *v.* esconder; ocultar.

hideous, *a.* horrible.

hide-out, *n.* escondite *m.*

hierarchy, *n.* jerarquía *f.*

high, *a.* alto, elevado; (in price) caro.

highbrow, *n.* erudito *m.*

high fidelity, de alta fidelidad.

highly, *adv.* altamente; sumamente.

high school, *n.* escuela secundaria *f.*

highway, *n.* carretera *f.;* camino real *m.*

hijacker, *n.* secuestrador, pirata de aviones *m.*

hike, *n.* caminata *f.*

hilarious, *a.* alegre, bullicioso.

hilariousness, hilarity, *n.* hilaridad *f.*

hill, *n.* colina *f.;* cerro *m.;* **down h.,** cuesta abajo. **up h.,** cuesta arriba.

hilt, *n.* puño *m.* **up to the h.,** a fondo.

him, *pron.* él; lo; le.

himself, *pron.* sí, sí mismo; se. **he h.,** él mismo. **with h.,** consigo.

hinder, *v.* impedir.

hindmost, *a.* último.

hindquarter, *n.* cuarto trasero *m.*

hindrance, *n.* obstáculo *m.*

hinge, 1. *n.* gozne *m.* 2. *v.* engoznar. **h. on,** depender de.

hint, 1. *n.* insinuación *f.;* indicio *m.* 2. *v.* insinuar.

hip, *n.* cadera *f.*

hippopotamus, *n.* hipopótamo *m.*

hire, *v.* alquilar.

his, 1. *a.* su. 2. *pron.* suyo, de él.

Hispanic, *a.* hispano.

hiss, *v.* silbar, sisear.

historian, *n.* historiador *m.*

historic, historical, *a.* histórico.

history, *n.* historia *f.*

histrionic, *a.* histriónico.

hit, 1. *n.* golpe *m.;* (coll.) éxito *m.* 2. *v.* golpear, dar.

hitch, *v.* amarrar; enganchar.

hither, *adv.* acá, hacia acá.

hitherto, *adv.* hasta ahora.

hive, *n.* colmena *f.*

hives, *n.* urticaria *f.*

hoard, 1. *n.* acumulación *f.* 2. *v.* acaparar; atesorar.

hoarse, *a.* ronco.

hoax, 1. *n.* engaño *m.* 2. *v.* engañar.

hobby, *n.* afición *f.,* pasatiempo *m.*

hobgoblin, *n.* trasgo *m.*

hobnob, *v.* tener intimidad.

hobo, *n.* vagabundo *m.*

hockey, *n.* hockey *m.* **ice-h.,** hockey sobre hielo.

hod, *n.* esparavel *m.*

hodgepodge, *n.* baturillo *m.;* mezcolanza *f.*

hoe, 1. *n.* azada *f.* 2. *v.* cultivar con azada.

hog, *n.* cerdo, puerco *m.*

hoist, 1. *n.* grúa *f.,* elevador *m.* 2. *v.* elevar, enarbolar.

hold, 1. *n.* presa *f.;* agarro *m.;*

(naut.) bodega f. **to get h. of,** conseguir, apoderarse de. **2.** v. tener; detener; sujetar; celebrar.

holder, n. tenedor m. **cigarette h.,** boquilla f.

holdup, n. salteamiento m.

hole, n. agujero; hoyo; hueco m.

holiday, n. día de fiesta.

holiness, n. santidad f.

Holland, n. Holanda f.

hollow, 1. a. hueco m. **2.** n. cavidad f. **3.** v. ahuecar; excavar.

holly, n. acebo m.

hollyhock, n. malva real f.

holocaust, n. holocausto m.

hologram, n. holograma m.

holography, n. holografía f.

holster, n. pistolera f.

holy, a. santo.

holy day, n. disanto m.

Holy See, n. Santa Sede f.

Holy Spirit, n. Espíritu Santo m.

Holy Week, n. Semana Santa f.

homage, n. homenaje m.

home, n. casa, morada f; hogar m. **at h.,** en casa. **to go h.,** ir a casa.

homeland, n. patria f.

homely, a. feo; casero.

home rule, n. autonomía f.

homesick, a. nostálgico.

homespun, a. casero; tocho.

homeward, adv. hacia casa.

homicide, n. homicida m. & f.

homily, n. homilía f.

homogeneous, a. homogéneo.

homogenize, v. homogenizar.

homosexual, n. & a. homosexual m.

Honduras, n. Honduras f.

hone, 1. n. piedra de afilar f. **2.** v. afilar.

honest, a. honrado, honesto; sincero.

honestly, adv. honradamente; de veras.

honesty, n. honradez, honestidad f.

honey, n. miel f.

honeybee, n. abeja obrera f.

honeymoon, n. luna de miel.

honeysuckle, n. madreselva f.

honor, 1. n. honra f.; honor m. **2.** v. honrar.

honorable, a. honorable; ilustre.

honorary, a. honorario.

hood, n. capota; capucha f.; (auto.) cubierta del motor.

hoodlum, n. pillo m., rufián m.

hoof, n. pezuña f.

hook, 1. n. gancho m. **2.** v. enganchar.

hoop, n. cerco m.

hop, 1. n. salto m. **2.** v. saltar.

hope, 1. n. esperanza f. **2.** v. esperar.

hopeful, a. lleno de esperanzas.

hopeless, a. desesperado; sin remedio.

horde, n. horda f.

horehound, n. marrubio m.

horizon, n. horizonte m.

horizontal, a. horizontal.

hormone, n. hormón m.

horn, n. cuerno m.; (music) trompa f.; (auto.) bocina f.

hornet, n. avispón m.

horny, a. córneo; calloso.

horoscope, n. horóscopo m.

horrendous, a. horrendo.

horrible, a. horrible.

horrid, a. horrible.

horrify, v. horrorizar.

horror, n. horror m.

horse, n. caballo m. **to ride a h.,** cabalgar.

horseback, n. **on h.,** a caballo. **to ride h.,** montar a caballo.

horsefly, n. tábano m.

horsehair, n. pelo de caballo m.; tela de crin f.

horseman, n. jinete m.

horsemanship, n. manejo m., equitación f.

horsepower, n. caballo de fuerza m.

horseradish, n. rábano picante m.

horseshoe, n. herradura f.

hortatory, a. exhortatorio.

horticulture, n. horticultura f.

hose, n. medias f.pl; (garden) manguera f.

hosiery, n. calcetería f.

hospitable, a. hospitalario.

hospital, n. hospital m.

hospitality, n. hospitalidad f.

hospitalization, n. hospitalización f.

hospitalize, v. hispitalizar.

host, n. anfitrión m., dueño de la casa; (rel.) hostia f.

hostage, n. rehén m.

hostel, n. hostería f.

hostelry, n. fonda f., parador m.

hostess, n. anfitriona f., dueña de la casa.

hostile, a. hostil.

hostility, n. hostilidad f.

hot, a. caliente; (sauce) picante. **to be h.,** tener calor; (weather) hacer calor.

hotbed, n. estercolero m. (fig.) foco m.

hotel, n. hotel m.

hot-headed, a. turbulente, alborotadizo.

hothouse, n. invernáculo m.

hound, 1. n. sabueso m. **2.** v. perseguir; seguir la pista.

hour, n. hora f.

hourglass, n. reloj de arena m.

hourly, 1. a. por horas. **2.** adv. a cada hora.

house, 1. casa f.; (theat.) público m. **2.** v. alojar, albergar.

housefly, n. mosca ordinaria f.

household, n. familia; casa f.

housekeeper, n. ama de llaves.

housemaid, n. criada f., sirvienta f.

housewife, n. ama de casa.

housework, n. tareas domésticas f.

hovel, n. choza f.

hover, v. revolotear.

hovercraft, n. hovercraft m.

how, adv. cómo. **h. much,** cuánto. **h. many,** cuántos. **h. far,** a qué distancia.

however, adv. como quiera; sin embargo.

howl, 1. n. aullido m. **2.** v. aullar.

hub, n. centro m.; eje m. **h. of a wheel,** cubo de la rueda m.

hubbub, n. alborota f., bulla f.

hue, n. matiz; color m.

hug, 1. n. abrazo m. **2.** v. abrazar.

huge, a. enorme.

hulk, n. casco de buque m.

hull, 1. n. cáscara f.; (naval) casco m. **2.** v. decascarar.

hum, 1. n. zumbido m. **2.** v. tararear; zumbar.

human, a. & n. humano -na.

humane, a. humano, humanitario.

humanism, n. humanidad f.; benevolencia f.

humanitarian, a. humanitario.

humanity, n. humanidad f.

humanly, a. humanamente.

humble, a. humilde.

humbug, n. farsa f., embaucador m.

humdrum, a. monótono.

humid, a. húmedo.

humidity, n. humedad f.

humiliate, v. humillar.

humiliation, n. mortificación f.; bochorno m.

humility, n. humildad f.

humor, 1. n. humor; capricho m. **2.** v. complacer.

humorist, n. humorista m.

humorous, a. divertido.

hump, n. joroba f.

humpback, n. jorobado m.

humus, n. humus m.

hunch, n. giba f.; (idea) corazonada f.

hunchback, n. jorobado m.

hundred, 1. a. & pron. cien, ciento. 200, doscientos. 300, trescientos. 400, cuatrocientos. 500, quinientos. 600, seiscientos. 700, setecientos. 800, ochocientos. 900, novecientos. **2.** n. centenar m.

hundredth, n. & a. centésimo m.

Hungarian, a. & n. húngaro -ra.

Hungary, Hungría f.

hunger, n. hambre f.

hungry, a. hambriento. **to be h.,** tener hambre.

hunt, 1. n. caza f. **2.** v. cazar. **h. up,** buscar.

hunter, n. cazador m.

hunting, n. caza f. **to go h.,** ir de caza.

hurdle, n. zarzo m., valla f.; dificultad f.

hurl, v. arrojar.

hurricane, n. huracán m.

hurry, 1. n. prisa f. to be in a h., tener prisa. 2. v. apresurar; darse prisa.

hurt, 1. n. daño, perjuicio m. 2. v. dañar; lastimar; doler; ofender.

hurtful, a. perjudicial, dañino.

hurtle, v. lanzar.

husband, n. marido, esposo m.

husk, 1. n. cáscara f. 2. v. descascarar.

husky, a. fornido.

hustle, v. empujar.

hut, n. choza f.

hyacinth, n. jacinto m.

hybrid, a. híbrido.

hydrangea, n. hortensia f.

hydraulic, a. hidráulico.

hydroelectric, a. hidroeléctrico.

hydrogen, n. hidrógeno m.

hydrophobia, n. hidrofobia. f.

hydroplane, n. hidroavión m.

hydrotherapy, n. hidroterapia f.

hyena, n. hiena f.

hygiene, n. higiene f.

hygienic, a. higiénico.

hymn, n. himno m.

hymnal, n. himnario m.

hypercritical, a. hipercrítico.

hyphen, n. guión m.

hyphenate, v. separar con guión.

hypnosis, n. hipnosis f.

hypnotic, a. hipnótico.

hypnotism, n. hipnotismo m.

hypnotize, v. hipnotizar.

hypochondria, n. hipocondría f.

hypochondriac, n. & a. hipocondríaco m.

hypocrisy, n. hipocresía f.

hypocrite, n. hipócrita m. & f.

hypocritical, a. hipócrita.

hypodermic, a. hipodérmico.

hypotenuse, n. hipotenusa f.

hypothesis, n. hipótesis f.

hypothetical, a. hipotético.

hysterectomy, n. histerectomía f.

hysteria, hysterics, n. histeria f.

hysterical, a. histérico.

I

I, pron. yo.

iambic, a. yámbico.

ice, n. hielo m.

iceberg, n. iceberg m.

icebox, n. refrigerador m.

ice cream, n. helado, mantecado m.; i.-c. cone, barquillo de helado.

ice skate, n. patín de cuchilla m.

icon, n. icón m.

icy, a. helado; indiferente.

idea. n. idea f.

ideal, a. ideal.

idealism, n. idealismo m.

idealist, n. idealista m. & f.

idealistic, a. idealista.

idealize, v. idealizar.

ideally, adv. idealmente.

identical, a. idéntico.

identifiable, a. identificable.

identification, n. identificación f. i. papers, cédula de identidad f.

identify, v. identificar.

identity, n. identidad f.

ideology, n. ideología f.

idiocy, n. idiotez f.

idiom, n. modismo m.; idioma m.

idiot, n. idiota m. & f.

idiotic, a. idiota, tonto.

idle, a. desocupado; perezoso.

idleness, n. ociosidad, pereza f.

idol, n. ídolo m.

idolatry, n. idolatría f.

idolize, v. idolatrar.

idyl, n. idilio m.

idyllic, a. idílico.

if, conj. si. even if, aunque.

ignite, v. encender.

ignition, n. ignición f.

ignoble, a. innoble, indigno.

ignominious, a. ignominioso.

ignoramus, n. ignorante m.

ignorance, n. ignorancia f.

ignorant, a. ignorante. to be i. of, ignorar.

ignore, v. desconocer, pasar por alto.

ill, a. enfermo, malo.

illegal, a. ilegal.

illegible, a. ilegible.

illegibly, a. ilegiblemente.

illegitimacy, n. ilegitimidad f.

illegitimate, a. ilegítimo; desautorizado.

illicit, a. ilícito.

illiteracy, n. analfabetismo m.

illiterate, a. & n. analfabeto -ta.

illness, n. enfermedad, maldad f.

illogical, a. ilógico.

illuminate, v. iluminar.

illumination, n. iluminación f.

illusion, n. ilusión f.; ensueño m.

illusive, a. ilusivo.

illustrate, v. ilustrar; ejemplificar.

illustration, n. ilustración f.; ejemplo; grabado m.

illustrative, a. ilustrativo.

illustrious, a. ilustre.

ill will, n. malevolencia f.

image, n. imagen, estatua f.

imagery, n. imaginación f.

imaginable, a. imaginable.

imaginary, a. imaginario.

imagination, n. imaginación f.

imaginative, a. imaginativo.

imagine, v. imaginarse, figurarse.

imam, n. imán m.

imbecile, n. & a. imbécil m.

imitate, v. imitar.

imitation, n. imitación f.

imitative, a. imitativo.

immaculate, a. inmaculado.

immanent, a. inmanente.

immaterial, a. inmaterial; sin importancia.

immature, a. inmaturo.

immediate, a. inmediato.

immediately, adv. inmediatamente.

immense, a. inmenso.

immerse, v. sumergir.

immigrant, n. & a. inmigrante m.

immigrate, v. inmigrar.

imminent, a. inminente.

immobile, a. inmóvil.

immoderate, a. inmoderado.

immodest, a. inmodesto; atrevido.

immoral, a. inmoral.

immorality, n. inmoralidad f.

immorally, adv. licenciosamente.

immortal, a. inmortal.

immortality, n. inmortalidad f.

immortalize, v. inmortalizar.

immune, a. inmune.

immunity, n. inmunidad f.

immunize, v. inmunizar.

impact, n. impacto m.

impair, v. empeorar, perjudicar.

impale, v. empalar.

impart, v. impartir, comunicar.

impartial, a. imparcial.

impatience, n. impaciencia f.

impatient, a. impaciente.

impede, v. impedir, estorbar.

impediment, n. impedimento m.

impel, v. impeler.

impenetrable, a. impenetrable.

impenitent, n. & a. impenitente m.

imperative, a. imperativo.

imperceptible, a. imperceptible.

imperfect, a. imperfecto.

imperfection, n. imperfección f.

imperial, a. imperial.

imperialism, n. imperialismo m.

imperious, a. imperioso.

impersonal, a. impersonal.

impersonate, v. personificar; imitar.

impersonation, n. personificación f.; imitación f.

impertinence, n. impertinencia f.

impervious, a. impermeable.

impetuous, a. impetuoso.

impetus, n. impetú m.; impulso m.

impinge, v. tropezar; infringir.

implacable, a. implacable.

implant, v. implantar; inculcar.

implement, n. herramienta f.

implicate, v. implicar; embrollar.

implication, n. inferencia f.; complicidad f.

implicit, a. implícito.

implied, a. implícito.

implore, v. implorar.

imply, v. significar; dar a entender.

impolite, *a.* descortés.
import, 1. *n.* importación *f.* **2.** *v.* importar.
importance, *n.* importancia *f.*
important, *a.* importante.
importation, *n.* importación *f.*
importune, *v.* importunar.
impose, *v.* imponer.
imposition, *n.* imposición *f.*
impossibility, *n.* imposibilidad *f.*
impossible, *a.* imposible.
impotence, *n.* impotencia *f.*
impotent, *a.* impotente.
impregnable, *a.* impregnable.
impregnate, *v.* impregnar; fecundizar.
impresario, *n.* empresario *m.*
impress, *v.* impresionar.
impression, *n.* impresión *f.*
impressive, *a.* imponente.
imprison, *v.* encarcelar.
imprisonment, *n.* prisión, encarcelación *f.*
improbable, *a.* improbable.
impromptu, *a.* extemporáneo.
improper, *a.* impropio.
improve, *v.* mejorar; progresar.
improvement, *n.* mejoramiento; progreso *m.*
improvise, *v.* improvisar.
impudent, *a.* descarada.
impugn, *v.* impugnar.
impulse, *n.* impulso *m.*
impulsive, *a.* impulsivo.
impunity, *n.* impunidad *f.*
impure, *a.* impuro.
impurity, *n.* impureza *f.;* deshonestidad *f.*
impute, *v.* imputar.
in, 1. *prep.* en; dentro de. **2.** *adv.* adentro.
inadvertent, *a.* inadvertido.
inalienable, *a.* inalienable.
inane, *a.* mentecato.
inaugural, *a.* inaugural.
inaugurate, *v.* inaugurar.
inauguration, *n.* inauguración *f.*
Inca, *n.* inca *m.*
incandescent, *a.* incandescente.
incantation, *n.* encantación *f.,* conjuro *m.*
incapacitate, *v.* incapacitar.
incarcerate, *v.* encarcelar.
incarnate, *a.* encarnado; personificado.
incarnation, *n.* encarnación *f.*
incendiary, *a.* incendiario.
incense, 1. *n.* incienso *m.* **2.** *v.* indignar.
incentive, *n.* incentivo *m.*
inception, *n.* cimienzo *m.*
incessant, *a.* incesante.
incest, *n.* incesto *m.*
inch, *n.* pulgada *f.*
incidence, *n.* incidencia *f.*
incident, *n.* incidente *m.*
incidental, *a.* incidental.
incidentally, *adv.* incidentalmente; entre paréntesis.
incinerator, *n.* incinerador *m.*
incipient, *a.* incipiente.

incision, *n.* incisión *f.;* cortadura *f.*
incisive, *a.* incisivo; mordaz.
incisor, *n.* incisivo *m.*
incite, *v.* incitar, instigar.
inclination, *n.* inclinación *f.;* declive *m.*
incline, 1. *n.* pendiente *m.* **2.** *v.* inclinar.
inclose, *v.* incluir.
include, *v.* incluir.
including, *prep.* incluso.
inclusive, *a.* inclusivo.
incognito, *n.* & *adv.* incógnito *m.*
income, *n.* renta *f.;* ingresos *m.pl.*
incomparable, *a.* incomparable.
inconvenience, 1. *n.* incomodidad *f.* **2.** *v.* incomodar.
inconvenient, *a.* incómodo.
incorporate, *v.* incoporar; dar cuerpo.
incorrigible, *a.* incorregible.
increase, *v.* crecer; aumentar.
incredible, *a.* increíble.
incredulity, *n.* incredulidad *f.*
incredulous, *a.* incrédulo.
increment, *n.* incremento *m.,* aumento *m.*
incriminate, *v.* incriminar.
incrimination, *n.* incriminación *f.*
incrust, *v.* incrustar.
incubator, *n.* incubadora *f.*
inculcate, *v.* inculcar.
incumbency, *n.* incumbencia *f.*
incumbent, *a.* obligatorio; colocado sobre.
incur, *v.* incurrir.
incurable, *a.* incurable.
indebted, *a.* obligado; adeudado.
indeed, *adv.* verdaderamente, de veras. **no i.,** de ninguna manera.
indefatigable, *a.* incansable.
indefinite, *a.* indefinido.
indefinitely, *adv.* indefinidamente.
indelible, *a.* indeleble.
indemnify, *v.* indemnizar.
indemnity, *n.* indemnificación *f.*
indent, 1. *n.* diente *f.,* mella *f.* **2.** *v.* indentar, mellar.
indentation, *n.* indentación *f.*
independence, *n.* independencia *f.*
independent, *a.* independiente.
in-depth, *adj.* en profundidad.
index, *n.* índice *m.;* (of book) tabla *f.*
India, *n.* India *f.*
Indian, *a.* & *n.* indio -dia.
indicate, *v.* indicar.
indication, *n.* indicación *f.*
indicative, *a.* & *n.* indicativo *m.*
indict, *v.* encausar.
indictment, *n.* (law) sumaria *m.;* denuncia *f.*
indifference, *n.* indiferencia *f.*
indifferent, *a.* indiferente.
indigenous, *a.* indígena.

indigent, *a.* indigente, pobre.
indigestion, *n.* indigestión *f.*
indignant, *a.* indignado.
indignation, *n.* indignación *f.*
indignity, *n.* indignidad *f.*
indirect, *a.* indirecto.
indiscreet, *a.* indiscreto.
indiscretion, *n.* indiscreción *f.*
indiscriminate, *a.* promiscuo.
indispensable, *a.* indispensable.
indisposed, *a.* indispuesto.
individual, *a.* & *n.* individuo *m.*
individuality, *n.* individualidad *f.*
individually, *adv.* individualmente.
indivisible, *a.* indivisible.
indoctrinate, *v.* doctrinar, enseñar.
indolent, *a.* indolente.
indoor, *a.* interior. **indoors,** *adv.* en casa; bajo techo.
indorse, *v.* endosar.
induce, *v.* inducir, persuadir.
induct, *v.* instalar, iniciar.
induction, *n.* introducción *f.;* instalación *f.*
inductive, *a.* inductivo; introductor.
indulge, *v.* favorecer. **i. in,** entregarse a.
indulgence, *n.* indulgencia *f.*
indulgent, *a.* indulgente.
industrial, *a.* industrial.
industrialist, *n.* industrial *m.*
industrious, *a.* industrioso, trabajador.
industry, *n.* industria *f.*
ineligible, *a.* inelegible.
inept, *a.* inepto.
inert, *a.* inerte.
inertia, *n.* inercia *f.*
inevitable, *a.* inevitable.
inexplicable, *a.* inexplicable.
infallible, *a.* infalible.
infamous, *a.* infame.
infamy, *n.* infamia *f.*
infancy, *n.* infancia *f.*
infant, *n.* nene *m.;* criatura *f.*
infantile, *a.* infantil.
infantry, *n.* infantería *f.*
infatuated, *a.* infatuado.
infect, *v.* infectar.
infection, *n.* infección *f.*
infectious, *a.* infeccioso.
infer, *v.* inferir.
inference, *n.* inferencia *f.*
inferior, *a.* inferior.
infernal, *a.* infernal.
inferno, *n.* infierno *m.*
infest, *v.* infestar.
infidel, 1. *n.* infiel *m.;* pagano *m.* **2.** *a.* infiel.
infidelity, *n.* infidelidad *f.*
infiltrate, *v.* infiltrar.
infinite, *a.* infinito.
infinitesimal, *a.* infinitesimal.
infinitive, *n.* & *a.* infinitivo *m.*
infinity, *n.* infinidad *f.*
infirm, *a.* enfermizo.
infirmary, *n.* hospital *m.,* enfermería *f.*
infirmity, *n.* enfermedad *f.*
inflame, *v.* inflamar.

inflammable, a. inflamable.
inflammation, n. inflamación f.
inflammatory, a. inflamante; (med.) inflamatorio.
inflate, v. inflar.
inflation, n. inflación f.
inflection, n. inflexión f.; (of the voice) modulación de la voz f.
inflict, v. infligir.
infliction, n. imposición f.
influence, 1. n. influencia f. **2.** v. influir en.
influential, a. influyente.
influenza, n. gripe f.
inform, v. informar. **i. oneself,** enterarse.
informal, a. informal.
information, n. informaciones f.pl.
infringe, v. infringir.
infuriate, v. enfurecer.
ingenious, a. ingenioso.
ingenuity, n. ingeniosidad; destreza f.
ingredient, n. ingrediente m.
inhabit, v. habitar.
inhabitant, n. habitante m. & f.
inhale, v. inhalar.
inherent, a. inherente.
inherit, v. heredar.
inheritance, n. herencia f.
inhibit, v. inhibir.
inhibition, n. inhibición f.
inhuman, a. inhumano.
inimical, a. hostil.
inimitable, a. inimitable.
iniquity, n. iniquidad f.
initial, a. & n. inicial f.
initiate, v. iniciar.
initiation, n. iniciación f.
initiative, n. iniciativa f.
inject, v. inyectar.
injection, n. inyección f.
injunction, n. mandato m.; (law) embargo m.
injure, v. herir; lastimar; ofender.
injurious, a. perjudicial.
injury, n. herida; afrenta f. perjuicio m.
injustice, n. injusticia f.
ink, n. tinta f.
inland, 1. a. interior. **2.** adv. tierra adentro.
inlet, n. entrada f.; ensenada f.; estuario m.
inmate, n. residente m.; (of a prison) preso m.
inn, n. posada f.; mesón m.
inner, a. interior. **i. tube,** cámara de aire.
innocence, n. inocencia f.
innocent, a. inocente.
innocuous, a. innocuo.
innovation, n. innovación f.
innuendo, n. insinuación f.
innumerable, a. innumerable.
inoculate, v. inocular.
inoculation, n. inoculación f.
input, n. aducto m.
inquest, n. indagación f.
inquire, v. preguntar; inquirir.
inquiry, n. pregunta; investigación f.

inquisition, n. escudriñamiento m.; (church) Inquisición f.
insane, a. loco. **to go i.,** perder la razón; volverse loco.
insanity, n. locura f.; demencia f.
inscribe, v. inscribir.
inscription, n. inscripción; dedicatoria f.
insect, n. insecto m.
insecticide, n. & a. insecticida f.
inseparable, a. inseparable.
insert, v. insertar, meter.
insertion, n. cosa insertada f.
inside, 1. a. & n. interior m. **2.** adv. adentro, por dentro. **i. out,** al revés. **3.** prep. dentro de.
insidious, a. insidioso.
insight, n. perspicacia f.; comprensión f.
insignia, n. insignias f.pl.
insignificance, n. insignificancia f.
insignificant, a. insignificante.
insinuate, v. insinuar.
insinuation, n. insinuación f.
insipid, a. insípido.
insist, v. insistir.
insistence, n. insistencia f.
insistent, a. insistente.
insolence, n. insolencia f.
insolent, a. insolente.
insomnia, n. insomnio m.
inspect, v. inspeccionar, examinar.
inspection, n. inspección f.
inspector, n. inspector m.
inspiration, n. inspiración f.
inspire, v. inspirar.
install, v. instalar.
installation, n. instalación f.
installment, n. plazo m.
instance, n. ocasión f. **for i.,** por ejemplo.
instant, a. & n. instante m.
instantaneous, a. instantáneo.
instantly, adv. al instante.
instead, adv. en lugar de eso. **i. of,** en vez de, en lugar de.
instigate, v. instigar.
instill, v. instilar.
instinct, n. instinto m.
instinctive, a. instintivo.
institute, 1. n. instituto m. **2.** v. instituir.
institution, n. institución f.
instruct, v. instruir.
instruction, n. instrucción f.
instructive, a. instructivo.
instructor, n. instructor m.
instrument, n. instrumento m.
instrumental, a. instrumental.
insufficient, a. insuficiente.
insular, a. insular; estrecho de miras.
insulate, v. aislar.
insulation, n. aislamiento m.
insulator, n. aislador m.
insulin, n. insulina f.
insult, 1. n. insulto m. **2.** v. insultar.
insuperable, a. insuperable.
insurance, n. seguro m.

insure, v. asegurar.
insurgent, a. & n. insurgente m.
insurrection, n. insurrección f.
intact, a. intacto.
intangible, a. intangible, impalpable.
integral, a. íntegro.
integrate, v. integrar.
integrity, n. integridad f.
intellect, n. intelecto m.
intellectual, a. & n. intelectual m. & f.
intelligence, n. inteligencia f.
intelligent, a. inteligente.
intelligible, a. inteligible.
intend, v. pensar; intentar; destinar.
intense, a. intenso.
intensify, v. intensificar.
intensity, n. intensidad f.
intensive, a. intensivo.
intent, n. intento m.
intention, n. intención f.
intentional, a. intencional.
intercede, v. interceder.
intercept, v. interceptar; detener.
intercourse, n. tráfico m.; comunicación f.; coito m.
interest, 1. n. interés m. **2.** v. interesar.
interesting, a. interesante.
interface, n. aparato o zona de contacto.
interfere, v. meterse; intervenir. **i. with,** estorbar.
interference, n. intervención f.; obstáculo m.
interior, a. interior.
interject, v. interponer; intervenir.
interjection, n. interjección f.; interposición f.
interlude, n. intervalo m.; (theat.) intermedio m.; (music) interludio m.
intermediary, n. intermediario m.
intermediate, a. intermedio.
interment, n. entierro m.
intermission, n. intermisión f.; (theat.) entreacto m.
intermittent, a. intermitente.
intern, 1. n. interno m. **2.** v. internar.
internal, a. interno.
international, a. internacional.
internationalism, n. internacionalismo m.
interne, n. practicante de hospital m.
interpose, v. interponer.
interpret, v. interpretar.
interpretation, n. interpretación f.
interpreter, n. intérprete m. & f.
interrogate, v. interrogar.
interrogation, n. interrogación f.; pregunta f.
interrogative, a. interrogativo.
interrupt, v. interrumpir.
interruption, n. interrupción f.
intersect, v. cortar.

intersection, *n.* intersección *f.;* (street) bocacalle *f.*
intersperse, *v.* entremezclar.
interval, *n.* intervalo *m.*
intervene, *v.* intervenir.
intervention, *n.* intervención *f.*
interview, 1. *n.* entrevista *f.* **2.** *v.* entrevistar.
intestine, *n.* intestino *m.*
intimacy, *n.* intimidad; familiaridad *f.*
intimate, 1. *a.* íntimo, familiar. **2.** *ñ.* amigo íntimo. **3.** *v.* insinuar.
intimidate, *v.* intimidar.
intimidation, *n.* intimidación *f.*
into, *prep.* en, dentro de.
intonation, *n.* entonación *f.*
intone, *v.* entonar.
intoxicate, *v.* embriagar.
intoxication, *n.* embriaguez *f.*
intravenous, *a.* intravenoso.
intrepid, *a.* intrépido.
intricacy, *n.* intrincación *f.;* enredo *m.*
intricate, *a.* intrincado; complejo.
intrigue, 1. *n.* intriga *f.* **2.** *v.* intrigar.
intrinsic, *a.* intrínseco.
introduce, *v.* introducir; (a person) presentar.
introduction, *n.* presentación; introducción *f.*
introductory, *a.* introductivo.
introvert, *n. & a.* introverso *m.*
intrude, *v.* entremeterse.
intruder, *n.* intruso -sa.
intuition, *n.* intuición *f.*
intuitive, *a.* intuitivo.
inundate, *v.* inundar.
invade, *v.* invadir.
invader, *n.* invasor *m.*
invalid, *a. & n.* inválido -da.
invariable, *a.* invariable.
invasion, *n.* invasión *f.*
invective, 1. *n.* invectiva *f.* **2.** *a.* ultrajante.
inveigle, *v.* seducir.
invent, *v.* inventar.
invention, *n.* invención *f.*
inventive, *a.* inventivo.
inventor, *n.* inventor *m.*
inventory, *n.* inventario *m.*
invertebrate, *n. & a.* invertebrado *m.*
invest, *v.* investir; (com.) invertir.
investigate, *v.* investigar.
investigation, *n.* investigación *f.*
investment, *n.* inversión *f.*
inveterate, *a.* inveterado.
invidious, *a.* difamatorio.
invigorate, *v.* vigorizar, fortificar.
invincible, *a.* invencible.
invisible, *a.* invisible.
invitation, *n.* invitación *f.*
invite, *v.* invitar, convidar.
invocation, *n.* invocación *f.*
invoice, *n.* factura *f.*
invoke, *v.* invocar.
involuntary, *a.* involuntario.

involve, *v.* envolver; implicar.
involved, *a.* complicado.
invulnerable, *a.* invulnerable.
inward, *adv.* hacia adentro.
inwardly, *adv.* interiormente.
iodine, *n.* iodo *m.*
irate, *a.* encolerizado.
Ireland, *n.* Irlanda *f.*
iris, *n.* (anat.) iris *m.;* (botany) flor de lis *f.*
Irish, *a.* irlandés.
irk, *v.* fastidiar.
iron, 1. *n.* hierro *m.;* (appliance) plancha *f.* **2.** *v.* planchar.
ironical, *a.* irónico.
irony, *n.* ironía *f.*
irrational, *a.* irracional; ilógico.
irregular, *a.* irregular.
irregularity, *n.* irregularidad *f.*
irrelevant, *a.* ajeno.
irresistible, *a.* irresistible.
irresponsible, *a.* irresponsable.
irreverent, *a.* irreverente.
irrevocable, *a.* irrevocable.
irrigate, *v.* regar; (med.) irrigar.
irrigation, *n.* riego *m.*
irritability, *n.* irritabilidad *f.*
irritable, *a.* irritable.
irritant, *n. & a.* irritante *m.*
irritate, *v.* irritar.
irritation, *n.* irritación *f.*
island, *n.* isla *f.*
isolate, *v.* aislar.
isolation, *n.* aislamiento *f.*
isosceles, *a.* isósceles.
issuance, *n.* emisión *f.;* publicación *f.*
issue, 1. *n.* emisión; edición; progenie *f.;* número *m.;* punto en disputa. **2.** *v.* emitir; publicar.
isthmus, *n.* istmo *m.*
it, *pron.* ello; él, ella; lo, la.
Italian, *n. & a.* italiano -na.
Italy, *n.* Italia *f.*
itch, 1. *n.* picazón *f.* **2.** *v.* picar.
item, *n.* artículo; detalle *m.;* inserción *f.;* (com.) renglón *m.*
itemize, *v.* detallar.
itinerant, 1. *n.* viandante *m.* **2.** *a.* ambulante.
itinerary, *n.* itinerario *m.*
its, *a.* su.
itself, *pron.* sí; se.
ivory, *n.* marfil *m.*
ivy, *n.* hiedra *f.*

J

jab, 1. *n.* pinchazo *m.* **2.** *v.* pinchar.
jack, *n.* (for lifting) gato *m.;* (cards) sota *f.*
jackal, *n.* chacal *m.*
jackass, *n.* asno *m.*
jacket, *n.* chaqueta *f.;* saco *m.*
jack-of-all-trades, *n.* estuche *m.*
jade, *n.* (horse) rocín *m.;*

(woman) picarona *f.;* (mineral) jade *m.*
jaded, *a.* rendido.
jagged, *a.* mellado.
jaguar, *n.* jaguar *m.*
jail, *n.* cárcel *f.*
jailer, *n.* carcelero *m.*
jam, 1. *n.* conserva *f.;* apretura *f.* **2.** *v.* apiñar, apretar; trabar.
janitor, *n.* portero *m.*
January, *n.* enero *m.*
Japan, *n.* Japón *m.*
Japanese, *a. & n.* japonés -esa.
jar, 1. *n.* jarro *m.* **2.** *v.* chocar; agitar.
jargon, *n.* jerga *f.*
jasmine, *n.* jazmín *m.*
jaundice, *n.* ictericia *f.*
jaunt, *n.* paseata *f.*
javelin, *n.* jabalina *f.*
jaw, *n.* quijada *f.*
jay, *n.* grajo *m.*
jazz, *n.* jazz *m.*
jealous, *a.* celoso. **to be j.,** tener celos.
jealousy, *n.* celos *m.pl.*
jeans, *n.* jeans *m.pl.*
jeer, 1. *n.* burla *f.,* mofa *f.* **2.** *v.* burlar, mofar.
jelly, *n.* jalea *f.*
jellyfish, *n.* aguamar *m.*
jeopardize, *v.* arriesgar.
jeopardy, *n.* riesgo *m.*
jerk, 1. *n.* sacudida *f.* **2.** *v.* sacudir.
jerky, *a.* espasmódico.
Jerusalem, *n.* Jerusalén *m.*
jest, 1. *n.* broma *f.* **2.** *v.* bromear.
jester, *n.* bufón *m.;* burlón *m.*
Jesuit, 1. *n.* jesuíta *m.* **2.** *a.* jesuítico.
Jesus Christ, *n.* Jesucristo *m.*
jet, *n.* chorro *m.;* (gas) mechero *m.*
jet lag, *n.* fatiga que sufre un viajero en avión, por causa del cambio de horas.
jetsam, *n.* echazón *f.*
jettison, *v.* echar mercancías al mar.
jetty, *n.* muelle *m.*
Jew, *n.* judío -día.
jewel, *n.* joya *f.*
jeweler, *n.* joyero *m.*
jewelry, *n.* joyería *f.* **j. store,** joyería *f.*
Jewish, *a.* judío.
jib, *n.* (naut.) foque *m.*
jiffy, *n.* instante *m.*
jig, *n.* jiga *f.* **j-saw,** sierra de vaivén *f.*
jilt, *v.* dar calabazas.
jingle, 1. *n.* retintín *m.;* rima pueril *f.* **2.** *v.* retiñir.
jinx, 1. *n.* aojo *m.* **2.** *v.* aojar.
jittery, *a.* nervioso.
job, *n.* empleo *m.*
jobber, *n.* destajista *m.,* remendero *m.*
jockey, *n.* jockey *m.*
jocular, *a.* jocoso.
jog, 1. *n.* empujoncito *m.* **2.** *v.* empujar; estimular. **to j. along,** ir a un trote corto.

join, v. juntar; unir.
joiner, n. ebanista m.
joint, n. juntura f.
jointly, adv. conjuntamente.
joke, 1. n. broma, chanza f.; chiste m. 2. v. bromear.
joker, n. bromista m. & f.
jolly, a. alegre, jovial.
jolt, 1. n. sacudido m. 2. v. sacudir.
jonquil, n. junquillo m.
jostle, v. rempujar.
journal, n. diario m.; revista f.
journalism, n. periodismo m.
journalist, n. periodista m. & f.
journey, 1. n. viaje m.; jornada f. 2. v. viajar.
journeyman, n. jornalero m., oficial m.
jovial, a. jovial.
jowl, n. carrillo m.
joy, n. alegría f.
joyful, joyous, a. alegre, gozoso.
jubilant, a. jubiloso.
jubilee, n. jubileo m.
Judaism, n. judaísmo m.
judge, 1. n. juez m. 2. v. juzgar.
judgment, n. juicio m.
judicial, a. judicial.
judiciary, a. judiciario.
judicious, a. juicioso.
jug, n. jarro m.
juggle, v. escamotear.
juice, n. jugo, zumo m.
juicy, a. jugoso.
July, n. julio m.
jumble, 1. n. revoltillo m. 2. v. arrebujar, revolver.
jump, 1. n. salto m. 2. v. saltar, brincar.
junction, n. confluencia f.; (railway) empalme m.
juncture, n. junta f.
June, n. junio m.
jungle, n. selva f.
junior, a. menor; más joven. Jr., hijo.
juniper, n. enebro m.
junk, n. basura f.
junket, 1. n. leche cuajado f. 2. v. festejar.
jurisdiction, n. jurisdicción f.
jurisprudence, n. jurisprudencia f.
jurist, n. jurista m.
juror, n. jurado m.
jury, n. jurado m.
just, 1. a. justo; exacto. 2. adv. exactamente; (only) sólo. j. now, ahora mismo. to have j., acabar de.
justice, n. justicia f.; (person) juez m.
justifiable, a. justificable.
justification, n. justificación f.
justify, v. justificar.
jut, v. sobresalir.
jute, n. yute m.
juvenile, a. juvenil.

K

kaleidoscope, n. calidoscopio m.

kangaroo, n. canguro m.
karakul, n. caracul m.
karat, n. quilate m.
karate, n. karate m.
keel, 1. n. quilla f. 2. v. to k. over, volcarse.
keen. a. agudo; penetrante.
keep, v. mantener, retener; guardar; preservar. k. on, seguir, continuar.
keeper, n. guardián m.
keepsake, n. recuerdo m.
keg, n. barrilito m.
kennel, n. perrera f.
kerchief, n. pañuelo m.
kernel, n. pepita f.; grano m.
kerosene, n. kerosén m.
ketchup, n. salsa de tomate f.
kettle, n. caldera, olla f.
kettledrum, n. tímpano m.
key, n. llave f.; (music) clave f.; (piano) tecla f.
keyhole, n. bocallave f.
khaki, a. caqui.
kick, 1. n. patada f. 2. v. patear; (coll.) quejarse.
kid, 1. n. cabrito m.; (coll.) niño -ña, chico, -ca. 2. v. (coll.) bromear.
kidnap, v. secuestrar.
kidnaper, n. secuestrador m.
kidney, n. riñón m.
kidney bean, n. frijol m.
kill, v. matar.
killer, n. matador m.
kiln, n. horno m.
kilogram, n. kilogramo m.
kilohertz, n. kilohertzio m.
kilometer, n. kilómetro m.
kilowatt, n. kilovatio m.
kin, n. parentesco m.; parientes m.pl.
kind, 1. a. bondadoso, amable. 2. n. género m.; clase f. k. of, algo, un poco.
kindergarten, n. kindergarten m.
kindle, v. encender.
kindling, n. encendimiento m. k.-wood, leña menuda f.
kindly, a. bondadoso.
kindness, n. bondad f.
kindred, n. parentesco m.
kinetic, a. cinético.
king, n. rey m.
kingdom, n. reino m.
kink, n. retorcimiento m.
kiosk, n. kiosco m.
kiss, 1. n. beso m. 2. v. besar.
kitchen, n. cocina f.
kite, n. cometa f.
kitten, n. gatito -ta.
kleptomania, n. cleptomanía f.
kleptomaniac, n. cleptómano m.
knack, n. don m., destreza f.
knapsack, n. alforja f.
knead, v. amasar.
knee, n. rodilla f.
kneecap, n. rodillera f.
kneel, v. arrodillarse.
knickers, n. calzón corto m., pantalones m.

knife, n. cuchillo m.
knight, n. caballero m.; (chess) caballo m.
knit, v. tejer.
knob, n. tirador m.
knock, 1. n. golpe m.; llamada f. 2. v. golpear; tocar, llamar.
knot, 1. n. nudo; lazo m. 2. v. anudar.
knotty, a. nudoso.
know, v. saber; (a person) conocer.
knowledge, n. conocimiento, saber m.
knuckle, n. nudillo m. k. bone, jarrete m. to k. under, ceder a.
Korea, n. Corea f.

L

label, 1. n. rótulo m. 2. v. rotular; designar.
labor, 1. n. trabajo m.; la clase obrera. 2. v. trabajar.
laboratory, n. laboratorio m.
laborer, n. trabajador, obrero m.
laborious, a. laborioso, difícil.
labor union, n. gremio obrero m.
labyrinth, n. laberinto m.
lace, 1. n. encaje m.; (of shoe) lazo m. 2. v. amarrar.
lacerate, v. lacerar, lastimar.
laceration, n. laceración f., desgarro m.
lack, 1. n. falta f. 2. v. faltar, carecer.
lackadaisical, a. indiferente; soñador.
laconic, a. lacónico.
lacquer, 1. n. laca f., barniz m. 2. v. laquear, barnizar.
lactic, a. láctico.
lactose, n. lactosa f.
ladder, n. escalera f.
ladle, 1. n. cucharón m. 2. v. servir con cucharón.
lady, n. señora, dama f.
ladybug, n. mariquita f.
lag, 1. n. retraso m. 2. v. quedarse atrás.
lagoon, n. laguna f.
laid-back, a. de buen talante.
laity, n. laicidad f.
lake, n. lago m.
lamb, n. cordero m.
lame, 1. a. cojo; estropeado. 2. v. estropear.
lament, 1. n. lamento m. 2. v. lamentar.
lamentable, a. lamentable.
lamentation, n. lamento m.; lamentación f.
laminate, a. laminado.
lamp, n. lámpara f.
lampoon, 1. n. pasquín m. 2. v. pasquinar.
lance, 1. n. lanza f. 2. v. (med.) abrir.
land, 1. n. país m.; tierra f. native l., patria f. 2. v. desembarcar; (plane) aterrizar.

landholder, n. hacendado m.

landing, n. (of stairs) descanso m.; (ship) desembarcadero m.; (airplane) aterrizaje m.

landlady, landlord, n. propietario -ria.

landmark, n. mojón m., señal f.; rasgo sobresaliente m.

landscape, n. paisaje m.

landslide, n. derrumbe m.

lane, n. senda f.

language, n. lengua f., idioma; lenguaje m.

languid, a. lánguido.

languish, v. languidecer.

languor, n. languidez f.

lanolin, n. lanolina f.

lantern, n. linterna f.; farol m.

lap, 1. n. regazo m.; falda f. 2. v. lamer.

lapel, n. solapa f.

lapse, 1. n. lapso m. 2. v. pasar; decaer; caer en error.

larceny, n. ratería f.

lard, n. manteca f.

large, a. grande.

largely, v. ampliamente; mayormente; muy.

largo, n. & a. (mus.) largo m.

lariat, n. lazo m.

lark, n. (bird) alondra f.

larva, n. larva f.

laryngitis, n. laringitis f.

larynx, n. laringe f.

lascivious, a. lascivo.

laser, n. láser m.

lash, 1. n. azote, latigazo m. 2. v. azotar.

lass, n. doncella f.

lassitude, n. lasitud f.

lasso, 1. n. lazo m. 2. v. enlazar.

last, 1. a. pasado; (final) último. at l., por fin. 2. v. durar.

lasting, a. duradero.

latch, n. aldaba f.

late, 1. a. tardío; (deceased) difunto. to be l., llegar tarde. 2. adv. tarde.

lately, adv. recientemente.

latent, a. latente.

lateral, a. lateral.

lather, 1. n. espuma de jabón. 2. v. enjabonar.

Latin, n. latín m.

Latin America, n. Hispanoamérica, América Latina f.

Latin American, a. & n. hispanoamericano -na.

latitude, n. latitud f.

latrine, n. letrina f.

latter, a. posterior. the l., éste.

lattice, n. celosía f.

laud, v. loar.

laudable, a. laudable.

laudanum, n. láudano m.

laudatory, a. laudatorio.

laugh, 1. n. risa, risotada f. 2. v. reír. l. at, reírse de.

laughable, a. risible.

laughter, n. risa f.

launch, 1. n. (naut.) lancha f. 2. v. lanzar.

launder, v. lavar y planchar la ropa.

laundry, n. lavandería f.

laundryman, n. lavandero m.

laureate, n. & a. laureado m.

laurel, n. laureado.

lava, n. lava f.

lavatory, n. lavatorio m.

lavender, n. lavándula f.

lavish, 1. a. pródigo. 2. v. prodigar.

law, n. ley f.; derecho m.

lawful, a. legal.

lawless, a. sin ley.

lawn, n. césped; prado m.

lawsuit, n. pleito m.

lawyer, n. abogado m.

lax, a. flojo, laxo.

laxative, n. purgante m.

laxity, n. laxidad f.; flojedad f.

lay, 1. a. secular. 2. v. poner.

layer, n. capa f.

layman, n. lego, seglar m.

lazy, a. perezoso.

lead, 1. n. plomo m.; (theat.) papel principal. to take the l., tomar la delantera. 2. v. conducir; dirigir.

leaden, a. plomizo; pesado; abatido.

leader, n. líder; jefe; director m.

leadership, n. dirección f.

leaf, n. hoja f.

leaflet, n. (bot.) hojilla f.; folleto m.

league, n. liga; (measure) legua f.

leak, 1. n. escape; goteo m. 2. v. gotear; (naut.) hacer agua.

leakage, n. goteo m., escape m., pérdida f.

leaky, a. llovedizo, resquebrajado.

lean, 1. a. flaco, magro. 2. v. apoyarse, arrimarse.

leap, 1. n. salto m. 2. v. saltar.

leap year, n. año bisiesto m.

learn, v. aprender; saber.

learned, a. erudito.

learning, n. erudición f., instrucción f.

lease, 1. n. arriendo m. 2. v. arrendar.

leash, 1. n. correa f. 2. v. atraillar.

least, a. menor; mínimo. the l., lo menos. at l., por lo menos.

leather, n. cuero m.

leathery, a. coriáceo.

leave, 1. n. licencia f. to take l., despedirse. 2. v. dejar; (depart) salir, irse. l. out, omitir.

leaven, 1. n. levadura f. 2. v. fermentar, imbuir.

lecherous, a. lujurioso.

lecture, n. conferencia f.

lecturer, n. conferencista m.; catedrático m.

ledge, n. borde m.; capa f.

ledger, n. libro mayor m.

lee, n. sotavento m.

leech, n. sanguijuela f.

leek, n. porro m.

leer, v. mirar de soslayo.

leeward, n. sotavento.

left, a. izquierdo. the l., la iz-

quierda. to be left, quedarse.

leftist, n. izquierdista m. & f.

leg, n. pierna f.

legacy, n. legado m., herencia f.

legal, a. legal.

legalize, v. legalizar.

legation, n. legación, embajada f.

legend, n. leyenda f.

legendary, a. legendario.

legible, a. legible.

legion, n. legión f.

legislate, v. legislar.

legislation, n. legislación f.

legislator, n. legislador m.

legislature, n. legislatura f.

legitimate, a. legítimo.

legume, n. legumbre f.

leisure, n. desocupación f.; horas libres.

leisurely, 1. a. deliberado. 2. adv. despacio.

lemon, n. limón m.

lemonade, n. limonada f.

lend, v. prestar.

length, n. largo m.; duración f.

lengthen, v. alargar.

lengthwise, adv. a lo largo.

lengthy, a. largo.

lenient, a. indulgente.

lens, n. lente m. or f.

Lent, n. cuaresma f.

Lenten, a. cuaresmal.

lentil, n. lenteja f.

leopard, n. leopardo m.

leper, n. leproso m.

leprosy, a. lepra.

lesbian, n. lesbiana f.

lesion, n. lesión f.

less, a. & adv. menos.

lessen, v. disminuir.

lesser, a. menor; más pequeño.

lesson, n. lección f.

lest, conj. para que no.

let, v. dejar; permitir; arrendar.

lethal, a. letal.

lethargic, a. letárgico.

lethargy, n. letargo m.

letter, n. carta; (of alphabet) letra f.

letterhead, n. membrete m.

lettuce, n. lechuga f.

leukemia, n. leucemia f.

levee, n. recepción f.

level, 1. a. llano, nivelado. 2. n. nivel m.; llanura f. 3. v. allanar; nivelar.

lever, n. palanca f.

levity, n. levedad f.

levy, 1. n. leva f. 2. v. imponer.

lewd, a. lascivo.

lexicon, n. léxico m.

liability, n. riesgo m.; obligación f.

liable, a. sujeto; responsable.

liaison, n. vinculación f., enlace m.; concubinaje m.

liar, n. embustero -ra.

libel, 1. n. libelo m. 2. v. difamar.

libelous, a. difamatorio.

liberal, a. liberal; generoso.

liberalism, *n.* liberalismo *m.*

liberality, *n.* liberalidad *f.*

liberate, *v.* libertar.

liberty, *n.* libertad *f.*

libidinous, *a.* libidinoso.

librarian, *n.* bibliotecario *m.*

library, *n.* biblioteca *f.*

libretto, *n.* libreto *m.*

license, *n.* licencia *f.;* permiso *m.*

licentious, *a.* licencioso.

lick, *v.* lamer.

licorice, *n.* regaliz *m.*

lid, *n.* tapa *f.*

lie, 1. *n.* mentira *f.* 2. *v.* mentir. **l. down,** acostarse, echarse.

lieutenant, *n.* teniente *m.*

life, *n.* vida *f.*

lifeboat, *n.* bote salvavidas *m.*

life buoy, *n.* buya *f.*

life insurance, *n.* seguro de vida *m.*

lifeless, *a.* sin vida.

life preserver, *n.* salvavidas *m.*

life style, *n.* modo de vida *m.*

lift, *v.* levantar, alzar, elevar.

ligament, *n.* ligamento *m.*

ligature, *n.* ligadura *f.*

light, 1. *a.* ligero; liviano; (in color) claro. 2. *n.* luz; candela *f.* 3. *v.* encender; iluminar.

lighten, *v.* aligerar; aclarar; iluminar.

lighter, *n.* encendedor *m.*

lighthouse, *n.* faro *m.*

lightness, *n.* ligereza; agilidad *f.*

lightning, *n.* relámpago *m.*

like, 1. *a.* semejante. 2. *prep.* como. 3. *v.* **I like . . .** me gusta, me gustan . . . **I should like,** quisiera.

likeable, *a.* simpático, agradable.

likelihood, *n.* probabilidad *f.*

likely, *a.* probable; verosímil.

liken, *v.* comparar; asemejar.

likeness, *n.* semejanza *f.*

likewise, *adv.* igualmente.

lilac, *n.* lila *f.*

lilt, 1. *n.* cadencia alegre *f.* 2. *v.* cantar alegremente.

lily, *n.* lirio *m.*

lily of the valley, *n.* muguete *m.*

limb, *n.* rama *f.*

limber, *a.* flexible. **to l. up,** ponerse flexible.

limbo, *n.* limbo *m.*

lime, *n.* cal *f.;* (fruit) limoncito *m.,* lima *f.*

limestone, *n.* piedra caliza *f.*

limewater, *n.* agua de cal *f.*

limit, 1. *n.* límite *m.* 2. *v.* limitar.

limitation, *n.* limitación *f.*

limitless, *a.* ilimitado.

limousine, *n.* limousine *f.*

limp, 1. *n.* cojera *f.* 2. *a.* flojo. 3. *v.* cojear.

limpid, *a.* límpido.

line, 1. *n.* línea; fila; raya *f.;* (of print) renglón *m.* 2. *v.* forrar; rayar.

lineage, *n.* linaje *m.*

lineal, *a.* lineal.

linear, *a.* linear, longitudinal.

linen, *n.* lienzo, lino *m.;* ropa blanca.

liner, *n.* vapor *m.*

linger, *v.* demorarse.

lingerie, *n.* ropa blanca *f.*

linguist, *n.* lingüista *m. & f.*

linguistic, *a.* lingüístico.

liniment, *n.* linimento *m.*

lining, *n.* forro *m.*

link, 1. *n.* eslabón; vínculo *m.* 2. *v.* vincular.

linoleum, *n.* linóleo *m.*

linseed, *n.* linaza *f.;* simiente de lino *f.*

lint, *n.* hilacha *f.*

lion, *n.* león *m.*

lip, *n.* labio *m.*

lipstick, *n.* lápiz de labios.

liqueur, *n.* cordial *m.*

liquid, *a. & n.* líquido *m.*

liquidate, *v.* liquidar.

liquidation, *n.* liquidación *f.*

liquor, *n.* licor *m.*

lisp, 1. *n.* ceceo *m.* 2. *v.* cecear.

list, 1. *n.* lista *f.* 2. *v.* registrar.

listen (to), *v.* escuchar.

listless, *a.* indiferente.

litany, *n.* letanía *f.*

liter, *n.* litro *m.*

literal, *a.* literal.

literary, *a.* literario.

literate, *a.* literato.

literature, *n.* literatura *f.*

litigant, *n. & a.* litigante *m.*

litigation, *n.* litigio, pleito *m.*

litter, 1. *n.* litera *f.;* cama de paja. 2. *v.* poner en desorden.

little, *a.* pequeño; (quantity) poco.

liturgical, *a.* litúrgico.

liturgy, *n.* liturgia *f.*

live, 1. *a.* vivo. 2. *v.* vivir.

livelihood, *n.* subsistencia *f.*

lively, *a.* vivo; rápido; animado.

liver, *n.* hígado *m.*

livery, *n.* librea *f.*

livestock, *n.* ganadería *f.*

livid, *a.* lívido.

living, 1. *a.* vivo. 2. *n.* sustento *m.* **to earn (make) a living,** ganarse la vida.

lizard, *n.* lagarto *m.,* lagartija *f.*

llama, *n.* llama *f.*

load, 1. *n.* carga *f.* 2. *v.* cargar.

loaf, 1. *n.* pan *m.* 2. *v.* holgazanear.

loam, *n.* marga *f.*

loan, 1. *n.* préstamo *m.* 2. *v.* prestar.

loathe, *v.* aborrecer, detestar.

lobby, *n.* vestíbulo *m.*

lobe, *n.* lóbulo *m.*

lobster, *n.* langosta *f.*

local, *a.* local.

locale, *n.* localidad *f.*

locality, *n.* localidad *f.,* lugar *m.*

localize, *v.* localizar.

locate, *v.* situar; hallar.

location, *n.* sitio *m.;* posición *f.*

lock, 1. *n.* cerradura *f.;* (pl.) cabellos *m.pl.* 2. *v.* cerrar con llave.

locker, *n.* cajón *m.;* ropero *m.*

locket, *n.* guardapelo *m.,* medallón *m.*

lockjaw, *n.* trismo *m.*

locksmith, *n.* cerrajero *m.*

locomotive, *n.* locomotora *f.*

locust, *n.* cigarra *f.,* saltamontes *m.*

locution, *n.* locución *f.*

lode, *n.* filón *m.,* vena *f.*

lodge, 1. *n.* logia; (inn) posada *f.* 2. *v.* fijar; alojar, morar.

lodger, *n.* inquilino *m.*

lodging, *n.* posada *f.*

loft, *n.* piso *m.,* sobrado *m.*

lofty, *a.* alto; altivo.

log, *n.* tronco de árbol; (naut.) barquilla *f.*

loge, *n.* palco *m.*

logic, *n.* lógica *f.*

logical, *a.* lógico.

loin, *n.* lomo *m.*

loiter, *v.* haraganear.

lone, *a.* solitario.

loneliness, *n.* soledad *f.;* tristeza *f.*

lonely, lonesome, *a.* solo y triste.

lonesome, *a.* solitario; triste.

long, 1. *a.* largo. **a l. time,** mucho tiempo. 2. *adv.* mucho tiempo. **how l.,** cuánto tiempo. **no longer,** ya no. 3. *v.* **l. for,** anhelar.

longevity, *n.* longevidad *f.*

longing, *n.* anhelo *m.*

longitude, *n.* longitud *m.*

look, 1. *n.* mirada *f.;* aspecto *m.* 2. *v.* parecer; mirar. **l. at,** mirar. **l. for,** buscar. **l. like,** parecerse a. **l. out!,** ¡cuidado! **l. up,** buscar; ir a ver, venir a ver.

looking glass, *n.* espejo *m.*

loom, 1. *n.* telar *m.* 2. *v.* asomar.

loop, *n.* vuelta *f.*

loophole, *n.* abertura *f.,* mirador *m.*

loose, *a.* suelto; flojo.

loosen, *v.* soltar; aflojar.

loot, 1. *n.* botín *m.,* saqueo *m.* 2. *v.* saquear.

lopsided, *a.* desequilibrado.

loquacious, *a.* locuaz.

lord, *n.* señor *m.;* (Brit. title) lord *m.*

lordship, *n.* señorío *m.*

lose, *v.* perder.

loss, *n.* pérdida *f.*

lost, *a.* perdido.

lot, *n.* suerte *f.* **building l.,** solar *m.* **a lot (of), lots of,** mucho.

lotion, *n.* loción *f.*

lottery, *n.* lotería *f.*

loud, 1. *a.* fuerte; ruidoso. 2. *adv.* alto.

loudspeaker, *n.* altavoz *m.*

lounge, *n.* sofá *m.;* salón de fumar *m.*

louse, *n.* piojo *m.*

love, 1. *n.* amor *m.* **in l.,** enamorado. **to fall in l.,** enamorarse. 2. *v.* querer; amar; adorar.

lovely, *a.* hermoso.
lover, *n.* amante *m.*
low, *a.* bajo; vil.
lower, *v.* bajar; (in price) rebajar.
lowly, *a.* humilde.
loyal, *a.* leal, fiel.
loyalist, *n.* lealista *m.* & *f.*
loyalty, *n.* lealtad *f.*
lozenge, *n.* pastilla *f.*
lubricant, *n.* lubricante *m.*
lubricate, *v.* engrasar, lubricar.
lucid, *a.* claro, lúcido.
luck, *n.* suerte; fortuna *f.*
lucky, *a.* afortunado. **to be l.**, tener suerte.
lucrative, *a.* lucrativo.
ludicrous, *a.* ridículo.
luggage, *n.* equipaje *m.*
lukewarm, *a.* tibio.
lull, **1.** *n.* momento de calma. **2.** *v.* calmar.
lullaby, *n.* arrullo *m.*
lumbago, *n.* lumbago *m.*
lumber, *n.* madera *f.*
luminous, *a.* luminoso.
lump, *n.* protuberancia *f.;* (of sugar) terrón *m.*
lunacy, *n.* locura *f.*
lunar, *a.* lunar.
lunatic, *a.* & *n.* loco -ca.
lunch, **luncheon**, **1.** *n.* merienda *f.*, almuerzo *m.* **2.** *v.* merendar, almorzar.
lung, *n.* pulmón *m.*
lunge, **1.** *n.* estocada *f.* **2.** *v.* dar un estocada.
lure, *v.* atraer.
lurid, *a.* rojizo; fantástico.
lurk, *v.* esconderse; espiar.
luscious, *a.* sabroso, delicioso.
lust, *n.* sensualidad; codicia *f.*
luster, *n.* lustre *m.*
lustful, *a.* sensual, lascivo.
lusty, *a.* vigoroso.
lute, *n.* laúd *m.*
Lutheran, *n.* & *a.* luterano *m.*
luxuriant, *a.* exuberante, frondoso.
luxurious, *a.* lujoso.
luxury, *n.* lujo *m.*
lying, *a.* mentiroso.
lymph, *n.* linfa *f.*
lynch, *v.* linchar.
lyre, *n.* lira *f.*
lyric, *a.* lírico.
lyricism, *n.* lirismo *m.*

M

macabre, *a.* macabre.
macaroni, *n.* macarrones *m.*
machine, *n.* máquina *f.*
machine gun, *n.* ametralladora *f.*
machinery, *n.* maquinaria *f.*
machinist, *n.* maquinista, mecánico *m.*
macho, *a.* machista.
mackerel, *n.* escombro *m.*
mad, *a.* loco; furioso.
madam, *n.* señora *f.*
mafia, *n.* mafia *f.*
magazine, *n.* revista *f.*

magic, **1.** *a.* mágico. **2.** *n.* magia *f.*
magician, *n.* mágico *m.*
magistrate, *n.* magistrado *m.*
magnanimous, *a.* magnánimo.
magnate, *n.* magnate *m.*
magnesium, *n.* magnesio *m.*
magnet, *n.* imán *m.*
magnetic, *a.* magnético.
magnificence, *n.* magnificencia *f.*
magnificent, *a.* magnífico.
magnify, *v.* magnificar.
magnitude, *n.* magnitud *f.*
mahogany, *n.* caoba *f.*
maid, *n.* criada *f.* **old m.**, solterona *f.*
maiden, *a.* soltero.
mail, **1.** *n.* correo *m.* **air m.**, correo aéreo. **by return m.**, a vuelta de correo. **2.** *v.* echar al correo.
mailbox, *n.* buzón *m.*
mailman, *n.* cartero *m.*
maim, *v.* multilar.
main, *a.* principal.
mainframe, *n.* componente central de una computadora.
mainland, *n.* continente *m.*
maintain, *v.* mantener; sostener.
maintenance, *n.* mantenimiento; sustento *m.;* conservación *f.*
maize, *n.* maíz *m.*
majestic, *a.* majestuoso.
majesty, *n.* majestad *f.*
major, **1.** *n.* mayor. **2.** *n.* (mil.) comandante *m.;* (study) especialidad *f.*
majority, *n.* mayoría *f.*
make, **1.** *n.* marca *f.* **2.** *v.* hacer; fabricar; (earn) ganar.
maker, *n.* fabricante *m.*
makeshift, *a.* provisional.
make-up, *n.* cosméticos *m.pl.*
malady, *n.* mal *m.,* enfermedad *f.*
malaria, *n.* paludismo *m.*
male, *a.* & *n.* macho *m.*
malevolent, *a.* malévolo.
malice, *n.* malicia *f.*
malicious, *a.* malicioso.
malign, **1.** *v.* difamar. **2.** *a.* maligno.
malignant, *a.* maligno.
malnutrition, *n.* desnutrición *f.*
malt, *n.* malta *m.* & *f.*
mammal, *n.* mamífero *m.*
man, *n.* hombre; varón *m.*
manage, *v.* manejar; dirigir; administrar; arreglárselas. **m. to**, lograr.
management, *n.* dirección, administración *f.*
manager, *n.* director *m.*
mandate, *n.* mandato *m.*
mandatory, *a.* obligatorio.
mandolin, *n.* mandolina *f.*
mane, *n.* crines *f.*
maneuver, **1.** *n.* maniobra *f.* **2.** *v.* maniobrar.
manganese, *n.* manganeso *m.*
manger, *n.* pesebre *m.*

mangle, **1.** *n.* planchadora mecánica. **2.** *v.* mutilar.
manhood, *n.* virilidad *f.*
mania, *n.* manía *f.*
maniac, *a.* & *n.* maniático *m.*
manicure, *n.* manicuro *m.*
manifest, **1.** *a.* & *n.* manifiesto *m.* **2.** *v.* manifestar.
manifesto, *n.* manifesto *m.*
manifold, **1.** *a.* muchos. **2.** *n.* (auto.) tubo múltiple.
manipulate, *v.* manipular.
mankind, *n.* humanidad *f.*
manly, *a.* varonil.
manner, *n.* manera *f.,* modo *m.*
manners, modales *m.pl.*
mannerism, *n.* manerismo *m.*
mansion, *n.* mansión *f.*
mantel, *n.* manto de chimenea.
mantle, *n.* manto *m.*
manual, *a.* & *n.* manual *m.*
manufacture, *v.* fabricar.
manufacturer, *n.* fabricante *m.*
manufacturing, *n.* fabricación *f.*
manure, *n.* abono, estiércol *m.*
manuscript, *n.* manuscrito *m.*
many, *a.* muchos. **how m.**, so m., tantos. **too m.**, demasiados, cuántos. **as m. as**, tantos como.
map, *n.* mapa *m.*
maple, *n.* arce *m.*
mar, *v.* estropear; desfigurar.
marble, *n.* mármol *f.*
march, **1.** *n.* marcha *f.* **2.** *v.* marchar.
mare, *n.* yegua *f.*
margarine, *n.* margarina *f.*
margin, *n.* margen *m.* or *f.*
marijuana, *n.* marijuana *f.*
marine, **1.** *a.* marino. **2.** *n.* soldado de marina.
mariner, *n.* marinero *m.*
marionette, *n.* marioneta *f.*
marital, *a.* marital.
maritime, *a.* marítimo.
mark, **1.** *n.* marca *f.* **2.** *v.* marcar.
market, *n.* mercado *m.* **meat m.**, carnicería *f.* **stock m.**, bolsa *f.*
marmalade, *n.* mermelada *f.*
maroon, *a.* & *n.* color rojo oscuro.
marquis, *n.* marqués *m.*
marriage, *n.* matrimonio *m.*
married, *a.* casado. **to get m.**, casarse.
marrow, *n.* medula *f.;* substancia *f.*
marry, *v.* casarse con; casar.
marsh, *n.* pantano *m.*
marshal, *n.* mariscal *m.*
marshmallow, *n.* malvarisco *m.;* bombón de altea *m.*
martial, *a.* marcial. **m. law**, gobierno militar.
martyr, *n.* mártir *m.* & *f.*
martyrdom, *n.* martirio *m.*
marvel, **1.** *n.* maravilla *f.* **2.** *v.* maravillarse.
marvelous, *a.* maravilloso.
mascot, *n.* mascota *f.*
masculine, *a.* masculino.

mash, v. majar. **mashed pota-toes,** puré de papas m.

mask, n. máscara f.

mason, n. albañil m.

masquerade, n. mascarada f.

mass, n. masa f.; (rel.) misa f. **to say m.,** cantar misa. m. **production,** producción en serie.

massacre, 1. n. carnicería, matanza f. 2. v. matar attrozmente, destrozar.

massage, 1. n. masaje m.; soba f. 2. v. sobar.

masseur, n. masajista m. & f.

massive, a. macizo, sólido.

mast, n. palo, árbol m.

master, 1. n. amo; maestro m. 2. v. domar, dominar.

masterpiece, n. obra maestra.

mastery, n. maestría f.

mat, 1. n. estera; palleta f. 2. v. enredar.

match, 1. n. igual m; fósforo m.; (sport) partida, contienda f.; (marriage) noviazgo; casamiento. 2. v. ser igual a; igualar.

mate, 1. n. consorte m. & f.; compañero -ra. 2. v. igualar; casar.

material, a. & n. material m. **raw materials,** materias primas.

materialism, n. materialismo m.

materialize, v. materializar.

maternal, a. materno.

maternity, n. maternidad f.

mathematical, a. matemático.

mathematics, n. matemáticas f.pl.

matinee, n. matiné f.

matrimony, n. matrimonio m.

matron, n. matrona; directora f.

matter, 1. n. materia f.; asunto m. **what's the m.?,** ¿qué pasa? 2. v. importar.

mattress, n. colchón m.

mature, 1. a. maduro. 2. v. madurar.

maturity, n. madurez f.

maudlin, a. sentimental en exceso; peneque.

maul, v. maltratar a golpes.

maxim, n. máxima f.

maximum, a. & n. máximo.

may, v. poder.

May, n. mayo m.

maybe, adv. quizá, quizás, tal vez.

mayonnaise, n. mayonesa f.

mayor, n. alcalde m.

maze, n. laberinto m.

me, pron. mí; me. **with me,** conmigo.

meadow, n. prado m.; vega f.

meager, a. magro; pobre.

meal, n. comida; (flour) harina f.

mean, 1. a. bajo; malo. 2. n. medio (see also means). 3. v. significar; querer decir.

meaning, n. sentido, significado m.

means, n.pl. medios, recursos. **by all m.,** sin falta. by no m., de ningún modo. **by m. of,** por medio de.

meanwhile, adv. mientras tanto.

measles, n. sarampión m.

measure, 1. n. medida f.; (music) compás m. 2. v. medir.

measurement, n. medida, dimensión f.

meat, n. carne f.

mechanic, n. mecánico m.

mechanical, a. mecánico.

mechanism, n. mecanismo m.

mechanize, v. mecanizar.

medal, n. medalla f.

meddle, v. meterse, entremeterse.

mediate, v. mediar.

medical, a. médico.

medicine, n. medicina f.

medieval, a. medioeval.

mediocre, a. mediocre.

mediocrity, n. mediocridad f.

meditate, v. meditar.

meditation, n. meditación f.

Mediterranean, n. Mediterráneo m.

medium, 1. a. mediano, medio. 2. n. medio m.

medley, n. mezcla f., ensalada f.

meek, a. manso; humilde.

meekness, n. modestia; humildad f.

meet, 1. a. propio. 2. n. concurso m. 3. v. encontrar; reunirse; conocer.

meeting, n. reunión f.; mitin m.

megahertz, n. megahertzio m.

megaphone, n. megáfono m.

melancholy, 1. a. melancólico. 2. n. melancolía f.

mellow, a. suave; blando; maduro.

melodious, a. melodioso.

melodrama, n. melodrama m.

melody, n. melodía f.

melon, n. melón m.

melt, v. derretir.

meltdown, n. fundición resultante de un accidente en un reactor nuclear.

member, n. socio -ia; miembro m.

membership, n. membrecía f.

membrane, n. membrana f.

memento, n. recuerdo m.

memoir, n. memoria f.

memorable, a. memorable.

memorandum, n. memorándum, volante m.

memorial, 1. a. conmemorativo. 2. n. memorial m.

memorize, v. aprender de memoria.

memory, n. memoria f.; recuerdo m.

menace, 1. n. amenaza f. 2. v. amenazar.

mend, v. reparar, remendar.

menial, 1. a. servil. 2. n. sirviente m.

menopause, n. menopausia f.

menstruation, n. menstruación f.

menswear, n. ropa de caballeros f.

mental, a. mental.

mentality, n. mentalidad f.

menthol, n. mentol m.

mention, 1. n. mención f. 2. v. mencionar.

menu, n. menú m., lista f.

mercantile, a. mercantil.

mercenary, a. & n. mercenario -ria.

merchandise, n. mercancía f.

merchant, n. mercante. 2. n. comerciante m.

merciful, a. misericordioso, compasivo.

merciless, a. cruel, inhumano.

mercury, n. mércurio m.

mercy, n. misericordia; merced f.

mere, a. mero, puro.

merely, adv. solamente; simplemente.

merge, v. unir, combinar.

merger, n. consolidación, fusión.

meringue, n. merengue m.

merit, 1. n. mérito m. 2. v. merecer.

meritorious, a. meritorio.

mermaid, n. sirena f.

merriment, n. regocijo m.

merry, a. alegre, festivo.

merry-go-round, n. caballitos m.

mesh, n. malla f.

mess, 1. n. lío m.; confusión f.; (mil.) salón comedor, rancho m. 2. v. m. up, ensuciar; enredar.

message, n. mensaje, recado m.

messenger, n. mensajero -ra.

messy, a. confuso, desarreglado.

metabolism, n. metabolismo m.

metal, n. metal m.

metallic, a. metálico.

metaphysics, n. metafísica f.

meteor, n. metéoro m.

meteorology, n. meteorología f.

meter, n. medidor; (measure) metro m.

method, n. método m.

meticulous, a. meticuloso.

metric, a. métrico.

metropolis, n. metrópoli f.

metropolitan, a. metropolitano.

Mexican, a. & n. mexicano -na.

Mexico, n. México m.

mezzanine, n. entresuelo m.

microbe, n. microbio m.

microfiche, n. microficha f.

microfilm, n. microfilm m.

microform, n. microforma f.

microphone, n. micrófono m.

microscope, n. microscopio m.
microscopic, a. microscópico.
mid, a. medio.
middle, a. & n. medio m. in the m. of, en medio de, a mediados de.
middle-aged, a. de edad madura.
Middle East, n. Medio Oriente m.
midget, n. enano -na.
midnight, n. medianoche f.
midwife, n. partera f.
might, n. poder m., fuerza f.
mighty, a. poderoso.
migraine, n. migraña f.; jaqueca f.
migrate, v. emigrar.
migration, n. emigración f.
migratory, a. migratorio.
mild, a. moderado, suave; templado.
mildew, n. añublo m., moho m.
mile, n. milla f.
militant, a. militante.
militarism, n. militarismo m.
military, a. militar.
militia, n. milicia f.
milk, 1. n. leche f. 2. v. ordeñar.
milkman, n. lechero m.
milky, a. lácteo; lechoso.
mill, 1. n. molino m.; fábrica f. 2. v. moler.
miller, n. molinero m.
millimeter, n. milímetro m.
milliner, n. modista m. & f.
millinery, n. sombrerería f.
million, n. millón m.
millionaire, n. millonario -ria.
mimic, 1. n. mimo m. 2. v. imitar.
mind, 1. n. mente; opinión f. 2. v. obedecer. never m., no se ocupe.
mindful, a. atento.
mine, 1. pron. mío. 2. n. mina f. 3. v. minar.
miner, n. minero m.
mineral, a. & n. mineral m.
mine sweeper, n. dragaminas f.
mingle, v. mezclar.
miniature, n. miniatura f.
miniaturize, v. miniaturizar.
minimize, v. menospreciar.
minimum, a. & n. mínimo m.
mining, n. minería f.
minister, 1. n. ministro; (rel.) pastor m. 2. v. ministrar.
ministry, n. ministerio m.
mink, n. visón m.; (fur) piel de visón m.
minor, 1. a. menor. 2. n. menor de edad.
minority, n. minoría f.
minstrel, n. juglar m.
mint, 1. n. menta f.; casa de moneda. 2. v. acuñar.
minus, prep. menos.
minute, 1. a. minucioso. 2. n. minuto, momento m.
miracle, n. milagro m.
miraculous, a. milagroso.
mirage, n. miraje m.
mire, n. lodo m.

mirror, n. espejo m.
mirth, n. alegría; risa f.
misbehave, v. portarse mal.
miscellaneous, a. misceláneo.
mischief, n. travesura, diablura f.
mischievous, a. travieso, dañino.
miser, n. avaro -ra.
miserable, a. miserable; infeliz.
miserly, a. avariento, tacaño.
misfortune, n. desgracia f., infortunio, revés m.
misgiving, n. recelo m., desconfianza f.
mishap, n. desgracia f., contratiempo m.
mislead, v. extraviar, despistar; pervertir.
misplaced, a. extraviado.
mispronounce, v. pronunciar mal.
miss, 1. n. señorita f. 2. v. perder; echar de menos, extrañar. be missing, faltar.
missile, n. proyectil m.
mission, n. misión; comisión f.
missionary, n. misionero -ra.
mist, n. niebla, bruma f.
mistake, 1. n. equivocación f.; error m. to make a m., equivocarse.
mistaken, a. equivocado.
mister, n. señor m.
mistletoe, n. muérdago m.
mistreat, v. maltratar.
mistress, n. ama; señora; concubina f.
mistrust, v. desconfiar; sospechar.
misty, a. nebuloso, brumoso.
misunderstand, v. entender mal.
misuse, v. maltratar; abusar.
mite, n. pizca f., blanca f.
mitten, n. mitón, confortante m.
mix, v. mezclar. m. up, confundir.
mixture, n. mezcla, mixtura f.
mix-up, n. confusión f.
moan, 1. n. quejido, gemido m. 2. v. gemir.
mob, n. muchedumbre f.; gentío m.
mobilization, n. movilización f.
mobilize, v. movilizar.
mock, v. burlar.
mockery, n. burla f.
mod, a. a la última; en boga.
mode, n. modo m.
model, 1. n. modelo m. 2. v. modelar.
moderate, 1. a. moderado. 2. v. moderar.
moderation, n. moderación; sobriedad f.
modern, a. moderno.
modernize, v. modernizar.
modest, a. modesto.
modesty, n. modestia f.
modify, v. modificar.
modulate, v. modular.
moist, a. húmedo.

moisten, v. humedecer.
moisture, n. humedad f.
molar, n. molar m.
molasses, n. molaza f.
mold, 1. n. molde; moho m. 2. v. moldar, formar; enmohecerse.
moldy, a. mohoso.
mole, n. lunar m.; (animal) topo m.
molecule, n. molécula f.
molest, v. molestar.
mollify, v. molificar.
moment, n. momento m.
momentary, a. momentáneo.
momentous, a. importante.
monarch, n. monarca m.
monarchy, n. monarquía f.
monastery, n. monasterio m.
Monday, n. lunes m.
monetary, a. monetario.
money, n. dinero m. m. order, giro postal.
mongrel, 1. n. mestizo m. 2. a. mestizo, cruzado.
monitor, n. amonestador m.
monk, n. monje m.
monkey, n. mono -na.
monocle, n. monóculo m.
monologue, n. monólogo m.
monopolize, v. monopolizar.
monopoly, n. monopolio m.
monosyllable, n. monosílabo m.
monotone, n. monotonía f.
monotonous, a. monótono.
monotony, n. monotonía f.
monsoon, n. monzón m.
monster, n. monstruo m.
monstrosity, n. monstruosidad f.
monstrous, a. monstruoso.
month, n. mes m.
monthly, a. mensual.
monument, n. momumento m.
monumental, a. monumental.
mood, n. humor m.; (gram.) modo m.
moody, a. caprichoso, taciturno.
moon, n. luna f.
moonlight, n. luz de la luna.
moor, 1. n. párano m. 2. v. anclar.
mop, 1. n. estropajo m. 2. v. fregar.
moped (vehicle), n. velomotor m.
moral, 1. a. moral. 2. n. moraleja f. morals, moralidad f.
morale, n. espíritu m.
moralist, n. moralista m. & f.
morality, n. moralidad, ética f.
morbid, a. mórbido.
more, a. & adv. más. m. and m., cada vez más.
moreover, adv. además.
morgue, n. necrocomio m.
morning, n. mañana f. good m., buenos días.
morose, a. malhumorado.
morphine, n. morfina f.
morsel, n. bocado m.
mortal, a. & n. mortal m.
mortality, n. mortalidad f.

mortar, n. mortero m.

mortgage, 1. n. hipoteca f. **2.** v. hipotecar.

mortify, v. mortificar.

mosaic, n. & a. mosaico m.

mosquito, n. mosquito m.

moss, n. musgo m.

most, 1. a. más. **2.** adv. más; sumamente. **3.** pron. **m.** of, la mayor parte de.

mostly, adv. principalmente; en su mayor parte.

moth, n. polilla f.

mother, n. madre f.

mother-in-law, n. suegra f.

motif, n. tema m.

motion, 1. n. moción f.; movimiento m. **2.** v. hacer señas.

motionless, a. inmóvil.

motion picture, n. película f.

motivate, v. motivar.

motive, n. motivo m.

motor, n. motor m.

motorboat, n. bote de gasolina.

motorcycle, n. motocicleta f.

motorist, n. motorista m. & f.

motto, n. lema m.

mound, n. terrón; montón m.

mount, 1. n. monte m.; (horse) montura f. **2.** v. montar; subir.

mountain, n. montaña f.

mountaineer, n. montañés m.

mountainous, a. montañoso.

mourn, v. lamentar, llorar; llevar luto.

mournful, a. triste.

mourning, n. luto; lamento m.

mouse, n. ratón, ratoncito m.

mouth, n. boca f.; (of river) desembocadura f.

movable, a. movible, movedizo.

move, 1. n. movimiento m.; mudanza f. **2.** v. mover; mudarse; emocionar conmover. **m. away,** quitar; alejarse; mudarse.

movement, n. movimiento m.

movie, n. película f. **m. theater,** movies, cine m.

moving, a. conmovedor; persuasivo.

mow, v. guadañar, segar.

Mr., title. Señor (Sr.)

Mrs., title. Señora (Sra.)

much, a. & adv. mucho. **how m.,** cuánto. **so m.,** tanto. **too m.,** demasiado. **as m. as,** tanto como.

mucilage, n. mucílago m.

mucous, a. mucoso.

mucous membrane, n. mucosa f.

mud, n. fango, lodo m.

muddy, 1. a. lodoso; turbio. **2.** v. ensuciar; enturbiar.

muff, n. manguito m.

muffin, n. panecillo m.

mug, n. cubilete m.

mulatto, n. mulato m.

mule, n. mula f.

mullah, n. mullah m.

multinational, a. multinacional.

multiple, a. múltiple.

multiplication, n. multiplicación f.

multiplicity, n. multiplicidad f.

multiply, v. multiplicar.

multitude, n. multitud f.

mummy, n. momia f.

mumps, n. poperas f.pl.

municipal, a. municipal.

munificent, a. munífico.

munition, n. municiones m.

mural, a. & n. mural m.

murder, 1. n. asesinato; homicidio m. **2.** v. asesinar.

murderer, n. asesino -na.

murmur, 1. n. murmullo m. **2.** v. murmurar.

muscle, n. músculo m.

muscular, a. muscular.

muse, 1. n. musa f. **2.** v. meditar.

museum, n. museo m.

mushroom, n. seta f., hongo m.

music, n. música f.

musical, a. musical; melodioso.

musician, n. músico m.

muslin, n. muselina f., percal m.

must, v. deber; tener que.

mustache, n. bigotes m.pl.

mustard, n. mostaza f.

muster, 1. n. (mil.) revista f. **2.** v. agregar.

mute, a. & n. mudo m.

mutilate, v. mutilar.

mutiny, 1. n. motín m. **2.** amotinarse.

mutter, v. refunfuñar, gruñir.

mutton, n. carnero m.

mutual, a. mutuo.

muzzle, 1. n. hocico m.; bozal m. **2.** v. embozar.

my, a. mi.

myriad, n. miríada f.

myrtle, n. mirto m.

myself, pron. mí, mí mismo; me. **I m.,** yo mismo.

mysterious, a. misterioso.

mystery, n. misterio m.

mystic, a. místico.

mystify, v. confundir.

myth, n. mito m.

mythical, a. mítico.

mythology, n. mitología f.

N

nag, 1. n. jaca f. **2.** v. regañar; sermonear.

nail, 1. n. clavo m.; (finger) uña f. **2.** v. clavar.

naïve, a. ingenuo.

naked, a. desnudo.

name, 1. n. nombre m.; reputación f. **2.** v. nombrar, mencionar.

namely, adv. a saber; es decir.

namesake, n. tocayo m.

nap, n. siesta f. **to take a n.,** echar una siesta.

naphtha, n. nafta f.

napkin, n. servilleta f.

narcissus, n. narciso m.

narcotic, a. & n. narcótico m.

narrate, v. narrar.

narrative, 1. a. narrativo. **2.** n. cuento, relato m.

narrow, a. estrecho, angosto. **n.-minded,** intolerante.

nasal, a. nasal.

nasty, a. desagradable; antipático.

nation, n. nación f.

national, a. nacional.

nationalism, n. nacionalismo m.

nationality, n. nacionalidad f.

nationalization, n. nacionalización f.

nationalize, v. nacionalizar.

native, 1. a. nativo. **2.** n. natural; indígena m. & f.

nativity, n. natividad f.

natural, a. natural.

naturalist, n. naturalista m.

naturalize, v. naturalizar.

naturalness, n. naturalidad f.

nature, n. naturaleza f.; índole f.; humor m.

naughty, a. travieso, desobediente.

nausea, n. náusea f.

nauseous, a. nauseoso.

nautical, a. náutico.

naval, a. naval.

nave, n. nave f.

navel, n. ombligo m.

navigable, a. navegable.

navigate, v. navegar.

navigation, n. navegación f.

navigator, n. navegante m.

navy, n. marina f.

near, 1. a. cercano, próximo. **2.** adv. cerca. **3.** prep. cerca de.

nearby, 1. a. cercano. **2.** adv. cerca.

nearly, adv. casi.

nearsighted, a. corto de vista.

neat, a. aseado; ordenado.

neatness, n. aseo m.

nebulous, a. nebuloso.

necessary, a. necesario.

necessity, n. necesidad f.

neck, n. cuello m.

necklace, n. collar m.

necktie, n. corbata f.

nectar, n. néctar m.

need, 1. n. necesidad; (poverty) pobreza f. **2.** v. necesitar.

needle, n. aguja f.

needless, a. innecesario, inútil.

needy, a. indigente, necesitado, pobre.

nefarious, a. nefario.

negative, 1. a. negativo. **2.** n. negativa f.

neglect, 1. n. negligencia f.; descuido m. **2.** v. descuidar.

negligee, n. negligee m., bata de casa f.

negligent, a. negligente, descuidado.

negligible, a. insignificante.

negotiate, v. negociar.

negotiation, n. negociación f.

Negro, n. negro -ra.

neighbor, n. vecino -na.

neighborhood, n. vecindad f.
neither, 1. a. & pron. ninguno de los dos. **2.** adv. tampoco. **3.** conj. neither ... nor, ni ... ni.
neon, n. neón m. **n. light,** tubo neón m.
nephew, n. sobrino m.
nerve, n. nervio m.; (coll.) audacia f.
nervous, a. nervioso.
nest, n. nido m.
net, 1. a. neto. **2.** n. red f. **hair n.,** albanega f. **3.** redar; (com.) ganar.
netting, n. red m.; obra de malla f.
network, n. (radio) red radiodifusora.
neuralgia, n. neuralgia f.
neurology, n. neurología f.
neurotic, a. neurótico.
neutral, a. neutral.
neutrality, n. neutralidad f.
neutron, n. neutrón m.
neutron bomb, bomba de neutrones f.
never, adv. nunca, jamás; **n. mind,** no importa.
nevertheless, adv. no obstante, sin embargo.
new, a. nuevo.
news, n. noticias f.pl.
newsboy, n. vendedor de periódicos.
newspaper, n. periódico m.
New Testament, n. Nuevo Testamento m.
new year, n. año nuevo m.
next, 1. a. próximo; siguiente; contiguo. **2.** adv. luego, después. **n. door,** al lado. **n. to,** al lado de.
nibble, v. picar.
nice, a. simpático, agradable; amable; hermoso; exacto.
nick, n. muesca f., picadura f. **in the n. of time,** apunto.
nickel, n. níquel m.
nickname, 1. n. apodo, mote m. **2.** v. apodar.
nicotine, n. nicotina f.
niece, n. sobrina f.
niggardly, a. mezquino.
night, n. noche f. **good n.,** buenas noches. **last n.,** anoche. **n. club,** cabaret m.
nightclub, n. cabaret m.
nightgown, n. camisa de dormir.
nightingale, n. ruiseñor m.
nightly, adv. todas las noches.
nightmare, n. pesadilla f.
nimble, a. ágil.
nine, a. & pron. nueve.
nineteen, a. & pron. diecinueve.
ninety, a. & pron. noventa.
ninth, a. noveno.
nipple, n. teta f.; pezón m.
nitrogen, n. nitrógeno m.
no, 1. a. ninguno. **no one,** nadie. **2.** adv. no.
nobility, n. nobleza f.
noble, a. & n. noble m.

nobleman, n. noble m.
nobody, pron. nadie.
nocturnal, a. nocturno.
nocturne, n. nocturno m.
nod, 1. n. seña con la cabeza. **2.** v. inclinar la cabeza; (doze) dormitar.
no-frills, a. sin extras.
noise, n. ruido m.
noiseless, a. silencioso.
noisy, a. ruidoso.
nominal, a. nominal.
nominate, v. nombrar.
nomination, n. nombramiento m., nominación f.
nominee, n. nombrado m.
nonaligned (in political sense) a. no alineado.
nonchalant, a. indiferente.
noncombatant, n. no combatiente m.
noncommittal, a. evasivo; reservado.
nondescript, a. difícil de describir.
none, pron. ninguno.
nonentity, n. nulidad f.
nonpartisan, a. sin afiliación.
non-proliferation, n. no proliferación m.
nonsense, n. tontería f.
noodle, n. fideo m.
noon, n. mediodía m.
noose, n. lazo corredizo m.; dogal m.
nor, conj. ni.
normal, a. normal.
north, n. norte m.
North America, n. Norte América f.
North American, a. & n. norteamericano -na.
northeast, n. nordeste m.
northern, a. septentrional.
North Pole, n. polo norte m.
northwest, n. noroeste m.
Norway, n. Noruega f.
Norwegian, a. & n. noruego -ga.
nose, n. nariz f.
nostalgia, n. nostalgia f.
nostril, n. ventana de la nariz; (pl.) narices.
not, adv. no. **n. at all,** de ninguna manera. **n. even,** ni siquiera.
notable, a. notable.
notary, n. notario m.
notation, n. notación f.
notch, n. muesca f.; corte m.
note, 1. n. nota f.; apunte m. **2.** v. notar.
notebook, n. libreta f., cuaderno m.
noted, a. célebre.
notepaper, n. papel de notas m.
noteworthy, a. notable.
nothing, pron. nada.
notice, 1. n. aviso m.; noticia f. **2.** v. observar, fijarse en.
noticeable, a. notable.
notification, n. notificación f.
notify, v. notificar.

notion, n. noción; idea f.; (pl.) novedades f.pl.
notoriety, n. notoriedad f.
notorious, a. notorio.
noun, n. nombre, sustantivo m.
nourish, v. nutrir, alimentar.
nourishment, n. nutrimento, alimento m.
novel, 1. a. nuevo, original. **2.** n. novela f.
novelist, n. novelista m. & f.
novelty, n. novedad f.
November, n. noviembre m.
novena, n. novena f.
novice, n. novicio -cia, novato -ta.
Novocaine, n. novocaína f.
now, adv. ahora. **n. and then,** de vez en cuando. **by n.,** ya. **from n. on,** de ahora en adelante. **just n.,** ahorita. **right n.,** ahora mismo.
nowhere, adv. en ninguna parte.
nozzle, n. boquilla f.
nuance, n. matiz m.
nuclear, a. nuclear.
nuclear warhead, cabeza nuclear f.
nuclear waste, desechos nucleares m.pl.
nucleus, n. núcleo m.
nude, a. desnudo.
nuisance, n. molestia f.
nuke, n. armamento o reactor nuclear.
nullify, v. anular.
number, 1. n. número m.; cifra f. **license n.,** matrícula f. **2.** v. numerar, contar.
numerical, a. numérico.
numerous, a. numeroso.
nun, n. monja f.
nuptial, a. nupcial.
nurse, 1. n. enfermera f.; (child's) ama, niñera f. **2.** v. criar, alimentar, amamantar; cuidar.
nursery, n. cuarto destinado a los niños; (agr.) plantel, criadero m.
nurture, v. nutrir.
nut, n. nuez f.; (mech.) tuerca f.
nutrition, n. nutrición f.
nutritious, a. nutritivo.
nylon, n. nilón m.
nymph, n. ninfa f.

O

oak, n. roble m.
oar, n. remo m.
oasis, n. oasis m.
oat, n. avena f.
oath, n. juramento m.
oatmeal, n. harina de avena f.
obedience, n. obediencia f.
obedient, a. obediente.
obese, a. obeso, gordo.
obey, v. obedecer.
obituary, n. obituario m.
object, 1. n. objeto m.; (gram.)

complemento *m.* **2.** *v.* oponerse; objectar.

objection, *n.* objección *f.*

objectionable, *a.* censurable.

objective, *a.* & *n.* objetivo *m.*

obligation, *n.* obligación *f.*

obligatory, *a.* obligatorio.

oblige, *v.* obligar; complacer.

oblique, *a.* oblicuo.

obliterate, *v.* borrar; destruir.

oblivion, *n.* olvido *m.*

oblong, *a.* oblongo.

obnoxious, *a.* ofensivo, odioso.

obscene, *a.* obsceno, indecente.

obscure, **1.** *a.* obscuro. **2.** *v.* obscurecer.

observance, *n.* observancia; ceremonia *f.*

observation, *n.* observación *f.*

observatory, *n.* observatorio *m.*

observe, *v.* observar; celebrar.

observer, *n.* observador -ra.

obsession, *n.* obsesión *f.*

obsolete, *a.* anticuado.

obstacle, *n.* obstáculo *m.*

obstetrician, *n.* obstétrico *m.*

obstinate, *a.* obstinado, terco.

obstruct, *v.* obstruir, impedir.

obstruction, *n.* obstrucción *f.*

obtain, *v.* obtener, conseguir.

obtuse, *a.* obtuso.

obviate, *v.* obviar.

obvious, *a.* evidente, obvio.

occasion, **1.** *n.* ocasión *f.* **2.** *v.* ocasionar.

occasional, *a.* ocasional.

occult, *a.* oculto.

occupant, *n.* ocupante *m.;* inquilino -na.

occupation, *n.* ocupación *f.;* empleo *m.*

occupy, *v.* ocupar; emplear.

occur, *v.* ocurrir.

occurrence, *n.* ocurrencia *f.*

ocean, *n.* océano *m.*

o'clock: it's one o., es la una. **it's two o.,** son las dos, etc. **at . . . o.,** a las . . .

octagon, *n.* octágono *m.*

octave, *n.* octava *f.*

October, *n.* octubre *m.*

octopus, *n.* pulpo *m.*

oculist, *n.* oculista *m.*

odd, *a.* impar; suelto; raro.

odious, *a.* odioso.

odor, *n.* olor *m.;* fragancia *f.*

of, *prep.* de.

off, *adv.* (see under verb: **stop off, take off,** etc.)

offend, *v.* ofender.

offender, *n.* ofensor -ra; delincuente *m.*

offense, *n.* ofensa *f.;* crimen *m.*

offensive, **1.** *a.* ofensivo. **2.** *n.* ofensiva *f.*

offer, **1.** *n.* oferta *f.* **2.** *v.* ofrecer.

offering, *n.* oferta *f.*

office, *n.* oficina *f.;* despacho *m.;* oficio, cargo *m.*

officer, *n.* oficial *m.* **police o.,** agente de policía.

official, **1.** *a.* oficial. **2.** *n.* oficial, funcionario *m.*

officiate, *v.* oficiar.

officious, *a.* oficioso.

offspring, *n.* hijos *m.pl.;* progenie *f.*

often, *adv.* muchas veces, a menudo. **how o.,** con qué frecuencia.

oil, **1.** *n.* aceite; óleo; petróleo *m.* **2.** *v.* aceitar; engrasar.

oily, *a.* aceitoso.

ointment, *n.* ungüento *m.*

okay, *adv.* bien; de acuerdo.

old, *a.* viejo; antiguo. **o. man, o. woman,** viejo -ja.

old-fashioned, *a.* fuera de moda.

Old Testament, *n.* Antiguo Testamento *m.*

olive, *n.* aceituna, oliva *f.*

ombudsman, *n.* ombudsman *m.*

omelet, *n.* tortilla de huevos.

omen, *n.* agüero *m.*

ominous, *a.* ominoso, siniestro.

omission, *n.* omisión *f.;* olvido *m.*

omit, *v.* omitir.

omnibus, *n.* ómnibus *m.*

omnipotent, *a.* omnipotente.

on, *prep.* en, sobre, encima de. **2.** *adv.* adelante.

once, *adv.* una vez. **at o.,** en seguida. **o. in a while,** de vez en cuando.

one, *a.* & *pron.* uno.

oneself, *pron.* sí mismo; se. **with o.,** consigo.

onion, *n.* cebolla *f.*

only, **1.** *a.* único, solo. **2.** *adv.* sólo, solamente.

onward, *adv.* adelante.

opal, *n.* ópalo *m.*

opaque, *a.* opaco.

open, **1.** *a.* abierto; franco. **o. air,** aire libre. **2.** *v.* abrir.

opening, *n.* abertura *f.*

opera, *n.* ópera *f.* **o. glasses,** anteojos de ópera; gemelos *m.pl.*

operate, *v.* operar.

operation, *n.* operación *f.* **to have an o.,** operarse, ser operado.

operative, *a.* eficaz, operativo.

operator, *n.* operario -ria. **elevator o.,** ascensorista *m.* & *f.* **telephone o.,** telefonista *m.* & *f.*

operetta, *n.* opereta *f.*

ophthalmic, *a.* oftálmico.

opinion, *n.* opinión *f.*

opponent, *n.* antagonista *m.* & *f.*

opportunism, *n.* oportunismo *m.*

opportunity, *n.* ocasión, oportunidad *f.*

oppose, *v.* oponer.

opposite, **1.** *a.* opuesto, contrario. **2.** *prep.* al frente de. **3.** *n.* contrario *m.*

opposition, *n.* oposición *f.*

oppress, *v.* oprimir.

oppression, *n.* opresión *f.*

oppressive, *a.* opresivo.

optic, *a.* óptico.

optician, *n.* óptico *m.*

optics, *n.* óptica *f.*

optimism, *n.* optimismo.

optimistic, *a.* optimista.

option, *n.* opción, elección *f.*

optional, *a.* discrecional, facultativo.

optometry, *n.* optometría *f.*

opulent, *a.* opulento.

or, *conj.* o, (before *o-, ho-*) u.

oracle, *n.* oráculo *m.*

oral, *a.* oral, vocal.

orange, *n.* naranja *f.*

oration, *n.* discurso *m.;* oración *f.*

orator, *n.* orador *m.*

oratory, *n.* elocuencia *f.;* (church) oratorio *m.*

orbit, *n.* órbita *f.*

orchard, *n.* huerto *m.*

orchestra, *n.* orquesta *f.* **o. seat,** butaca *f.*

orchid, *n.* orquídea *f.*

ordain, *v.* ordenar.

ordeal, *n.* prueba *f.*

order, **1.** *n.* orden, *m.* or *f.;* clase *f.;* (com.) pedido *m.* **in o. that,** para que. **2.** *v.* ordenar; mandar; pedir.

orderly, *a.* ordenado.

ordinance, *n.* ordenanza *f.*

ordinary, *a.* ordinario.

ordination, *n.* ordenación *f.*

ore, *n.* mineral *m.*

organ, *n.* órgano *m.*

organdy, *n.* organdí *m.*

organic, *a.* orgánico.

organism, *n.* organismo *m.*

organist, *n.* organista *m.* & *f.*

organization, *n.* organización *f.*

organize, *v.* organizar.

orgy, *n.* orgía *f.*

orient, **1.** *n.* oriente *m.* **2.** *v.* orientar.

Oriental, *a.* oriental.

orientation, *n.* orientación *f.*

origin, *n.* origen *m.*

original, *a.* & *n.* original *m.*

originality, *n.* originalidad *f.*

ornament, **1.** *n.* ornamento *m.* **2.** *v.* ornamentar.

ornamental, *a.* ornamental, decorativo.

ornate, *a.* ornado.

ornithology, *n.* ornitología *f.*

orphan, *a.* & *n.* huérfano -na.

orphanage, *n.* orfanato *m.*

orthodox, *a.* ortodoxo.

ostentation, *n.* ostentación *f.*

ostentatious, *a.* ostentoso.

ostrich, *n.* avestruz *m.*

other, *a.* & *pron.* otro. **every o. day,** un día sí otro no.

otherwise, *adv.* de otra manera.

ought, *v.* deber.

ounce, *n.* onza *f.*

our, ours, *a.* & *pron.* nuestro.

ourselves, *pron.* nosotros mismos; nos.

oust, *v.* desalojar.

ouster, *n.* desahuco *m.*

out, **1.** *adv.* fuera, afuera. **out of,** fuera de. **2.** *prep.* por.

outbreak, *n.* erupción *f.*

outcast, *n.* paria *m. & f.*

outcome, *n.* resultado *m.*

outdoors, *adv.* fuera de casa; al aire libre.

outer, *a.* exterior, externo.

outfit, 1. *n.* equipo; traje *m.* **2.** *v.* equipar.

outgrowth, *n.* resultado *m.*

outing, *n.* paseo *m.*

outlaw, 1. *n.* bandido *m.* **2.** *v.* proscribir.

outlet, *n.* salida *f.*

outline, 1. *n.* contorno; esbozo *m.;* silueta *f.* **2.** *v.* esbozar.

outlive, *v.* sobrevivir.

out-of-date, *a.* pasado.

outpost, *n.* puesto avanzado.

output, *n.* capacidad *f.;* educto *m.*

outrage, 1. *n.* ultraje *m.;* atrocidad *f.* **2.** *v.* ultrajar.

outrageous, *a.* atroz.

outrun, *v.* exceder.

outside, 1. *a. & n.* exterior *m.* **2.** *adv.* afuera, por fuera. **3.** *prep.* fuera de.

outskirt, *n.* borde *m.*

outward, *adv.* hacia afuera.

outwardly, *adv.* exteriormente.

oval, 1. *a.* oval, ovalado. **2.** *n.* óvalo *m.*

ovary, *n.* ovario *m.*

ovation, *n.* ovación *f.*

oven, *n.* horno *m.*

over, 1. *prep.* sobre, encima de; por. **2.** *adv.* o. **here,** aquí. **o. there,** allí, por allí. **to be o.,** estar terminado.

overcoat, *n.* abrigo, sobretodo *m.*

overcome, *v.* superar, vencer.

overdue, *a.* restrasado.

overflow, 1. *n.* inundación *f.* **2.** *v.* inundar.

overhaul, *v.* repasar.

overhead, *adv.* arriba, en lo alto.

overkill, *n.* efecto mayor que el pretendido.

overlook, *v.* pasar por alto.

overnight, *adv.* **to stay or stop o.,** pasar la noche.

overpower, *v.* vencer.

overrule, *v.* predominar.

overrun, *v.* invadir.

oversee, *v.* superentender.

oversight, *n.* equivocación *f.*

overt, *a.* abierto.

overtake, *v.* alcanzar.

overthrow, 1. *n.* trastorno *m.* **2.** *v.* trastornar.

overture, *n.* obertura *f.*

overturn, *v.* trastornar.

overview, *n.* visión de conjunto *f.*

overweight, *a.* demasiado pesado.

overwhelm, *v.* abrumar.

overwork, *v.* trabajar demasiado.

owe, *v.* deber. **owing to,** debido a.

owl, *n.* lechuza *f.*

own, 1. *a.* propio. **2.** *v.* poseer.

owner, *n.* dueño -ña.

ox, *n.* buey *m.*

oxygen, *n.* oxígeno *m.*

oxygen tent, *n.* tienda de oxigeno *f.*

oyster, *n.* ostra *f.*

P

pace, 1. *n.* paso *m.* **2.** *v.* pasearse. **p. off,** medir a pasos.

pacific, *a.* pacífico.

pacifier, *n.* pacificador *m.;* (baby p.) chupete *m.*

pacifism, *n.* pacifismo *m.*

pacifist, *n.* pacifista *m. & f.*

pacify, *v.* pacificar.

pack, 1. *n.* fardo; paquete *m.;* (animals) muta *f.* **p. of cards,** baraja *f.* **2.** *v.* empaquetar; (baggage) empacar.

package, *n.* paquete, bulto *m.*

pact, *n.* pacto *m.*

pad, 1. *n.* colchoncillo *m.* **p. of paper,** bloc de papel. **2.** *v.* rellenar.

paddle, 1. *n.* canalete *m.* **2.** *v.* remar.

padlock, *n.* candado *m.*

pagan, *a. & n.* pagano -na.

page, *n.* página *f.;* (boy) paje *m.*

pageant, *n.* espectáculo *m.;* procesión *f.*

pail, *n.* cubo *m.*

pain, 1. *n.* dolor *m.* **to take pains,** esmerarse.

painful, *a.* doloroso; penoso.

paint, 1. *n.* pintura *f.* **2.** *v.* pintar.

painter, *n.* pintor -ra.

painting, *n.* pintura *f.;* cuadro *m.*

pair, 1. *n.* par *m.;* pareja *f.* **2.** *v.* parear. **p. off,** emparejarse.

pajamas, *n.* pijama *m.*

palace, *n.* palacio *m.*

palatable, *a.* sabroso, agradable.

palate, *n.* paladar *m.*

palatial, *a.* palaciego, suntuoso.

pale, *a.* pálido. **to turn pale,** palidecer.

paleness, *n.* palidez *f.*

palette, *n.* paleta *f.*

pallbearer, *n.* andero *m.*

pallid, *a.* pálido.

palm, *n.* palma *f.* **p. tree,** palmera *f.*

palpitate, *v.* palpitar.

paltry, *a.* miserable.

pamper, *v.* mimar.

pamphlet, *n.* folleto *m.*

pan, *n.* cacerola *f.*

panacea, *n.* panacea *f.*

Pan-American, *a.* panamericano.

pane, *n.* hoja *f.,* cuadro *m.*

panel, *n.* tablero *m.*

pang, *n.* dolor; remordimiento *m.*

panic, *n.* pánico *m.*

panorama, *n.* panorama *m.*

pant, *v.* jadear.

panther, *n.* pantera *f.*

pantomine, *n.* pantomima *f.;* mímica *f.*

pantry, *n.* despensa *f.*

pants, *n.* pantalones, *m.pl.*

panty hose, *n.* pantyhose *m.* (medias hasta la cintura).

papal, *a.* papal.

paper, *n.* papel; periódico; artículo *m.*

paperback, *n.* libro en rústica *m.*

paper hanger, *n.* empapelador *m.*

par, *n.* paridad *f.;* (com.) par *f.*

parable, *n.* parábola *f.*

parachute, *n.* paracaídas *m.*

parade, 1. *n.* desfile *m.,* procesión *f.* **2.** *v.* desfilar.

paradise, *n.* paraíso *m.*

paradox, *n.* paradoja *f.*

paraffin, *n.* parafina *f.*

paragraph, *n.* párrafo *m.*

parakeet, *n.* perico *m.*

parallel, 1. *a.* paralelo. **2.** *v.* correr parejas con.

paralysis, *n.* parálisis *f.*

paralyze, *v.* paralizar.

paramedic, *n.* paramédico *m.*

parameter, *n.* parámetro *m.*

paramount, *a.* supremo.

paraphrase, 1. *n.* paráfrasis *f.* **2.** *v.* parafrasear.

parasite, *n.* parásito *m.*

parcel, *n.* paquete *m.* **p. of land,** lote de terreno.

parchment, *n.* pergamino *m.*

pardon, 1. *n.* perdón *m.* **2.** *v.* perdonar.

pare, *v.* pelar.

parentage, *n.* origen *m.;* extracción *f.*

parenthesis, *n.* paréntesis *f.*

parents, *n.* padres *m.pl.*

parish, *n.* parroquia *f.*

Parisian, *a. & n.* parisiense *m. & f.*

park, 1. *n.* parque *m.* **2.** *v.* estacionar.

parkway, *n.* bulevar *m.*

parley, *n.* conferencia *f.;* (mil.) parlamento *m.*

parliament, *n.* parlamento *m.*

parliamentary, *a.* parlamentario.

parlor, *n.* sala *f.,* salón *m.*

parochial, *a.* parroquial.

parody, 1. *n.* parodia *f.* **2.** *v.* parodiar.

parole, 1. *n.* palabra *f.;* (mil.) santo y seña. **2.** *v.* poner en libertad bajo palabra.

paroxysm, *n.* paroxismo *m.*

parrot, *n.* loro, papagayo *m.*

parsimony, *n.* parsimonia *f.*

parsley, *n.* perejil *m.*

parson, *n.* párroco *m.*

part, 1. *n.* parte *f.;* (theat.) papel *m.* **2.** *v.* separarse; partirse. **p. with,** desprenderse de.

partake, *v.* tomar parte.

partial, *a.* parcial.

participant, *n.* participante *m.* & *f.*

participate, *v.* participar.

participation, *n.* participación *f.*

participle, *n.* participio *m.*

particle, *n.* partícula *f.*

particular, *a.* & *n.* particular *m.*

parting, *n.* despedida *f.*

partisan, *a.* & *n.* partidario -ria.

partition, *n.* tabique *m.*

partly, *adv.* en parte.

partner, *n.* socio -cia; compañero -ra.

partridge, *n.* perdiz *f.*

party, *n.* tertulia, fiesta *f.;* grupo *m.;* (political) partido *m.*

pass, 1. *n.* pase; (mountain) paso *m.* 2. *v.* pasar. **p. away,** fallecer.

passable, *a.* transitable; regular.

passage, *n.* pasaje; (corridor) pasillo *m.*

passé, *a.* anticuado.

passenger, *n.* pasajero -ra.

passerby, *n.* transeúnte *m.* & *f.*

passion, *n.* pasión *f.*

passionate, *a.* apasionado.

passive, *a.* pasivo.

passport, *n.* pasaporte *m.*

past, 1. *a.* & *n.* pasado *m.* 2. *prep.* más allá de; después de.

paste, 1. *n.* pasta *f.* 2. *v.* empastar; pegar.

pasteurize, *v.* pasteurizar.

pastime, *n.* pasatiempo *m.;* diversión *f.*

pastor, *n.* pastor *m.*

pastry, *n.* pastelería *f.*

pastuer, 1. *n.* pasto *m.;* pradera *f.* 2. *v.* pastar.

pat, 1. *n.* golpecillo *m.* **to stand p.,** mantenerse firme. 2. *v.* dar golpecillos.

patch, 1. *n.* remiendo *m.* 2. *v.* remendar.

patent, 1. *a.* & *n.* patente *m.* 2. *v.* patentar.

patent leather, *n.* charol *m.*

paternal, *a.* paterno, paternal.

paternity, *n.* paternidad *f.*

path, *n.* senda *f.*

pathetic, *a.* patético.

pathology, *n.* patología *f.*

pathos, *n.* rasgo conmovedor *m.*

patience, *n.* paciencia *f.*

patient, 1. *a.* paciente. 2. *n.* enfermo, paciente *m.*

patio, *n.* patio *m.*

patriarch, *n.* patriarca *m.*

patriot, *n.* patriota *m.*

patriotic, *a.* patriótico.

patriotism, *n.* patriotismo *m.*

patrol, 1. *n.* patrulla *f.* 2. *v.* patrullar.

patrolman, *n.* vigilante *m.;* patrullador *m.*

patron, *n.* patrón *m.*

patronize, *v.* condescender; patrocinar; ser cliente de.

pattern, *n.* modelo *m.*

pauper, *n.* indigent *m.* & *f.*

pause, 1. *n.* pausa *f.* 2. *v.* pausar.

pave, *v.* pavimentar. **p. the way,** preparar el camino.

pavement, *n.* pavimento *m.*

pavilion, *n.* pabellón *m.*

paw, 1. *n.* pata *f.* 2. *v.* patear.

pawn, 1. *n.* prenda *f.;* (chess) peón de ajedrez *m.* 2. *v.* empeñar.

pay, 1. *n.* pago; sueldo, salario *m.;* 2. *v.* pagar. **p. back,** pagar; vengarse de.

payment, *n.* pago *m.;* recompensa *f.*

pea, *n.* guisante *m.*

peace, *n.* paz *f.*

peaceable, *a.* pacífico.

peaceful, *a.* tranquilo.

peach, *n.* durazno, melocotón *m.*

peacock, *n.* pavo real *m.*

peak, *n.* pico, cumbre; máximo *m.*

peal, *n.* repique; estruendo *m.* **p. of laughter,** risotada *f.*

peanut, *n.* maní, cacahuete *m.*

pear, *n.* pera *f.*

pearl, *n.* perla *f.*

peasant, *n.* campesino -na.

pebble, *n.* guija *f.*

peck, 1. *n.* picotazo *m.* 2. *v.* picotear.

peculiar, *a.* peculiar.

pecuniary, *a.* pecuniario.

pedagogue, *n.* pedagogo *m.*

pedagogy, *n.* pedagogía *f.*

pedal, *n.* pedal *m.*

pedant, *n.* pedante *m.*

peddler, *n.* buhonero *m.*

pedestal, *n.* pedestal *m.*

pedestrian, *n.* peatón -na.

pediatrician, *n.* pediatra *m.* & *f.*

pedigree, *n.* genealogía *f.*

peek, 1. *n.* atisbo *m.* 2. *v.* atisbar.

peel, 1. *n.* corteza *f.;* (fruit) pellejo *m.* 2. *v.* descortezar; pelar.

peep, *n.* ojeada *f.*

peer, 1. *n.* par *m.* 2. *v.* mirar fijamente.

peg, *n.* clavija; estaquilla *f.;* gancho *m.*

pelt, 1. *n.* pellejo *m.* 2. *v.* apedrear; (rain) caer con fuerza.

pelvis, *n.* pelvis *f.*

pen, *n.* pluma *f.;* corral *m.* **fountain p.,** pluma fuente.

penalty, *n.* pena; multa *f.;* castigo *m.*

penance, *n.* penitencia *f.* **to do p.,** penar.

penchant, *n.* propensión *f.*

pencil, *n.* lápiz *m.*

pending, *a.* pendiente. **to be p.,** pender.

penetrate, *v.* penetrar.

penetration, *n.* penetración *f.*

penicillin, *n.* penicilina *f.*

peninsula, *n.* península *f.*

penitent, *n.* & *a.* penitente *n.*

penknife, *n.* cortaplumas *f.*

penniless, *a.* indigente.

penny, *n.* penique *m.*

pension, *n.* pensión *f.*

pensive, *a.* pensativo.

penury, *n.* penuria *f.*

people, 1. *n.* gente *f.;* (of a nation) pueblo *m.* 2. *v.* poblar.

pepper, *n.* pimienta *f.;* (plant) pimiento *m.*

per, *prep.* por.

perambulator, *n.* cochecillo de niño *m.*

perceive, *v.* percibir.

percent, *adv.* por ciento.

percentage, *n.* porcentaje *m.*

perceptible, *a.* perceptible.

perception, *n.* percepción *f.*

perch, *n.* percha *f.;* (fish) perca *f.*

perdition, *n.* perdición *f.*

peremptory, *a.* perentorio, terminante.

perennial, *a.* perenne.

perfect, 1. *a.* perfecto. 2. *v.* perfeccionar.

perfection, *n.* perfección *f.*

perforation, *n.* perforación *f.*

perform, *v.* hacer; ejecutar; (theat.) representar.

performance, *n.* ejecución *f.;* (theat.) representación *f.*

perfume, 1. *n.* perfume *m.;* fragancia *f.* 2. *v.* perfumar.

perfunctory, *a.* perfunctorio, superficial.

perhaps, *adv.* quizá, quizás, tal vez.

peril, *n.* peligro *m.*

perilous, *a.* peligroso.

perimeter, *n.* perímetro *m.*

period, *n.* periodo *m.;* (punct.) punto *m.*

periodic, *a.* periódico.

periodical, *n.* revista *f.*

periphery, *n.* periferia *f.*

perish, *v.* perecer.

perishable, *a.* perecedero.

perjury, *n.* perjurio *m.*

permanent, *a.* permanente. **p. wave,** ondulado permanente.

permeate, *v.* penetrar.

permissible, *a.* permisible.

permission, *n.* permiso *m.*

permit, 1. *n.* permiso *m.* 2. *v.* permitir.

pernicious, *a.* pernicioso.

perpendicular, *n.* & *a.* perpendicular *m.*

perpetrate, *v.* perpetrar.

perpetual, *a.* perpetuo.

perplex, *v.* confundir.

perplexity, *n.* perplejidad *f.*

persecute, *v.* perseguir.

persecution, *n.* persecución *f.*

perseverance, *n.* perseverancia *f.*

persevere, *v.* perseverar.

persist, *v.* persistir.

persistent, *a.* persistente.

person, *n.* persona *f.*

personage, *n.* personaje *m.*

personal, *a.* personal.

personality, *n.* personalidad *f.*

personnel, *n.* personal *m.*

perspective, *n.* perspectiva *f.*

perspiration, *n.* sudor *m.*

perspire, *v.* sudar.

persuade, v. persuadir.

persuasive, a. persuasivo.

pertain, v. pertenecer.

pertinent, a. pertinente.

perturb, v. perturbar.

peruse, v. leer con cuidado.

pervade, v. penetrar; llenar.

perverse, a. perverso.

perversion, n. perversión f.

pessimism, n. pesimismo m.

pestilence, n. pestilencia f.

pet, 1. n. favorito -ta. 2. v. mimar.

petal, n. pétalo m.

petition, 1. n. petición, súplica f. 2. v. pedir, suplicar.

petrify, v. petrificar.

petroleum, n. petróleo m.

petticoat, n. enagua f.

petty, a. mezquino, insignificante.

petulant, a. quisquilloso.

pew, n. banco de iglesia m.

pewter, n. peltre m.

phantom, n. espectro, fantasma m.

pharmacist, n. farmacéutico, boticario m.

pharmacy, n. farmacia, botica f.

phase, n. fase f.

pheasant, n. faisán m.

phenomenal, a. fenomenal.

phenomenon, n. fenómeno f.

philanthropy, n. filantropía f.

philately, n. filatelia f.

philosopher, n. filósofo m.

philosophical, a. filosófico.

philosophy, n. filosofía f.

phlegm, n. flema f.; frialdad de ánimo f.

phobia, n. fobia f.

phonetic, a. fonético.

phonograph, n. fonógrafo m.

phosphorus, n. fósforo m.

photocopier, n. fotocopiadora f.

photocopy, 1. n. fotocopia f. 2. v. fotocopiar.

photoelectric, a. fotoeléctrico.

photogenic, a. fotogénico.

photograph, 1. n. fotografía f. 2. v. fotografiar; retratar.

photography, n. fotografía f.

Photostat, n. fotocopia f.

phrase, 1. n. frase f. 2. v. expresar.

physical, a. físico.

physician, n. médico m.

physics, n. física f.

physiology, n. fisiología f.

physiotherapy, n. fisioterapia f.

physique, n. físico m.

pianist, n. pianista m. & f.

piano, n. piano m.

picayune, a. insignificante.

piccolo, n. flutín m.

pick, 1. n. pico m. 2. v. escoger. **p. up,** recoger.

picket, n. piquete m.

pickle, 1. n. salmuera f.; encurtido m. 2. v. escabechar.

pickpocket, n. cortabolsas m. & f.

picnic, n. picnic m.

picture, 1. n. cuadro; retrato m.; fotografía f.; (movie) película f. 2. v. imaginarse.

picturesque, a. pintoresco.

pie, n. pastel m.

piece, n. pedazo m.; pieza f.

pier, n. muelle m.

pierce, v. perforar; pinchar; traspasar.

piety, n. piedad f.

pig, n. puerco, cerdo, lechón m.

pigeon, n. paloma f.

pigeonhole, n. casilla f.

pigment, n. pigmento m.

pile, 1. n. pila f.; montón m.pl.; (med.) hemorroides f.pl. 2. v. amontonar.

pilfer, v. ratear.

pilgrim, n. peregrino -na, romero -ra.

pilgrimage, n. romería f.

pill, n. píldora f.

pillage, 1. n. pillaje m. 2. v. pillar.

pillar, n. columna f.

pillow, n. almohada f.

pillowcase, n. funda de almohada f.

pilot, 1. n. piloto m. 2. v. pilotear.

pimple, n. grano m.

pin, 1. n. alfiler; broche m.; (mech.) clavija f. 2. v. prender. **p. up,** fijar.

pinch, 1. n. pellizco m. 2. v. pellizcar.

pine, 1. n. pino m. 2. v. **p. away,** languidecer. **p. for,** anhelar.

pineapple, n. piña f., ananá m.

pink, a. rosado.

pinnacle, n. pináculo m.; cumbre f.

pint, n. pinta f.

pioneer, n. pionero -ra.

pious, a. piadoso.

pipe, n. pipa f.; tubo; (of organ) cañón m.

piper, n. flautista m. & f.

piquant, a. picante.

pirate, n. pirata m.

pistol, n. pistola f.

piston, n. pistón m.

pit, n. hoyo m.; (fruit) hueso m.

pitch, 1. n. brea f.; grado de inclinación; (music) tono m.; 2. v. lanzar; (ship) cabecear.

pitchblende, n. pechblenda f.

pitcher, n. cántaro m.; (baseball) lanzador m.

pitchfork, n. horca f.; tridente m.

pitfall, n. trampa f., hoya cubierta f.

pitiful, a. lastimoso.

pitiless, a. cruel.

pity, 1. n. compasión, piedad f. **to be a p.,** ser lástima. 2. v. compadecer.

pivot, 1. n. espiga f., pivote m.; punto de partido m. 2. v. girar sobre un pivote.

pizza, n. pizza f.

placard, 1. n. cartel m. 2. v. fijar carteles.

placate, v. aplacar.

place, 1. n. lugar, sitio, puesto m. 2. v. colocar, poner.

placid, a. plácido.

plagiarism, n. plagio m.

plague, 1. n. plaga, peste f. 2. v. atormentar.

plain, 1. a. sencillo; puro; evidente. 2. n. llano m.

plaintiff, n. demandador -ra.

plan, 1. n. plan, propósito m. 2. v. planear; pensar. **p. on,** contar con.

plane, 1. n. plano; (tool) cepillo m. 2. v. allanar; acepillar.

planet, n. planeta m.

planetarium, n. planetario m.

plank, n. tablón m.

plant, 1. n. mata, planta f. 2. v. sembrar, plantar.

plantation, n. plantación f. **coffee p.,** cafetal m.

planter, n. plantador; hacendado m.

plasma, n. plasma m.

plaster, 1. n. yeso; emplasto m. 2. v. enyesar; emplastar.

plastic, a. plástico.

plate, 1. n. plato m.; plancha de metal. 2. v. planchear.

plateau, n. meseta f.

platform, n. plataforma f.

platinum, n. platino m.

platitude, n. perogrullada f.

platter, n. fuente f.; platel m.

plaudit, n. aplauso m.

plausible, a. plausible.

play, 1. n. juego m.; (theat.) pieza f. 2. v. jugar; (music) tocar; (theat.) representar. **p. a part,** hacer un papel.

player, n. jugador -ra; (music) músico m.; (theat.) actor m., actriz f.

playful, a. juguetón.

playground, n. campo de deportes; patio de recreo.

playmate, n. compañero -ra de juego.

playwright, n. dramaturgo m.

plea, n. ruego m.; súplica f.; (legal) declaración f.

plead, v. suplicar; declararse. **p. a case,** defender un pleito.

pleasant, a. agradable.

please, 1. v. gustar, agradar. **Pleased to meet you,** Mucho gusto en conocer a Vd. 2. adv. por favor. **Please . . .** Haga el favor de . . ., Tenga la bondad de . . ., Sírvase . . .

pleasure, n. gusto, placer m.

pleat, 1. n. pliegue m. 2. v. plegar.

plebiscite, n. plebiscito m.

pledge, 1. n. empeño m. 2. v. empeñar.

plentiful, a. abundante.

plenty, n. abundancia f. **p. of,** bastante. **p. more,** mucho más.

pleurisy, n. pleuritis f.

pliable, pliant, a. flexible.

pliers, *n.pl.* alicates *m.pl.*
plight, *n.* apuro, aprieto *m.*
plot, 1. *n.* conspiración; (of a story) trama; (of land) parcela *f.* **2.** *v.* conspirar; tramar.
plow, 1. *n.* arado *m.* **2.** *v.* arar.
pluck, 1. *n.* valor *m.* **2.** *v.* arrancar; desplumar.
plug, 1. *n.* tapón; (elec.) enchufe *m.* **spark p.,** bujía *f.* **2.** *v.* tapar.
plum, *n.* ciruela *f.*
plumage, *n.* plumaje *m.*
plumber, *n.* plomero *m.*
plume, *n.* pluma *f.*
plump, *a.* regordete.
plunder, 1. *n.* botín *m.;* despojos *m.pl.* **2.** *v.* saquear.
plunge, *v.* zambullir; precipitar.
plural, *a.* & *n.* plural *m.*
plus, *prep.* más.
plutocrat, *n.* plutócrata *m.* & *f.*
pneumatic, *a.* neumático.
pneumonia, *n.* pulmonía *f.*
poach, *v.* (eggs) escalfar; invadir; cazar en vedadado.
pocket, 1. *n.* bolsillo *m.* **2.** *v.* embolsar.
pocketbook, *n.* cartera *f.*
podiatry, *n.* podiatría *f.*
poem, *n.* poema *m.*
poet, *n.* poeta *m.*
poetic, *a.* poético.
poetry, *n.* poesía *f.*
poignant, *a.* conmovedor.
point, 1. *n.* punta *f.;* punto *m.* **2.** *v.* apuntar. **p. out,** señalar.
pointed, *a.* puntiagudo; directo.
pointless, *a.* inútil.
poise, 1. *n.* equilibrio *m.;* serenidad *f.* **2.** *v.* equilibrar; estar suspendido.
poison, 1. *n.* veneno *m.* **2.** *v.* envenenar.
poisonous, *a.* venenoso.
poke, *v.* empuje *m.,* hurgonada *f.* **2.** *v.* picar; haronear.
Poland, *n.* Polonia *f.*
polar, *a.* polar.
pole, *n.* palo; (geog.) polo *m.*
police, *n.* policía *f.*
policeman, *n.* policía *m.*
policy, *n.* política *f.* **insurance p.,** póliza de seguro.
Polish, *a.* & *n.* polaco *m.*
polish, 1. *n.* lustre *m.* **2.** *v.* pulir, lustrar.
polite, *a.* cortés.
politic, political, *a.* político.
politician, *n.* político *m.*
politics, *n.* política *f.*
poll, *n.* encuesta *f.;* (pl.) urnas *f.pl.*
pollen, *n.* polen *m.*
pollute, *v.* contaminar.
polo, *n.* polo *m.*
polygamy, *n.* poligamia *f.*
polygon, *n.* polígono *m.*
pomp, *n.* pompa *f.*
pompous, *a.* pomposo.
poncho, *n.* poncho *m.*
pond, *n.* charca *f.*
ponder, *v.* ponderar, meditar.

ponderous, *a.* ponderoso, pesado.
pontiff, *n.* pontífice *m.*
pontoon, *n.* pontón *m.*
pony, *n.* caballito *m.*
pool, *n.* charco *m.* **swimming p.,** piscina *f.*
poor, *a.* pobre; (not good) malo.
pop, *n.* chasquido *m.*
popcorn, *n.* maíz tostado *m.*
pope, *n.* papa *m.*
popular, *a.* popular.
popularity, *n.* popularidad *f.*
population, *n.* población *f.*
porcelain, *n.* porcelana *f.*
porch, *n.* pórtico *m.;* galería *f.*
pore, *n.* poro *m.*
pork, *n.* carne de puerco.
pornography, *n.* pornografía *f.*
porous, *a.* poroso, esponjoso.
port, *n.* puerto; (naut.) babor **m. p. wine,** oporto *m.*
portable, *a.* portátil.
portal, *n.* portal *m.*
portend, *v.* pronosticar.
portent, *n.* presagio *m.,* portento *m.*
porter, *n.* portero *m.*
portfolio, *n.* cartera *f.*
porthole, *n.* porta *f.*
portion, *n.* porción *f.*
portly, *a.* corpulento.
portrait, *n.* retrato *m.*
portray, *v.* pintar.
Portugal, *n.* Portugal *m.*
Portuguese, *a.* & *n.* portugués - sa.
pose, 1. *n.* postura; actitud *f.* **2.** *v.* posar. **p. as,** pretender ser.
position, *n.* posición *f.*
positive, *a.* positivo.
possess, *v.* poseer.
possession, *n.* posesión *f.*
possessive, *a.* posesorio.
possibility, *n.* posibilidad *f.*
possible, *a.* posible.
post, 1. *n.* poste; puesto *m.* **2.** *v.* fijar; situar; echar al correo.
postage, *n.* porte de correo. **p. stamp,** sello *m.*
postal, *a.* postal.
post card, tarjeta postal.
poster, *n.* cartel, letrero *m.*
posterior, *a.* posterior.
posterity, *n.* posteridad *f.*
postgraduate, *a.* postgraduado.
postmark, *n.* matasellos *m.*
post office, casa de correos.
postpone, *v.* posponer, aplazar.
postscript, *n.* posdata *f.*
posture, *n.* postura *f.*
pot, *n.* olla, marmita; (marijuana) marijuana, hierba *f.* **flower p.,** tiesto *m.*
potassium, *n.* potasio *m.*
potato, *n.* patata, papa *f.* **sweet p.,** batata *f.*
potent, *a.* potente, poderoso.
potential, *a.* & *n.* potencial *f.*
potion, *n.* poción *f.,* pócima *f.*
pottery, *n.* alfarería *f.*
pouch, *n.* saco *m.;* bolsa *f.*
poultry, *n.* aves de corral.

pound, 1. *n.* libra *f.* **2.** *v.* golpear.
pour, *v.* echar; verter; llover a cántaros.
poverty, *n.* pobreza *f.*
powder, 1. *n.* polvo *m.;* (gun) pólvora *f.* **2.** *v.* empolvar; pulverizar.
power, *n.* poder *m.;* potencia *f.*
powerful, *a.* poderoso, fuerte.
powerless, *a.* impotente.
practical, *a.* prático.
practically, *adv.* casi; prácticamente.
practice, 1. *n.* prática; costumbre; clientela *f.* **2.** *v.* practicar; ejercer.
practiced, *a.* experto.
practitioner, *n.* practicante *m.*
pragmatic, *a.* pragmática.
prairie, *n.* llanura; (So. Amer.) pampa *f.*
praise, 1. *n.* alabanza *f.* **2.** *v.* alabar.
prank, *n.* travesura *f.*
pray, *v.* rezar; (beg) rogar.
prayer, *n.* oración; súplica *f.;* ruego *m.*
preach, *v.* predicar; sermonear.
preacher, *n.* predicador *m.*
preamble, *n.* preámbulo *m.*
precarious, *a.* precario.
precaution, *n.* precaución *f.*
precede, *v.* preceder, anteceder.
precedent, *a.* & *n.* precedente *m.*
precept, *n.* precepto *m.*
precinct, *n.* recinto *m.*
precious, *a.* precioso.
precipice, *n.* precipicio *m.*
precipitate, *v.* precipitar.
precise, *a.* preciso, exacto.
precision, *n.* precisión *f.*
preclude, *v.* evitar.
precocious, *a.* precoz.
predatory, *a.* de rapiña, rapaz.
predecessor, *n.* predecesor, antecesor *m.*
predicament, *n.* dificultad *f.;* apuro *m.*
predict, *v.* pronosticar, predecir.
predilection, *n.* predilección *f.*
predispose, *v.* predisponer.
predominant, *a.* predominante.
prefabricate, *v.* fabricar de antemano.
preface, *n.* prefacio *m.*
prefer, *v.* preferir.
preferable, *a.* preferible.
preference, *n.* preferencia *f.*
prefix, 1. *n.* prefijo *m.* **2.** *v.* prefijar.
pregnant, *a.* preñada.
prehistoric, *a.* prehistórico.
prejudice, *n.* prejuicio *m.*
prejudiced, *a.* prejuiciado.
preliminary, *a.* preliminar.
prelude, *n.* preludio *m.*
premature, *a.* prematuro.
premeditate, *v.* premeditar.
premier, *n.* premer ministro.
première, *n.* estreno *m.*
premise, *n.* premisa *f.*

premium, n. premio m.

premonition, n. presentimiento m.

prenatal, a. prenatal.

preparation, n. preparativo m.; preparación f.

preparatory, a. preparatorio. p. to, antes de.

prepare, v. preparar.

preponderant, a. preponderante.

preposition, n. preposición f.

preposterous, a. prepóstero, absurdo.

prerequisite, n. requisito previo.

prerogative, n. prerrogativa f.

prescribe, v. prescribir; (med.) recetar.

prescription, n. prescripción; (med.) receta f.

presence, n. presencia f.; porte m.

present, 1. a. presente. to be present at, asistir a. 2. n. presente; (gift) regalo m. at p., ahora. for the p., por ahora. 3. v. presentar.

presentable, a. presentable.

presentation, n. presentación; introducción f.; (theat.) representación f.

presently, adv. luego; dentro de poco.

preservative, a. & n. preservativo m.

preserve, 1. n. conserva f.; (hunting) vedado m. 2. v. preservar.

preside, v. presidir.

presidency, n. presidencia f.

president, n. presidente -ta.

press, 1. n. prensa f. 2. v. apretar; urgir; (clothes) planchar.

pressing, a. urgente.

pressure, n. presión f.

pressure cooker, n. cocina de presión f.

prestige, n. prestigio m.

presume, v. presumir; suponer.

presumptuous, a. presumtuoso.

presuppose, v. presuponer.

pretend, v. fingir. p. to the throne, aspirar al trono.

pretense, n. pretensión f.; fingimiento m.

pretension, n. pretensión f.

pretentious, a. presumido.

pretext, n. pretexto m.

pretty, 1. a. bonito, lindo. 2. adv. bastante.

prevail, v. prevalecer.

prevailing, prevalent, a. predominante.

prevent, v. impedir; evitar.

prevention, n. prevención f.

preventive, a. preventivo.

preview, n. vista previa f.

previous, a. anterior, previo.

prey, n. presa f.

price, n. precio m.

priceless, a. sin precio.

prick, 1. n. punzada f. 2. v. punzar.

pride, n. orgullo m.

priest, n. sacerdote, cura m.

prim, a. severamente modesto.

primary, a. primario, principal.

prime, 1. a. primero. 2. n. flor f. 3. v. alistar.

prime minister, n. primer ministro m.

primitive, a. primitivo.

prince, n. príncipe m.

princess, n. princesa f.

principal, 1. a. principal. 2. n. principal; director m.

principle, n. principio m.

print, 1. n. letra f.; (art) grabado m. 2. v. imprimir, estampar.

printing, n. imprenta f.

printing press, n. prensa f.

printout, n. impreso producido por una computadora.

priority, n. prioridad, precedencia f.

prism, n. prisma m.

prison, n. prisión, cárcel f.

prisoner, n. prisionero, preso m.

privacy, n. soledad f.

private, 1. a. particular. 2. n. soldado raso. in p., en particular.

privation, n. privación f.

privet, n. ligustro m.

privilege, n. privilegio m.

privy, n. letrina f.

prize, 1. n. premio m. 2. v. apreciar, estimar.

probability, n. probabilidad f.

probable, a. probable.

probate, a. testamentario.

probation, n. prueba f.; probación f.; libertad condicional f.

probe, 1. n. indagación f. 2. v. indagar; tentar.

probity, n. probidad f.

problem, n. problema m.

procedure, n. procedimiento m.

proceed, v. proceder; proseguir.

process, n. proceso m.

procession, n. procesión f.

proclaim, v. proclamar, anunciar.

proclamation, n. proclamación f.; decreto m.

procrastinate, v. dilatar.

procure, v. obtener, procurar.

prodigal, n. & a. pródigo m.

prodigy, n. prodigio m.

produce, v. producir.

product, n. producto m.

production, n. producción f.

productive, a. productivo.

profane, 1. a. profano. 2. v. profanar.

profanity, n. profanidad f.

profess, v. profesar; declarar.

profession, n. profesión f.

professional, a. & n. profesional m.

professor, n. profesor -ra; catedrático m.

proficient, a. experto, proficiente.

profile, n. perfil m.

profit, 1. n. provecho m.; ventaja f.; (com.) ganancia f. 2. v. aprovechar; beneficiar.

profitable, a. provechoso, ventajoso, lucrativo.

profiteer, 1. n. explotador m. 2. v. explotar.

profound, a. profundo, hondo.

profuse, a. pródigo, profuso.

prognosis, n. pronóstico m.

program, n. programa m.

progress, 1. n. progresos m.pl. in p., en marcha. 2. v. progresar; marchar.

progressive, a. progresivo; progresista.

prohibit, v. prohibir.

prohibition, n. prohibición f.

prohibitive, a. prohibitivo.

project, 1. n. proyecto m. 2. v. proyectar.

projectile, n. proyectil m.

projection, n. proyección f.

projector, n. proyector m.

proliferation, n. proliferación f.

prolific, a. prolífico.

prologue, n. prólogo m.

prolong, v. prolongar.

prominent, a. prominente; eminente.

promiscuous, a. promiscuo.

promise, 1. n. promesa f. 2. v. prometer.

promote, v. fomentar; estimular; adelantar.

promotion, n. promoción f.; adelanto m.

prompt, 1. a. pronto; puntual. 2. v. impulsar; (theat.) apuntar.

promulgate, v. promulgar.

pronoun, n. pronombre m.

pronounce, v. pronunciar.

pronunciation, n. pronunciación f.

proof, n. prueba f.

proofread, v. corregir pruebas.

prop, 1. n. apoyo, m. 2. v. sostener.

propaganda, n. propaganda f.

propagate, v. propagar.

propel, v. propulsar.

propeller, n. hélice f.

propensity, n. tendencia f.

proper, a. propio; correcto.

property, n. propiedad f.

prophecy, n. profecía f.

prophesy, v. predecir, profetizar.

prophet, n. profeta m.

prophetic, a. profético.

propitious, a. propicio.

proponent, n. & a. proponente m.

proportion, n. proporción f.

proportionate, a. proporcionado.

proposal, n. propuesta; oferta f.; (marriage) declaración f.

propose, v. proponer; pensar; declararse.

proposition, n. proposición f.

proprietor, *n.* propietario, dueño *m.*

propriety, *n.* corrección *f.,* decoro *m.*

prosaic, *a.* prosaico.

proscribe, *v.* proscribir.

prose, *n.* prosa *f.*

prosecute, *v.* acusar, procesar.

prospect, *n.* perspectiva; esperanza *f.*

prospective, *a.* anticipado, presunto.

prosper, *v.* prosperar.

prosperity, *n.* prosperidad *f.*

prosperous, *a.* próspero.

prostitute, 1. *n.* prostituta *f.* **2.** *v.* prostituir. **3.** *a.* prostituido.

prostrate, 1. *a.* postrado. **2.** *v.* postrar.

protect, *v.* proteger; amparar.

protection, *n.* protección *f.;* amparo *m.*

protective, *a.* protector.

protector, *n.* protector *m.*

protégé, *n.* protegido -da.

protein, *n.* proteína *f.*

protest, 1. *n.* protesta *f.* **2.** *v.* protestar.

Protestant, *a. & n.* protestante *m.*

protocol, *n.* protocolo *m.*

proton, *n.* protón *m.*

protract, *v.* alargar, demorar.

protrude, *v.* salir fuera.

protuberance, *n.* protuberancia *f.*

proud, *a.* orgulloso.

prove, *v.* comprobar.

proverb, *n.* proverbio, refrán *m.*

provide, *v.* proporcionar; proveer.

provided, *conj.* con tal que.

providence, *n.* providencia *f.*

province, *n.* provincia *f.*

provincial, 1. *a.* provincial. **2.** *n.* provinciano -na.

provision, 1. *n.* provisión *f.;* (pl.) comestibles *m.pl.* **2.** *v.* abastecer.

provocation, *n.* provocación *f.*

provoke, *v.* provocar.

prowess, *n.* proeza *f.*

prowl, *v.* rondar.

proximity, *n.* proximidad *f.*

proxy, *n.* delegado *m.* **by p.,** mediante apoderado.

prudence, *n.* prudencia *f.*

prudent, *a.* prudente, cauteloso.

prune, *n.* circuela pasa.

pry, *v.* atisbar; curiosear; (mech.) alzaprimar.

psalm, *n.* salmo *m.*

pseudonym, *n.* seudónimo *m.*

psychedelic, *a.* psiquedélico.

psychiatrist, *n.* psiquiatra *m.*

psychiatry, *n.* psiquiatría *f.*

psychoanalysis, *n.* psicoanálisis *m.* or *f.*

psychological, *a.* psicológico.

psychology, *n.* psicología *f.*

psychosis, *n.* psicosis.

ptomaine, *n.* tomaína *f.*

public, *a. & n.* público *m.*

publication, *n.* publicación; revista *f.*

publicity, *n.* publicidad *f.*

publish, *v.* publicar.

publisher, *n.* editor *m.*

pudding, *n.* pudín *m.*

puddle, *n.* charco, lodazal *m.*

Puerto Rico, *n.* Puerto Rico *m.*

Puerto Rican, *a. & n.* puertorriqueño -ña.

puff, 1. *n.* soplo *m.;* (of smoke) bocanada *f.* **powder p.,** polvera *f.* **2.** *v.* jadear; echar bocanadas. **p. up,** hinchar; (fig.) engreír.

pugnacious, *a.* pugnaz.

pull, 1. *n.* tirón *m.;* (coll.) influencia *f.* **2.** *v.* tirar; halar.

pulley, *n.* polla *f.,* motón *m.*

pulmonary, *a.* pulmonar.

pulp, *n.* pulpa; (of fruit) carne *f.*

pulpit, *n.* púlpito *m.*

pulsar, *n.* pulsar *m.*

pulsate, *v.* pulsar.

pulse, *n.* pulso *m.*

pump, 1. *n.* bomba *f.* **2.** *v.* bombear. **p. up,** inflar.

pumpkin, *n.* calabaza *f.*

pun, *n.* juego de palabras.

punch, 1. *n.* puñetazo; (mech.) punzón; (beverage) ponche *m.* **2.** *v.* dar puñetazos; punzar.

punctual, *a.* puntual.

punctuate, *v.* puntuar.

puncture, 1. *n.* pinchazo *m.,* perforación *f.* **2.** *v.* pinchar, perforar.

pungent, *a.* picante, pungente.

punish, *v.* castigar.

punishment, *n.* castigo *m.*

punitive, *a.* punitivo.

puny, *a.* encanijado.

pupil, *n.* alumno -na; (anat.) pupila *f.*

puppet, *n.* muñeco *m.*

puppy, *n.* perrito *m.*

purchase, 1. *n.* compra *f.* **2.** *v.* comprar.

pure, *a.* puro.

purée, *n.* puré *m.*

purge, *v.* purgar.

purify, *v.* purificar.

puritanical, *a.* puritano.

purity, *n.* pureza *f.*

purple, 1. *a.* purpúreo. **2.** *n.* púrpura *f.*

purport, 1. *n.* significación *f.* **2.** *v.* significar.

purpose, *n.* propósito *m.* **on p.,** de propósito.

purse, *n.* bolsa *f.*

pursue, *v.* perseguir.

pursuit, *n.* caza; busca; ocupación *f.* **p. plane,** caza *m.*

push, 1. *n.* empuje; impulso *m.* **2.** *v.* empujar.

put, *v.* poner, colocar. **p. away,** guardar. **p. in,** meter. **p. off,** dejar. **p. on,** ponerse. **p. out,** apagar. **p. up with,** aguantar.

putrid, *a.* podrido.

puzzle, 1. *n.* enigma; rompecabe-

zas *m.* **2.** *v.* dejar perplejo. **p. out,** descifrar.

pyramid, *n.* pirámide *f.*

pyromania, *n.* piromanía *f.*

Q

quadrangle, *n.* cuandrángulo *m.*

quadraphonic, *a.* cuadrafónico.

quadruped, *a. & n.* cuadrúpedo *m.*

quail, 1. *n.* codorniz *f.* **2.** *v.* descorazonarse.

quaint, *a.* arcaico y curioso.

quake, 1. *n.* temblor *m.* **2.** *v.* temblar.

qualification, *n.* requisito *m.;* (pl.) preparaciones.

qualified, *a.* calificado, competente; preparado.

qualify, *v.* calificar, modificar; llenar los requisitos.

quality, *n.* calidad *f.*

quandary, *n.* incertidumbre *f.*

quantity, *n.* cantidad *f.*

quarantine, *n.* cuarentena *f.*

quarrel, 1. *n.* riña, disputa *f.* **2.** *v.* reñir, disputar.

quarry, *n.* cantera; (hunting) presa *f.*

quarter, *n.* cuarto *m.;* (pl.) vivienda *f.*

quarterly, 1. *a.* trimestral. **2.** *adv.* por cuartos.

quartet, *n.* cuarteto *m.*

quartz, *n.* cuarzo *m.*

quasar, *n.* quasar *m.*

quaver, *v.* temblar.

queen, *n.* reina *f.;* (chess) dama *f.*

queer, *a.* extraño, raro.

quell, *v.* reprimir.

quench, *v.* apagar.

query, 1. *n.* pregunta *f.* **2.** *v.* preguntar.

quest, *n.* busca *f.*

question, 1. *n.* pregunta; cuestión *f.* **q. mark,** signo de interrogación. **2.** *v.* preguntar; interrogar; dudar.

questionable, *a.* dudoso.

questionnaire, *n.* cuestionario *m.*

quick, *a.* rápido.

quicken, *v.* acelerar.

quicksand, *n.* arena movediza.

quiet, 1. *a.* quieto, tranquilo; callado. **to be q., keep q.,** callarse. **2.** *n.* calma; quietud *f.* **3.** *v.* tranquilizar. **q. down,** callarse; calmarse.

quilt, *n.* colcha *f.*

quinine, *n.* quinina *f.*

quintet, *n.* (mus.) quinteto *m.*

quip, 1. *n.* pulla *f.* **2.** *v.* echar pullas.

quit, *v.* dejar; renunciar a. **q. doing** (etc.) dejar de hacer (etc.).

quite, *adv.* bastante; completamente. **not q.,** no precisamente; no completamente.

quiver, 1. n. aljabe f.; temblor m. **2.** v. temblar.

quixotic, a. quijotesco.

quorum, n. quórum m.

quota, n. cuota f.

quotation, n. citación; (com.) cotización f. **q. marks,** comillas f.pl.

quote, v. citar; (com.) cotizar.

R

rabbi, n. rabí, rabino m.

rabbit, n. conejo m.

rabble, n. canalla f.

rabid, a. rabioso.

rabies, n. hidrofobia f.

race, 1. n. raza; carrera f. **2.** v. echar una carrera; correr de prisa.

rack, 1. n. (cooking) pesebre m.; (clothing) colgador m. **2.** v. atormentar.

racket, n. (noise) ruido m.; (tennis) raqueta f.; (graft) fraude organizado.

radar, n. radar m.

radiance, n. brillo m.

radiant, a. radiante.

radiate, v. irradiar.

radiation, n. irradiación f.

radiator, n. colorifero m.; (auto.) radiador m.

radical, a. & n. radical m.

radio, n. radio m. or f. **r. station,** estación radiodifusora.

radioactive, a. radioactivo.

radish, n. rábano m.

radium, n. radio m.

radius, n. radio m.

raffle, 1. n. rifa, lotería f. **2.** v. rifar.

raft, n. balsa f.

rafter, n. viga f.

rag, n. trapo m.

ragamuffin, n. galopín m.

rage, 1. n. rabia f. **2.** v. rabiar.

ragged, a. andrajoso; desigual.

raid, n. (mil.) correría f.

rail, n. baranda f.; carril m. **by r.,** por ferrocarril.

railroad, n. ferrocarril m.

rain, 1. n. lluvia f. **2.** v. llover.

rainbow, n. arco iris m.

raincoat, n. impermeable m.

rainfall, n. precipitación f.

rainy, a. lluvioso.

raise, 1. n. aumento m. **2.** v. levantar, alzar; criar.

raisin, n. pasa f.

rake, 1. n. rastro m. **2.** v. rastrillar.

rally, 1. n. reunión f. **2.** v. reunirse.

ram, n. carnero m.

ramble, v. vagar.

ramp, n. rampa f.

rampart, n. terraplén m.

ranch, n. rancho m.

rancid, a. rancio.

rancor, n. rencor m.

random, a. fortuito. **at r.,** a la ventura.

range, 1. n. extensión f.; alcan-

ce m.; estufa; sierra f.; terreno de pasto. **2.** v. recorrer; extenderse.

rank, 1. a. espeso; rancio. **2.** n. fila f.; grado, rango m. **3.** v. clasificar.

ransack, v. saquear.

ransom, 1. n. rescate m. **2.** v. rescatar.

rap, 1. n. golpecito m. **2.** v. golpear.

rapid, a. rápido.

rapport, n. armonía f.

rapture, n. éxtasis m.

rare, a. raro.

rascal, n. pícaro, bribón m.

rash, 1. a. temerario. **2.** n. erupción f.

raspberry, n. frambuesa f.

rat, n. rata f.

rate, 1. n. velocidad; tasa f.; precio m.; (of exchange; of interest) tipo m. **at any r.,** de todos modos. **2.** v. valuar.

rather, adv. bastante; más bien, mejor dicho.

ratify, v. ratificar.

ratio, n. razón; proporción f.

ration, 1. n. ración f. **2.** v. racionar.

rational, a. racional.

rattle, 1. n. ruido m.; matraca f. **r. snake,** culebra de cascabel. **2.** v. matraquear; rechinar.

raucous, a. ronco.

ravage, v. pillar; destruir; asolar.

rave, v. delirar; entusiasmarse.

ravel, v. deshilar.

raven, n. cuervo m.

ravenous, a. voraz.

raw, a. crudo; verde.

ray, n. rayo m.

rayon, n. rayón m.

razor, n. navaja de afeitar. **r. blade,** hoja de afeitar.

reach, 1. n. alcance m. **2.** v. alcanzar.

react, v. reaccionar.

reaction, n. reacción f.

reactionary, 1. a. reaccionario. **2.** n. (pol.) retrógrado m.

read, v. leer.

reader, n. lector m.; libro de lectura.

readily, adv. fácilmente.

reading, n. lectura f.

ready, a. listo, preparado; dispuesto.

real, a. verdadero; real.

realist, n. realista m. & f.

reality, n. realidad f.

realization, n. comprensión; realización f.

realize, v. darse cuenta de; realizar.

really, adv. de veras; en realidad.

realm, n. reino; dominio m.

reap, v. segar, cosechar.

rear, 1. a. posterior. **2.** n. parte posterior. **3.** v. criar; levantar.

reason, 1. n. razón; causa f.; motivo m. **2.** v. razonar.

reasonable, a. razonable.

reassure, v. calmar, tranquilizar.

rebate, n. rebaja f.

rebel, 1. n. rebelde m. & f. **2.** v. rebelarse.

rebellion, n. rebelión f.

rebellious, a. rebelde.

rebirth, n. renacimiento m.

rebound, v. repercutir; resaltar.

rebuff, 1. n. repulsa f. **2.** v. rechazar.

rebuke, 1. n. reprensión f. **2.** v. reprender.

rebuttal, n. refutación f.

recalcitrant, a. recalcitrante.

recall, v. recordar; acordarse de; hacer volver.

recapitulate, v. recapitular.

recede, v. retroceder.

receipt, n. recibo m.; (com., pl.) ingresos m.pl.

receive, v. recibir.

receiver, n. receptor m.

recent, a. reciente.

recently, adv. recién.

receptacle, n. receptáculo m.

reception, n. acogida; recepción f.

receptionist, n. recepcionista m. & f.

receptive, a. receptivo.

recess, n. nicho; retiro; recreo m.

recipe, n. receta f.

recipient, n. receptor, recipiente m.

reciprocate, v. corresponder; reciprocar.

recite, v. recitar.

reckless, a. descuidado; imprudente.

reckon, v. contar; calcular.

reclaim, v. reformar; (leg.) reclamar.

recline, v. reclinar; recostar.

recognition, n. reconocimiento m.

recognize, v. reconocer.

recoil, 1. n. culatada f. **2.** v. recular.

recollect, v. recordar, acordarse de.

recommend, v. recomendar.

recommendation, n. recomendación f.

recompense, 1. n. recompensa f. **2.** v. recompensar.

reconcile, v. reconciliar.

recondition, v. reacondicionar.

reconsider, v. considerar de nuevo.

reconstruct, v. reconstruir.

record, 1. n. registro; (sports) record m. **phonograph r.,** disco m. **2.** v. registrar.

record player, n. tocadiscos m.

recount, v. relatar; contar.

recover, v. recobrar; restablecerse.

recovery, n. recobro m.; recuperación f.

recruit, 1. n. recluta m. **2.** v. reclutar.

rectangle, *n.* rectángulo *m.*
rectify, *v.* rectificar.
recuperate, *v.* recuperar.
recur, *v.* recurrir.
recycle, *v.* reciclar.
red, *a.* rojo; colorado.
redeem, *v.* redimir, rescatar.
redemption, *n.* redención *f.*
reduce, *v.* reducir.
reduction, *n.* reducción *f.*
reed, *n.* caña *f.*, (S.A.) bejuco *m.*
reef, *n.* arrecife, escollo *m.*
reel, 1. *n.* aspa *f.*, carrete *m.* 2. *v.* aspar.
refer, *v.* referir.
referee, *n.* árbitro *m.*
reference, *n.* referencia *f.*
refill, 1. *n.* relleno *m.* 2. *v.* rellenar.
refine, *n.* refinar.
refinement, *n.* refinamiento *m.*; cultura *f.*
reflect, *v.* reflejar; reflexionar.
reflection, *n.* reflejo *m.*; reflexión *f.*
reflex, *a.* reflejo.
reform, 1. *n.* reforma *f.* 2. *v.* reformar.
reformation, *n.* reformación *f.*
refractory, *a.* refractorio.
refrain, 1. *n.* estribillo *m.* 2. *v.* abstenerse.
refresh, *v.* refrescar.
refreshment, *n.* refresco *m.*
refrigerator, *n.* refrigerador *m.*
refuge, *n.* refugio *m.*
refugee, *n.* refugiado -da.
refund, 1. *n.* reembolso *m.* 2. *v.* reembolsar.
refusal, *n.* negativa *f.*
refuse, 1. *n.* basura *f.* 2. *v.* negarse, rehusar.
refute, *v.* refutar.
regain, *v.* recobrar.
regal, *a.* real.
regard, 1. *n.* aprecio; respeto *m.* **with r. to,** con respecto a. 2. *v.* considerar; estimar.
regarding, *prep.* en cuanto a, acerca de.
regardless (of), a pesar de.
regent, *n.* regente *m.*
regime, *n.* régimen *m.*
regiment, 1. *n.* regimiento *m.* 2. *v.* regimentar.
region, *n.* región *f.*
register, 1. *n.* registro *m.* **cash r.,** caja registradora. 2. *v.* registrar; matricularse; (a letter) certificar.
registration, *n.* registro *m.*; matrícula *f.*
regret, 1. *n.* pena *f.* 2. *v.* sentir, lamentar.
regular, *a.* regular; ordinario.
regularity, *n.* regularidad *f.*
regulate, *v.* regular.
regulation, *n.* regulación *f.*
regulator, *n.* regulador *m.*
rehabilitate, *v.* rehabilitar.
rehearse, *v.* repasar; (theat.) ensayar.
reign, 1. *n.* reino, reinado *m.* 2. *v.* reinar.

reimburse, *v.* reembolsar.
rein, 1. *n.* rienda *f.* 2. *v.* refrenar.
reincarnation, *n.* reencarnación *f.*
reindeer, *n.* reno *m.*
reinforce, *v.* reforzar.
reinforcement, *n.* refuerzo *m.*; armadura *f.*
reiterate, *v.* reiterar.
reject, *v.* rechazar.
rejoice, *v.* regocijarse.
rejoin, *v.* reunirse con; replicar.
rejuvenate, *v.* rejuvenecer.
relapse, 1. *n.* recaída *f.* 2. *v.* recaer.
relate, *v.* relatar, contar; relacionar. **r. to,** llevarse bien con.
relation, *n.* relación *f.*; pariente *m.* & *f.*
relative, 1. *a.* relativo. 2. *n.* pariente *m.* & *f.*
relativity, *n.* relatividad *f.*
relax, *v.* descansar; relajar.
relay, 1. *n.* relevo *m.* 2. *v.* retransmitir.
release, 1. *n.* liberación *f.* 2. *v.* soltar.
relent, *v.* ceder.
relevant, *a.* pertinente.
reliability, *n.* veracidad *f.*
reliable, *a.* responsable; digno de confianza.
relic, *n.* reliquia *f.*
relief, *n.* alivio; (sculpture) relieve *m.*
relieve, *v.* aliviar.
religion, *n.* religión *f.*
religious, *a.* religioso.
relinquish, *v.* abandonar.
relish, 1. *n.* sabor; condimento *m.* 2. *v.* saborear.
reluctant, *a.* renuente.
rely, *v.* **r. on,** confiar en; contar con; depender de.
remain, 1. *n.* (pl.) restos *m.pl.* 2. *v.* quedar, permanecer.
remainder, *n.* resto *m.*
remark, 1. *n.* observación *f.* 2. *v.* observar.
remarkable, *a.* notable.
remedial, *a.* reparador.
remedy, 1. *n.* remedio *m.* 2. *v.* remediar.
remember, *v.* acordarse de, recordar.
remembrance, *n.* recuerdo *m.*
remind, *v.* **r. of,** recordar.
reminisce, *v.* pensar en o hablar de cosas pasadas.
remiss, *a.* remiso; flojo.
remit, *v.* remitir.
remorse, *n.* remordimiento *m.*
remote, *a.* remoto.
removal, *n.* alejamiento *m.*; eliminación *f.*
remove, *v.* quitar; remover.
renaissance, *n.* renacimiento *m.*
rend, *v.* hacer pedazos; separar.
render, *v.* dar; rendir; (theat.) interpretar.

rendezvous, *n.* cita *f.*
rendition, *n.* interpretación, rendición *f.*
renege, *v.* renunciar.
renew, *v.* renovar.
renewal, *n.* renovación; (com.) prórroga *f.*
renounce, *v.* renunciar a.
renovate, *v.* renovar.
renown, *n.* renombre *m.*, fama *f.*
rent, 1. *n.* alquiler *m.* 2. *v.* arrendar, alquilar.
repair, 1. *n.* reparo *m.* 2. *v.* reparar.
repatriate, *v.* repatriar.
repay, *v.* pagar; devolver.
repeat, *v.* repetir.
repel, *v.* repeler, repulsar.
repent, *v.* arrepentirse.
repentance, *n.* arrepentimiento *m.*
repercussion, *n.* repercusión *f.*
repertoire, *n.* repertorio *m.*
repetition, *n.* repetición *f.*
replace, *v.* reemplazar.
replenish, *v.* rellenar; surtir de nuevo.
reply, 1. *n.* respuesta *f.* 2. *v.* replicar; contestar.
report, 1. *n.* informe *m.* 2. *v.* informar, contar; denunciar; presentarse.
reporter, *n.* repórter, reportero *m.*
repose, 1. *n.* reposo *m.* 2. *v.* reposar; reclinar.
reprehensible, *a.* reprensible.
represent, *v.* representar.
representation, *n.* representación *f.*
representative, 1. *a.* representativo. 2. *n.* representante *m.*
repress, *v.* reprimir.
reprimand, 1. *n.* regaño *m.* 2. *v.* regañar.
reprisal, *n.* represalia *f.*
reproach, 1. *n.* reproche *m.* 2. *v.* reprochar.
reproduce, *v.* reproducir.
reproduction, *n.* reproducción *f.*
reproof, *n.* censura *f.*
reprove, *v.* censurar, regañar.
reptile, *n.* reptil *m.*
republic, *n.* república *f.*
republican, *a.* & *n.* republicano -na.
repudiate, *v.* repudiar.
repulsive, *a.* repulsivo, repugnante.
reputation, *n.* reputación; fama *f.*
repute, 1. *n.* reputación *f.* 2. *v.* reputar.
request, 1. *n.* súplica *f.*, ruego *m.* 2. *v.* pedir; rogar, suplicar.
require, *v.* requerir; exigir.
requirement, *n.* requisito *m.*
requisite, 1. *a.* necesario. 2. *n.* requisito *m.*
requisition, *n.* requisición *f.*
rescind, *v.* rescindir, anular.
rescue, 1. *n.* rescate *m.* 2. *v.* rescatar.

research, *n.* investigación *f.*

resemble, *v.* parecerse a, asemejarse a.

resent, *v.* resentirse de.

reservation, *n.* reservación *f.*

reserve, 1. *n.* reserva *f.* **2.** *v.* reservar.

reservoir, *n* depósito; tanque *m.*

reside, *v.* residir, morar.

residence, *n.* residencia, morada *f.*

resident, *n.* residente *m. & f.*

residue, *n.* residuo *m.*

resign, *v.* dimitir; resignar.

resignation, *n.* dimisión, resignación *f.*

resist, *v.* resistir.

resistance, *n.* resistencia *f.*

resolute, *a.* resuelto.

resolution, *n.* resolución *f.*

resolve, *v.* resolver.

resonant, *a.* resonante.

resort, 1. *n.* recurso; expediente **summer r.,** lugar de veraneo. **2.** *v.* acudir, recurrir.

resound, *v.* resonar.

resource, *n.* recurso *m.*

respect, 1. *n.* respeto *m.* **with r. to,** con respecto a. **2.** *v.* respetar.

respectable, *a.* respetable.

respectful, *a.* respetuoso.

respective, *a.* respectivo.

respiration, *n.* respiración *f.*

respite, *n.* pausa, tregura *f.*

respond, *v.* responder.

response, *n.* respuesta *f.*

responsibility, *n.* responsabilidad *f.*

responsible, *a.* responsable.

responsive, *a.* respondiente, sensible.

rest, 1. *n.* descanso; reposo *m.;* (music) pausa *f.* **the r.,** el resto, lo demás; los demás. **2.** *v.* descansar; rocostar.

restaurant, *n.* restaurante *m.*

restful, *a.* tranquilo.

restitution, *n.* restitución *f.*

restless, *a.* inquieto.

restoration, *n.* restauración *f.*

restore, *v.* restaurar.

restrain, *v.* refrenar.

restraint, *n.* limitación, restricción *f.*

restrict, *v.* restringir, limitar.

result, 1. *n.* resultado *m.* **2.** *v.* resultar.

resume, *v.* reasumir; empezar de nuevo.

resurgent, *a.* resurgente.

resurrect, *v.* resucitar.

retail, *n.* at **r.,** al por menor.

retain, *v.* retener.

retaliate, *v.* vengarse.

retard, *v.* retardar.

retention, *n.* retención *f.*

reticent, *a.* reticente.

retire, *v.* retirar.

retort, 1. *n.* réplica; (chem.) retorta *f.* **2.** *v.* replicar.

retreat, 1. *n.* retiro *m.;* (mil.) retirada, retreta *f.* **2.** *v.* retirarse.

retribution, *n.* retribución *f.*

retrieve, *v.* recobrar.

return, 1. *n.* vuelta *f.,* regreso; retorno *m.* **by r. mail,** a vuelta de correo. **2.** *v.* volver, regresar; devolver.

reunion, *n.* reunión *f.*

reveal, *v.* revelar.

revelation, *n.* revelación *f.*

revenge, *n.* venganza *f.* **to get r.,** vengarse.

revenue, *n.* renta *f.*

revere, *v.* reverenciar, venerar.

reverence, 1. *n.* reverencia *f.* **2.** *v.* reverenciar.

reverend, 1. *a.* reverendo. **2.** *n.* pastor *m.*

reverent, *a.* reverente.

reverse, 1. *a.* inverso. **2.** *n.* revés, inverso *m.* **3.** *v.* invertir; revocar.

revert, *v.* revertir.

review, 1. *n.* repaso *m.;* revista *f.* **2.** *v.* repasar; revistar.

revise, *v.* revisar.

revision, *n.* revisión *f.*

revival, *n.* reavivamiento *m.*

revive, *v.* avivar; revivir.

revoke, *v.* revocar.

revolt, 1. *n.* rebelión *f.* **2.** *v.* rebelarse.

revolution, *n.* revolución *f.*

revolutionary, *a. & n.* revolucionario -ria.

revolve, *v.* girar; dar vueltas.

revolver, *n.* revólver *m.*

reward, 1. *n.* pago *m.;* recompensa *f.* **2.** *v.* recompensar.

rhetoric, *n.* retórica *f.*

rheumatism, *n.* reumatismo *m.*

rhinoceros, *n.* rinoceronte *m.*

rhyme, 1. *n.* rima *f.* **2.** *v.* rimar.

rhythm, *n.* ritmo *m.*

rhythmical, *a.* rítmico.

rib, *n.* costilla *f.*

ribbon, *n.* cinta *f.*

rice, *n.* arroz *m.*

rich, *a.* rico.

rid, *v.* librar. **get r. of,** deshacerse de, quitarse.

riddle, *n.* enigma; rompecabezas *m.*

ride, 1. *n.* paseo (a caballo o en coche) *m.* **2.** *v.* cabalgar; ir en coche.

ridge, *n.* cerro *m.;* arruga *f.;* (of a roof) caballete *m.*

ridicule, 1. *n.* ridículo *m.* **2.** *v.* ridiculizar.

ridiculous, *a.* ridículo.

rifle, 1. *n.* fusil *m.* **2.** *v.* robar.

rig, 1. *n.* aparejo *m.* **2.** *v.* aparejar.

right, 1. *a.* derecho; correcto. **to be r.,** tener razón. **2.** *adv.* bien, correctamente. **r. here,** etc., aquí mismo, etc. **all r.,** está bien, muy bien. **3.** *n.* derecho *m.;* justicia *f.* **to the r.,** a la derecha. **4.** *v.* corregir; enderezar.

righteous, *a.* justo.

rigid, *a.* rígido.

rigor, *n.* rigor *m.*

rigorous, *a.* riguroso.

rim, *n.* margen *m. or f.;* borde *m.*

ring, 1. *n.* anillo *m.;* sortija *f.;* círculo; campaneo *m.* **2.** *v.* cercar; sonar; tocar.

rinse, *v.* enjuagar, lavar.

riot, *n.* motín; alboroto *m.*

rip, 1. *n.* rasgadura *f.* **2.** *v.* rasgar; descoser.

ripe, *a.* maduro.

ripen, *v.* madurar.

ripoff, *n.* robo, atraco *m.*

ripple, 1. *n.* onda *f.* **2.** *v.* ondear.

rise, 1. *n.* subida *f.* **2.** *v.* ascender; levantarse; (moon) salir.

risk, 1. *n.* riesgo *m.* **2.** *v.* arriesgar.

rite, *n.* rito *m.*

ritual, *a. & n.* ritual *m.*

rival, *n.* rival *m. & f.*

rivalry, *n.* rivalidad *f.*

river, *n.* río *m.*

rivet, 1. *n.* remache, roblón *m.* **2.** *v.* remachar, roblar.

road, *n.* camino *m.;* carretera *f.*

roam, *v.* vagar.

roar, 1. *n.* rugido, bramido *m.* **2.** *v.* rugir, bramar.

roast, 1. *n.* asado *m.* **2.** *v.* asar.

rob, *v.* robar.

robber, *n.* ladrón -na.

robbery, *n.* robo *m.*

robe, *n.* manto *m.*

robin, *n.* petirrojo *m.*

robust, *a.* robusto.

rock, 1. *n.* roca *f.;* (music) rock *m.,* musica (de) rock *f.* **2.** *v.* mecer; oscilar.

rocker, *n.* mecedora *f.*

rocket, *n.* cohete *m.*

rocky, *a.* pedregoso.

rod, *n.* varilla *f.*

rodent, *n.* roedor *m.*

rogue, *n.* bribón, pícaro *m.*

roguish, *a.* pícaro.

role, *n.* papel *m.*

roll, 1. *n.* rollo *m.;* lista *f.;* panecillo *m.* **to call the r.,** pasar lista. **2.** *v.* rodar. **r. up,** enrollar.

roller, *n.* rodillo, cilindro *m.*

Roman, *a. & n.* romano -na.

romance, 1. *a.* romántico. **2.** *n.* romance *m.;* amorío *m.*

romantic, *a.* romántico.

romp, *v.* retozar; jugar.

roof, 1. *n.* techo *m.;* **2.** *v.* techar.

room, 1. *n.* cuarto *m.,* habitación *f.;* lugar *m.* **2.** *v.* alojarse.

roommate, *n.* compañero -ra de cuarto.

rooster, *n.* gallo *m.*

root, *n.* raíz *f.* **to take r.,** arraigar.

rope, *n.* cuerda, soga *f.*

rose, *n.* rosa *f.*

rosy, *a.* róseo, rosado.

rot, 1. *n.* putrefacción *f.* **2.** *v.* pudrirse.

rotary, *a.* giratorio; rotativo.

rotate, *v.* girar; alternar.

rotation, *n.* rotación *f.*

rotten, *a.* podrido.

rouge, *n.* colorete *m.*

rough, a. áspero; rudo; grosero; aproximado.

round, 1. a. rodondo. **r. trip,** viaje de ida y vuelta. **2.** n. ronda f.; (boxing) asalto m.

rouse, v. despertar.

rout, 1. n. derrota f. **2.** v. derrotar.

route, n. ruta, vía f.

routine, 1. a. rutinario. **2.** n. rutina f.

rove, v. vagar.

rover, n. vagabundo -da.

row, 1. n. fila; pelea f. **2.** v. (naut.) remar.

rowboat, n. bote de remos.

rowdy, a. alborotoso.

royal, a. real.

royalty, n. realeza f.; (pl.) regalías f.pl.

rub, v. frotar. **r. against,** rozar. **r. out,** borrar.

rubber, n. goma f.; caucho m.; (pl.) chanclos m.pl., zapatos de goma.

rubbish, n. basura f.; (nonsense) tonterías f.pl.

ruby, n. rubí m.

rudder, n. timón m.

ruddy, a. colorado.

rude, a. rudo; grosero; descortés.

rudiment, n. rudimento m.

rue, v. deplorar; lamentar.

ruffian, n. rufián, bandolero m.

ruffle, 1. n. volante fruncido. **2.** v. fruncir; irritar.

rug, n. alfombra f.

rugged, a. áspero; robusto.

ruin, 1. n. ruina f. **2.** v. arruinar.

ruinous, a. ruinoso.

rule, 1. n. regla f. **as a r., by** regla general. **2.** v. gobernar; mandar; rayar.

ruler, n. gobernante; soberano m.; regla f.

rum, n. ron m.

rumble, v. retumbar.

rumor, n. rumor m.

run, v. correr; hacer correr. **r. away,** escaparse. **r. into,** chocar con.

runner, n. corredor -ra; mensajero -ra.

rupture, 1. n. rotura; hernia f. **2.** v. reventar.

rural, a. rural, campestre.

rush, 1. n. prisa f.; (bot.) junco m. **2.** v. ir de prisa.

Russia, n. Rusia f.

Russian, a. & n. ruso -sa.

rust, 1. n. herrumbre m. **2.** v. aherrumbrarse.

rustic, a. rústico.

rustle, 1. n. susurro m. **2.** v. susurrar.

rusty, a. mohoso.

rut, n. surco m.

ruthless, a. cruel, inhumano.

rye, n. centeno m.

S

saber, n. sable m.

saber, n. sable m.

sable, n. cebellina f.

sabotage, n. sabotaje m.

sachet, n. perfumador m.

sack, 1. n. saco m. **2.** v. (mil.) saquear.

sacred, a. sagrado, santo.

sacrifice, 1. n. sacrificio m. **2.** v. sacrificar.

sacrilege, n. sacrilegio m.

sad, a. triste.

saddle, 1. n. silla de montar. **2.** v. ensillar.

safe, 1. a. seguro; salvo. **2.** n. caja de caudales.

safeguard, 1. n. salvaguardia m. **2.** v. proteger, poner a salvo.

safety, n. seguridad, protección f.

safety pin, n. imperdible m.

sage, 1. a. sabio, sagaz. **2.** n. sabio m.; (bot.) salvia f.

sail, 1. n. vela f.; paseo por mar. **2.** v. navegar; embarcarse.

sailboat, n. barco de vela.

sailor, n. marinero m.

saint, n. santo -ta.

sake, n. for the s. of, por; por el bien de.

salad, n. ensalada f. **s. bowl,** ensaladera f.

salary, n. sueldo, salario m.

sale, n. venta f.

salesman, n. vendedor m.; viajante de comercio.

sales tax, impuesto sobre la venta.

saliva, n. saliva f.

salmon, n. salmón m.

salt, 1. a. salado. **2.** n. sal f. **3.** v. salar.

salute, 1. n. saludo m. **2.** v. saludar.

salvage, v. salvar; recobrar.

salvation, n. salvación; redención f.

salve, n. emplasto, ungüento m.

same, a. & pron. mismo. **it's all the s.,** lo mismo da.

sample, 1. n. muestra f. **2.** v. probar.

sanatorium, n. sanatorio m.

sanctify, v. santificar.

sanction, 1. n. sanción f. **2.** v. sancionar.

sanctity, n. santidad f.

sanctuary, n. santuario, asilo m.

sand, n. arena f.

sandal, n. sandalia f.

sandwich, n. sandwich m.

sandy, a. arenoso; (color) rufo.

sane, a. cuerdo; sano.

sanitary, a. higiénico, sanitario.

sanitation, n. saneamiento m.

sanity, n. cordura f.

sap, 1. n. savia f.; (coll.) estúpido, bobo m. **2.** v. agotar.

sapphire, n. zafiro m.

sarcasm, n. sarcasmo m.

sardine, n. sardina f.

sash, n. cinta f.

satellite, n. satélite m.

satin, n. raso m.

satire, n. sátira f.

satisfaction, n. satisfacción; recompensa f.

satisfactory, a. satisfactorio.

satisfy, v. satisfacer. **be satisfied that . . . ,** estar convencido de que.

saturate, v. saturar.

Saturday, n. sábado m.

sauce, n. salsa; compota f.

saucer, n. platillo m.

saucy, a. descarado, insolente.

sausage, n. salchicha f.

savage, a. & n. salvaje m.

save, 1. v. salvar; guardar; ahorrar, economizar. **2.** prep. salvo, excepto.

savings, n. ahorros m.pl.

savior, n. salvador m.

savor, 1. n. sabor m. **2.** v. saborear.

savory, a. sabroso.

saw, 1. n. sierra f. **2.** v. aserrar.

say, v. decir; recitar.

saying, n. dicho, refrán m.

scaffold, n. andamio; (gallows) patíbulo f.

scald, v. escaldar.

scale, 1. n. escala; (of fish) escama f.; (pl.) balanza f. **2.** v. escalar; escamar.

scalp, 1. n. pericráneo m. **2.** v. escalpar.

scan, v. hojear, repasar; (poetry) escandir.

scandal, n. escándalo m.

scant, a. escaso.

scar, n. cicatriz f.

scarce, a. escaso; raro.

scarcely, adv. & conj. apenas.

scare, 1. n. susto m. **2.** v. asustar. **s. away,** espantar.

scarf, n. pañueleta, bufanda f.

scarlet, n. escarlata f.

scatter, v. esparcir; dispersar.

scavenger, n. basurero m.

scenario, n. escenario m.

scene, n. vista f., paisaje m.; (theat.) escena f. **behind the scenes,** bajo cuerda.

scenery, n. paisaje m.; (theat.) decorado m.

scent, 1. n. olor, perfume; (sense) olfato m. **2.** v. perfumar; (fig.) sospechar.

schedule, 1. n. programa, horario m. **2.** v. fijar la hora para.

scheme, 1. n. proyecto; esquema m. **2.** v. intrigar.

scholar, n. erudito; becado -da.

scholarship, n. beca; erudición f.

school, 1. n. escuela f.; colegio m.; (of fish) banco m. **2.** v. enseñar.

sciatica, n. ciática f.

science, n. ciencia f.

science fiction, n. ciencia ficción f.

scientific, a. científico.

scientist, n. científico -ca.

scissors, *n.* tijeras *f.pl.*

scoff, *v.* mofarse, burlarse.

scold, *v.* regañar.

scoop, 1. *n.* cucharón *m.;* cucharada *f.* 2. *v.* **s. out**, recoger, sacar.

scope, *n.* alcance; campo *m.*

scorch, 1. *n.* tantos *m.pl.;* (music) partitura *f.* 2. *v.* marcar, hacer tantos.

scorn, 1. *n.* desprecio *m.* 2. *v.* despreciar.

scornful, *a.* desdeñoso.

Scotch, *a.* escocés.

Scotland, *n.* Escocia *f.*

scour, *v.* fregar, estregar.

scourge, *n.* azote *m.;* plaga *f.*

scout, 1. *n.* explorador *m.* 2. *v.* explorar, reconocer.

scramble, 1. *n.* ribatiña *f.* 2. *v.* bregar. **scrambled eggs**, huevos revueltos.

scrap, 1. *n.* migaja *f.;* pedacito *m.;* (coll.) riña *f.* **s. metal**, hierro viejo. **s. paper**, papel borrador. 2. *v.* desechar; (coll.) reñir.

scrape, 1. *n.* lío, apuro *m.* 2. *v.* rascar; (feet) restregar.

scratch, 1. *n.* rasguño *m.* 2. *v.* rasguñar; rayar.

scream, 1. *n.* grito, chillido *m.* 2. *v.* gritar, chillar.

screen, *n.* biombo *m.;* (for window) tela metálica; (movie) pantalla *f.*

screw, 1. *n.* tornillo *m.* 2. *v.* atornillar.

screwdriver, *n.* destornillador *m.*

scribble, *v.* hacer garabatos.

scroll, *n.* rúbrica *f.;* rollo de papel.

scrub, *v.* gregar, estregar.

scruple, *n.* escrúpulo *m.*

scrupulous, *a.* escrupuloso.

sculptor, *n.* escultor *m.*

sculpture, 1. *n.* escultura *f.* 2. *v.* esculpir.

scythe, *n.* guadaña *f.*

sea, *n.* mar *m. or f.*

seabed, *n.* lecho marino *m.*

seal, 1. *n.* sello *m.;* (animal) foca *f.* 2. *v.* sellar.

seam, *n.* costura *f.*

seaport, *n.* puerto de mar.

search, 1. *n.* registro *m.* **in s. of**, en busca de. 2. *v.* registrar. **s. for**, buscar.

seasick, *a.* mareado. **to get s.**, marearse.

season, 1. *n.* estación; sazón, temporada *f.* 2. *v.* sazonar.

seasoning, *n.* condimento *m.*

seat, 1. *n.* asiento *m.;* residencia, sede *f.;* (theat.) localidad *f.* 2. *v.* sentar. **be seated**, sentarse.

second, 1. *a. & n.* segundo *m.* 2. *v.* apoyar, segundar.

secondary, *a.* secundario.

secret, *a. & n.* secreto *m.*

secretary, *n.* secretario -ria; (govt.) ministro *m.;* (furniture) papelera *f.*

sect, *n.* secta *f.;* partido *m.*

section, *n.* sección, parte *f.*

sectional, *a.* regional, local.

secular, *a.* secular.

secure, 1. *a.* seguro. 2. *v.* asegurar; obtener, conseguir; (fin.) garantizar.

security, *n.* seguridad; garantía *f.*

sedative, *a. & n.* sedativo *m.*

seduce, *v.* seducir.

see, *v.* ver; comprender. **s. off**, despedirse de. **s. to**, encargarse de.

seed, 1. *n.* semilla *f.* 2. *v.* sembrar.

seek, *v.* buscar. **s. to**, tratar de.

seem, *v.* parecer.

seep, *v.* colarse.

segment, *n.* segmento *m.*

segregate, *v.* segregar.

seize, *v.* agarrar; apoderarse de.

seldom, *adv.* rara vez.

select, 1. *a.* escogido, selecto. 2. *v.* elegir, seleccionar.

selection, *n.* selección *f.*

selective, *a.* escogedor.

selfish, *a.* egoísta.

selfishness, *n.* egoísmo *m.*

sell, *v.* vender.

semester, *n.* semestre *m.*

semicircle, *n.* semicírculo *m.*

senate, *n.* senado *m.*

senator, *n.* senador -ra.

send, *v.* mandar, enviar; (a wire) poner. **s. away**, despedir. **s. back**, devolver. **s. for**, mandar buscar. **s. off**, expedir. **s. word**, mandar recado.

senile, *a.* senil.

senior, *a.* mayor; más viejo. Sr., padre.

senior citizen, persona de edad.

sensation, *n.* sensación *f.*

sensational, *a.* sensacional.

sense, 1. *n.* sentido; juicio *m.* 2. *v.* percibir; sospechar.

sensible, *a.* sensato, razonable.

sensitive, *a.* sensible; sensitivo.

sensual, *a.* sensual.

sentence, 1. *n.* frase; (gram.) oración; (leg.) sentencia *f.* 2. *v.* condenar.

sentiment, *n.* sentimiento *m.*

sentimental, *a.* sentimental.

separate, 1. *a.* separado; suelto. 2. *v.* separar, dividir.

separation, *n.* separación *f.*

September, *n.* septiembre *m.*

sequence, *n.* serie *f.* **in s.**, seguidos.

serenade, 1. *n.* serenata *f.* 2. *v.* dar serenata a.

serene, *a.* sereno; tranquilo.

sergeant, *n.* sargento *m.*

serial, *a.* en serie, de serie.

series, *n.* serie *f.*

serious, *a.* serio; grave.

sermon, *n.* sermón *m.*

serpent, *n.* serpiente *f.*

servant, *n.* criado -da; servidor -ra.

serve, *v.* servir.

service, 1. *n.* servicio *m.* **at the s. of**, a las órdenes de. **to be of s.**, servir; ser útil. 2. *v.* (auto.) reparar.

session, *n.* sesión *f.*

set, 1. *a.* fijo. 2. *n.* colección *f.;* (of a game) juego; (mech.) aparato; (theat.) decorado *m.* 3. *v.* poner, colocar; fijar; (sun) ponerse. **s. forth**, exponer. **s. off**, **s. out**, salir. **s. up**, instalar; establecer.

settle, *v.* solucionar; arreglar; establecerse.

settlement, *n.* caserío; arreglo; acuerdo *m.*

settler, *n.* poblador -ra.

seven, *a. & pron.* siete.

seventeen, *a. & pron.* diecisiete.

seventh, *a.* séptimo.

seventy, *a. & pron.* setenta.

sever, *v.* desunir; romper.

several, *a. & pron.* varios.

severe, *a.* severo; grave.

severity, *n.* severidad *f.*

sew, *v.* coser.

sewer, *n.* cloaca *f.*

sex, *n.* sexo *m.*

sexism, *n.* sexismo *m.*

sexist, *a. & n.* sexista.

sexton, *n.* sacristán *m.*

sexual, *a.* sexual.

shabby, *a.* haraposo, desalineado.

shade, 1. *n.* sombra *f.;* tinte *m.;* (window) transparente *m.* 2. *v.* sombrear.

shadow, *n.* sombra *f.*

shady, *a.* sombroso; sospechoso.

shaft, *n.* columna; (mech.) asta *f.*

shake, *v.* sacudir; agitar; temblar. **s. hands with**, dar la mano a.

shallow, *a.* poco hondo; superficial.

shame, 1. *n.* vergüenza *f.* **to be a s.**, ser una lástima. 2. *v.* avergonzar.

shameful, *a.* vergonzoso.

shampoo, *n.* champú *m.*

shape, 1. *n.* forma *f.;* estado *m.* 2. *v.* formar.

share, 1. *n.* parte; (stock) acción *f.* 2 *v.* compartir.

shark, *n.* tiburón *m.*

sharp, *a.* agudo; (blade) afilado.

sharpen, *v.* aguzar; afilar.

shatter, *v.* estrellar; hacer pedazos.

shave, 1. *n.* afeitada *f.* 2. *v.* afeitarse.

shawl, *n.* rebozo, chal *m.*

she, *pron.* ella *f.*

sheaf, *n.* gavilla *f.*

shear, *v.* cizallar.

shears, *n.* cizallas *f.pl.*

sheath, *n.* vaina *f.*

shed, 1. *n.* cobertizo *m.* 2. *v.* arrojar, quitarse.

sheep, *n.* oveja *f.*

sheet, n. sábana; (of paper) hoja f.

shelf, n. estante, m., repisa f.

shell, 1. n. cáscara; (sea) concha f.; (mil.) proyectil m. 2. v. desgranar; bombardear.

shellac, n. laca f.

shelter, 1. n. albergue; refugio m. 2. v. albergar; amparar.

shepherd, n. pastor m.

sherry, n. jerez m.

shield, 1. n. escudo m. 2. v. amparar.

shift, 1. n. cambio; (work) turno m. 2. v. cambiar, mudar. s. **for oneself,** arreglárselas.

shine, 1. n. brillo, lustre m. 2. v. brillar; (shoes) lustrar.

shiny, a. brillante, lustroso.

ship, 1. n. barco m., nave f. 2. v. embarcar; (com.) enviar.

shipment, n. envío, embarque m.

shirk, v. faltar a.

shirt, n. camisa f.

shiver, 1. n. temblor m. 2. v. temblar.

shock, 1. n. choque m. 2. v. chocar.

shoe, n. zapato m.

shoelace, n. lazo m.; cordón de zapato.

shoemaker, n. zapatero m.

shoot, v. tirar; (gun) disparar. s. **away, s. off,** salir disparado.

shop, n. tienda f.

shopping, n. **to go s.,** hacer compras, ir de compras.

shore, n. orilla; playa f.

short, a. corto; breve; (in stature) pequeño, bajo. **a s. time,** poco tiempo. **in s.,** en suma.

shortage, n. escasez; falta f.

shorten, v. acortar, abreviar.

shortly, adv. en breve, dentro de poco.

shorts, n. calzoncillos m.pl.

shot, n. tiro, disparo m.

shoulder, 1. n. hombro m. 2. v. asumir; cargar con.

shout, 1. n. grito m. 2. v. gritar.

shove, 1. n. empujón m. 2. v. empujar.

shovel, 1. n. pala f. 2. v. traspalar.

show, 1. n. ostentación f.; (theat.) función f.; espectáculo m. 2. v. enseñar, mostrar; verse. s. **up,** destacarse; (coll.) asomar.

shower, n. chubasco m.; (bath) ducha f.

shrapnel, n. metralla f.

shrewd, a. astuto.

shriek, 1. n. chillido m. 2. v. chillar.

shrill, a. chillón, agudo.

shrimp, n. camarón m.

shrine, n. santuario m.

shrink, v. encogerse, contraerse, s. **from,** huir de.

shroud, 1. n. mortaja f. 2. v. (fig.) ocultar.

shrub, n. arbusto m.

shudder, 1. n. estremecimiento m. 2. v. estremecerse.

shun, v. evitar, huir de.

shut, v. cerrar. s. **in,** encerrar. s. **up,** (coll.) callarse.

shutter, n. persiana f.

shy, a. tímido, vergonzoso.

sick, a. enfermo. s. **of,** aburrido de, cansado de.

sickness, n. enfermedad f.

side, 1. n. lado; partido m.; parte f.; (anat.) costado m. v. s. **with,** ponerse del lado de.

sidewalk, n. acera, vereda f.

siege, n. asedio m.

sieve, n. cedazo m.

sift, v. cerner.

sigh, 1. n. suspiro m. 2. v. suspirar.

sight, n. vista f.; punto de interés. **to lose s. of,** perder de vista. 2. v. divisar.

sign, 1. n. letrero; señal, seña f. 2. v. firmar. s. **up,** inscribirse.

signal, 1. n. señal f. 2. v. hacer señales.

signature, n. firma f.

significance, n. significación f.

significant, a. significativo.

signify, v. significar.

silence, 1. n. silencio m. 2. v. hacer callar.

silent, a. silencioso; callado.

silk, n. seda f.

silken, silky, a. sedoso.

sill, n. umbral de puerta m., solera f.

silly, a. necio, tonto.

silo, n. silo m.

silver, n. plata f.

silverware, n. artículos de plata.

similar, a. semejante, parecido.

similarity, n. semejanza f.

simple, a. sencillo, simple.

simplicity, n. sencillez f.

simplify, v. simplificar.

simulate, v. simular.

simultaneous, a. simultáneo.

sin, 1. n. pecado m. 2. v. pecar.

since, 1. adv. desde entonces. 2. prep. desde. 3. conj. desde que; puesto que.

sincere, a. sincero.

sincerely, adv. sinceramente.

sincerity, n. sinceridad f.

sinew, n. tendón m.

sinful, a. pecador.

sing, v. cantar.

singe, v. chamuscar.

singer, n. cantante m. & f.

single, a. solo; (room) sencillo; (unmarried) soltero.

singular, a. & n. singular m.

sinister, a. siniestro.

sink, 1. n. fregadero m. 2. v. hundir; (fig.) abatir.

sinner, n. pecador -ra.

sinuous, a. sinuoso.

sinus, n. seno; hueco m.

sip, 1. n. sorbo m. 2. v. sorber.

siphon, n. sifón m.

sir, title. señor.

siren, n. sirena f.

sirloin, n. solomillo m.

sisal, n. henequén m.

sister, n. hermana f.

sister-in-law, n. cuñada f.

sit, v. sentarse; posar. **be sitting,** estar sentado. s. **down,** sentarse. s. **up,** incorporarse; quedar levantado.

site, n. sitio, local m.

sitting, n. sesión f.

situate, v. situar.

situation, n. situación f.

six, a. & pron. seis.

sixteen, a. & pron. dieciseis.

sixth, a. sexto.

sixty, a. & pron. sesenta.

size, n. tamaño; (of shoe, etc.) número m.

sizing, n. aderezo m.

skate, 1. n. patín m. 2. v. patinar.

skateboard, n. monopatín m.

skein, n. madeja f.

skeleton, n. esqueleto m.

skeptic, n. escéptico -ca.

skeptical, a. escéptico.

sketch, 1. n. esbozo m. 2. v. esbozar.

ski, 1. n. esquí m. 2. v. esquiar.

skid, 1. v. resbalar. 2. n. varadera f.

skill, n. destreza, habilidad f.

skillful, a. diestro, hábil.

skim, v. rasar; (milk) desnatar. s. **over, s. through,** hojear.

skin, 1. n. piel; (of fruit) corteza f. 2. v. desollar.

skip, 1. n. brinco m. 2. v. brincar. s. **over,** pasar por alto.

skirmish, n. escaramuza f.

skirt, n. falda f.

skull, n. cráneo m.

skunk, n. zorrillo m.

sky, n. cielo m.

skylight, n. tragaluz m.

skyscraper, n. rascacielos m.

slab, n. tabla f.

slack, a. flojo; descuidado.

slacken, v. relajar.

slacks, n. pantalones flojos.

slam, 1. n. portazo m. 2. v. cerrar de golpe.

slander, 1. n. calumnia f. 2. v. calumniar.

slang, n. jerga f.

slant, 1. n. sesgo m. 2. v. sesgar.

slap, 1. n. bofetada, palmada f. 2. v. dar una bofetada.

slash, 1. n. cuchillada f. 2. v. acuchillar.

slat, 1. n. tablilla f. 2. v. lanzar.

slate, 1. n. pizarra f.; lista de candidatos. 2. n. destinar.

slaughter, 1. n. matanza f. 2. v. matar.

slave, n. esclavo -va.

slavery, n. esclavitud f.

Slavic, a. eslavo.

slay, v. matar, asesinar.

sled, n. trineo m.

sleek, a. liso.

sleep, 1. n. sueño m. **to get much s.,** dormir mucho. 2. v. dormir.

sleeper, sleeping car, n. coche cama.

sleepy, *a.* soñoliento. **to be s.,** tener sueño.

sleet, 1. *n.* cellisca *f.* 2. *v.* cellisquear.

sleeve, *n.* manga *f.*

sleigh, *n.* trineo *m.*

slender, *a.* delgado.

slice, 1. *n.* rebanada; (of meat) tajada *f.* 2. *v.* rebanar; tajar.

slide, *v.* resbalar, deslizarse.

slide rule, *n.* regla de cálculo *f.*

slight, 1. *n.* desaire *m.* 2. *a.* pequeño; leve. 3. *v.* desairar.

slim, *a.* delgado.

slime, *n.* lama *f.*

sling, 1. *n.* honda *f.;* (med.) cabestrillo *m.* 2. *v.* tirar.

slink, *v.* escabullirse.

slip, 1. *n.* imprudencia; (garment) combinación *f.;* (of paper) trozo *m.;* ficha *f.* 2. *v.* resbalar; deslizar. **s. up,** equivocarse.

slipper, *n.* chinela *f.*

slippery, *a.* resbaloso.

slit, 1. *n.* abertura *f.* 2. *v.* cortar.

slogan, *n.* lema *m.*

slope, 1. *n.* declive *m.* 2. *v.* inclinarse.

sloppy, *a.* desaliñado, chapucero.

slot, *n.* ranura *f.*

slot machine, *n.* máquina de servicio automático *f.*

slouch, 1. *n.* patán *m.* 2. *v.* estar gacho.

slovenly, *a.* desaliñado.

slow, 1. *a.* lento; (watch) atrasado. 2. *v.* **s. down, s. up,** retardar; ir más despacio.

slowly, *adv.* despacio.

slowness, *n.* lentitud *f.*

sluggish, *a.* perezoso, inactivo.

slum, *n.* barrio bajo *m.*

slumber, *v.* dormitar.

slur, 1. *n.* estigma *m.* 2. *v.* menospreciar.

slush, *n.* fango *m.*

sly, *a.* taimado. **on the s.** a hurtadillas.

smack, 1. *n.* manotada *f.* 2. *v.* manotear.

small, *a.* pequeño.

smallpox, *n.* viruela *f.*

smart, 1. *a.* listo; elegante. 2. *v.* escocer.

smash, *v.* aplastar; hacer pedazos.

smear, 1. *n.* mancha; difamación *f.* 2. *v.* manchar; difamar.

smell, 1. *n.* olor; (sense) olfato *m.* 2. *v.* oler.

smelt, 1. *n.* eperlano *m.* 2. *v.* fundir.

smile, 1. *n.* sonrisa *f.* 2. *v.* sonreír.

smite, *v.* afligir; apenar.

smock, *n.* camisa de mujer *f.*

smoke, 1. *n.* humo *m.* 2. *v.* fumar; (food) ahumar.

smokestack, *n.* chimenea *f.*

smolder, *v.* arder sin llama.

smooth, 1. *a.* liso; suave; tranquilo. 2. *v.* alisar.

smother, *v.* sofocar.

smug, *a.* presumido.

smuggle, *v.* pasar de contrabando.

snack, *n.* bocadillo *m.*

snag, *n.* nudo *m.*, obstáculo *m.*

snail, *n.* caracol *m.*

snake, *n.* culebra, serpiente *f.*

snap, 1. *n.* trueno *m.* 2. *v.* tronar, romper.

snapshot, *n.* instantánea *f.*

snare, *n.* trampa *f.*

snarl, 1. *n.* gruñido *m.* 2. *v.* gruñir; (hair) enredar.

snatch, *v.* arrebatar.

sneak, *v.* ir, entrar, salir (etc.) a hurtadillas.

sneaker, *n.* sujeto ruín *m.*

sneer, 1. *n.* mofa *f.* 2. *v.* mofarse.

sneeze, 1. *n.* estornudo *m.* 2. *v.* estornudar.

snicker, *n.* risita *m.*

snob, *n.* esnob *m.*

snore, 1. *n.* ronquido *m.* 2. *v.* roncar.

snow, 1. *n.* nieve *f.* 2. *v.* nevar.

snowdrift, *n.* ventisquero *m.*

snub, *v.* desairar.

snug, *a.* abrigado y cómodo.

so, 1. *adv.* así; (also) también. **so as to,** para. **so that,** para que. **so . . . as,** tan . . . como. **so . . . that,** tan . . . que. 2. *conj.* así es que.

soak, *v.* empapar.

soap, 1. *n.* jabón *m.* 2. *v.* enjabonar.

soar, *v.* remontarse.

sob, 1. *n.* sollozo *m.* 2. *v.* sollozar.

sober, *a.* sobrio; pensativo.

sociable, *a.* sociable.

social, 1. *a.* social. 2. *n.* tertulia *f.*

socialism, *n.* socialismo *m.*

socialist, *a.* & *n.* socialista *m.*

society, *n.* sociedad; compañía *f.*

sociology, *n.* sociología *f.*

sock, 1. *n.* calcetín; puñetazo *m.* 2. *v.* dar un puñetazo a.

socket, *n.* cuenca *f.;* (elec.) enchufe *m.*

sod, *n.* césped *m.*

soda, *n.* soda; (chem.) sosa *f.*

sodium, *n.* sodio *m.*

sofa, *n.* sofá *m.*

soft, *a.* blando; fino; suave.

soft drink, *n.* bebida no alcohólica *m.*

soften, *v.* ablandar; suavizar.

soil, 1. *n.* suelo *m.;* tierra *f.* 2. *v.* ensuciar.

sojourn, *n.* morada *f.*, estandia *f.*

solace, 1. *n.* solaz *m.* 2. *v.* solazar.

solar, *a.* solar.

solar system, *n.* sistema solar *m.*

solder, 1. *v.* soldar. 2. *n.* soldadura *f.*

soldier, *n.* soldado *m.*

sole, 1. *n.* suela; (of foot) planta *f.;* (fish) lenguado *m.* 2. *a.* único.

solemn, *a.* solemne.

solemnity, *n.* solemnidad *f.*

solicit, *v.* solicitar.

solicitous, *a.* solícito.

solid, *a.* & *n.* sólido *m.*

solidify, *v.* solidificar.

solidity, *n.* solidez *f.*

solitary, *a.* solitario.

solitude, *n.* soledad *f.*

solo, *n.* solo *m.*

soloist, *n.* solista *m.*

soluble, *a.* soluble.

solution, *n.* solución *f.*

solve, *v.* solucionar; resolver.

solvent, *a.* solvente.

somber, *a.* sombrío.

some, *a.* & *pron.* algo (de), un poco (de); alguno; (pl.) unos, unos.

somebody, someone, *pron.* alguien.

somehow, *adv.* de algún modo.

someone, *n.* alguien o alguno.

somersault, *n.* salto mortal *m.*

something, *pron.* algo, alguna cosa.

sometime, *adv.* alguna vez.

sometimes, *adv.* a veces, algunas veces.

somewhat, *adv.* algo, un poco.

somewhere, *adv.* en (or a) alguna parte.

son, *n.* hijo *m.*

song, *n.* canción *f.*

son-in-law, *n.* yerno *m.*

soon, *adv.* pronto. **as s. as possible,** cuanto antes. **sooner or later,** tarde o temprano. **no sooner . . . than,** apenas . . . cuando.

soot, *n.* hollín *m.*

soothe, *v.* calmar.

soothingly, *adv.* tiernamente.

sophisticated, *a.* sofisticado.

sophomore, *n.* estudiante de segundo año *m.*

soprano, *n.* soprano *m.* & *f.*

sorcery, *n.* encantamiento *m.*

sordid, *a.* sórdido.

sore, 1. *n.* llaga *f.* 2. *a.* lastimado; (coll.) enojado. **to be s.,** doler.

sorority, *n.* hermandad de mujeres *f.*

sorrow, *n.* pesar, dolor *m.*, aflicción *f.*

sorrowful, *a.* doloroso; afligido.

sorry, *a.* **to be s.,** sentir, lamentar. **to be s. for,** compadecer.

sort, 1. *n.* tipo *m.;* clase, especie *f.* **s. of,** algo, un poco. 2. *v.* clasificar.

soul, *n.* alma *f.*

sound, 1. *a.* sano; razonable; firme. 2. *n.* sonido *m.* 3. *v.* sonar; parecer.

soup, *n.* sopa *f.*

sour, *a.* agrio; ácido; rancio.

source, *n.* fuente *f.;* causa *f.*

south, *n.* sur *m.*

South America, *n.* Sud América, América del Sur.

South American, *a. & n.* sudamericano -na.

southeast, *n.* sudeste *m.*

southern, *a.* meridional.

South Pole, *n.* polo sur *m.*

southwest, *n.* sudoeste *m.*

souvenir, *n.* recuerdo *m.*

sovereign, *n.* soberano *m.*

sovereignty, *n.* soberanía *f.*

Soviet Russia, *n.* Rusia Soviética *f.*

sow, 1. *n.* puerca *f.* **2.** *v.* sembrar.

space, 1. *n.* espacio *m.* **2.** *v.* espaciar.

space shuttle, *n.* vehículo que comunica a dos naves espaciales.

spacious, *a.* espacioso.

spade, 1. *n.* laya; (cards) espada *f.* **2.** *v.* layar.

spaghetti, *n.* fideo *m.*

Spain, *n.* España *f.*

span, 1. *n.* tramo *m.* **2.** *v.* extenderse sobre.

Spaniard, *n.* español -la.

Spanish, *a. & n.* español *m.*

spank, *v.* pegar.

spanking, *n.* tunda, zumba *f.*

spar, *v.* altercar.

spare, 1. *a.* de respuesto. **2.** *v.* perdonar; ahorrar; prestar. **have . . . to s.,** tener . . . de sobra.

spark, *n.* chispa *f.*

sparkle, 1. *n.* destello *m.* **2.** *v.* chispear. **sparkling wine,** vino espumoso.

spark plug, *n.* bujía *f.*

sparrow, *n.* gorrión *m.*

sparse, *a.* esparcido.

spasm, *n.* espasmo *m.*

spasmodic, *a.* espasmódico.

spatter, *v.* salpicar; manchar.

speak, *v.* hablar.

speaker, *n.* conferencista *m. & f.*

spear, *n.* lanza *f.*

special, *a.* especial. **s. delivery,** entrega inmediata, entrega urgente.

specialist, *n.* especialista *m. & f.*

specialty, *n.* especialidad *f.*

species, *n.* especie *f.*

specific, *a.* específico.

specify, *v.* especificar.

specimen, *n.* espécimen *m.;* muestra *f.*

spectacle, *n.* espectáculo *m.;* (pl.) lentes, anteojos *m.pl.*

spectacular, *a.* espectacular, aparatoso.

spectator, *n.* espectador -ra.

spectrum, *n.* espectro *m.*

speculate, *v.* especular.

speculation, *n.* especulación *f.*

speech, *n.* habla *f.;* lenguaje; discurso *m.* **part of s.,** parte de la oración.

speechless, *a.* mudo.

speed, 1. *n.* velocidad; rapidez

f. **2.** *v.* **s. up,** acelerar, apresurar.

speedometer, *n.* velocímetro *m.*

speedy, *a.* veloz, rápido.

spell, 1. *n.* hechizo; rato; (med.) ataque *m.* **2.** *v.* escribir; relevar.

spelling, *n.* ortografía *f.*

spend, *v.* gastar; (time) pasar.

spendthrift, *n.* pródigo; manirroto *m.*

sphere, *n.* esfera *f.*

spice, 1. *n.* especia *f.* **2.** *v.* especiar.

spider, *n.* araña *f.*

spike, *n.* alcayata *f.*

spill, *v.* derramar.

spillway, *n.* vertedero *m.*

spin, *v.* hilar; girar.

spinach, *n.* espinaca *f.*

spine, *n.* espinazo *m.*

spinet, *n.* espineta *m.*

spinster, *n.* solterona *f.*

spiral, *a. & n.* espiral *m.*

spire, *n.* caracol *m.,* espira *f.*

spirit, *n.* espíritu; ánimo *m.*

spiritual, *a.* espiritual.

spiritualism, *n.* espiritismo *m.*

spit, *v.* escupir.

spite, *n.* despecho *m.* **in s. of,** a pesar de.

splash, 1. *n.* salpicadura *f.* **2.** *v.* salpicar.

splendid, *a.* espléndido.

splendor, *n.* esplendor *m.*

splice, 1. *v.* empalmar. **2.** *n.* empalme *m.*

splint, *n.* tablilla *f.*

splinter, 1. *n.* astilla *f.* **2.** *v.* astillar.

split, 1. *n.* división *f.* **2.** *v.* dividir, romper en dos.

splurge, 1. *v.* fachendear. **2.** *n.* fachenda *f.*

spoil, 1. *n.* (pl.) botín *m.* **2.** *v.* echar a perder; (a child) mimar.

spoke, *n.* rayo (de rueda) *m.*

spokesman, *n.* interlocutor *m.*

sponge, *n.* esponja *f.*

sponsor, 1. *n.* patrocinador *m.* **2.** *v.* patrocinar; costear.

spontaneity, *n.* espontaneidad *f.*

spontaneous, *a.* espontáneo.

spool, *n.* carrete *m.*

spoon, *n.* cuchara *f.*

spoonful, *n.* cucharada *f.*

sporadic, *a.* esporádico.

sport, *n.* deporte *m.*

sportsman, 1. *a.* deportivo. **2.** *n.* deportista *m.*

spot, 1. *n.* mancha *f.;* lugar, punto *m.* **2.** *v.* distinguir.

spouse, *n.* esposo (o esposa) *m.* or *f.*

spout, 1. *n.* chorro; (of teapot) pico *m.* **2.** *v.* correr a chorro.

sprain, 1. *n.* torcedura *f.* **2.** *v.* torcerse.

sprawl, *v.* tenderse.

spray, 1. *n.* rociada *f.* **2.** *v.* rociar.

spread, 1. *n.* propagación; ex-

tensión; (for bed) colcha *f.* **2.** *v.* propagar; extender.

spree, *n.* parranda *f.*

sprig, *n.* ramita *f.*

sprightly, *a.* garboso.

spring, *n.* resorte, muelle *m.;* (season) primavera *f.;* (of water) manantial *m.*

springboard, *n.* trampolín *m.*

sprinkle, *v.* rociar; (rain) lloviznar.

sprint, *n.* carrera *f.*

sprout, *n.* retoño *m.*

spry, *a.* ágil.

spun, *a.* hilado.

spur, 1. *n.* espuela *f.* **on the s. of the moment,** sin pensarlo. **2.** *v.* espolear.

spurious, *a.* espurio.

spurn, *v.* rechazar, despreciar.

spurt, 1. *n.* chorro *m.;* esfuerzo supremo. **2.** *v.* salir en chorro.

spy, 1. *n.* espía *m. & f.* **2.** *v.* espiar.

squabble, 1. *n.* riña *f.* **2.** *v.* reñir.

squad, *n.* escuadra *f.*

squadron, *n.* escuadrón *m.*

squalid, *a.* escuálido.

squall, *n.* borrasca *f.*

squalor, *n.* escualidez *f.*

squander, *v.* malgastar.

square, 1. *a.* cuadrado. **2.** *n.* cuadrado *m.;* plaza *f.*

square dance, *n.* contradanza *f.*

squat, *v.* agacharse.

squeak, 1. *n.* chirrido *m.* **2.** *v.* chirriar.

squeamish, *a.* escrupuloso.

squeeze, 1. *n.* apretón *m.* **2.** *v.* apretar; (fruit) exprimir.

squirrel, *n.* ardilla *f.*

squirt, 1. *n.* chisguete *m.* **2.** *v.* jeringar.

stab, 1. *n.* puñalada *f.* **2.** *v.* apuñalar.

stability, *n.* estabilidad *f.*

stabilize, *v.* estabilizar.

stable, 1. *a.* estable, equilibrado. **2.** *n.* caballeriza *f.*

stack, 1. *n.* pila *f.* **2.** *v.* apilar.

stadium, *n.* estadio *m.*

staff, *n.* personal *m.* **editorial s.,** cuerpo de redacción. **general s.,** estado mayor.

stag, *n.* ciervo *m.*

stage, 1. *n.* etapa *f.;* (theat.) escena *f.* **2.** *v.* representar.

stagger, *v.* tambalear.

stagnant, *a.* estancado.

stagnate, *v.* estancarse.

stain, 1. *n.* mancha *f.* **2.** *v.* manchar.

staircase, stairs, *n.* escalera *f.*

stake, 1. *n.* estaca; (bet) apuesta *f.* **at s.,** en juego; en peligro.

stale, *a.* rancio.

stalemate, *n.* estancación *f.,* tablas.

stalk, *n.* caña *f.;* (of flower) tallo *m.*

stall, 1. *n.* tenderete; (for

horse) pesebre *m.* **2.** *v.* demorar; (motor) atascar.

stallion, *n.* garañon *m.*

stalwart, *a.* fornido.

stamina, *n.* vigor *m.*

stammer, *v.* tartamudear.

stamp, 1. *n.* sello *m.,* estampilla *f.* **2.** *v.* sellar.

stampede, *n.* estampida *f.*

stand, 1. *n.* puesto *m.;* posición; (speaker's) tribuna; (furniture) mesita *f.* **2.** *v.* estar; estar de pie; aguantar. **s. up,** pararse, levantarse.

standard, 1. *a.* normal, corriente. **2.** *n.* norma *f.* **s. of living,** nivel de vida.

standardize, *v.* uniformar.

standing, *a.* fijo; establecido.

standpoint, *n.* punto de vista *m.*

staple, *n.* materia prima *f.*

star, *n.* estrella *f.*

starboard, *n.* estribor *m.*

starch, 1. *n.* almidón *m.;* (in diet) fécula *f.* **2.** *v.* almidonar.

stare, *v.* mirar fijamente.

stark, 1. *a.* severo. **2.** *adv.* completamente.

start, 1. *n.* susto; principio *m.* **2.** *v.* comenzar, empezar; salir; poner en marcha; causar.

startle, *v.* asustar.

starvation, *n.* hambre *f.*

starve, *v.* morir de hambre.

state, 1. *n.* estado *m.* **2.** *v.* declarar, decir.

statement, *n.* declaración *f.*

stateroom, *n.* camarote *m.*

statesman, *n.* estadista *m.*

static, 1. *a.* estático. **2.** *n.* estática *f.*

station, *n.* estación *f.*

stationary, *a.* estacionario, fijo.

stationery, *n.* papel de escribir.

statistics, *n.* estadística *f.*

statue, *n.* estatua *f.*

stature, *n.* estatura *f.*

status, *n.* estado legal *m.*

statute, *n.* ley *f.*

staunch, *a.* fiel; constante.

stay, 1. *n.* estancia; vista *f.* **2.** *v.* quedar, permanecer; parar; alojarse. **s. away,** ausentarse. **s. up,** velar.

steadfast, *a.* inmutable.

steady, 1. *a.* firme; permanente; regular. **2.** *v.* sostener.

steak, *n.* biftec, bistec *m.*

steal, 1. *n.* plagio *m.* **2.** *v.* robar. **s. away,** escabullirse.

stealth, *n.* cautela *f.*

steam, *n.* vapor *m.*

steamboat, steamer, steamship, *n.* vapor *m.*

steel, 1. *n.* acero *m.* **2.** *v.* **s. oneself,** fortalecerse.

steep, *a.* escarpado, empinado.

steeple, *n.* campanario *m.*

steer, 1. *n.* buey *m.* **2.** *v.* guiar, manejar.

stellar, *a.* astral.

stem, 1. *n.* tallo *m.* **2.** *v.* parar. **s. from,** emanar de.

stencil, 1. *n.* estarcidor. **2.** *v.* estarcir.

stenographer, *n.* estenógrafo -fa.

stenography, *n.* taquigrafía *f.*

step, 1. *n.* paso *m.;* medida *f.;* (stairs) escalón *m.* **2.** *m.* *v.* pisar. **s. back,** retirarse.

stepladder, *n.* escalera de mano *f.*

stereophonic, *a.* estereofónico.

stereotype, *n.* estereotipo. **2** *v.* estereotipar.

sterile, *a.* estéril.

sterilize, *v.* esterilizar.

sterling, *a.* esterlina, genuino.

stern, 1. *n.* popa *f.* **2.** *a.* duro, severo.

stethoscope, *n.* estetoscopio *m.*

stevedore, *n.* estibador *m.*

stew, 1. *n.* guisado *m.* **2.** *v.* estofar.

steward, *n.* camarero.

stewardess, *n.* azafata *f.,* aeromoza *f.*

stick, 1. *n.* palo, bastón *m.* **2.** *v.* pegar; (put) poner, meter.

sticky, *a.* pegajoso.

stiff, *a.* tieso; duro.

stiffness, *n.* tiesura *f.*

stifle, *v.* sofocar; (fig.) suprimir.

stigma, *n.* estigma *m.*

still, 1. *a.* quieto; silencioso. **to keep s.,** callarse. **2.** *adv.* todavía, aún; no obstante. **3.** *n.* alambique *m.*

stillborn, *n.* & *a.* nacido muerto *m.*

still life, *n.* naturaleza muerta *f.*

stillness, *n.* silencio *m.*

stilted, *a.* altisonante.

stimulant, *a.* & *n.* estimulante *m.*

stimulate, *v.* estimular.

stimulus, *n.* estímulo *m.*

sting, 1. *n.* picadura *f.* **2.** *v.* picar.

stingy, *a.* tacaño.

stipulate, *v.* estipular.

stir, 1. *n.* conmoción *f.* **2.** *v.* mover. **s. up,** conmover; suscitar.

stitch, 1. *n.* puntada *f.* **2.** *v.* coser.

stock, 1. *n.* surtido *f.;* raza *f.;* (finance) acciones. *f.pl.* **in s.,** en existencia. **to take s. in,** tener fe en.

stock exchange, *n.* bolsa *f.*

stockholder, *n.* corredor de bolsa *m.*

stocking, *n.* media *f.*

stockyard, *n.* corral de ganado *m.*

stodgy, *a.* pesado.

stoical, *a.* estoico.

stole, *n.* estola *f.*

stolid, *a.* impasible.

stomach, *n.* estómago *m.*

stone, *n.* piedra *f.*

stool, *n.* banquillo *m.*

stoop, *v.* encorvarse; (fig.) rebajarse.

stop, 1. *n.* parada *f.* **to put a s. to,** poner fin a. **2.** *v.* parar; suspender; detener; impedir. **s. doing** (etc.), dejar de hacer (etc.).

stopgap, *n.* subterfugio *m.*

storage, *n.* almacenaje *m.*

store, 1. *n.* tienda; provisión *f.* **department s.,** almacén *m.* **2.** *v.* guardar; almacenar.

storm, *n.* tempestad, tormenta *f.*

stormy, *a.* tempestuoso.

story, *n.* cuento; relato *m.;* historia *f.* **short s.,** cuento.

stout, *a.* corpulento.

stove, *n.* hornilla; estufa *f.*

straight, 1. *a.* recto; derecho. **2.** *adv.* directamente.

straighten, *v.* enderezar. **s. out,** poner en orden.

straightforward, *a.* recto, sincero.

strain, 1. *n.* tensión *f.* **2.** *v.* colar.

strainer, *n.* colador *m.*

strait, *n.* estrecho *m.*

strand, 1. *n.* hilo *m.* **2.** *v.* **be stranded,** encallarse.

strange, *a.* extraño; raro.

stranger, *n.* extranjero -ra. forastero -ra; desconocido -da.

strangle, *v.* estrangular.

strap, *n.* correa *f.*

stratagem, *n.* estrategama *f.*

strategic, *a.* estratégico.

strategy, *n.* estrategia *f.*

stratosphere, *n.* estratosfera *f.*

straw, *n.* paja *f.*

strawberry, *n.* fresa *f.*

stray, 1. *a.* vagabundo. **2.** *v.* extraviarse.

streak, *n.* racha; raya *f.;* lado *m.* **2.** *v.* rayar.

stream, *n.* corriente *f.*

street, *n.* calle *f.*

streetcar, *n.* tranvía *m.*

strength, *n.* fuerza *m.*

strengthen, *v.* reforzar.

strenuous, *a.* estrenuo.

streptococcus, *n.* estreptococo *m.*

stress, 1. *n.* tensión *f.;* énfasis *m.* **2.** *v.* recalcar; acentuar.

stretch, 1. *n.* trecho *m.* **at one s.,** de un tirón. **2.** *v.* tender; extender; estirarse.

stretcher, *n.* camilla *f.*

strew, *v.* esparcir.

stricken, *a.* agobiado.

strict, *a.* estricto; severo.

stride, 1. *n.* tranco *m.;* (fig., pl.) progresos. **2.** *v.* andar a trancos.

strife, *n.* contienda *f.*

strike, 1. *n.* huelga *f.* **2.** *v.* pegar; chocar con; (clock) dar.

string, *n.* cuerda *f.;* cordel *m.*

string bean, *n.* habichuela *f.*

stringent, *a.* estricto.

strip, 1. *n.* tira *f.* **2.** despojar; desnudarse.

stripe, *n.* raya *f.;* (mil.) galón *m.*

strive, *v.* esforzarse.

stroke, n. golpe m.; (swimming) brazada f.; (med.) ataque m. **s. of luck**, suerte f.

stroll, 1. n. paseo m. 2. v. pasearse.

stroller, n. vagabundo m.

strong, a. fuerte.

stronghold, n. fortificación f.

structure, n. estructura f.

struggle, 1. n. lucha f. 2. v. luchar.

strut, 1. n. pavonada f. 2. v. pavonear.

stub, 1. n. cabo; (ticket) talón m. 2. v. **s. one's toe on**, tropezar con.

stubborn, a. testarudo.

stucco, 1. n. estuco. 2. v. estucar.

student, n. alumno -na, estudiante -ta.

studio, n. estudio m.

studious, a. aplicado; estudioso.

study, 1. n. estudio m. 2. v. estudiar.

stuff, 1. n. cosas f.pl. 2. v. llenar; rellenar.

stuffing, n. relleno m.

stumble, v. tropezar.

stump, n. tronco m.

stun, v. aturdir.

stunt, 1. n. suerte f. 2. v. impedir crecimiento.

stupendous, a. estupendo.

stupid, a. estúpido.

stupidity, n. estupidez f.

stupor, n. estupor m.

sturdy, a. robusto.

stutter, 1. v. tartamudear. 2. n. tartamudeo m.

sty, n. pocilga f.

style, n. estilo m.; moda f.

stylish, a. elegante; a la moda.

suave, a. afable, suave.

subconscious, a. subconsciente.

subdue, v. dominar.

subject, 1. a. sujeto. 2. n. tema m.; (of study) materia f.; (pol.) súbdito -ta; (gram.) sujeto m. 3. v. someter.

subjugate, v. sojuzgar, subjugar.

subjunctive, a. & n. subjuntivo m.

sublimate, v. sublimar.

sublime, a. sublime.

submarine, a. & n. submarino m.

submerge, v. sumergir.

submission, n. sumisión f.

submit, v. someter.

subnormal, a. subnormal.

subordinate, 1. a. & n. subordinado m. 2. v. subordinar.

subscribe, v. aprobar; abonarse.

subscription, n. abono m.

subsequent, a. subsiguiente.

subservient, a. servicial.

subside, v. apaciguarse.

subsidy, n. subvención f.

substance, n. substancia f.

substantial, a. substancial; considerable.

substitute, 1. a. substitutivo. 2. n. substituto m. 3. v. substituir.

substitution, n. substitución f.

subterfuge, n. subterfugio m.

subtle, a. sutil.

subtract, v. substraer.

suburb, n. suburbio m.; (pl.) afueras f.pl.

subversive, a. subversivo.

subway, n. metro m.

succeed, v. lograr, tener éxito; (in office) suceder a.

success, n. éxito m.

successful, a. próspero; afortunado.

succession, n. sucesión f.

successive, a. sucesivo.

successor, n. sucesor -ra; heredero -ra.

succor, 1. n. socorro m. 2. v. socorrer.

succumb, v. sucumbir.

such, a. tal.

suck, v. chupar.

suction, n. succión f.

sudden, a. repentino, súbito. **all of a s.**, de repente.

suds, n. jabonaduras f.

suffer, v. sufrir; padecer.

suffice, v. bastar.

sufficient, a. suficiente.

suffocate, v. sofocar.

sugar, n. azúcar m.

suggest, v. sugerir.

suggestion, n. sugerencia f.

suicide, n. suicidio m.; (person) suicida m. & f. **to commit s.**, suicidarse.

suit, 1. n. traje; (cards) palo; (law) pleito m. 2. v. convenir a.

suitable, a. apropiado; que conviene.

suitcase, n. maleta f.

suite, n. serie f., séquito m.

suitor, n. pretendiente m.

sullen, a. hosco.

sum, 1. n. suma f. 2. v. **s. up**, resumir.

summarize, v. resumir.

summary, n. resumen m.

summer, n. verano m.

summon, v. llamar; (law) citar.

summons, n. citación f.

sumptuous, a. suntuoso.

sun, 1. n. sol m. 2. v. tomar el sol.

sunburn, n. quemadura de sol.

sunburned, a. quemado por el sol.

Sunday, n. domingo m.

sunken, a. hundido.

sunny, a. asoleado. **s. day**, día de sol. **to be s.**, (weather) hacer sol.

sunshine, n. luz del sol.

superb, a. soberbio.

superficial, a. superficial.

superfluous, a. superfluo.

superhuman, a. sobrehumano.

superintendent, n. superinten-

dente m.; (of building) conserje m.; (of school) director general.

superior, a. & n. superior m.

superiority, n. superioridad f.

superlative, a. superlativo.

supernatural, a. sobrenatural.

supersede, v. reemplazar.

superstar, n. superstar m.

superstition, n. superstición f.

superstitious, a. supersticioso.

supervise, v. supervisar.

supper, n. cena f.

supplement, 1. n. suplemento m. 2. v. suplementar.

supply, 1. n. provisión f.; (com.) surtido m.; (econ.) existencia f. 2. v. suplir; proporcionar.

support, 1. n. sustento; apoyo m. 2. v. mantener; apoyar.

suppose, v. suponer. **be supposed to**, deber.

suppress, v. suprimir.

suppression, n. supresión f.

supreme, a. supremo.

sure, a. seguro, cierto. **for s.**, con seguridad. **to make s.**, asegurarse.

surety, n. garantía f.

surf, n. marejada f.

surface, n. superficie f.

surge, v. surgir.

surgeon, n. cirujano m.

surgery, n. cirujía f.

surmise, 1. n. conjetura f. 2. v. suponer.

surmount, v. vencer.

surname, n. apellido m.

surpass, v. superar.

surplus, a. & n. sobrante m.

surprise, 1. n. sorpresa 2. v. sorprender. **I am surprised . . .**, me extraña . . .

surrender, 1. n. rendición f. 2. v. rendir.

surround, v. rodear, circundar.

surveillance, n. vigilancia f.

survey, 1. n. examen estudio m. 2. v. examinar, estudiar; (land) medir.

survival, n. supervivencia f.

survive, v. sobrevivir.

susceptible, a. susceptible.

suspect, v. sospechar.

suspend, v. suspender.

suspense, n. incertidumbre f. **in s.**, en suspenso.

suspension, n. suspensión f.

suspension bridge, n. puente colgante m.

suspicion, n. sospecha f.

suspicious, a. sospechoso.

sustain, v. sustentar; mantener.

swallow, 1. n. trago m.; (bird) golondrina f. 2. v. tragar.

swamp, 1. n. pantano m. 2. v. (fig.) abrumar.

swan, n. cisne m.

swap, 1. n. trueque m. 2. v. cambalachear.

swarm, n. enjambre m.

sway, 1. n. predominio m. 2. v. bambolearse; (fig.) influir en.

swear, v. jurar. **s. off,** renunciar a.

sweat, **1.** sudor m. **2.** v. sudar.

sweater, n. suéter m.

Swede, n. sueco -ca.

Sweden, n. Suecia f.

Swedish, a. sueco.

sweep, v. barrer.

sweet, **1.** a. dulce; amable, simpático. **2.** n. (pl.) dulces m.pl.

sweetheart, n. amante m.

sweetness, n. dulzura f.

swell, **1.** a. (coll.) estupendo, excelente. **2.** n. (mar.) oleada f. **3.** v. hincharse; aumentar.

swelter, v. sofacar.

swift, a. rápido, veloz.

swim, **1.** n. nadada f. **2.** v. nadar.

swindle, **1.** n. estafa. **2.** v. estafar.

swine, n. puercos m.pl.

swing, **1.** n. columpio m. **in full s.,** en plena actividad. **2.** v. mecer; balancear.

swirl, **1.** n. remolino m. **2.** v. arremolinar.

Swiss, a. & n. suizo -za.

switch, **1.** n. varilla f.; (elec.) llave f., conmutador m.; (railway) cambiavía m. **2.** v. cambiar; trocar.

switchboard, n. cuadro conmutador m.

Switzerland, n. Suiza f.

sword, n. espada f.

syllable, n. sílaba f.

symbol, n. símbolo m.

sympathetic, a. compasivo. **to be s.,** tener simpatía.

sympathy, n. lástima; condolencia f.

symphony, n. sinfonía f.

symptom, n. síntoma m.

synchronize, v. sincronizar.

syndicate, n. sindicato m.

syndrome, n. sindroma m.

synonym, n. sinónimo m.

synthetic, a. sintético.

syringe, n. jeringa f.

syrup, n. almíbar; (cough) jarabe m.

system, n. sistema m.

systematic, a. sistemático.

T

tabernacle, n. tabernáculo m.

table, n. mesa; (list) tabla f.

tablespoon, n. cuchara f.

tablespoonful, n. cucharada f.

tablet, n. tableta; (med.) pastilla f.

tack, n. tachuela f.

tact, n. tacto m.

tag, n. etiqueta f., rótulo m.

tail, n. cola f., rabo m.

tailor, n. sastre m.

take, v. tomar; llevar. **t. away,** quitar. **t. off,** quitarse. **t. out,** sacar. **t. long,** tardar mucho.

tale, n. cuento m.

talent, n. talento m.

talk, **1.** n. plática, habla f.; discurso m. **2.** v. hablar.

talkative, a. locuaz.

tall, a. alto.

tame, **1.** a. manso, domesticado. **2.** v. domesticar.

tamper, v. **t. with,** entremeterse en.

tan, **1.** a. color de arena. **2.** v. curtir; tostar.

tangible, a. tangible.

tangle, **1.** n. enredo m. **2.** v. enredar.

tank, n. tanque m.

tap, **1.** n. golpe ligero. **2.** v. golpear ligeramente; decentar.

tape, n. cinta f.

tape recorder, n. magnetófono m.

tapestry, n. tapiz m.; tapicería f.

tar, **1.** n. brea f. **2.** v. embrear.

target, n. blanco m.

tarnish, **1.** n. deslustre m. **2.** v. deslustrar.

task, n. tarea f.

taste, **1.** n. gusto; sabor m. **2.** v. gustar; progar. **t. of,** saber a.

tasty, a. sabroso.

taut, a. tieso.

tavern, n. taberna f.

tax, **1.** n. impuesto m. **2.** v. imponer impuestos.

taxi, n. taxi, taxímetro m.

tea, n. té m.

teach, v. enseñar.

teacher, n. maestro -tra, profesor -ra.

team, n. equipo m.; pareja f.

tear, **1.** rasgón m.; lágrima f. **2.** v. rasgar, lacerar; separar.

tease, v. atormentar; embromar.

teaspoon, n. cucharita f.

technical, a. técnico.

technique, n. técnica f.

tedious, a. tedioso.

telegram, n. telegrama m.

telegraph, **1.** n. telégrafo m. **2.** v. telegrafiar.

telephone, **1.** n. teléfono m. **t. book,** directorio telefónico. **2.** v. telefonear; llamar por teléfono.

telescope, **1.** n. telescopio m. **2.** v. enchufar.

television, n. televisión f.

tell, v. decir; contar; distinguir.

temper, **1.** n. temperamento, genio m. **2.** v. templar.

temperament, n. temperamento m.

temperamental, a. sensible, emocional.

temperance, n. moderación, sobriedad f.

temperate, a. templado.

temperature, n. temperatura f.

tempest, n. tempestad f.

tempestuous, a. tempestuoso.

temple, n. templo m.

temporary, a. temporal, temporario.

tempt, v. tentar.

temptation, n. tentación f.

ten, a. & pron. diez.

tenant, n. inquilino -na.

tend, v. tender. **t. to,** atender.

tendency, n. tendencia f.

tender, **1.** a. tierno. **2.** v. ofrecer.

tenderness, n. ternura f.

tennis, n. tenis m.

tenor, n. tenor m.

tense, **1.** a. tenso. **2.** n. tiempo m.

tent, n. tienda, carpa f.

tenth, a. décimo.

term, **1.** n. término; plazo m. **2.** v. llamar.

terrace, n. terraza f.

terrible, a. terrible, espantoso.

territory, n. territorio m.

terror, n. terror, espanto m.

test, **1.** n. prueba f.; examen m. **2.** v. probar, examinar.

testament, n. testamento m.

testify, v. atestiguar, testificar.

testimony, n. testimonio m.

text, n. texto; tema m.

textile, **1.** a. textil. **2.** n. tejido m.

texture, n. textura f.; tejido m.

than, conj. que; de.

thank, v. agradecer, dar gracias; **thanks, th. you,** gracias.

thankful, a. agradecido; grato.

that, **1.** a. ese, aquel. **2.** dem. pron. ése, aquél; eso, aquello. **3.** rel. pron. & conj. que.

the, art. el, la, los, las; lo.

theater, n. teatro m.

theft, n. robo m.

their, a. su.

theirs, pron. suyo, de ellos.

them, pron. ellos, ellas; los, las; les.

theme, n. tema m.; (mus.) motivo m.

themselves, pron. sí, sí mismos -as. **they th.,** ellos mismos, ellas mismas. **with th.,** consigo.

then, adv. entonces, después; pues.

thence, adv. de allí.

theology, n. teología f.

theory, n. teoría f.

there, adv. allí, allá, ahí. **there is, there are,** hay.

therefore, adv. por lo tanto, por consiguiente.

thermometer, n. termómetro m.

they, pron. ellos, ellas.

thick, a. espeso, grueso, denso; torpe.

thicken, v. espesar, condensar.

thief, n. ladrón -na.

thigh, n. muslo m.

thimble, n. dedal m.

thin, **1.** a. delgado; raro; claro; escaso. **2.** v. enrarecer; adelgazar.

thing, n. cosa f.

think, v. pensar; creer.

thinker, n. pensador -ra.

third, a. tercero.

Third World, n. Tercer Mundo m.

thirst, n. sed f.

thirsty, a. sediento. **to be th.,** tener sed.

thirteen, a. & pron. trece.

thirty, a. & pron. treinta.

this, 1. a. este. 2. pron. éste; esto.

thorough, a. completo; cuidadoso.

though, 1. adv. sin embargo. 2. conj. aunque. **as th.,** como si.

thought, n. pensamiento m.

thoughtful, a. pensativo; considerado.

thousand, a. & pron. mil.

thread, n. hilo m.; (of screw) rosca f.

threat, n. amenaza f.

threaten, v. amenazar.

three, a. & pron. tres.

thrift, n. economía, frugalidad f.

thrill, 1. n. emoción f. 2. v. emocionar.

thrive, v. prosperar.

throat, n. garganta f.

throne, n. trono m.

through, 1. prep. por; a través de; por medio de. 2. a. continuo. **th. train,** tren directo. **to be th.,** haber terminado.

throughout, 1. prep. por todo, durante todo. 2. adv. en todas partes; completamente.

throw, 1. n. tiro m. 2. v. tirar, lanzar. **th. away,** arrojar. **th. out,** echar.

thrust, 1. n. lanzada f. 2. v. empujar.

thumb, n. pulgar m.

thunder, 1. n. trueno m. 2. v. tronar.

Thursday, n. jueves m.

thus, adv. así, de este modo.

thwart, v. frustrar.

ticket, 1. n. billete, boleto m. **t. window,** taquilla f. **round trip t.,** billete de ida y vuelta.

tickle, 1. n. cosquilla f. 2. v. hacer cosquillas a.

ticklish, a. cosquilloso.

tide, n. marea f.

tidy, 1. a. limpio, ordenado. 2. v. poner en orden.

tie, 1. n. corbata f.; lazo; (game) empate m. 2. v. atar; anudar.

tier, n. hilera f.

tiger, n. tigre m.

tight, a. apretado; tacaño.

tighten, v. estrechar, apretar.

tile, n. teja f., azulejo m.

till, 1. prep. hasta. 2. conj. hasta que. 3. n. cajón m. 4. v. cultivar, labrar.

tilt, 1. n. inclinación; justa f. 2. v. inclinar; justar.

timber, n. madera f.; (beam) madero m.

time, n. tiempo m.; vez f.; (of day) hora f.

timetable, n. horario, itinerario m.

timid, a. tímido.

timidity, n. timidez f.

tin, n. estaño m.; hojalata f. **t. can,** lata f.

tint, 1. n. tinte m. 2. v. teñir.

tiny, a. chiquito, pequeñito.

tip, 1. n. punta; propina f. 2. v. inclinar; dar propina a.

tire, 1. n. llanta, goma f., neumático m. 2. v. cansar.

tired, a. cansado.

tissue, n. tejido m. **t. paper,** papel de seda.

title, 1. n. título m. 2. v. titular.

to, prep. a; para.

toast, 1. n. tostada f.; (drink) brindis m. 2. v. tostar; brindar por.

tobacco, n. tabaco m.

today, adv. hoy.

toe, n. dedo del pie.

together, 1. a. juntos. 2. adv. juntamente.

toil, 1. n. trabajo m. 2. v. afanarse.

toilet, n. tocado; excusado, retrete m. **t. paper,** papel higiénico.

token, n. señal f.

tolerance, n. tolerancia f.

tolerate, v. tolerar.

tomato, n. tomate m.

tomb, n. tumba f.

tomorrow, adv. mañana. **day after t.,** pasado mañana.

ton, n. tonelada f.

tone, n. tono m.

tongue, n. lengua f.

tonic, n. tónico m.

tonight, adv. esta noche.

tonsil, n. amígdala f.

too, adv. también; demasiado. **t. much,** demasiado. **t. many,** demasiados.

tool, n. herramienta f.

tooth, n. diente m.; (back) muela f.

toothache, n. dolor de muela.

toothbrush, n. cepillo de dientes.

top, 1. n. parte de arriba. 2. v. cubrir; sobrepasar.

topic, n. tópico m.

topical, a. tópico.

torch, n. antorcha f.

torment, 1. n. tormento m. 2. v. atormentar.

torrent, n. torrente m.

torture, 1. n. tortura f. 2. v. torturar.

toss, v. tirar; agitar.

total, 1. a. total, entero. 2. n. total m.

totalitarian, a. totalitario.

touch, 1. n. tacto m. **in t.,** en comunicación. 2. v. tocar; conmover.

tough, a. tosco; tieso; fuerte.

tour, 1. n. viaje m., jira f. 2. v. viajar.

tourist, n. turista m. & f.

tournament, n. torneo m.

tow, 1. n. remolque m. 2. v. remolcar.

toward, prep. hacia.

towel, n. toalla f.

tower, n. torre f.

town, n. pueblo m.

toy, 1. n. juguete m. 2. v. jugar.

trace, 1. n. vestigio; rastro m. 2. v. trazar; rastrear; investigar.

track, 1. n. huella, pista f. **race t.,** hipódromo m. 2. v. rastrear.

tract, n. trecho, tracto; tratado m.

tractor, n. tractor m.

trade, 1. n. comercio, negocio; oficio; canje m. 2. v. comerciar, negociar; cambiar.

trader, n. comerciante f.

tradition, n. tradición f.

traditional, a. tradicional.

traffic, 1. n. tráfico m. 2. v. traficar.

tragedy, n. tragedia f.

tragic, a. trágico.

trail, 1. n. sendero; rastro m. 2. v. rastrear; arrastrar.

train, 1. n. tren m. 2. v. enseñar; disciplinar; (sport) entrenarse.

traitor, n. traidor m.

tramp, 1. n. caminata f.; vagabundo m. 2. v. patear.

tranquil, a. tranquilo.

tranquillity, n. tranquilidad f.

transaction, n. transacción f.

transfer, 1. traslado m.; boleto de transbordo. 2. v. trasladar, transferir.

transform, v. transformar.

transfusion, n. transfusión f.

transition, n. transición f.

translate, v. traducir.

translation, n. traducción f.

transmit, v. transmitir.

transparent, a. transparente.

transport, 1. n. transporte m., transportación f. 2. v. transportar.

transportation, n. transporte m.

transsexual, a. transexual.

transvestite, n. travesti m.

trap, 1. n. trampa f. 2. v. atrapar.

trash, n. desecho m.; basura f.

travel, 1. n. tráfico m.; (pl.) viajes m.pl. 2. v. viajar.

traveler, n. viajero -ra.

traveler's check, n. cheque de viaje m.

tray, n. bandeja f.

tread, 1. n. pisada f.; (of a tire) cubierta f. 2. v. pisar.

treason, n. traición f.

treasure, n. tesoro m.

treasurer, n. tesorero -ra.

treasury, n. tesorería f.

treat, v. tratar; convidar.

treatment, n. trato, tratamiento m.

treaty, n. tratado, pacto m.

tree, n. árbol m.

tremble, v. temblar.

tremendous, a. tremendo.

trench, n. foso m.; (mil.) trinchera f.

trend, 1. *n.* tendencia *f.* **2.** *v.* tender.

trespass, *v.* traspasar; violar.

triage, *n.* clasificación de los heridos después del combate.

trial, *n.* prueba *f.;* (leg.) proceso, juicio *m.*

triangle, *n.* triángulo *m.*

tribulation, *n.* tribulación *f.*

tributary, *a. &* *n.* tributario *m.*

tribute, *n.* tributo *m.*

trick, 1. *n.* engaño *m.;* maña *f.;* (cards) baza *f.* **2.** *v.* engañar.

trifle, 1. *n.* pequeñez *f.* **2.** *v.* juguetear.

trigger, *n.* gatillo *m.*

trim, 1. *a.* ajustado, acicalado. **2.** *n.* adorno *m.* **3.** *v.* adornar; ajustar; cortar un poco.

trinket, *n.* bagatela, chuchería *f.*

trip, 1. *n.* viaje *m.* **2.** *v.* tropezar.

triple, 1. *a.* triple **2.** *v.* triplicar.

trite, *a.* banal.

triumph, 1. *n.* triunfo *m.* **2.** *v.* triunfar.

triumphant, *a.* triunfante.

trivial, *a.* trivial.

trolley, *n.* tranvía *m.*

troop, *n.* tropa *f.*

trophy, *n:* trofeo *m.*

tropical, *a.* trópico.

tropics, *n.* trópico *m.*

trot, 1. *n.* trote *m.* **2.** *v.* trotar.

trouble, 1. *n.* apuro *m.;* congoja; aflicción *f.* **2.** *v.* molestar; afligir.

troublesome, *a.* penoso, molesto.

trough, *n.* artesa *f.*

trousers, *n.* pantalones, calzones *m.pl.*

trout, *n.* trucha *f.*

truce, *n.* tregua *f.*

truck, *n.* camión *m.*

true, *a.* verdadero; cierto, verdad.

trumpet, *n.* trompeta, trompa *f.*

trunk, *n.* baúl *m.;* (of a tree) tronco *m.*

trust, 1. *n.* confianza *f.* **2.** *v.* confiar.

trustworthy, *a.* digno de confianza.

truth, *n.* verdad *f.*

truthful, *a.* veraz.

try, 1. *n.* prueba *f.;* ensayo *m.* **2.** *v.* tratar; probar; ensayar; (leg.) juzgar. **t. on,** probarse.

T-shirt, *n.* camiseta *f.*

tub, *n.* tina *f.*

tube, *n.* tubo *m.*

tuberculosis, *n.* tuberculosis, tisis *f.*

tuck, 1. *n.* recogido *m.* **2.** *v.* recoger.

Tuesday, *n.* martes *m.*

tug, 1. *n.* tirada *f.;* (boat) remolcador *m.* **2.** *v.* tirar.

tuition, *n.* matrícula, colegiatura *f.*

tumble, 1. *n.* caída *f.* **2.** *v.* caer; tumbar; voltear.

tumult, *n.* tumulto, alboroto *m.*

tune, 1. *n.* tono *m.;* melodía, canción *f.* **2.** *v.* templar.

tunnel, *n.* túnel *m.*

turf, *n.* césped *m.*

Turkey, *n.* Turquía *f.*

Turkish, *a.* turco.

turmoil, *n.* disturbio *m.*

turn, 1. *n.* vuelta *f.;* giro; turno *m.* **2.** *v.* volver, tornear, girar; transformar. **t. around,** volverse. **t. on,** encender; abrir. **t. off, t. out,** apagar.

turnip, *n.* nabo *m.*

turret, *n.* torrecilla *f.*

turtle, *n.* tortuga *f.*

tutor, 1. *n.* tutor *m.* **2.** *v.* enseñar.

twelve, *a. &* *pron.* doce.

twenty, *a. &* *pron.* veinte.

twice, *adv.* dos veces.

twig, *n.* varita, ramita *f.;* vástago *m.*

twilight, *n.* crepúsculo *m.*

twin, *n.* gemelo -la.

twine, 1. *n.* guita *f.* **2.** *v.* torcer.

twinkle, *v.* centellear.

twist, *v.* torcer.

two, *a. &* *pron.* dos.

type, 1. *n.* tipo *m.* **2.** *v.* escribir a máquina.

typewriter, *n.* máquina de escribir.

typhoid fever, fiebre tifoidea.

typical, *a.* típico.

typist, *n.* mecanógrafo -fa.

tyranny, *n.* tiranía *f.*

tyrant, *n.* tirano *m.*

U

udder, *n.* ubre *f.*

ugly, *a.* feo.

ulcer, *n.* úlcera *f.*

ulterior, *a.* ulterior.

ultimate, *a.* último.

umbrella, *n.* paraguas *m.* **sun u.,** quitasol *m.*

umpire, *n.* árbitro *m.*

unable, *a.* incapaz. **to be u.,** no poder.

unanimous, *a.* unánime.

uncertain, *a.* incierto, inseguro.

uncle, *n.* tío *m.*

unconscious, *a.* inconsciente; desmayado.

uncover, *v.* descubrir.

under, 1. *adv.* debajo, abajo. **2.** *prep.* bajo, debajo de.

underestimate, *v.* menospreciar, subestimar.

undergo, *v.* sufrir.

underground, *a.* subterráneo.

underline, *v.* subrayar.

underneath, 1. *adv.* por debajo. **2.** *prep.* debajo de.

undershirt, *n.* camiseta *f.*

understand, *v.* entender, comprender.

undertake, *v.* emprender.

underwear, *n.* ropa interior.

undo, *v.* deshacer; desatar.

undress, *v.* desnudar, desvestir.

uneasy, *a.* inquieto.

uneven, *a.* desigual.

unexpected, *a.* inesperado.

unfair, *a.* injusto.

unfit, *a.* incapaz; inadecuado.

unfold, *v.* desplegar; revelar.

unforgettable, *a.* inolvidable.

unfortunate, *a.* desafortunado, desgraciado.

unhappy, *a.* infeliz.

uniform, *a. &* *n.* uniforme *m.*

unify, *v.* unificar.

union, *n.* unión *f.* **labor u.,** sindicato de obreros.

unique, *a.* único.

unisex, *a.* unisex.

unit, *n.* unidad *f.*

unite, *v.* unir.

unity, *n.* unidad *f.*

universal, *a.* universal.

universe, *n.* universo *m.*

university, *n.* universidad *f.*

unleaded, *a.* sin plomo.

unless, *conj.* a menos que, si no es que.

unlike, *a.* disímil.

unload, *v.* descargar.

unlock, *v.* abrir.

untie, *v.* desatar, soltar.

until, 1. *prep.* hasta. **2.** *conj.* hasta que.

unusual, *a.* raro, inusitado.

up, 1. *adv.* arriba. **2.** *prep.* **u. the street,** *etc.* calle arriba, etc.

uphold, *v.* apoyar, defender.

upholster, *v.* entapizar.

upon, *prep.* sobre, encima de.

upper, *a.* superior.

upright, *a.* derecho, recto.

uproar, *n.* alboroto, tumulto *m.*

upset, 1. *n.* trastorno *m.* **2.** *v.* trastornar.

uptight, *a.* (psicológicamente) tenso, tieso.

upward, *adv.* hacia arriba.

urge, 1. *n.* deseo *m.* **2.** *v.* instar.

urgency, *n.* urgencia *f.*

urgent, *a.* urgente. **to be u.,** urgir.

us, *pron.* nosotros -as; nos.

use, 1. *n.* uso *m.* **2.** *v.* usar, emplear. **u. up,** gastar, agotar. **be used to,** ser acostumbrado a.

useful, *a.* útil.

useless, *a.* inútil.

usher, 1. *n.* acomodador *m.* **2.** *v.* introducir.

usual, *a.* usual.

utensil, *n.* utensilio *m.*

utmost, *a.* sumo, extremo.

utter, 1. *a.* completo. **2.** *v.* proferir; dar.

utterance, *n.* expresión *f.*

V

vacancy, *n.* vacante *f.*

vacant, *a.* desocupado, libre.

vacation, *n.* vacaciones *f.pl.*

vaccinate, *v.* vacunar.

vacuum, *n.* vacuo, vacío *m.* **v. cleaner,** aspirador *m.*

vagrant, *n.* vagabundo.

vague, *a.* vago.

vain, *a.* vano; vanidoso. **in v.,** en vano.

valiant, *a.* valiente.

valid, *a.* válido.

valley, *n.* valle *m.*

valor, *n.* valor *m.*, valentía *f.*

valuable, *a.* precioso. **to be v.,** valer mucho.

value, **1.** *n.* valor, importe *m.* **2.** *v.* valorar; estimar.

vandal, *n.* vándalo *m.*

vanish, *v.* desaparecer.

vanity, *n.* vanidad *f.* **v. case,** polvera *f.*

vanquish, *v.* vencer.

vapor, *n.* vapor *m.*

variation, *n.* variación *f.*

variety, *n.* variedad *f.*

various, *a.* varios, diversos.

varnish, **1.** *n.* barniz *m.* **2.** *v.* barnizar.

vary, *v.* variar; cambiar.

vase, *n.* vaso, jarrón *m.*

vasectomy, *n.* vasectomía *f.*

vassal, *n.* vasallo *m.*

vast, *a.* vasto.

vat, *n.* tina *f.*, tanque *m.*

vault, *n.* bóveda *f.*

vegetable, *n.* & *n.* vegetal *m.*; (pl.) legumbres, verderas *f.pl.*

vehement, *a.* vehemente.

vehicle, *n.* vehículo *m.*

veil, **1.** *n.* velo *m.* **2.** *v.* velar.

vein, *n.* vena *f.*

velocity, *n.* velocidad *f.*

velvet, *n.* terciopelo *m.*

vengeance, *n.* venganza *f.*

vent, *n.* apertura *f.*

ventilate, *v.* ventilar.

venture, *n.* ventura *f.*

verb, *n.* verbo *m.*

verbose, *a.* verboso.

verdict, *n.* veredicto, fallo *m.*

verge, *n.* borde *m.*

verify, *v.* verificar.

versatile, *a.* versátil.

verse, *n.* verso *m.*

version, *n.* versión *f.*

vertical, *a.* vertical.

very, **1.** *a.* mismo. **2.** *adv.* muy.

vessel, *n.* vasija *f.*; barco *m.*

vest, *n.* chaleco *m.*

veteran, *a.* & *n.* veterano -na.

veto, *n.* veto *m.*

vex, *v.* molestar.

via, *prep.* por la vía de; por.

viaduct, *n.* viaducto *m.*

vibrate, *v.* vibrar.

vibration, *n.* vibración *f.*

vice, *n.* vicio *m.*

vicinity, *n.* vecindad *f.*

vicious, *a.* vicioso.

victim, *n.* víctima *f.*

victor, *n.* vencedor *m.*

victorious, *a.* victorioso.

victory, *n.* victoria *f.*

videodisc, *n.* videodisco *m.*

videotape, *n.* vídeo *m.*, magnetoscopio *m.*

view, **1.** *n.* vista *f.* **2.** *v.* ver.

vigil, *n.* vigilia, vela *f.*

vigilant, *a.* vigilante.

vigor, *n.* vigor *m.*

vile, *a.* vil, bajo.

village, *n.* aldea *f.*

villain, *n.* malvado *m.*

vindicate, *v.* vindicar.

vine, *n.* parra, vid *f.*

vinegar, *n.* vinagre *m.*

vintage, *n.* vendimia *f.*

violate, *v.* violar.

violation, *n.* violación *f.*

violence, *n.* violencia *f.*

violent, *a.* violento.

violin, *n.* violín *m.*

virgin, *n.* virgen *f.*

virile, *a.* viril.

virtual, *a.* virtual.

virtue, *n.* virtud *f.*

virtuous, *a.* virtuoso.

virus, *n.* virus *m.*

visa, *n.* visa *f.*

visible, *a.* visible.

vision, *n.* visión *f.*

visit, **1.** *n.* visita *f.* **2.** *v.* visitar.

visitor, *n.* visitante *m.* & *f.*

visual, *a.* visual.

vital, *a.* vital.

vitality, *n.* vitalidad *f.*

vitamin, *n.* vitamina *f.*

vivacious, *a.* vivaz.

vivid, *a.* vivo; gráfico.

vocabulary, *n.* vocabulario *m.*

vocal, *a.* vocal.

vogue, *n.* boga; moda *f.*

voice, **1.** *n.* voz *f.* **2.** *v.* expresar.

void, **1.** *a.* vacío. **2.** *n.* vacío *m.* **3.** *v.* invalidar.

volume, *n.* volumen, tomo *m.*

voluntary, *a.* voluntario.

volunteer, **1.** *n.* voluntario *m.* **2.** *v.* ofrecerse.

vomit, *v.* vomitar.

vote, **1.** *n.* voto *m.* **2.** *v.* votar.

voter, *n.* votante *m.* & *f.*

vouch, *v.* **v. for,** garantizar.

vow, **1.** *n.* voto *m.* **2.** *v.* jurar.

vowel, *n.* vocal *f.*

voyage, *n.* viaje *m.*

vulgar, *a.* vulgar; común.

vulnerable, *a.* vulnerable.

W

wade, *v.* vadear.

wag, *v.* menear.

wage, **1.** *n.* (pl.) sueldo, salario *m.* **2.** *v.* **w. war,** hacer guerra.

wagon, *n.* carreta *f.*

wail, **1.** *n.* lamento, gemido *m.* **2.** *v.* lamentar, gemir.

waist, *n.* cintura *f.*

wait, **1.** *n.* espera *f.* **2.** *v.* esperar. **w. for,** esperar. **w. on,** atender.

waiter, waitress, *n.* camarero -ra.

wake, *v.* **w. up,** despertar.

walk, **1.** *n.* paseo *m.;* vuelta; caminata *f.* modo de andar. **2.** *v.* andar; caminar; ir a pie.

wall, *n.* pared; (outdoor) tapia; muralla *f.*

wallcovering, *n.* tapizado de pared *m.*

wallet, *n.* cartera *f.*

wallpaper, *n.* empapelado *m.*

walnut, *n.* nuez *f.*

waltz, *n.* vals *m.*

wander, *v.* vagar.

want, **1.** *n.* necesidad *f.* **2.** *v.* querer.

war, *n.* guerra *f.*

ward, **1.** *n.* (pol.) barrio *m.;* (hospital) cuadra *f.* **2.** *v.* **w. off,** parar.

wares, *n.* mercancías *f.pl.*

warlike, *a.* belicoso.

warm, **1.** *a.* caliente; (fig.) caluroso. **to be w.,** tener calor; (weather) hacer calor. **2.** *v.* calentar.

warmth, *n.* calor *m.*

warn, *v.* advertir.

warp, *v.* alabear.

warrant, *v.* justificar.

warrior, *n.* guerrero *m.*

warship, *n.* navío de guerra.

wash, *v.* lavar.

wasp, *n.* avispa *f.*

waste, **1.** *n.* gasto *m.;* desechos *m.pl.* **2.** *v.* gastar, perder.

watch, **1.** *n.* reloj *m.;* (mil.) guardia *f.* **2.** *v.* observar, mirar. **w. for,** esperar. **w. out for,** tener cuidado con. **w. over,** guardar; velar por.

watchful, *a.* desvelado.

watchmaker, *n.* relojero *m.*

watchman, *n.* sereno *m.*

water, **1.** *n.* agua *f.* **w. color,** acuarela *f.* **2.** *v.* aguar.

waterbed, *n.* cama de agua *f.*

waterfall, *n.* catarata *f.*

waterproof, *a.* impermeable.

wave, **1.** *n.* onda; ola *f.* **2.** *v.* ondear; agitar; hacer señas.

waver, *v.* vacilar.

wax, **1.** *n.* cera *f.* **2.** *v.* encerar.

way, *n.* camino; modo *m.,* manera *f.* **in a w.,** hasta cierto punto. **a long w.,** muy lejos. **by the w.,** a propósito. **this w.,** por aquí. **that w.,** por allí. **which w.,** por dónde.

we, *pron.* nosotros -as.

weak, *a.* débil.

weaken, *v.* debilitar.

weakness, *n.* debilidad *f.*

wealth, *n.* riqueza *f.*

wealthy, *a.* rico.

weapon, *n.* arma *f.*

wear, **1.** *n.* uso, desgaste *m.;* (clothes) ropa *f.* **2.** *v.* usar, llevar. **w. out,** gastar; cansar.

weary, *a.* cansado, rendido.

weather, *n.* tiempo *m.*

weave, *v.* tejer.

weaver, *n.* tejedor -ra.

web, *n.* tela *f.*

wedding, *n.* boda *f.*

wedge, *n.* cuña *f.*

Wednesday, *n.* miércoles *m.*

weed, *n.* maleza *f.*

week, *n.* semana *f.* **w. end,** fin de semana.

weekday, *n.* día de trabajo.

weekly, *a.* semanal.

weep, *v.* llorar.

weigh, *v.* pesar.

weight, n. peso m.

weird, a. misterioso, sobrenatural.

welcome, 1. a. bienvenido. **you're w.,** de nada, no hay de qué. **2.** n. acogida, bienvenida f. **3.** v. acoger, recibir bien.

welfare, n. bienestar m.

well, 1. a. sano, bueno. **2.** adv. bien; pues. **3.** n. pozo m.

well-known, a. bien conocido.

west, n. oeste, occidente m.

western, a. occidental.

westward, adv. hacia el oeste.

wet, 1. a. mojado. **to get w.,** mojarse. **2.** v. mojar.

whale, n. ballena f.

what, 1. a. qué; cuál. **2.** interrog. pron. qué. **3.** rel. pron. lo que.

whatever, 1. a. cualquier. **2.** pron. lo que; todo lo que.

wheat, n. trigo m.

wheel, n. rueda f. **steering w.,** volante m.

when, 1. adv. cuándo. **2.** conj. cuando.

whenever, conj. siempre que, cuando quiera que.

where, 1. adv. dónde, adónde. **2.** conj. donde.

wherever, conj. dondequiera que, adondequiera que.

whether, conj. si.

which, 1. a. qué. **2.** interrog. pron. cuál. **3.** rel. pron. que; el cual; lo cual.

whichever, a. & pron. cualquiera que.

while, 1. conj. mientras; mientras que. **2.** n. rato m. **to be worth w.,** valer la pena.

whip, 1. n. látigo m. **2.** v. azotar.

whirl, v. girar.

whirlpool, n. vórtice m.

whirlwind, n. torbellino m.

whisk broom, n. escobilla f.

whisker, n. bigote m.

whiskey, n. whisky m.

whisper, 1. n. cuchicheo m. **2.** v. cuchichear.

whistle, 1. n. pito; silbido m. **2.** v. silbar.

white, 1. a. blanco. **2.** n. (of egg) clara f.

who, whom, 1. interrog. pron. quién. **2.** rel. pron. que; quien.

whoever, whomever, pron. quienquiera que.

whole, 1. a. entero. **the wh.,** todo el. **2.** n. totalidad f. **on the wh.,** por lo general.

wholesale, n. **at wh.,** al por mayor.

wholesome, a. sano, saludable.

wholly, adv. enteramente.

whose, 1. interrog. adj. de quién. **2.** rel. adj. cuyo.

why, adv. por qué; para qué.

wicked, a. malo, malvado.

wickedness, n. maldad f.

wide, 1. a. ancho; extenso. **2.**

adv. **w. open,** abierto de par en par.

widen, v. ensanchar; extender.

widespread, a. extenso.

widow, n. viuda f.

widower, n. viudo m.

width, n. anchura f.

wield, v. manejar, empuñar.

wife, n. esposa, señora, mujer f.

wig, n. peluca f.

wild, a. salvaje; bárbaro.

wilderness, n. desierto m.

wildlife, n. fauna silvestre f.

will, 1. n. voluntad f.; testamento m. **2.** v. querer; determinar; (leg.) legar.

willful, a. voluntarioso; premeditado.

willing, a. **to be w.,** estar dispuesto.

willingly, adv. de buena gana.

wilt, v. marchitar.

win, v. ganar.

wind, 1. viento m. **2.** v. torcer; dar cuerda a.

window, n. ventana; (of car) ventanilla f.

windy, a. ventoso. **to be w.,** (weather) hacer viento.

wine, n. vino m.

wing, n. ala f.; (theat.) bastidor m.

wink, 1. n. guiño m. **2.** v. guiñar.

winner, n. ganador -ra.

winter, n. invierno m.

wipe, v. limpiar; (dry) secar. **w. out,** destruir.

wire, 1. n. alambre; hilo; telegrama m. **2.** v. telegrafiar.

wireless, n. telégrafo sin hilos.

wisdom, n. juicio m.; sabiduría f.

wise, a. sensato, juicioso; sabio.

wish, 1. n. deseo; voto m. **2.** v. desear; querer.

wit, n. ingenio m., sal f.

witch, n. bruja f.

with, prep. con.

withdraw, v. retirar.

wither, v. marchitar.

withhold, v. retener, suspender.

within, 1. adv. dentro, por dentro. **2.** prep. dentro de; en.

without, 1. adv. fuera, por fuera. **2.** prep. sin.

witness, 1. n. testigo; testimonio m. **2.** v. presenciar; atestar.

witty, a. ingenioso, gracioso.

wizard, n. hechicero m.

woe, n. dolor m.; pena f.

wolf, n. lobo m.

woman, n. mujer f.

womb, n. entrañas f.pl., matriz f.

wonder, 1. n. maravilla; admiración f. **for a w.,** por milagro. **no w.,** no es extraño. **2.** v. preguntarse; maravillarse.

wonderful, a. maravilloso; estupendo.

woo, v. cortejar.

wood, n. madera; (for fire) leña f.

wooden, a. de madera.

wool, n. lana f.

word, 1. n. palabra f. **the words** (of a song), la letra. **2.** v. expresar.

work, 1. n. trabajo m.; (of art) obra f. **2.** v. trabajar; obrar; funcionar.

worker, n. trabajador -ra; obrero -ra.

workman, n. obrero m.

world, n. mundo m. **w. war,** guerra mundial.

worldly, a. mundano.

worldwide, a. mundial.

worm, n. gusano m.

worn, a. usado. **w. out,** gastado, cansado, rendido.

worry, 1. n. preocupación f. **2.** v. preocupar.

worse, a. peor. **to get w.,** empeorar.

worship, 1. n. adoración f. **2.** v. adorar.

worst, a. peor.

worth, 1. a. **to be w.,** valer. **2.** n. valor m.

worthless, a. sin valor.

worthy, a. digno.

wound, 1. n. herida f. **2.** v. herir.

wrap, 1. v. (pl.) abrigos m.pl. **2.** n. envolver.

wrapping, n. cubierta f.

wrath, n. ira, cólera f.

wreath, n. guirnalda; corona f.

wreck, 1. n. ruina f.; accidente m. **2.** v. destrozar, arruinar.

wrench, n. llave f. **monkey w.,** llave inglesa.

wrestle, v. luchar.

wretched, a. miserable.

wring, v. retorcer.

wrinkle, 1. n. arruga f. **2.** v. arrugar.

wrist, n. muñeca f. **w. watch,** reloj de pulsera.

write, v. escribir. **w. down,** apuntar.

writer, n. escritor -ra.

writhe, v. contorcerse.

wrong, 1. a. equivocado; incorrecto. **to be w.,** equivocarse; no tener razón. **2.** adv. mal, incorrectamente. **3.** n. agravio m. **right and w.,** el bien y el mal. **4.** v. agraviar, ofender.

X, Y, Z

x-ray, n. rayo X m.

xylophone, n. xilófono m.

yacht, n. yate m.

yard, n. patio, corral m.; (measure) yarda f.

yarn, n. hilo.

yawn, 1. n. bostezo m. **2.** v. bostezar.

year, n. año m.

yearly, a. anual.

yearn, *v.* anhelar.
yell, 1. *n.* grito *m.* **2.** *v.* gritar.
yellow, *a.* amarillo.
yes, *adv.* sí.
yesterday, *adv.* ayer.
yet, *adv.* todavía, aún.
yield, *v.* producir; ceder.
yoke, *n.* yugo *m.*
yolk, *n.* yema *f.*
you, *pron.* usted, (pl.) ustedes; lo, la, los, las; le, les; (famil-iar) tú, (pl.) vosotros -as; ti; te, (pl.) os. **with y.,** contigo.
young, *a.* joven.
your, *a.* su; (familiar) tu; (pl.) vuestro.
yours, *pron.* suyo; (familiar) tuyo; (pl.) vuestro.
yourself, -selves, *pron.* sí; se; (familiar) ti; te. **with y.,** con-sigo; contigo. **you y.,** usted mismo, ustedes mismos; tú mismo, vosotros mismos.

youth, *n.* juventud *f.;* (person) joven *m.*
youthful, *a.* juvenil.
zap, *v.* desintegrar, aniquilar.
zeal, *n.* celo, fervor *m.*
zealous, *a.* celoso, fervoroso.
zero, *n.* cero *m.*
zest, *n.* gusto *m.*
zip code, *n.* número de distrito postal.
zone, *n.* zona *f.*
zoo, *n.* jardín zoológico.